The New Adapted Physical Education

The New Adapted Physical Education:

A Developmental Approach

Janet A. Seaman
California State University, Los Angeles

Karen P. DePauw
Washington State University, Pullman

 MAYFIELD PUBLISHING COMPANY

Library of Congress Catalog Card Number: 81-84691
International Standard Book Number: 0-87484-524-6

Manufactured in the United States of America
Mayfield Publishing Company
285 Hamilton Avenue
Palo Alto, California 94301

Sponsoring editor: C. Lansing Hays
Special projects editor: Liz Currie
Manuscript editor: Naomi Lucks
Designer: Nancy Sears
Illustrators: Cindy Clark-Huegel, Wayne Clark, and Mary Burkhardt
Cover designer: William Dunn
Production manager: Cathy Willkie
Compositor: Computer Typesetting Services, Inc.
Printer and binder: R. R. Donnelley

Table 5-13, ``Behavior disorders of childhood and adolescence''
(p. 117), is used by permission of the American Psychiatric
Association.

Table 6-3, ``Age of onset and presumptive cause of epilepsy''
(p. 127), is reproduced from J. C. Chusid, *Correlative
Neuroanatomy and Functional Neurology*, 17th ed., 1979, with
permission of Lange Medical Publications.

Cover Photo Credits

Top row: Greg Fulton. *Second row:* Ben Esparza. *Third row:* Lyonel
Avance (left), Janet A. Seaman (right). *Bottom row:* Lyonel Avance
(left), Janet A. Seaman (middle and right).

Chapter-Opening Photo Credits

Chapter 1: City of Anaheim. *Chapters 2-3:* Janet A. Seaman.
Chapters 4-6: Lyonel Avance. *Chapters 7-13:* Janet A. Seaman.
Chapter 14: Karen DePauw. *Chapter 15:* Janet A. Seaman. *Chapter
16:* Alameda County School Department Photographer Al Scheuller.
Chapter 17: Layne Hackett, Santa Clara County Superintendent of
Schools. *Chapters 18-19:* Janet A. Seaman.

In the text, photos not otherwise credited have been taken by
Janet A. Seaman.

Contents

Preface

Through the medium of movement, physical educators (generalists in physical education and specialists in adapted physical education) can challenge all children—handicapped and nonhandicapped—to achieve their maximum potential in the motor domain. But helping a special child to expand his or her skills is an especially rewarding experience. To see a boy smile after successfully lifting his head, rolling over, or grasping an object, to see a girl's pleasure in catching a ball, running a race, or playing a game—such triumphs make teaching most worthwhile.

By some standards, the steps of progress made by handicapped children may seem small, but to the children, their parents, and their teachers they are major accomplishments. By evaluating performance on an individual basis, we learn to appreciate the achievements of exceptional individuals more fully. The developmental approach taken by this text is a means of viewing children singly and tailoring instruction to each individual with special needs. Years of observing and interacting with handicapped and nonhandicapped children have convinced us of its value.

The developmental approach changes one's perspective. By focusing on characteristics that should occur naturally in the course of growth and maturing, the developmental model helps the physical educator to recognize and understand atypical development and performance. It lets the teacher challenge a student to progress along a natural continuum. It also gives rise to flexible and creative programming. Physical educators must look beyond educational classification and medical diagnoses of handicapped children. We must focus on ability rather than on disability. By means of the developmental approach, future physical educators will be better prepared to identify sources of poor motor performance and to plan, implement, and evaluate effective physical education programs for handicapped individuals.

The New Adapted Physical Education is divided into four parts. Part One, "The Developmental Approach" (Chapters 1 through 6), introduces students to adapted physical education. The developmental approach is described in detail in this section. Etiology, characteristics, and legal classifications of educational categories are presented to help students understand handicapping conditions, but emphasis is placed on individuals' developmental needs, limitations, and capacities.

Part Two, "Assessment of Developmental Levels of Performance" (Chapters 7 through 12), stresses assessment techniques, the selection and appropriateness of tests, and the significance of results for establishing the individualized education program. Assessment, ways of collecting, interpreting, and evaluating data, and other factors influencing motor performance are discussed.

Part Three, "Application of the Developmental Approach" (Chapters 13 through 17), examines theoretical concepts and practical instructional strategies, including modification of the learning environment, activities, and approach; task analysis; observational techniques; behavior management; and alternatives for communication. This section presents techniques and activities for effective programming based on the developmental model. Also discussed are the planning, equipment, and facilities needed for an effective program and the use of physical activity to promote cognitive learning and language development.

Part Four, "Toward Fruition of the Developmental Approach" (Chapters 18 and 19), looks at the expanding role of the physical educator in the school, home, and community. Chapter 18, "The Team Approach: Working with Educational Personnel," covers various forms of team interaction, in-service training, concepts related to mainstreaming, and the role of the physical educator as a resource person. The concluding chapter discusses the expanding role of the physical educator "beyond the schoolyard fence" — in the community and in related service agencies as well as with parents and guardians.

We have supplemented the text with several special features to provide additional information and resources:

- "Guiding Questions" at the beginning of each chapter identify major topics.
- Chapter summaries help the reader recall key points.
- Bibliographies at the end of each chapter provide lists of references.
- Boxed material elaborates on topics introduced within chapters.

- Examples of forms used by physical educators for gathering data, recording progress, and documenting students' status have been included.
- Seven appendixes provide a virtual treasure chest of resource materials for the future teacher — guidelines for adapted physical education, a developmental schedule, accounts of several testing procedures, bibliographies of perceptual-motor theory and articles on physical education and recreation for the handicapped from *JOPER*, the names and addresses of sports organizations for the handicapped, and examples of materials available to parents for use at home.
- The Instructor's Manual contains chapter overviews and outlines, behavioral objectives, test questions, an assortment of projects and discussion topics, annotated lists of readings, and information about sources of films and equipment to be used in adapted physical education classes.

No project of this magnitude is possible without the cooperation and support of numerous friends and colleagues. At the risk of excluding someone, we wish to extend our gratitude to the following people who rose to the occasion to help us meet deadlines and preserve our sanity. Many thanks to Joan Gunnell and Rozanne LaRusso for the preparation of the manuscript and to Pat Klein, Ernst J. Kiphard, and Ted Baumgartner for their expert input. A very warm thank you to the "cast of thousands" who helped complete the very lengthy list of photographs. Facilitators for this process included Lyonel Avance, Joanne Betts, Jodi Critz, Ben Esparza, Dorothy Franks, Ed Greaves, Layne Hackett, Ed Kinney, Kim Morton, and Lou Stewart. The agencies and school districts these people are affiliated with also did their part: the Los Angeles Unified School District, El Monte Elementary School District, Educational Studies Center for Adapted Physical Education, Cajon Valley Union School District, Santa Clara County Superintendent of

Schools, Long Beach Veterans Administration Medical Center, and the Southern California Diagnostic School.

We would also like to thank our colleagues who reviewed the manuscript in various stages of its development: Larry Ankenbrand, Eastern Illinois University; Peter Aufsesser, San Diego State University; Lee Burkett, Arizona State University; Gail Dummer, University of Maryland; Sue Gavron, Bowling Green State University; Donald Kallen, Eastern Washington University; William Karper, University of North Carolina; and Wendell Liemohn, University of Tennessee.

J.A.S.
K.P.D.

Part One

The Developmental Approach

1   What Is Adapted Physical Education?

Guiding Questions

1. What is the definition of adapted physical education?
2. What are the history and scope of adapted physical education?
3. What are the legal mandates for adapted physical education?
4. What sorts of jobs are available, and what is the professional preparation required by the field?
5. What are the history and current status of competencies required by adapted physical education?

Throughout history, physical activity has been accepted as a remedial technique. More recently, physical activity has been seen to have preventative value as well. Currently, a widespread emphasis has been placed on total mental and physical fitness as a worthwhile goal for all members of society. Handicapped people are no exception.

The benefits of physical education for the handicapped are many. A well-designed program of physical education can contribute to their lives through (1) the development of physical and motor skills necessary for the activities of daily living and participation with peers, family, and friends; (2) the development of a more positive self-image and feeling of self-worth; and (3) the development of skills and abilities that will enable them to participate in enjoyable leisuretime activities and recreational pursuits. To this end, the field of adapted physical education has been developed.

Adapted physical education—the physical educa-tion of students who have special needs—is a diversified program that incorporates a variety of individual programs. Developmental activities, games, sports, and rhythms are considered appropriate and feasible activities for the handicapped population, and all programming is suited to the interests, capacities, and limitations of these students.

HISTORY AND SCOPE OF ADAPTED PHYSICAL EDUCATION

It was not until 1952 that the scope of adapted physical education was clearly and consistently defined. This definition, which is the basis for this text, established a much broader application of kinesiological principles and learning theory than had been used in earlier programs. The statement of the committee of the American Alliance for Health, Physical Education, Recreation, and Dance (AAHPERD)* defined adapted physical education as

> [A] diversified program of developmental activities, games, sports, and rhythms, suited to the interests, capacities, and limitations of students with disabilities who may not safely or successfully engage in unrestricted participation in the vigorous activities of the general physical education program (AAHPERD, 1952).

The first new thought advanced by the committee was that programs should be diversified. They should not consist exclusively of rehabilitative or therapeutic exercise, as implemented by early physician-educators, but should mirror or parallel the concepts and structures of physical education programs for nonhandicapped students.

Second, to ensure that such programs would be diversified, the committee specified what diversification should entail. Developmental activities were to include the broad range of activities geared to the improvement of movement parameters: strength, flexibility, motor ability, endurance, perceptual-motor function, skills, and so on. Through developmental activities, students could profit from rehabilitative exercise as well as from activities designed to bring them to age level in perceptual-motor functioning, if such activities were appropriate to their needs.

The suggestion that games, sports, and rhythms should be included in programs for students with special needs took physical education into uncharted territory. It wasn't until after World War II, when disabled veterans began playing wheelchair basketball, practicing archery, and square dancing, that physical

educators in the schools realized how numerous were the possibilities for furthering the development of handicapped children. With the growth of special education in the past twenty-five years, these newly found applications have become part of the curriculum for the mentally retarded, learning-disabled, and other handicapped individuals, who have had new experiences as a result of appropriately modified physical education programs.

Third, in creating its definition of adapted physical education, the committee suggested the needs that could be met by a diversified program. The program should be "suited to the interests, capacities, and limitations of students with disabilities . . ." As a result, the age-determined interests of handicapped students were being considered for the first time. Also for the first time, the committee was suggesting that students should be challenged to reach their capacities.

Finally, the committee identified the segment of the school population that could profit from such an all-encompassing program as "students . . . who may not safely or successfully engage in unrestricted participation in the . . . general physical education program." Although early programs had been concerned with safety and the possibility of aggravating certain existing conditions, the committee again ventured into uncharted waters in suggesting that students who could not be successful in the general physical education program could profit from the application of the principles of adapted physical education.

The committee's definition is general enough to allow for a multifaceted approach to physical education for exceptional individuals, yet specific enough to focus the field upon the challenge and uniqueness of its application. This view of adapted physical education has persisted through an age of rapid change. More recently, physical education's potential contribution to children with special needs was given new impetus. In 1975, physical education was included in the Education for All Handicapped Children Act (Public Law [PL]

*Although the word "Dance" was not added to the name of the American Alliance for Health, Physical Education, and Recreation until 1979, the organization will be referred to by the initials AAHPERD throughout the text. Prior to 1973, it was known as the American Association for Health, Physical Education, and Recreation.

94–142), the first piece of federal legislation to acknowledge this discipline as important to the overall education of handicapped children.

In addition to mandating physical education as part of special education, PL 94–142 defines handicapped children as those who are mentally retarded, hard of hearing, deaf, speech- and language-impaired, visually handicapped, seriously emotionally disturbed, orthopedically impaired, otherwise health-impaired, deaf-blind, multihandicapped, and learning-disabled. It puts on public record the fact that the nation's lawmakers recognize physical education as a right and as a valuable addition to the curriculum for *all* handicapped children, not just the physically handicapped.

The regulations of PL 94–142 include a definition of physical education that bears striking resemblance to the definition written in 1952 by the AAHPERD:

Physical education is defined as follows:
(I) The term means the development of:
  A. Physical and motor fitness
  B. Fundamental motor skills and patterns, and
  C. Skills in aquatics, dance, and individual and group games and sports (including intramural and lifetime sports).
(II) The term includes special physical education, adapted physical education, movement education, and motor development.

With the passage of PL 94–142, it appeared that Congress intended to apply the concepts laid down in the earlier definition of adapted physical education. Accordingly, it would be incorrect to view adapted physical education as a specific regimen of rehabilitative activities or as an explanation for "what goes on" in a particular area or room in the physical education building. Rather, adapted physical education should be thought of as a state of mind. It is not a program that contributes exclusively to the physical and motor development of children; it is not a program intended solely for the remediation of disabilities; nor is it a pro-

gram of table games for students who cannot match skills with their peers. Rather, it is all of these and much more. Remediation of conditions is important only where it is appropriate. Modification of activities is important for building wanted leisuretime skills and for promoting socialization and peer interaction; but there are other objectives as well. Students with special needs in motor performance often require finitely sequenced instructional plans to accommodate their styles of learning; others need to be allowed to proceed at their own pace; still others need modified facilities or teaching methods in order to circumvent their limitations.

Origin and Evolution of Adapted Physical Education

The roots of adapted physical education can be traced back to the curative physical regimens found in China in 2700 B.C. The ancients relied on activities such as medical gymnastics, preventive exercise, and therapeutic exercise to alleviate physical disorders and illnesses.

The European cultures influenced the development of adapted physical education primarily through medical gymnastics. A large part of medical gymnastics was taken up with prescribed exercises to remediate specific disorders, since exercise was considered the best medicine. During the late eighteenth century, recreational therapy and adapted sports for the disabled were developed in Europe.

In the nineteenth century in the United States, the medical gymnastics model for physical education continued to be applied. Preventive and corrective exercise was still emphasized. Little changed until after World War I, when the needs of returning war veterans caused the structure of programs that had previously been labeled "corrective physical education" to be altered. The successes of physical therapists and corrective therapists in hospitals inspired a new line of thought and, as we have seen, the way opened for physical education to contribute to the enjoyment of physical activity among handicapped children as well.

During this period, which lasted from the 1920s to the 1950s, corrective physical education developed as a separate entity from physical education. Additional changes were needed as the field's emphasis shifted to service for handicapped children. The definition of adapted physical education adopted in 1952 expanded upon the concept of corrective physical education. Currently, the terms *developmental, special,* and *adapted physical education* are in common use.

Adapted physical education has been undergoing radical changes in the 1980s. As more scientific evidence of the beneficial effects of physical education for the handicapped is generated and tested, adapted physical education is emerging as a viable subdiscipline.

Scope of Adapted Physical Education

The emergence of adapted physical education as a viable entity is a new direction of the 1980s. The extent to which it will affect the whole of education depends upon the leadership and common goals of adapted physical education professionals. Just as leaders in general physical education have attempted to identify the body of knowledge unique to that discipline, so must leaders in adapted physical education clarify the content of the subdiscipline. In this regard, it is useful to have a set of criteria against which progress of the subdiscipline can be measured.

In his article "The Criteria of a Discipline," Nixon (1967) identified the following seven criteria:

1. A discipline has an identifiable domain, a body of knowledge.
2. A discipline is characterized by substantial history and tradition.
3. A discipline has a conceptual structure.

4. A discipline possesses a unique integrity.
5. A discipline is recognized by the procedures and methods it employs.
6. A discipline is recognized as a process as well as noted for its product.
7. A discipline relies on accurate language.

How does adapted physical education stand up to these criteria? First, it certainly can be said to have an identifiable domain: physical education for the exceptional population. As do other applied areas, its body of knowledge borrows principles from the generic base of natural and behavioral sciences, with unique applications of its parent disciplines, physical and special education.

Second, as has been noted, the use of adapted physical education can be traced back to ancient China and eighteenth-century Europe. Although there have been changes in its name, emphasis, and scope over the years, the history and tradition of the rehabilitative aspects of adapted physical education is substantial. However, as an applied discipline in the habilitative arena, its history is admittedly quite short.

The third criterion, a conceptual structure, can be seen to emerge from adapted physical education's unique application of the principles and knowledge of its contributing disciplines. Biology, physics, and psychology have contributed principles to kinesiology, biomechanics, and motor learning in much the same way that physical and special education have contributed to the conceptual framework of adapted physical education.

Possession of a unique integrity and an arbitrary quality is the fourth criterion of a discipline. As previously stated, although adapted physical education does borrow from a generic base, it possesses an arbitrary quality and unique integrity of its own. Modifications are generated from within the field, thus preserving the "wholeness" of adapted physical education.

Nixon's fifth criterion states that a discipline is recognized by the procedures and methods it employs. Adapted physical education clearly utilizes methods that set it apart from general physical education. For example, human movement is used to generate learning. The methods for creating movement experiences for the exceptional population result in a student-centered program rather than the group-centered program common in general physical education.

As for the sixth criterion, adapted physical education tends by definition to be a process-oriented program. A program suited to the interests, capacities, and limitations of students nearly dismisses a commitment to product, whereas general physical education uses performance criteria to strive for a specified product. This is not to say that adapted physical education is not noted for its product: witness the performances of handicapped children who have had the benefits of such a program, as compared with their adult counterparts. The positive influence of adapted physical education is markedly evident.

Reliance on accurate language, Nixon's final criterion, is slowly being achieved. Since adapted physical education is emerging from a wide base of knowledge, constituents within the field must establish common terminology. As its scope broadens, its longevity increases, and the integrity of adapted physical education persists, a unique and accurate language system will evolve. It is the responsibility of current and future teachers and leaders to ensure that the emergence of adapted physical education as a sub-discipline within physical education does, in fact, come to pass.

LEGAL MANDATES

Just as there are laws that affect society at large, so are there laws that affect the handicapped. The two most powerful and comprehensive such laws are PL 94–142, the Education for All Handicapped Children Act of 1975, and PL 93–112, Section 504 of the Rehabilitation Act of 1973.

Public Law 94–142

More so than any other legislation enacted to date, PL 94–142 identifies and outlines the federal government's commitment to the education of all handicapped individuals. Also outlined is the plan for ensuring the rights of handicapped children to a free, appropriate public education in the least restrictive environment. An emphasis has also been placed on providing services for those not previously served, and for the severely handicapped who are receiving inadequate public education. Since the major intent of the law was to provide full educational opportunities for all handicapped children, the states were required to find and serve all handicapped children ages three to eighteen years by 1978, and all handicapped individuals ages three to twenty-one years by 1980.

PL 94–142 has one basic mandate that encompasses several other key issues: it calls for a free, appropriate public education in the least restrictive environment. The education mandated by the law is special education; that is, specially designed instruction to meet the unique needs of a handicapped child. Special education is defined to include the following direct services: classroom instruction, instruction in physical education, home instruction, and instruction in hospitals and institutions. A direct service is one that *must* be provided for the child, whereas related services may be provided only if required to assist a handicapped child to benefit from special education. Related services include physical therapy, occupational therapy, recreation therapy, social services, counseling, audiology, speech therapy, and so on. Consequently, PL 94–142 has a significant impact on physical education for the handicapped, which is mandated as a direct service.

Under the law, physical education or specially designed physical education, if necessary, must be made available to every handicapped child receiving a free, appropriate public education. Each handicapped child must be afforded the opportunity to participate in regular physical education unless (1) the child is enrolled in a separate facility, or (2) the child needs an adapted physical education program as specified in the individualized education program. If specially designed physical education is prescribed, the public educational agency is responsible for providing such service, either directly or through other public or private agencies.

Section 504 of the Rehabilitation Act of 1973

This section of PL 93–112 implies much of the same educational mandate as PL 94–142, along with many all-encompassing civil rights issues. In fact, PL 94–142 is sometimes unofficially referred to as the education amendment of PL 93–112. Section 504, a federal civil rights law protecting the rights of handicapped persons, reflects the government's commitment to end discrimination on the basis of handicap and to bring handicapped people into the mainstream of society.

The regulations of Section 504 apply to all recipients of federal financial assistance, including state departments of education, school districts, and colleges and universities. All federally assisted programs and activities must be operated without discrimination on the basis of handicap. The regulations also forbid employment discrimination against qualified handicapped individuals. Reasonable accommodation is expected, which means that both the facilities and the recipients' programs must be accessible to the handicapped.

Intent of the Laws

Section 504 specifically mentions physical education, intramurals, and interscholastic athletics, stating that where these services are provided for nonhandi-

capped individuals, the handicapped must also be afforded the opportunity to participate, without discrimination on the basis of handicap. Often, however, the letter and spirit of legislation are not the same when full implementation is reached. There is always room for various interpretations, because enabling legislation at the state level includes more precise language to meet unique characteristics of each state. However, in the case of PL 94–142 and Section 504 of PL 93–112 the basic intents are present in the federal legislation and the mandates must be met.

Free, Appropriate Public Education

Free, appropriate public education is mentioned in both pieces of federal legislation. As discussed in Section 504, subpart D, the provision of a free education means the provision of educational services without cost to the handicapped children or their parents. The definition of free education in PL 94–142 is quite similar. Special education, including physical education and related services, are to be provided at public expense under public supervision and direction.

Appropriate public education, as defined by PL 94–142, must meet the standards of the state educational agency. This education includes preschool, elementary school, and secondary school education, and must conform to the specific requirements of an individualized education program. In PL 93–112, appropriate education means that the needs of handicapped children must be met and be equal to the quality of educational services provided for the nonhandicapped.

Free, appropriate public education, in terms of both laws, means that handicapped children are entitled to an individualized education program at the public agency's expense. It is the responsibility of the public school district to provide the appropriate education. If this cannot be done, it may be deemed appropriate for the school district to pay the expense

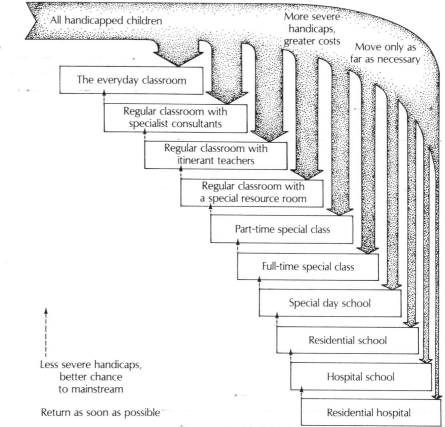

Figure 1-1. The "cascade" system of services available to the handicapped. SOURCE: Reproduced from the publication *One Out of Ten* and used by permission of Educational Facilities Laboratories, New York, N.Y.

All handicapped children

More severe handicaps, greater costs

Move only as far as necessary

The everyday classroom

Regular classroom with specialist consultants

Regular classroom with itinerant teachers

Regular classroom with a special resource room

Part-time special class

Full-time special class

Special day school

Residential school

Hospital school

Residential hospital

Less severe handicaps, better chance to mainstream

Return as soon as possible

for other than public school education, depending upon the requirements of the individualized educational program. If the handicapped student chooses to enroll in other than the public school, where appropriate services are available, then the family must be prepared to bear the expense.

Least Restrictive Environment

Under both laws, the intent of the least restrictive environment is to establish procedures that would

ensure, to the maximum extent possible, that handicapped individuals would be educated with those who are not handicapped. PL 94-142 specifically presents a continuum of alternative placements available to handicapped people, ranging from regular school placement to institutions (See Figure 1-1).

As can be seen in this diagram, decisions regarding the environment for delivering educational services are no longer based upon segregated or integrated alternatives. Rather, many alternatives based upon each child's needs must be made available. PL 94-142 stresses that, in determination of the appropriate, least restrictive environment, consideration must be given to any potentially harmful effect on the child and to the quality of services needed. Section 504 places emphasis upon the comparability of quality facilities for the handicapped and nonhandicapped.

Mainstreaming is a term most frequently associated with PL 94–142; however, it should be noted that "mainstreaming" and "least restrictive environment" are not synonymous terms. The mandate is for education in the least restrictive environment, one alternative of which is the mainstream of education. In actual practice, mainstreaming is often a byproduct of the implementation of federal regulations. It must always be the handicapped child, not the letter of the law, whose needs, limitations, capacities, and interests dictate the appropriate educational placement.

Individualized Education Program (IEP)

PL 94–142 states that the free, appropriate public education in the least restrictive environment must include an individualized education program (IEP) for every handicapped child served. The IEP is defined as a written statement, developed and implemented in accordance with federal regulations, which must be developed for any handicapped child who is served in regular education, as well as for a child placed in a private school by a state or local educational agency.

The IEP is an educational program jointly prepared by a number of people who are directly concerned with the education of the handicapped child. The members of the IEP committee must include a representative of the public education agency other than the child's teacher; the child's teacher; one or both of the parents; the child, when appropriate; and other individuals, at the discretion of the parent or agency. When physical education services are included, the adapted physical educator or regular physical educator should be present.

The written statement of the IEP includes documentation of decisions reached about the objectives, content, implementation, and evaluation of the child's educational program. There are specified regulations regarding timelines in establishing and reviewing the IEP. The IEP is not intended to be a binding contract, inasmuch as certain objectives for the child may not be met or goals and objectives may need to be revised as the child's needs change. It does, however, commit the local educational agency to the provision of services delineated in the IEP.

Accountability

Accountability in the education of handicapped children is either implied or specifically stated within the context of both PL 94–142 and Section 504. Certain policies and procedures are guaranteed under these laws, but what is not guaranteed is the child's progress at a specified rate. The teachers and public agencies are still held accountable for making good faith efforts to assist the child in achieving the objectives and goals listed in the IEP. If stated goals and objectives are not being met, the IEP committee has the option to review and restate them at any time. Thus the impact of implementation of these laws is that more accountability and responsibility rests on teachers and public agencies than ever before.

Additionally, due process safeguards for the handicapped children and their families are implicit, and many forms of appeal and due process procedures are specifically outlined in both laws. Although it is beyond the purview of this book to identify those procedures, it is important to realize that due process safeguards are positive means toward the end of achieving the goal of quality education for all handicapped children.

BECOMING A PROFESSIONAL IN ADAPTED PHYSICAL EDUCATION

The constantly changing issues and trends in our society inevitably shape the environment in which adapted physical education must operate. The implementation of federal and state legislation places increasing demands on the field, and increases the variety of roles and teaching environments in which both adapted physical educators and regular physical educators must function.

Jobs in Adapted Physical Education

Because of the recent popularity of mainstreaming, handicapped individuals may be present in regular physical education classes. Thus general physical educators must have a basic knowledge and understanding of the exceptional population, as well as the competencies, skills, techniques, and resources needed to face the challenges of teaching these students.

Adapted physical education specialists work in a variety of teaching environments. Some, trained as specialists, teach in the mainstream of education, working with both the handicapped and nonhandicapped. Others, itinerant teachers, are assigned to more than one school in a given area where various special education classes are conducted, and must travel daily or weekly to teach adapted physical education. Still others work in a single special education school, instructing and providing service in physical education for the exceptional population. Two or three adapted physical education teachers may be assigned to one special school, although in most states this is quite rare. Adapted physical educators are also employed in residential facilities or institutions in many states.

All adapted physical education teachers, no matter what the working environment, must be capable of working with handicapped people aged three to twenty-one years, ranging in degree from mildly involved to the most severely handicapped. This includes not only physically handicapped but emotionally disturbed and learning-disabled as well. In some states, pregnant teens and the socially deviant are also included in adapted physical education programs.

The duties of adapted physical education teachers may include evaluating and advising the regular physical education and classroom teachers, meeting as members of the interdisciplinary IEP committee, and teaching and assessing handicapped children. Additionally, they may be required to provide inservices, demonstrations, and community or liaison services.

Adapted physical education specialists may also become program specialists, consultants, coordinators, supervisors, and administrators of adapted physical education programs. University and community college teaching is a growing area of need for trained adapted physical education specialists, both for applied service and teaching academic courses.

Professional Preparation

Professional preparation programs in adapted physical education have existed for the past twenty years, and more programs continue to be developed as the need for specialists grows. Currently, more than two hundred colleges and universities throughout the United States and U.S. territories offer some coursework in adapted physical education; over fifty colleges and universities offer specialization programs at the undergraduate, masters, or doctoral levels. The coursework offered in these programs includes the following areas: dimensions of physical education for the learning-disabled, mentally retarded, physically handicapped, and severely handicapped; assessment and evaluation; planning and implementing appropriate physical education programs; and an interdisciplinary approach. In addition, fundamental coursework and practical experience are included in most professional preparation programs (DePauw, 1979).

As the state of the art and the environment for adapted physical education change, so must professional preparation programs change. Implementation of PL 94–142 and other federal and state laws demands qualified physical educators to provide physical education for exceptional individuals.

COMPETENCIES IN ADAPTED PHYSICAL EDUCATION

The foremost goal of adapted physical education is the adequate preparation of competent physical educators for teaching exceptional children. As the inevitable standardization of professional preparation evolves, the issue of competencies must be addressed. Specifically: (1) competencies appropriate to the variety of environments in which adapted physical education is implemented must be identified; and (2) professional preparation programs capable of teaching those competencies must be developed.

Historical Perspective

The first identification of competencies related to physical education for the handicapped was investigated in the late 1940s by Davies (1950), specifically in relation to corrective physical education for the orthopedically handicapped. Between 1950 and 1973, several studies investigating professional preparation in adapted physical education were conducted (Hooley, 1964; Winnick, 1969; Ersing and Wheeler, 1971). The results and recommendations of these studies seemed to reflect the state of the art at the time and included some mention of the need for adequately prepared adapted physical educators, but without

mention of specific competencies. From 1973 to the present, updated studies have been done on professional preparation of adapted physical educators (Hooley, 1974; Keogh, 1975; Vodola and Daniel, 1976; Bird, 1976; Browne, 1977; DePauw, 1979). Again, although these reports may not have specifically included or identified competencies, they did provide further support of the need for adequately prepared adapted physical education teachers. During this six-year span, the literature did include several articles specific to competencies in adapted physical education (Stein, 1969; AAHPERD, 1976; Moseley, 1971; Geddes and Seaman, 1978; California State Task Force on Standards for Professional Preparation in Adapted Physical Education, 1978). These articles have been valuable in identifying the competencies necessary for professional performance and providing curricular guidelines in adapted physical education.

Current Status

Much of the recent work on competencies has been and is continuing to be done at the state level. Several states have accepted the specific challenge of establishing standards and identifying competencies in adapted physical education. Currently, five states (California, Louisiana, Georgia, Kansas, and New Mexico) require written certification of teachers of adapted physical education. The majority of the rest of the states have the requirements of at least certification in physical education, if not the requirement of coursework in adapted physical education. A few states are still without any requirements, but this situation is changing. Because a need for standards of professional preparation had been previously identified and has gained national emphasis, action has been taken specifically and swiftly in response to the growing demand for adequately trained physical educators of the handicapped.

Although many states have been prompted into action, the AAHPERD has also been involved since 1973 in the process of identifying competencies and providing national leadership and direction. Recently, three AAHPERD structures – the Adapted Physical Education Academy, the Therapeutics Council, and the Unit on Programs for the Handicapped – ventured into a joint project designed to develop and distribute information and materials focusing upon competencies, with implications for certification of individuals responsible for physical education programs and activities involving students with special needs. The roles of particular focus included the generalist in regular physical education, and adapted physical education personnel.

The Competency Identification Project was undertaken by the Adapted Physical Education Competencies Committee, with representatives from each of the AAHPERD structures named above. The goal of the committee, established in June 1979, was to identify guidelines and competencies necessary to the instruction of physical education to handicapped individuals in both the integrated and special class/adapted physical education setting. Two years later, the guidelines and competencies were approved by AAHPERD (see Appendix A).*

SUMMARY

The definition, terminology associated with, and emphasis of adapted physical education for the

handicapped have changed over the years. In general, the evolution has been from curative through rehabilitation to habilitation – from a medical model to an educational model. The first definition of adapted physical education in 1952 and recent federal legislation (PL 94–142 and Section 504 of PL 93–112) each support the educational model. The scope of adapted physical education is still evolving.

The federal legislation provides a strong mandate for physical education services to handicapped individuals. The interpretation and implementation of these laws continue to shape the environment for physical education for the handicapped, as well as the roles and responsibilities of such physical education personnel as generalists, specialists, resources teachers, and administrators. Thus colleges and universities must continue to change their professional preparation programs to adequately prepare those instructors for work in physical education for the handicapped.

Over the last decade, the need for standardized professional preparation in adapted physical education has been well-established. The trend is toward adequately prepared, competent adapted physical education personnel, and toward establishing competencies at the national, state, and local levels. Future changes may include national registration or certification as well as state certification or credentialling in adapted physical education. This has already taken place in some states. Currently, adapted physical educators are taking a stand, making a firm commitment to the profession, and striving for adequately prepared, competent professionals who can provide quality service to exceptional children.

*Only the competencies for the specialist in adapted physical education were approved by the AAHPERD Board of Governors; the competencies for the generalist were sent to an appropriate structure within AAHPERD for inclusion in the competencies being established for the undergraduate in physical education.

BIBLIOGRAPHY

American Alliance for Health, Physical Education, Recreation, and Dance. "Guiding Principles for Adapted Physical Education." *Journal of Health, Physical Education, and Recreation* 23 (April 1952): 15.

American Alliance for Health, Physical Education, Recreation, and Dance. *Professional Preparation in Adapted Physical Education, Therapeutic Recreation and Corrective Therapy.* Washington, D.C.: American Alliance for Health, Physical Education, Recreation, and Dance, 1976.

Bird, P. J. *Program Assistance Grant for the Preparation of Personnel at the Master of Education Level in Physical Education for the Handicapped.* Charlottesville, Virginia: University of Virginia, 1976. Mimeographed.

Browne, R. J. *An Informal Survey of Self-Perceived Competencies of Physical Education and Special Education Teachers.* Syracuse, New York: 1977. Mimeographed.

California State Task Force on Standards for Professional Preparation in Adapted Physical Education. *Scope and Content Statement in Adapted Physical Education.* Los Angeles: California State University, Los Angeles, 1978. Mimeographed.

Davies. E. A. "An Analysis of Corrective Physical Education in Schools with Implications for Teacher Education." Ed.D. dissertation, Columbia University, 1950.

DePauw, K. P. "Nationwide Survey of Professional Preparation in Adapted Physical Education." *California Association for Health, Physical Education, and Recreation Journal.* November 1979.

Ersing, W. F., and Wheeler, R. "The Status of Professional Preparation in Adapted Physical Education." *American Corrective Therapy Journal* 25, vol. 4 (1971): 111–118.

Geddes, D., and Seaman, J. A. *Competencies of Adapted Physical Educators in Special Education.* Washington, D.C.: IRUC, American Alliance for Health, Physical Education, Recreation, and Dance, 1978.

Hooley, A. M. *A Study of Certification, and Course-Work Practices in the Preparation of Teachers for the Area of Adapted Physical Education.* Bowling Green, Ohio: Bowling Green State University, 1964. Mimeographed.

Hooley, A. M. "A Survey of Practices in the Fifty States of the United States, concerning State Requirement or Recommendation, with regard to Training in Adapted Physical Education, for Those Who Would Teach Physical Education in a Given State." Bowling Green, Ohio: Bowling Green State University, 1974.

Keogh, J. F., Stiehl, J., and Gordon, L. "Remedial Physical Education Programs in California, 1973–1974." Los Angeles: Prepared under contract no. 5893 between the California State Department of Education and the University of California at Los Angeles, September, 1975. Mimeographed.

Moseley, M. L. *TPSPE: A Proposed CBTE Curriculum for the Teacher Preparation of Special Physical Educator at the Undergraduate Level.* Cortland, New York: SUNY Press, 1977.

Nixon, J. "The Criteria of a Discipline." *Quest* 19 (December 1967): 42–48.

Stein, J. U. "Professional Preparation in Physical Education and Recreation for the Mentally Retarded." *Education and Training of the Mentally Retarded* 4 (1969): 101–108.

Vodola, T. M., and Daniel, A. *The State of Development and Adapted Physical Education in the New Jersey Public and Private School Systems.* Trenton, New Jersey: New Jersey Youth Commissioners Subcommittee on Youth Fitness, 1976. Mimeographed.

Winnick, J. P. ''Professional Preparation in Adapted Physical Education in the State of New York.'' *New York Journal of Health, Physical Education and Recreation* 21, vol. 3 (1969): 23–26.

2   The Developmental Approach

Guiding Questions

1. What is meant by the "developmental approach"?
2. How are the levels of education, current terminology, and perceptual-motor theory related to the developmental approach?
3. What are the sensory and motor systems that comprise the developmental model?
4. How does the sensory-integrative-motor-sensory-feedback system receive, process, and use sensory input and motor output?

The developmental approach enables the teacher of adapted physical education to look at the whole child—the way the child talks, plays, learns, walks, throws a ball, jumps, and so forth. The whole child has an ever-changing profile of developmental levels, needs, capacities, and limitations, which require an approach that is flexible enough to continually challenge the child to perform at maximum capacity. Because the developmental approach is not restricted to use in a special class, it can serve students in any learning environment. Embracing the developmental approach as a philosophy ensures equal access to programs for all students.

WHAT IS THE DEVELOPMENTAL APPROACH?

The developmental approach is _a vehicle that employs myriad methods and techniques in a predetermined, systematic way to facilitate growth and development among individuals with performance disorders, so that these individuals may approximate the_ _norm and achieve their maximum potential_.* This definition contains several key words that deserve close attention.

First, the developmental approach is a _vehicle_ for delivering a service; it is not a sequence of activities that can be used as a recipe for the correction, remediation, or compensation of performance disorders. Rather, it provides a foundation on which theory can be put into practice.

Second, the developmental approach is not itself a method or technique. It uses _myriad methods and techniques_ applied in a _predetermined, systematic manner_—that is, developmentally.

Third, the developmental approach is used to _facilitate growth and development_. General physical educators often do not think in these terms, since most motor patterns have developed by school age (see Appendix B). Children and young adults who have

---

*Although no specific reference is made in this definition to motor performance, this text will deal primarily with the use of the developmental approach in the psychomotor domain.

special needs, however, often have psychomotor development at preschool or even infantile levels; hence facilitation of normal developmental levels is in order. This does not mean simply an incremental change in conditions or criteria for performance; rather, it implies the process of generating a motor response with increasing complexity, appropriateness, accuracy, and specificity along the entire developmental continuum (see Figure 2-1).*

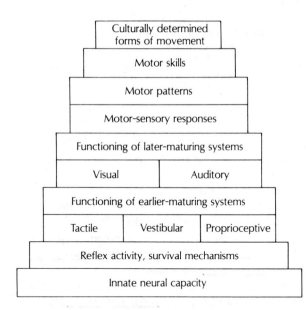

Figure 2-1. The developmental model.

A confusing plethora of terminology currently surrounds the process of development as it relates to physical education programming. The developmental model, however, demonstrates how terms, levels, and other aspects of physical education — rather than

*The terminology used in Figure 2-1, the developmental model, will be discussed throughout Chapters 2 and 3.

being discrete entities — are actually parts of the motor domain as a whole. Four important aspects are: (1) levels of educational programming; (2) current terminology; (3) perceptual-motor theory; and perceptual motor theorists.

Levels of Educational Programming

In order to provide physical education activities and experiences appropriate for the individual, and to encourage progress through the medium of movement, the teacher must be fully cognizant of the spectrum of the motor domain. The following levels of educational programming will be discussed in this text: (1) infant stimulation; (2) early childhood education/preschool play; (3) elementary physical education; (4) junior and senior high school physical education; and (5) college/university physical education. In addition, athletic experience and physical education for the handicapped will also be briefly discussed (see Figure 2-2).

The goal of any adapted or general physical education program is for the children to achieve their maximum potential in the motor domain through physical education experiences. Each level of the model provides a means to that end, not the end in itself. Especially when teaching culturally determined forms of movement, the physical educator must remember to teach "individuals" rather than "games and sports."

The starting point for any given level of educational programming is, of necessity, somewhat arbitrary. The instructor should begin with activities and experiences at the lowest specified level of the developmental model, and progress upward.

Only the first levels of the model are appropriate in an *infant stimulation* program. Infants function primarily in the sensorimotor period of development (Piaget, 1936). This period relies heavily upon sensory input, and motor development is dominated by reflex activity and motor-sensory responses. The goal of in-

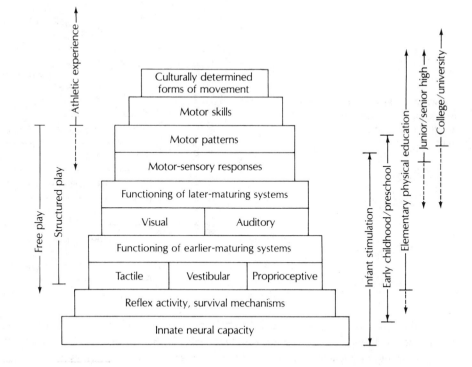

Figure 2-2. Levels of educational programming.

fant stimulation programs should be to enhance the processing of sensory input and integration with motor output, laying the foundation for further development.

Early childhood education programs usually include free play, because formally structured physical education instruction is unnatural to the preschool child. *Preschoolers* must be actively involved in movement experiences, especially large muscle activity. Sensory stimulation remains quite important during this time. The child is growing rapidly and exploring new ways of moving. Activities for this level should include those designed for the development or use of sensory stimulation, motor sensory responses, and motor patterns.

Elementary physical education programs range from sensory stimulation activities to culturally determined forms of movements. The primary emphasis should be placed upon the development of motor-sensory response, motor patterns, and basic motor skills. Games and some sports should be played, but as a culmination of physical education programming and

not as the focus of the program. Too often, participation in games and sports is paramount, without any regard for development of the prerequisite abilities and skills. The elementary physical educator must be able to task analyze the motor performance of young children to determine their needs and abilities in the motor domain. If necessary, activities may have to include those for reflex integration and sensory stimulation.

Although many differences are noticed between *junior and senior high school* students, a similar general trend exists in both physical education programs. Generally speaking, physical education programming at these levels assumes acquisition of motor skills. Although such programming seems appropriate, not all individuals may be functioning at this motor skill level. The focus of programs need not necessarily be changed if activities that allow for the refinement of basic motor skills and motor patterns can be included.

College and university physical education is primarily an elective program. Experiences are usually

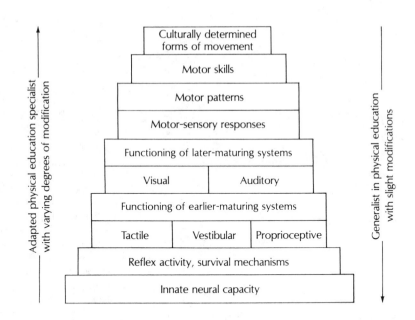

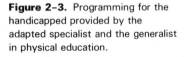

Figure 2-3. Programming for the handicapped provided by the adapted specialist and the generalist in physical education.

gained through athletics or in pursuit of recreational sports such as tennis, racquetball, or golf. Dance, weight training, physical fitness, yoga, and the like are pursued for similar reasons. Culturally determined forms of movement such as sports, dance, aquatics, and other physical activities comprise the majority of the physical education program at this level. Although, in the vast majority of cases, the motor skills and culturally determined levels of the pyramid can be safely assumed to be present, this assumption does not preclude knowledge and ability in the analysis of deficits in motor performance and assistance in skill acquisition on the part of the physical education instructor.

Athletic experience must be predicated upon motor skills and culturally determined forms of movement. The age of the beginning athletic experience is variable, and depends on a high level of skill acquisition. The athletic experience extends well beyond the top level of this model into quality or refined motor performance. The developmental nature of the model applies to athletics in that the learning process is sequentially ordered, hierarchical in nature, and results in skill acquisition; however, it does not imply quality or refinement of execution.

Physical education programming for the handicapped is certainly aided by the developmental model.

The levels of educational programming and activities are applicable to both handicapped and normal children. The severity of the handicapping condition will dictate educational placement and appropriate physical education services. Handicapped children may be served by a generalist in physical education, who will work with them in regular education; or by a specialist in adapted physical education; or by both.

The specialist in adapted physical education must be able to provide services throughout the entire model, with varying degrees of modification. Specialists will primarily work with the more severely involved children, but must also be able to offer consultation on the mildly impaired. Generalists in physical education must have a basic understanding of all the levels of the model, but will, in most instances, only plan and implement programs at the motor-sensory response/motor pattern level and above. Slight modifications will have to be included in the physical education program provided by the generalist (see Figure 2-3).

Current Terminology

The terms defined below are used quite commonly today. Unfortunately, they are used interchangeably by some authors, while others draw distinctions be-

Figure 2-4. Terminology and the developmental model.

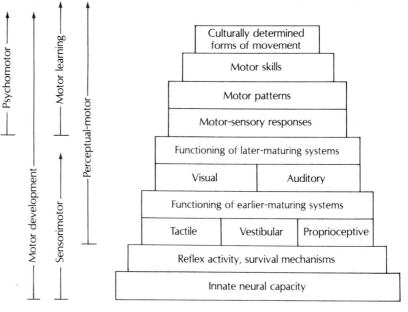

tween the terms. The authors of this text believe that these terms are parts of a whole, differentiated only by the aspect they tend to emphasize. For example, _motor development_ is the development of abilities essential to movement and necessary to the acquisition of motor skills; _motor learning_ takes the prerequisite motor abilities and turns them into skilled, controlled, consistent motor behavior. _Perceptual-motor_ and _sensorimotor_ are specialty areas within the motor domain; the former emphasizes the perceptual process, the latter emphasizes sensory stimulation.

Current terminology can be depicted in relation to the developmental model, although the terms tend to overlap levels. While drawing precise lines of demarcation between terms may be an academic exercise, understanding the conceptual relationship between the terms is of unquestionable value (see Figure 2-4).

Motor development encompasses (1) development of abilities that are essential to movement; and (2) the acquisition and refinement of motor skills. It is an extensive, lifelong process. Growth and maturation are terms usually associated, and sometimes used synonymously, with motor development. Specifically, _growth_ refers to measurable physical and biological changes; _maturation_ is the achievement of genetically endowed, developmental milestones. Motor develop-

ment is commonly thought of as occurring early in life, but should be considered to be an ongoing process.

Motor learning refers to one specific type of learning: the lessening of unpredictability resulting in more consistency in motor efficiency. Lockhart (1964:12) stated that motor learning "refers to actions instigated through sensory receptors, integrated through the nervous system, and modulated through the response mechanisms into controlled motor behavior." Motor learning is often thought of as occurring relative to the acquisition of motor skills, and this is its most common usage.

Perceptual-motor includes the interpretation and response made by an individual to a stimulus. _Perception_ refers to consciousness or awareness through the senses; the meaning or interpretation placed by the learner upon sensory stimulation; the selection, organization, and interpretation of sensory stimulation; and the precursor of action. Perceptual-motor is thought by some to be the learning of overt motor responses that result from primarily nonverbal stimuli. Under the terminology of perceptual-motor, motor responses generally cannot be easily separated from the perceptual stimuli.

The term _psychomotor_ (which is decreasing in

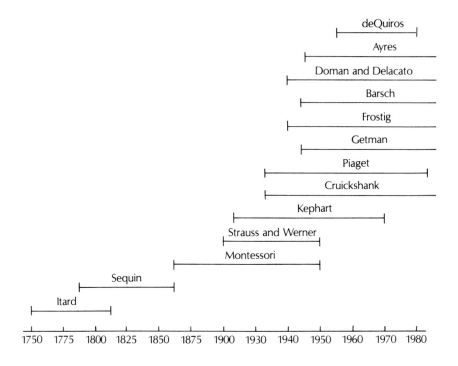

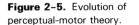

Figure 2-5. Evolution of perceptual-motor theory.

usage) refers to observable voluntary human movement and excludes involuntary reflex activity. Harrow (1972) stated that psychomotor refers to manipulative skills, motor skills, and other acts requiring neuromuscular coordination.

Sensorimotor refers to activities involving both sensory and motor components: sensory stimulation and the resulting motor response. The emphasis is placed upon sensory discrimination, integration, and organization. Although sensorimotor development is usually considered to take place within the first decade of life, the utilization of sensory information for motor output is an ongoing process.

Perceptual-Motor Theory

Although a developmental approach has been espoused by many authors and professionals in physical education over the last three decades, the impetus toward an understanding and acceptance of this approach has primarily been provided by professionals from the subdisciplines of motor development, motor learning, elementary physical education, and

adapted physical education. An understanding of the developmental model requires knowledge of a broad spectrum of development and learning within the motor domain, including information on the process of organizing, integrating, and utilizing sensory and perceptual stimuli. The following discussion is intended to assist the reader in synthesizing information basic to understanding the developmental approach (see Figure 2-5).

Much work has been done strictly in perceptual-motor theory, mostly outside of the physical education profession. The foundations can be traced to Jean Marc Itard, one of the first to work with the retarded — who, until then, had been locked up. Itard (1801) wrote about the retarded boy named Victor, "the wild boy of Averyon." In the early 1800s, Itard postulated the concepts of (1) progressive stages of individual development; (2) modification and adjustment by the teacher to meet the needs of the student; and (3) a relaxed yet stimulating environment as a potential factor in education.

Edouard Seguin, a French physician who studied under Itard and worked with Victor, is considered to be the founder of perceptual-motor theory. He developed a neurophysiological approach to teaching, which recognized the relationship between motor activity and sensory perception (1971).

Maria M. Montessori was much influenced by Seguin's work. Montessori's educational system, developed in 1912, emphasized sensorimotor processes. Her motto, "Help Me to Help Myself," became most evident in her individualized, experiential, self-paced, and independently oriented education programs.

During the 1930s, Swiss psychologist Jean Piaget began emphasizing the importance of early sensorimotor learning as fundamental building blocks for later, more complex perceptual and cognitive development. At the same time, two German immigrants to America, Alfred A. Strauss and Heinz Werner, were conducting experiments at Wayne County Training School that dealt with perception and perceptual-motor functions of mentally retarded individuals.

The early work of Strauss and Werner (1939) laid the foundation for other investigators, such as William Cruickshank and Newell C. Kephart. Cruickshank (1967) conducted many perceptual-motor studies with exogenous mentally retarded subjects (i.e., neurologically impaired) and cerebral palsied individuals. Kephart's most significant contribution was the publication of his book *Slow Learner in the Classroom* (1960), which presented a discourse on his perceptual-motor theory.

A more specifically neurologically oriented approach to perceptual-motor theory was expounded by G. Doman and C. H. Delacato in the 1960s (Delacato, 1963; Doman, 1974). Their theory of neurological organization — ontogeny recapitulates phylogeny — was brought to the forefront through work at the Institute for Development of Human Potential in the treatment of brain-damaged individuals.

The perceptual-motor theories of Gerald Getman and Ray Barsch (both of whom were influenced by their association with Kephart) and Marianne Frostig (who was indirectly influenced by the work of Werner and Strauss) gained prominence and acceptance in the 1960s. Getman (1968) proposed a visually oriented theory of treatment, while Barsch espoused a theory involving a spatial orientation (1967; 1968).

At about the same time, Bryant J. Cratty wrote of the perceptual-motor behavior of normal infants and children (1970). He was the first physical educator to become involved with perceptual-motor theory. Also during the 1960s, A. Jean Ayres and Julio B. deQuiros were developing their respective neurologically oriented theories of perceptual-motor learning and development. The initial publication of Ayres' emerging theory used the term "perceptual motor development" (1964), but it has recently been changed to the theory of "sensory integration" (1972). DeQuiros's approach has only recently gained exposure in the United States. DeQuiros and his coworkers in Argentina espouse a neuropsychological approach to intervention and understanding of learning problems (1978).

While some theories are remarkably similar and others are quite different from one another, all of the authors involved in the evolution of perceptual-motor theory include aspects of sensory input, perceptual processing, and motor output in their theories. The early theorists postulated generally regarding perceptual-motor function, its existence, and its relationship to growth, development, and learning. Most of the later theorists (including Ayres, Barsch, Doman and Delacato, Frostig, Getman, and Kephart) not only have postulated theory, but have also developed some sort of screening or assessment tool, remediation principles and techniques, and suggestions for perceptual-motor activities.

Perceptual-Motor Theorists

Because all perceptual-motor theories and approaches are strongly developmental in nature, one

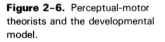

Figure 2-6. Perceptual-motor theorists and the developmental model.

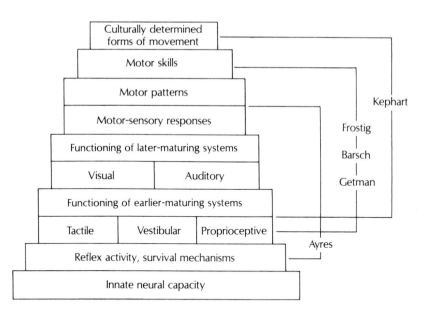

may follow any single theory and its prescribed methods and find that it is progressively sequenced. Each of the theorists fits into the developmental model at somewhat different levels (see Figure 2-6).

The lowest levels are represented by the theory of sensory integration proposed by Ayres, an occupational therapist. Sensory integration therapy is based on the child's needs, and consists of experiences with controlled sensory input resulting in increased neurological organization. Such experiences include activities for tactile stimulation through rubbing the skin with materials of different textures, and discriminatory touch perception by identifying and matching textures, shapes, and the like. Activities for vestibular stimulation include spinning and swinging, in addition to other proprioceptive stimulation from scooterboard riding. Kinesthetic stimulation and motor-planning demands are made using novel scooterboard activities, tasks while swinging, and numerous other motor-sequencing tasks both with and without vision. Visual perception per se is stimulated as it relates to the systems that subserve vision, and is addressed independently only when it has been determined that the child has a visual form and space dysfunction that is discrete from a dysfunction in any of the underlying systems or atypical reflex behavior.

In contrast to Ayres, Barsch, a special educator, has developed a movement theory known as *movigenics,* a learning system based on the efficiency of movement. Like other theorists, he believes that motor skills should be sequentially learned, with one motor skill based upon the learning of earlier skills until the desired level of motor functioning has been attained. Barsch considers movigenics as basic to thinking, and movement as basic to efficient cognitive processing. Movigenics is proposed as a precise system for assisting the child with spatial orientation, which in turn assists the child as a learner. Movigenics employs many different activities for reaching the goals of proprioceptive awareness, spatial diversity, movement synchrony, and shifting capacity. Unlike Ayres, Barsch tends to use common motor patterns and skills in rather uncommon ways to assist children in attaining total movement efficiency.

Frostig, a psychologist, maintains that most learning is acquired through the visual channel and, if development in visual perception is hindered, some cognitive deficits will result. She points out that a disability in visual perception may be the result either of delayed maturation, actual cerebral injury, or genetic and environmental factors. A variety of visual perception skills are addressed in Frostig's training program, including eye-hand coordination, perception and identification of specified figures placed against increasingly complex backgrounds, recognition of a variety of geometric shapes in varying positions, and copying of designs.

Getman, an optometrist, believes that perception — primarily visual perception — can be developed through motor training. According to Getman, visual perception is learned in a developmental sequence. He developed the theory of a visual-motor complex, in which visual perception is developed from the infant's earliest reflex behavior, progressing through locomotion, to the more sophisticated human responses of eye coordination, ocular-motor systems, and speech systems, until cognition and intelligence are developed. Getman suggests that visual perception can be developed by special training in general coordination, balance, eye-hand coordination, eye movements, form recognition, and visual memory. Unlike Ayres or Barsch, he is less concerned with movement for total development than with its specific effect on visual perception. His prescribed program uses the walking beam, chalkboard, and templates together with specific exercises for developing eye control and hand-eye coordination.

Newell Kephart, a psychologist, was one of the pioneers of the use of perceptual-motor training to increase a child's academic potential and for the remediation of learning disorders. Like the previously discussed theorists, Kephart believed that a child's behavior is based on early motor responses and that more complex behavior evolves out of less complex behavior. Kephart, who subscribed to the learning and memory theories of D. O. Hebb (1949), felt that if learning is to take place effectively, perception and movement must be matched — a process that occurs through a wide variety of sensory experiences and movement opportunities. As a result, movement and perception are joined and function as one. Kephart considered posture to be the primary pattern of movement, and vision the primary mode of percep-

tion, and that all other motor patterns and perceptions are based upon these. He conceived of learning as being dependent upon three additional basic movement generalizations: locomotion, contacting and receiving objects, and propelling objects. According to Kephart, laterality, directionality, body awareness, figure-ground discrimination, and symbol recognition are necessary for movement efficiency. Kephart also stressed ocular training for other activities in which the eye is required to pursue and fixate on specific objects. Kephart's perceptual-motor training program requires the use of walking boards, balance boards, trampolines, dance, games, and rhythmical activities.*

THE DEVELOPMENTAL MODEL

In order to understand the developmental model, a basic understanding of the terms *sensory* and *motor* is imperative. The word sensory first brings to mind the senses of sight, smell, taste, hearing, and touch. For the purposes of this text, however, sensory will refer to the systems most used in education: (1) tactile; (2) vestibular; (3) proprioceptive; (4) visual; and (5) auditory.

According to Moore, *sensory* implies the neurological "perception or perceiving of a stimulus" (1969:8). Sage wrote that "sensation may be viewed as the first stage in a multi-stage process of bringing order and organization out of the kaleidoscopic environment" (1971:67). *Sensation*, or the reception of sensory stimuli, provides the raw data through which the nervous system can organize and interpret the stimuli. The reaction to sensory stimuli is commonly referred to as the *motor response*. There is an inseparable link between sensory stimuli (*input*) and the motor response (*output*): for every sensory input, there is motor output. Therefore "all movement . . . is

*An annotated bibliography of selected perceptual-motor theorists is included in Appendix C.

the motor result of some preceding (sensory) stimuli'' (Sage, 1971:10).

These basic concepts of development, which are commonly accepted as facts, are fundamental to understanding of the developmental model:

1. Development is sequential.
2. The brain (central nervous system) needs sensory stimulation to function adequately.
3. An ''X'' (unknown) amount of sensory input, unique to each individual, is necessary for adequate functioning.
4. The brain tends to function as a whole.
5. The organization of the structure and function of the central nervous system is hierarchical.
6. A human being functions as a sensory-integrative-motor-sensory-feedback system.

It is generally accepted that each developmental step depends on a certain degree of maturation at previous steps. Piaget (1952) stressed early sensori-motor development as critical to the origins of intelligence. Ames and Ilg (1964) also emphasized the sequential manner of development. Herrick (1956) spoke of the evolutionary development of higher intellectual functions. Humphrey (1969) refers to early developmental stages as building blocks for later stages. A child inherits some innate behavior patterns, but maturation and expression depend on individual experience. As the brain develops along normal lines, growth follows a smooth, generally sequential, developmentally progressive pattern.

The brain needs sensory stimulation to function adequately. In cases of sensory deprivation, when the brain fails to receive the necessary stimulation, function is impaired (Solomon, 1961; Levine and Alpert, 1959; Melzack, 1962). Learning in and interacting with one's environment is a function of the brain; and one of the most basic demands of existence is the interpretation of and response to sensory stimuli, which is the primary task of the nervous system.

The quality of function depends on the type and amount of sensory stimulation. According to Moore (1975), an ''X'' or ''unknown'' amount of sensory input is unique to each individual and is needed for adequate brain function. Some people may need more sensory stimulation in all of their sensory systems, while others may need more sensory stimulation in selected systems.

In the process of receiving and then responding to stimuli, the human organism strives to maintain *homeostasis* — the ability of the human organism to maintain a state of neurological balance. As stimuli enter the sensory systems, they act as stressors and disturb homeostasis, which must then be gained anew by means of a respective, appropriate motor response. The drive toward homeostasis is inherent in human beings and reflects adequate neurological function.

It is generally accepted that the brain tends to function as a whole. Moore writes that, for ''normal function, the entire organism must work as an integrated whole'' (1973:35). She adds:

Without being facetious, one can state that intelligence resides in the total nervous system with emphasis on the higher centers and that it is totally dependent upon the proper functioning of the entire organism in its environment (1973:78).

As the nervous system evolved to meet the expanding needs of existence, the newer structures tended to duplicate older structures and functions and improve upon them. However, the higher levels still remained dependent upon the older, lower structures. A process of interaction with the environment and sensations that act upon the nervous system led to this evolutionary development (Ayres, 1972) (see Figure 2-7).

The organization of structure and function of the nervous system is hierarchical; that is, some structures and functions rank higher than others. The phyletically or evolutionarily older structures are found at the anatomically lowest and least complex level. The newer and phyletically later-maturing structures are found in the highest position. For optimum functioning, the higher levels of the brain depend upon adequate lower-level function. Additionally, this arrangement of structure and function implies an interdependence between the brain structures and their associated functions. In progressing from lowest to highest centers, the following general concepts apply (taken from Moore, 1973):

1. Growth, development and maturation begin in the spinal cord and end in the cortex.
2. Hierarchy of control and complexity of function increase with higher central nervous system structures.
3. Inhibitory centers tend to predominate over excitatory centers.
4. Reflexes and feedback loops (servomechanisms) become progressively more complex with higher structures.

The spinal cord is the lowest anatomical level, and is structurally and functionally the simplest in the central nervous system. Its importance lies in its mediation of spinal cord reflexes and conduction of neural impulses. Located anatomically higher, the brain stem receives sensory input from many sources, handles significant and massive integration, and has widespread influence over the rest of the brain. Just as human beings would not function without spinal reflexes, they would function less well without the complex sensory stimulation, integration, and motor responses mediated by the brain stem.

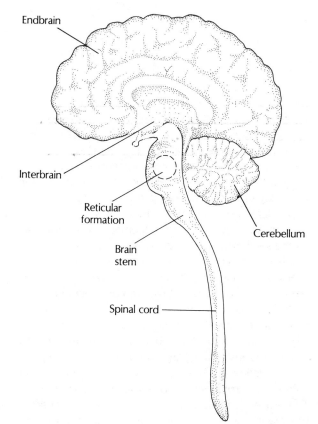

Figure 2-7. Parts of the brain.

Within the brain stem is found the *reticular formation*, considered to be the master control mechanism in the central nervous system. The reticular formation serves a general arousal and alerting function, and a central integrative role (e.g., inhibition, facilitation, augmentation, synthesis). It is also a selective network that decides upon information to be perceived and focused upon.

The *cerebellum* is a huge integration center, the primary function of which is that of integration and regulation. Its action has been linked most frequently to motor output acting to smooth and coordinate action and influence muscle tone.

The *diencephalon* (or *interbrain*) and *encephalon* respectively comprise the next to highest and highest levels of the central nervous system. Their respective functions are most complex. The *telencephalon* (or *endbrain*) includes the basal ganglia, limbic lobe system, and cerebral cortex. The limbic lobe system, or "old cortex," is the primary memory storage area of the brain. These higher centers organize sensory activity at their respective levels and influence integration at the lower levels. Processing at the cortical level is dependent upon subcortical processes. As the level of function increases, behavior becomes less stereotyped. As the level of sensory organization increases, more emphasis is placed upon analysis and precise interpretation; as the level of organization decreases, more emphasis is placed upon sensorimotor integration.

Tactile, vestibular, proprioceptive, visual, and auditory input continually impinge upon the human organism, placing demands that help determine the growth of the nervous system. An individual's innate neural capacity influences responses that allow for interaction with the environment and promote development. The process begins with enhancing development at the lower, less complex levels of structure and response and, in turn, enables the individual to become more competent at the higher, more complex levels.

Sensory Systems

Sequential development is inherent in the sensory systems. The sequence is also hierarchical, inasmuch as the later-maturing sensory systems (visual and auditory) are dependent upon the earlier-maturing sensory systems (vestibular, tactile, and proprioceptive). According to Trevarthen and others, "vestibular, tactile and proprioceptive systems may all receive stimulation before birth . . ." (1974:99–100). At birth the vestibular, tactile, and proprioceptive systems are almost completely mature and functional, whereas the visual and auditory systems are not as mature and consequently not as fully functional (see Figure 2–8).

Vestibular System

The vestibular system responds to the influences of gravity and accelerated or decelerated movements (Ayres, 1978). The vestibular receptors are specialized proprioceptors that are specifically housed in nonauditory organs in the inner ear (i.e., semicircular canals, utricle, and saccule) and are dedicated to posture, equilibrium, muscular tone, and spatial orientation. Vestibular information is obtained through the eyes, proprioceptors throughout the body, and the vestibular membranous labyrinth (i.e., the semicircular ducts, utricle, saccule, and cochlear duct of the middle ear). The vestibular system acts chiefly through the vestibular-spinal tracts and vestibular-oculomotor pathways, sending impulses to the rest of the central nervous system via the coordinating structure known as the cerebellum (deQuiros and Schrager, 1978).

The vestibular system develops early in life and is a highly mature system that functions well before birth (Klosovskii, 1963; Korner and Thoman, 1972). Humphrey wrote that the vestibular system is "unquestionably functional at twenty-one weeks of gestation" (1965:51). It contributes to the development of postural responses and equilibrium by preserving head position on a constant plane; it is a determinant in spatial orientation to the environment by directing the gaze of the eyes (deQuiros and Schrager, 1978; Leach, 1960); it modifies muscle tone contributing to physical growth and development (Kantner, 1976); and promotes cortical arousal (Ayres, 1972; deQuiros and Schrager, 1978).

The vestibular system is also thought to be more influential during early development than the other sensory systems (Klosovskii, 1963; Korner and Thoman, 1972). Clark, Kreutzberg, and Chee (forthcoming) and Gregg and others (1976) found that, by providing additional vestibular stimulation, the rate of motor development can be increased and the ability of the eyes to follow objects can be improved.

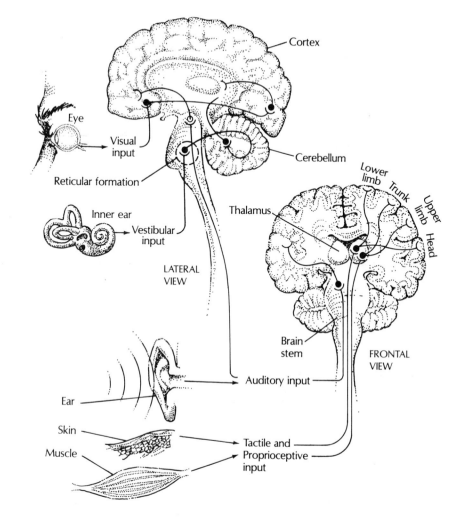

Figure 2-8. The central nervous system, showing the main flow of sensory information from each system's receptors to the brain.

The vestibular system is a special proprioceptive system that functions to maintain equilibrium, muscle tone, position of the head in space, and an awareness of motion. It provides widespread influence throughout the central nervous system and contributes to the coordination and timing of all sensory input for enhancement of perception.

Tactile System

The tactile system, also known as the touch-pressure or tactile-touch system, receives stimuli from the receptors beneath the skin. This system can be divided into two levels: *touch and tactile*. Touch refers to the primary or older sense, characterized by nondiscriminating, nonlocalized, and generalized information. Knowing that one's clothing is in place or that one is being touched in a crowded elevator comes from information provided at this first level. Tactile is the newer, later-developing sense, able to discriminate among and localize tactile stimuli. Distinguishing the type of fabric in one's clothing and on what body parts the elevator crowd is pressing are examples of tactile-level information. Both are important for growth and development.

The tactile sense is a predominant one throughout

life, critical to life support and related to development. Several studies have been undertaken with exceptional individuals to investigate these aspects. McCracken (1975) investigated the tactile perception ability of educable mentally retarded children and found that they were significantly inferior to normal children in tactile discrimination. Rice (1975) found that premature infants responded to sensory stimulation and made significant gains in weight, neurological development, and mental functioning. Additional studies by Bauer (1977a and b) of tactile sensitivity, and Ayres (1964) of tactile function, conclude that a positive relationship exists between the tactile system and human behavior. Huss (1977) discussed the premise that sensory input, especially tactile stimulation, can influence motor output. The development of tactile functions is closely linked with general neural development in that, up to eight or nine years of age, the degree of integration of the tactile system is indicative of the degree of adequate functioning of the nervous system (Ayres, 1972).

Since its primary receptors are located in the skin, the primary function of the tactile system is to receive information from the environment. It helps in maintaining stability of the central nervous system through continuous bombardment of the brain by the tactile stimulation. It also serves an arousal and inhibitory role.

Proprioceptive System

The proprioceptive system receives information from receptors in the muscles, joints, ligaments, and bones. Most of these sensations do not reach a conscious awareness level. Proprioception has tremendous importance to motor development, since it is critical to the motor action of reflexes, automatic responses, and planned movement. *Kinesthesia*, the more commonly used term in physical education, is the awareness of joint positions and movement. Kinesthesia uses proprioceptive information for planned movement.

Proprioception involves a basic subcortical awareness of body parts and their locations. Kinesthesia, then, consciously uses specific proprioceptive input to move and regulate a body segment appropriately. In physical education, the kinesthetic sense is employed in the acquisition of motor patterns, motor skills, and culturally determined forms of movement.

The importance of proprioception to the developmental approach is threefold: (1) it helps to maintain normal muscle contraction; (2) it influences muscle tone; and (3) it aids in visual space perception. Proprioception results in a basic awareness of the body's position in space and provides information for the conscious, purposeful, and planned movement needed for kinesthesia. The continuous flow of proprioceptive stimulation supports the motor component in maintaining muscle contraction and muscle tone. The flow of proprioceptive information through the integrative structures of the brain also contributes to visual space perception by supplying concrete information regarding the size and shape of the environment.

Auditory System

The auditory system is the hearing sense, which receives stimuli through the ear. This is a very intricate and complex system. The stimuli enter at the ear and are represented bilaterally almost as soon as they enter. As input passes through the nervous system, it makes many different connections and travels directly or indirectly to the cortex. The indirect path leads through brain structures that contribute to the general arousal and inhibition of the central nervous system at the cerebellar level. As impulses travel through integrative brain structures, the auditory system becomes closely associated with the visual system. The auditory system also has a close association with the vestibular system, since the receptors are in proximity to one another in the inner ear and they share the same cranial nerve (vestibulocochlear).

Visual System

The visual system processes stimuli received through the eyes, and needs light stimulation in order to develop and to ensure maturation of vision through myelination (neurological maturation) of the optic nerve. Vision is reflexive in nature at the lower neurological levels, and becomes increasingly complex and intricate as the system matures and reaches the higher, cortical levels of functioning. Each eye sends impulses to both cerebral hemispheres, a factor that contributes to the complexity of the system. Each eye has a visual field that is divided into halves. The right visual field of each eye transmits information to the left hemisphere, and the left visual field transmits to the right hemisphere. This phenomenon, which results in accurate visual system function, necessarily involves communication between the two hemispheres of the brain. For the most part, humans are extremely dependent upon adequate functioning of the complex and intricate visual system.

Human Development

A thorough understanding of human development is imperative for the teacher of adapted physical education. Human beings rely implicitly on a series of relative values; and unless one understands the criteria for acceptable standards, deviations from those standards are indiscernible or, at best, difficult to evaluate. A great deal of data has been gathered both empirically and experimentally for the purpose of understanding human development.

A few basic principles of human development will help to explain the overall process of motor development:

1. Motor development occurs in a cephalo-caudal fashion; that is, development proceeds from head to foot.

2. Motor development occurs in a proximo-distal fashion; that is, from the center of the body outward.

3. Function influences structure of the human body; that is, the use or activity of the human organism determines to a large extent the physical growth of the body.

4. Motor development proceeds from massed, undifferentiated movements to automatic, specific, volitional motor control.

5. Among normal children, there is a great deal of variation in the age at which developmental milestones are achieved; development does occur sequentially, however, and ages of accomplishment should be considered average.

Motor development follows a sequential order and refers to the acquisition and refinement of motor behavior. An individual will normally pass through the various stages of motor development, achieving the milestones along the way. (See Appendix B for a comprehensive listing of developmental milestones and motor behavior exhibited in normal growth and development.)

The relationship between sensory and motor functions has been studied and commented upon in the literature since the late nineteenth century, when Munsterberg (1899) and others developed theories to explain the marriage between the sensory and motor systems. The early twentieth century saw more theories reported in the literature, with Sherrington (1906) and Montessori (1912) lending their unique rationales to the functioning of the whole organism.

Piaget (1936), using empirical evidence for his developmental theory, emphasized the importance of early sensorimotor learning as "fundamental building blocks" for later more complex perceptual and cognitive development. Herrick (1956:315) reiterated the evolutionary process of the brain's development and described its primary function as one of transforming patterns of sensory experiences into patterns of motor responses. This notion has been clearly documented in more sophisticated brain research over the past twenty-five years, producing more convincing evidence that, in reality, we cannot deal with, teach, or treat the motor component of human performance separate from the sensory component.

Moore (1973) pointed out that only when working with animals in a lab can one fractionate an organism in order to study only one component of the whole. In contrast, a human being functions as a sensorimotor organism or, as Moore puts it, as a "sensori-integrative-motor-sensory-feedback system" (1973:22). Frostig summed it up this way:

> All movement is best understood as [sensorimotor] activity. Conscious, controlled movement depends on sensory input; therefore all movement education can be considered to be [sensorimotor] training, whatever form it takes. The teacher needs to study both the sensory and the motor aspects of movement, and these should also be considered equally in educational programs (1971:73).

Innate Neural Capacity

The developmental model reflects the relationship and interdependence of motor development and sensory systems. Each individual, handicapped or not, is born with an innate neural capacity. This predetermined capacity undergirds development and has a potential that is influenced by experiences to which the organism is exposed. Since function and structure are interrelated, the structural potential of the human nervous system, impinged upon by environmental experiences, determines whether the functional potential of that innate neural capacity will be realized.

Reflex Activity

Early motor activity is comprised of dominating reflexive responses to various forms of sensory stimuli. The early reflexes are vital to the human organism's drive for survival. An individual is born with primitive reflexes that are necessary for survival, and which later become inhibited or integrated into the central nervous system for future use. Other reflexes remain with the individual throughout life, and still others must be developed in order for the organism to achieve full potential. All reflex activity is important for the further development of neuromuscular function (see Figure 2–9).

Earlier-Maturing Systems

Practically at birth, the earlier-maturing sensory systems are functioning with incredible precision. The infant's violent reactions to the tactile stimulation of wetness, cold, and heat are testimony that the tactile system is delivering adequate quantities of meaningful stimuli to the brain. In turn, the brain is sending impulses to motor effectors, resulting in responses of crying, leg thrusting, and circular arm movements.

The vestibular system has conclusively demonstrated its maturity within the first week of life among infants studied by deQuiros (1961) and others. Axial rotation of an individual as slow as two degrees per second can be recognized by this sensitive system. Tests of middle and inner ear structures (i.e., otological tests) are used to determine normal function of the vestibular system. These include caloric and linear acceleration tests (described in Part II), which generate nystagmus — movement of the eyeballs elicited by stimulation of the semicircular canals of the vestibular system (deQuiros, 1978:156; Ayres, 1975:1).

Rather sophisticated proprioception is also demonstrated quite early in life. Since reflex activity underlies these early maturing systems and most postural "reflexes are elicited by stimulation of the sensory end organs in the muscles and joints" (Bobath, 1965:9), it is clear that the very young infant is capable of perceiving and responding to proprioceptive stimuli. The

Figure 2–9. Interfering reflexes. This boy has an interfering reflex that causes his head and hips to flex when he kicks (left). A residual reflex that should have disappeared between four and six months of age causes this boy's right arm to flex when he turns his head to catch the beanbag (right).

functioning of these earlier-maturing sensory systems depends, at least in part, on the innate neural capacity and the reflex activity of the newborn child. Thus if the innate neural capacity of an individual precludes normal reflex activity or perception of some forms of stimuli to these earlier-maturing systems (by damage or disease), functioning of the organism will be disturbed.

Later-Maturing Systems

The immature functioning of the visual system early in neonatal life is well documented in the literature. Kephart (1971) refers to what infants see in their visual fields as "blobs." Regardless of the accuracy of this description, it is common knowledge that the quality of visual stimuli entering the central nervous system during infancy far from matches the sophistication of that received from the earlier-maturing systems. The interdependence of the visual system with the earlier-maturing systems is pointed out by Gesell and Armatruda. They noted that infants move their hands, the active explorers, and watch them with their eyes, the learners. In this way, the eye is taught where an object is located in space. Through proprioceptive information from the hand, arm, and extraocular muscles, and through tactile information from the hand, the texture, shape, and size of the object are learned. "The

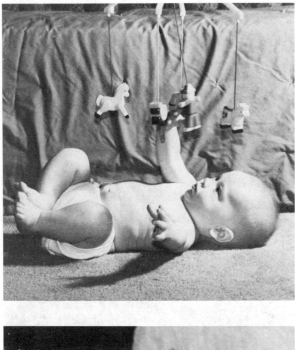

Figure 2-10. Eye-hand interaction. The infant sees the mobile (above left) and guides hand to make contact (above right). Once the coordination between visual and proprioceptive information is learned, only proprioception is needed to enable the infant to "steer" itself through its environment (left).

eye learns under the active tutelage of the hand" (Gesell and Armatruda, 1941). Thus, according to Kephart, eye-hand coordination develops by achieving this first step of hand-eye coordination (1971:21) (see Figure 2-10).

The interaction between the visual and vestibular systems, one of the earlier-maturing systems, is dramatically demonstrated by the reception of a certain type of visual stimuli. For example, if you were to watch a rapidly rotating object such as a merry-go-round, or a person moving under a flashing strobe light, even though you were stationary, you would probably feel as though you were in motion. This sensation demonstrates the phenomenon described by Jung, Kornhuber, and Da Fonseca (1963), in which the authors suggest that the convergence of visual and vestibular stimuli probably occurs in the brain stem before it ever reaches cortical levels and, therefore, the brain perceives vestibular input even though the stimuli are coming from the visual modality.

The relationship between the auditory system and the earlier-maturing systems is probably not as well understood as the corresponding bond between the visual system and the others. Hearing, like vision, does not show an early level of sophistication. The perception of undifferentiated sounds in infants is evident when an infant shows the startle reaction; but the ability to distinguish the meaning of familiar sounds, such as mother's voice, is not reported by developmentalists until at least four months of age. Presumably, the infants' own undifferentiated sounds at this age are representative of what they are perceiving auditorily. Again, the proprioceptive system is called upon to "teach" the ears to make auditory-motor associations. According to Kephart (1971:260), a baby's rattle probably serves this purpose. At about three to four months, infants use proprioceptive information to vary the pitch of their vocalizations by tensing and relaxing the muscles of the vocal folds. A very close relationship also exists between the auditory and vestibular systems, in that stimuli entering one system influence the other through their shared neural structures.

Motor-Sensory Responses

As the infant continues to develop, more complex, appropriate motor-sensory responses are observed. Although movement has been observed in the infant from birth, most of these have been reflexive responses to stimuli from the earlier-maturing sensory systems. As the visual and auditory systems become more sophisticated, greater quantities and increased quality of sensory input are made available to the central nervous system for its use. As this occurs, more complex, appropriate, and purposeful movements are noted in the infant. These are voluntary motor responses. Piaget (1936) described an increasing ability in the infant to interact with objects and show repetitive movements that later develop into motor patterns. Responses to the external environment that appear at this stage, such as reach and grasp, are evidence that integration of sensory stimuli is taking place and praxis or motor planning is evolving. The initial signs of volitional reaching, grasping, and manipulating are examples of the most primitive functioning of human

beings as sensory-integrative-motor-sensory-feedback systems. It is not until an infant's movements become purposeful and willful that we can say the infant is demonstrating a true motor-sensory response.

Motor-sensory responses are observable motor behaviors that specifically require much use of sensory input, and that provide the basis for and are requisite to the development of motor patterns. These responses include eye-hand interaction, eye-foot interaction, the ability to use each side of the body together and in opposition, the ability to isolate body segments for use, the ability to cross the midline of the body, the ability to plan and execute purposeful, nonhabitual movement (praxis), as well as the ability to maintain balance.

Motor Patterns

As mentioned earlier, motor patterns evolve out of and are more accurate forms of motor-sensory responses. As infants repeatedly use a motor response as a result of sensory feedback, they demonstrate patterns such as reaching, twisting, or pulling. These patterns serve a functional purpose for development, such as obtaining an object, rolling over, or creeping. "Motor patterns are the foundation for more complex learnings because the motor pattern provides the basis for meaningful orientation" (Roach and Kephart, 1966:7).

Motor patterns are those major motor milestones that develop within the natural sequence of events in a child's life, are common to normal individuals, and represent simple, purposeful movement. Motor patterns include head raising, rolling over, crawling, creeping, climbing, walking, sliding, running, throwing, jumping, hopping, leaping, kicking, and striking. Skipping and galloping are not considered motor patterns, but combinations of patterns — skipping is made up of walking (stepping) and hopping, while galloping combines walking and leaping.

Motor Skills

Motor skills, which emanate out of motor patterns, represent a much more accurate and specific use of motor patterns and combinations of patterns. They also represent a much higher level of integration between the sensory and motor systems. Walking, an infantile pattern, evolves into walking on a line, in a specified direction, or with a specific amount of speed — a skill. Stepping and hopping are patterns that, when combined, become the skill of skipping, a

much more complex, accurate and specific motor response. Catching emanates from the motor-sensory responses of reaching, grasping, and eye-hand interaction, and may involve the patterns of walking, sliding or running (see Figure 2-11).

Forms of Movement

Culturally determined forms of movement are exceedingly more complex refinements of motor skills. Receiving a forward pass in football requires appropri-

Figure 2-11. This girl is just developing the catching pattern.

Figure 2–12. Culturally determined forms of movement depend on refinements of motor skills. Only limited success is possible for this physically handicapped student (left); execution of this yoga posture depends on knowing where one's body parts are in space (right).

ate reflex behavior, incredibly complex integration of sensory stimuli, and increased specificity of motor responses and patterns for successful completion of the task. An individual who has never played football, or whose development is impaired at any level of development or stage of this process, would probably be unsuccessful at this task (see Figure 2–12).

Functions at each level of this model are dependent upon adequate functioning at each of the lower levels of the model. For example, free-kicking a soccer ball first requires innate neural capacity that determines the capability of the kicker to conceptualize and plan the kick. Appropriate reflex activity, such as assistance from ocular, head, and neck-righting reflexes, is also needed. In addition, there can be no interference from the tonic labyrinthine or symmetrical tonic neck reflexes. Adequate functioning of earlier-maturing systems such as proprioceptive (telling where the body parts are in space), vestibular (telling when the kicker is in motion), and tactile (giving information about when the ball is contacted) are all needed. Visual fixation supports the motor response of eye-foot interaction, while auditory stimuli verify the contact with the ball. The patterns of walking, running, and kicking are further supported by the motor-sensory response of balance. Kicking in a specified direction is a skill further refined to the culturally determined skill of free-kicking a soccer ball. Unless functioning at each level is appropriate, more complex, accurate, and specific functions at higher levels of the developmental model will be impaired. Thus motor performance can be seen to be truly complex; not as motor behavior, per se, but as an observable manifestation of the inner workings of the human organism in motion.

SENSORY-INTEGRATIVE-MOTOR-SENSORY-FEEDBACK SYSTEM

A human being cannot have just motor behavior or just perception; thus a more descriptive term such as sensorimotor or perceptual-motor would represent the true functional capabilities of the total nervous system. Sensory-integrative-motor-sensory-feedback sys-

---

The following principles underlying the sensory-integrative-motor-sensory-feedback system are suggested for advanced study:

1. Sequential development is inherent in neurology, the sensory systems, and the motor system.
2. There is functional interdependence between the structures and related functions in the brain.
3. There is intersensory modality association.
4. There is an inseparable link between the sensory input and motor output.
5. A very plastic (or nonrigid) nervous system enables human beings to be one of the least specialized and most versatile species on earth (Moore, 1973).
6. The individual-environment interaction is the basis for growth, development, and learning.
7. Movement is one of the most powerful organizers of sensory input (Ayres, 1972).

---

tem is an all-encompassing term, based on sound neurological principles, that provides the basis for understanding the developmental model.

Each stage of this system will be discussed in detail, in order to clarify the interaction between the sensory and motor systems. Having a global picture of how the human organism responds to and utilizes sensory information should also be useful to the adapted physical educator in using the developmental model.

Sensory Input

The functions of the sensory systems discussed above — tactile, vestibular, proprioceptive, visual, and auditory — along with gustatory (taste) and olfactory (smell) — constitute the full complement of ways through which information can reach the central nervous system. They are sources of *input;* that is, as with a computer, the information is *put into* the central nervous system (central core), where it is processed.

The normal human organism is subject to auditory and visual stimuli during most of the waking hours, and the forms of sensory input do not enter the central nervous system one at a time. Movement results in proprioceptive and vestibular stimuli entering the system, with tactile stimulation emanating from the environment (e.g., air, clothing, equipment, and so on). The normal human organism can receive and process this complexity of stimuli with little difficulty. When the organism is dysfunctioning, however, or the stimuli reaches unusual levels of quantity (intensity) or quality, extreme demands for adaptation are placed on the central nervous system. This adaptation normally occurs when a new skill is learned. The "snowplow" maneuver in downhill skiing, for example, requires that the body be placed in unusual postures, giving proprioceptive input that is intense and, at first, unusual. As learning proceeds, the position "feels more comfortable" or "more natural" as the central nervous system adapts to this new quality and quantity of sensory (proprioceptive) input.

Integration

A variety of terms and descriptors have been used in conjunction with discussions of the processing of sensory input, although the basic conceptualizations are similar. Sage uses the term *perception*, and defines it as "the process of organizing and giving meaning to sensory input, [which] therefore serves a useful function as a guide to behavior" (1971:67). Moore (1969) discusses this function as one of the *interpretations* by the nervous system of sensory input. Ayres has chosen the term *sensory integration*, and defines it as "the ability to organize sensory information for use" (1972:1). She further states that the sensory integrative processes "result in perception and other types of synthesis of sensory data that enable man to interact effectively with the environment" (1972:1).

Kephart writes that perception "supplies the information upon which behavior is based" (1971:19), whereas Marianne Frostig (1970) uses the term *associative process*. Based upon what is known about central nervous system function, there seem to be many steps through which this incoming sensory input is processed.

The first step is *reception*. The sensory input is first received or recorded at some level of the central nervous system as a sensation. This is not to imply that the individual is consciously (cortically) aware of the reception, but that some structure or structures of the central nervous system must be aware in order for the input to be processed. Another step is *mediation*. Only the important information is conveyed to the higher levels of the central nervous system. *Modulation* is another step in which present input from several sources serves to regulate or bring meaning to the collective input. *Association*, which requires retrieval from memory in order to make the necessary

comparisons, takes place between present input and past input. *Sequencing* (putting the information in appropriate order), *motor planning*, and *imagery* ("picturing" what the response should look or feel like) are also parts of this process. Thus the input is treated through a highly sophisticated mechanism and process, the end result of which is integration—bringing together all the parts to form a whole in preparation for a motor response.

Motor Output

Continuing the computer analogy, once the central core of the computer has treated the input data, there is output from this process. In a computer, this output is usually in the form of printed pages, but may be displayed on a screen or stored elsewhere in the computer for later use. In human beings, all observable behavior is motor behavior or motor output. As with the computer, the central nervous system sends messages through efferent neural pathways to motor effectors in order to create it. Whether the output is in the form of throwing a ball, writing a sentence, or speaking, the central processing is the same and the result is motor output.

For example, the physical educator may give the command to Mark, a student, to "Step up onto the balance beam, walk to the other end, and step off." Mark must first *receive* or hear the command, and must visually *receive* or see the beam somewhere in his visual field. There may be other sounds in the gymnasium and other objects in the field of vision, but his central nervous system *mediates* the input and allows only that related to the task to go to higher centers for processing. At the same time, *association* is taking place. The words used in the verbal command must be associated with the meaning of the words retrieved from the brain's memory bank in order for Mark to understand the required task. This is coupled with treatment of the visual input to associate the words "balance beam" with the visual stimulus. Mark's brain then _modulates these_ two primary sources of input in order to sequence and plan what the output will be. His brain is also using imagery to picture what the output will look like and feel like before there is any observable response from Mark at all. These final stages prepare the central nervous system to utilize later feedback. Once the input is _integrated,_ messages are sent to the appropriate muscle groups for _motor output_ and Mark performs the task.

Feedback

"Feedback is the information that an individual receives as a result of some response" (Sage, 1971:336). It is a vital aspect in the sensory-integrative-motor-sensory-feedback system, because if this link (or any other link) in the system is deleted, the human organism ceases to exist as such (Moore, 1973). According to Moore (1973), there are many feedback loops within the nervous system vital to maintaining integration and homeostasis within the organism. These feedback loops exist at all levels of the central nervous system, becoming increasingly intricate and complex when progressing from the lowest to the highest levels of the central nervous system.

Sage (1971) states that one of the most critical variables affecting the efficiency and effectiveness of motor skill learning and performance is feedback. Kephart (1971) writes of feedback creating a closed system of control, which becomes self-monitoring. As the feedback reenters on the input end of the system, becoming in itself a part of input, it continues to do so until the "feedback exactly matches the input" (1971:113). He calls this process _perceptual-motor match._ Ayres uses the term _sensory feedback,_ and states that the "execution of an adaptive response is dependent upon continual sensory feedback", (1972:32). She goes on to say that hazy or vague feedback interferes with functions that enable develop-

ment. Moore (1969) views feedback as an important function in learning. Normal feedback would perpetuate the normal learning cycle; but with abnormal central nervous systems, the "faulty feedback perpetuates the cycle causing abnormal input resulting in exaggerated faulty feedback" (1969:92). The quality of feedback becomes vitally important in this cycle, since it becomes the new input used in continual central processing.

Mark's walk on the balance beam uses the visual, vestibular, proprioceptive, and tactile input received while on the beam for processing. The challenge is not only to receive this new input, but also to modulate and associate it with the auditory input (i.e., the command) in order to generate the appropriate output — a match between what is requested and what is performed. Another function of feedback is to provide information to the brain's memory bank for future use. Had Mark not recognized the language symbols used in the command or the visual stimulus of the beam, or had he not been able to associate that information with previous experience (information retrieved from memory), he would have had difficulty planning the motor output and using the feedback (see Figures 2–13 and 2–14).

As can be seen from the figure, without the feedback, a performer would have no way of knowing whether or not the performance is correct. There are many situations in motor performance, however, in which the output appears to be the product of an open loop system rather than a closed loop system, as pictured here. Swinging a bat and missing a breaking pitch, making a typographical error, or missing a tennis ball that has top-spin are all examples of motor output that the performer "knows" are incorrect. These performances are all products of the closed loop system, but the feedback from the output modulated with the new input cannot be integrated rapidly enough for the adaptation in the output to be made. Therefore the output is incorrect. The performer

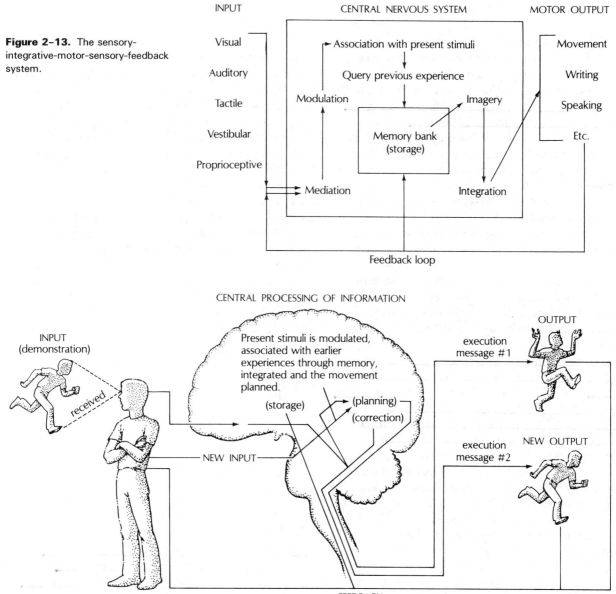

Figure 2–13. The sensory-integrative-motor-sensory-feedback system.

INPUT   CENTRAL NERVOUS SYSTEM   MOTOR OUTPUT

Visual
Auditory
Tactile
Vestibular
Proprioceptive

Association with present stimuli
Query previous experience
Modulation   Imagery
Memory bank (storage)
Mediation   Integration

Movement
Writing
Speaking
Etc.

Feedback loop

CENTRAL PROCESSING OF INFORMATION

INPUT (demonstration)

received

NEW INPUT

Present stimuli is modulated, associated with earlier experiences through memory, integrated and the movement planned.

(storage)
(planning)
(correction)

OUTPUT

execution message #1

NEW OUTPUT

execution message #2

FEEDBACK

Figure 2–14. Example of how the sensory-integrative-motor-sensory-feedback system promotes learning new skills.

knows it is incorrect and the audience knows it is incorrect. The system simply cannot respond any faster.

The influence of the quality and quantity of sensory input on motor performance has been previously discussed. It is the individual's central nervous system that determines what that influence will be. If sensory input is adequate, integrated, and appropriate, and impulses are transmitted accurately to motor effectors, then appropriate, correct motor responses will be observed. On the other hand, if one stage of this process is disordered, then some degree of motor dysfunction will result.

One of the factors that can interfere with the integrity of this process is the central nervous system's responsivity to sensory input. As with all aspects of human behavior, there is a range of response within which normal functioning is observed. This range is the quality that accounts for the uniqueness of each human being. Outside these normal limits, human behavior is said to be atypical.

Certain minimum and maximum criteria must be met in order to generate an appropriate motor response. Generally speaking, these criteria are based on the sensitivity of a nerve fiber to the stimulus, the rate of central processing, and the rate at which an impulse can travel along that fiber or circuit of fibers. The limits set by these criteria allow the organism to function at a level of homeostasis. That is, if the stimuli stay within the limits set by these criteria, the central nervous system can mediate, modulate, and integrate the stimuli for appropriate and effective use. For example, Chris can sit in a college class and listen to a lecture, effectively utilizing, for her purposes, all the auditory and visual stimuli that she needs for learning. At the same time, many other forms of sensory stimuli are entering her central nervous system — voices in the hall, paper shuffling in the classroom, discomfort in her muscles from a tennis game. These sources of auditory, tactile, and proprioceptive input are considered by Chris's central nervous system to be unim-

portant and unrelated to her learning experience at the time. Her central nervous system mediates and masks out the extra information as unimportant, thus allowing her to attend only to the lecture. In this way, Chris is functioning at a level of homeostasis and, with the help of her central nervous system, is keeping her level of responsivity to sensory stimuli and her observable motor output (behavior) within normal, accepted limits.

On the other hand, people with disordered central nervous systems may display behaviors that fall outside these normal limits as a result of variance in responsivity to the sensory stimuli impinging on their central nervous systems. Each of our central nervous systems could be plotted along a responsivity continuum. A normal individual is in the middle, at a state of homeostasis. Individuals whose systems cannot appropriately use irrelevant stimuli are outside the parentheses, or at either end of this continuum (see Figure 2–15).

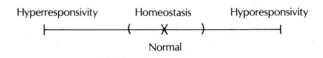

Figure 2–15. The responsivity continuum.

SUMMARY

The developmental approach is a vehicle that employs a myriad of methods and techniques in a predetermined, systematic way to facilitate growth and development among individuals with performance disorders, so that these individuals may approximate the norm and achieve their maximum potential. Application of the model puts into perspective the interrelatedness of levels of educational programming, current terminology, and perceptual-motor theories. The developmental model describes the emergence of culturally determined forms of movement based upon the innate neural capacity of an individual. Through understanding the developmental sequence evolving from the integrity of the central nervous system and reflex activity, the adapted physical educator can learn to consider students with special needs in terms of the functioning of sensory and motor systems rather than in terms of an educational classification that may or may not imply the students' levels of motor performance. With an understanding of how motor patterns and skills are acquired as a result of input and functioning of the sensory-integrative-motor-sensory-feedback system, deviations from normal responsivity to sensory input can be identified.

BIBLIOGRAPHY

Ames, L. B., and Ilg, F. L. "The Developmental Point of View with Special Reference to the Principle of Reciprocal Neuromotor Interweaving." *Journal of Genetic Psychology* 105 (1964): 195–209.

Ayres, A. J. "Tactile Functions: Their Relationship to Hyperactive and Perceptual-Motor Behavior." *American Journal of Occupational Therapy* 18 (1964): 6–11.

Ayres, A. J. *Sensory Integration and Learning Disorders.* Los Angeles: Western Psychological Services, 1972.

Ayres, A. J. *Southern California Postrotary Nystagmus Test Manual.* Los Angeles: Western Psychological Services, 1975.

Ayres, A. J. "Learning Disabilities and the Vestibular System." *Journal of Learning Disabilities* 11 (1978): 30–41.

Bauer, B. A. "Tactile Sensitivity." *American Journal of Occupational Therapy* 31 (1977a): 357–361.

Bauer, B. A. "Tactile-Sensitive Behavior in Hyperactive and Nonhyperactive Children." *American Journal of Occupational Therapy* 31 (1977b): 447–453.

Bobath, B. *Abnormal Postural Reflex Activity Caused by Brain Lesions.* London: William Heinemann Medical Books, Ltd., 1965.

Clark, D. L., Kreutzberg, J. R., and Chee, F. K. W. "Vestibular Stimulation Influence on Motor Development in Infants." Forthcoming.

Cratty, B. J. *Perceptual and Motor Development in Infants and Children.* Los Angeles: Macmillan Co., 1970.

Cruickshank, W. M. *The Brain-Injured Child in Home, School, and Community.* Syracuse, New York: Syracuse University Press, 1967.

Delacato, C. H. *The Diagnosis and Treatment of Speech and Reading Problems.* Springfield, Illinois: Charles C. Thomas, 1963.

Doman, G. *What to Do About Your Brain-Injured Child.* Garden City, New York: Doubleday, 1964.

Frostig, M., and Maslow, P. *Movement Education: Theory and Practice.* Chicago: Follett, 1970.

Frostig, M. "Program for Sensory-Motor Development at the Marianne Frostig Center for Educational Therapy." *Foundations and Practices in Perceptual-Motor Learning — A Quest for Understanding*. Washington, D.C.: American Alliance for Health, Physical Education, and Recreation, 1971.

Gesell, A., and Armatruda, C. S. *Development Diagnosis*. New York: Harper and Bros., 1941.

Gregg, C. L., Haffner, M. E., and Korner, A. F. "The Relative Efficacy of Vestibular-Proprioceptive Stimulation and the Upright Position in Enhancing Visual Pursuit in Neonates." *Child Development* 47 (1976): 309-314.

Harrow, A. J. *Taxonomy of the Psychomotor Domain*. New York: D. McKay, 1972.

Hebb, D. O. *The Organization of Behavior*. New York: John Wiley & Sons, 1949.

Herrick, C. J. *The Evolution of Human Nature*. Austin, Texas: University of Texas Press, 1956.

Humphrey, T. "The Embryologic Differentiation of the Vestibular Nuclei in Man Correlated with Functional Development." *International Symposium on Vestibular and Oculomotor Problems*, vol. 51, Tokyo: Nippon-Hoechst, 1965.

Humphrey, T. "Postnatal Repetition of Human Prenatal Activity Sequences with Some Suggestions of their Neuroanatomical Basis." In *Brain and Early Behavior: Development in the Fetus and Infant*, edited by R. J. Robinson. New York: Academic Press, 1969.

Huss, A. J. "Touch with Care or a Caring Touch?" *American Journal of Occupational Therapy* 31 (1977): 11-18.

Itard, J. M. *Wild Boy of Averyon*. New York: Appleton-Century-Crofts, 1801.

Jung, R., Kornhuber, H. H., and Da Fonseca, J. S. "Multi-sensory Convergence on Cervical Neurons." In *Progress in Brain Research*, vol. I, edited by G. Moruzzi, A. Fessard, and H. H. Jasper. New York: Elsevier, 1963.

Kanter, R., et al. "Effects of Vestibular Stimulation on Nystagmus Response and Motor Performance in the Developmentally Delayed Infant." *Physical Therapy* 56 (1976): 414-421.

Kephart, N. C. *The Slow Learner in the Classroom*. 2d ed. Columbus: Charles E. Merrill, 1971.

Klosovskii, B. *The Development of the Brain and Its Disturbances by Harmful Effects*. New York: Macmillian Co., 1963.

Korner, A. F., and Thoman, E. B. "Relative Efficacy of Contact and Vestibular Proprioceptive Stimulation in Soothing Neonates." *Child Development* 43 (1972): 445-453.

Leach W. W. "Nystagmus: An Integrative Neural Deficit in Schizophrenia." *Journal of Abnormal and Social Psychology* 60 (1960): 305-309.

Levine, S., and Alpert, M. "Differential Maturation of the Central Nervous System as a Function of Early Experience." *AMA Archives of General Psychiatry* 1 (1959): 403-405.

Lockhart, A. S. "What's in a Name?" *Quest* monograph II (1964): 9-13.

McCracken, A. "Tactile Function of Educable Mentally Retarded Children." *American Journal of Occupational Therapy* 29 (1975): 397-402.

Melzack, R. "Effects of Early Perceptual Restriction on Simple Visual Discrimination." *Science* 137 (1962): 978-979.

Montessori, M. M. *The Montessori Method.* Cambridge, Massachussetts: Robert Bentley, 1965.

Montessori, M. M. *The Absorbent Mind.* New York: Holt, Rinehart and Winston, 1967.

Moore, J. C. *Neuroanatomy Simplified.* Dubuque, Iowa: Kendall-Hunt Publishing Company, 1969.

Moore, J. C. *Concepts from the Neurobehavioral Sciences.* Dubuque: Kendall-Hunt, 1973.

Moore, J. C. "Hemispheric Specialization." Lecture presented at the Hemispheric Specialization: Workshop on Brain Function at the University of California at San Diego Medical School, June 1975.

Munsterberg, H. *Psychology and Life.* Boston: Houghton Mifflin, 1899.

Piaget, J. *The Origins of Intelligence in the Child.* New York: Penguin Books, 1936.

Piaget, J. *The Origins of Intelligence in Children.* New York: International Universities Press, 1952.

deQuiros, J. B., Coriat, L. F., and Benasayag, L. "Hacia el Encuentro del Esquema Corporal a traves de las Respuestas Neurologicas Vestibulares." *Fonoaudiologica* (Buenos Aires) 7 (1961): 27–55.

deQuiros, J. B., and Schrager, O. L. *Neuropsychological Fundamentals in Learning Disabilities.* San Rafael, California: Academic Therapy Publications, 1978.

Rice, R. D. "Premature Infants Respond to Sensory Stimulation." *American Psychological Association Monitor* (November 1975).

Sage, G. H. *Introduction to Motor Behavior.* Menlo Park, California: Addison-Wesley, 1971.

Seguin, E. *Idiocy and Its Treatment by the Physiological Method.* New York: A. M. Kelley, 1971. (Reprint of the 1866 edition with bibliographical note by Harold Ruvin and Francesco Cordasco.)

Sherrington, C. S. *The Integrative Action of the Nervous System.* New Haven: Yale University Press, 1906.

Solomon, P., et al. *Sensory Deprivation.* Cambridge, Massachussetts: Harvard University Press, 1961.

Trevarthen, C. B. "Behavioral Embryology." In *Handbook of Perception,* vol. III, edited by E. C. Carterette and M. P. Freidman. New York: Academic Press, 1974.

Werner, H., and Strauss, A. A. "Problems and Methods of Functional Analysis in Mentally Deficient Children." *Journal of Abnormal and Social Psychology* 34 (1939): 37–62.

3   Disorders of Development

Guiding Questions

1. What is the difference between process disorders and developmental disorders?
2. What are the four possible sites of processing breakdown in the sensory-integrative-motor-sensory-feedback system?
3. What is the significance of abnormal reflex behavior to motor behavior?

Within the general population, there are two major types of disorders: process disorders and developmental disorders. Process disorders are related to impaired learning resulting from a breakdown in the sensory-integrative-motor-sensory-feedback system and responsivity. Although developmental disorders are often associated with process disorders, as in blindness or brain damage, this is not necessarily the case.*

PROCESS DISORDERS

A process disorder in the sensory-integrative-motor-sensory-feedback system may have as its source any one or a combination of four possible breakdown sites. Figure 3–1 shows a simplified version of this system.

Structural or functional impairment may prevent sensory stimuli from ever reaching the central nervous system (shown on Figure 3–1 as Breakdown Site #1).

*It should also be noted that, although these disorders do not always result in impairment of learning, this text focuses on the disorders as they result in the identification of children with special educational needs.

The neural impulses, as a result of damaged or dysfunctioning transmission routes, may not be transmitted or may be transmitted in such poor quantity or quality that the central nervous system cannot effectively utilize the information. Thus the learner is expected to perform based on inadequate sensory information. Some forms of blindness or deafness are extreme examples of breakdown at this site (see Figure 3–2).

Breakdown Site #2 symbolizes a breakdown in central processing. The information is reaching the central nervous system, but is not being effectively processed or integrated for an appropriate motor response. An extreme example of breakdown at this site is brain damage. Students with the learning disability known as dyslexia were once thought to have minimal brain damage or dysfunction because they saw letters in reverse. This transposition actually occurs in the central processing of information, even though the input is being received and transmitted to the central nervous system intact.

At Breakdown Site #3, the efferent pathways (those going from the brain to the muscles) are damaged or dysfunctional. Even though the individual knows what the task is and how to complete it, neural

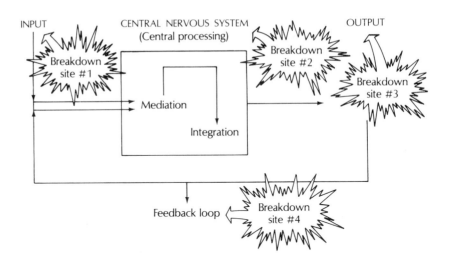

Figure 3-1. Possible sites of breakdown in the sensory-integrative-motor-sensory-feedback system.

transmission is inadequate to stimulate the muscles needed to do the task. This is commonly the case with incomplete paraplegics or quadraplegics.

Breakdown Site #4 occurs in the feedback loop. Faulty transmission of feedback results in poor quality and quantity of new input, and will assuredly decrease the ability of the performer to make progressively more adaptive responses to input. Dysfunction in afferent pathways (those going from the muscles to the brain) among clumsy children is an example of this problem. Even though all the anatomical structures needed to perform are intact, clumsy children cannot correct their movement errors. Faulty transmission of proprioceptive information prevents them from "feeling" their body's position in space and correcting or making an adjustment to the correct position.

Responsivity Disorders

A process disorder of responsivity may manifest itself in one of three ways: (1) hyperresponsivity; (2) hyporesponsivity; or (3) vacillating responsivity.

Hyperresponsivity

Individuals whose systems are hyperresponsive to any form of sensory stimulation demonstrate dramatic reactions to that stimuli. Hyperactive children, for example, are often described as "not paying attention," when they are actually paying too much attention. For example, Paul — a hyperactive child — simultaneously hears the voice of his teacher, the conversation of people in the hall, and the sounds of his classmate shuffling paper. Within the space of a few seconds, Paul may look at his teacher, run to the hallway, and turn to watch his classmate. His central nervous system is being overloaded with information that it cannot integrate. Just as water must overflow when poured into a bucket that is already full, these children's responses must also "overflow." Many children will show this type of response when several forms of stimuli enter the system simultaneously; other children will show this reaction only to specific forms of stimuli.

One variation of hyperresponsivity is described as "summating input." In this disorder, the child is able to respond appropriately to normal quantities and qualities of input for awhile, and therefore function within the limits of homeostasis. Due to intermittent central nervous system dysfunction, however, after a period of time the system seems to allow the input to add up or "summate," and the individual is thrown into a state of overloading. The reaction to stimuli then becomes hyperresponsive, and behavior is observed to be hyperactive (see Figure 3-3a).

Figure 3-2. Organic examples of breakdown sites.

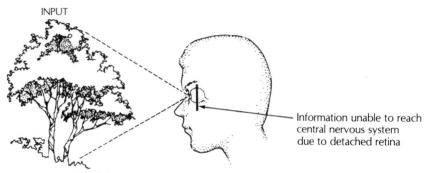

Information unable to reach central nervous system due to detached retina

a. Breakdown at site #1: example of input breakdown of visual system due to detached retina.

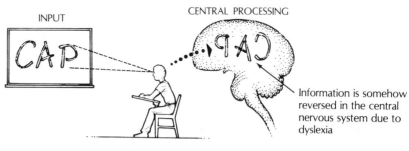

Information is somehow reversed in the central nervous system due to dyslexia

b. Breakdown at site #2: example of processing breakdown in visual system due to dyslexia.

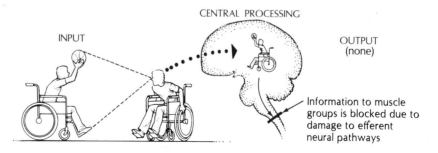

Information to muscle groups is blocked due to damage to efferent neural pathways

c. Breakdown at site #3: example of output breakdown of proprioceptive system due to quadraplegia.

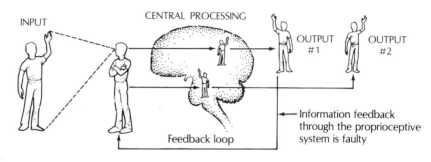

Information feedback through the proprioceptive system is faulty

d. Breakdown at site #4: example of feedback breakdown of proprioceptive system in clumsy child.

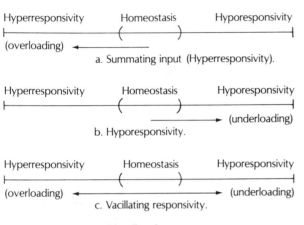

a. Summating input (Hyperresponsivity).

b. Hyporesponsivity.

c. Vacillating responsivity.

Figure 3-3. Responsivity disorders.

Hyporesponsivity

Hyporesponsive individuals are on the other end of the continuum from those who are hyperresponsive. Severely multihandicapped and brain-damaged individuals, as well as individuals with peripheral nerve damage, often display little or no response to the stimuli around them. For example, the severance of afferent peripheral nerves (as may be seen in paraplegia) precludes perception and hence responsivity, since no nerve impulses reach the brain. Although they may be capable of receiving stimuli, those individuals with higher lesions in the central nervous system or who have abnormally high thresholds require exceedingly large quantities of stimuli in order to generate a response. Because their sensory systems are underloaded, they need greater quantities or improved quality of input in order to activate neural structures. As opposed to the "full bucket" analogy of the hyperresponsive individual, stimuli entering the hyporesponsive system can be compared to pouring water into a bucket that has a hole in the bottom (see Figure 3-3b).

The following discussion is offered as further explanation of vacillating responsivity for the advanced student. Differences in responsivity appear to be due to some sort of breakdown in the inhibitory process. This process, when working in reverse, results in excitation of neural structures and is precipitated by neural impulses causing release of an inhibitory transmitter in the synapse. This inhibitory transmitter then acts on the postsynaptic neuron, hyperpolarizing the membrane and thus raising the threshold and making it more difficult for the postsynaptic neuron to fire (Sage, 1971:56). According to Abuladze (1968), there are no predetermined inhibitory patterns in the central nervous system, but the process of inhibition is always associated with stimulation. It is logical to assume that, in the case of individuals with atypical responsivity to sensory stimulation, one of three types of disruptions may be occurring in the inhibitory process:

1. The inhibitory transmitter is not being secreted; thus the postsynaptic neuron continues to fire, resulting in hyperresponsivity.
2. The inhibitory transmitter is being secreted all the time as a result of unknown stimuli; thus hyporesponsivity to sensory stimuli is observed.
3. There is irregularity in the secretion of the inhibitory transmitter; thus a vacillation of responsivity is observed.

Vacillating Responsivity

In vacillating responsivity, the individual's central nervous system seems to vacillate in its ability to mediate, modulate, or integrate sensory information. This disorder is often seen in individuals with autistic-like behaviors. Their systems seem to be overloading sometimes and underloading at other times. Goldfarb (1963) and others have observed that autistic children both overrespond and underrespond to sensory stimuli. Children with special needs may demonstrate this vacillation on a day-to-day, minute-to-minute basis, or may be hyporesponsive to some forms of stimuli and hyperresponsive to others. There is some speculation that variations in responsivity are the end result of the central nervous system's attempt to find homeostasis (see Figure 3–3c).

DEVELOPMENTAL DISORDERS

Every human being is born with an innate neural capacity — an inherent capacity for neurological development. Development is taking place even before birth. Thus a child is born "adequately programmed to cope with the demands of the environment" (Moore, 1973:27).

This is not to say that each person is born with the same neural capacity, nor does this imply normal neural capacity. Obviously, there are differences in neural capacities. This is most evident when normal individuals are compared with individuals who are mentally retarded, cerebral palsied, or learning disabled. Individuals with cerebral palsy, or those who have experienced prenatal or postnatal brain trauma, have more obvious limitations to their innate neural capacities based upon the extent and type of brain damage. Speech, physical coordination, and mental functioning, for example, may all be impaired in the cerebral palsied. Individuals with nonorganic causes of mental retardation or learning disabilities will manifest

more subtle, less discrete differences in neural capacity. It should be noted that variance exists not only *between* normal and exceptional individuals, but also *within* each of these two populations.*

Reflex Activity

Reflex activity is a normal part of development. Some reflexes exist from birth, while other reflexes must develop later. Reflexes are inborn, genetically endowed, and remain "functional or potentially functional" (Moore, 1973:25) throughout life. Although several authors (Bobath, 1965; Bobath and Bobath, 1971, 1975; Fiorentino, 1963, 1972; Moore, 1973) discuss a great number of reflexes, this text will discuss only those reflexes thought to impinge most on motor performance: (1) spinal reflexes (grasp, startle, crossed extension); (2) brain stem reflexes (tonic neck, tonic labyrinthine, associated reactions, positive and negative support); (3) midbrain reflexes and reactions (righting reactions); (4) automatic movement reactions (protective extension); and (5) cortical-equilibrium reactions (protective reaction in prone and supine).

Reflexes emerge and are integrated or inhibited in the same sequence as neurological development proceeds. Reflex behavior controlled by the older, lower structures of the central nervous system (spinal cord) emerge and are integrated or inhibited first. As the development of the central nervous system proceeds upward toward the cortex, there is an emergence of reflexes controlled by those higher, newer structures. Developmental disorders of reflex behavior take one of two forms: (1) interference from dominating reflexes that should have been integrated or inhibited

---

*The adapted physical educator should not impose additional limitations or restrictions upon expected performance other than those existing as a direct result of certain handicapping conditions. Rather, innate neural capacity should be accepted as a foundation from which to proceed through the developmental model.

but are not; and (2) lack of assistance from reflexes that should have emerged during development but never have.

Interference from Dominating Reflexes

An example of this form is the grasp reflex, which is present at birth and becomes integrated at about three to six months of age (Fiorentino, 1972). Grasping during this stage is nonvolitional but, when integrated, allows voluntary grasp and release. Sometimes, as in dangerous situations, it again dominates to prevent possible injury. However, when this reflex remains dominant beyond six months of age, it interferes with motor responses (such as release of an object); with motor patterns (such as throwing); and with motor skills of throwing for distance and accuracy (such as the sport skill of throwing a javelin) (see Figure 3–4).

Another example of interference is interference from the tonic labyrinthine reflex. Because the reflex pulls the ends of the body toward the ground, a child who has this problem cannot remain tucked while doing a forward roll (see Figure 3–5).

Lack of Assistance from Reflexes

An assistive reflex, such as protective extension, is an example of this second form of disordered reflex behavior. This reflex emerges at about six to nine months of age (Fiorentino, 1972) and, under normal conditions, remains present throughout life. When one loses one's balance, it comes into play to "break the fall." If this reflex does not emerge during the normal course of development, its impact on motor performance is global. Children who do not have assistance from this reflex soon learn that when they play, they fall; and when they fall, they get hurt. Early childhood programs contain many children who have already learned the

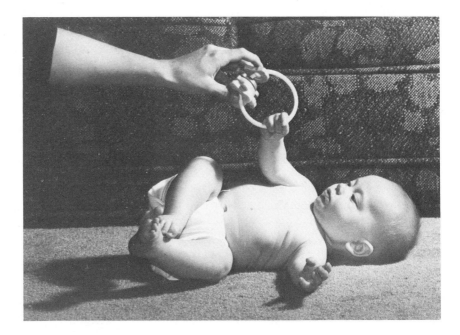

Figure 3–4. The grasp reflex is normal in infants to approximately three to six months of age.

Figure 3-5. Interference from the tonic labyrinthine reflex prevents this girl from completing a forward roll in the tucked position.

Figure 3-6. Protective extension emerges at about six months and remains throughout life.

"safe" games to play, and who avoid experience with activities that will enhance the normal course of development of motor patterns, skills, and other forms of movement. In these cases, lack of assistive reflexes tends to interfere as much, although indirectly, as the direct interference of dominating residual reflexes (see Figure 3-6).

Sensory Systems

DeQuiros and Schrager (1978:93) have noted that:

If sensory integration fails, all sequences (maturational, functional, experimental) will be disrupted according to the degree of the handicap, thus determining an unusual developmental pattern. If only one sensory modality is disturbed, development is not halted but it is distorted because other sensory modalities must help construct an abnormal model which at least must try in some way to compensate the primary unisensorial deficit. It is obvious that the case in which two or more sensory modalities are disturbed is far more serious.

Vestibular System

The vestibular system is stimulated whenever an individual moves in response to gravity. The widespread influence of the vestibular system has far-reaching effects within every aspect of human movement.* While the vestibular system can enhance organization, if it is functioning inadequately it can also create disorganization. Disorders in this system are observable in behavior and motor performance. The following is a list of some of the many signs and characteristics of vestibular disorders:

1. Abnormal muscle tone.
2. Poor balance and equilibrium responses with and without vision.
3. Poor postural responses.
4. Poor cocontraction — that is, inability to simultaneously contract antagonist muscle groups or "fixate" two or more body parts about a joint.
5. Lack of reflex integration.
6. Postural insecurity — that is, adverse reaction to sudden movements.
7. Poor eye pursuits.
8. Lack of fully established hand preference.
9. Short attention span.
10. Distractibility.
11. Aversive reaction to sound.

12. Disorders in arousal state, such as excitability or lethargy.
13. Vestibular seeking activities, such as swinging, spinning, and twirling.
14. Avoidance of swinging, spinning, or twirling.
15. Motion sickness.

Muscle tone is directly affected by the vestibular system. Consequently, both too much (hypertonia) and too little (hypotonia, flaccidity) muscle tone may be the result of vestibular dysfunction. Hypotonicity and hypertonicity can, in turn, adversely affect motor development and motor performance. Abnormal muscle tone can affect strength, muscular fitness, flexibility, agility, cardiovascular functions, endurance, perseverance (sustaining a movement), ease of movement, and the ability to perform coordinated movements.

Balance and equilibrium responses can also be affected by dysfunctioning of the vestibular system. Signs of this dysfunction are evidenced by difficulty in achieving and maintaining balance, a decreased ability in regaining balance, an inability to adjust quickly to changes in equilibrium, and an inability to avoid falling. Individuals will often assume awkward postures to compensate for the lack of fully functional balance and equilibrium responses. The "clumsy child," the "motor moron," and the more subtly handicapped — as well as more obviously handicapped individuals who exhibit signs of poor balance and equilibrium responses by having constantly skinned knees, clumsiness, and disorientation — should be assessed for adequate vestibular function.

Before human beings can respond to stimuli, they must receive the input that neurologically arouses, excites, and prepares them in readiness for movement. Often, individuals with disordered vestibular systems do not adequately receive this stimuli; as a result, their systems are not in an arousal or readiness state. When the central nervous system is not aroused, there

---

*The vestibular system carries out a specific type of proprioception. However, due to its widespread influence throughout the nervous system, initial discussion will be independent of proprioception.

is little feedback with which to respond further to the demands of the environment. Consequently, there is an inappropriate motor response that hinders motor performance. In terms of the computer analogy, there is more feedback, but it is of poor quality; and it is quality of feedback, not quantity, which enhances integration or adequate functioning of the vestibular system.

Most researchers agree that there is a range of nystagmus response considered to reflect normal functioning of the vestibular system (Leach, 1960; Kantner, et al., 1976; Korner and Thoman, 1972). Tibbling (1969) and Van der Laan and Oosterveld (1974) presented normative data for evaluation of the nystagmus response to vestibular stimulation. Responses falling outside the accepted limits of normal variation are considered abnormal.

These abnormal responses, which differ markedly, reflect some degree of dysfunction within the entire vestibular system (Jongkees, 1948). Hyporesponsive reaction, characterized by short duration and inconsistent nystagmus, is more often considered to be originating in the peripheral nervous system (Fredrickson, et al., 1969). Ayres (1978) states that another source of hyporesponsivity may be overinhibition of the vestibular nuclei from the cerebellum.

Hyperresponsivity, indicated by long duration, consistency, and little vertigo, is considered to be originating in the central nervous system and to be indicative of central vestibular syndromes and possible lesions (Rosenberg and Toglia, 1972; Fredrickson, 1969). According to Ayres (1972), hyperresponsive nystagmus may reflect less than normal inhibition from higher levels of the central nervous system. Vestibular disorders may also result from dysfunction or damage in both the central and peripheral systems.

Evidence regarding the patterns of responsivity of exceptional individuals is inconclusive. Kantner, et al. (1976) found hyperactive vestibular responses in children with Down's syndrome before a treatment program of vestibular stimulation. Chee, Clark, and Kreutzberg (1976) also reported prolonged postrotary nystagmus in cerebral palsied children. In a study completed by Leach (1960), a schizophrenic group showed diminished nystagmic reactivity to rotation and other measures of response to vestibular stimulation. Ritvo, et al. (1969) found diminished response to vestibular stimulation in autistic children. Ayres (1978) found that a selected sample of learning disabled children tended to have reduced nystagmus. Although the response to vestibular stimulation varies between and within exceptionalities, vestibular disorders have been found in exceptional individuals and those disorders were found to interfere with their behavior and performance.

Proprioceptive System

Disorders in this sensory system are often closely related to vestibular disorders. However, since the proprioceptive input deals with stimuli received through the muscles, joints, ligaments, and bones, there are specific types of proprioceptive disorders. An understanding of the responsivity continuum is important for an understanding of this system. Too little proprioceptive input will fail to fully activate the system, and will provide little information from which the individual can respond. Sensory overload of the proprioceptive system is possible, but sensory underloading is more commonly observed. Without enough proprioceptive information and inadequate processing of that information, the following signs and characteristics of disorders may be observed:

1. Abnormal muscle tone.
2. Inadequate muscle contraction for maintenance of postures.
3. Poor cocontraction.
4. Lack of body awareness — that is, knowing internally where the body parts are.
5. Inability to use body parts appropriately.

6. Inability to coordinate movement.
7. Difficulty in spatial maneuverability.

Individuals exhibiting signs of proprioceptive disorders may have difficulty attaining and maintaining certain postures or positions. Performing certain movements or assuming novel positions would be difficult for the individual whose proprioceptive system was not providing the necessary input and feedback for successful completion. Other signs include lack of body part awareness (especially without vision); inability to push or pull objects; and inability to maintain the arms held in a static position opposing the influence of gravity.

Proprioceptive system disorders adversely affect both static and dynamic balance. Without adequate support through the joints, muscles, and ligaments, the individual's movements appear jerky or aborted. Such an individual would have difficulty in executing smooth, coordinated movements. Proprioceptive system disorders can be found in all types of exceptional individuals.

Tactile System

The tactile system functions maturely throughout life. It is through this sense (as well as the vestibular and proprioceptive senses) that humans learn about their environment and provide the feedback through which they can cope with and respond to the demands of their environment. The responsivity continuum is important here, also, because individuals may show hyporesponsive or hyperresponsive reactions. Disorders in the tactile system may also be due to lack of adequate interpretation, assimilation, and organization of the incoming and outgoing tactile information. The following are common signs and characteristics of tactile disorder:

1. Tactile defensiveness — that is, negative response to touch.

2. Tactile-seeking behaviors — that is, touching anything and everything.
3. Inability to locate where on the body one has been touched.
4. Complete lack of response to touch.
5. Inability to discriminate between different tactile sensations.
6. Inability to perceive stimuli simultaneously.
7. Hyperactivity.
8. Emotional instability.
9. Distractibility.
10. Inability to motor plan effectively — that is, difficulty in planning and executing nonhabitual, purposeful movement.

Depending upon the type of responsivity to tactile stimulation, characteristics of disordered tactile function — which represent the individual nervous system's attempt to normalize or reach homeostasis — will vary. Hyperresponsivity to tactile stimulation results in a negative response to touch called *tactile defensiveness*. Individuals who are tactilly defensive often show negative response to touch, sensitivity to light, and difficulty in concentrating. Behaviors such as wearing the same clothes continuously, fighting while waiting in line, needing wide personal space, lacking affection, and withdrawal are often misinterpreted but can be indicative of an overload on the tactile system (see Figure 3–7). Hyporesponsivity generally results in *tactile-seeking* behaviors. Tactile-seekers exhibit signs of a disordered tactile system in other ways. They may be described as "clinging vines," who are compelled to touch everything and everybody. They often have bruises without knowing where, when, or how they got them. There are also tactile-seekers who do not respond at all to tactile stimulation. Diminished, or lack of, response is exhibited by not knowing where one has been touched, an inability to distinguish hot and cold stimuli, or an inability to tactilly discriminate between textures. Individuals in all handicapping categories exhibit signs of tactile system disorders.

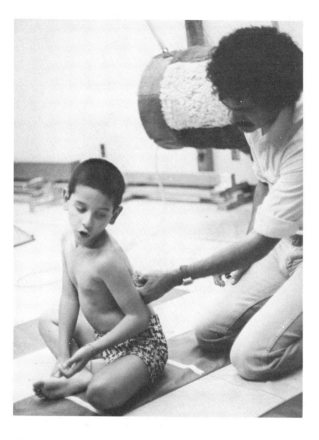

Figure 3-7. This child cannot tolerate tactile input and thus pulls away.

Visual System

The visual system, which develops in stages, demonstrates three basic functions early in life: *fixation, accommodation, and convergence*. These functions are not established until about the second or third month of postnatal life, long before maturation of the function known as *visual perception*, which is not thought to be fully mature until about seven years of age (deQuiros and Schrager, 1978). Therefore the distinction between visual acuity (the ability to see clearly) and visual perception (the capacity to organize and interpret what is seen) is quite clear. Disorders of visual acuity can be identified early in neonatal life, since around the third month of life observable behav-

iors include ocular pursuits (Shirley, 1933), holding a rattle and glancing at it (Gesell, 1940), and reaching for dangling objects (Shirley, 1933) (see Appendix B). Neither the visual nor the motor systems are prepared for these tasks before this period. Thus infants who are hyporesponsive to visual stimuli, primarily illumination, are suspected to have acuity disorders.

Disorders of visual perception are not easily detectable, nor can they be detected as early as disorders of other sensory systems. Therefore they present a variety of challenges to the physical educator. This is not to say that blind or partially sighted children are free from visual perception disorders, as the vast majority of individuals in these categories have some degree of usable vision. All other disorders of the visual system, therefore, are placed under the broad heading of visual perception.

Individuals who have visual perception disorders, regardless of the amount of useful vision, will demonstrate considerably different motor responses than individuals without disorders in the visual system. Some of these observable characteristics of significance to the physical educator are:

1. Poor attending behavior and distractibility for visual stimuli.
2. Inability to follow a visual sequence or maintain eye fixation on a moving object.
3. Inability to discriminate visual objects in the field of vision.
4. Inability to maintain spatial orientation either at rest or while in motion.
5. Inability to recall visual sequences, spatial relations, forms, or other visual features.

Hyporesponsivity to visual stimuli is seen in all educational classifications, including the regular classroom. Individuals who are hyporesponsive or unable to make use of visual stimuli are likely to demonstrate inaccurate or inappropriate motor responses to the visual input. Children who are struck by a ball before

Figure 3–8. Figure-ground confusion. Is it any wonder that children with visual perception disorders avoid situations such as climbing this jungle gym?

they have a chance to strike it, and children who cannot catch or show delayed reactions to an object moving toward them, may be having difficulty following the moving object (visual tracking), fixating on it, or discriminating it from the other stimuli in their field of vision (see Figure 3–8).

Children who seem confused about where they are or are supposed to be on the playing court, children who run or throw in the wrong direction, or children who cannot replicate a motor pattern they have seen demonstrated, may be experiencing quite different disorders. Spatial orientation is needed in order to know one's placement on a court, and visual memory is required for recalling and "reconstructing" a movement sequence that has gone before.*

*It should be apparent that many of these tasks require good vestibular, proprioceptive, and tactile input as well as visual perception. Thus the interrelatedness between the visual and the early developing systems can be readily seen. Vestibular organs play a fundamental role in the regulation of the head and eyes, with information from proprioceptors in the neck and ocular muscles serving as both primary and feedback input. Disorders in either of these two systems, or in the transmission of information from them to the visual cortex, will result in visual perception deficits. Conversely, inadequate quantity and quality of visual stimuli, including information resulting from poor fixation, accommodation, and convergence, is likely to affect adequate functioning of the earlier-developing systems as well.

Children who show hyperresponsivity to visual stimuli may also be found in any educational classification; in its most basic form, however, overreactive motor responses are more likely to be observed in the autistic, severely handicapped, severely emotionally disturbed, and hyperactive populations. Fearful reaction to illumination or changes in illumination (Barnes, 1977), covering the eyes, or running to turn out the lights are behaviors observed in autistic or autistic-like children. Hyperactive children, although demonstrating more subtle motor responses, may attempt to respond simultaneously to all visual stimuli within their field of vision and hence be unable to attend to a single task. This type of reaction presents obvious challenges to the physical educator for structuring the environment in such a way that learning can take place.

A child whose visual system seems to vacillate in its need for visual input may show seeking behaviors such as gazing at a light or bright object, flashing the lights off and on in a room, or hand-flapping in front of the eyes and then masking out all visual stimuli by covering the eyes, hiding in a closet, or in other ways withdrawing from the stimulus. The accompanying disorders of muscle tone and equilibrium among the population of individuals with visual perception disorders are, understandably, varied.

Auditory System

The auditory system is capable of two distinct functions: (1) auditory acuity (hearing); and (2) auditory perception (audition). Hearing disorders, which range from hearing loss to total deafness, will be discussed only briefly here, as this dysfunction limits the individual's ability to adequately receive auditory input for use. As hearing losses influence the organization and utilization of this input, or as other disorders intervene in this process, they are said to be disorders in audition — auditory perception.

Children who have loss of auditory acuity present two major challenges to the physical educator: (1) to modify their methods and techniques for communicating information to the learner; and (2) to plan appropriate activities for the learner whose hearing loss may be due to damage to parts of the hearing mechanism that also serve the vestibular system.

Children who have disorders of audition are not as easily recognized nor understood as those having acuity disorders. The most important characteristics of auditory perception disorders for the physical educator are:

1. Inability to grasp the meaning of words.
2. Inability to use language creatively by conceptualizing the message, associating the appropriate language symbols for use, and sequencing the motor response (expressive language).
3. Inability to recall language structures for use.
4. Inability to discriminate different sounds from one another.
5. Inability to detect variations in sound, including pitch, volume, direction, and rhythm.

For the physical educator, most disorders in audition that impinge on motor performance center in the perception of language and musical sounds. Individuals with severe oral language handicaps, childhood aphasia, mental retardation, or autism will demonstrate a wide variation in their abilities to perceive these two sound sources. Lack of response or inappropriate responses to language may stem from the inability to associate language symbols (words) with their meanings. In other cases, the child may understand what is said but cannot organize the words into appropriate linguistic patterns of phrases and sentences; or the child may not be able to recall the meaningful action components. An example of an inappropriate response is a child who brings you a ball when you have asked for a bat, or who does not act at all. Associations with other forms of stimuli, such as the differences in texture and weight between the bat and the ball, are perceptions that must be taught an individual who is seemingly hyporesponsive to auditory input when it takes the form of language. Results of hyporesponsivity to music and rhythmic sounds will take the form of arrhythmic motor responses, uncoordinated movements, and general motor clumsiness. Unless proprioceptive stimuli is perceived, these children have difficulty making use of the feedback from their motor responses and thus perpetuate inaccurate motor responses. These individuals tend to have poor muscle tone, reflective of the close relationship between the auditory and proprioceptive systems (deQuiros and Schrager, 1978).

Individuals who are hyperresponsive to auditory input may be identified in the same categorical populations mentioned above. Attending to all of the auditory input entering the system is characteristic of hyperactive individuals who cannot discriminate between the sounds that should have their attention and the sounds that should not. Children whose systems cannot modulate or mask unnecessary auditory stimuli appear to be intolerant in their behavior. Autistic and autistic-like individuals are often seen withdrawing from auditory stimuli by covering their ears or hiding. In other cases, in which the auditory system seems to be vacillating between seeking input and avoiding input, the individual may be observed clapping, pounding, or head-banging—seemingly, to create stimuli—then withdraw, cover the ears, or hide—seemingly, to avoid the input. Individuals whose behavior suggests that they are seeking auditory stimuli also often have disorders of the vestibular system and demonstrate disequilibrium (deQuiros, 1976).

Motor-Sensory Responses

Adequate functioning of the sensory systems, the interrelatedness of these systems, and the relationship to the motor system subserve and give rise to motor-sensory responses. The motor-sensory responses serve to identify some of the early integration of the sensory and motor systems resulting in observable, planned motor behavior. The focal point is the motor response predicated upon previous sensory-motor interaction. Deficits in the motor-sensory responses can be identified by (1) deficits in praxis or motor planning; and (2) integration of both sides of the body.

Praxis

Praxis is the ability to plan and execute purposeful movement or, according to deQuiros and Schrager, "the ability to perform a series of purposeful movements" (1978:252). Praxis is primarily built upon functioning of the tactile, vestibular, proprioceptive, and visual systems for the necessary input and an appropriate motor output. Disorders in praxis imply that an individual is having difficulty in successful execution of nonhabitual, purposeful movement. Disorders in the sensory systems can interfere with the ability to move efficiently, and have been discussed earlier. Disorders in interpretation, assimilation, organization, and transmission of motor-sensory information result in some observable signs and characteristics of disordered praxis:

1. Clumsiness.
2. Difficulty when approaching new tasks.

3. Lack of kinesthetic awareness.
4. Messy handwriting.
5. Poor tactile perception.
6. Poor ocular control.
7. Difficulty in imitation of movements.
8. Lack of body awareness.
9. Observable, slow, deliberately sequenced movements (calculated).
10. Extraneous movements.
11. Rapid, inappropriate movements.
12. Poor fine motor coordination.
13. Poor gross motor coordination.
14. Poor eye-hand or eye-foot coordination.
15. Uneven or hesitant gait.

If the sensory input is disordered, difficulty in motor planning will result. Disorganization, or lack of integration somewhere in the process of planning and execution of movement, will also result in praxis disorders. This can also adversely affect the end product of motor-sensory responses and motor patterns. All motor responses beyond the reflexive level initially require some degree of motor planning. Individuals throughout the range of exceptionality may exhibit signs of a praxis disorder.

The very clumsy child who falls a lot may be exhibiting signs of apraxia (i.e., without praxis). Messy handwriting, lack of body awareness, uneven gait, and inability to imitate movements are indicative of a disorder in praxis. In motor performance, there may be difficulty in motor sequencing a task such as climbing, going through an obstacle course, or getting onto a one-legged (T) stool. Motor-planning deficits can also appear at a higher skill level, as evidenced by children who have difficulty in sequencing a dance routine or karate move, who show an inability to coordinate their bodies sufficiently to run the hurdles successfully, or who have difficulty in performing a complex trampoline routine. Learning must always take place prior to and in conjunction with the acquisition of motor patterns and motor skills. Motor planning is a part of

Figure 3-9. To imitate a movement, processing of visual input, integration, and motor planning are required to give the correct response.

Figure 3-10. Lack of body integration. This girl cannot yet isolate one body side from the other. Notice the associated reaction in the left arm as she throws the beanbag with her right arm.

that process. When difficulty persists, it is then thought to have implications for disorders in motor planning (see Figure 3-9).

Integration of Both Sides of the Body

Integration of the two sides of the body is both a process and product. It has been discussed by Moore (1973) as *bilaterality;* Kephart (1971) as *differentiation;* Gesell, et al. (1941) as *reciprocal interweaving;* Ayres (1972) as *bilateral integration;* Frostig (1970) as *body schema;* and Barsch (1968) as *biomechanical economy.* Simply, integration of both sides of the body is the

established ability to use both sides of the body together and in opposition resulting in efficient motor performance. Developmentally, use of both sides together develops first with reciprocation following. Both are necessary to further growth in motor development and motor performance (see Figure 3-10).

Disorders can be characterized by the following:

1. Difficulty in jumping with both feet.
2. Unequal stance.
3. Inability to or hesitancy in crossing midline of the body.
4. Poor rhythmical activities.

5. Poor coordination of both sides of the body.
6. An inability to isolate one body part for use.
7. Slow balance reactions.
8. Differences between body sides in muscle tone and use.
9. Disturbances in laterality (knowing body sides) and directionality (projecting body sides into space — e.g., front to forward, side to sideways).
10. Appearance of residual reflexes.
11. Poor modulation of vestibular and proprioceptive stimulation.
12. Problems with spatial orientation.
13. Lack of hemisphere specialization or inter-hemisphere communication.

Individuals who lack integration of both sides of the body will demonstrate abnormalities in motor performance and acquisition of skill (see Figure 3-11).

In this example, the child is pointing to her nose, but the index finger of her opposite hand is also pointing! She is unable to isolate the one body part necessary for the movement.

For smooth, efficient movement, the individual must be able to respond to the demands of the environment. Integration of the two sides of the body necessitates the establishment of the ability to use one body part in isolation without associated reactions in other parts, the ability to cross the midline of the body, and the ability to differentiate between muscles and between movements; and requires communication between the sides of the body for normal motor performance.

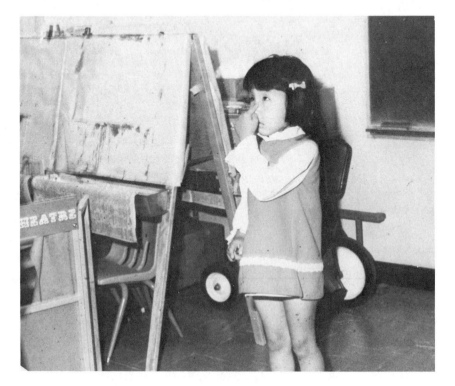

Figure 3-11. This child's right hand is mirroring the left, showing lack of integration of the two body sides.

Motor Patterns, Motor Skills, and Culturally Determined Forms of Movement

The emergence of patterns and skills needed for participation in physical education activities is directly related to age, and inversely related to reflex activity. As the human organism matures and receives functionally more assistance from later-maturing systems, responses become more complex and skills become increasingly more specific.

Earlier, this text discussed ways in which atypical reflex activity and disorders of earlier- and later-maturing systems and motor responses can adversely affect motor performance. These underlying components, integral parts of motor performance, should be considered as potential sources of disorders in skill acquisition, retention, execution, and refinement. When supportive functions are in order, then the focal point for adapted physical education becomes the normalization, or approximation to normal, of patterns and skills.

Children whose supportive functions are in order, at least within the scope of their neural capacities, may be demonstrating atypical motor patterns or skills due to one or a combination of the following reasons:

1. Lack of experience.
2. Mechanically ineffective body structure.
3. Limitations in cognitive function, interfering with the ability to master concepts related to the movement parameters.
4. Loss of the use of body structures.
5. Inadequately functioning physiological systems for providing the nutritional ingredients needed to support movement.
6. Superimposed emotional disorders interfering with utilization of the body.
7. Asocial behavior restricting the appropriate use of motor behavior.

Children who have such physical limitations as loss of sight, limbs, and hearing, or the effective use of these, will usually be able to develop motor patterns, skills, and other culturally determined forms of movement to their maximum potential within the scope of limitations imposed by the disability. Given the opportunity to learn in a sequenced instructional program, children with physical impositions on pattern development will achieve success. Children who have mechanically ineffective body structures may need the assistance of trained professionals in adapted physical education to identify mechanical principles they can use.

SUMMARY

The developmental approach as a vehicle for teaching adapted physical education provides myriad opportunities for students who have dysfunctions in innate neural capacity, reflex behavior, sensory and motor systems, and their interaction. Disorders of development can be classified into two categories: process disorders and developmental disorders. Process disorders often take the form of responsivity disorders, in that individuals overrespond, underrespond, or vary in their response to sensory input. Developmental disorders may be seen in abnormal reflex behavior, dysfunctions in the various sensory systems, or dysfunctions in the integration of sensory information for appropriate motor responses. Although breakdowns may occur in the sensory-integrative-motor-sensory-feedback system, resulting in inadequate motor output, the developmental approach allows the physical educator to approach the learner in a systematic way. When physiological or anatomical mechanisms are functioning inadequately or not at all, the adapted physical educator must use methods and techniques for structuring movement experiences that are compatible with the body's ability to respond. The developmental approach gives rise to appropriate methods and techniques.

BIBLIOGRAPHY

Abuladze, K. S. "Central Inhibition of Reflexes and the Problem of the Coupled Activity of Cerebral Hemispheres." In *Progress in Brain Research,* edited by E. A. Asratyan. New York: Elsevier, 1968.

Ayres, A. J. *Sensory Integration and Learning Disorders.* Los Angeles: Western Psychological Services, 1972.

Ayres, A. J. "Learning Disabilities and the Vestibular System." *Journal of Learning Disabilities* 11 (1978): 30-41.

Barnes, D. W. *Sensory Integrative Dysfunction and the Atypical Behaviors of Autistic and Autistic-Like Children: A Factorial Analysis.* Ph.D. dissertation, Brigham Young University, April 1977.

Barsch, R. H. *Enriching Perception and Cognition.* Seattle: Special Child Publications, 1968.

Bobath, B. *Abnormal Postural Reflex Activity Caused by Brain Lesions.* London: William Heinemann Medical Books, Ltd., 1965.

Bobath, B., and Bobath, K. *Abnormal Postural Reflex Activity Caused by Brain Lesions.* London: William Heinemann Medical Books, Ltd., 1971.

Bobath, B., and Bobath, K. *Motor Development in the Different Types of Cerebral Palsy.* London: International Ideas, 1975.

Chee, F. K. W., Clark, D. L., and Kreutzberg, J. R. "Comparison of Vestibular Function in Normal and Cerebral Palsy Children." Paper presented at the 89th Annual Session of the American Association of Anatomists, April 20-23, 1976, Louisville, Kentucky.

Clarke, D. L., Kreutzberg, J. R., and Chee, F. K. W. "Vestibular Stimulation Influence on Motor Development in Infants." *Science* 196 (1977): 1228-1229.

Fiorentino, M. R. *Reflex Testing Methods for Evaluating C.N.S. Development.* Springfield, Illinois: Charles C. Thomas, 1963.

Fiorentino, M. R. *Normal and Abnormal Development.* Springfield, Illinois: Charles C. Thomas, 1972.

Fredrickson, J. M., et al. "Nystagmus: Diagnostic Significance of Recent Observations." *Archives of Otolaryngology* 89 (1969): 504-511.

Frostig, M., and Maslow, P. *Movement Education: Theory and Practice.* Chicago: Follett, 1970.

Gesell, A., et al. *The First Five Years of Life.* New York: Harper & Row, 1940.

Gesell, A., Ilg, F. L., and Bullis, G. E. *Vision — Its Development in Infant and Child.* New York: Paul B. Hoeber, 1941.

Goldfarb, W. "Self-awareness in Schizophrenic Children." *Archives of General Psychiatry* 8 (1963): 47-60.

Jongkees, L. B. "Origin of the Caloric Reaction of the Labyrinth." *Archives of Otolaryngology* 48 (1948): 645-657.

Kantner, R., et al. "Effects of Vestibular Stimulation on Nystagmus Response and Motor Performance in the Developmentally Delayed Infant." *Physical Therapy* 56 (1976): 414-421.

Kephart, N. C. *Slow Learner in the Classroom.* 2d. ed. Columbus: Charles E. Merrill, 1971.

Korner, A. F., and Thoman, E. B. "Relative Efficacy of Contact and Vestibular Proprioceptive Stimulation in Soothing Neonates." *Child Development* 43 (1972): 445-453.

Leach, W. W. "Nystagmus: An Integrative Neural Deficit in Schizophrenia." *Journal of Abnormal and Social Psychology* 60 (1960): 305–309.

Moore, J. C. *Concepts from the Neurobehavioral Sciences.* Dubuque: Kendall-Hunt, 1973.

deQuiros, J. B. "Diagnosis of Vestibular Disorders in the Learning Disabled." *Journal of Learning Disabilities* 9 (1976): 30–41.

deQuiros, J. B., and Schrager, O. L. *Neuropsychological Fundamentals in Learning Disabilities.* San Rafael, California: Academic Therapy Publications, 1978.

Ritvo, E. R., et al. "Decreased Post-rotary Nystagmus in Early Infantile Autism." *Neurology* 19 (1969): 653–658.

Rosenberg, P. E., and Toglia, J. U. "Electronystagmography in Clinical Audiology." *Journal of Speech and Learning Disorders* 17 (1972).

Sage, G. H. *Introduction to Motor Behavior.* Menlo Park, California: Addison-Wesley, 1971.

Shirley, M. "The First Two Years: A Study of 25 Babies." *Institute of Child Welfare Monograph Series* 7 (1933): 2.

Tibbling, L. "The Rotary Nystagmus Response in Children." *Acta Otolarynogol* 68 (1969): 459–467.

Van Der Laan, F. L., and Oosterveld, W. J. "Age and Vestibular Function." *Clinical Aviation and Aerospace Medicine* 45 (1947): 45.

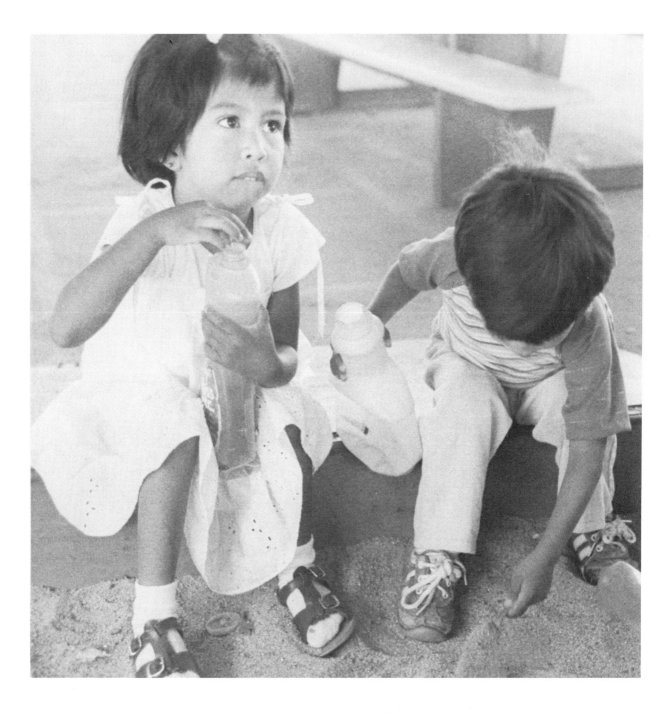

4   Teaching the Whole Child

Guiding Questions

1. In physical education programming for the whole child, what areas of development (in addition to motor) are important?
2. How are developmental profiles useful to physical education programming?
3. The developmental approach allows for individualization. Why and how is this possible?

The ever-changing needs of the whole child are of utmost importance and value in the developmental approach. Thus an understanding of human growth and development is imperative for the developmentalist.

DEVELOPMENTAL PARAMETERS

The adapted physical educator should have a thorough knowledge of motor development and a working knowledge of social, language, and intellectual development, as integrated and embodied in the child. With this background, the instructor becomes an educator, who uses the medium of movement as a vehicle for education.

Language Development

Sometime between the last quarter of the first year and the middle of the second year of life, the child begins to speak. But even before the onset of speech acquisition, language development has begun. The development of language is a continuous process throughout life, with comprehension preceding and exceeding language production from the beginning to the end of life. A child will normally pass through a series of stages of language development (see Table 4-1).

The first stage, undifferentiated crying, is primarily reflexive in nature. The cries are undifferentiated in that they are indistinguishable to the listener; the cry is essentially the same no matter what the cause.

Differentiated crying or differentiated vocalization includes comfort sounds, cries, coos, gurgles, and other sounds that approximate consonant sounds. During this period, the cries or sounds become discernible and may be in direct response to a given stimuli, person, or object.

A considerable increase in vocalization occurs during the ages of three to six months, and includes identifiable sounds characterized by babbling. Many of the sounds or combinations of sounds are duplicated, such as "ga-ga" or "bah-bah." Normally, babbling occurs in response to environmental stimuli.

Lalling and echolalia characterize the last two stages of prelingual language development. Lalling specifically refers to a great amount of self-imitation in such utterances as "ga-ga," "da-da," and "ma-ma." Intonation patterns tend to accompany lalling, and there is seemingly more control in the amount and

Table 4–1. Language development

Age	Language development milestones
0–6 months	Exhibits undifferentiated crying, begins to make differentiated sounds, attends to person's voice, experiments with voice, turns head to sounds.
6–12 months	Babbles, imitates sounds, says "da-da," "ma-ma," responds to "no," shakes head "no," says one word, knows names, gestures, three-word vocabulary at one year, responds to "give it to me."
12–18 months	Points to things wanted, shows variety of emotions, five-word vocabulary, knows three body parts, imitates talking, uses words to indicate needs and wants, ten-word vocabulary.
18–24 months	Tries to follow directions, knows five body parts, twenty-word vocabulary, follows simple command, refers to self by name, names objects, uses two- or three-word sentences.
2–4 years	Uses plurals, knows simple songs, gives full name, knows sex, counts to three, can tell a story, uses five- to six-word sentences, name colors, 800 word vocabulary.
5–6 years	Acquires sounds and structure needed for life, can follow three commands in sequence, lacks sensitivity to listener in giving information.
7–11 years	Masters sound patterns, utilizes complex sentence structure, reads, learns multiple word meanings.
11–15 years	Acquires adult language structures, uses socially oriented language, masters peer language, adult language, and foreign language.

type of vocalization. Echolalia is also characterized by imitation of sounds. At this stage, the child begins to imitate the speech, gestures, and intonation of others, but still with very little understanding.

A child who produces a verbal signal with an intended meaning is considered to have spoken a word. Usually by the beginning of the second year, the child has many words with which to identify objects or people. Echolalic utterances still occur, but have more meaning. The utterances or words of this stage are mainly responsive in nature, and are not yet used to bring about an event.

A child who uses words to bring about an event or to get something is said to be using true speech or anticipatory language. Between the ages of eighteen and twenty-four months, comprehension is much greater than the child's productive vocabulary of three to fifty words would indicate.

Syntactic speech occurs at approximately two years of age, when the child has a vocabulary of fifty to one hundred words. The words used are becoming intelligible, and are primarily nouns along with some adjectives and a few verbs. The child is also combining words into two-word sentences in order to convey meaning. During this stage, the child may reveal an ability to generalize from a familiar phrase to an unfamiliar phrase.

Functional words such as prepositions, articles, and conjunctions occur within the child's vocabulary around the second half of the second year of life. The child begins to speak grammatically, in a manner similar to the environment. Three- to four-word sentences

Table 4–2. Social and intellectual development

Age	Social development	Intellectual development
Birth to 2 years	Gratification of body needs, egocentricity, solitary play, responsive to people and objects, plays peek-a-boo and pat-a-cake, smiles, seeks attention.	Learns through the senses, perceives objects in immediate sensorimotor-visual field, reflex activity, no object permanence.
2 years to 4 years	Preference of playmates, strong attachment to one other child, parallel play, imitates other children's play, takes turns, plays aggressively, may have an imaginary playmate.	Pre-operational thought through sensorimotor activity, focuses on one characteristic only, has primary classification ability, is not concerned with contradictions, is able to distinguish vertical from horizontal lines.
4 years to 7 years	Participates in cooperative play, accepts adult authority, boasts, uses favorite expressions, seeks group approval, plays in groups of three.	Learns colors, classifies by emotions, uses symbols to represent concrete world, makes intuitive judgments about relationships.
7 years to 11 years	Identifies with persons of same sex, is loyal to gang, rejects adult authority, participates in large group activities.	Organizes environment through direct experiences, perceives consequences of own actions, uses logic, classifies by two characteristics, begins addition and subtraction.
11 years to 15 years	Seeks peer acceptance, develops personality type, is influenced by peer pressure, becomes intrinsically motivated.	Comprehends abstract concepts; handles contradictions, thoughts, direct observations; works with theories and abstractions; sees logical relationships; solves problems.

are frequent, and the intent of language is for communication. Language development is quite rapid during this time, and articulation becomes clear. Complex sentences are spoken, and speech with conventional syntax has become the norm. At the age of four, the child becomes a mature user of basic language and speaks in a unique manner.

The continuous development and refinement of language includes phonemic development (the acquisition of sounds), an increase in vocabulary (morphology), syntactic proficiency, and discriminatory use of language. The individual continues to increase comprehension and production of language through which

to derive meaning, formulate thought, speak intelligently, and communicate.

Intellectual Development

As discussed earlier, each individual has an innate neural capacity that is determined by heredity and shaped by experience and environment. A neural pattern for learning must be established early as a basis for further intellectual development. The first six years of the child's life are crucial in the development of cognitive/intellectual functions (see Table 4–2).

A child begins to learn at birth, and the process

Figure 4-1. This child is performing a Piagetian task of conservation of mass.

continues throughout life. Piaget (1952) has suggested that there are different types and levels of intellectual development, and has postulated ages coinciding with the various levels (see Figure 4-1).

From birth to two years of age comprises the period of sensorimotor intelligence, during which information is acquired by sensory systems and movements interacting with the environment. Practical intelligence acquired during this period provides a foundation for higher forms of learning.

During the pre-operational period, from ages two to seven years, the child begins to make intuitive judgments about relationships. Language becomes increasingly important, and the child begins to use symbols to represent the concrete world. The child learns of properties and attributes of the world. Thinking during this stage is dominated by perception.

From ages seven to eleven years, understanding of the environment comes through concrete operations.

Thoughts are shaped by experiences, in that they are dependent upon concrete objects that are understood and manipulated. The concrete operations represent the child's first attempts at reasoning or logic. The child is able to classify and order to show relationships, becomes capable of applying operational thinking to practical problems and concrete situations, and develops the ability to adapt knowingly to a changing environment. The child can also perceive consequences of actions and is able to systematize and organize thoughts.

The formal operations period, ages eleven to fifteen years, is the one during which the child develops an ability to deal with the abstract. Thoughts can now direct observations instead of the inverse, which was true at earlier stages of intellectual development. The child is capable of working with theories, logical relationships, and abstractions, without having to return to concrete operations or manipulation of

Figure 4-2. These children are engaged in parallel play—that is, they are each "doing their own thing" in the same play space. SOURCE: Photo by Lyonel Avance.

concrete objects for the answers. This period represents a generalized presentation to problem solving activities.

Academic skills are acquired throughout the stages of intellectual development. Academic skills, the product of a child's learning, are reflective of attained levels of intellectual development. The process through which the child acquires these academic skills is vitally important in the developmental understanding of the whole child as a functioning human being.

Social Development

Even from the beginnings of life, a child can be considered a social being. Play, socialization, and adaptive behavior all influence the course of social development.

The first six months of a child's life represent a time of complete dependence. Infancy is characterized by egocentricity and solitary play, and the first social gratification is the satisfaction of biological needs. Thus the infant relates first to the mother figure, and then to the father figure and siblings. At four months of age, the infant notices another infant, and by eleven months prefers an infant to a toy. Smiling, crying, and eye movements in response to people or objects are among the first social responses.

Between the ages of two to four years, the child learns to relate positively or negatively to social groups, shows a preference of playmates, and forms a strong attachment with one other child. Parallel play is most common during this time, along with the emergence of symbolic play and dramatic play. The beginnings of group play are evidenced by sharing and taking turns. At this time, the child still has difficulty handling altered circumstances. Guidelines and rules imposed upon the child by other people help the child to learn discipline and self-control (see Figure 4-2).

The four- to seven-year-old learns to interact in new social groups, seeking group approval and developing social patterns that remain throughout life. Adult authority is accepted, primarily without question. The child develops an awareness of self, which often results in boasting. Cooperative play occurs most frequently, including game-like situations, although game rules are not known or followed except in the mind of the child (see Figure 4-3).

The seven- to eleven-year-old child identifies with others of the same sex. Due to societal teaching and influence, the child begins to notice sex differences in activities. The child participates in large group activities with codified rules, and evolves into a social being who can give and take graciously, and who can follow, lead, and interact in social situations. Gang loyalty and seeming rejection of adult standards characterize this period of growth.

Peer acceptance soon becomes uppermost in the thoughts and actions of the adolescent. Individual personality is sought, and the adolescent attempts to gain acceptance from people of the opposite sex as well as from the group. Peer pressure strongly influences social behavior, although simple social reinforcement loses some impact as the child becomes intrinsically motivated. Self-consciousness may also be noticed in the learning of new skills. Social development continues as the social environments and types of social interactions vary, thus placing demands upon the individual.

Integration of Developmental Parameters

Because communication is fostered through verbal and nonverbal language, it is important for the physical educator to be able to ascertain both the level of lan-

Figure 4-3. Cooperative play is exhibited as this group of children works together in order to perform a parachute stunt successfully.

guage and the means of communication used by each child. In the developmental approach, the adapted physical education program includes encouragement and reinforcement of language development.

The level of intellectual development is at times closely related to language development, but this is not always the case. For example, a mentally retarded child exhibits language development commensurate with intellectual development, while an aphasic, language-disabled, or deaf child exhibits levels of language development that are frequently below intellectual development. Even though receptive language normally functions at a higher level than expressive language, a significant discrepancy between expressive and receptive language is often noticed with the aphasic, language-disabled, or deaf child. Thus the physical educator should communicate with the speech therapist, classroom teacher, and school psychologist in ascertaining the levels of language and intellectual development.

It is also best if the levels of functioning ascertained are in a usable form. Knowing that the child has a given score on a given language or intelligence test, for example, is not as helpful as the same information expressed as "_____ years or _____ months delay," or "functioning at a _____-year-old level." These forms provide the necessary facts, which can then be compared with normal growth and development patterns. Such a comparison enables the adapted physical educator to accurately pinpoint the ability levels of the child, and to teach at that level.

The level of social development of the exceptional child should not be assumed to coincide with the other levels of development. It is important to know at what social level the child is functioning, in order to help determine the most appropriate learning environment and level of interaction.

Normally, the levels of development in motor, social, language, and intellectual parameters fall within a small range of months. The variability of the levels of

development among the handicapped, however, is often much greater than in the normal population. Inconsistency within the categories of handicapping conditions is also noted (see Figure 4–4).

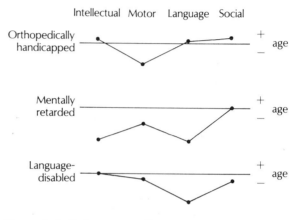

Figure 4–4. Performance profiles.

Determination of the levels of functioning affords the adapted physical education teacher the opportunity to better understand the exceptional individual, to deal with the child through appropriate methodology, and to plan, implement, and evaluate appropriate and effective programs. It can be demonstrated that, through an understanding of the whole child, the adapted physical education teacher can better individualize the program to foster maximum growth.

APPLYING THE DEVELOPMENTAL APPROACH

Because the developmental approach is a means whereby theory is translated into practice, it (1) allows for individualization from assessment through instruction; (2) provides a foundation for understanding the symptoms and characteristics of atypical performance by addressing the sources of the dysfunction; (3) provides a natural sequence of experiences in motor, learning, which enhances the growth and development of exceptional children; and (4) is noncategorical, placing emphasis on the individual's needs, capacities, and limitations.

In physical education programming for the exceptional child, the instructor should be aware of the specifics of the handicapping condition. Although these specifics must of course be dealt with in evaluating and programming, they should be viewed as aspects of functioning rather than used for categorization. Because much variation is noted within and among the categories of handicapping conditions, it is imperative that assessment and programming reflect individualization. A synthesis of information is sought, which includes the child's motor, social, language, and intellectual development.

The developmental model presented in Chapter 2 reflects sequential organization. Because optimal functioning at each level depends on adequate functioning at the lower levels, a breakdown at a lower level will cause less than optimum performance at each succeeding level. Understanding and working within the model provides guidelines for determining the appropriate level at which to begin programming. When the instructor seeks to assess the performance of the child, the model can be used to specifically address sources of atypical performance, and to provide a natural sequence of experiences in motor learning.

Sources of Atypical Performance

Because successful performance in games and sports is dependent upon adequate motor skills, difficulties encountered by an exceptional child during game and sport activities should be analyzed according to the motor skills necessary for successful participation. If the child's motor skills are deficient, it then becomes necessary to analyze the deficit in light of the prerequisite motor patterns and motor responses (see Figure 4–5).

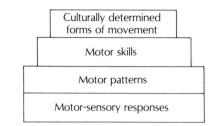

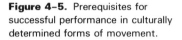

Figure 4–5. Prerequisites for successful performance in culturally determined forms of movement.

For example, Joanne is having difficulty in successful participation in the game of baseball, because she experiences an inability to hit a pitched ball or to catch a batted ball. She performs adequately as a baserunner. Once the ball is fielded, however, she has little or no difficulty in throwing to the appropriate base or person. The difficulty, then, is in batting and catching. The motor skills of batting and catching can be analyzed in terms of the adequacy of the motor patterns and motor responses. It is observed that Joanne exhibits an adequate swinging motion and can assume the appropriate position for catching, indicative of adequate motor patterns. But upon analyzing the motor-sensory responses of motor planning, balance, integration of the two sides of the body, and eye-hand coordination, she is found to show a deficit in eye-hand coordination. Batting and catching each require adequate eye-hand coordination for successful performance. By descending through the levels of the developmental pyramid, it is possible to ascertain that a deficit in the motor-sensory response of eye-hand coordination adversely affected batting and catching as a part of Joanne's inability to perform well in baseball (see Figure 4–6).

When a deficit in motor sensory responses or motor patterns is noticed, the functioning of the various sensory systems should be investigated. Continuing with the example of an eye-hand coordination

Figure 4-6. Deficits in eye-hand interaction can contribute to unsuccessful batting (above). The use of an oversized bat can help a child with this problem connect with the ball (right).

problem, the adequate functioning of the visual and proprioceptive sensory systems should be specifically assessed. For example, Joanne may show poor figure-ground discrimination (visual system) and a lack of body awareness (proprioceptive system), both of which can contribute to poor eye-hand coordination. If necessary, the adequacy of reflex integration should also be ascertained (see Figure 4-7).

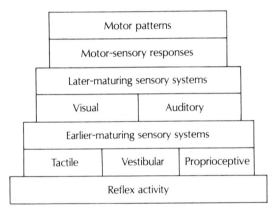

Figure 4-7. Prerequisite levels for adequate motor patterns.

Natural Sequence of Experiences in Motor Learning

Just as descending through the model serves to address sources of atypical performance, ascending the pyramid provides for a natural sequence of motor experiences. Each preceding level provides the foundation for the next level of motor experiences.

Each child is born with an innate neural capacity that is unique to that child, but basic to all humans. Reflex activity and survival mechanisms are the first observable movements of an infant. The sensory systems are functioning at birth, but must mature. Re-

flex integration and sensory-stimulating activities comprise much of the early sensorimotor experiences and learning, as reflected by the first levels of the model (see Figure 4-8).

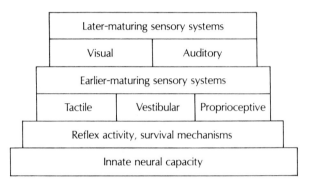

Figure 4-8. Importance of sensory stimulation as reflected by the lower level of the developmental model.

As reflexes become integrated and the tactile, vestibular, and proprioceptive systems mature, further motor experiences include additional challenges in the visual and auditory systems. Built upon a firm foundation of adequately functioning sensory systems, motor-sensory responses and motor patterns emerge and continue to develop. Motor skills follow sequentially, and ultimately result in culturally determined forms of movement.

SUMMARY

In addition to motor development, the physical educator should understand the child's social, language, and intellectual development — the whole child must be taken into account when determining a developmental profile. In programming for exceptional children, experiences should be sequentially ordered, using the levels of the developmental model as guidelines. After determining the fundamental sources of dysfunction, activities can be designed to foster growth at that level and help the child progress. Since the model is developmentally based, each succeeding level adds to the child's previous motor experiences, placing new demands on the child that challenge the adaptive responses necessary for development.

BIBLIOGRAPHY

Eisenson, J., and Ogilvie, M. *Speech Correction in the Schools.* New York: Macmillan Co., 1971.

Gesell, A., and Ilg, F. C. *Child Development.* New York: Harper & Row, 1947.

Kaluger, G., and Kolson, C. J. *Reading and Learning Disabilities.* Columbus: Charles E. Merrill, 1969.

Knobloch, H., and Pasamanick, B. *Gesell and Armatruda's Developmental Diagnosis.* New York: Harper & Row, 1974.

Piaget, J. *The Origins of Intelligence.* New York: W. W. Norton, 1952.

Weiss, C. E., and Lillywhite, H. S. *Communicative Disorders.* St. Louis: C. V. Mosby, 1976.

5 Exceptional Individuals: Mental, Physical, and Emotional Impairments

Guiding Questions

1. How are the terms "impaired," "exceptional," "disabled," and "handicapped" defined?
2. What are the most common causes of mental retardation?
3. What are the major causes of orthopedic impairment?
4. Who are "exceptional individuals" and what are the implications for physical education?
5. What is included under the category "seriously emotionally disturbed?"
6. What is meant by "severely handicapped" and "multihandicapped"?

Our society tends to impose labels, particularly upon individuals who have various physical, mental, emotional, and social conditions. Such terms as impaired, disabled, handicapped, and exceptional are often used synonymously and interchangeably, allowing for no real understanding of the individual's strengths and limitations. Too often, only lip service is given to a child's potential — what the child *can* do — while programs, activities, and efforts focus upon the disability and deficiency, and thus upon what the child *cannot* do. Although attention must be given to the disabilities or deficiencies, the individual ability of each child should be of prime importance when planning an educational program.

DEFINITION OF TERMS

Impaired individuals have identifiable organic or functional conditions; that is, some part of the body is actually missing, a portion of an anatomical structure is gone, or one or more parts of the body do not function properly or adequately. The condition may be permanent, as in the case of amputation, cerebral palsy, or congenital heart defect; or it may be temporary, as in the case of temporary paralysis, some learning disabilities, various emotional problems, certain social maladjustments, or specific movement deficiencies.

Individuals who are *disabled* because of impairments are limited or restricted in executing some skills, doing specific jobs or tasks, or performing certain activities. People with certain impairments should not be automatically excluded from activities because the condition makes it appear that they cannot participate safely, successfully, or with satisfaction. Indeed, some impaired people attain high levels of excellence in activities in which they are not supposed to be able to perform or participate. There is a growing number of success stories concerning highly motivated disabled individuals who are willing to put forth the extra effort for progress and achievement. Some of these individuals include Harry Condellos, a blind Boston Marathon runner; Wilma Rudolph, a congenital birth defect and polio victim who won three Olympic gold medals; Catfish Hunter, a severe diabetic and major league baseball player; Pete Gray, a single-arm amputee and major league centerfielder; Tom Dempsey, who is a professional football player although missing half of his foot; Yancy Sutton, a deaf linebacker; Patty Wilson, an epileptic long-distance runner; Jim Ryan, an asthmatic world-class distance runner; and George Murray and Curt Brinkman who, although confined to wheelchairs, finished the Boston Marathon before the first able-bodied runners.

Exceptional and _handicapped_ are terms that are currently used synonymously in reference to an individual with an impairment of functioning. For clarity and consistency, _handicapped person_ and _handicapping condition_ are defined as follows:

1. A handicapped person is "one who because of a physical or mental disability is at a disadvantage in functioning in one or more major life activities" (Office of Handicapped Individuals in the Department of Health, Education and Welfare).

2. "A handicapping condition is one where a . . . condition exists which is liable to persist over a long period of time and which impairs the normal functions of the individual to a significant degree" (White House Conference on Handicapped Individuals, 1977: 49).

Current estimates of the number of handicapped individuals (adults and children) are somewhat variable. According to leading authorities in attendance at the 1977 White House Conference on Handicapped Individuals, there were at that time an estimated seven million children with mental or physical handicaps — 10 percent of the school-aged population. An additional one million preschool children are considered handicapped in any of the following categories: deaf, blind, mentally retarded, speech-impaired, motor-impaired, emotionally disturbed, multihandicapped, learning-disabled, and other health-impaired (see Table 5–1).

Table 5–1. Prevalence of handicapped children

	Percent of population	_Number of children_
Visually impaired	0.1	55,000
Hearing impaired	0.6–0.8	330,000–440,000
Speech handicapped	3.4–5.0	1,925,000–2,750,000
Physically handicapped	0.5	275,000
Emotionally disturbed	2.0–3.0	1,100,000–1,650,000
Mentally retarded	2.5–3.0	1,375,000–1,650,000
Learning-disabled	2.0–4.0	1,100,000–2,200,000
Total	11.2–16.4	6,160,000–9,020,000

SOURCE: Adapted from T. M. Skrtic, _Instructor's Resource Manual: Exceptional Children and Youth_ (Denver: Love Publishing Co., 1978), p. 27. Reprinted by permission of the publisher.

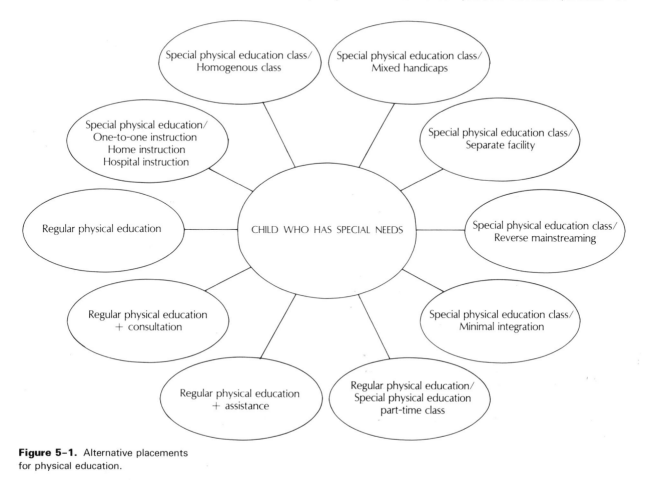

Figure 5–1. Alternative placements
for physical education.

Not all handicapped children will be placed in the regular education setting; the more severely handicapped, or those who specifically need a separate placement, will be more appropriately placed in one of the special education settings. With the implementation of PL 94–142, those who can safely and successfully function in the mainstream of regular education will do so; consequently, the number of handicapped children in regular education settings shall increase. The alternative placements for physical education services are many. (Figure 5–1 clearly identifies the various education settings available to handicapped individuals. Each alternative represents a possible least restrictive environment dependent upon the extent to which a child has special needs.)

THE NONCATEGORICAL APPROACH TO EDUCATIONAL PROGRAMMING

Traditionally, impaired, disabled, and handicapped individuals have been classified, categorized, and programmed according to specific physical, mental, emotional, or social conditions. Basic to this categorical approach is the false assumption that all people with a given condition have identical needs, interests, and abilities. Failure to recognize the uniqueness of each person negates the concept of individual differences. In fact, there is as much diversity among those with the same condition as there is between these individuals as a group and those who have other conditions or who have no impairment, disability, or handicap. Planning and programming on the basis of handicapping condition must be reevaluated in deference to planning and programming for the individual.

Specifically applied to physical education and recreation programs, the noncategorical approach focuses upon children as they function in various types and levels of programs and activities. Physical, mental, emotional, and social characteristics influence involvement, success, achievement, and satisfaction from physical education and recreation activities. The noncategorical approach deals with the whole child, not with a condition that may or may not affect the child's ability to perform certain movements, skills, and activities.

Thus categories and conditions per se should not be the major criteria in programs of physical education, although knowledge of these handicapping conditions does provide necessary information pertinent to a working knowledge of the handicapped child. Categories, educational, and legal classifications do provide the physical educator with knowledge of the specific characteristics of the various handicapping conditions, but do not provide more than generalizations when applied to a given handicapped individual. For example, the category of mental retardation includes below-average general intelligence, below-average language development, delayed motor development, and deficits in adaptive behavior. Within a given characteristic lies a range of variability that then can only be applied generally to the individual. Within below-average general intelligence, the mentally retarded child may be functioning at the mildly retarded end of the continuum, at the severely retarded end, or anywhere in between. In this case, the categorical label by itself does not provide adequate information.

Although the characteristics of the categories of handicapping conditions should be used in understanding, evaluating, and programming, this information should be regarded as providing guidelines only. The emphasis should be placed upon the child's needs and capabilities, with attention paid to possible limitations. Categories can and have sometimes been used to place undue limitations upon an individual's potential performance. The categories, and the characteristics thereof, must be employed in the fashion that best serves the exceptional individual.

Categories of handicapping conditions have existed for many years. Throughout the years, the actual categorical labels have varied as societal trends and legislation have precipitated changes. Current legislation, PL 94–142, has once again altered the categorical titles. Although the names may change in the future, it is believed that, for the most part, the categories of today have evolved into fairly discrete descriptions of handicapping conditions.

PL 94–142, Section 121a.5, offers a definition of handicapped children that includes the categories of handicapping conditions. Those categories and combinations thereof have provided the basis for the following classification system to be used in this text: (1) mentally retarded; (2) orthopedically impaired; (3) severely emotionally disturbed and behaviorally disordered; (4) multihandicapped and severely handicapped; (5) speech- and/or language-disabled; (6) other health-impaired; (7) deaf-blind; (8) blind/visually handicapped, (9) deaf/hard of hearing; and (10) specific learning-disabled.

The discussion of the various handicapping conditions in the balance of this chapter is intended to provide the reader with a basic understanding and workable knowledge of exceptional individuals. Each handicapping condition is identified by a legal definition, an overview of the etiology, and a discussion of the condition's characteristics. It cannot be stressed too often that, just as there is variability within the normal population, much variability exists within the handicapped population and also within handicapping conditions.

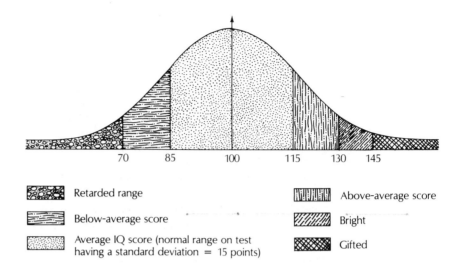

Figure 5-2. Range of IQ scores.

▨ Retarded range	▧ Above-average score
▤ Below-average score	▨ Bright
▨ Average IQ score (normal range on test having a standard deviation = 15 points)	▨ Gifted

MENTALLY RETARDED

Legal Classification

According to PL 94-142, Section 121a.5(b) (4),

"Mentally retarded" means significantly sub-average general intellectual functioning, existing concurrently with deficits in adaptive behavior and manifested during the developmental period, which adversely affects a child's educational performance.

The above definition is based on the 1973 definition of mental retardation offered by the American Association on Mental Deficiency (AAMD), and is the most comprehensive and widely used description of the mentally retarded population.

"Subaverage general intellectual functioning" means that the individual's assessed level is two or more standard deviations (S.D.) from the mean on a standardized intelligence test (see Figure 5-2). The Stanford-Binet and the Revised Wechsler Intelligence Scale for Children (WISC-R) are tests commonly used in schools for the determination of mental retardation (see Table 5-2).

The AAMD's classification system is obviously based on the severity of the retardation, and has definable IQ limits. The educational classification system is based not only on severity of retardation, but also is intended to be descriptive of the educational needs of the retarded individual. Currently, it appears as if the educational classification system is aligned more with the medical classification. In general, the *mildly mentally*

Table 5-2. Classification systems associated with IQ scores

AAMD classification	Stanford-Binet IQ	WISC-R IQ	Educational classification
Mildly retarded	68-52	69-55 ⎫	Educable mentally retarded
Moderately retarded	51-36	54-40 ⎬	
Severely retarded	35-20	39-25	Trainable mentally retarded
Profoundly retarded	<20	<25	Custodial

SOURCE: Adapted from H. J. Grossman, *Manual on Terminology and Classification in Mental Retardation* (Washington, D.C.: American Association on Mental Deficiency, 1977), p. 19.

retarded can be considered to be educable, inasmuch as they can be taught the basics of academic subjects. These individuals usually can achieve maximum performance at the sixth-grade level. The mildly retarded individual shows an ability to socially adjust to various situations, and can seek gainful employment.

The *moderately* to *severely mentally retarded* individual can be considered trainable, but the educational program must concentrate upon the functional or basic skills with emphasis on self-help and vocational skills. The moderately to severely retarded individual can be expected to achieve a maximum of second-grade level of educational performance. This individual shows potential for training in self-help skills, social adjustment, and economic usefulness (Gearheart and Litton, 1975). The truly custodial retarded, usually referred to as *profoundly retarded,* are more often found in institutions than public schools, but not exclusively. Most are in need of nearly complete care and supervision throughout life. Approximately 3 percent of the total population meet the criteria to be classified as retarded (see Table 5–3).

"Adaptive behavior" refers to the individual's ability to "meet the standards of his [or her] age and cultural group in personal independence and social responsibility" (Gearheart and Litton, 1975: 22). This adaptive behavior varies, and is relative to age and situation. The AAMD has specified adaptive behavior skills within various age-groups (see Table 5–4).

The "developmental period" has an upper limit of eighteen years. Consequently, according to the current definition, to be classified as mentally retarded an individual must be measured as having below-average general intelligence and deficits in adaptive behavior that have been manifest before eighteen years of age (during the developmental period) (see Figure 5–3).

Etiology

The causes of mental retardation are numerous and may be the results of either a single factor or multiple factors. Often, the causes fall into one of two broad

Table 5–3. Prevalence of retardation by age and level

1970 Census	Population	Under 21 years	21 years and over
Total population	203.3 million	80.5 million	122.7 million
Retarded population	6.1 million	2.4 million	3.7 million
Profoundly retarded about 1.5%	92,000	36,000	56,000
Severely retarded 3.5%	214,000	84,000	130,000
Moderately retarded 6%	366,000	144,000	222,000
Mildly retarded 89%	5.4 million	2.1 million	3.7 million

SOURCE: Adapted from National Association for Retarded Citizens, *Facts on Mental Retardation* (Arlington, Texas: National Association for Retarded Citizens, 1973).

Table 5-4. Adaptive behavior skills

Infancy and early childhood	Childhood and early adolescence	Late adolescence and adulthood
■ sensory-motor abilities ■ self-help skills ■ communication skills ■ socialization skills	■ academic skills ■ mastery of environment ■ interpersonal social skills	■ vocational skills ■ social responsibilities

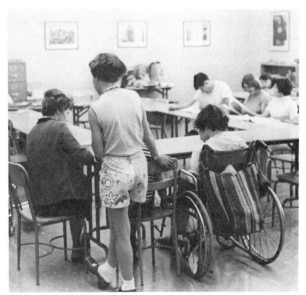

Figure 5-3. Adaptive behavior skills throughout life: sensorimotor ability of the young child (above left); retarded adolescents doing academic work (above right); and a retarded adult employing skills in a sheltered workshop (right). SOURCE: Photos by Ben Esparza (top left) and Lyonel Avance (top right).

categories: (1) brain-damaged (exogenous) and (2) cultural-familial (endogenous). Brain damage refers to mental retardation due to accident or injury before, during, or after birth. Cultural-familial refers to mental retardation due to environmental or possible genetic factors. Although the AAMD has identified ten general causal groupings for mental retardation, some causes are as yet unknown. The following categories will be discussed (the reader is referred to Robinson and Robinson [1976] and Grossman [1977] for a detailed listing of mental retardation syndromes and their causes):

1. Infections and intoxicants.
2. Metabolism or nutrition.
3. Gross brain disease.
4. Unknown prenatal influence.
5. Chromosomal abnormality.
6. Gestational disorders.
7. Other causes: environmental influences, trauma or physical agents, retardation following psychiatric disorder, other conditions.

Infections and Intoxicants

Infections and intoxicants can lead to retardation by their occurrence in either the mother-to-be, the infant, or the young child after birth. Rubella (German measles) and syphilis are examples of infections of the mother that affect the fetus.

Rubella infection during the first trimester of pregnancy may result in abnormalities in 50 percent of the infants, including cataracts, cardiac anomalies, deafness, blindness, microcephaly, and mental retardation. *Syphilis*, which is passed from mother to fetus as a transplacental infection, often results in rashes, severe rhinitis (snuffles), lesions of mouth, pseudo-paralysis of limbs, convulsions, and mental retardation.

Postnatal cerebral infections resulting from viruses, bacteria, parasites, and fungi have been known to cause mental retardation. *Meningitis*, an infection of the covering of the brain, and *encephalitis*, an inflammation of the brain, are two examples of infections that can affect mental development (see Figure 5–4).

A hemolytic or blood disease, such as *Rh incompatibility*, is another factor in which a toxic substance buildup in the fetus contributes to brain damage that causes mental retardation. *Poisoning*, in either the mother or the young child, can result in mental retardation. Possible poisons include lead, mercury, alcohol, manganese, arsenic, carbon monoxide, tobacco, heroin, food additives, and other drugs and narcotics (Hallahan and Kauffman, 1978; Gearheart and Litton, 1975).

Metabolism and Nutrition

This category includes metabolic, nutritional, endocrine, and mineral dysfunction as possible causes of retardation. Genetically determined metabolic disorders include PKU (phenylketonuria), Tay-Sachs disease, and Hurler's disease (gargoylism). *PKU* is the inability of the body to convert phenylamine (a common dietary substance found in milk) to tryosine, causing an accumulation of phenylpyruvic acid, a poison that causes damage to the brain. PKU is easily detected by a blood test. If untreated, children with PKU will suffer from mental retardation; however, if a specialized milk-free diet is started early (from two to four months of age), there is a good prognosis of little or no retardation.

Tay-Sachs disease, a disturbance of lipid metabolism, is a serious progressive degenerative disorder that results in death before eight or nine years of age. The majority of all known cases occur in Jewish families. *Hurler's disease* (gargoylism) is characterized by abnormal deposits of carbohydrates containing sugar throughout the body, especially in the tissues of the liver, heart, lungs, and brain. Progressive physical and mental deterioration result, with death occurring near the age of twelve.

Other common metabolic or nutritional disorders

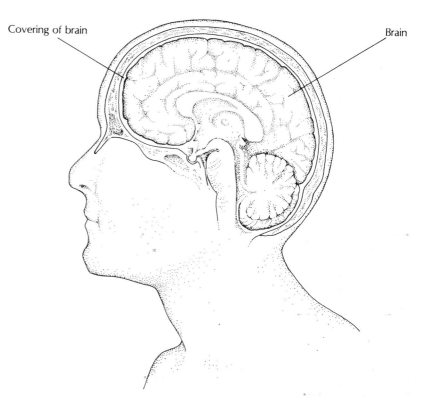

Covering of brain

Brain

Figure 5–4. Areas of the brain affected by meningitis and encephalitis.

include cretinism (hypothyroidism), Wilson's disease, and Prader-Willi syndrome. *Cretinism,* the most common endocrine problem, results from a thyroid gland disorder. The clinical features of cretinism include short, thick hands and neck; fine, thin, straight hair; delayed bone development; coarse voice; large tongue; and heart problems (see Figure 5–5).

Wilson's disease is a mineral disorder resulting from abnormal copper metabolism. If untreated by a special low-copper diet, progressive mental deterioration (due to degeneration of the gray matter of the brain) and death will occur. Prader-Willi syndrome is characterized by hypotonia and extreme obesity. People who are affected with this syndrome are obsessive overeaters; in some cases, padlocks must be placed on refrigerators and kitchen cupboards to prevent continual eating. Diabetes is often present in this syndrome.

Dietary imbalances of the child can result in slow development and retardation. Improper nutrition resulting in mental retardation can be caused by a

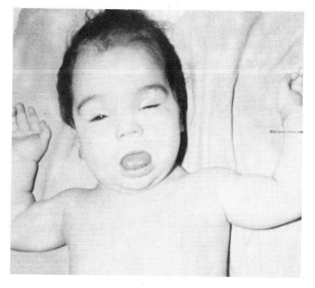

Figure 5–5. Infant exhibiting clinical features of cretinism. SOURCE: © L. V. Bergman & Assoc., Inc., Cold Spring, N.Y.

malnourished expectant mother or a malnourished child. Such problems may arise from inadequate diets, excessive intake of vitamins, disease, and various feeding problems.

Gross Brain Disease

Gross brain disease refers to postnatal mental retardation resulting from heredegenerative disorders. Three examples of inherited disorders are tuberous sclerosis, Stärge-Weber-Dimitri's syndrome, and Recklinghausen's disease (neurofibromatosis).

Tuberous sclerosis is a dominant genetic disorder characterized by potato-like nodules on the bridge of the nose and the cheeks, tumors in various parts of the body (especially the kidneys, heart, and brain), and progressive mental retardation. Stärge-Weber-Dimitri's syndrome is an inherited condition characterized by a "port wine stain" resulting from vascular malformation over the meninges of the parietal and occipital lobes of the brain. Although seizure activity is frequent, the range of intelligences does vary from normal to severe retardation. Recklinghausen's disease (neurofibromatosis) is a dominant, genetic, progressively degenerative disease characterized by yellow and brown pigmentations on the skin (café-au-lait spots), skin tumors, and tumors affecting the brain, spinal cord, meninges, and the roots of the cranial and spinal nerves (see Figure 5-6).

Unknown Prenatal Influence

No definitive cause has been found for the types of retardation in this category. Examples include microcephalus and hydrocephalus (see Figure 5-7), Apert's syndrome, and Cornelia deLange syndrome.

Microcephalus is characterized by an abnormally small head (2 S.D. below the mean). Lack of brain tissue formation and destruction of brain processes ac-

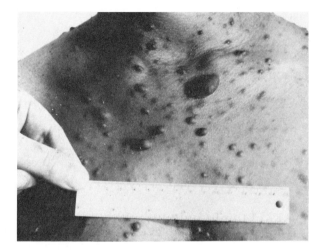

Figure 5-6. Note the café-au-lait spots and skin tumors characteristic of neurofibromatosis. SOURCE: © L. V. Bergman & Assoc., Inc., Cold Spring, N.Y.

company this condition. Hydrocephalus can be caused by an infection, trauma, or a developmental disorder resulting in excessive accumulation of cerebrospinal fluid under increased pressure. This increases the head size in children whose skull sutures have not fused, and increases intracranial pressure in those whose skulls are fully formed. Apert's syndrome is characterized by a narrowing of the skull such that improper brain development occurs. Severe mental retardation, skeletal abnormalities, and syndactyly (webbing) of hands and feet accompany Apert's syndrome. Cornelia deLange syndrome is a cranio-facial (head-face) anomaly characterized by severe mental retardation, excessive amounts of body hair, bushy eyelashes and eyebrows, and self-mutilative behavior (see Figure 5-8).

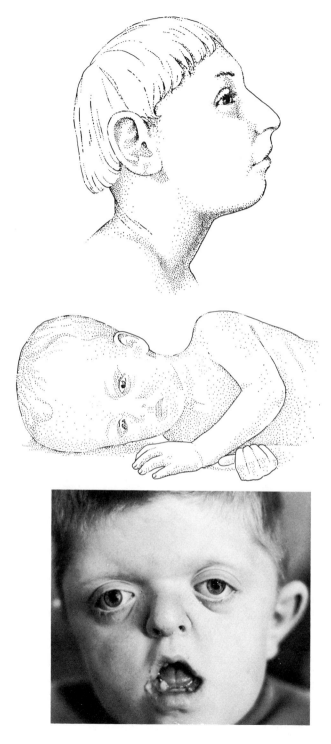

Figure 5–7. Retardation caused by unknown prenatal influences can result in microcephaly, or small head (upper left), and hydrocephaly, often characterized by an enlarged head (lower left). SOURCE: Lower left drawing adapted from an original painting by Frank H. Netter, M.D., from *The CIBA Collection of Medical Illustrations*, copyright by CIBA Pharmaceutical Company, Division of CIBA-GEIGY Corporation.

Chromosomal Abnormality

All aberrations of chromosomes (numerical, structural, or multiple) resulting in retardation are included in this category. Chromosomal disorders can be caused by abnormalities found in both regular autosomes and sex chromosomes. Possible causes of aberrations include gene mutation, radiation, drugs, viruses, and geographic locale; socioeconomic factors are sometimes considered to be at the root of factors such as poor nutrition, poor prenatal care, and so on. (Grossman, 1973).

Down's syndrome (mongolism), the most common type of chromosomal abnormality, is specifically associated with chromosome 21 and can result in one of the following three types: (1) trisomy, an extra chromosome 21; (2) translocation, the attachment of chromosome 21 to one of the other chromosomes;

Figure 5–8. Apert's syndrome— narrowing of the skull—is another result of unknown prenatal influences. SOURCE: Claudine Sherrill, *Adapted Physical Education and Recreaton: A Multidisciplinary Approach*, 2d ed © 1976, 1981 Wm. C. Brown Company Publishers, Dubuque, Iowa. Reprinted by permission.

Table 5-5. Clinical features and characteristics of Down's Syndrome

Physical features:

- short, broad neck, hands, feet
- short extremities
- pear-shaped abdomen (protruding)
- short fingers
- flat nose
- small mouth
- large tongue
- almond-shaped, closely set eyes
- small teeth
- straight, fine, sparse hair
- elastic, rough skin

Related aspects:

- congenital heart disorders
- poor muscle tone (hypotonia)
- increased flexibility
- overweight
- stunted growth
- slow, delayed development

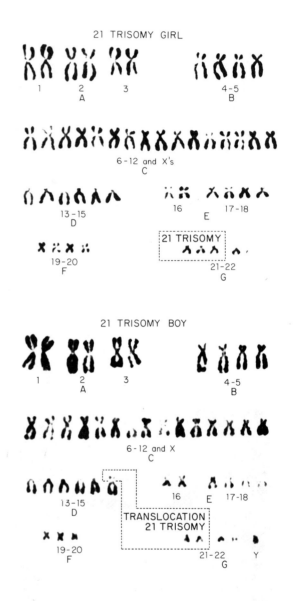

Figure 5-9. Two examples of karotype for Down's syndrome male and female. SOURCE: D. W. Smith and A. A. Wilson, *The Child with Down's Syndrome* (Philadelphia: W. B. Saunders, 1973), used with permission.

Figure 5-10. Two Down's syndrome children participating in an arts and crafts project. Note the clinical features exhibited.

and (3) <u>mosaicism,</u> resulting in some cells having the normal number of chromosomes (forty-six) and others having cells of forty-seven or forty-five chromosomes (see Figures 5-9 and 5-10, and Table 5-5).

   <u>Cri-du-chat syndrome (cat-cry syndrome)</u> is associated with a partial deletion of chromosome 5, resulting in many deformities. The most striking feature of this syndrome is a high-pitched, cat-like cry, along with severe retardation.

   Two sex chromosome abnormalities are Klinefelter's syndrome, occurring in males, the Turner's syndrome, occurring in females. The males with <u>Klinefelter's syndrome have an XXY</u> sex chromosome composition instead of the normal XY composition, and are characterized by retardation, sexual disorders, and psychotic disorders. <u>Turner's syndrome,</u> the absence of an X chromosome, results in more masculine-appearing features in females. Although it sometimes results in retardation, this condition more commonly results in learning disabilities.

Gestational Disorders

These disorders are limited to those in which the period of pregnancy or gestation was atypical; either too short (prematurity), or too long (postmaturity). Pre-maturity refers to birth before thirty-seven weeks and/or weight at birth under 5½ pounds. Postmaturity refers to infants who are born several days after the normal gestational period limits. A high incidence of defects is related to atypical gestation, many of which result in mental retardation.

Other Causes

Probably the largest number of mentally retarded individuals fall under this general heading. <u>Environmental influences</u> such as sensory deprivation, neglect, or other adverse conditions may result in retardation without apparent evidence of brain damage or genetic abnormalities. <u>Trauma or physical agents</u> can also cause mental retardation. These include injuries to the brain before, during, or after birth, as well as brain injury resulting from child abuse and battery. Retardation may also result *following psychiatric disorder* when there is no evidence of cerebral pathology. The AAMD lists one additional category of retardation, <u>other conditions,</u> which includes retardation of unknown etiology. In these cases, there is no evidence of structural defect, physical cause, or associated psychosocial factor, and no history of subnormal functioning of parents and siblings.

Table 5-6. Developmental milestones of the mentally retarded

	Preschool age: 0−5 Maturation and development	School age: 6−21 Training and education	Adult: 21− Social and vocational
Level I Profound	Gross retardation; minimal capacity for functioning in sensorimotor areas; needs nursing care.	Some motor development present; cannot profit from training in self-help; needs total care.	Some motor and speech development; totally incapable of self-maintenance; needs complete care and supervision.
Level II Severe	Poor motor development; speech is minimal; generally unable to profit from training in self-help; little or no communication skills.	Can talk or learn to communicate; can be trained in elemental health habits; cannot learn functional academic skills; profits from systematic training ("trainable").	Can contribute partially; self-support under complete supervision; can develop self-protection skills to a minimum useful level in controlled environment.
Level III Moderate	Can talk or learn to communicate; poor social awareness, fair development; may profit from self-help; can be managed with moderate supervision.	Can learn functional academic skills to approximately fourth-grade level by late teens if given "special education" ("educable").	Capable of self-maintenance in unskilled or semiskilled occupations; needs supervision and guidance when under mild social or economic stress.
Level IV Mild	Can develop social and communication skills; minimal retardation in sensorimotor areas; rarely distinguished from normal until later age.	Can learn academic skills to approximately sixth-grade level by late teens. Cannot learn general high school subjects. Needs special education, particularly at secondary school age level ("educable").	Capable of social and vocational adequacy with proper education and training. Often needs supervision and guidance under serious social or economic stress.

SOURCE: Rick Heber, *A Manual on Terminology and Classification in Mental Retardation* (Springfield, Illinois: Monograph Supplement to American Journal of Mental Deficiency, 2d ed., American Association on Mental Deficiency, 1961, pp. 20–43, 61).

Characteristics

Characteristics have been identified as common to the category known as mentally retarded, although an individual mentally retarded child may not show these characteristics. Most often, the appearance of or the likelihood of the appearance of these characteristics is related to the severity of the retardation (see Table 5-6).

One of the <u>most obvious characteristics of the retarded is the *reduced ability to learn*</u>. The mentally re-

tarded child is deficient in comparison to normal children in the areas of learning and memory (Estes, 1970; Robinson and Robinson, 1970, 1976; Hallahan and Kauffman, 1978). The mentally retarded individual often exhibits difficulty in attending to a variety of stimuli; delay in mastering tasks; short attention span; poor short-term memory; and difficulty in employing appropriate learning strategies.

Language difficulties are frequently encountered with mentally retarded children. <u>Typically, the retarded child's developmental language level is below the</u>

child's general mental age level (Smith, 1974). Some of the common characteristics include delayed language development, articulation problems, voice disorders, stuttering, and decreased level of language usage.

The mentally retarded individual is obviously _delayed in academic achievement,_ but the degree depends on the level of retardation. _Social development is also delayed,_ but a mentally retarded individual may display relatively normal social interaction. Depending on the severity of the condition, a mildly mentally retarded individual can show adequate occupational success, and marital and community adjustment.

Although an individual may not physically look retarded, _a delay in physical and motor development_ is often present. The mentally retarded individual is slower to develop motor patterns and movement abilities. The physical educator who considers IQ to be

an indication of rate of learning rather than amount to be learned will have a workable guideline for planning individualized programs. The motor skill levels attained by the mentally retarded are often less than the attained skill levels of normal individuals, but the range of capabilities and levels of attainment is exemplified by the achievements of the highly skilled Special Olympic athletes (see Figures 5–11 and 5–12, and Table 5–7).

ORTHOPEDICALLY IMPAIRED

Legal Classification

The term "orthopedically impaired" has, at least legally, replaced the term "physically handicapped." Approximately 3.5 percent of school-age children are physically handicapped due to orthopedic or neu-

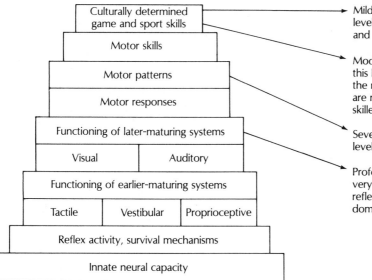

Figure 5-11. Achievement levels of mentally retarded individuals.

Table 5-7. Physical and motor characteristics of the mentally retarded

---

- awkward movement ability
- clumsy
- often flat-footed
- toe-heel shuffle gait
- difficulty in control of movement
- slow reaction time
- poor fine motor coordination
- poor posture, rounded shoulders
- easily fatigued
- poor muscle tone
- poor balance
- poor body awareness
- poor spatial, temporal awareness

---

rological impairment. According to PL 94-142, Section 121a.5(b) (6),

> "Orthopedically impaired" means a severe orthopedic impairment which adversely affects a child's educational performance. The term includes impairments caused by congenital anomaly, impairments caused by disease, and impairments from other causes.

This section of the chapter will deal specifically with orthopedic impairments that affect school-age children. Orthopedic problems affect the use of the body, especially the skeletal system, including the spine, muscles, bones, and joints. These impairments have a variety of causes. Three main sources of orthopedic impairments presented here are: (1) neurological impairment; (2) musculoskeletal conditions; and (3) trauma. Orthopedically impaired individuals are so diverse in etiology and characteristics that discus-

Figure 5-12. Mentally retarded youngsters participating in 50-yard dash at the Special Olympics.

sion of each of the three above-mentioned sources will focus upon the etiological factors and characteristics unique to that source and condition.

Neurological Impairment

Neurological impairment implies damage or deterioration to the central nervous system — the brain or spinal cord. The causes of and symptoms resulting from brain damage are many and varied and will only be discussed in conjunction with the specific disorder. It should be kept in mind that, whenever the central nervous system suffers damage, muscular weakness or paralysis are almost always present. For the purposes of this text, three types of neurological impairment will be discussed: (1) cerebral palsy; (2) poliomyelitis; and (3) multiple sclerosis.

Cerebral Palsy

Cerebral palsy is a condition or group of conditions characterized by paralysis, weakness, incoordination, or other motor dysfunction due to damage to the motor areas of the brain. Cerebral palsy was originally known as Little's disease, based upon a report by an English orthopedic surgeon, W. J. Little. In the 1930s, the name was changed to congenital spastic paralysis; in the 1940s, the term cerebral palsy was accepted. Cerebral palsy is not commonly referred to as a disease because it is not contagious or progressive, and there are no remissions.

Anything that results in oxygen deprivation (anoxia), poisoning, cerebral bleeding, or direct trauma to the brain before, during, or shortly after birth, can be a possible cause of cerebral palsy (Hallahan and Kauffman, 1978). Maternal infections, chronic diseases, physical trauma, maternal exposure to toxic substances (including x-rays), or direct trauma or anoxia during the birth process can cause damage to the brain. Premature birth or anoxia, high fevers, infections, poisoning, hemorrhaging, or direct head injury shortly after birth can also cause cerebral palsy.

There are six types of cerebral palsy (see Table 5–8):

1. *Spasticity* is characterized by a significant increase in muscle tone to the point of hypertonicity, and

Table 5-8. Types of cerebral palsy

Type of cerebral palsy	% of cases	Common associated disorders
Spasticity	50–60%	Mental retardation (full range); perceptual impairment (visual and/or auditory); speech disorders (articulation, stuttering).
Athetosis	20–30%	Hearing loss; speech disorders; visual disorders.
Ataxia	8%	Speech disorders; perceptual impairment.
Rigidity	4%	Severe mental retardation.
Tremor	2%	Mental retardation; perceptual disorders.
Mixed	Category used infrequently.	Usually severe involvement; multiple handicaps.

Figure 5-13. Three cerebral palsied children: rigid (left), athetoid (center), spastic (right).

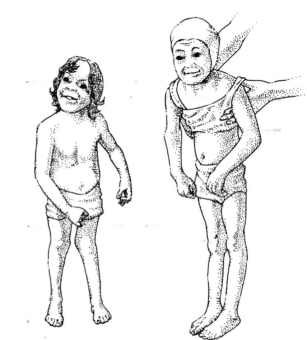

by exaggerated stretch reflexes. The muscles involuntarily contract when suddenly stretched, which results in a marked inability to perform precise voluntary movements. Tenseness and difficult, inaccurate voluntary movement results. This is by far the most common type of cerebral palsy (see Figure 5-13).

2. _Athetosis_ refers to involuntary, jerky, writhing movements. The continuous contraction of successive groups of muscles results in slow, uncontrollable, unpredictable, and purposeless motion of the involved body parts.

3. _Ataxia_ is characterized by awkwardness of fine and gross motor movements. It is a disorder of balance and posture, resulting from proprioceptive and vestibular inadequacies. The resulting movements are slow and deliberate, yet awkward, which cause the individual to appear to be functioning in a "drunken" state. When combined with spasticity and athetosis, these three types constitute 78 to 98 percent of all cerebral palsy.

4. _Rigidity_ refers to diffuse, continuous muscle tension and, consequently, generalized inelasticity and stiffness. Diminished motion and hyperextension characterize this type of cerebral palsy.

5. _Tremor_ refers to rhythmic, involuntary vibrating movements. The tremor is increased with voluntary movements.

6. _Mixed_ refers to the combination of several types of cerebral palsy in any one individual.

Another method of classifying cerebral palsy, as well as other motor disabilities or paralysis, is by topographical classification. This involves the identification by affected extremities as follows (Denoff, 1967):

1. *Hemiplegia:* one half of the body is involved. The arm and the leg on the same side are affected. (35 to 40 percent of the cases).
2. *Diplegia:* legs are involved to a greater extent than the arms (10 to 20 percent).
3. *Quadraplegia:* all four limbs are involved (15 to 20 percent).
4. *Paraplegia:* only the legs are involved (10 to 20 percent).
5. *Monoplegia:* one arm or limb is involved (rarely occurs).
6. *Triplegia:* three limbs are involved (rarely occurs).
7. *Double Hemiplegia:* both halves of the body are involved but, unlike quadraplegia, the sides are affected differently (rarely occurs).

Poliomyelitis

Poliomyelitis is an infectious disease caused by the polio virus, which attacks the nerve tissue in the spinal cord and/or brain, most commonly attacking the motor cells in the anterior horn of the spinal cord. Before the perfection of the Salk vaccine in the 1950s, polio was a leading crippler of children and young adults in the United States. Although only 6 percent of those who contract polio die, 14 percent have severe paralysis, 30 percent suffer mild paralysis or aftereffects, and 50 percent recover completely (see Figures 5–14 and 5–15).

The postpolio victim is usually not intellectually affected, but is left with severe muscular weakness, spasticity, and complete paralysis or skeletal deformities. Due to damage to affected nerve cells, impulses to muscles are not transmitted. Lack of stimulation to muscles results in loss of muscle function, movement, and strength, due to muscle hypotonicity and atrophy.

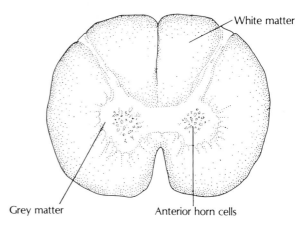

Figure 5–14. Cross-section of spinal cord. Polio virus usually attacks the motor cells in the anterior horn.

Multiple Sclerosis

Multiple sclerosis is a chronic and degenerative neurological disease primarily affecting older adolescents and adults. It is a chronic, slowly progressive disease of the central nervous system leading to the disintegration of the myelin coverings of nerve fibers, which results in hardening or scarring of the tissue that replaces the disintegrated protective myelin sheath. The cause of this demyelinating disease and others, such as amyotrophic lateral sclerosis (ALS, or Lou Gehrig's disease), is not known (see Figure 5–16).

Multiple sclerosis generally appears between the ages of twenty and forty, and results in incapacitation and eventual death. The symptoms include a variety of sensory problems, tremors, muscle weakness, spasticity, speech difficulties, dizziness, mild emotional disturbances, partial paralysis, and motor difficulties.

Figure 5-15. Post-polio victim walking. Note the apparent loss of muscle tone in legs as evidenced by hyperextended knees (side view); exaggerated rotation of hips, swing-through action of legs, and plantar flexion of feet (front view). SOURCE: R. Ducroquret et al., *Walking and Limping* (Philadelphia: Lippincott, 1968); used by permission of Lippincott/Harper & Row.

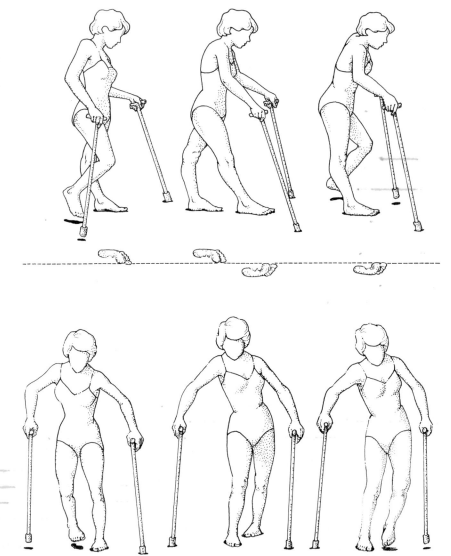

Musculoskeletal Conditions

Some children are physically handicapped due to defects or diseases of the muscles or bones. The condition of the musculature or skeletal system, or both, affects these children's ability to move. Problems arising from musculoskeletal conditions, without neurological impairment, may be congenital or acquired after birth. The causes of these conditions may include genetic defects, infectious disease, accidents, or developmental disorders. In the majority of individuals, intellectual functioning is not affected.

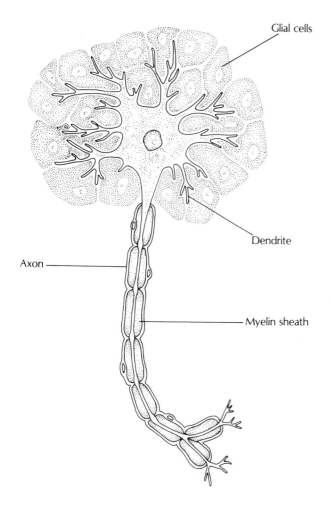

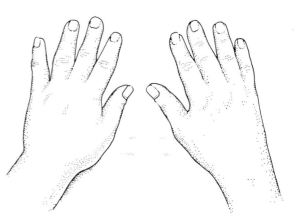

Arthritis

Simply stated, <u>arthritis means joint inflammation</u> that causes great pain in and around the joints. Arthritis may be found in people of any age, including young children. It is estimated that there are 35 million individuals in the U.S., including 250,000 children under sixteen years of age, affected with arthritis.

Rheumatoid arthritis, the most common form, has been defined as a <u>systematic</u> (i.e., affecting the entire skeletal system) <u>disease, with the major symptoms being the involvement of the muscles and joints.</u> *Juvenile rheumatoid arthritis*, also known as *Still's Disease*, attacks children before the age of seven years. Females are affected more often than males. The cause and cure of rheumatoid arthritis and juvenile rheumatoid arthritis are unknown at this time (see Figure 5–17).

Figure 5–16. The neuron with myelin sheath covering of axon. The myelin sheath disintegrates in multiple sclerosis.

Figure 5–17. The joints of these arthritic hands are swollen, making movement painful.

Figure 5-18. Common types of clubfoot.

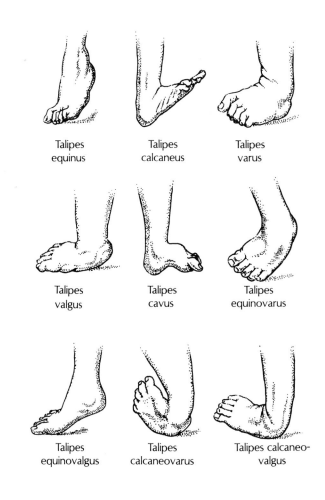

Talipes equinus   Talipes calcaneus   Talipes varus

Talipes valgus   Talipes cavus   Talipes equinovarus

Talipes equinovalgus   Talipes calcaneovarus   Talipes calcaneovalgus

Arthritis, in any form, varies greatly in severity from relatively mild inflammation, to swelling and stiffness in the joints and connective tissues, to extreme debilitation in the form of atrophy and joint deformity. The arthritic involvement is usually symmetrical, and is commonly found initially in the small joints of the hands and feet. Tenderness and pain usually accompany arthritis.

Arthrogryposis

Arthrogryposis is a congenital condition in which muscles of the limbs are missing, or are smaller and weaker than normal, resulting in stiffness and/or deformity of the limbs and trunk (Hallahan and Kauffman, 1978). Due to this condition, several joints may become fixed at birth, which has precipitated the use of the term "multiple congenital contractures." Arthrogryposis is similar to arthritis in the awkwardness of joint positions and mechanics, but dissimilar in that it causes no pain.

Clubfoot (Talipes)

Clubfoot (talipes) is a common foot deformity that occurs two times per 10,000 births. This orthopedic defect can be either acquired or congenital. *Acquired clubfoot* develops from spastic paralysis, found in neuromuscular disorders such as cerebral palsy. The causes of *congenital clubfoot* are not known, but are thought to include defective cells, muscle imbalance, and position in utero. Bracing, casting, and surgery are utilized in the correction of clubfoot. Many types of clubfoot exist, and are identified by the direction of the deformity (see Figure 5-18):

1. *Talipes equinus:* forefoot plantar-flexed (heels drawn up).
2. *Talipes calcaneus:* forefoot dorsiflexed (toes drawn up).
3. *Talipes varus:* inverted heel and forefoot (sole of foot turned in).
4. *Talipes valgus:* everted heel and forefoot (sole of foot turned out).
5. *Talipes cavus:* hollow foot, high arch.
6. *Talipes equinovarus* (most common): inverted foot, forefoot adducted, forefoot plantarflexed.
7. *Talipes equinovalgus:* everted forefoot and heel, forefoot plantarflexed.
8. *Talipes calcaneousvarus:* forefoot dorsiflexed, inverted heel and forefoot.
9. *Talipes calcaneovalgus:* foot dorsiflexed, everted forefoot and heel.

Congenital Amputations

Children born with a limb or part of a limb missing are said to have a congenital amputation, otherwise

Figure 5-19. This boy, a congenital amputee, was born without legs and with feet attached at the thighs.

known as skeletal anomalies. Thalidomide babies, born after World War II, are commonly associated with this type of musculoskeletal impairment (see Figure 5-19).

Congenital Malformations

Congenital defects of malformations include those of the heart, head, and face (craniofacial abnormalities); extremities; and hip. Congenital malformations of the heart, head, and face (eyes, ears, nose, mouth) and the extremities (webbing of fingers, an extra toe, deformity of a limb) are correctable by plastic, corrective, and reconstructive surgery. Congenital dislocation of the hip (dysplasia), a fairly common affliction in eight times more females than males, is a condition usually corrected with the use of casts and braces until the hip socket grows properly.

Dwarfism

Dwarfism results from retarded physical growth (retarded growth is that which is more than three S.D. below the mean for any given age group). The dwarf most commonly seen is a victim of achondroplasia, a congenital skeletal anomaly caused by an autosomal (i.e., a chromosome other than a sex chromosome) dominant gene abnormality. The dwarf is quite physically capable, except for the limitations imposed by disproportionately short arms and legs relative to a normal sized trunk and head. There is no mental retardation directly associated with dwarfism.

Legg-Calve-Perthes (Coxa Plana)

Legg-Calve-Perthes (coxa plana) is a condition of the hip usually occurring more frequently in boys than girls

from three to eleven years of age. It is characterized by a flattening of the head of the femur resulting from death of local tissue, degeneration, and fragmentation of the growing end of the bone (epiphysis). Trauma and infection are among the causes most frequently hypothesized (see Figure 5–20).

Regeneration of bone and tissue and replacement of the femoral head depends on the amount of stress that is relieved by inhibiting weight bearing via crutches, braces, casts, and slings. Regeneration takes approximately two to three years. Restricted motion, muscular spasm, limping, tenderness, and some atrophy are common symptoms during the early stages of the disorder (see Figure 5–21).

Muscular Dystrophy

According to the Muscular Dystrophy Association of America, muscular dystrophy is a "general designation for a group of chronic diseases whose most prominent characteristic is the progressive degeneration of the skeletal or voluntary musculature." The various types of muscular dystrophy are caused by transmission of a recessive gene carried by an unaffected female (Duchenne type) or genetically transmitted by either or both parents. Muscular dystrophy is always progressive and genetically determined. Often, the ulti-

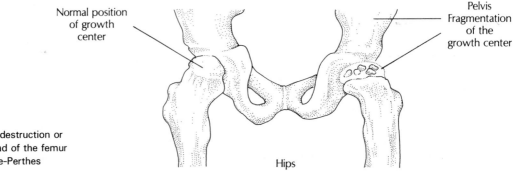

Normal position of growth center

Pelvis
Fragmentation of the growth center

Hips

Figure 5–20. The destruction or flattening of the head of the femur occurs in Legg-Calve-Perthes disease.

mate death of an individual with muscular dystrophy is not due to the disease itself, but rather to associated respiratory infections or pneumonia.

The most severe and prevalent type is _Duchenne muscular dystrophy_, which is sex-linked (i.e., X-chromosome linked, carried by the mother and passed to the son). The degeneration of the muscles becomes apparent before the age of three years. The hip girdle and thigh muscles are first affected, and the shoulder muscles later become involved. The disease progresses, and usually the affected male is in a wheelchair before his teen years. Death often occurs before the age of twenty-five (see Table 5–9 and Figures 5–22 and 5–23).

Facio-scapulo-humeral muscular dystrophy is also quite common, occurring more often in adolescent females than males. This type, transmitted as an autosomal dominant trait, does not shorten the life span,

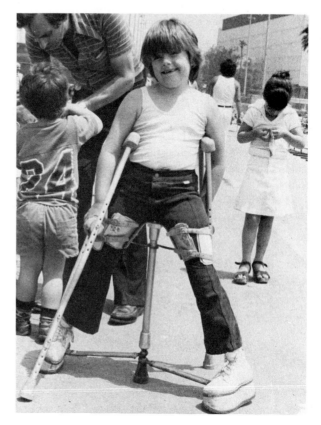

Figure 5–21. Weight bearing, achieved through the use of braces and crutches, is designed to relieve stress and allow regeneration of bone and tissue in Legg-Calve-Perthes disease. These pictures show a Toronto Legg-Calve-Perthes brace.

Table 5-9. Characteristics of Duchenne muscular dystrophy

- decreased physical activity with age
- limited and decreased muscular endurance
- waddling gait with legs wide apart
- toe walking
- "walking up" one's body (Gower's sign)
- moves to all fours when changing from prone to standing
- gradually weakening abdominal muscles
- gradual weakening of neck muscles
- lordosis
- gradual weakening of lower extremities
- muscle imbalance

progresses slowly with plateaus occurring, and includes much variability in severity. The muscles of the face (facio), shoulder-girdle (scapulo), and arm (humeral) are primarily affected. Forward-sloping shoulders, winged scapula, lordosis, difficulty in raising the arms above the head, and limited facial mobility are common characteristics of this type of muscular dystrophy (see Figure 5-22).

Limb-girdle muscular dystrophy is an autosomal recessive gene disorder (both parents must carry the defective gene) that occurs equally in males and females. The onset is usually between the middle teens and early twenties. This type bears similarity to facio-

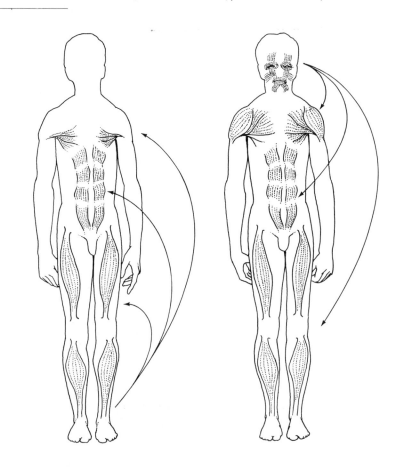

Figure 5-22. Two types of muscular dystrophy. The figure on the left shows the progression of Duchenne muscular dystrophy from the lower limbs to the upper limbs. The figure on the right shows the progression of weakness in facio-scapulo-humeral type muscular dystrophy: the face first, then shoulder girdle, and finally lower limbs.

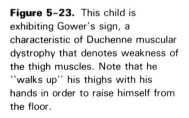

Figure 5-23. This child is exhibiting Gower's sign, a characteristic of Duchenne muscular dystrophy that denotes weakness of the thigh muscles. Note that he "walks up" his thighs with his hands in order to raise himself from the floor.

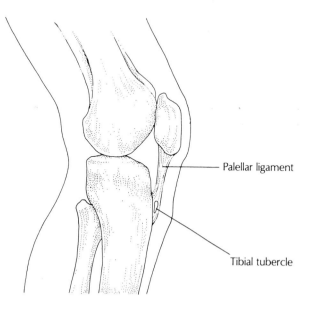

scapulo-humeral muscular dystrophy, with the exception of the involvement of the facial muscles. Individuals with limb-girdle muscular dystrophy exhibit some of the characteristic behaviors (waddling gait and lordosis), but usually have a normal life span.

Osgood-Schlatter's Condition

Osgood-Schlatter's condition is not a disease entity, although it is commonly referred to as Osgood-Schlatter's disease. The condition results from either partial or complete separation of the tibial tubercle at the epiphyseal junction, and may be caused by tendon strain, direct injury or abnormal alignment of the leg. The condition is quite painful because there is swelling around the knee. It occurs most frequently in boys eleven to fifteen years of age, and is curable by medical treatment. In general, individuals with Osgood-Schlatter's condition should abstain from all knee movements for approximately five weeks, and possibly up to nine months of undemanding physical activity (see Figure 5-24).

Palellar ligament

Tibial tubercle

Figure 5-24. Osgood-Schlatter's condition is characterized by separation of the tibial tubercle at the epiphyseal junction.

Osteomyelitis

Osteomyelitis is a <u>bone infection</u>, prevalent in the western hemisphere, which is frequently called a childhood disease. It may be caused by staphylococcus, streptococcus, or pneumococcus organisms. Osteomyelitis most often affects the tibia, femur, or humerus of only one limb — the arm or the leg — and results in some crippling. The infection can be acute or chronic (lasting over several years), with the symptoms and severity varying accordingly.

Osteogenesis Imperfecta (Brittle Bones)

A <u>dominant mutant gene</u> is the cause of this inherited condition, in which the bones are soft and brittle as a result of decreased bone density. A brittle-bone child may be born with bone fractures that recur throughout life. Deformities may occur as a result of these fractures. The child also bruises quite easily, but the bruising and breakage lessen after adolescence. The affected child is often below average in height.

Spina Bifida

<u>Spina bifida</u> is a <u>congenital midline defect of the spinal column</u> that can occur anywhere between the head and lumbar region of the spine. The defect results from the failure of one or more neural arches of the spinal vertebrae to close completely during fetal development. The nature and magnitude of the nerve damage and paralysis depends on the severity and location of the defect.

The primary cause of spina bifida is unknown; however, it is known that when the neural tube fails to develop completely and to close within the first thirty days of pregnancy, spina bifida occurs (Bleck and Nagel, 1975). There are several different forms of spina bifida, the most common of which are (1) spina bifida occulta; (2) meningocele; and (3) myelomeningocele (see Figure 5–25).

In *spina bifida occulta*, the defect is small and marked only by a dimple, mole, or tuft of hair. In its mildest form, spina bifida occulta may go undetected, for there is no neurological disability or retardation associated with this form. More serious forms of occulta may be characterized by slight deviations in posture and muscle tone leading to muscle weakness and mild deformities of the hips, legs, and feet.

Meningocele is distinguished by a tumor-like, sacular protrusion along the backbone. The sac contains cerebrospinal fluid, but the spinal cord and nerve roots (nerve tissue) remain in normal position. The sac is usually removed either shortly after birth or in infancy.

Figure 5–25. Three types of spina bifida, exemplifying degrees of severity. SOURCE: Adapted from an original painting by Frank H. Netter, M.D., from *The CIBA Collection of Medical Illustrations,* copyright by CIBA Pharmaceutical Company, Division of CIBA-GEIGY Corporation.

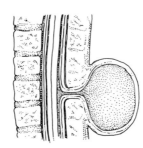

a. Meningocele

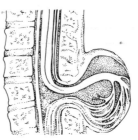

b. Myelomeningocele

c. Spina bifida occulta

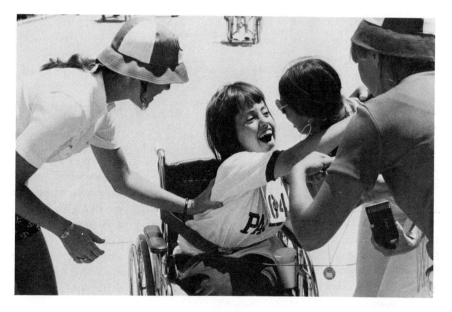

Figure 5-26. This girl, who has spina bifida, is happy because she has finished a race at Exceptional Games for the physically handicapped.

Rarely do neurological impairments or mental retardation occur with this type of spina bifida.

The most common and severe type of spina bifida is _myelomeningocele_. This type is also distinguished by a sac protruding from the backbone; in this case however, the sac contains the meninges (coverings of the spinal cord), portions of the spinal cord, cerebrospinal fluid, and nerve fibers. Although usually surgically closed shortly after birth, the defect is such that neurological impairment, hydrocephalus, and mental retardation almost always accompany this condition. Paralysis or partial paralysis, disturbance of sphincter function, and lack of sensation result from myelomeningocele spina bifida. The paralysis, disturbance of sphincter function, and loss of sensation occur below the site of the defect and can be either partial or complete. The child with myelomeningocele most commonly utilizes some sort of bowel and bladder drainage system, from catheters (collecting bags) to diapers. Braces, crutches, or a wheelchair are commonly employed to increase support and enhance ambulation (see Figure 5-26).

Postural Deviations

Based upon acquisition, two types of postural deviations can be identified: (1) functional; and (2) structural.

Functional deviations emerge as a result of the way in which the body is used. The source of the deviation is muscle and connective tissue imbalance; the bony tissue is not affected. Repetitive, habitual sitting, standing, and moving postures may result in functional deviations. Examples of these include sitting on one foot; carrying books on one side; and continuous work on a given skill, such as the butterfly stroke in swimming. As long as the soft tissue is involved, functional conditions can be lessened through therapeutic exercise, elimination of the habitual postures, and counterbalancing activities.

Structural deviations are those in which the bony tissue or structure of the body are affected. These may result from ignored functional deviations, trauma, congenital anomalies, or infection of the growth centers of the bone. Structural deviations are correctable only through surgery.

Scoliosis

Scoliosis is a roto-lateral curvature of the spine, which may be either congenital or acquired from poor posture, disease, or muscular weakness. Scoliosis is more prevalent among females and can be associated with other disorders, such as cerebral palsy, poliomyelitis, and arthrogryposis. The early stages of scoliosis describe a C curve, which may develop into an S curve if not given appropriate treatment (see Table 5-10 and Figures 5-27 and 5-28).

Lordosis

<u>Lordosis (sway or hollow back)</u> is an exaggeration of the normal curvature of the spine in the lumbar region. Only the five lumbar vertebrae and the pelvis are affected. The exaggerated concave curve results in a forward and downward tilt of the pelvis. Both weak muscles (e.g., abdominals, gluteals, hamstrings) and tight muscles (e.g., lumbar extensors, lower erector

Table 5-10. Observable characteristics associated with scoliosis

- difference in shoulder height
- head slightly tilted to one side
- spinous processes deviated from midline
- trunk displaced to one side
- ribs bulge out on one side
- possible difference in leg length
- difference in hip height
- muscle imbalance between the sides of the body
- difference in scapular prominence

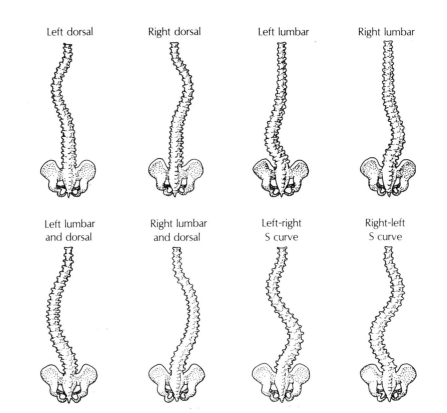

Figure 5-27. Possible C-curves and S-curves of the spine.

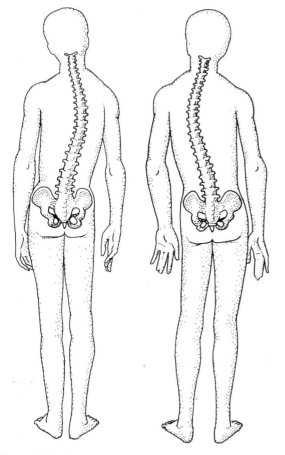

Figure 5-28. Scoliosis—a lateral curvature of the spine.

Figure 5-29. Typical postural profile of individual who has lordosis (increased lumbar curvature).

spinae or sacrospinalis, iliopsoas, rectus femoris, hip flexors) contribute to pelvic tilting and possible hyperextension of the knees. Compensatory posturing often results. In most cases, lordosis is correctable through therapeutic exercises and counterbalancing activities that promote muscle strengthening (shortening) or loosening (stretching) (see Figure 5-29).

Kyphosis

Kyphosis (hunchback, humpback) is an abnormal amount of flexion (convexity) in the upper spine, dorsal or thoracic regions. This condition is similar to lordosis in that it is often correctable. Kyphosis is characterized by weak erector spinae, weak upper back

extensors, weak trapezius, tight pectorals, and tight anterior intercostals. Round shoulders, forward head, and winged scapula often accompany this condition (see Figure 5-30).

Winged Scapula

This condition is characterized by the abduction and projection of the shoulder blades; the inferior angles of the scapula are prominent. The slower developing nature or general weakness of the rhomboids and serratus anterior muscles is considered to contribute to winged scapula. This condition is normal in preschool and elementary school children, and is more commonly found among females than males. It can be

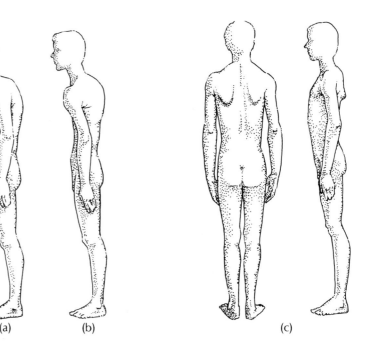

Figure 5-30. Kyphosis—increased dorsal curvature—(a) is often accompanied by round shoulders (b) and winged scapula (c).

(a)   (b)   (c)

ameliorated through exercise and counterbalancing activities.

Trauma-Caused Physical Impairments

For the purposes of this text, "trauma" refers to those accidents or mishaps that occur after birth to an otherwise normal individual.

Accidents

Fractures, dislocations, sprains, bruises, contusions, poisoning, and various other wounds can result in temporary or permanent physical and neurological impairment. The ensuing problem, be it physical, neurological, psychological, or educational, ranges from insignificant to profound.

Acquired Amputations

Amputation is the removal of some member or body part. *Acquired amputation* includes all elective or traumatic amputations, but excludes congenital amputations. *Elective amputation* is surgery performed to ameliorate a disease condition (e.g., infection, tumor) or to correct a congenital or traumatic condition. *Traumatic amputation* occurs as a result of some violence or accident to the body that causes the severance of a body part. Anxiety, psychological problems, "phantom pains" in the missing limb, and obvious physical impairment are all associated with acquired amputation.

Prosthetic devices or appliances are considered in most cases of amputations, for both children and adults. Prosthetic appliances for lower extremities include the above-knee (AK) and below-knee (BK) types. The lower limb prosthesis consists of a socket for the stump and, if appropriate, an artificial knee joint, ankle joint, and segmented foot. Prostheses for upper extremity amputations are quite variable, depending on the level of the amputation and the requirements for function desired (e.g., cosmetic, heavy labor, skilled dexterous work). A shoulder harness and steel cables are provided for control of the artificial limb. Common prosthetic hand devices are (1) a cosmetic prosthesis with some prehension (grasp); and (2) the split-hooks prosthesis, which is adjustable and offers more prehension. (See Figure 5-31.)

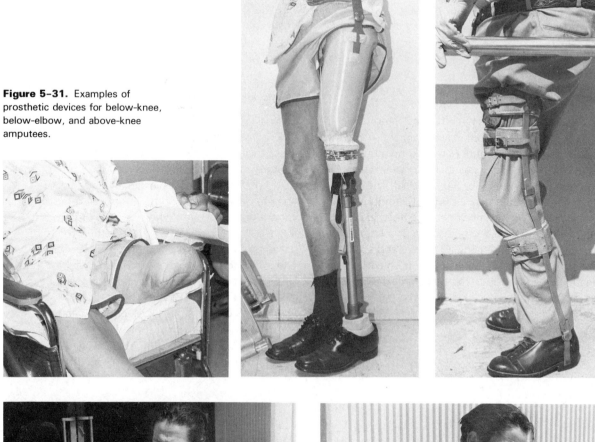

Figure 5–31. Examples of prosthetic devices for below-knee, below-elbow, and above-knee amputees.

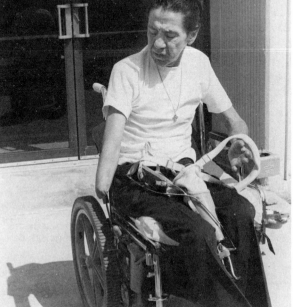

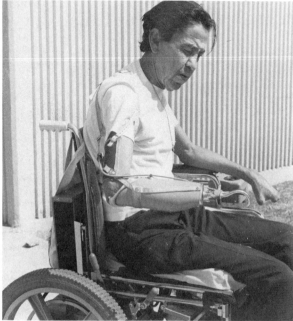

Battery

Since the 1960's there has been national interest in the "battered child syndrome" and child abuse in general. The causes of child abuse are unknown but are not confined to any particular socioeconomic class, family size, cultural group, or type of child. The consequences of child abuse may include: (1) temporary or permanent neurological impairment, (2) internal injuries, (3) skeletal deformities, (4) broken or fractured bones, (5) facial disfigurement, (6) bruises and scars, (7) sensory impairments, (8) psychological problems, or (9) death. Dependent upon the type and extent of injury, problems in the education of the battered child are addressed in various sections of this chapter under trauma.

Thermal Injuries (Burns)

Thermal injuries (burns) are damage to the skin and underlying structures that are caused by fire, chemicals, or electricity. Prolonged contact with extreme temperatures of hot or cold liquids can also cause thermal injury. Thermal injuries are evaluated in terms of extent and degree of the burn. The extent refers to the amount of surface area where the burn is located; the degrees of the burn refer to the depth of the burn (see Figure 5–32).

In a *first-degree burn,* only the outer layer of the skin (epidermis) is affected. The skin surface appears fiery red and is quite sensitive to the touch. A *second-degree burn* destroys both the epidermal and the dermal (cutaneous) layers. Exposed nerve endings

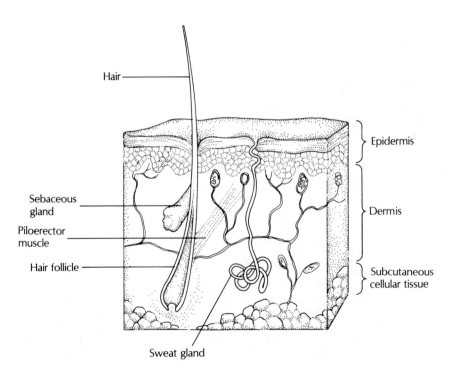

Figure 5–32. Cross-sectional view of layers of skin and subcutaneous tissue.

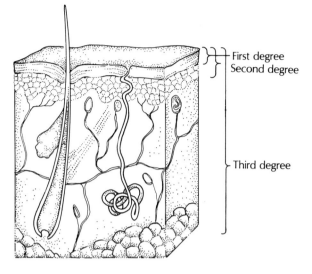

Figure 5-33. Degrees of burns and layers of skin affected.

cause extreme pain when touched. Blister formation, blanching, and redness are apparent in varying degrees. The most serious burn is the *third-degree burn,* in which both layers of skin and subcutaneous tissue are affected. The affected surface is dry and white, with little or no associated sensitivity to touch or pain due to the destruction of nerve endings. Thick scar tissue, resulting contractures, and scar hypertrophy contribute to limited range of motion and minor physical impairment. Elective amputation may sometimes be indicated (see Figure 5-33).

SERIOUSLY EMOTIONALLY DISTURBED AND BEHAVIORALLY DISORDERED

Legal Classification

According to PL 94-142, Section 121a.5(b)(8),

"Seriously emotionally disturbed" is defined as follows:

(i) The term means a condition exhibiting one or more, of the following characteristics over a long period of time and to a marked degree, which adversely affects educational performance.

(A) An inability to learn which cannot be explained by intellectual, sensory, or health factors.

(B) An inability to build or maintain satisfactory interpersonal relationships with peers and teachers.

(C) Inappropriate types of behavior or feelings under normal circumstances.

(D) A general pervasive mood of unhappiness or depression; or

(E) A tendency to develop physical symptoms or fears associated with personal or school problems.

(ii) The term includes children who are schizophrenic or autistic. The term does not include children who are socially maladjusted, unless it is determined that they are seriously emotionally disturbed.

The prevalence figures of emotionally disturbed and behaviorally disordered school-age children range from 2 to 22 percent (Kirk, 1972). The estimates of 2 percent, or one million seriously emotionally disturbed children requiring special education, are considered conservative. It is generally agreed that any child in this category can be identified by extremes of behavior, chronic problems, and socially or culturally unacceptable behavior (Hallahan and Kauffman, 1978). Within this broad category are the subdivisions of (1) autism; (2) behavior disorders of childhood and adolescence; (3) depression; (4) mental illness; and (5) schizophrenia.

Autism

Kanner (1943) was the first person to describe a type of schizophrenia associated with childhood. Kanner's term, *early infantile autism,* included such characteristics and descriptors as extreme aloneness; inability or refusal to communicate; often beautiful-looking children who appear to be intelligent, but who are functioning at retarded levels; and having an isolated area of excellence. Many theories and approaches have been postulated since the mid-1900s regarding early infantile autism, but there has been no consensus

Table 5–11. Clusters of disturbances in autism

Cluster	Behavioral characteristics
Relating	■ pathological need to be alone ■ lack of aversive reaction to strangers (7 to 9 months of age) ■ lack of playing baby games (peek-a-boo) ■ unusual need for sameness ■ disinterest in others, looks past or through others ■ poor or deviant eye contact ■ disinterest in learning experiences
Motility	■ hand-flapping ■ stereotyped behavior — lunging and darting movements ■ body rocking and head banging to great degree ■ toe walking ■ whirling, spinning objects and self ■ perseveration (continuing contact with one activity or object)
Perception and regulation of sensory input	■ underactivity, under-reactivity, unresponsive — lack of startle reaction — lack of response to sensory stimulation ■ over-reactivity, heightened awareness and sensitivity — agitation by certain sounds — intolerance of rough fabric — oversensitive to sensory stimulation — postural insecurity — intolerant of lifting off ground, elevators ■ sensory-stimulating seeking behaviors — over-attending to objects or behavior — self-stimulating activities
Language	■ many remain mute ■ echolalic speech (repeats words and phrases) ■ inappropriate use of personal pronoun ■ atonal, arrhythmical speech ■ delayed speech ■ speech lacking in emotion and affect
Developmental rate	■ irregularities in passing major developmental milestones ■ discontinuities in development ■ perseverative or unusual use of normal, transitory behaviors.

SOURCE: Adapted from E. Ornitz, "Childhood Autism: A Review of the Clinical Experimental Literature (Medical Progress)," *California Medicine* 18 (1973): 21–57.

regarding etiology and treatment. The causes of autism are rather speculative at this time.

The National Society for Autistic Children (1980) describes autism as a severely incapacitating lifelong developmental disability that usually appears during the first three years of life. It is a rare condition, occurring in five of every ten thousand births, which is characterized by severe problems in communication and behavior and an inability to relate to people in a normal manner. Autism is four times more common in males than females, and has been found throughout the world in families of all racial, ethnic, and social backgrounds.

Throughout all the literature on autism, authorities agree on only two basic criteria for classification as autistic: (1) early onset of clinical symptoms; and (2) profound inability to relate to others. Ornitz (1973) has identified five clusters of disturbances found in autistic children and has described the clinical course of autism (see Tables 5-11 and 5-12).

Behavior Disorders of Childhood and Adolescence

The American Psychiatric Association (1968) has one of the best-known and most comprehensive classification systems of mental disorders. The system describes psychosis, neurosis, personality disorders, and behavior disorders of childhood and adolescence.

Behavior disorders of childhood and adolescence are divided into seven categories. The causes of these disorders are speculative, and are not agreed upon among professionals. Factors affecting or influencing behavior disorders are (1) heredity; (2) organic causes; and (3) environmental or functional factors (see Table 5-13).

Depression

Severe depression is a specific type of mental illness.

It can affect any age group, and seems to be on the rise among children as well as teenagers. The symptoms of depression in the child are (1) social withdrawal; (2) loss of initiative; (3) decrease in appetite; (4) difficulty in sleeping; and (5) a self-deprecating attitude. Disobedience, self-destructive behavior, truancy, and even suicide attempts characterize severe depression.

Mental Illness

The American Psychiatric Association (1968) has identified three major types of mental illness — psychosis, neurosis, and personality disorders. The prevalence of these types of mental illness in children and adolescents is quite high.

Neuroses are characterized by anxieties, phobias, obsessive ideas, distortions of reality, compulsive rituals, and other benign personality disturbances. Neuroses do not cause serious personality disorganization. The neurotic tends to ignore reality, whereas the psychotic denies it.

Psychoses are diagnosed when the individual's mental functioning is so impaired that the daily routines and ordinary demands of life are no longer met. Psychoses are characterized by loss of contact with reality; failure to attend and relate appropriately within one's own environment; a tendency to withdraw into one's own world; and deficits in perception, language, and memory. Schizophrenia, the most common, and manic depression are examples of psychoses.

Personality disorders are those in which the chronic maladaptive behavior exists without anxiety or guilt. Socially or culturally unacceptable behavior patterns become so fully ingrained in the individual that they become the norm for that individual. Alcoholism, drug addiction, and sexual deviance are included in this category.

Table 5-12. Clinical course of autism

Time	Behaviors
Neonatal period	■ infrequent crying ■ limpness or rigidity when being held ■ abnormal posturing ■ flaccid muscle tone ■ undemanding of companionship
First half-year	■ failure to notice coming and going of mother ■ lack of responsive smiling ■ unresponsive to toys ■ overreactive to sounds ■ failure to make earliest vocalizations
Second half-year	■ refusal of rough-textured foods ■ ignoring toys ■ motor milestones occurring in spurts and lags ■ unaffectionate ■ lack of stranger anxiety ■ failure to play baby games ■ distressful reactions to changes in sensory-stimuli
Second and third years	■ repetitive and stereotyped mannerisms with hands ■ preoccupation with spinning objects ■ use of others as an extension of self
Fourth and fifth year	■ severe reactions to sensory stimuli ■ unusual speech ■ echolalia ■ misuse of personal pronouns
Middle childhood	■ flat affect ■ emotionally detached ■ possible decrease in unusual responses to stimulation ■ impulsivity ■ lack of emotional control ■ hyperactivity ■ irritability ■ restlessness

SOURCE: Adapted from E. Ornitz, "Childhood Autism: A Review of the Clinical Experimental Literature (Medical Progress)," *California Medicine* 18 (1973): 21-57.

Table 5-13. Behavior disorders of childhood and adolescence

Behavior	Characteristics
Hyperkinetic reaction (Hyperkinetic syndrome disorder)	■ overactivity ■ restlessness ■ distractibility ■ short attention span
Withdrawal reaction	■ seclusiveness ■ detachment ■ sensitivity ■ shyness ■ timidity ■ inability to form close personal relationships
Overanxious reaction	■ chronic anxiety ■ excessive, unrealistic fears ■ sleeplessness ■ nightmares
Runaway reaction	■ frequently runs away from home ■ feelings of rejection at home ■ immature ■ timid
Aggressive reaction	■ hostile disobedience ■ physical or verbal aggression ■ frequent temper tantrums ■ steals ■ frequently tells lies ■ vengeful ■ destructive
Group delinquent reaction	■ holds group values ■ group delinquency ■ group stealing/shoplifting
Other reaction	■ unclassified behavior disorders

SOURCE: Adapted from American Psychiatric Association, *Diagnostic and Statistical Manual of Mental Disorders* (Washington, D.C.: American Psychiatric Association, 1968, pp. 49–51).

Schizophrenia

Schizophrenia is defined as <u>abnormal behavior patterns involving some degree of personality disorganization with less than adequate contact with reality</u>. Psychotic behavior manifested by loss of contact with reality, bizarre thought processes, and inappropriate actions are characteristics of schizophrenia. While there are at least four identifiable types of schizophrenia, symptoms common to all exist and are identified as *splits*. The types of splits include (<u>1</u>) split of affect — lack of integration between thoughts and feelings; (<u>2</u>) split of association — thoughts isolated from logical associations or reasoning; (<u>3</u>) split of attention — inability to focus on one topic; and (<u>4</u>) split sense of reality — retreating from real world to make-believe world (see Table 5–14).

MULTIHANDICAPPED AND SEVERELY HANDICAPPED

Legal Classification

According to PL 94–142, Section 121a.5(b)(5),

"Multihandicapped" <u>means concomitant impairments (such as mentally retarded-blind, mentally retarded-orthopedically impaired)</u>, the combination of which causes such severe educational problems that they cannot be accommodated in special education programs solely for one of the impairments. The term does not include deaf-blind children.

Multihandicapped

The multihandicapped child is afflicted with <u>two or more handicapping conditions</u>. These conditions may include physical, mental, sensory, neurological, and emotional handicaps. Each multihandicapped child is unique in etiology and characteristics, and the combination of handicapping conditions and the severity of

Table 5–14. Characteristics associated with schizophrenia

- feelings of loneliness and depression
- withdrawal and complete seclusion
- bizarre thoughts
- rambling, incoherent, emotionally flat speech
- neologisms (words devised by patient)
- echolalia
- disturbed neuromuscular coordinations
- inaccurate and awkward movements
- slow reaction time
- poor posture
- lethargy
- poor physical fitness

impairment dictate the nature of necessary intervention or programming.

Many multihandicapped children have orthopedic impairment as one of the handicapping conditions. A majority of <u>cerebral palsied children</u>, for example, have <u>multiple handicaps. Mental retardation, strabismus (wandering or crossed eyes), hearing loss, seizure activity, "soft" neurological signs, and speech problems may accompany cerebral palsy</u>. The severely and profoundly mentally retarded have multiple handicaps primarily in the form of physical or motor, sensory, and/or language impairments.

Severely Handicapped

As early as 1975, the following definition of severely handicapped appeared in the February 20 issue of the Federal Register:

"Severely handicapped children" are those who because of the intensity of their physical, mental, or emotional problems, or a combination of such problems, need educational, social, psychological, and medical services beyond those which are traditionally offered by regular and special educational programs, in order to maximize their full potential for useful and meaningful participation in society and for self-fulfillment.

(A) The term includes those children who are classified as seriously emotionally disturbed (including children who are schizophrenic or autistic), profoundly and severely mentally retarded, and those with two or more serious handicapping conditions, such as the mentally-retarded blind, and the cerebral palsied deaf.

(B) "Severely handicapped children" (1) may possess severe language and/or perceptual-cognitive deprivations, and evidence abnormal behaviors such as: (I) failure to respond to pronounced social stimuli, (II) self mutilation, (III) self-stimulation, (IV) manifestation of intense and prolonged temper tantrums, and (V) the absence of rudimentary forms of verbal control, and (2) may also have extremely fragile physiological conditions.

"Severely handicapped" individuals exist across all special education categories, but the expression generally refers to a very low level of intellectual functioning. According to Baker (1979), a severely handicapped individual is "one whose ability to provide for his or her own basic life-sustaining and safety needs is so limited, relative to proficiency expected on the basis of chronological age, that it could pose a serious threat to his or her survival." Although these individuals tend to be a homogeneous group at a young age, individual potentials vary (see Figure 5–34).

A recent investigation into the developmental characteristics of severely handicapped individuals was undertaken in California. Although the findings are based solely upon the available population in California, the large number of individuals sampled — 2938 — and the extensive nature of the inquiry lend themselves nicely to summary (Levine, Elzey, and Fiske-Rollins (1979):

1. The majority of the individuals were males (55 percent).

Figure 5–34. This severely handicapped young man enjoys participating in a target game.

2. The ages ranged from three to twenty-one years; mean age was 10.34.

3. The majority were living at home (59 percent) although 22 percent were living in foster homes and 19 percent in institutions.

4. More than one-third of the individuals were taking some kind of medication.

5. At least 20 percent of the individuals were known to have a history of seizures.

6. The majority (73 percent) functioned at the severe and profound levels of cognitive ability.

7. More than half of the individuals had no deficit in visual (60 percent) or auditory acuity (80 percent).

8. Many (88 percent) of the individuals had less than one-word utterances.

9. One third of the individuals had no ambulation; those under eight years had less ambulation, those nine to fourteen years had average ambulation, and those fourteen years and older had good ambulation.
10. Approximately two-thirds of the individuals had fair to good head and hand control, both tended to increase with age.
11. Generally, the younger the child the more severe the disability; the older the individual, the more capable of independent function.

SUMMARY

In order to individualize instruction in physical education, a workable knowledge and understanding of physical, mental, and emotional impairments is necessary. Mental retardation refers to below-average general intellectual functioning. Mentally retarded individuals are delayed in development but are capable of varying degrees of learning. Orthopedic or physical impairments are quite diverse. The continuum of physical involvement ranges from mild to severe limitation, some temporary, and some permanent conditions. Some conditions warrant specific intervention, while others require modifications or adaptations of normal physical activities. Emotional disturbances are quite varied and may be easily misunderstood and misinterpreted. When mental, physical, emotional, and other impairments occur in combination, the individual is said to be multihandicapped; if the severity is great enough, the individual can be considered severely handicapped. To understand these individuals, the physical educator must understand each of the conditions and the cumulative effect. This background knowledge will provide the base for programming in physical education.

BIBLIOGRAPHY

American Psychiatric Association. *Diagnostics and Statistical Manual of Mental Disorders.* Washington, D.C.: American Psychiatric Association, 1968.

Baker, D. B. "Severely Handicapped: Toward an Inclusive Definition." *American Association for the Education of the Severely and Profoundly Handicapped Review* 4 (1) (1979): 52–63.

Benda, C. E. *The Child with Mongolism.* New York: Grune and Stratton, 1960.

Bleck, E. E., and Nagel, D. A. (eds.). *Physically Handicapped Children: A Medical Atlas for Teachers.* New York: Grune and Stratton, 1975.

Bourne, C. H., and Golarz, M. N. *Muscular Dystrophy in Man and Animals.* New York: Hafner, 1963.

Caillet, R. *Foot and Ankle Pain.* Philadelphia: F. A. Davis, 1976.

Carter, C. O., and Fairbanks, T. J. *The Genetics of Locomotor Disorders.* New York: Oxford University Press, 1974.

Chusid, J. C. *Correlative Neuroanatomy and Functional Neurology.* Los Altos, California: LANGE Medical Publications, 1976.

Cratty, B. J. *Motor Activity and the Education of Retardates.* Philadelphia: Lea and Febiger, 1974.

Denoff, E. *Cerebral Palsy, the Preschool Years.* Springfield, Illinois: Charles C. Thomas, 1967.

Estes. W. K. *Learning Theory and Mental Development.* New York: Academic Press, 1970.

Gearheart, B. R., and Litton, F. W. *The Trainable Retarded*. St. Louis: C. V. Mosby, 1975.

Gibson, D. *Down's Syndrome, the Psychology of Mongolism*. New York: Cambridge University Press, 1978.

Gray, H. *Anatomy: Descriptive and Surgical*. Philadelphia: Running Press, 1974.

Grossman, H. (ed.). *Manual on Terminology and Classification in Mental Retardation*. Baltimore: American Association of Mental Deficiency, 1977.

Hallahan, D. P., and Kauffman, J. M. *Exceptional Children*. Englewood Cliffs, New Jersey: Prentice-Hall, 1978.

Kanner, L. ``Autistic Disturbances of Affective Contact.'' *Nervous Child* (1943): 217–250.

Kirk, S. A. *Educating Exceptional Children*. Boston: Houghton Mifflin, 1972.

Levine, S., Elzey, F. F., and Fiske-Rollin, B. ``Developmental Characteristics of Severely and Profoundly Handicapped.'' *AAESPH Review* 4(1) (1979): 36–51.

Muscular Dystrophy Association of America, Inc. *Muscular Dystrophy Fact Sheet*. New York: Muscular Dystrophy Association of American, Inc., n.d.

National Association for Retarded Citizens. *Facts on Mental Retardation*. Arlington, Texas: National Association for Retarded Citizens, 1973.

National Society for Autistic Children. *Fact Sheet: Autism*. Washington, D.C.: National Society for Autistic Children, 1980.

Netter, F. H. *Ciba Collection of Medical Illustrations*. New York: Case-Hoyt, 1977.

Office of Handicapped Individuals. Definition of Handicapped Person. In ``White House Conference on Handicapped Individuals.'' Washington, D.C.: Government Printing Office, 1977.

Ornitz, E. ``Childhood Autism: A Review of the Clinical Experimental Literature (Medical Progress).'' *California Medicine* 18 (1973): 21–57.

Robinson, H. B., and Robinson, N. M. ``Mental Retardation.'' In *Carmichael's Manual of Child Psychology*, 3rd ed., vol. 11, edited by P. H. Mussen. New York: John Wiley & Sons, 1970.

Robinson, N. M., and Robinson, H. B. *The Mentally Retarded Child: A Psychological Approach*. New York: McGraw-Hill 1976.

Smith, D. W., and Wilson, A. A. *The Child with Down's Syndrome*. Philadelphia: W. B. Saunders, 1973.

Smith, R. M. *Clinical Teaching: Methods of Teaching for the Retarded*, 2d ed. New York: McGraw-Hill, 1974.

Turek, S. L. *Orthopedics: Principles and Their Application*. Philadelphia: J. B. Lippincott, 1967.

The White House Conference on Handicapped Individuals. Washington, D.C.: Government Printing Office, 1977.

6

Exceptional Individuals: Health, Sensory, and Learning Impairments

Guiding Questions

1. What does the category "other health-impaired" include?
2. What are some of the causes and characteristics of sensory impairments?
3. What is meant by "specific learning disability" and what are its causes?
4. What are the types of speech and language impairment?

In addition to the more easily observed handicapping conditions discussed in Chapter 5, the physical education teacher should understand the less obvious conditions, such as health-impaired, sensory-disordered, and language- and learning-disabled.

OTHER HEALTH-IMPAIRED

Legal Classification

According to PL 94–142, Section 121a.5(b)(7):

"Other health impaired" means limited strength, vitality or alertness, due to chronic or acute health problems such as a heart condition, tuberculosis, rheumatic fever, nephritis, asthma, sickle cell anemia, hemophilia, epilepsy, lead poisoning, leukemia, or diabetes, which adversely affects a child's educational performance.

The physical educator must be aware of the many health impairments that exist, and the extent to which

the various conditions are physically limiting. Because children may be affected mildly, moderately, or severely, appropriate placements for the health-impaired include both regular and adapted physical education.

Asthma

Asthma is a chronic respiratory condition in which the individual experiences repeated episodes of difficulty in breathing (dyspnea). This condition of the lungs is characterized by spasms of the bronchial tubes, swelling of the linings of the bronchial tubes and excessive secretion of mucus, which results in coughing, wheezing, difficulty in breathing, and a feeling of constriction in the chest. The majority of asthma sufferers are under the age of fifteen, with a slightly higher incidence among boys than girls.

Asthma is caused by deficient homeostatic function at the cellular level. Normally, there is a balance (i.e., homeostasis) between the releasing of adrenalin (epinephrine) and acetylcholine. Any change in this balance causes changes in the lining of the bronchial

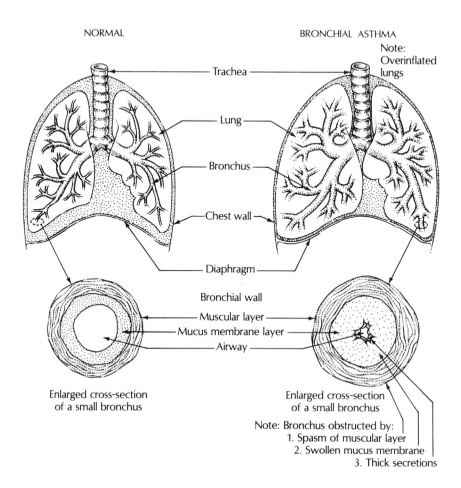

NORMAL

BRONCHIAL ASTHMA

Note: Overinflated lungs

Trachea

Lung

Bronchus

Chest wall

Diaphragm

Bronchial wall
Muscular layer
Mucus membrane layer
Airway

Enlarged cross-section of a small bronchus

Enlarged cross-section of a small bronchus

Note: Bronchus obstructed by:
1. Spasm of muscular layer
2. Swollen mucus membrane
3. Thick secretions

Figure 6-1. Changes in the bronchii and lungs during an asthmatic attack.

tubes. This deficiency increases the irritability of the bronchii to a variety of stimuli. Heightened sensitivity to environmental stimuli (e.g., cigarette smoking, changes in weather, changes in body temperature, air pollutants, allergens), infections, and emotions (e.g., excitement, fear, anxiety, stress) contribute to changes in the homeostatic function, which can cause an asthma attack (see Figure 6-1).

Asthmatics tend to be introspective and ultrasensitive to criticism, but eager to please. They also tend to set unrealistic goals and standards for themselves and then give an all-out effort to achieve their goals. The asthmatic may or may not be self-limiting in physical activity.

Cardiovascular Disorders

Cardiovascular disorders include all diseases of the heart and blood vessels. Rheumatic and congenital heart conditions, coronary heart disease (arteriosclerosis), hypertensive heart disease, and cerebrovascular disease (stroke) are included in this category. Congenital heart conditions and rheumatic heart disease are primarily associated with children. Stroke, although primarily associated with adults, is also possible with children, adolescents, and young adults (see Figure 6-2).

Rheumatic heart disease results in about 10 percent of the cases following rheumatic fever (discussed

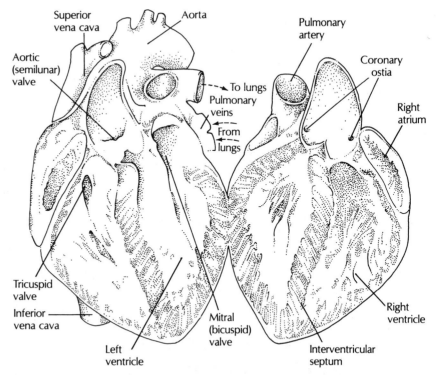

Superior vena cava

Aorta

Pulmonary artery

Aortic (semilunar) valve

Coronary ostia

To lungs

Pulmonary veins

From lungs

Right atrium

Tricuspid valve

Inferior vena cava

Left ventricle

Mitral (bicuspid) valve

Interventricular septum

Right ventricle

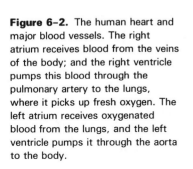

Figure 6-2. The human heart and major blood vessels. The right atrium receives blood from the veins of the body; and the right ventricle pumps this blood through the pulmonary artery to the lungs, where it picks up fresh oxygen. The left atrium receives oxygenated blood from the lungs, and the left ventricle pumps it through the aorta to the body.

later in this chapter). The disease damages the heart and its valves, muscles, and blood vessels. *Stroke* victims of any age may recover completely; may show any degree of paralysis, muscle weakness, aphasia, and primitive reflex activity; or die as a result of the hemorrhage within the brain.

A *congenital heart condition* is a malfunction of the heart that occurs during fetal life. The range in severity of congenital heart conditions is great, from minimal dysfunction to death. More than half of the congenital heart disorders are caused by one of the following three conditions: (1) ventricular septal defect (22 percent); (2) patent ductus arteriosis (17 percent); and (3) tetralogy of Fallot (11 percent) (see Table 6-1).

Ventricular septal defects are small openings (holes) in the septum (the wall between the ventricles). These openings, if considered to adversely affect pulmonary circulation, are usually surgically repaired. *Patent ductus arteriosus* refers to the lack of closure or incomplete closure of the ductus, a passageway used only as a part of fetal circulation before birth. *Tetralogy of Fallot* is a combination of four abnormalities that

results in the birth of "blue babies." The four abnormalities are: (1) ventricular septal defect; (2) pulmonary stenosis; (3) enlarged right ventricle; and (4) an abnormal positioning of the aorta. This defect results in unoxygenated blood (bluish in color) being circulated throughout the body, which may cause the infant to become cyanotic. Tetralogy of Fallot is surgically correctable after the age of four years.

Cystic Fibrosis

Cystic fibrosis is an inherited childhood disease characterized by chronic respiratory and digestive problems. Abnormal secretion (thick and sticky mucus) of the membranes that line internal organs is the primary disorder in cystic fibrosis. The mucus clogs the bronchial tubes, resulting in a chronic cough, difficulty in breathing, and frequent respiratory infections; mucus also clogs the pancreatic ducts, resulting in excessive bowel movements. Excessive salt loss in perspiration is an ever-present danger. Until recently, most children with cystic fibrosis died before reaching adolescence.

Table 6-1. Two classification systems of cardiac diseases

System 1.

Class I:	People with heart disease who do not have physical limitations.
Class II:	People with heart disease who have slight limitation of physical activity. Ordinary physical activity results in fatigue, difficulty in breathing, and pain.
Class III:	People with heart disease who have marked limitation of physical activity. Less than normal physical activity causes fatigue, difficulty in breathing, and pain.
Class IV:	People with heart disease resulting in severe limitations of physical activity. Inability to participate in any physical activity without discomfort and pain.

System 2.

Class A:	Ordinary physical activity need not be restricted.
Class B:	Ordinary physical activity need not be restricted, but severe or competitive physical efforts are contraindicated.
Class C:	Ordinary physical activity moderately limited. Strenuous efforts discontinued.
Class D:	Ordinary physical activity restricted considerably.
Class E:	Complete bed rest, confined to bed or chair. No physical activity.

Table 6-2. Common clinical features of diabetic coma and insulin shock

Diabetic coma	*Insulin shock*
Onset: gradual, over a period of days	sudden
Symptoms:	
■ nausea	■ fatigue
■ vomiting	■ weakness
■ abdominal pain	■ sweating
■ constipation	■ tremor
■ dyspnea (difficulty breathing)	■ sudden hunger
■ dim vision	■ diplogia (double vision)
■ high sugar in urine	■ sugar absent from urine

Treatment: both diabetic coma and insulin shock are serious medical conditions requiring prompt treatment by a doctor.

Diabetes

Diabetes, a metabolic disturbance, is a hereditary or developmental problem of sugar metabolism resulting in insufficient insulin in the blood stream. Diabetes can be remediated through diet, exercise, and insulin treatment. A critical balance is necessary, and each factor must be strictly controlled.

Insulin shock or insulin coma are two results of the diet-exercise-insulin imbalance. *Insulin shock* (too much insulin) may be caused by skipping meals, overexercising, and too large an insulin dosage. Characteristics of insulin shock include sluggish thinking, muscle weakness, drowsiness, blurred or double vision, unconsciousness, and convulsions.

Diabetic or *insulin coma* is caused by too little insulin, the onset of infection or mild illness, overeating, excessive drinking of alcoholic beverages, and emotional stress. Symptoms of impending coma include extreme thirst, loss of appetite, nausea, cramping, leg cramps, and blurring of vision. Temporary blindness may accompany a diabetic coma (see Table 6-2).

Epilepsy

Epilepsy refers to sudden, transient alterations of brain functions and consciousness, characterized by seizures. Epilepsy is a syndrome rather than a specific disease entity, and there is much variability among individuals with epilepsy.

Epilepsy can be caused by or may accompany any of the following: (1) genetic and birth factors; (2) infectious disorders; (3) toxic factors; (4) trauma or physical agents; (5) circulatory disturbances; (6) metabolic and nutritional disturbances; (7) neoplasms; (8) heredofamilial and degenerative diseases; (9) psychogenic causes; and (10) unknown etiology. For further description, the reader is referred to Robb (1965) (see Table 6-3).

Factors that can trigger seizures in epileptics in-

Table 6-3. Age of onset and presumptive cause of epilepsy

Age of onset	Presumptive cause
Infancy (0–2 years)	Birth injury, congenital
Childhood (2–10 years)	Birth injury, trauma
Adolescence (10–20 years)	Trauma, obscure causes
Youth (20–35 years)	Trauma, neoplasm
Middle age (35–55 years)	Neoplasm, trauma, arteriosclerosis
Senescence (55–70 years)	Neoplasm, arteriosclerosis

SOURCE: Adapted from J. C. Chusid, *Correlative Neuroanatomy and Functional Neurology* (Los Altos, California: LANGE Medical Publications, 1979).

clude changes in alkalinity of blood, excessive intake of alcoholic beverages, psychogenic stimulus (e.g., anger, fright, stress), hyperventilation, chronic recurrent head trauma, and excessive sensory stimulation. Seizures can be controlled by such drugs as dilantin, phenobarbital, librium, and valium.

A seizure specifically occurs as a result of abnormal discharge of electrical energy in the brain; why the brain tissues discharge abnormally is unknown. The five most common types of seizures are: (1) grand mal; (2) Jacksonian; (3) petit mal; (4) psychomotor; and (5) mixed (see Table 6-4).

Hemophilia

Hemophilia is a rare, sex-linked disorder of the blood. It is transmitted through a recessive gene that is carried by the mother and passed to the son. A deficiency of a clotting factor in the blood is the principal characteristic of hemophilia. The afflicted individual may hemorrhage internally or externally from even the slightest scratch. Blood transfusions are frequently a part of treatment.

Table 6-4. Types of seizures and characteristics

Type of seizure	Behavior characteristics, symptoms
Grand mal (with Jacksonian, 45%)	
Aura phase	■ vague feeling, certain smell, a sinking feeling, flashing of lights
Tonic phase	■ continuous contraction of muscles, inane utterances, loss of consciousness
Clonic phase	■ intermittent contraction and relaxation of muscles
Sleep/coma phase	■ semiconsciousness, then deep sleep, no memory of seizure
Jacksonian (with grand mal, 45%)	■ similar to grand mal but without the aura or tonic phases ■ Clonic contraction begins in one part of the body (hand or foot) and spreads throughout the limb ■ loss of consciousness
Petit mal (8%)	■ does not lose consciousness ■ child seems dazed ■ eyes roll up ■ momentary silence

Psychomotor (5%)	■ short-term changes in behavior
	  — temper tantrums
	  — incoherent chatter
	  — repetitious phrases
	  — daydreaming
	■ no memory of seizures

Mixed (35–40%)	■ usually refers to grand mal and petit mal types of seizures. Any two or more types of seizures

Obesity

Obesity is often determined by percentage of body fat. Body fat is defined as the amount of total body weight that is fatty tissue, and is usually expressed in terms of percentage of actual body weight (Edington and Cunningham, 1975). Body fat standards for Americans range from 12 to 19 percent for males and 20 to 25 percent for females. Generally speaking, children who are 10 to 20 percent above their desired weight are considered overweight; persons over 20 percent of desired weight are obese; and those over 50 percent are super-obese.

There are several ways of determining obesity. Height, weight, and age tables can be used as screening devices for further in-depth evaluation, which take into consideration body type, distribution of fat, muscle development, sexual maturation, and sex. Obesity can result from either endocrine or nonendocrine causes (see Table 6-5).

No matter what the cause, the management of obesity must be undertaken. Getting and keeping a balance between food intake and energy output must be a priority in the management of obesity. Obesity, by itself, is a problem to control, and since it often accompanies other handicapping conditions, the problems are compounded. In fact, obesity itself can become an orthopedic problem because excessive weight may ultimately result in physical deformities, motor difficulties, and postural faults.

Vigorous activity is beneficial to the obese, but not without consideration of certain physical characteristics. Sherrill (1976) has identified the following ten physical characteristics commonly found among obese children:

1. *Distended abdomen* — anatomical difference in stomach position that affects vital processes and flexibility.
2. *Excessive perspiration* — obese persons become hot and sweaty quickly.
3. *Rolls of fat* — excessive fat causes pain and discomfort during physical activity.
4. *Chafing of skin areas that rub* — painful irritation of skin areas, such as between thighs, which may be slow to heal.
5. *Postural faults* — knock knees, pronation, flat feet, sagging abdomen, dropped shoulders, and round back adversely affect mechanical efficiency.
6. *Skeletal immaturity* — growth centers of bones are much more highly susceptible to injury.
7. *Edema* — retention of fluids causes swelling and pain and limits movement.
8. *Wide stance in locomotion* — postural problems and chafing between thighs result in slow, inefficient locomotor patterns.
9. *Fear of falling* — due to excessive weight and lack of mobility, falling is feared as being quite painful and dangerous.
10. *Excessive buoyancy in water* — presents difficulties in mastering swimming strokes.

Rheumatic Fever

Rheumatic fever, a disease that school-age children may contract, usually follows strep throat or scarlet fever. Painful swelling and inflammation of the joints are caused by an allergic reaction to the antibodies the body produces to fight the streptococcus bacteria, the inflammation can spread to the brain or heart. There is a good chance of recurrence of rheumatic fever in previously afflicted children, which may result in more serious and permanent heart damage (i.e., rheumatic heart disease).

Sickle Cell Anemia

Sickle cell anemia is a severe blood disease that occurs when the child inherits defective hemoglobin-forming genes from both parents. This disease is found almost exclusively among blacks. There is no known cure at this time, and affected children usually die before twenty years of age. People who have this disease are anemic, suffer crises of severe pain, and are prone to infection. Poor appetite, paleness, weakness, pain in legs and back, fatigue, and skin ulcers are often the first symptoms noticed.

Table 6-5. Causes of obesity

Endocrine obesity	Nonendocrine obesity
■ cerebral-hypothalamic	■ overeating and/or underexercising
■ pituitary gland disorder	■ familial and genetic patterns
■ thyroid disorder	■ environmental influences
■ adrenocortical disorder	■ metabolic sluggishness
	■ psychogenic causes

Tuberculosis

Although tuberculosis is most commonly referred to as a disease of the lungs (pulmonary tuberculosis) the tuberculosis bacterium can infect nearly any organ or system in the body. The most common type, pulmonary tuberculosis, can affect anyone of any age. Poor nutrition and hygiene, a chronic debilitating disease and a physical lowering of resistance, or a combination of these factors predispose to tuberculosis. The disease is medically curable through bed rest, nutritious diet, and progressive physical activity.

BLIND/VISUALLY HANDICAPPED

Legal Classification

According to PL 94–142, Section 121a.5(b)(11):

"Visually handicapped" means a visual impairment which, even with correction, adversely affects a child's educational performance. The term includes both partially seeing and blind children.

There are several different definitions or classifications of visual impairment. The American Medical Association proposed in 1934 what the American Foundation for the Blind (1963) has now accepted as the definition of a *legally blind* person:

A legally blind person is said to be one who has visual acuity of 20/200 or less in the better eye even with correction or whose field of vision is narrowed so that the widest diameter of his visual field subtends an angular distance no greater than 20 degrees.

Partially sighted is legally defined as visual acuity that falls between 20/70 and 20/200 in the better eye, with correction. The educational definition of *blind* includes those who are so severely visually impaired that they must be taught to read by braille. The partially

Table 6-6. Classification of visual impairments

Level	Description
Legal blindness 20/200	The ability to see at 20 feet what the normal eye can see at 200 feet.
Travel vision 5/200 to 10/200	The ability to see at 5 to 10 feet what the normal eye can see at 200 feet.
Motion perception 3/200 to 5/200	The ability to see at 3 to 5 feet what the normal eye can see at 200 feet. This ability is limited almost entirely to motion.
Light perception less than 3/200	The ability to distinguish a strong light at a distance of 3 feet from the eye what the normal eye would see at 200 feet. Motion of the hand at 3 feet would be undetected.
Total blindness	The inability to recognize or respond to a strong light shone directly into the eye.

sighted, as defined for educational purposes, are those who can read print even though they need to use large-print books or assorted magnifying devices.

Visual handicaps are usually classified in terms of visual acuity as measured by a Snellen chart. A person who is classified as legally blind can have, and in the majority of cases does have, usable vision (see Table 6-6 and Figure 6-3).

Etiology

Visual impairments and blindness are caused primarily by *birth defects, tumors,* and *injuries.* Common causes include *congenital cataracts,* characterized by clouding of the lens resulting in blurred vision; *diabetic*

Figure 6-3. This blind girl is learning to negotiate a jungle gym. SOURCE: Photo by Lyonel Avance.

retinopathy, associated with diabetes and a result of interference of the blood supply to the retina; *coloboma,* a congenital degenerative condition in which the central and/or peripheral areas of the retina are affected; *retinitis pigmentosa,* a hereditary degenerative disease of the retina; and visual impairments or blindness caused by *rubella* and *syphilis. Retrolental fibroplasia,* caused by too-high levels of oxygen administered at birth, can also result in blindness.

Other conditions can adversely affect visual function. *Strabismus,* caused by improper muscle function-ing, is a condition in which the eyes are directed inward (crossed eyes) or outward. Another condition caused by improper muscle function is *continuous nystagmus,* continuous and rapid involuntary horizontal eye movements. Refractory errors affecting visual acuity include *myopia* (nearsightedness), *hyperopia* (farsightedness), and *astigmatism* (blurred vision).

Extraordinary movement characteristics of the blind, *blindisms,* are thought by some to result from the need for sensory stimulation through movement. Blindisms include body rocking, putting fists or fingers into the eyes, twirling or spinning of the body, finger waving, and bending the head forward. Physical characteristics include the following:

1. Poor posture.
2. Retarded physical growth and maturation (small body size for age).
3. Head held forward.
4. Tense body.
5. Cautious locomotion.
6. Stumbling.
7. Expressionless face.
8. Tendency to be overweight.
9. Tendency to be physically unfit.
10. Easily fatigued.
11. Discharge from eyes.
12. Frequent rubbing of eyes.
13. Eyelids crusted, red, and swollen.
14. Squinting.
15. Inability to distinguish colors.
16. Heightened sensitivity to normal light levels.

DEAF/HARD OF HEARING

Legal Classification

According to PL 94-142:

"Deaf" means a hearing impairment which is so severe that the child is impaired in processing linguistic information through hearing, with or without amplification, which adversely affects educational performance (Section 121a.5[b] [1]) . . . "Hard of hearing" means a hearing impairment, whether permanent or fluctuating, which adversely affects a child's educational performance but which is not included under the definition of deaf in this section (Section 121a.5[b] [3]).

Definitions of hearing impairments proposed by various organizations include such variables as speaking ability, functional hearing ability, and the time of onset of the hearing loss. The following definitions were proposed in 1975 by the Conference of Executives of American Schools for the Deaf (Ad Hoc Committee, 1975):

1. *Hearing impairment* — a generic term indicating a hearing disability that may range in severity from mild to profound; it includes the subsets of deaf and hard of hearing.
2. *Deaf* — a person whose hearing disability precludes successful processing of linguistic information through audition, with or without a hearing aid.
3. *Hard of hearing* — a person who, generally with the use of a hearing aid, has residual hearing sufficient to enable successful processing of linguistic information through audition.
4. *Prelingual deafness* — deafness present at birth or occurring early in life, at an age prior to the development of speech or language.
5. *Postlingual deafness* — deafness occurring at an age following the development of speech and language.

The 1975 committee also specified threshold level classifications of the severity of the hearing loss, in which hearing sensitivity is measured in terms of decibels (units of relative loudness of sounds) (see Table 6-7).

Etiology and Characteristics

The four categories of deafness are:

1. *Psychogenic deafness* — no damage to the central nervous system and receptive organs function adequately; for emotional reasons, the individual does not respond to sound.
2. *Central deafness* — receiving mechanisms are functioning properly, but abnormality in central nervous system prevents processing of the information.
3. *Perceptive or sensorineural deafness* — defect of

Table 6-7. Classification of hearing loss

Hearing loss	Effect of hearing loss
Mild: 26-54 DB*	■ may have difficulty hearing faint or distant speech ■ may have some problems with language arts ■ understands conversational speech ■ may have limited vocabulary and slight speech problems
Moderate: 55-69 DB	■ can understand loud conversation ■ difficulty in group discussion ■ speech deficits ■ deficits in language usage and comprehension ■ limited vocabulary
Severe: 70-89 DB	■ hears voices 1 foot from ear ■ can identify environmental sounds ■ can discriminate vowels but not consonants ■ speech and language problems
Extreme: 90 DB and more	■ may hear some loud sounds ■ aware of vibrations more than tones ■ relies on vision rather than hearing ■ speech and language problems

SOURCE: *Adapted from Report of a Committee for a Comprehensive Plan for Children* (Office of the Superintendent of Public Instruction — Title VI — Elementary and Secondary Education Act, and the University of Illinois, Division for Services for Crippled Children, 1968).

*DB = decibels

inner ear or auditory nerve, which prevents transmission of impulse to brain.

4. *Conductive loss* — the intensity of the sound is drastically reduced before reaching the inner ear and the auditory nerve.

Deafness can occur before, during, or after birth. Some hearing defects are acquired and others are inherited, and still other causes of deafness or hearing impairment are yet unknown. Causes of deafness or hearing impairment include: personality inadequacies associated with neurosis or psychosis; cerebral tumor or abscess; arteriosclerosis; cerebral hemorrhage; multiple sclerosis; rubella; lesion in the cortex and association pathways (auditory aphasia); infections in the various portions of the ear (e.g., otitis media, mastoiditis); mumps; scarlet fever; diphtheria; whooping cough; viral infections; and mixed etiology.

Hearing-impaired children vary greatly. Some characteristics are common to the severe and profoundly

Table 6-8. Characteristics of the deaf and hearing-impaired

Domain	Characteristics
Socialization	■ voice is monotonous, guttural, and highly fluctuating in pitch range ■ distorted tonal quality, difficult to understand ■ often left out of group play ■ may develop solitary play interests ■ withdraws ■ unable to grasp and understand social situations
Language	■ expressive language problems ■ derives no pleasure from laughing ■ crying is normal
Hyperactivity	■ tends to be overly active or hyperactive at times
Postures	■ abnormal tilts and rotations of head ■ forward lean
Movement	■ impaired balance ■ slow in performing motor tasks ■ shuffling gait
Academic achievement	■ delayed

deaf who were born deaf or acquired the hearing impairment before the development of speech and language. Hearing-impaired individuals are somewhat delayed in their educational achievement, but this is not necessarily related to intellectual functioning (see Table 6-8).

DEAF/BLIND

Legal Classification

According to PL 94-142, (Section 121a.5(b)(2):

"Deaf/blind" means concomitant hearing and visual impairments, the combination of which causes such severe communication and other developmental and educational problems that they cannot be accommodated in special education programs solely for deaf or blind children.

Etiology and Characteristics

Individuals who have hearing impairment serious enough to be classified as deaf and a visual impairment debilitating enough to fit within the category of blind are identified as deaf/blind. This condition may be inherited or acquired. Diseases such as *rubella, scarlet fever,* and *meningitis* can leave a person deaf and blind. *Usher's syndrome*, a genetic condition resulting in congenital deafness and progressive blindness, is the leading cause of deaf/blindness.

The combination of deafness and blindness is a serious condition. Approximately 2,500 children are considered to be deaf/blind, and special regional Deaf/Blind Centers have been established throughout the country to offer guidance and assistance in the care and education of these persons. Mental retardation is not always associated with the deaf/blind, and the gamut of intellectual functioning is possible. Helen

Figure 6-4. Deaf/blind children are not prevented from participating in physical activities by the nature of their handicap. SOURCE: Photo by Lyonel Avance.

Keller, a brilliant woman who graduated cum laude from Radcliffe, represents one end of the continuum of capabilities; those babies born of mothers who had rubella during pregnancy (rubella babies) are usually deaf/blind and retarded, representing the other end (see Figure 6-4).

Because both deafness and blindness are measured on a continuum, deaf/blind individuals show variability from each other in their limited ability in either or both sensory systems. One child might have total blindness and severe but not total deafness, and would be classified as deaf/blind. A deaf/blind child could also be completely deaf with motion perception. Although the educational problems presented are similar, each deaf/blind individual is unique.

SPEECH AND/OR LANGUAGE IMPAIRED

Legal Classification

According to Public Law 94-142, Section 121a.5(b)(10):

"Speech impaired" means a communication disorder, such as stuttering, impaired articulation, a language impairment, or a voice impairment, which adversely affects a child's educational performance.

Language is the communication of ideas through symbols we call words; speech is the behavior of forming and sequencing the sounds of oral language. A child who has difficulty communicating thought and ideas, or in forming or sequencing sounds, is said to have speech and/or language deficits.

Speech Disorders

Speech disorders are divided into three categories: articulation, voice, and speech flow. These types are not mutually exclusive.

Articulatory disorders are related to the intelligibility of an individual's speech. There are four types of articulation disorders.

1. Omissions — the consistent omissions of a sound or letter, which results in only parts of words being pronounced.
2. Substitutions — these include errors made by substituting one letter for another, such as saying "bery" for "very."
3. Additions — extra sounds added to words.
4. Distortions — sounds that are only approximations of what is "correct."

The development of correct articulation is a function of each child's fine motor development, auditory discrimination, and speech models in the child's environment. Articulation differences from adult speech, therefore, are a normal part of development. These, however, should not persist beyond the age of school entrance.

Voice disorders are "characteristics of pitch, loudness, and/or quality that are abusive of the larynx, hamper communication, or are aesthetically displeasing to the speaker or listener" (Hallahan and Kauffman, 1978: 234). Monotone speech, stereotyped inflections, and breaks or cracks of the voice are considered disorders of pitch. Speaking too loudly, too softly, or vacillating between loud and soft are examples of loudness disorder. Nasality and hoarseness are two examples of disorders of the quality of voice.

Speech flow dimensions include sequencing, duration, rate, rhythm, and fluency (Perkins, 1971). Disorders of speech flow include stuttering and cluttering. Stuttering consists of "abnormal repetitions, hesitations, or prolongations of speech sounds, syllables, or movements required for articulation" (Hallahan and Kauffman, 1978: 237). Cluttering involves "excessive speed of speaking plus disorganized sentence structure and articulation problems as well as difficulty in initiating speech sounds . . . " (Hallahan and Kauffman, 1978: 237).

Language Disorders

Language disorders include problems in receptive language — deriving meaning from what is heard; and in expressive language — expressing oneself in a meaningful way with words. Two types of language disorders are delayed language and childhood aphasia.

Delayed language is the inability to use spoken language well beyond an age at which normal children learn to talk. Children who do not develop language at the expected times or who are having difficulties understanding or expressing language may be delayed in their language ability.

Aphasia is the loss or impairment of the ability to understand or formulate language. It can be of the receptive, expressive, or mixed type. Aphasia commonly is used to refer to language disability in adults as a result of brain damage such as stroke. Childhood aphasia, congenital aphasia, or developmental aphasia are language disorders of children similar to that experienced by stroke victims.

Children diagnosed as having developmental aphasia are not mentally retarded, deaf, nor severely autistic (Eisenson, 1972). Besides the obvious language impairment, children with aphasia may have perceptual dysfunctions in one or more of the sensory modalities, disorders of attention, problems with laterality, disorders in sequencing speech sounds or parts of speech, and delayed motor development.

SPECIFIC LEARNING DISABILITY

Legal Classification

According to PL 94-142, Section 121a.5(b)(9):

"Specific learning disability" means a disorder in one or more of the basic psychological processes involved in understanding or in using language spoken or written, which may manifest itself in an imperfect ability to listen, think, speak, read, write, spell, or to do mathematical calculations. The term includes such conditions as perceptual handicaps, brain injury, minimal brain dysfunction, dyslexia, and developmental aphasia. The term does not include children who have learning problems which are primarily a result of visual, hearing, or motor handicaps, mental retardation, or of environmental, cultural or economic disadvantage.

The above legal definition is based upon the definition proposed by the National Advisory Committee on Handicapped Children in 1968. Several other definitions have been suggested over the past decade. Hallahan and Kauffman (1976) have listed five common factors regarding learning disabilities, which are included in most definitions:

1. An academic retardation or academic discrepancy exists.
2. An uneven pattern of development exists.
3. Central nervous system dysfunction may or may not exist.
4. Learning problems are not due to environmental disadvantage.
5. Learning problems are not due to mental retardation or emotional disturbance.

Etiology and Characteristics

Academic retardation is a discrepancy between a child's academic potential and actual academic achievement — that is, the child is not working up to his or her potential. *Uneven pattern* of development may refer to developmental imbalances, or to a wide range of abilities and disabilities found in any one individual. The child may be high in one area of development, such as reading, and low in others, such as spelling.

A learning-disabled individual may or may not have *central nervous system dysfunction.** Learning-disabled individuals who have actual brain damage are verified by the results of a neurological examination or electroencephalogram (EEG).

The learning problems of the learning-disabled cannot, by definition, be the result of *environmental disadvantage, mental retardation, or emotional disturbance.* The environment may be a contributing factor, but may not be the sole factor. Mentally retarded and emotionally disturbed individuals may have learning problems, but these would be considered to be secondary problems. The learning problems of the mentally retarded or emotionally disturbed stem from different causes, and may require different intervention techniques. The mental retardation or emotional disturbance must be treated additionally, and therefore is excluded from the definition of specific learning disability.

The vast majority of causes of learning disabilities is unknown. The causal factors fit into three general categories: (1) organic and biological; (2) genetic; and (3) environmental factors. There is very little documented evidence to support any specific etiology. *Organic and biological* factors refer primarily to soft neurological signs that are indicative of brain dysfunction. *Genetic* factors causing or contributing to learning disabilities are highly speculative. It is now accepted that learning disabilities tend to run in families, and some indications of subtle chromosomal abnormalities

*The term "dysfunction" refers to a malfunctioning of the brain, and is replacing such terms as "injury" or "damage."

Table 6-9. Common characteristics of the learning-disabled

Perceptual, perceptual-motor,
and general coordination problems

- visual perceptual disabilities
- auditory perceptual disabilities
- perceptual-motor dysfunction
- immature body image
- poor spatial orientation
- clumsiness, uncoordinated
- motor-planning problems, inaccurate motor responses
- poor fine motor coordination
- poor balance
- poor eye-hand coordination

Disorders of attention and hyperactivity

- short attention span
- distractible
- hyperactivity
- impulsivity
- perseveration
- hyporesponsive

Language problems

- expressive language problems
- receptive language problems

Disorders of memory and thinking

- memory deficit
- impulsivity
- lacking in concept development
- dissociation

Emotional lability

- lacking in emotion
- frequent changes in mood
- social maladjustment
- low self-esteem

Neurological problems

- EEG irregularities
- "soft" neurological signs

Academic achievement

- achievement-potential discrepancy
- developmental imbalance
- problems in reading, writing, spelling, arithmetic

have been identified. Inadequate learning experiences and inappropriate teaching techniques in addition to a disadvantaged environment are considered as possible *environmental factors* contributing to specific learning disabilities.

Almost one hundred different symptoms of the learning-disabled child have been reported in the literature (Clements, 1966) (see Table 6-9).

SUMMARY

Health-impaired, sensory-disordered, and language- and learning-disabled individuals exist in relatively large numbers in the school-age population. The physical educator must be aware of the many health impairments that exist and the extent to which the various conditions are physically limiting. These health conditions (both chronic and acute problems), include asthma, cardiovascular disorders, cystic fibrosis, di-

abetes, epilepsy, hemophilia, obesity, rheumatic fever, sickle cell anemia, and tuberculosis. Sensory disorders include deaf, hard-of-hearing, blind, visually impaired, and deaf/blind individuals. Each individual presents a unique set of limitations and abilities that must be reckoned with. Language and learning disabilities also come in a variety of forms. There are those children whose problems are quite specific, limited to a type of speech or language problem; others manifest a more generalized learning disability. These individuals often exhibit deficits in motor function. As would be expected, each handicapped person brings a unique set of needs, abilities, and limitations into the physical education setting. Thus, with an understanding of handicapping conditions, the physical educator is better able to translate information regarding the uniqueness of each individual into a viable physical education experience that focuses on ability and its further development.

BIBLIOGRAPHY

Ad Hoc Committee to Define Deaf and Hard of Hearing. ``Report of the Ad Hoc Committee to Define Deaf and Hard of Hearing.'' *American Annals of the Deaf* (1975): 120, 150.

American Diabetes Association. *Facts about Diabetes.* New York: American Diabetes Association, 1966.

American Foundation for the Blind. *Blindness: Some Facts and Figures.* New York: American Foundation for the Blind, 1963.

American Heart Association. *Heart Disease in Children.* New York: American Heart Association, 1963.

American Heart Association. *If Your Child Has a Congenital Heart Defect.* New York: American Heart Association, 1970.

Buell, C. E. *Physical Education for the Blind.* Springfield, Illinois: Charles C. Thomas, 1974.

Clements, S. D. ``Minimal Brain Dysfunction in Children: Terminology and Identification.'' *NINDB Monograph, No. 3.* Washington, D.C.: U.S. Department of Health, Education, and Welfare, 1966.

Edington, D. W., and Cunningham, L. *Biological Awareness.* Englewood Cliffs, New Jersey: Prentice-Hall, 1975.

Eisenson, J. *Aphasia in Children.* San Francisco: Harper & Row, 1972.

Hallahan, D. P., and Cruickshank, W. M. *Psychoeducational Foundations of Learning Disabilities.* Englewood Cliffs, New Jersey: Prentice-Hall, 1973.

Hallahan, D. P., and Kauffman, J. M. *Introduction to Learning Disabilities: A Psychobehavioral Approach.* Englewood Cliffs, New Jersey: Prentice-Hall, 1976.

Hallahan, D. P., and Kauffman, J. M. *Exceptional Children.* Englewood Cliffs, New Jersey: Prentice-Hall, 1978.

Mayer, J. *Overweight: Causes, Cost, and Control.* Englewood Cliffs, New Jersey: Prentice-Hall, 1968.

Perkins, W. H. *Speech Pathology: An Applied Behavioral Science.* St. Louis: C. V. Mosby, 1971.

Robb, P. ``Epilepsy.'' *NINDB Monograph No. 1.* Washington, D.C.: U.S. Department of Health, Education, and Welfare, USPHS Publication No. 1356, 1965.

Sherrill, C. S. *Adapted Physical Education and Recreation: A Multidisciplinary Approach.* Dubuque: William C. Brown, 1976.

Steiner, M. K. *Clinical Approach to Endocrine Problems in Children.* St. Louis: C. V. Mosby, 1970.

Part Two

Assessment of Developmental Levels of Performance

7

The Process of Assessment

Guiding Questions

1. What are the differences between testing, measurement, assessment, and evaluation?
2. What are the respective purposes of evaluation and assessment as they affect the adapted physical educator?
3. What are the advantages and disadvantages of using such measurement concepts as central tendency, variability, class rank, and percentile rank?
4. How are graphing and correlation used?
5. What are the four levels of assessment?
6. What are some forms and techniques of data collection?

Most students of physical education have had an introduction to quantifying motor performance through a course dealing with measurement and evaluation. Few, however, have had courses in the *assessment* of motor performance, particularly as it pertains to children who have special needs. Although a basic course in measurement serves as a good foundation for understanding the concepts presented in this chapter, it is certainly not essential.

DEFINITION OF TERMS

Four basic concepts are presented and defined in this section: (1) testing, (2) measurement, (3) evaluation, and (4) assessment. Each term is defined and graphically represented in its relationship to the others in Figure 7–1.

Testing

Testing, as defined for use in this text, is a data-gathering technique that uses tools or specific procedures for systematizing observations. Testing may be either formal or informal, objective or subjective. Formal testing usually involves setting aside a special time, using a preplanned set of procedures (often published in printed form), using a predetermined space and equipment, and recording scores.

Informal testing may take the form of observation, may be done at any time and under any conditions, and may or may not require recording scores. For example, in a formal test of endurance, one would time the number of seconds a student takes to run 600 yards (AAHPERD Youth Fitness Test, 1975). This example also demonstrates *objective testing*, because it is not up to the teacher to judge whether the student

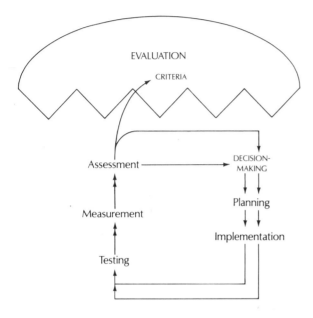

Figure 7-1. The relationship between testing, measurement, assessment, and evaluation.

runs "fast" or runs "slowly." Rather, the precise number of seconds is recorded and would be scored the same by any other examiner. An informal test of endurance may take the form of observing that, after three minutes of play in a soccer game, the student appears fatigued and cannot keep up with the other students. The observation that the student "appears fatigued" is clearly judgmental and is an example of *subjective testing*.

Measurement

The technique of testing nets a result known as measurement, which is a procedure of placing symbols (i.e., scores) on characteristics. It helps to determine the degree to which a person possesses a defined characteristic (Baumgartner and Jackson, 1981). For example, measurement of the characteristic of weight is usually determined by weighing the person to determine the degree or amount of weight possessed. The running test mentioned above nets a measurement of endurance in terms of the number of seconds required to cover the distance; the number of minutes the student is able to play soccer nets a measurement of endurance in terms of physical appearance, regardless of the accuracy of that judgment.

Evaluation

Adapted physical education specialists and general physical educators have different needs in the use of measurement results. As discussed in Chapter 1, enabling legislation requires the educator of students with special needs to assess each student's current level of performance for the purpose of planning an individualized education program. The generalist in physical education, on the other hand, most often uses measurement for assigning grades, determining effectiveness of instruction, and providing motivation. These different uses of measurement results warrant the use of two distinctly different terms. Evaluation is the process used most often by the generalist, and assessment is the process used most often by the adapted physical educator.

Some authors, however, use the terms evaluation and assessment interchangeably. (Barrow and McGee, 1979; Dizney, 1971; Ebel, 1972). Evaluation is generally defined as the process that uses the result of measurement to compare with predetermined standards to facilitate rational decisions. Often, these standards are extrinsic to the needs, capacities, and limitations of the individual student. Comparing a throwing pattern with the known standard for mechanical efficiency (a criterion-referenced standard),* comparing the number of sit-ups performed with age-group norms (a norm-referenced standard), or comparing a score on a written test with the maximum number of points possible are all examples of evaluation in which the standards have little relationship to the current level of performance, needs, capacities, or limitations of the student. Most authors agree that evaluation, like assessment, serves the purpose of providing information for decision-making (Safrit, 1980; Baumgartner and Jackson, 1981), but the decisions in these cases usually revolve around what particular skills or components of the performance must be developed in order to achieve the ideal standard.

When used for student evaluation, the term takes on a summative form because (1) the measurement results are most often compared with norm-referenced standards (that is, a student's performance is compared with a table of norms of ''typical'' performance of a well-defined group [e.g, twelve-year-old boys]); (2) it tells the teacher and student what must yet be done to accomplish a specific, usually ideal, level of performance; and (3) it is usually used at the end of an instructional unit, semester, or course. The use of evaluation, as a summative process, will seldom be used by the adapted physical educator serving

students in segregated classes. In adapted physical education, the annual goals will usually serve as the standard and are part of the ongoing assessment process. Evaluation will most likely be used by specialists in adapted physical education to determine the appropriateness of placing exceptional students into regular classes, since it is this extrinsic standard against which all other students in regular classes are compared.

Program Evaluation

Another use of evaluation is in program evaluation — determining the overall effectiveness of a program (or service) on the performance of a group of students rather than on individuals within the group. This process is becoming increasingly important in making decisions in regard to the physical education of exceptional students. Program evaluation is generally considered to involve three basic considerations: (1) the learning environment; (2) the learners; and (3) learning.

The learning environment — which includes the quantity and quality of facilities, supplies and equipment; the teaching staff; and the class size — is exceedingly important to the education of students with special needs. Wittrock and others discount the learning environment as the least important of the considerations for the regular educational setting; but for the exceptional student, it can be critical. Although it may be argued that the availability of a swimming pool will not ensure that students will learn to swim, the absence of a pool or some substitute will assuredly preclude the students from acquiring those skills. Without the minimal space, supplies, and equipment required to allow exceptional students to have a variety of movement experiences, learning will not occur.

The teaching staff is also critical to the facilitation of learning among students with special needs. The possession of the needed competencies among the

---

*It is important to understand the difference between criterion-referenced and norm-referenced standards. *Norm-referenced standards* are determined by gathering data on a large number of individuals who have specifically defined characteristics (e.g., age, sex, and socioeconomic status). The data are statistically analyzed, and performance standards called ''norms'' are constructed based upon this analysis. Comparing a performance with norms results in a hierarchical ordering of individuals. *Criterion-referenced standards* state an explicit definition of a task. Any given performance is described in terms of the degree to which the task is mastered. Comparing a performance to the criterion results in a description of the student's approximation to the criterion rather than a hierarchical ordering of that student's performance relative to other, similar students.

available staff should be considered not only as part of the program evaluation, but also as part of the decision when considering the most appropriate placement for any given student. Seaman (1970) found that class administration and conduct was the most significant factor in developing negative attitudes toward physical education among handicapped students. A physical educator who does not have the needed competencies, knowledge, and understanding of a handicapped student's needs not only can destroy the student's interest in motor activities, but can also do harm to the student. For example, a teacher who lacks the competencies for teaching language-disabled students can contribute to the frustration and impaired learning of those students. Teachers who have inadequate knowledge of such handicapping conditions as "brittle bones" (osteogenesis imperfecta) can actually aggravate the condition through class conduct or activities.

Class size can also be a significant factor. The very existence of special education is based, at least in part, on the demonstration of increased learning among some segments of the handicapped population when they are placed in small classes that use specialized learning materials and aids and that are conducted by specially prepared teachers.

Evaluation of the learners involves the relative strengths and weaknesses of students when compared with selected characteristics. Although delivering physical education services to groups of students classified according to traditional educational categories is not advocated in this text, there is much to be said for the learning that can take place when students are homogeneously grouped according to their motor needs. This is not to imply that students who have low fitness levels should all be grouped into one class, or students who need work on ball handling skills should be placed into another. Rather, students who have needs at specific levels of the developmental model could more readily have their needs met if grouped according to those levels. Also, the students' style of learning, capacities, and limitations should be among the "selected characteristics" being considered. A trainable mentally retarded (TMR) student does not learn in the same way as a mentally normal student. Thus a program evaluation would most likely reveal that placement of the TMR student into a regular class has not brought about the desired learning results. This student is too different and has learning needs so diverse from the group that the program is ineffective. A child functioning at Piaget's sensorimotor level of development would be inappropriately placed in a program that emphasizes game and sport skills. Thus the program would be evaluated as ineffective.

There is a nationwide movement to comply with PL 94–142 by mainstreaming students into regular physical education programs and removing students from specially designed programs, allowing them to acquire motor skills in the same context as nonhandicapped students. Unless adequate evaluation of the program considerations are made, this movement can prove disastrous to the acquisition of movement skills among the handicapped. When determining placement or reevaluating placement of a student with special needs, ask the following questions about the program under consideration:

1. Are the facilities adequate in quantity and quality to provide this student with a variety of movement experiences?
2. Are the supplies and equipment of appropriate quantity and quality for the unique needs and learning characteristics of this student?
3. Does the teacher in this program have the needed competencies, knowledge, and human qualities to create a successful learning experience for this student?
4. Is the size of the class conducive to this student's learning?
5. Do the other students in this program have similar motor learning needs?

6. Are the students (and is this student) making reasonable progress toward the learning goals of the program?

Evaluation of learning includes the demonstration of permanent changes in behavior as a result of the experience with the program. Since programs for students with special needs are developed on an individual basis, and the measurement of permanent changes in motor behavior is usually made through the performance objectives and annual goals, this aspect of program evaluation is little use to the adapted specialist.

Assessment

In contrast to evaluation, assessment involves *interpreting* the results of measurement for the purpose of making decisions about placement, program planning, and performance objectives. As used with students with special needs, assessment is formative in nature: (1) it uses measurement results for the purpose of immediate decision-making in program modification and individual program planning; (2) it is criterion-referenced; (3) it helps the teacher identify the fundamental areas of dysfunction rather than specific skills; and (4) it is an ongoing process used consistently throughout the instructional process. Comparing a student's standing balance with that student's previous performance, comparing the head-raising skills of a nine-year-old with a developmental sequence, or comparing the amount of space used by a blind child during a dance lesson are all examples of assessment in which the standard or criteria against which the measurement results are compared describe either the student's previous performance, the student's level of development, or a previously identified area of dysfunction. This is in contrast to the evaluation process of comparing performance with norms for nine-year-olds or space used by sighted children (see Table 7-1).

PURPOSES OF EVALUATION AND ASSESSMENT

Since the outcome of measurement leads to a process enhancing decision-making for both the generalist

Table 7-1. Comparison of norm-referenced and criterion-referenced standards

Performance	Norm-referenced	Criterion-referenced
Walking	Walks with heel-toe gait (32–35 months).	Walks distance of 10 feet.
Running	50-yard dash (9.3 seconds for 11-year-old boys).	Runs stiffly.
Throwing	Throws ball 5–7 feet in a vertical pattern (28–31 months).	Throws overhand.
Jumping	Vertical jump (7 inches for 6.6–6.11-year-olds).	Jumps with feet together.

SOURCE: For walking and throwing, D. Sue Schafer and Martha S. Moersch, eds., *Developmental Programming for Infants and Young Children*, vol. 2 (Ann Arbor, Michigan: University of Michigan Press, n.d.). For running and jumping, Los Angeles Unified School District (Janet A. Seaman, consultant), *Adapted Physical Education Assessment Scale* (Los Angeles: Los Angeles Board of Education, 1979).

and the adapted physical education specialist, it makes sense that some of the purposes of evaluation and assessment will overlap. Four general purposes have similar value for both the generalist and the adapted physical education specialist and are widely accepted in measurement circles (Educational Testing Service, 1958; McCloy, 1954): (1) placement/classification, (2) diagnosis, (3) prediction, and (4) measuring achievement. Two additional purposes of assessment, unique to adapted physical education, are (5) program planning and (6) determining further testing/related services.

Placement/Classification

One of the first purposes of the testing and measurement of a student with special needs is to determine whether the student should be placed in a segregated adapted physical education class, a regular physical education class, or some combination of the two. Both criterion-referenced and norm-referenced standards may be used. For both the generalist and the specialist, measurement results may be used to further classify or ability-group students within a given class. Criterion-referenced standards are more useful for the purpose of classification, while norm-referenced standards tend to be more helpful in making placement decisions.

Diagnosis

Measurement can be used to diagnose weaknesses of students in both regular and special classes. For the assessment process, this is the heart of planning individualized education programs. For the evaluation process, diagnosis serves to help identify students who should be referred to adapted physical education or those for whom specific units of instruction should be stressed. For assessment, diagnosis uses criterion-referenced standards; for evaluation, norm-referenced standards should be used.

Prediction

Assessment is used by the specialist in adapted physical education to predict a student's achievement level at the beginning of a specified instructional period. Since assessment employs quantitative as well as qualitative measurements and theory (Baumgartner and Jackson, 1981:3), it allows the specialist to consider all factors impinging on the student for the duration of the instructional period. Criterion-referenced standards should be used when prediction is the purpose of assessment. For the generalist, norm-referenced standards should be used when predicting such things as potential success in interscholastic athletics. Far more predictive value is derived from knowing that a given student's vertical jump is equal to or better than 99 percent of her age-peers (i.e., norm-referenced) than knowing that she jumped two inches higher today than she did last week (i.e., criterion-referenced).

Measuring Achievement

For either the generalist or the specialist, one of the most important purposes of measurement is to determine whether a student has achieved instructional objectives (Baumgartner and Jackson, 1981). Whether the evaluation process of the generalist is being used to assign grades, or the assessment process of the specialist is being used to review a student's educational plan, a most important reason to measure is to determine whether there has been any change in performance since the last time a measurement was taken. Criterion-referenced or norm-referenced standards are suggested, depending on whether the process is assessment or evaluation.

Program Planning

Individualized educational plans must be made at least yearly for all students who have special needs. These plans must be based upon the current level of performance, including a prediction of the student's achievement level at the end of one year of instruction or less. Unlike the traditional method of curriculum development, in which specific units of instruction are provided all students at any given grade level, program planning for students with special needs is based upon the results of the assessment process. Therefore criterion-referenced standards are appropriate.

Determining Further Testing/Related Services

Although the primary purpose of motor assessment for the adapted physical educator would never be to determine a need for further testing or related services, this is very often an outcome. Because the adapted physical educator uses movement as the medium for testing and measurement, the resultant assessment may provide some qualitative data that has not been gathered before. Implications for muscle or reflex testing may suggest the need for physical or occupational therapy testing services, and may only be revealed through measurement of motor performance. Either criterion-referenced or norm-referenced standards would generate this information.

MEASUREMENT CONCEPTS

Basic concepts involved in the measurement of motor performance will be covered in this section. For students who have experience in measurement or statistics, much of the material will be a review. Students who desire more in-depth coverage of these concepts are referred to any one of the excellent texts already cited in this chapter (Barrow and McGee, 1979; Baumgartner and Jackson, 1981; Ebel, 1972; Safrit, 1980).

Types of Scores

Measurement occurs when symbols are placed on characteristics. In physical education, these symbols usually take the form of scores. The two types of scores most commonly used are continuous and discrete. *Continuous scores* have a potentially infinite number of values (i.e., along a continuum) depending on the ability or accuracy of the tool used in the measurement. A 50-yard dash score, for example, is usually measured in tenths of a second; however, if a more sophisticated watch were available, the dash could be measured in hundredths or even thousandths of a second. In contrast, *discrete scores* have a limited number of specific values and usually have no obtainable scores between these values. Possible scores on an archery target, for example, are 9-7-5-3-1; it is not possible for an archer to score 8 or 6 in any single hit.

Further, scores can be classified as ratio, interval, ordinal, or nominal. *Ratios* have a common unit of measure between each score and a true zero point. The number of sit-ups, pull-ups, or balls caught are examples of ratios. *Interval* scores have a common unit of measure between each score, but do not have a true zero point. Intelligence or knowledge tests generate interval scores because each score reflects one more question answered correctly than the next lower score, but a zero score does not reflect absolute lack of intelligence or knowledge. A zero score, in this instance, simply means that no questions were answered correctly. *Ordinal* scores do not have a common unit of measure. Class rankings are ordinal because the best-skilled student in class is given a rank of 1, the second best a rank of 2, and so on. The student ranked number 1 may be exceedingly more skilled than anyone else in class, yet this rank is as close to number 2 as the second student is to number 3. Most scores used in adapted physical education are ratio, interval, or ordinal. *Nominal* scores cannot be hierarchically ordered, but can provide useful information for the adapted physical educator in the assessment process. Students can be classified as right-handed or left-handed, or as subject to seizures or not, with neither of the categories in each pair valued as better than the other. The adapted physical educator is advised to collect such nominal data, however, as an aid to assessment and a help in program planning.

Organization of Scores

Once scores have been gathered on a group of students, a representation of each group of students on each variable or performance measured can be devised. This can be done most easily in one of two ways: (1) simple frequency distribution; or (2) graphing.

A *simple frequency distribution* is a table with all the scores (x) listed in descending order from best to worst. Opposite each score is the frequency (f) or number of times that score occurs (i.e., the number of students making each score). The highest score is usually the best score (except in running events, in which the lowest score is best). (Table 7-2 demonstrates the use of a frequency table with scores made on the softball throw of the Special Fitness Test for the Mentally Retarded.)

If this table represented a group of students at a school who were being considered for Special Olympics competition, it would be easy to see from the organization of scores which students would be the most likely candidates to compete in the softball throw. Since the softball throw test item is suggested as a measure of shoulder strength and arm speed, this table also helps identify students who need work in those areas. (Table 7-3 shows the distribution of scores on the 50-yard dash.) Since the 50-yard dash is a running event, the lowest score (i.e., fewer seconds) is the best score. Again, it is easy to get a picture of this group of students in terms of running speed. The teacher can readily identify students who need work in this area.

Another simple method of organizing scores is by *graphing*. This method gives a literal picture of the similarities and differences within a group on any given measure. For example, to graph the softball throw

Table 7-2. Softball throw measured in feet

X	F	X	F	X	F
169	1	115	2	87	5
154	1	112	2	85	3
152	2	110	5	70	2
149	3	109	7	65	2
130	1	105	12	64	1
128	1	103	10	50	3
127	1	100	5	41	1
125	2	98	3	30	1
123	3	95	2	27	1
120	1	91	2	15	1

SOURCE: American Alliance for Health, Physical Education, Recreation, and Dance, *Special Fitness Test for the Mentally Retarded* (Washington, D.C.: AAHPERD, 1968).

Table 7-3. 50-Yard dash measured in seconds

X	F	X	F	X	F
7.2	1	8.1	10	9.1	1
7.3	1	8.2	13	9.3	2
7.5	1	8.4	10	9.5	1
7.6	1	8.6	10	9.6	1
7.7	2	8.7	7	9.9	1
7.9	1	8.8	2	10.1	1
8.0	2	8.9	1	10.3	1

SOURCE: American Alliance for Health, Physical Education, Recreation, and Dance, *Special Fitness Test for the Mentally Retarded* (Washington, D.C.: AAHPERD, 1968).

scores represented on Table 7-2, scores are listed on the horizontal axis and frequencies on the vertical axis. A dot is placed on the graph above each score and corresponding with the number of students making that score. By connecting the dots with lines, a frequency polygon is completed. A smooth line drawn through the majority of the scores gives an even better picture of distribution (see Figure 7-2).

A graph of the 50-yard dash (shown on Table 7-3) gives a different picture of this group of students. The long, low tail of the curve to the left of the graph, which shows that relatively few students obtained low

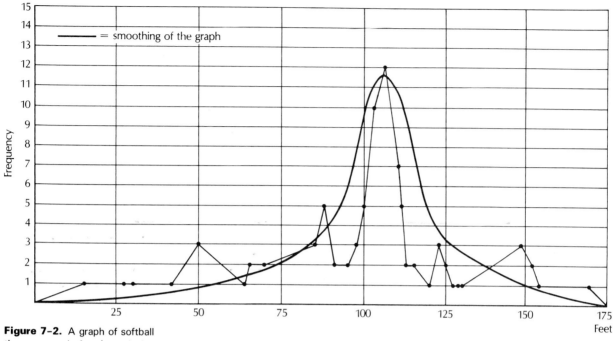

Figure 7-2. A graph of softball throw scores in feet (negatively skewed).

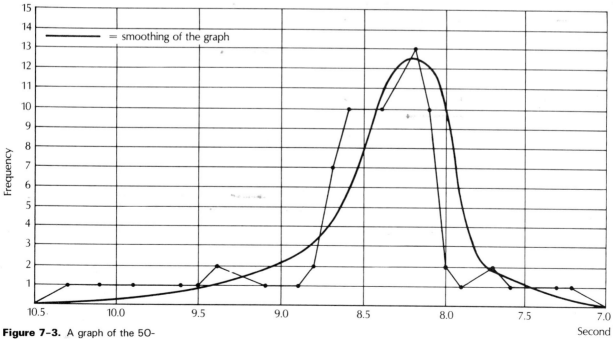

Figure 7-3. A graph of the 50-yard dash in seconds (leptokurtic).

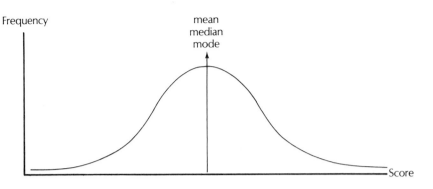

Figure 7–4. Normal or bell-shaped curve.

scores, is said to be *negatively skewed.* If the long tail were to the right, it would be positively skewed (see Figure 7–3).

A normal or bell-shaped curve, which has tails of equal lengths, describes a group of scores that consists of neither exceedingly high scores nor exceedingly low scores, and with the majority of students obtaining scores around the middle of the distribution (see Figure 7–4).

A curve such as the one in Figure 7–3, which is more sharply peaked than a normal curve, is called *leptokurtic.* It describes a rather homogeneous group of scores. As can be seen in Table 7–3 and Figure 7–3, the vast majority of scores on the 50-yard dash fell between 8.0 and 9.0 seconds. This means that students in this group are quite similar to one another in running speed. A curve that is flatter or less peaked than a normal curve is called *platykurtic.* This curve represents a group that is quite heterogeneous in nature. The implications of these various distributions for program planning will be discussed more fully in later chapters.

Measures of Central Tendency

Whether the adapted physical educator is analyzing scores for the purpose of individual assessment, planning group activities, developing a test, or comparing a group with another similar group, it is important to be able to describe the scores. Although the frequency table and polygon help to characterize the group, other descriptive values are significant when describing specific characteristics. One such descriptive value is

the measure of central tendency. There are three measures of central tendency: (1) mean, (2) median, and (3) mode.

The *mean* is the arithmetic average score of all the scores, and is influenced by the position and value of any single score in the group. It is usually the best measure of central tendency, and is reported the most often in ready-made tests of motor performance. The mean is derived by adding all the scores in the group and dividing that sum by the number of scores in the group. For example, the sum of the scores in Table 7–2 divided by the number of scores is 8,708 ÷ 86 = 101.26 for the average or mean score.

The *median* is the absolute middle score; half the scores fall above this score and half the scores fall below. It cannot be found unless all the scores are listed from best to worst. The median of the scores in Table 7–2 is 105, since out of eighty-six scores, forty-three scores are equal to or greater than 105, and forty-three scores are equal to or less than 105. Notice that the median is affected only by the position of each score and not the value.

The *mode* is the score in a group that is most frequently obtained. It is seldom used in test development and reporting. In the softball throw scores in Table 7–2, the mode is 105. The mode is the least stable measure of central tendency, since the change in one score (in some cases) would change its value.

In a normal curve (i.e., frequency polygon), the mean, median, and mode are the same, as on Figure 7–4. In a negatively skewed curve, such as Figure 7–2, the mean would be less than the median and the mode, because its value is influenced by the extremely low scores. In a positively skewed curve, the situation would be reversed.

Measures of Variability

Another descriptive value often used in describing a group of scores is a measure of variability. Measures of variability indicate the spread of the scores; the homogeneity or heterogeneity of the group. Three measures of variability are discussed here: (1) standard deviation; (2) interquartile deviation; and (3) range.

The *standard deviation*, used with the mean, is the most common measure of variability reported in ready-made tests. It describes the average amount by which all the scores differ or deviate from the mean. When looking at the two frequency polygons in Figures 7–2 and 7–3, it is easy to see that the standard deviation for the softball throw is going to be much larger than for the 50-yard dash, because this visual picture (Figure 7–2) shows that the scores are much more spread. A large standard deviation describes a rather heterogeneous group of scores; a small one describes a homogeneous group — considering, of course, the differences in units of measure.

The *interquartile deviation* is used with the median, and describes the variability of the middle 50 percent of the scores. It is seldom reported and serves no useful purpose in describing the performance of a group of students.

The *range* is used with the mode, and is the easiest to determine. The range is the difference between the lowest and highest scores, and tells much about impending challenges to a teacher planning group activities. Like the mode, it is not a very stable measure, because a change in either of the extreme scores could significantly affect the range. It can be readily determined that the range for the scores listed in Table 7–2 is 154 (i.e., a high score of 169 and a low score of 15) and therefore it is used quite often by teachers because of the ease of calculation.

Position in a Group

Whether assessing for placement, diagnosis, prediction, or achievement, it is important to determine each student's position within a group. The group may be the student's own class at school, or a national group of students on whose performance ready-made test norms are based. A student's score is meaningless without the orientation provided by the group. The score takes on more meaning when the mean, the standard deviation, and sometimes the frequency polygon are shown. Since these values represent the group of which the student is a part, a parent or professional can see generally how the student compares. More precise methods are used in ready-made tests for explaining the position of a given score, and it is important for the adapted physical educator to be familiar with them in order to use these tests.

Class Rank

The most basic indicator of position in a group is class rank. Any teacher can rank-order — that is, list scores from best to worst, and assign a position to a student based on a single measurement or a group of measurements. The student with the best score is assigned a rank of 1; the next best 2, and so on. In the case of tied scores, the ranks that would be given to each student involved in the tie would be averaged, and that score assigned to all students involved. In Table 7–3, the ranking would go smoothly until the time of 7.7 seconds. Since the two runners involved are equal in ability (at least this time the test was given), they cannot be assigned different ranks. Instead, it is necessary to take the average or mean rank of the positions they share (which is 5.5) and assign that rank to both students. The student timed at 7.9 seconds would then be ranked seventh in this group. It should be remembered that group rank has very little meaning unless the number of scores in the group is known. The two runners ranked 5.5, above, appear very good because there was a total of seventy students in the group. Had there been only seven students in the group, their performance would look quite poor.

Another problem with group ranking, especially when used with exceptional students, revolves around the fact that these students are usually ability-grouped, categorized, or classified on any number of educational criteria exclusive of motor performance. Therefore a special education class of fifteen students may be very similar in their ability to grasp concepts in the classroom, but may be very dissimilar in motor performance. For example, a particular student may be ranked number 1 in his special education class on a motor performance measure. However, if his class is the lowest functioning in the entire school, he may still be ranked 716 in a school of 730 students (i.e., fifteenth from the bottom).

Percentile Rank

A better indicator of a student's position relative to a group is a percentile rank. Because a percentile rank describes the percentage of the group that scored below a given score, it doesn't require reporting the number of scores in the group. The runner in Table 7–3, who is ranked number 7, has a percentile rank of 90, since 90 percent of the students (i.e., sixty-three) in the group of seventy ran slower, and 10 percent ran equal to or better. Percentile ranks are ordinal scores, cannot be used in calculations, and are totally dependent upon the other scores in the group. Percentile ranks do not change at the same rate as the actual or raw scores. For example, if the runner with the time of 7.9 seconds could have run the distance one-tenth second faster (i.e., 7.8 seconds) the percentile rank would not have changed at all.

Ready-made tests that use percentile ranks for norms are usually expressed as *percentiles.* A percentile is a point (i.e., score) in a distribution, below which falls the percent of scores indicated by the percentile.

Hence, in the above example, the ninetieth percentile is the point (score) below which 90 percent of the scores fall. That point in the distribution in Table 7–3 is 7.9 seconds; or, the percentile rank of 7.9 is 90. Since a percentile is a point rather than a segment in the distribution, the score is always reported as being *at* (not in) a given percentile. Most ready-made fitness test norms are given in percentiles.

Standard Scores

Norms on some tests appropriate for use in adapted physical education are given in the form of standard scores. Standard scores, categorically, are scores on a scale that have been generated by "transforming" the raw scores. They are often used for convenience, comparability, ease, and value for interpretation. The standard scores most commonly used are: (1) stanine, (2) z score, and (3) T-score. If a teacher gives two performance tests, such as the 50-yard dash and sit-ups, there is no way a total score for the two tests can be combined or compared, since they each have a different unit of measure and a different orientation (that is, on the 50-yard dash, a small score is good; but for sit-ups, a large score is good). By converting to standard scores, the unit of measure is "transformed" from seconds and number of sit-ups to a common, standard score unit. The scores can then be combined, compared, or interpreted to parents with relative ease.

The standard-nine or *stanine* scale is a 9-point scale having values of 1 to 9, with a mean of 5 and a standard deviation of 2. Stanines require use of a lot of fractional values. Given the range of scores in Table 7–2 of 154 feet, it can easily be seen that transforming those raw scores from feet to a 9-point stanine value will result in many scores being expressed in fractions (decimals).

The *z score* scale has a mean of 0 and a standard deviation of 1. This implies that all the scores below the mean are negative, and that those above are posi-

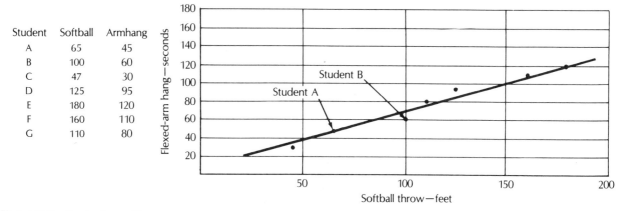

Student	Softball	Armhang
A	65	45
B	100	60
C	47	30
D	125	95
E	180	120
F	160	110
G	110	80

Figure 7-5. Graph of a positive relationship.

tive numbers. Like stanines, transformation to z scores results in having to handle a lot of fractional values. The fact that the mean on the z scale is 0 usually requires some explanation when reporting these scores to parents or others who are unfamiliar with measurement concepts. Another disadvantage to this scale is that, since half of the scores on a normal curve fall below the mean, the teacher using z scores will be working with negative numbers.

T scores are on a scale of 20 to 80, with a mean of 50 and a standard deviation of 10. Like percentiles, T-scores are easier to understand and are expressed in whole numbers. Unlike percentiles, z and T-scores can be used in calculations. Most ready-made tests in physical education in general are normed in T-scores or percentiles, although tests normed on students with special needs use a variety of standard scales.

Relationships Between Scores

Determining the relationships between scores is also done so that the interpretation of measurements will net a quality assessment. Two different techniques that can be used to determine the relationship between scores are: (1) graphing and (2) correlation.

Graphing

Graphing is easier and, for many purposes, adequate; but it is not as precise as the mathematically derived correlation. In graphing, a coordinate system is used (as

in the frequency polygon) with one measure on the horizontal axis and one on the vertical axis. In graphing the softball throw, for the score student A made, a dot is placed on the graph above the score (i.e., 65) and opposite student A's flexed arm hang score. After all the students' scores are plotted, a trend line (a line showing the trend of the relationship) is drawn between them. Figure 7-5 shows a near perfect (*positive*) relationship. As one score gets larger, the other score *tends to get larger.* The closer the dots are to the trend line, the higher or nearer perfect the relationship (see Figure 7-5).

A graph can also show a high, nearly perfect relationship that is *negative.* In graphing body weight, for example, as the students get heavier their high jump scores tend to decrease. Because the lower score in running events is the better score, a negative trend would also exist when running scores are plotted against most other physical measures (see Figure 7-6).

If the plotted dots resemble a circle, and no trend line can be drawn through them, a very low or *no* relationship at all exists (see Figure 7-7).

Correlation

Correlation is the mathematical technique for determining the trend or relationship between two measures. It is more precise because a fractional value between -1.0 and $+1.0$ is derived from the calculation. The relationship in Figure 7-5 is nearly perfect; since it is positive, its correlation value would be very

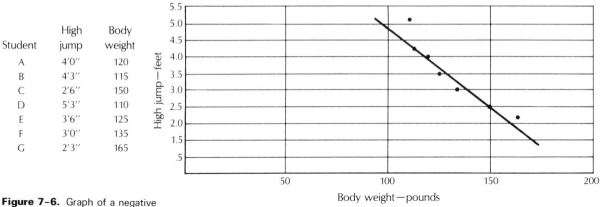

Student	High jump	Body weight
A	4'0"	120
B	4'3"	115
C	2'6"	150
D	5'3"	110
E	3'6"	125
F	3'0"	135
G	2'3"	165

Figure 7-6. Graph of a negative relationship.

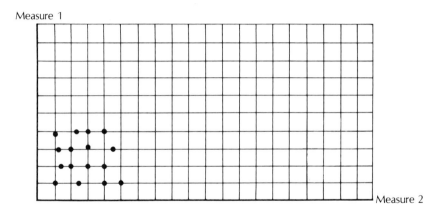

Figure 7-7. Graph of no relationship.

near +1.0. The actual correlation is +0.99, which for most purposes is not enough of a difference to warrant doing the calculations. Nonetheless, there is a difference.

Correlations are used by test makers to express the reliability and validity of ready-made tests. The potential user must be aware of these qualities of ready-made tests, and must have a good understanding of correlation.

LEVELS OF ASSESSMENT

Using the developmental approach requires not only a good understanding of motor development, but also a firm grasp of the levels of assessment that are appropriate at each developmental stage. For purposes

of assessment, the developmental model has been condensed into four levels: (1) reflex behavior; (2) sensory systems; (3) motor patterns; and (4) movement skills. Measurement of parameters at each level may be done using a variety of data collection tools or techniques as indicated below.

Reflex Behavior

Reflex testing involves the sampling of primitive reflex behavior that supports automatic postural and adaptive reactions and makes higher activities possible (Fiorentino, 1972). The presence of some residual reflex behavior, which should have been inhibited during infancy, tends to interfere with the development of motor patterns and movement skills in school-age children. Inversely, the absence of some reflex behavior,

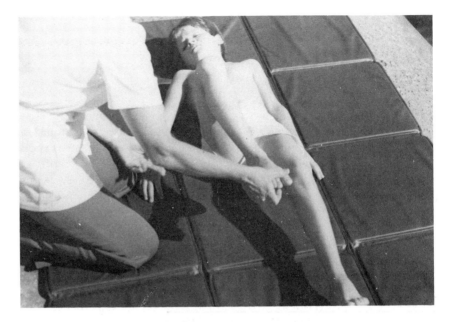

Figure 7-8. Sample of testing for crossed extension reflex.

which should have developed during infancy, can have similar interfering effects on motor behavior. An indication of reflex behavior can be obtained through observation or performance testing by an occupational or physical therapist (see Figure 7-8).

Sensory Systems

Testing of the sensory systems focuses on the functioning of those systems that most directly support motor performance. The three systems of greatest interest to the physical educator are the vestibular, tactile, and proprioceptive. Functioning of the visual and auditory systems are important to program planning for the adapted physical educator, but are not directly within the usual purview of assessment. Functioning of the sensory systems is usually measured in education by sensorimotor tests (see Figure 7-9), discussed in Chapter 8.

Motor Patterns

Motor patterns are functional units of movement that occur in the normal course of development as a result of sensory feedback. Testing at this level also involves

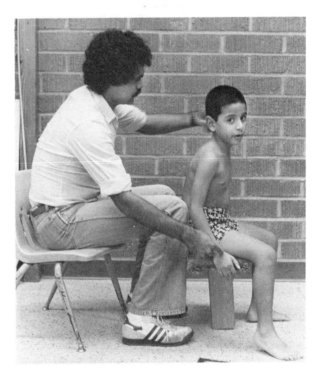

Figure 7-9. This child's tactile system is being tested by a double tactile stimulation test.

testing motor responses, since they are approximations of motor patterns. Motor patterns include all patterns learned experientially for functional purposes (e.g., rolling, twisting, and walking). Motor patterns are most commonly measured through motor development profiles, motor ability tests, or comprehensive motor performance tests.

Movement Skills

Movement skills include all skills learned through modeling (i.e., copying the behavior of others) or formal instruction, the purpose for which is external to the individual's functional needs. Testing at this level includes specific applications of simple and compound motor patterns as well as skills involved in culturally determined forms of movement (see Figure 7-10).

Movement skills are most often measured through the use of motor skills and sports skills tests, but may also be measured through motor ability and comprehensive motor performance tests. Other components of culturally determined forms of movement, such as strength, flexibility, agility, endurance, and body alignment, may be measured through the use of direct measures of these parameters or physical fitness tests.

DATA COLLECTION

Data collection can take many forms. To the beginning student in adapted physical education, the task may seem insurmountable. For an average specialist in adapted physical education, serving from eighty to one hundred students daily (Geddes and Seaman,

Figure 7-10. Volleyball playing ability can be measured by a volleyball skills test. SOURCE: Photo by Ben Esparza.

1978), a total assessment and diagnostic workup on each student would take the entire school year! Obviously, neither school districts, parents, nor students could tolerate this loss in instructional time.

Two major keys can help to streamline the assessment process to net the most information in the least amount of time invested: (1) adequate sampling and (2) use of available resources.

Adequate Sampling

Adequate sampling of motor performance is probably the most critical key, since it is totally within the control of the adapted physical educator. In a self-contained special education class, the classroom teacher has opportunities for data collection from approximately three to four hours each day. Most physical educators see each student approximately thirty to sixty minutes each day, and in some programs as little as thirty minutes each week. The adapted physical educator must be realistic about what can be accomplished in the time available and use as many data sources as possible to compensate for a restricted schedule.

In an educational setting, it is usually only possible (at least initially) to sample motor performance, because time does not allow a total diagnostic process to be completed. Rather, "diagnosis" must be projected from measuring aspects or components of motor performance. A good instrument that samples several aspects of motor performance would solve this problem, but few such tools exist in the ready-made test market. A student's educational classification, a classroom teacher's or nurse's "reason for referral" to adapted physical education, and the specialist's own observations should lend valuable information regarding possible areas of dysfunction. Careful planning of the assessment program and astute observations during the process can help keep the student-teacher contact time to a minimum. Generally, thirty to forty-

five minutes of pupil contact time should be allowed for testing. This would require approximately fifteen to twenty school days for eighty students, assuming all students needed to be tested. Since complete assessments are required by law only every three years, and only assessment of current levels of performance relative to performance objectives are required yearly, it is clear that this formula fits well within the timelines for identifying educational needs.

Once the initial observations, reasons for referral, educational classification (if any), and the like are known, the adapted physical educator should have a fairly good idea of what performance parameters or aspects should be measured formally. Preplanning of the assessment program is not only expedient, it is required since, by law, parental permission must be obtained in order to proceed.

Forms of Data Collection

Three forms of data collection most often comprise the student-teacher contact phase of the assessment process: (1) observation; (2) formal testing; and (3) self-report.

Observation should always be structured by the time the teacher gets to this point of the assessment process. Based on preliminary information gathered on the student, the adapted physical education teacher should have in mind specific motor behaviors for which they are looking.

Whether the activity is planned to require the motor behaviors of interest, or whether the adapted physical educator watches for the behaviors of interest to occur spontaneously, a clear picture of the data or information desired is essential. This distinguishes a trained observer from one who is untrained. Untrained observers can "look" without really "seeing," because they have no clear idea of what they are looking for. The American soccer movement offers a good example of this. The untrained or naive American spectator can watch a soccer game without knowing the significance of a given play in terms of strategy or skill. More experience and knowledge is needed. Until that spectator has learned the skills and rules of the game that are the criteria with which to measure the quality of a performance, observation of the game may be unsatisfying and will produce no real set of useful information.

Formal testing usually implies the use of a specified instrument or tool, a specified protocol or set of procedures, and criterion-referenced or norm-referenced standards. This is not to say that once formal testing begins, observation ceases. The best examiner is first a skilled observer.

Self-report is the third form of data collection requiring student-teacher contact. This form of data collection is obviously limited to use with those students who have language expression, and who can be considered reliable reporters of their own behavior. Information on attitude, habits, and interests may be gathered in this way. A questionnaire requiring little teacher time could be used in some cases, but interviews or planned questions usually comprise the bulk of data gathered through self-report.

Use of Available Resources

The second key in streamlining the assessment process is the effective use of available resources. A great deal of data that can be used by the adapted physical educator is usually already available. Observations of other professionals, formal test results, and anecdotal and health records often provide valuable information to the decision-making process. Cumulative files maintained by the school district usually include grade or progress reports, anecdotal records, and teacher observations. Sometimes in this file or in separate files are records of physical examinations; medications used (if any); history of various health-related problems, such as seizures, visual or hearing losses, childhood diseases, prenatal and perinatal complications, and the like. The results of psychological and language evaluations may also be available.

This data can help the adapted physical educator make decisions regarding instrument selection, selection of parameters to be measured, interpretation of the data collected by the specialist, and recommendations for program planning and further testing. A more detailed coverage of these forms of data collection and their use is given in Chapters 8 and 9.

SUMMARY

In order to measure a student's current level of performance, the adapted physical educator must consider sampling all levels of the developmental continuum in order to get a clear picture of the student's functioning. Reflex behavior, sensory system function, development of motor patterns, and the application of those patterns to movement skills must be considered. Each level of performance must be sampled with enough information before the data can be considered valid. This does not mean that the physical educator must gather all data; rather, other professionals can provide useful information about the motor performance of a student that enables the physical educator to write an appropriate educational program.

BIBLIOGRAPHY

American Alliance for Health, Physical Education, Recreation, and Dance. *Youth Fitness Test.* Washington, D.C.: AAHPERD, 1975.

American Alliance for Health, Physical Education, Recreation, and Dance. *Special Fitness Test for the Mentally Retarded.* Washington, D.C.: AAHPERD, 1968.

Barrow, H. M., and McGee, R. *A Practical Approach to Measurement in Physical Education.* 3d ed. Philadelphia: Lea and Febiger, 1979.

Baumgartner, T. A., and Jackson, A. S. *Measurement for Evaluation in Physical Education.* 2d ed. Boston: Houghton Mifflin, 1981.

Dizney, H. *Classroom Evaluation for Teachers.* Dubuque: Wm. C. Brown, 1971.

Ebel, R. L. *Essentials of Educational Measurement.* Englewood Cliffs, New Jersey: Educational Testing Service, 1978.

Educational Testing Service. *Selecting an Achievement Test: Principles and Procedures.* Princeton, New Jersey: Educational Testing Service, 1958.

Fiorentino, M. R. *Normal and Abnormal Development.* Springfield, Illinois: Charles C. Thomas, 1972.

Geddes, D., and Seaman, J. A. *Competencies of Adapted Physical Educators in Special Education.* Washington, D.C.: Information and Research Utilization Center, AAHPERD, 1978.

McCloy, C. H., and Young, N. D. *Tests and Measurements in Health and Physical Education.* New York: Appleton-Century-Crofts, 1954.

Safrit, M. J. *Evaluation in Physical Education: Assessing Motor Behavior.* 2d ed. Englewood Cliffs, New Jersey: Prentice-Hall, 1980.

Seaman, J. A. ``Attitudes of Physically Handicapped Students Toward Physical Education.'' *The Research Quarterly* 41 (1970): 439–445.

Wittrock, M. C. ``The Evaluation of Instruction: Cause-and-Effect Relations in Naturalistic Data.'' In *The Evaluation of Instruction: Issues and Problems,* edited by M. C. Wittrock and D. E. Wiley. New York: Holt, Rinehart and Winston, 1970, pp. 3–21.

8 Data Collection: Informal Observation, Performance Testing, and Direct Measures

Guiding Questions

1. What are the applications of observation, performance testing, and direct methods?
2. What are the fundamentals of test administration?
3. What are some key elements in generating useful data through the use of observational techniques?
4. What are some important criteria to be met when selecting an instrument or procedure for measuring the motor performance of students who have special needs?
5. What are two tests for measuring each of the following: function, motor patterns, movement skills, and physical fitness?

PL 94–142 requires that the current level of performance of all individuals identified as having special needs be determined, in order to aid the development of an individualized educational plan (IEP) for every student, and to assure that the plan is based upon the current needs of each student. This is a rather new concept for physical educators. Historically, measurement and evaluation have been used for screening and classifying students, measuring achievement, and grading. Sometimes, measurement for diagnosis of deficiencies has also been used. Furthermore, educational programs have traditionally been planned on the basis of categorical, age-related characteristics; predetermined curricular content; or seasonal interests and resources.

Because of this, the content of many adapted, remedial, special, or modified physical education programs has paralleled regular physical education, with modifications or omissions of content to fit within the limitations of students in these programs. In contrast, current legislation and social trends call for the identification of individual strengths and weaknesses of each student, and the eventual planning of program content that will enhance those strengths and reduce, if not eliminate, the weaknesses.

The use of physical fitness, motor ability, and skill proficiency tests has only limited value to the adapted physical educator, since they are typically norm-referenced tests that have been standardized on school-age populations that exclude students with special needs.

Further, these tests underscore the performances that a student *cannot do,* but leave much to the imagination regarding what a student *can do.* Norm-referenced tests will have ultimate application in the evaluation process when considering placement or progress of a student in the mainstream. For individualized program planning, however, they tend to give inadequate quantity and quality of information.

Although qualitative and diagnostic techniques generate more useful data, they are often impractical for school use due to the time needed to administer them and the level of training needed to become a proficient examiner. Other tools, however, can be used efficiently in the school environment to gather the needed data for program planning. These tools include (1) informal observation, (2) performance tests, (3) direct measures, (4) self-report, and (5) unobtrusive measures. The first three will be discussed here, and the others will be discussed in Chapter 9.

INFORMAL OBSERVATION

The total process of gathering data and interpretation of that data for the purpose of program planning is the process of *assessment.* Data gathering alone does not complete the assessment process. In fact, the assessment process should be ongoing or cyclical, with data collection and comparison with long-range goals and performance objectives occurring constantly. The most commonly used tool for implementing this process is observation.

Observational Techniques

Valid observational techniques rely mainly on five basic competencies. The observer must have (1) a solid understanding of developmental milestones for the parameter or performance being observed, (2) knowledge of the elements or dimensions of the target performance, (3) the ability to identify deviations

Figure 8-1. This teacher is gathering data on a student playing T-ball.

from the norm in the observed performance, (4) the ability to describe the observed performance in performance terms, and (5) the ability to make sense out of the relationships among several performances (i.e., interpretation) for the purpose of planning or modifying individual programs (see Figure 8-1).

The normal course of growth and development forms the basis of valid observations. A good examiner and diagnostician is first of all a good observer. Knowing when a child would normally be expected to skip, hop, or throw a ball, and knowing when a child would be expected to participate in group games, understand language concepts, or conceptualize spatial relationships, is all part of knowing whether or not a particular child's motor performance deviates significantly enough to warrant special physical education services. It is not enough to know that a child would be expected to sit up unsupported at six months, walk at one year, and go upstairs using alternate feet at three years. In order to teach children with special needs, it is important to have knowledge of sensory, language, cognitive, and social development as well as motor development. A nine-year-old who has age-appropriate motor skills, but who has a three-year lag in social skills, will almost assuredly fail unless the physical educator understands both the implications of the child's social development and the adequacy of the motor skills.

Knowledge of the elements or dimensions of the target performance helps the observer to better understand the quality of the performance that should be expected. For children seven years of age and older, mature patterns should be expected. Basic physical education courses in physical growth and development, motor learning, kinesiology, and measurement of motor performance should provide insight into the elements or criteria for what constitutes quality or "correct form" for a given performance. What are lacking in physical education literature, in this regard, are the entry criteria or performances needed at each level of development for any given task. This is where the skilled observer will use an "internal yardstick" of developmental progressions and truly see what the child is *doing,* rather than seeing only that the child is *not doing* the target performance.

Once the observer knows what motor performance to expect at any given age and what the criterion is for a mature or good quality performance, identification of deviations in the observed performance becomes possible. Deviations usually take one or more of three forms: (1) omissions, (2) substitutions, and (3) additions. Children with motor dysfunction are identified as such due to these irregularities. *Omissions* (e.g., no backswing or follow-through in throwing, no flight-phase while running, no arm-swing while jumping) often lead to inefficient and hence poor performance. *Substitutions* occur when one or more elements of a pattern are replaced by elements not normally a part of that pattern (e.g., running with the arms held overhead rather than swinging at the side; swinging the arms vigorously while jumping rather than getting lift from the legs). *Additions* are often used to compensate for mechanical, perceptual or muscular deficiencies (e.g., flailing the arms while walking — seen in some cerebral palsied individuals;

thrusting upward onto the toes while walking — sometimes seen in the emotionally disturbed population).

Once this yardstick for measurement is well in mind, the next most important task for the observer is to describe the observed performance. Any casual observer should be able to conclude that a performance is "awkward," "clumsy," or "funny." It takes a trained observer to describe those patterns or elements of patterns that would result in the untrained observer's conclusion of "clumsy." The trained observer should ask "What do I see the individual *doing* that results in the label 'awkward'? What is the child adding, substituting, or omitting from the gait pattern that results in the statement that 'he walks funny'?" (see Figure 8-2). Descriptors such as "poor," "inadequate," or "immature" do not describe the performance either. Knowing that a child can only balance two seconds on one foot, rotates the entire trunk while throwing, or fails to get full body extension while jumping describes specific, identifiable elements of these patterns that can be addressed in an IEP. It is far more accurate to describe a performance in performance terms than in qualitative terms (e.g., poor balance, immature throwing pattern, inadequate jumping ability). Performance terms also assist in making interpretations and writing objectives.

The ability to "make sense out of" or interpret the meaning of several deviant elements or patterns is probably the most difficult aspect of the assessment process. Herein lies the basis for program planning and program modification. The observer must be able to find the link between or among all the deviations observed. The observer must ask, "What do these elements or patterns have in common? Do they all require balance, eye-hand coordination, muscular endurance, ocular control, flexibility, etc?" Once tasks or performances are analyzed in terms of their elements (i.e., sensory and motor demands), a funneling process can help ferret out the common element or elements. The end-product is the area or areas of

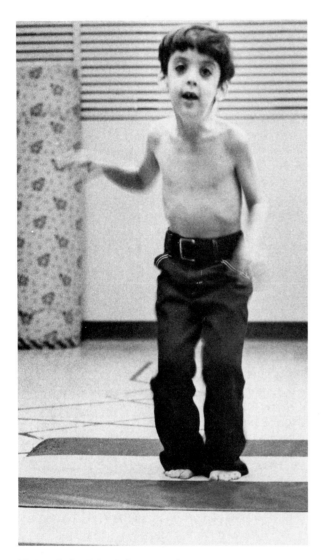

Figure 8-2. Trained observers ask such questions as, ''What am I seeing in this picture? What elements of jumping has this child added or omitted?'' SOURCE: Photo by Ben Esparza.

dysfunction most likely at the source of inefficient motor performance.

Interpretation

Interpretation, whether of formal test scores or observational data, usually takes one of two forms: (1) comparison with accepted criteria and/or norms; or (2) in terms of commonalities among test items. Accepted norms usually are expressed in developmental expectations, criterion-referencing, or standard scores. The observer has age expectations and criterion-referencing available without any extensive formal testing. Concluding that a particular child is two years below age level in running because her base of support is wide, the swing of her leg is short, and her arms swing stiffly outward gives solid information that can later be used to write performance objectives and plan individualized programs.

Interpreting data on the basis of commonalities among items is also widely used. During fitness testing, if a student does poorly on sit-ups, pull-ups, or broad-jump — all items measuring strength — the student is said to be ''weak.'' Once the elements of motor dysfunction are discovered, the commonalities may be expressed as agility, flexibility, balance, visual tracking, gross motor or fine motor control, and so on. Some test makers do this type of factor-analysis for us; but with observational data, the observer must find these commonalities.

PERFORMANCE TESTING AND DIRECT MEASURES

Although observation is the most commonly used tool for data collecting, performance testing and direct measurement should never be excluded from the assessment process. *Performance tests* measure movement parameters indirectly, by having the student perform a motor response, pattern, or skill. Both criterion-referenced and norm-referenced performance tests give the physical educator information about a student in relation to a group of students.

Like a developmental scale, *direct measures* give reference to known quantities or parameters, and have a high degree of credibility. Direct measures, in contrast to performance tests, measure movement parameters directly through the use of instrumentation, which seldom requires the performance of a skill or pattern. A flexometer measuring flexibility, a grip dynamometer for measuring hand-grip strength, and a spirometer for measuring lung capacity are examples of direct measures. Performance tests measuring these same parameters might include a toe touch for flexibility, a pull-up for strength, and a 12-minute run for endurance as a function of lung capacity. When selecting an appropriate tool for measurement, it is important to apply specific criteria in order to be certain of selecting the right one.

Criteria for Selecting an Instrument

One criterion a test or test item should meet is *validity*. A valid tool or item measures what it is claimed to measure. Just as a yardstick measures distance and a watch measures the passage of time, any motor performance test should measure what it purports to measure. Validity is determined by finding the relationship between two measures of a single parameter using a correlation. Usually one tool used to measure the parameter is a well-accepted, often direct measure of that parameter. A dynamometer, for example, is an accepted way to measure strength directly, whereas pull-ups may be used indirectly to measure upper body strength. The relationship or correlation between those two tests reflects the validity of the pull-up test for measuring strength. The relationship between the two may or may not be strong; hence the pull-up test may or may not be a valid test of strength.

A second criterion is *reliability*. That is, the test can be relied on to measure the same each time it is used. A test of abdominal strength, such as sit-ups, is usually quite reliable, in that a student will probably be able to do as many sit-ups on one day as on another. On the other hand, ratings of gymnastic performance not only vary — sometimes considerably — from one judge to the next, but also from one performance to the next. Reliability is also determined by finding a correlation or relationship between two scores. Gymnastic ratings would be considered ordinal scores; like interval scores and nominal data, they tend to be generated by tests that are not as reliable as tests generating ratios. Therefore multiple sets of these scores should be gathered to improve the reliability of this type of data.

A test should also be *objective*. That is, two examiners should be able to obtain the same score for any given performance. As in the examples above, the dynamometer, pull-ups, and sit-ups are objective measures because two examiners would obtain approximately the same scores on each measure. Ratings of gymnastic performance are not objective; hence judges' ratings often tend to differ.

Validity, reliability, and objectivity can all be greatly influenced by the mere fact that the student being tested is a student who has special needs. The validity of an endurance run, for example, can be reduced by the fact that an exceptional student does not comprehend what an "all-out" effort means. Therefore, such a test may be as much a measurement of cognitive function as it is of endurance. The reliability of performance tests can be reduced as a result of an exceptional student's inability to understand the task, or as a result of lack of experience. Any student who has never performed a shuttle-run, a standing broad jump, or a vertical jump may perform significantly better on the second administration than on the first simply because the student has "learned" how the task is to be performed. Many exceptional students have never had the opportunity to use their bodies in the way required by these tests; hence familiarity with the task nets improved performance. Objectivity can be reduced by several factors. Many of the parameters of interest and tests made for use with the exceptional population generate qualitative rather than quantitative data. This data, therefore, is often interval, ordinal, or nominal. The very nature of this type of data tends to reduce the objectivity of the test. When ratings are used, for example, even though the criteria for a given rating may be extensive, there may still be room for two raters to assign different scores. The interaction or rapport between the examiner and the student can reduce objectivity. One examiner who is skillful and insightful into the problems of the handicapped may be able to elicit a much better performance from such a student than an examiner who lacks such qualities.

Most motor performance tests make the following assumptions: (1) the student is already familiar with the performance task, or will become familiar with it in a minimum number of practice trials; (2) the student understands the concepts of "doing your best"; (3) the student is internally motivated or can be externally motivated to "do his or her best"; and (4) the student is positively reinforced by the knowledge of his or her performance, especially if it compares favorably with earlier performances or the performance of others.

When testing students who have special needs, these assumptions cannot be safely made because the experience, intellectual functioning, associative language, or motivation may not be equal to the task. Therefore, measures of motor performance tend to be confounded or confused by elements of cognition, language, social or emotional development, and achievement. When selecting a ready-made measurement tool, it is desirable to select an instrument that has elements capable of reducing the impact of exceptionalities on validity, reliability, and objectivity. These elements are discussed further in the following criteria.

The fourth criterion for selecting a measurement tool is *appropriateness*. If the test is a norm-referenced test, the norming sample or individuals upon whom the norms are based should be the same or include the same type of student who will be tested in terms of age, sex, and handicapping conditions. The *AAHPERD Youth Fitness Test* (1975) is not an appropriate test for a class of moderately retarded teens, for example, because there were no moderately retarded individuals included in the norming sample. There is sufficient information in the research literature that concludes that the moderately retarded will perform poorer than their chronologically aged peers. Using such a test will elicit no new information. If a criterion-referenced instrument is being considered, the tasks should be appropriate to the needs, interests, and capacities of students with whom the test is to be used. Norm-referenced tests, which exclude the handicapped from the norming sample, would only be appropriate for use with exceptional individuals when placement is the purpose of testing.

The test should *discriminate* adequately among a broad range of performances. It cannot be too easy for the best performers in the group nor too difficult for the poorest performers. For assessment, it serves no useful purpose to find that all students score below the norms, since that information has no interpretive value. Since the educational classification of students seldom considers the motor performance of those students, it is quite common to find among students in a special education class a range of motor performance from motor patterns to culturally determined game and sport skills. Thus a single instrument used to measure performance within such a group must be able to discriminate between the extremes of this range as well as among students in the middle of the range.

The next criterion is ease of *administration*. PL 94–142 requires that assessments must be completed within thirty-five days of the date of parental permission. Thus lengthy, cumbersome diagnostic instruments are not practical for public school use. In addition, as mentioned before, administrative procedures should allow ample practice trials to assure that lack of familiarity or learning will not interfere with the validity and reliability of the test. Furthermore, the scoring should be easy to compute and should provide scores that are useful to the examiner. Many norm-referenced tests are scored using discrete, ratio-type data such as time, distance, or number of repetitions. These are often converted to percentile ranks. Ratings, when used, usually have no more than five points, since it is difficult to distinguish levels of a performance accurately beyond that number of categories. Criterion-referenced tests often use check marks, pluses, or minuses to designate capability to complete a task with effort or with ease. Although these scoring methods provide less interpretive value, they do describe the performances the student is and is not able to do. The reader is cautioned to note that the tasks required on the criterion-referenced test must be realistic and meaningful in light of the capabilities of the student; otherwise, the teacher is again left with no useful information for program planning.

Finally, the test should be *economical.* That is, cost of materials, time, and personnel should be minimal. A test that requires expensive or elaborate equipment and takes more than about forty to forty-five minutes per student is impractical for school use. Since the average adapted physical education specialist serves eighty to one hundred students daily (Geddes and Seaman, 1978), extensive time spent in testing is not possible. An instrument that can be administered in a group setting is desirable.

Test Administration

In contrast to the freedom allowed by observational techniques and direct measurement methods, the administration of performance tests presents unique constraints to the examiner. The following discussion covers some general and specific points relative to data collection that tend to give physical educators the greatest problems.

Conditions of Testing

In physical education, the term *standardized* is generally used to refer to tools having an accompanying set of norm- or criterion-referenced standards called ``norms.'' The *norm* or standard for performance (e.g., percentage of body fat, acquisition of developmental milestones) is determined through compilation and analysis of data gathered on a given population to serve as a guide for what to expect from individuals of certain descriptions. Most standardized tests will give a description of the *norming sample* or group of individuals upon whom the standards are based. For example, the Basic Motor Ability Test (BMAT) is based on the performances of 1,563 children from four to twelve years of age and of various ethnic, cultural, and socioeconomic backgrounds; Cooper's (1978) norms for the 12-minute test/1.5 mile run test are based on males and females ages thirteen to over sixty; and the Bayley Scales of Motor Development are based on 1,262 normal children from two to thirty months of age.

This form of standardization should not be confused with *standardized administration procedures.* Many tools, especially diagnostic tests, have a specifically described set of physical conditions, equipment to be used, and instructions for the examiner, in order to assure that the test is administered in precisely the same way each time it is given. It is important that these procedures be accurately followed in order to assure valid results. Although these tools usually have a set of norms accompanying them, they may not.

When administering any test, it is important that the examiner precisely follows the procedures accompanying the test. If the equipment list includes a six by six-inch bean bag, a thirty-second stopwatch, or an eight-inch ball, then these should be used — with no substitutions. If the procedures require that the examiner gives specific instructions to the student, such as, "Close your eyes, raise this foot, and balance until I tell you to stop" (Seaman, 1979), then these should be used precisely. Any deviation from the prescribed procedures may render the results invalid for the student's performance or for comparison with the test norms. A further discussion of the language used in testing can be found later in this section.

Be sure the test is appropriate for the students in terms of expected performance and understanding. Language and cognitive development can play a major role in obtaining valid results. Tests that do not allow the examiner to demonstrate the required performance are inappropriate for youngsters of some disability groups. The score in these cases often reflects the level of the students' understanding rather than their true performance capabilities. Be certain the setting in which the test is being administered is not interfering with performance. If the student is easily distracted, the setting should be free from distractions and interruptions. When the test is readministered, (e.g., for an annual review), be certain the setting and conditions are the same as for the earlier administration. This also includes being aware of the student's personal environment (e.g., when medication has been taken relative to the testing time; home and school conditions) that may influence performance. All of these factors should be as much the same as possible from one testing session to the next.

Procedures for Testing

Besides the specific procedures provided for each test, a few elemental procedures are applicable to all tests. It is important for the examiner to be fully aware of the purpose of each test item. Understanding the purpose often gives a clue as to the additional data that can be gathered through observation and the

position of the examiner during the performance. If the purpose of a throwing item is throwing accuracy, then noting the quality of the throwing pattern and the hand used is incidental and the examiner should stand behind the thrower in clear view of the target so an accurate score can be obtained. On the other hand, if the item's purpose is to qualitatively measure the development of the throwing pattern, then the examiner should stand in front of and to the side of the thrower in order to clearly see the mechanics of the throw. A skilled examiner can obtain both types of information from one position or, if practice trials are allowed, obtain the qualitative data at this point and the quantitative data (accuracy score) during the actual test trials.

Examiners must take their cues from the student. How the student approaches a task often provides as much useful information as the score itself. On a task that produces a permanent product, such as reproducing figures on paper or a chalkboard, the accuracy of the reproduction can be observed after the performance is over. Therefore the examiner should be in position to observe signs of overflow of movement (e.g., the tongue sticking out of the mouth, opposite hand movements, changing hands at midline). If the student is constantly asking, "Are we almost finished?" or "When can I go back to my room?" a quick check with the classroom teacher should reveal whether this is typical or whether this behavior suggests that the student is having a "bad day." If the behavior is atypical, the testing should perhaps be resumed at another time.

Getting Language Out of Testing

The speech-language pathologist and classroom teacher concern themselves with measuring speech and language parameters. The goal of the physical educator is to circumvent any speech or language disorders so they do not interfere with getting a valid account of a student's motor performance. Certainly tools that allow the examiner to demonstrate or that provide for testing several children at one time will help, since the student can see the expected performance even though he or she may not understand the instructions. There is some information, however, that the physical educator can gather through observation or from other professionals, and which can serve to assure the validity of motor performance scores. Below is a list of possible signs of speech and language problems to be used as guidelines.

Hearing

1. Do the students hear you?
2. Are the students looking for visual cues?
3. Do the students ask you to repeat instructions?

Auditory skills

1. Can the students discriminate sounds? When you say "touch your toes," do they touch their noses?
2. Do the students seem to "forget" a sequence of commands? Or do they perform only the first or last part of the sequence?
3. Do the students repeat the examiner's command?
4. Do the students wait several seconds before initiating action?

Expressive language

1. How do the students speak? Do they lisp, omit parts of words, misuse incorrect sounds, get words or sounds in the wrong sequence?
2. How do the students use language? Do they speak in complex sentences, fast, slow, misuse plurals, ask questions, label objects, use words inappropriately?

The list below gives point-by-point suggestions for ways in which the physical educator can circumvent these disorders. This is not an exhaustive list of guidelines or solutions, but is merely intended as a starting point. A speech-language pathologist should be consulted for advice on specific children and problems.

Hearing

1. Verify students' hearing acuity with the speech-language pathologist or audiologist.
2. Provide visual cues, demonstrations, pictures or information through other modalities or learning channels.
3. Repeat instructions only after students ask or have had a reasonable period of time to perform. (Students may be "buying time" to process the information. Thus repeating the instructions too soon may be overloading, and they will have to begin the language processing again.)

Auditory skills

1. Use pictures or demonstrations to clarify the meaning of words that have similar sounds.
2. Reduce the length of the command or give only one or two commands at a time.
3. If students repeat the command, they are probably experiencing a processing delay or problem with keeping the command in memory. Let them do this.
4. Speed up the command or omit unimportant words in order to give students less interfering information and more time in which to process it. (E.g., "Step up onto the beam, walk to the other end, and then walk backwards." Shorten to: "Step up, walk beam, walk back.")

Expressive language

1. Take your cues from the students. Ask them to repeat what they have been asked to do to verify the sequence of the task.
2. Analyze the level of your language relative to the way the students use language and simplify or change the rate of your command. Use words that have lower semantic content levels (i.e., words that mean the same thing as words commonly used in testing, but that are understood at developmentally earlier ages). If the student seems not to

understand the command, try using a lower level word (see Table 8-1).

Reflex Testing

Although reflex activity is a normal part of development, reflex testing is not normally within the purview of the adapted physical educator's responsibilities. However, in the absence of physical or occupational therapy evaluations, knowledge of appropriate reflex activity is important to the assessment process.* Several authors (Bobath, 1965; Bobath and Bobath, 1975; Fiorentino, 1972) have identified numerous reflexes, but only those that have implications for motor performance will be discussed here.

The reflexes considered most important to the physical educator are: (1) spinal; (2) brain stem; (3) midbrain; (4) automatic movement reactions; and (5) cortical equilibrium reactions.

Spinal level reflexes are present at birth and become integrated into the system at two months of age. *Brain stem* reflexes are inhibited after four to six months of age. *Midbrain* reflexes slowly mature until ten or twelve months of age, then succumb to cortical control at about five years. The *cortical equilibrium* reactions begin appearing at about six to eight months, and gradually bring the child to an upright posture (Fiorentino, 1972). Just as the lack of appearance of protective extension or righting reactions (i.e., automatic responses) can interfere with normal motor development, the persistence of spinal and brain stem reflexes can also delay motor development (Fiorentino, 1972:43).

A continuum rather than an "all-or-nothing" law of reflex development and inhibition is typical of reflex activity. Generally, reflexes that are present at birth be-

*The examples presented in this section are partial explanations for understanding of the reflex or reaction under discussion, and are not meant to imply the entire interpretation for the specific examples of abnormalities in motor performance.

Table 8-1. Changing words for better understanding

Words found commonly in motor tests	Lower level words
like (alike)	same
gently	soft
different	not same
difficult	hard
over	on top of
into	in
on top of	on
first	in front of
beside	next to
last	in back of
behind	in back of
as long as . . .	until I say STOP
left/right	this side/that side (Point.)
forward	toward me (Examiner stands in front.)
large	big
small	little

SOURCE: Adapted from C. E. Weiss and H. S. Lillywhite, *Communicative Disorders* (St. Louis: C. V. Mosby, 1976).

come inhibited as the individual grows. Reflexes that are not present at birth may follow one of two paths: (1) development of the reflex; or (2) development and then inhibition. Once the paths of the reflexes are complete, there is said to be reflex integration, which is a prerequisite to full maturity of the central nervous system (see Figure 8-3).

Adapted physical educators more commonly see responses that are indicative of partially developed reflexes, or of those developed in stages. The best example here is the initial appearance of the protective extension reflex as evidenced by partial extension of arm and forearm, a stage before the fully extended arms. A child may show protective extension on one side and not the other, which may also be indicative of a partially developed reflex. Reflex inhibition, not disappearance, is accomplished in stages; not discretely designated, but individually, developmentally sequenced. Consequently, throughout growth, residuals — levels of inhibition — of various reflexes may

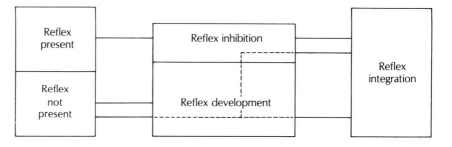

Figure 8-3. Reflex integration.

become evident in motor performance and, if not fully integrated, may interfere with performance. Residuals of the tonic neck or tonic labyrinthine reflexes would adversely affect the developmental sequence leading to motor responses and motor patterns. For example, a child who lacks a fully integrated asymmetrical tonic neck reflex will have difficulty catching a ball or a bean bag with one hand—for whenever turning the head

is involved, one arm will tend to extend and the other to flex (see Table 8-2).

Spinal Reflexes

Grasp reflex. Retention of the grasp reflex past six months of age will adversely affect voluntary release, which in turn would restrict or limit the prehension

Table 8-2. Timetable of reflex emergence and integration

Responses	Weeks 1-4	2	3	4	5	6	7	8	9	10	11	12	2-3	3-5	After 5	Source
Moro	+	+	+	±	±	±	±	±	±	−						Peiper
Asymmetrical TNR	+	±	±	±	±	±	−									Peiper
Symmetrical TNR	+	+	+	+	+	+	−									Fiorentino
Tonic labyrinthine	+	+	+	+	−											Fiorentino
Grasp	+	+	+	±	±	±										Peiper
Neck righting	+	+	+	±	±	±	±	±	±	±	±	±	±			Bobath
Labyrinthine righting		+	+	+	+	+										Bobath
Optical righting						+	+	+	+	+	+	+	+	+	+	Fiorentino
Body righting on the body						+	+	+	+	+	+	+	±	±		Bobath
Protective extension of the arms						+	+	+	+	+	+	+	+	+	+	Fiorentino
Equilibrium reactions in																
Prone						+	+	+	+	+	+	+	+	+	+	Bobath
Supine							+	+	+	+	+	+	+	+	+	Bobath
Sitting								+	+	+	+	+	+	+	+	Bobath
Quadrupedal												+	+	+	+	Bobath
Standing												+	+	+	+	Bobath

SOURCE: Adapted from B. S. Banus, et al., *The Developmental Therapist* (Thorofare, New Jersey: Charles B. Slack, 1971).

Key: + = age at which reflex is present; ± = age at which reflex is beginning to be integrated; − = reflex would normally be expected to be integrated; blank = reflex would not normally be expected to be present at these ages.

Figure 8-4. A normal grasp reflex results when something is placed in an infant's hand.

development necessary for hand use in such elementary tasks as stacking blocks all the way through to the skill of javelin throwing. A strong grasp reflex prevents a child from voluntarily releasing an object. Difficulty in voluntary release or intermittently active grasp-release response, often found in individuals with cerebral palsy, could be attributable to a residual of the grasp reflex. Observable signs of a persistent grasp reflex include a rapid, automatic grasping of objects, a tightly closed hand, difficulty in opening the hand, and an inconsistent pattern of grasp-release. The adapted physical educator should consider the safety aspect of the grasp reflex residual and its effect upon motor skill acquisition when planning activities that require voluntary release (e.g., manipulation of objects, throwing, catching). (See Figure 8-4.)

Startle response. The startle reflex is an automatic reaction characteristic of infant behavior that results first in abduction then adduction of the limbs, and hyperextension of the neck. It may be stimulated by such things as sudden noise, sudden movement of the child, or any abrupt change in the environment. The persistence of a strong startle reflex will interfere with the development of equilibrium and support reactions. As the startle response diminishes, there may be only a reaction of the arms; but even that response can interfere with the development of motor patterns, motor skills, and acquisition of sport skills. Imagine a

child who has a persistent startle reflex trying to perform a gymnastic activity that consists of many sudden movements, running in a foot race started by the sound of a gun, or using the trampoline for the first time. This reflex is not reserved for any specific handicapping condition, but appears throughout the range of exceptionalities (see Figure 8-5).

Crossed extension. The crossed extension reflex serves a useful purpose in walking and running, but must be integrated and cannot dominate motor performance. In the young infant, when one leg is flexed, the opposite leg extends. Later, developing skills such as jumping do not allow for each leg to extend independently. Youngsters who cannot jump because only one leg at a time extends are often called ''earth bound,'' because they never get both feet off the ground at the same time.

Brain Stem Reflexes

Tonic neck reflexes. The tonic neck reflexes, asymmetrical (ATNR) and symmetrical (STNR), are evoked by changes in the position of the head in space. The ATNR, elicited by rotation of the head to one side, results in extension of the arm on the face side and flexion on the skull side. This reflexive response, when it persists, interferes with rolling over, segmental trunk rotation, self-feeding, use of the hands at midline, and perhaps the maintenance of a hands-and-knees position. By analyzing the head and limb positions of motor patterns, and motor and sports skills such as crawling, catching, throwing, javelin throwing, and so on, it becomes apparent that the ATNR could interfere with the smooth execution of these patterns and skills (see Figure 8-6).

The position held in fencing, and perhaps the

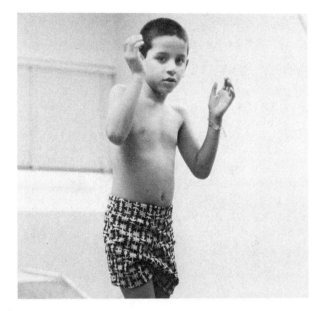

Figure 8-5. This student is showing a normal startle response.

short pass in football, are two of the very few skills that are not as adversely affected by the presence of the ATNR, because position needed for successful execution of the skills actually utilizes the ATNR position. This is an example of potential functioning of a reflex whenever it might be needed.

The STNR is elicited by flexion or extension of the head. When the head is in flexion, the upper limbs flex and the lower limbs extend. Extension of the head causes the upper arms to extend, and the lower limbs to flex. Presence of this reflex prevents segmental trunk rotation, interferes with creeping (i.e., quadraped position), and prevents reciprocation of the extremities. The commonly seen bunny-hopping or scooting activity performed prior to creeping represents the presence of STNR. The persistence of this reflex can interfere with kicking and catching, as well as other activities involving movement of the head in space and reciprocation of extremities (see Figure 8-7). STNR interferes with tumbling activities, catching, throwing, and springboard diving. All of these activities involve changes in head position that could effect changes in muscle tone, and could ultimately interfere with the motor performance.

Tonic labyrinthine reflex. The tonic labyrinthine reflex (TLR) is evoked by changes in the position of the head in space causing increased trunk flexion when prone, and increased trunk extension when supine. With persistence of a strong TLR, the child has extreme difficulty in raising the head in prone position, in rolling over, and in attaining an upright posture. Although a child may have developed some motor patterns, residuals of TLR may interfere with coordination and refinement of motor skills. In learning a forward or backward roll, the interference by the TLR results in the back arching at the vertical upside

Figure 8-6. This asymmetrical tonic neck reflex, which causes the boy's right arm to flex and the left to extend, should have been inhibited at about four months. SOURCE: Photo by Ben Esparza.

down position. Thus the student cannot maintain a tucked position, which ultimately results in poorly executed somersaults. The lack of TLR inhibition can also adversely affect crawling (on the stomach), due to the increase in flexion of the trunk and hips while prone. Even sitting in a chair with stimulation to the back can result in increased trunk extension. Infants and individuals in all categories of handicapping conditions have been known to slide right out of a chair due to a strong residual of TLR. The interference by the TLR, if strong enough, can impinge on any level of activity in which changes in head position are involved (see Figure 8–8).

Associated reactions. Sympathetic, bilateral muscular contractions are associated reactions that interfere with motor performance. A student grasping an object, throwing a ball, or swinging a tennis racquet will have difficulty executing the task if the opposite arm is mirroring the arm involved in the task. Even in bilateral skills, such as swinging a softball bat, the batter executes two different patterns with each arm as the bat swings through. This mirroring is sometimes referred to as "overflow"; besides interfering with unilateral skill execution, it uses energy unnecessarily.

Positive and negative support reactions. The *positive support* reaction, in standing, produces extension of the legs and plantar flexion of the feet. Persistence of this reflex will adversely affect the normal extension-abduction pattern utilized initially in weight bearing. Residuals, or lack of an integrated positive support reflex, can hinder the child's ability to reciprocate the legs and will additionally affect equilibrium reactions while standing. Observable signs include (1) the extension of both legs simultaneously with toes pointed towards the ground; (2) an inability to move one leg without an associated reaction in the other leg; and (3) an awkward looking position. The individual who has a strong residual of this reflex will not be able to stand unsupported. This is more commonly seen in cerebral palsied individuals, but can also be apparent in other handicapping conditions.

Negative support, or lack of weight bearing, is usually seen in transition from supporting reactions to normal weight bearing. Persistence of negative support reactions past approximately four months is indicative of delayed reflexive maturation (Fiorentino, 1972). Developmentally delayed, mentally retarded, multihandicapped, or relatively inactive individuals may all exhibit signs of residual negative support in motor performance. The child's response might vary from complete lack of bearing weight on legs, to momentary weight bearing, to momentary lack of weight bearing. These are obviously restrictions and limitations to attainment of the upright position.

Figure 8-7. Child with symmetrical tonic neck reflex. When head is down, arms flex and legs extend (photos on page 176). When head is up, arms extend and legs flex (photos above).

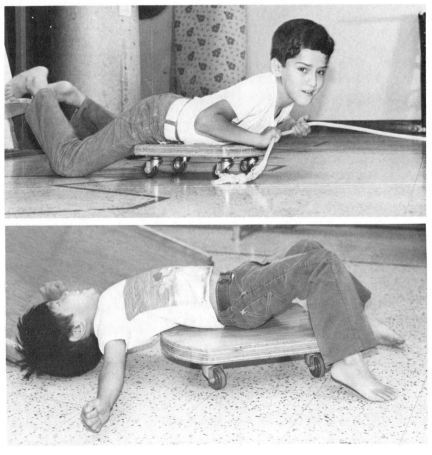

Figure 8-8. The child in the photo above has a residual tonic labyrinthine reflex in prone position. Notice the flexion in his hips. The child in the photo at right has a residual tonic labyrinthine reflex in supine position. Notice the total hyperextension of his back and neck. SOURCE: Photo by Ben Esparza (right).

Stepping reflex. The automatic stepping reflex normally appears during the first one and one-half months of postnatal life. It is characterized by high stereotypic steps, which if persistent can cause interference with attainment of the upright position and the development of walking. Persistence of this reflex is most commonly seen in cerebral palsied individuals, but also appears in the motor responses of other physically handicapped, multihandicapped, and mentally retarded individuals.

Midbrain Reflexes and Reactions

Righting reactions. Righting reactions develop shortly after birth but do not reach maximal function until ten to twelve months. They allow the individual to move against gravity, maintain positions against gravity, and are considered the bases for developing equilibrium responses. Generally, these are reactions with and without vision that (1) allow the head to turn without the body rotating as a whole; (2) lead to segmental rolling; and (3) allow the head to assume a normal position toward either the horizontal (optical righting) or the vertical (labyrinthine righting). If the righting reactions have not yet fully matured, the child will exhibit signs of interference with good postural alignment and maintenance of body positions. Immature righting reactions interfere with a child's ability to run and then rapidly change directions. Without fully established righting reactions, the child might be unable, through head position, to rapidly regain and maintain adequate alignment necessary to the flow of movement. Immature righting reactions can also interfere with recovery from any airborne position, or other positions requiring equilibrium responses.

Automatic Movement Reactions

Protective extension. The protective extension reflex first appears around six months of age (Bobath, 1963) and should remain throughout life. Immediate extension of arms with abduction and extension of fingers is the response elicited by a sudden change in the body against gravity (falling) in an attempt to protect itself. Many individuals in all the categories of exceptionality show lack of fully developed protective extension. Cerebral palsied, multihandicapped, mentally retarded, and many learning-disabled individuals may show no protective extension at all. Without a protective mechanism, they have no ability to break a fall nor to protect the head when falling. Protective extension appears when an individual has passed beyond the endpoint of balance in any direction—forward, backward, sideways, and downward (see Figure 8-9).

The degree of development of protective extension can be seen in the places that young children hurt themselves at play. As the reflex develops, children are observed to have progressively skinned chins, skinned elbows, and then skinned hands. This reflex must become automatic, so that higher levels of performance can be built on a firm foundation. Protective extension is obviously important for safety. As the protective reflex becomes more automatic, protection becomes more of a natural response, and there are fewer unnecessary injuries.

Other important aspects of full development of protective extension are seen in social-psychological implications of the "clumsy child" who avoids activity because of fear of getting hurt; this is at least partially due to lack of adequate protection. Participants in sports activities need to learn how to fall, which is easier if the protective reaction is automatic. Certain gymnastic skills such as handsprings and vaulting should have fully integrated protective extension as a prerequisite. This also applies to expressive movements in dance and free exercise.

The following two checklists for identifying residual reflexes are appropriate for educators to use as observational tools.

Figure 8-9. This child is showing a protective extension reflex to avoid falling off the large ball.

MILANI-COMPARETTI TEST OF REFLEX DEVELOPMENT

Available: A. Milani-Comparetti and E. A. Gidoni, *Developmental Medicine and Child Neurology*, 9 (5) (October 1967).

Validity: none reported.

Reliability: none reported.

Scoring: check-off by months.

Population: infants 0–24 months, functioning at that age, those suspected of having residuals of reflexes.

Performances measured: primitive reflexes, righting reactions, parachute reactions, tilting reactions, postural control, active movement.

Economy: individual administration.

Norms: expressed in months that reflex should be present.

REFLEX INTEGRATION TEST

Available: P. Montgomery, and E. Richter, *Sensorimotor Integration Program: Preliminary Assessment Forms*. Los Angeles: Western Psychological Services.

Validity: none reported.

Reliability: none reported.

Scoring: check-off by age in months (0–48 months).

Population: children (0–48 months), those functioning between 0 and 48 months, or those suspected of having residuals of reflexes.

Performances measured: 15 reflexes including grasp, neck righting, body righting, ATNR, STNR, TLR, head righting, protective extension, equilibrium.

Norms: expressed in months that reflex should be present.

Cortical-Equilibrium Reactions

Prone and supine. When prone or supine, a student whose equilibrium is changed by tilting or moving the surface should show a protective reaction by extending and abducting the arms and legs. Laying the student on a trampoline bed or air flow mattress allows the adapted physical educator to observe this reaction. When the student is on hands and knees, sitting or kneeling, and loses balance, the head should right itself and the limbs on the side away from the fall should extend and abduct while the other limbs protect in the direction of the fall. These reactions appear at about ten to twelve months and persist throughout life.

Hopping in all directions as a result of loss of balance emerges at about fifteen to eighteen months and supports motor performance throughout life. Individuals who do not have this equilibrium reaction get knocked down easily from the slightest bump. Children who avoid activities that involve close physical contact with other children, or youngsters who get knocked down when lining up to go somewhere with their class may lack this equilibrium reaction.*

*Throughout this section, the examples presented are partial explanations for understanding of the reflex or reaction being discussed, and are not meant to imply the entire interpretation for the specific examples of abnormalities in motor performance. Adapted physical educators are not typically expected to test reflexes, but knowledge of their integration can improve communication with therapists and enhance analysis of movement deficiencies.

Sensorimotor Testing

Sensorimotor or perceptual-motor instruments sample (more or less directly) the functioning of the sensory systems as they support or contribute to efficient movement. Since sensory system functioning (at least among the earlier maturing systems) cannot be sampled by performance tests without movement, it is sometimes difficult to separate the movement of the performance from the manifestation of a sensory system dysfunction. Therefore it is essential to understand the interplay between the movements of the required tasks in the test and the subservient sensory systems. It is also important to be aware of the potential assistive or interfering influence of abnormal reflex behavior. Finally, in selecting a test for assessment of sensorimotor function, the physical educator should know first what parameters are to be measured, and then select a test that purportedly measures those parameters. Only tests that would be of primary interest to the physical educator will be presented in this section. Instruments designed solely for measuring aspects of visual or auditory function will be presented later in this text.

Commonly Used Performance Tests

Sensorimotor, or perceptual-motor testing, samples the functions of the underlying sensory systems through observable motor performance (see Appendix D for performance testing examples).

Abbreviations used by test-makers in the following descriptions are:

CH = communicatively handicapped
ED = emotionally disturbed
EMR = educable mentally retarded
LD = learning disabled
LH = learning handicapped
MR = mentally retarded
NI = neurologically impaired
SED = seriously emotionally disturbed
TMR = trainable mentally retarded.

PERCEPTUAL-MOTOR SURVEY

Available: Matthew E. Sullivan, Physical Education Consultant
           Special School District of St. Louis County
           12100 Clayton Road, Town and Country, Missouri 63125
Validity: none reported.
Reliability: none reported.
Scoring (objectivity): 5-point rating scale.
Population (norming sample): elementary school age children.
Performances (parameters) measured: static and dynamic balance, awareness of self, spatial orientation.
Economy: administered in groups or individually; required equipment includes a stopwatch, balance beam, erasers, fiber barrel, pictures of animals or objects, mats, ordinary stairs, rung ladder, horizontal bar, large area the size of half a basketball court, footprints, several playground balls, several beach balls, string, safety pins, rubber bands, crayons, and ropes. Time undetermined.
Norms: none reported.

PURDUE PERCEPTUAL MOTOR SURVEY

Available: Charles E. Merrill Publishing Company
           1300 Alum Creek Drive, Columbus, Ohio 43216
Validity: .65 between teacher ratings and PPMS.

Reliability: .95 test-retest with 30 children one week apart.

Scoring (objectivity): 4-point rating scale with criteria.

Population (norming sample): 200 randomly selected children grades 1–4 with 50 from each grade; 97 nonachievers, no motor defects, no retardation, IQ $\geq$ 80.

Performance (parameters) measured: balance and posture, body image and differentiation, perceptual-motor match, ocular control, form perception.

Economy: administered individually in 45 minutes; required equipment includes chalkboard and chalk, penlight, yardstick or dowel, visual achievement forms, standardized administration procedures (manual).

Norms: grades 1–4; reported means and standard deviations (see Figure 8–10).

QUICK NEUROLOGICAL SCREENING TEST

Available: Academic Therapy Publications
20 Commercial Blvd., Novato, California 94949

Validity: with educational classification for 88 pairs of learning-disabled and normal children.

Reliability: .41–.93 for items on test/retest basis 1 month apart.

Scoring (objectivity): rating scale with criteria.

Population (norming sample): based on 2,239 normal, LD and undifferentiated children 6.5 to 18.3 years of age.

Performances (parameters) measured: 15 tasks measuring motor development, large and small muscle control, motor planning and sequencing, sense of rate and rhythm, spatial organization, visual and auditory perceptual skills, balance and cerebellar-vestibular function and disorders of attention.

Economy: individually administered in approximately 20 minutes; equipment required includes data collection sheet, recording form, ballpoint pen, pencil, stopwatch.

Norms: criterion-referenced; tables showing age at which 25, 50, and 75% of norming sample met criterion per item.

DEVELOPMENTAL TEST OF VISUAL-MOTOR INTEGRATION (VMI)

Available: Follett Educational Corporation
1018 West Washington Blvd., Chicago, Illinois 60607

Validity: 0.89 between VMI scores and chronological age.

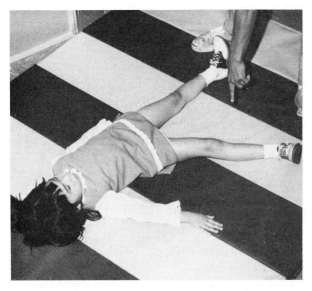 

Figure 8-10. Two test items from the Purdue Perceptual Motor Survey: angels-in-the-snow (left) and chalkboard double circles (right).

Reliability: See: *Visual-Motor Integration* (monograph) by Keith E. Beery, Follett Publishing Co., 1967.

Scoring (objectivity): discrete scores on 15 items.

Population (norming sample): children ranging in ages from 2–15 years.

Performances (parameters) measured: ability to imitate drawings of various forms (e.g., copying vertical lines, horizontal lines, circles, vertical horizontal cross, right oblique line, square, left oblique line, etc.).

Economy: administered individually or in groups in 15–20 minutes; required equipment includes test booklet for each child, administration and scoring manual, pencils.

Norms: expressed in age-equivalents for children 4–15 years.

FROSTIG DEVELOPMENTAL TEST OF VISUAL PERCEPTION (DTVP)

Available: Consulting Psychologist Press, Inc.
577 College Avenue, Palo Alto, California 94360

Validity: .44, .50, .50 between DTVP and teacher ratings of classroom adjustment, motor coordination, and intellectual functioning.

Reliability: ≥.80 test-retest of kindergarteners and first-graders tested 2–3 weeks apart; ≥.70 when subtests were compared to total test scores.

Scoring (objectivity): raw scores with criteria provided; convert to perceptual quotient (PQ) and perceptual age (PA).

Population (norming sample): 2,116 unselected caucasian school children from middle-class homes.

Performances (parameters) measured: eye-motor coordination, figure ground, constancy of shape, perception of position in space, perception of spatial relations.

Economy: administered to a group in about 50 minutes and individually in 30–45 minutes; required materials include test booklet for each child, administration and scoring manual, enlarged models for group administration, pencils, colored pencils.

Norms: children aged 4–7.11 years.

SOUTHERN CALIFORNIA SENSORY INTEGRATION TESTS

Available: Western Psychological Services
13081 Wilshire Blvd., Los Angeles, California 90025

Validity: .48–.50 with Bender-Gestalt.

Reliability: wide range of test-retest correlation coefficients with scores on younger children tending to be most stable; 0.92 test-retest on 41 pairs of scores on motor accuracy subtest was best.

Scoring (objectivity): raw scores with criteria; convert to standard z scores.

Population (norming sample): 30–125 unselected children in 0.5-year age categories from 4.0–10.11 years.

Performances (parameters) measured: figure-ground, position in space, design copying, kinesthesia, manual form perception, tactile discrimination, midline crossing, bilateral motor control, right-left discrimination, standing balance.

Economy: administered individually in 1 to 1½ hours; required equipment includes protocol booklet, test kit, stopwatch, administration and scoring manual, pencils, ballpoint pen.

Norms: expressed in standard z scores in 6-month intervals; visual tests: age 4.0–10.11 years; others: 4.0–8.11 years.

MVPT MOTOR-FREE VISUAL PERCEPTION TEST

Available: Academic Therapy Publications
20 Commercial Blvd., Novato, California 94949

Validity: median correlation of .49 for construct validity determined by age differentiation, within and among parameters measured.

Reliability: .86 on test-retest basis.

Scoring (objectivity): dichotomous raw scores (right or wrong); convert to perceptual age.

Population (norming sample): 883 children 4–9 years.

Performances (parameters) measured: 36 items measure spatial relationships, visual discrimination, figure-ground, visual closure, visual memory (child points to multiple-choice selection).

Economy: individually administered in less than 10 minutes; required materials include multiple-choice templates, score sheet.

Norms: expressed in perceptual age scores.

Direct Measures of Sensory System Function

The following tests give direct measurement of sensory system function.

CALORIC TEST OF VESTIBULAR FUNCTION

Available: In J. B. deQuiros and O. L. Schrager, *Neuropsychological Fundamentals in Learning Disabilities*. Novato, California: Academic Therapy, 1978.

Validity: none reported.

Reliability: none reported.

Scoring (objectivity): duration of nystagmus.

Population (norming sample): normal individuals.

Performances (parameters) measured: vestibular system function.

Economy: administered individually by physician by irrigating ear with warm or cold water and observing saccadic movements of the eyes (nystagmus).

Norms: normal responses in newborn infants reported in deQuiros and Schrager, p. 163.

DIRECT PRESSURE TEST OF TACTILE DISCRIMINATION

Available: In Nancy B. Taylor, "A Stereognostic Test for Screening Tactile Sensation." *The American Journal of Occupational Therapy* 26 (5) (1972): 256–260.

Validity: face.

Reliability: −.20–.28 for 2-year-olds; .69 for 3-year-olds; 1.0 for 3–6-year-olds; test-retest.

Scoring (objectivity): tactile identification of familiar items; verbal response required.

Population (norming sample): normal children 1.8–4.7 years (N = 78).

Performances (parameters) measured: tactile discrimination.

Economy: individually administered in 10 minutes; small equipment needed includes cap, ball, penny, spoon, chair, button, stuffed animal.

Norms: none reported.

Motor Development Profiles

Tests of motor development basically measure the emergence of motor responses and motor patterns that develop naturally as a result of physical growth, reflex and sensory system function, and development and interaction of the organism with the environment. As can be seen in the description of tests included here, many developmental profiles do not distinguish between naturally emerging responses and patterns and the functioning of the sensory systems or the acquisition of skills. In selecting a developmental profile, therefore, it is important for the physical educator to know which responses and patterns emerge naturally and which ones are learned, so as to distinguish between developmental differences and differences or deficits manifest from lack of experience or learning. Chapter 2 and the motor development schedule in Appendix B document the natural emergence (up to about four years of age) of motor responses and patterns that would be of interest to the physical educator involved in measuring the motor development of the children.

DENVER DEVELOPMENTAL SCREENING TEST

Available: University of Colorado Medical Center
Denver, Colorado 80220

Validity: .97 with Yale Developmental Examination.

Reliability: ranges from .66–.93 on test-retest for four parameters.

Scoring (objectivity): tasks are scored ''pass,'' ''fail,'' ''refusal'' or ''no opportunity for child to perform''; some items may be scored by report of parent.

Population (norming sample): 1,043 children from birth to 6 years.

Performances (parameters) measured: 105 tasks representing personal-social, fine motor-adaptive, language, and gross motor development; identifies developmental delays.

Economy: time needs depend on age of child and number of items passed; administered individually; equipment required includes small toy, rattle, piece of yarn, paper and pencil for scribbling and drawing, box of raisins, 8 small cubes, small bottle, pictures of familiar objects, small ball.

Norms: charts showing at what age level 10, 25, 50, 75, and 90 percent of children can perform specific tasks.

PEABODY DEVELOPMENTAL MOTOR SCALES (IMRID BEHAVIORAL SCIENCE MONOGRAPH NO. 25)

Available: IMRID, George Peabody College
P. O. Box 163, Nashville, Tennessee 37203

Validity: face with literature.

Reliability: none reported.

Scoring (objectivity): 5-point rating with criteria provided.

Population (norming sample): normal children birth through 7 for gross motor development and birth through 6 for fine motor development.

Performances (parameters) measured: 205 gross motor tasks and 130 fine motor tasks.

Economy: equipment includes common items found in home and school; time undetermined.

Norms: expressed in age equivalents for each task birth through 7 years.

Note: accompanying program of motor activities available.

CALIFORNIA STATE UNIVERSITY MOTOR DEVELOPMENT CHECKLIST (see Appendix D)

Available: Janet A. Seaman
California State University
5151 State University Drive, Los Angeles, California 90032

Validity: face with literature.

Reliability: .96 between physical educator and classroom teacher.

Scoring (objectivity): 3-point rating scale; "adequate, inadequate, cannot do."

Population (norming sample): normal children 3 months–7 years.

Performances (parameters) measured: 31 locomotor patterns, motor skills, and game skills.

Economy: administered in a group activity setting; time undeterminable; equipment required includes obstacles for walking over, under, between, footprints, jump rope, 10-inch ball, box.

Norms: associated with developmental tasks reported in literature.

KOONTZ CHILD DEVELOPMENT PROGRAM

Available: Western Psychological Services
13081 Wilshire Blvd., Los Angeles, California 90025

Validity: validity of program reported percentage of change over time; no validity of screening instrument reported.

Reliability: .73 to .82 between classroom and head teachers for four parameters screened.

Scoring (objectivity): dichotomous pass/fail for each item.

Population (norming sample): normal children between 0–48 months.

Performances (parameters) measured: 550 items measuring gross motor, fine motor, social, and language development.

Economy: administered informally through observation; time undeterminable; equipment needed includes common items such as tricycle, ball, shoe, pull-toy, etc.

Norms: associated with developmental tasks reported in the literature.

Note: accompanying program of motor activities available.

BAYLEY SCALES OF MOTOR DEVELOPMENT

Available: Psychological Corporation
757 Third Avenue
New York, New York 10017

Validity: none reported.

Reliability: .68–.92 split half (median .84).

Scoring (objectivity): items scored pass/fail; allows omit, refuse, parent report.

Population (norming sample): 1,262 normal children, 2–30 months old.

Performances (parameters) measured: gross motor development; sensory perception.

Economy: 45 minutes for individually administered motor portion. Kit available from publisher.

Norms: expressed as ratios in a psychomotor index score.

Note: requires special training.

Motor Ability Tests

Motor ability tests have historically been used in physical education as predictors of and synonymously with athletic ability (Mathews, 1978). They tend to include novel tasks, some of which have more or less of a direct relationship to sports performance such as high jump, broad jump, dashes, and basketball and baseball throws for distance. The distinctive place of motor ability in a developmental hierarchy is not clear, however, as McCloy (1940) reported that, among other parameters, motor ability requires muscular strength, ability to change direction, flexibility, peripheral vision, concentration, timing, rhythm, and coordination, all of which have requirements for adequate functioning at several levels of the developmental model. Tests selected for treatment in this section, therefore, are representative of instruments that sample the broad spectrum of parameters listed and implied by McCloy. The particular placement at this point in the discussion implies that innate neural capacity, reflex behavior, functioning of the sensory systems, and motor development have progressed to the point of being able to support the tasks included in motor ability tests. This placement is not meant to imply that extensive learning or acquisition of motor skills has taken place.

✓SIX CATEGORY GROSS MOTOR TEST

Available: In B. J. Cratty, *Perceptual-Motor Behavior and Educational Processes*. Springfield, Illinois: Charles C. Thomas, 1969.

Validity: none reported.

Reliability: .91 test-retest on 83 children.

Scoring (objectivity): 5-point rating scale with criteria.

Population (norming sample): 200 children.

Performances (parameters) measured: body perception, gross agility, balance, locomotor agility, ball throwing, ball tracking.

Economy: administered in about 30 minutes individually; required equipment includes 8-inch ball, rubber softball with 18-inch string attached, 4-foot by 6-foot mat marked off in 12-inch squares, clipboard, scoring sheet, stopwatch.

Norms: reported in deciles for children between the ages of 5–24 years trainable mentally retarded (TMR), 6–20 years educable mentally retarded (EMR), 4–11 years (normal IQ).

LINCOLN-OSERETSKY MOTOR DEVELOPMENT SCALE (LINCOLN ADAPTATION OF OSERETSKY TESTS OF MOTOR PROFICIENCY)

Available: American Guidance Service, Inc.
Publisher's Building, Circle Pines, Minnesota 55014

Validity: .32 with Brace Motor Ability Test; .37 with Cowan-Pratt Test.

Reliability: .96 and .97 for males and females respectively using split-half method.

Scoring (objectivity): items scored on pass/fail basis.

Population (norming sample): 380 males and 369 females between the ages of 6 and 14 years, randomly selected from rural-urban schools of middle-class socioeconomic status.

Performances (parameters) measured: 36 items measuring static coordination, dynamic manual coordination of hands, general dynamic coordination, motor speed, simultaneous movement, synkinesia.

Economy: administered individually in about 45 minutes; required equipment includes test kit containing ball, mazes, scissors, balance rod, matchbook, coins, small boxes, thread, spool, playing cards, matchsticks, ballpoint pen, paper.

Norms: expressed in percentiles by sex and age from 6–14 years.

PROJECT ACTIVE

Available: Township of Ocean School District
Dow Avenue, Oakhurst, New Jersey 07755
Validity: motor ability with panel of experts; fitness (level 2) with Roger's PFI
= .87.
Reliability: test-retest within one week — motor ability (level 2) = .53-.65;
(level 3) = .82-.86; fitness (level 2) = .70-.99.
Scoring (objectivity): rating scale with criteria.
Population (norming sample): normal, CH, NI, ED, EMR 5-17 years.

Performances: gross body coordination, balance/posture orientation, eye-
hand coordination, eye-foot accuracy, arm strength, abdominal
strength, leg strength, endurance.
Economy: administered individually in about 20 minutes.
Norms: expressed in percentiles and stanines by age.

TRAMPOLINE SCREENING TEST

Available: Dr. Ernst J. Kiphard
Ginnheimer Stadtweg 119
D-6000 Frankfurt 50, West Germany
Validity: .53 with balancing backward on Body Coordination Test (BCTC).
Reliability: test-retest = .85.
Scoring (objectivity): rating scale.
Population (norming sample): brain-damaged children (LH, EMR, SED, autistic)
but intended for use with school children of all ages.
Performances (parameters) measured: balance, gross motor abilities, fine
motor abilities, total body coordination.
Economy: administered in 2-3 minutes per child; equipment needed: tram-
poline, scoring sheet; administered individually within group.
Norms: none established as yet.

GEDDES PSYCHOMOTOR INVENTORY (GPI)

Available: In D. Geddes, *Psychomotor Individualized Educational Programs
for Intellectual, Learning and Behavioral Disabilities*. Rockleigh, New
Jersey: Allyn and Bacon, 1981.
Validity: none reported.
Reliability: none reported.
Scoring (objectivity): ratings.

Population (norming sample): intended for use with normal, LD, MR, behavioral disorders, autistic-like children.

Performances (parameters) measured: balance, visual skills, eye-hand coordination, eye-foot coordination, kinesthetic awareness, tactile discrimination, throwing, gross motor abilities, fine motor abilities, 30-yard dash, 600-yard walk-run, softball throw, etc.

Economy: varies in time according to section selected; average time 30–45 minutes for short form; administered individually.

Norms: age range standards charted on profile sheets.

STOTT-MOYES-HENDERSON TEST OF MOTOR IMPAIRMENT

Available: Brook Educational Publishing, Ltd.
Box 1171, Guelph, Ontario, Canada N1H-6N3

Validity: .85 with teacher assessment/referral.

Reliability: .91–.99 test/retest with 24 children tested 2 days apart; .66–.87 inter-rater reliability on 28–39 children.

Scoring (objectivity): 3-point rating scale for pass, fail, or fail on one body side.

Population (norming sample): children ages 5–16 years, except physically handicapped.

Performances (parameters) measured: control and balance while immobile, speed, eye-hand coordination, eye-foot coordination, throwing, kinesthetic awareness, bilateral control, gross motor abilities, fine motor abilities, neurological dysfunction.

Economy: administered individually in 20 minutes to nonimpaired and 45 minutes to impaired children; test kit available from publisher.

Norms: expressed in percentiles based on normal population.

THE O.S.U. SCALE OF INTRA GROSS MOTOR ASSESSMENT (O.S.U. SIGMA)

Available: Mohican Textbook Publishing Co.
Loudonville, Ohio 44842

Validity: face with literature.

Reliability: none reported.

Scoring (objectivity): rating based on approximation to criterion.

Population (norming sample): intended for use with children having suspected motor dysfunction.

Performances (parameters) measured: 11 fundamental skills: walking, stair climbing, running, throwing, catching, jumping, hopping, skipping, striking, kicking, ladder climbing.

Economy: undeterminable administration time, since data can be gathered in formal testing or free play; equipment required includes: bench, stationary rail, steps, 6-inch ball, tennis ball, 8-inch step, paper, plastic bat, 6-inch suspended ball, ladder.

Norms: criterion-referenced by levels.

Note: accompanying performance based curriculum (PBC) available.

PRESCHOOL TEST BATTERY (EXPERIMENTAL VERSION)

Available: Arlene M. Morris, Ph.D.
Dept. of Physical Education, University of Arizona, Tucson, Arizona

Validity: none reported.

Reliability: .27–.94 range by item, age, and sex on a test-retest basis; testing on 2 days, 1–10 days apart.

Scoring (objectivity): 14 items generate ratios; 1 item, 4-point rating.

Population (norming sample): 269 normal caucasian children 3–6 years.

Performances (parameters) measured: 7 fundamental motor patterns, including: balance, agility, catching, speed, long jump, throw for distance; and 8 anthropometric measures including: height, weight, leg length, diameter, girth, and skin fold.

Economy: experimental version administered individually in 45 minutes at 8 stations; equipment required includes: stopwatch, fleece ball, 8½-inch ball, tape measure, Harpenden skinfold calipers, anthropometric tape.

Norms: raw scores for performances at 10, 50, and 90 percentile reported by sex and age for each item; anthropometric norms expressed in mean and standard deviation units by age and sex.

BRUNINKS-OSERETSKY TEST OF MOTOR PROFICIENCY

Available: American Guidance Service
Circle Pines, Minnesota 55014

Validity: .57 to .78 with age; item relationship to subtest .65 to .87 for internal consistency.

Reliability: .60 to .89 for items on long form; .86 for short form on test-retest basis for 126 children.

Figure 8–11. Two test items from the Bruninks-Oseretsky Test of Motor Proficiency: upper limb speed and dexterity—placing pennies in a box (left); and upper limb coordination—touching nose (right).

Scoring (objectivity): ratios generated for time, repetitions, and errors; some items scored pass/fail.

Population (norming sample): 800 normal children; 80 in each age group 4.5–14.5 years.

Performances (parameters) measured: running speed, agility, balance, bilateral coordination, strength, upper limb coordination, response speed, visual-motor coordination, upper limb speed, and dexterity.

Economy: individually administered in approximately 45–60 minutes for complete 46-item battery; 15–20 minutes for 14 item short form; required equipment for standardized administration included in test kit, stopwatch not included.

Norms: expressed in standard scores converted from z scores, percentile ranks and stanines (see Figure 8–11).

BASIC MOTOR ABILITY TEST—REVISED

Available: In D. Arnheim and A. Sinclair, *The Clumsy Child.* St. Louis: C. V. Mosby, 1979.

Validity: none reported.

Reliability: undefined random samples from norming sample established .93 test-retest correlation coefficient.

Scoring (objectivity): four test items generate continuous; seven generate discrete scores.

Population (norming sample): 1,563 children of various ethnic, cultural, social and economic groups.

Performances (parameters) measured: 11 tests designed to evaluate selected motor responses of small- and large-muscle control, static and dynamic balance, eye-hand coordination, and flexibility.

Figure 8-12. Two test items from the Basic Motor Ability Test: bead stringing (left) and ball striking (right).

Economy: individually administered in 15–20 minutes; administered to groups of up to five children in 30–40 minutes.

Norms: expressed in percentiles for children 4–12 years of age (see Figure 8–12).

BODY COORDINATION TEST FOR CHILDREN (BCTC)

Available: Beltz Test GmbH
         Weinheim, West Germany

Validity: none reported.

Reliability: .90 of motor quotient and .97 of raw data on test-retest.

Scoring (objectivity): 3 items generate ratios, one item interval.

Population (norming sample): 1,228 normal children between ages 5–14 years.

Performances (parameters) measured: body coordination is measured using 4 items requiring backward beam walking, monopedal hopping over, lateral jumping back and forth, lateral moving.

Economy: may be administered individually or in groups in about 15 minutes per child; equipment required includes quiet test room, free of distractions, measuring about 16 feet square; 3 balance beams of various lengths, ranging in width from 3 cm to 6 cm; 12 rectangular foam rubber plates measuring 50 × 20 × 5 cm; 2 plywood plates 50 × 60 × 0.8 cm, with a ridge in the middle 4 cm wide and 2 cm high; 2 platforms, 25 × 25 × 1.5 cm of pressboard with 4 rubber door-stoppers, each 3.7 cm high.

Norms: expressed in motor quotients (mean = 100) for males and females ages 5–14 years.

Motor Skills Tests

Tests of motor skills tend to measure specific applications and combinations of motor patterns. To distinguish between tests of motor skills and developmental profiles, the former usually require performance of a motor pattern under specific conditions such as walking (on a line) or crawling (through a maze). Motor skills tests also require combinations of patterns such as skipping, which is a combination of stepping and hopping. Separate from motor ability tests, motor skills tests tend to sample performances that have more global application to movement proficiency rather than specific application to athletic ability. The selection of an instrument to measure motor skills should rely heavily on knowledge of the student's abilities and opportunities for learning and experience, since motor skills are learned.

PHYSICAL ABILITY RATING SCALE

Available: IRUC, c/o AAHPERD
1900 Association Drive
Reston, Virginia 22091
Validity: none determined; subjective, based on field use.
Reliability: none determined.
Scoring (objectivity): ratings of number of items performed successfully.
Population (norming sample): physically handicapped hospitalized children from birth through 72 months.
Performances (parameters) measured: 238 items measure toilet habits, ability to lift glass, grip, dressing, self-feeding, variety of physical and motor skills, including building towers, copying, drawing, jumping, hopping, skipping, running, galloping, balancing, walking, climbing, throwing, catching, etc.
Economy: administered informally through observation; time undeterminable.
Norms: criterion-referenced, based on successful completion of tasks.

A PSYCHOEDUCATIONAL INVENTORY OF BASIC LEARNING

Available: Fearon Publishers
6 Davis Drive, Belmont, California 94002
Validity: none reported.
Reliability: none reported.
Scoring (objectivity): 5-point rating scale.
Population (norming sample): primary school-age children.

Performances (parameters) measured: 53 items measuring gross motor development, sensorimotor integration, perceptual-motor skills, language development, conceptual skills, social skills.

Economy: administered individually to children with suspected learning disabilities, in as much time as needed to provide valid information; required materials include workbook, teaspoon, beads, texture ball, old newspapers, softball, jump rope, records and record player, hand mirror, brick, playing cards, books, paper bag, nail, sticks, wood blocks, etc.

Norms: criterion-referenced.

MOVE-GROW-LEARN: MOVEMENT SKILLS SURVEY

Available: Follett Educational Corporation
            1018 W. Washington Blvd., Chicago, Illinois 60607

Validity: no correlation with criterion variable (an existing test).

Reliability: .44–.88 minimum estimate of subtest reliability.

Scoring (objectivity): 5-point rating scale.

Population (norming sample): 744 caucasian children 6–12 years of age.

Performances (parameters) measured: coordination and rhythm, gross motor, fine motor, eye motor, agility, flexibility, strength, speed, static, dynamic and object balance, endurance, body awareness.

Economy: administered informally through observation; time undeterminable; required equipment includes materials for drawing, coloring, writing and cutting, beads, beanbags, ball for kicking and catching, tetherball, target.

Norms: scaled scores for 6–12 year old males and females.

Note: accompanying program of motor activities available.

Physical Fitness Tests

Testing for physical fitness is, understandably, <u>an area of measurement</u> with which physical educators feel most comfortable. The development of appropriate and adequate levels of fitness is an unique contribution to the life of handicapped individuals that the physical educator should never ignore. Although the definition of physical fitness may take many forms in physical education literature, tests designed to measure its pa-

rameters, directly or indirectly, tend to have several similarities:

1. They tend to be highly reliable both on a test-retest basis and on scores obtained between two or more examiners. Scoring tends to be objective, usually using ratios expressing time, distance, repetitions, force, and the like.

2. They tend to use a few items to sample the major parameters or factors that have been documented

by research to contribute to overall fitness for life. These factors are: strength, power, agility, flexibility, muscular and cardiorespiratory endurance, speed, balance, and general coordination.

3. They usually tend to be normed on large numbers of normal school-age children (exclusive of the primary grades, ages 5 to 7 or 8), with the norms expressed in percentile ranks.

4. They tend to be designed for administration to groups, an obvious advantage for the physical educator.

5. They tend to require an "all-out" effort, and assume each student's ability to understand the meaning of that concept.

Although measurement of physical fitness represents a unique contribution to the total data-gathering process needed in appropriate programming for exceptional students, it should not constitute the major focus for decision-making. All major physical fitness tests systematically exclude children with identified physical, mental, emotional, and sensory handicaps in their norming samples. Most performance tests discussed in this section, although normed on specific segments of the exceptional population, represent a much wider range of abilities, since specific handicapping conditions have varying degrees of impact on motor performance. Therefore the reader is cautioned to consider such factors as physical and organic limitations of performance, innate neural capacity, emotional capacity, the presence of interfering reflexes and the development or acquisition of prerequisite functions, responses, and skills before interpreting the results of physical fitness testing. Selection of a physical fitness test should rely as much on its appropriateness for the group of students being tested as on parameters measured.

Physical Fitness Performance Tests

PHYSICAL FITNESS TEST BATTERY FOR MENTALLY RETARDED CHILDREN

Available: Hollis Fait, School of Physical Education
University of Connecticut, Storrs, Connecticut 06268
Validity: reportedly the same as for normal children.
Reliability: .90<.
Scoring (objectivity): ratios generated on distance, time, and repetitions.
Population (norming sample): moderately and mildly retarded children between the ages of 9–20 years.
Performances (parameters) measured: speed, static muscular endurance of arm and shoulder girdle, muscular endurance of leg and abdominal muscles, static balance, agility, cardiorespiratory endurance.
Economy: can be administered in one day to groups using six stations; required equipment includes hanging bar, stopwatch, mats or other padded surface, sufficient space for running, score cards.
Norms: low, average and good performance scales established for males and females for moderately and mildly retarded in 9–12, 13–16, and 17–20 year age groups.

MR. PEANUT'S GUIDE TO PHYSICAL FITNESS

Available: Standard Brands Education Service
P.O. Box 2695, Grand Central Station,
New York, New York 10017
Validity: none reported.
Reliability: none reported.
Scoring (objectivity): ratios generated on time and distance.
Population (norming sample): normal children ages 7–9 years.
Performances (parameters) measured: arm and shoulder strength, flexibility, abdominal strength and endurance, explosive leg power, speed, coordination, cardiorespiratory endurance.
Economy: supplements AAHPERD Youth Fitness Test and can be administered individually or in groups during two physical education periods; required equipment includes bench and horizontal bar, 20-inch ruler, tape measure or yardstick, stopwatch, softballs, stakes for marking throws, sufficient room for running.
Norms: expressed in percentiles for males and females ages 7–9 years.
Note: incentive awards available.

PHYSICAL FITNESS FOR THE MENTALLY RETARDED

Available: Metropolitan Toronto Association for Retarded Children
186 Beverley St., Toronto 2B, Ontario, Canada
Validity: none reported.
Reliability: none reported.
Scoring (objectivity): ratios generated on time, distance, and repetitions.
Population (norming sample): moderately retarded males and females between the ages of 8–17 years.
Performances (parameters) measured: muscular fitness of arms and shoulders, back flexibility, leg power, abdominal endurance, hamstring flexibility, cardiorespiratory endurance, physique.
Economy: administered individually or in groups during two regular physical education periods; required equipment includes horizontal bar, medicine ball, yardstick and 6-inch ruler, gym mat, stopwatch, scale marked at ½-inch intervals mounted on wall, block of wood 10 inches, scale for determining body weight, sufficient area for running.
Norms: percentiles expressed for male and female moderately retarded children ages 8–17 years.
Note: accompanying program of motor activities available.

ELEMENTARY SCHOOL PHYSICAL FITNESS TEST FOR BOYS AND GIRLS

Available: State Department of Public Instruction
Olympia, Washington 98501
Validity: .81 with AAHPERD Youth Fitness Test.
Reliability: .76-.84 on test-retest of 100 children.
Scoring (objectivity): ratios generated for distance, repetitions, and time.
Population (norming sample): normal children ages 6-12 years.
Performances (parameters) measured: leg power, strength and endurance of forearm, arm and shoulder girdle, strength and endurance of trunk flexor muscles, strength and endurance of trunk and leg extensor muscles, speed.
Economy: administered individually or in groups in one testing period; required equipment includes stopwatches, measuring tape, mats, chairs, yardstick, score sheets, manual.
Norms: by age and sex for males and females ages 6-12 years.
Note: accompanying program of motor activities available.

SPECIAL FITNESS TEST MANUAL FOR THE MENTALLY RETARDED

Available: American Alliance for Health, Physical Education, Recreation, and Dance
1900 Association Drive, Reston, Virginia 22091
Validity: none reported.
Reliability: none reported.
Scoring (objectivity): ratios generated for time, repetitions, and distance.
Population (norming sample): 4,200 mildly retarded children ages 8-18 years.
Performances (parameters) measured: arm-shoulder endurance, abdominal endurance, agility, leg power, speed, coordination, cardiorespiratory endurance, arm/shoulder power.
Economy: administered in groups during two physical education periods; required equipment includes horizontal bar, stopwatch, mat, two wooden blocks or erasers, tape measure, softball, sufficient space for running.
Norms: percentiles for male and female mildly retarded children ages 8-18 years.
Note: incentive awards available for achievement of 50th, 75th, and 85th percentiles (see Figure 8-13).

Figure 8-13. Two test items from the Special Fitness Test for the Mentally Retarded: the 30-second sit-up test (left); the flexed arm hang test (right).

MOTOR FITNESS TESTING MANUAL FOR THE MODERATELY MENTALLY RETARDED

Available: American Alliance for Health, Physical Education, Recreation, and Dance
  1900 Association Drive, Reston, Virginia 22091
Validity: none reported.
Reliability: .60-.90 on test-retest basis.
Scoring (objectivity): ratios generated for time, repetitions and distance.
Population (norming sample): 1,097 moderately retarded institutionalized (TMR) children ages 6-20 years.
Performances (parameters) measured: arm-shoulder endurance, abdominal endurance, leg power, speed, coordination, cardiorespiratory endurance, arm/shoulder power, height, weight, flexibility, hopping, skipping, throwing accuracy.
Economy: administered in groups during two physical education periods; required equipment includes horizontal bar, stopwatch, mat, two wooden blocks or erasers, tape measure, softball, sufficient space for running.
Norms: percentiles for male and female moderately retarded children ages 6-20 years.
Note: incentive awards available for achievement.

AAHPERD YOUTH FITNESS TEST ADAPTATION FOR THE BLIND

Available: In AAHPERD, *Physical Education and Recreation for Visually Handi-
capped,* 1974.
American Alliance for Health, Physical Education, Recreation, and
Dance
1900 Association Drive, Reston, Virginia 22091
(See also AAHPERD Youth Fitness Test, AAHPERD, 1975, available at
the above address.)
Validity: not reported for adaptation.
Reliability: not reported for adaptation.
Scoring (objectivity): ratios generated for time, repetitions and distance.
Population (norming sample): not reported.
Performances (parameters) measured: arm/shoulder power, abdominal en-
durance, speed, agility, leg power, cardiorespiratory endurance.
Economy: administered individually or in a group in two physical education
class periods; required equipment includes hanging bar, mats,
stopwatch, adequate space for running.
Norms: special norms designed for blind and partially sighted students 6–20
years for 50-yard dash and 600-yard run-walk; regular norms used
for students 8–18 years for pull-ups, flexed arm hang, sit-ups, standing long jump.
Note: incentive awards available for scoring at the 50th and 80th percentiles.

LIFETIME HEALTH RELATED FITNESS TEST

Available: The American Alliance for Health, Physical Education, Recreation
and Dance
1900 Association Drive, Reston, Virginia 22091
Validity: sit and reach = .80–.90 with several other types of flexibility tests;
skinfold = .70–.90 with hydrostatic weighing.
Reliability: sit-up = .68–.94 for test-retest; sit and reach = .70 +; skinfold = .95 with experienced testers.
Scoring (objectivity): see: *Technical Manual: AAHPERD Health Related Physical Fitness Test,* AAHPERD Publications for details.; ratios and discrete scores generated on 4 measures.

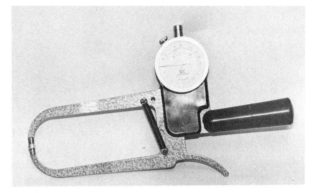

Figure 8-14.
An adjustable skinfold caliper for measuring body fat.

Population (norming sample): 12,000 children and youths ranging in age from 6–17 years, living in 13 states.

Performances (parameters) measured: cardiorespiratory function, body composition, abdominal and low back-hamstring musculoskeletal function.

Economy: equipment needed includes: stopwatch, Harpenden or Lange skinfold calipers, specially constructed box (measurements for construction included in test manual); time to administer = 2–3 class periods, depending on equipment available; can be administered in groups.

Norms: percentiles for 1-mile run, 9-minute run, sit-ups, sit and reach for ages 5–17+; percentiles for 1.5 mile/12 minute run for ages 13–18; percentiles for skinfold measurement ages 6–17.

Direct Measures of Fitness Components

DETERMINING BODY FAT FROM SKINFOLD MEASUREMENTS

Available: K. H. Cooper, *The Aerobics Way.* New York: M. Evans, 1978, pp. 278–279.

Validity: (w/underwater weighing) .80–.87 for males; .68–.87 for females.

Reliability: .90–.96 on test-retest for experienced examiners.

Scoring (objectivity): measurement of skin and subcutaneous tissue measured in millimeters.

Population (norming sample): normal males and females.

Performances (parameters) measured: skinfold of suprailiac crest and triceps for women; axilla, chest, and tricep for men.

Economy: 5–10 minutes per individual; required equipment includes skinfold calipers and calculator.

Norms: 15% or less for men and 18–20% for women ages 30–60 years (see Figure 8–14).

Figure 8-15.
The Leighton flexometer
for flexibility testing.

12-MINUTE TEST/1.5-MILE RUN TEST

Available: K. H. Cooper, *The Aerobics Way.* New York: M. Evans, 1978, pp.
282–283.
Validity: w/laboratory treadmill test; .90 with max. O_2 consumption.
Reliability: .94 on test-retest basis.
Scoring (objectivity): distance covered in 12 minutes or time to run 1.5 miles.
Population (norming sample): normal males and females ages 13–60+ years.
Performances (parameters) measured: maximum oxygen consumption.
Economy: may be administered individually or in groups in 20–30 minutes
depending on age and warm-up time needed; required equipment
includes stopwatch or sweep second hand, running area measured
to 1.5 miles, data recording forms.
Norms: expressed in time and distance for males and females ages 13–60+
years.

FLEXIBILITY MEASURED BY THE LEIGHTON FLEXOMETER

Available: In Jack Leighton, ``An Instrument and Technique for the Measure-
ment of Joint Motion.'' *Archives of Physical Medicine* (1955).
Validity: face with literature.
Reliability: .91–.99 on test-retest basis with 120 males.
Scoring (objectivity): ratios based upon degrees of movement about a joint.
Population (norming sample): normal 16-year-old males (N = 50) (Mathews,
1978).
Performances (parameters) measured: range of movement about a joint
(flexibility).
Economy: individually administered in undetermined amount of time dependent upon number of joints measured; required equipment
includes flexometer, projecting wall corner, long bench or table,
low-backed armchair.
Norms: expressed in means and standard deviations for fifty 16-year-old
males (Mathews, 1978: 363) (see Figure 8-15).

WELLS SIT AND REACH TEST (WELLS 1952)

Available: In K. F. Wells and E. K. Dillon, "The Sit and Reach — A Test of Back and Leg Flexibility." *The Research Quarterly* (March 1952).

Validity: .90 with standing bobbing test.

Reliability: .98 on test-retest basis given 3 preliminary bobs.

Scoring (objectivity): ratio data expressed as maximum reach in inches.

Population (norming sample): 100 college freshmen and sophomore women.

Performances (parameters) measured: back and leg flexibility.

Economy: administered individually in less than 5 minutes per individual; required equipment includes a specially designed calibrated "bench" (Mathews, 1978), scoring sheets.

Norms: none reported.

STRENGTH INDEX

Available: In D. K. Mathews, *Measurement in Physical Education*. New York: Holt, Rinehart and Winston, 1978, pp. 93–107 (part of Physical Fitness Index).

Validity: .76–.81 with other measures of general athletic ability.

Reliability: .96 for boys and .95 for girls 2.6–6.5 years of age, and .82–.92 for children 4 years to high school age on test-retest basis using manuometer (Metheny, 1940).

Scoring (objectivity): ratios of height and weight; hand, back, and leg strength measured in pounds.

Population (norming sample): normal males and females 8–18 years of age.

Performances (parameters) measured: hand, back, and leg strength.

Economy: administered individually in 15–20 minutes per individual spread over 2–3 physical education class periods; required equipment includes scale for measuring body weight and height, back and leg dynamometer (back and leg strength), manuometer (grip strength).

Norms: Obtained Strength Index calculated by adding lung capacity (measured using a spirometer in milliliters) to back and leg strength and grip strength; expressed in mean SI for males and females ages 8–18 years.

HEATH-CARTER ANTHROPOMETRIC SOMATOTYPING

Available: In B. H. Heath and J. E. L. Carter, "A Modified Somatotype Method." *American Journal of Physical Anthropology* (1967).

Validity: .76–.84 when skinfolds were compared with body density.

Reliability: height and weight = .98, girths and diameters = .92–.98, skin-folds = .90–.96 on test-retest basis.

Scoring (objectivity): ratios of height, weight, skinfolds, diameters, and girths expressed in inches, pounds, millimeters, and centimeters.

Population (norming sample): 59 males, 61 females, 17–23 years.

Performances (parameters) measured: height, weight, body fat, bone diameters, muscle girths to determine body type (somatotype).

Economy: administered individually in 3–5 minutes; required equipment includes wall scale and Broca plane, balance scale, skinfold caliper, sliding steel caliper for bone diameters.

Norms: scales of mean dimensions and somatotype components based upon height.

Body Alignment Tests

Posture testing or screening is probably one of the most commonly used methods traditional to adapted physical education. Early physical educators such as Ling and Sargeant developed physical education curricula around medical gymnastics and movement experiences as preventive measures to ill health and other "afflictions" of the body. There are, perhaps, as many tools developed for posture evaluation as there are professionals who have tried to solve the problem of gathering useful data. Instruments and techniques for the evaluation of body alignment tend to cluster into two categories: (1) subjective, observational screening tests and (2) objective, refined tests.

It should be noted that the measurement of body alignment is only as useful in decision-making as the physical, emotional, and mental limitations of the stu-dent allow. Structural deviations that can only be maintained and do not interfere with the student's ability to perform to potential could probably be managed in the mainstream of physical education. Functional deviations resulting from a true imbalance in musculature and body alignment could probably best be treated in a separate adapted physical education class with the goal being to restore criterion body alignment and efficient body mechanics. The physical educator must consider the interaction of reflex behavior and sensory system function as it relates to postural mechanisms. Once sensorimotor dysfunction and potential interference of abnormal reflexes have been ferreted out, then deviations in body alignment can be identified. The format of this section has been altered to accommodate the unique nature of posture evaluation techniques, procedures, and instruments.

Screening Tests

CSULA GROUP POSTURE SCREENING

Description: group scoring sheet with list of deviations; entire class is evaluated for further individual analysis.

Scoring (objectivity): check mark used to indicate deviations observed.

Parameters measured: static and dynamic body alignment (anterior, posterior, and lateral views); gait; back symmetry; foot and ankle deviations.

Procedure: students walk toward examiner and stand behind posture screen or in front of plumb line; lateral and posterior views are made; students walk toward examiner and assume Adam's position on pedioscope (flexed at hips and waist with arms and head hanging freely); students then walk at right angles to examiner for gait evaluation.

Economy: administered to a group of 30–40 students in one physical education class period; required equipment includes posture screen or plumb line, pedioscope, group score sheet (see Figure 8-16).

PLUMB LINE

Description: a plumb line test requires a string with a weight on the end, hung freely from the ceiling or other overhead support.

Scoring (objectivity): instructor notes, in narrative form, any deviations of the line from anatomical landmarks.

Parameters measured: posterior and anterior body alignment.

Procedure: student stands in gym clothes, bathing suit or underwear behind the plumb line so string falls between the student and the instructor; plumb line should be aligned about 1–1½ inches in front of the lateral malleolus (ankle bone); landmarks for correct posture when viewed from the side are: plumb line falls 1–1½ inches in front of ankle bone, just behind the knee cap (patella), through the center of the hip, through the center of the shoulder (acromial process) and through the lobe of the ear. From the front (anterior view), the plumb line should fall midpoint between the ankles (medial malleoli) between the knees, through the center of the pubic symphysis (crotch), center of the umbilicus (navel), the center of the linea alba, the middle of the chin, center of the nose and forehead. The back view (posterior) has the plumb line intersecting the following landmarks: midpoint between medial malleoli and knees, cleft of the buttocks, center of the spinous processes of spine, and center of the back of the head.

Economy: can be used to screen anterior and posterior deviations in a class of 30–40 students in one class period: equipment needed includes: plumb line, paper, pencil, and writing surface.

Figure 8-16. CSULA Group
Posture Screening checklist.

Class _____

	Name	1	2	3	4	5	6	7	8	9	10
A. Gait											
B. Anterior view (ft. together)											
1. Overweight											
2. Underweight											
3. Lateral head tilt											
4. Shoulders uneven											
5. Knock-knees											
6. Bow-legs											
C. Ant. view (arms overhead)											
1. Restricted range of movement											
2. Upper extremity deformity											
D. Posterior view											
1. Scoliosis											
2. Winged scapula											
3. Hips uneven											
4. Achilles deviation											
5. Foot pronation											
6. Foot supination											
E. Adam position (posterior)											
1. Upper back-asymmetry											
2. Flat back											
3. Restricted range of movement											
F. Lateral view											
1. Forward head											
2. Round shoulders											
3. Kyphosis											
4. Lordosis											
G. Medical records (code)											
H. General appearance (check if poor)											
I. Check if individual screening needed											

Examiner _____

Norms: see anthropometric landmarks above; slight, moderate, and marked deviations from the above landmarks can be noted for further postural analysis, referral or programming.

POSTURE SCREEN

Description: a 4 × 6 foot rectangular frame mounted on feet or casters; the frame is laced with string making a 2-inch grid pattern; the center vertical line should be a different color to serve as a plumb line reference point (see above); all vertical strings are parallel to this and all horizontal strings are perpendicular to the vertical strings.

Scoring (objectivity): same as plumb line.

Parameters measured: same as plumb line; also the horizontal references allow measurement of evenness of shoulders and hips.

Procedure: student stands behind screen aligning ankle bone with colored center string the same as in the use of the plumb line; all vertical reference points are the same landmarks as above for lateral, anterior, and posterior views; the 2-inch squares allow the instructor to quantify the deviations from landmark criteria; horizontally, the shoulders and iliac crests (hip bones) should be intersected by the same horizontal string.

Norms: see anatomical landmarks under plumb line (above); deviations from vertical and horizontal landmarks can be reported in inches.

Note: photographic records can be made of each student's posture test and progress noted by comparing photos over a period of time. Photos must be handled confidentially and should be kept in a locked cabinet.

PEDIOSCOPE

Description: a wooden box 14–16 inches square made of ¾-inch thick wood; the top is ¾-inch thick plate glass and the front is left open; under the glass, a mirror is mounted at a 45 degree angle in a wooden frame, which is adjustable so the student can view his or her own feet when standing in front of a wall mirror (see Figure 8-17).

Scoring: instructor notes in narrative form: shape and height of longitudinal and transverse arches; areas of support should be the toes, ball of the foot, outer margin of the sole and heel; areas of support other than these (indicated by light coloration from the blood being

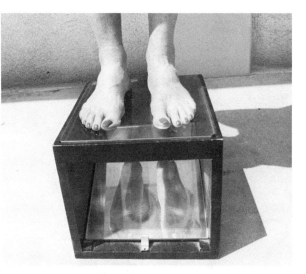

Figure 8-17.
A pedioscope in use.

pressed away from the area); areas of stress indicated by dark coloration and calluses; toes straight and bearing weight.

Parameters measured: longitudinal and transverse arch integrity, weight distribution on weight-bearing surfaces, areas of stress.

Procedure: student stands barefooted on glass; instructor stands in front to note deviations.

Economy: notes can be made on 30–40 students in one class period.

Norms: see areas of support above.

ADAMS TEST

Description: student assumes position below for evaluation.

Scoring (objectivity): narrative of observations.

Parameters measured: scoliosis in order to determine whether previously identified deviation is functional or structural.

Procedure: student stands with back toward instructor then gradually bends head and trunk forward with arms hanging freely; instructor observes symmetry of back.

Economy: no equipment needed; individually administered in groups; 1–2 minutes per student.

Norms: if back is symmetrical in Adam's position, scoliosis is functional; if asymmetrical, scoliosis is structural and student should be referred for further orthopedic testing.

CURETON-GUNBY CONFORMATEUR

T. K. Cureton, et al., "Reliability and Objectivity of Springfield Postural Measurements," Supplement to *The Research Quarterly* (2 May 1935).

Description: pictures taken of the standing posture of students are measured and analyzed.

Scoring (objectivity): angles of deviation from proper alignment.

Parameters measured: head tilt, trunk-hip flexion, thigh-leg flexion.

Procedure: photographs of students are marked for measurement of angles of relationship between body segments (13 measurements); anatomical landmarks are used to define angles; protractor used to measure angles; measurements are weighted then summed.

Economy: equipment required includes: ruler, protractor, pencil, camera, film, time for measurement and calculations undeterminable.

Norms: degrees of summed deviation are graded by letter grades on 5-point scale.

Movement Skills

Measurement of a child's ability to perform socially acceptable, age-appropriate game, sport and other movement skills often serves as the criterion by which students are placed either in the mainstream or in a separate adapted physical education class. Sports skill testing has historically been used in physical education for ability grouping (i.e., classification), determining progress, and grading. Many good sports skill tests are available on the market and referenced in measurement texts in physical education (Safrit, 1980; Baumgartner and Jackson, 1981; Barrow and McGee, 1979; Mathews, 1978). These norm-referenced tests are appropriate for students with special needs who have been placed in the mainstream of physical education. For exceptional students who either do not have the skills or the subservient sensory functions, responses, patterns, and fundamental skills to learn the sport skills, criterion-referenced instruments would be more useful. As discussed earlier in this chapter, criterion-referenced skill tests can help the physical educator identify what skills or components of skills the student *can do*, rather than underscoring performances the student cannot do. A sample of five criterion-referenced instruments have been included to give the reader an idea of how game and sport performances can be analyzed for effective measurement, as well as generating useful information for program planning. These instruments measure skills in roller skating, aquatics, bowling, stunts-tumbling-gymnastics, and rhythms (see Figures 8-18, 8-19, 8-20, 8-21, and 8-22). (See the bibliography at the end of this chapter for a selected list of sport skills tests commonly available in physical education resources.)

Comprehensive Motor Performance Tests

Comprehensive motor performance tests span several categories of motor performance testing previously discussed, and thus belong in a category by themselves. As discussed earlier, the factors of economy of time and adequate sampling of performance may necessitate obtaining measures of several aspects of motor performance not measured by any single tool previously listed. Comprehensive motor performance tests can generate data that can serve as indicators of areas of dysfunction requiring further testing, or may provide adequate information by themselves for making the necessary decisions in program planning . Two such tests are listed below.

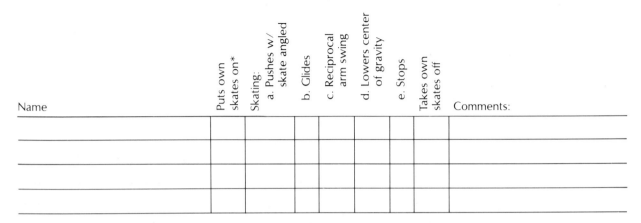

Name	Puts own skates on*	Skating: a. Pushes w/ skate angled	b. Glides	c. Reciprocal arm swing	d. Lowers center of gravity	e. Stops	Takes own skates off	Comments:

*Check skills or skill components student is able to do independently

Figure 8–18. Roller skating rating sheet. SOURCE: Developed by Lou Stewart, A.P.E. Specialist, County Superintendent of Schools, Los Angeles.

ADAPTED PHYSICAL EDUCATION ASSESSMENT SCALE
(Field Test Draft) (APEAS)

Available: Los Angeles Unified School District
450 No. Grand Ave., Los Angeles, California

Validity: face with literature.

Reliability: variable per item; 10 items > 0.70 on test-retest basis.

Scoring (objectivity): 8 items use ratios representing distance or repetitions, 8 items use ratings and 2 items generate categorical data; 0.39–0.96 with median = 0.63.

Population (norming sample): stratified random sample of LAUSD students ages 5–18 years based on age, disability and ethnicity.

Performances (parameters) measured: motor development, perceptual motor function, motor achievement, posture, and physical fitness.

Economy: administered individually or in small groups in about 20–30 minutes per student; required equipment includes 8½-inch rubber ball, 18-inch ruler or yardstick, 5 bean bags 6 × 6 inch, stopwatch, test manual, chalk, masking tape, score sheets (see Figure 8–23).

Norms: expressed in percentile ranks at 6 month intervals for 5–7.11 years and one year intervals for 8.0–18 years.

Note: Additional information about this test can be found in Appendix D.

BASIC MOTOR FITNESS

Available: Donald A. Hilsendager, Dept. of Physical Education
Temple University, Philadelphia, Pennsylvania 19122

Validity: face with two-year field test.

Reliability: none reported.

Scoring (objectivity): some items scored pass/fail, others generate ratios.

Figure 8-19. Adapted aquatics checklist. SOURCE: Developed by Karen P. DePauw, California State University, Los Angeles.

	Name					
I. Water adjustment						
A. On deck: wading pool						
1. sit in water						
2. splash water						
3. wash face with water						
4. water play: pour water with bucket, squeeze sponges						
5. retrieve objects (chips) from water						
B. In water: swimming pool						
1. sit on step						
2. splash water on body and face						
3. move down steps into water						
4. wade in waist deep assisted						
5. wade in waist deep unassisted						
6. wade in chest deep assisted						
7. wade in chest deep unassisted						
8. move forward, backward & sideways unassisted						
9. bend knees & submerge to chin						
10. put parts of head (chin, ears, cheeks, forehead, nose, mouth, eyes) into water						
11. quickly place nose and mouth into water						
12. place whole face into water						
13. submerge body to ears						
14. submerge with head under water						
II. Breath control						
1. out of water: inhale — exhale						
2. with body in chest deep water — *easy* inhale, slow exhale						
3. blow ping pong ball across pool						
4. with mouth in water — *slow exhale* into water, making bubbles						
5. with face in water, blow bubbles						

	Name					
6. submerge and blow bubbles						
7. rhythmic bobbing at 3–4 second intervals						
8. exhale through nose into water						
III. Body control						
1. walk slowly through water						
2. walk fast through water						
3. jump while in water						
4. squat under water						
5. sit on bottom of pool						
6. kneel on bottom of pool						
7. lie prone on bottom						
8. lie supine on bottom						
9. roll over while on bottom						
10. combination of movements (knees to sitting, sitting to prone, etc.) while on bottom						
11. with hands on steps, bring legs up to floating position, unassisted recovery						
12. hands on steps, prone float position, unassisted recovery						
13. with hands on steps, prone float position, "kick" with legs						
14. hands on steps, kick fast						
15. hands on steps, kick slowly						
16. while held in prone position in chest deep water, recover to standing with assistance						
17. while held in prone position, recover without assistance						
18. while held in supine position in chest deep water, recover to standing with assistance						
19. while held in supine, recover to standing without assistance						
20. while being pulled in prone position, maintain relaxed body position						
21. retrieve objects (diving rings, chips) from 2–3 feet of water						
22. jellyfish float — arms & legs hang & float						
23. turtle float — grab legs, feet off bottom & float						

Figure 8–19. (continued)

Name					
24. prone float & recovery					
25. supine float (knees bent & recovery					
26. roll over from prone float to supine float					
27. roll from supine float to prone float					
IV. Basic skills					
1. steamboat — kicking while being pulled through water					
2. prone glide with assistance					
3. prone glide to steps & recover					
4. prone glide to instructor (3 feet away from steps), assisted recovery					
5. prone glide to instructor (3-4 feet from steps), unassisted recovery					
6. prone glide — width of pool (6-10 feet)					
7. kick glide to steps (3 feet)					
8. kick glide to instructor (3-4 feet) assisted recovery					
9. kick glide (3-4 feet) unassisted recovery					
10. kick glide the width of pool (6-10 feet)					
11. while in supine position, finning and sculling with hands					
12. beginning armstroke with underwater recovery of arms					
13. armstroke — hand over hand					
14. beginner's stroke with kick					
15. front crawl without breathing					
16. change directions while swimming					
17. swim 2 widths of pool (15-20 feet)					
18. jump into chest deep water					
19. jump into head deep water and swim 15-20 feet					
V. Swimming skills					
1. front crawl with breathing					
2. swim under water (5-8 ft.)					
3. jump into deep water & swims 30 feet					
4. tread water with arms and legs					

Name					
5. dive into pool from sitting position					
6. dive into pool from one knee					
7. dive into pool from crouch position					
8. dive from standing position					
9. elementary backstroke					
10. breaststroke					
11. back crawl					
12. side stroke					
13. dive from low board					
VI. Creative movement					
1. somersaults (forward) in water					
2. backward somersaults in water					
3. log rolls in water					
4. egg rolls in water					
5. hand stands in shallow water					
6. elbow stands in shallow water					
7. walk on hands in shallow water					
8. corkscrew swimming					
9. shark swim (swim in circle with one hand on hip — elbow out of water)					
10. swim without arms, legs only					
11. swim without legs, arms only					
12. swim without legs or arms					
13. swim through hula hoops					
14. retrieve objects from bottom					
15. rhythmic bobbing in deep water					

Figure 8-20. Individual bowling skills checklist. SOURCE: Developed by Janet A. Seaman as part of practicum course P.Ed. for Women, Indiana University.

Date _____   Name _____

Below are listed bowling-skill components and two levels of proficiency — "self" and "with help." Please check "self" if the child has learned the skill or component and is able to perform it entirely by himself. Check "with help" if he can perform the component but needs some assistance in its execution. A brief comment as to the type of assistance needed such as patterning, prompting, positioning, etc. should be entered in the comments column.

Skills and their components	Comments	Self	w/help
Ball release			
1. Pushes ball			
2. Holds ball with one hand			
3. Keeps thumb on top of ball			
4. Swings arm			
5. Places opposite foot forward at line			
6. Follows through			
Approach			
1. Slides into delivery			
2. Steps into delivery			
3. Takes two steps			
4. Takes three steps			
5. Takes four steps			
6. Coordinates armswing w/feet			
7. Pushes ball away on 1st step			
Other skills			
1. Carries own ball to line			
2. Counts pins remaining			
3. Deduces # of pins knocked down			
4. Writes numbers on scoresheet			
5. Recognizes numerals			
6. Writes name on scoresheet			
7. Adds in keeping score			
8. Spot bowls			
9. Pushes reset button when appropriate			

Population (norming sample): 240 children, 4–18 years (ED, BI, MR).

Performances (parameters) measured: walking, balance, crawling, creeping, coordination, stair climbing, hopping, skipping, marching, ball handling, flexibility, leg power, abdominal strength and endurance, upper arm and shoulder strength and endurance, hand grip strength, speed, agility, cardiorespiratory endurance, overall endurance.

Economy: 13 qualitative and 13 quantitative items are administered individually; required equipment includes balance beam, mat, stopwatch, 18-inch bench, stairs, soft cloth ball, 8-inch playground ball, flexibility tester, 2 tapered balance beams, medicine ball (5 lb.), Jamar Manuometer, sufficient space for running.

Norms: expressed in Hull scores for each test item by sex and grade level.

A chart for "Quick Reference to Tests on the Market" is included in Appendix D. The chart includes all the performance tests covered in this chapter except for sports skills tests. A somewhat condensed set of parameters is listed across the top of the chart so that a tool can easily be found to measure the movement elements of interest.

SUMMARY

There are several procedures for collecting motor performance data on students with special needs. These include: informal observation, performance testing, and direct measures. Skillful observation is the foundation upon which all other forms of data collection are based. The observer must have a solid understanding of developmental milestones, knowledge of the dimensions of the target performance, the ability to identify deviations from the performance norm or standard, the ability to describe the observed performance, and the ability to make sense out of the relationships among performances for the purpose of program planning.

Formal performance testing and direct measures require not only the skill to validly and reliably administer the test, but also the ability to select an appropriate tool that will generate useful information. Qualities of a useful instrument include validity, reliability, objectivity, appropriateness to the student and performances measured, discriminating ability, and administrative ease and economy in terms of time, equipment, and personnel needed.

Some data collected by people other than the physical educator can be useful in test administration and interpretation. Although physical educators can usually rely on other professionals to provide needed information, they should have a working knowledge of the elements involved and the limitations imposed by abnormal reflex behavior in order to make the best use of this information when provided.

Numerous tools are available on the market for measuring the motor performance of students with special needs. These are categorized according to their titles or parameters measured. Categories of tests included in Chapter 8 are: Sensorimotor, Motor Development, Motor Ability, Motor Skills, Physical Fitness, Body Alignment, and Movement Skills. A quick reference chart of these tools is found in Appendix D.

Figure 8-21. Stunts-tumbling-
gymnastics checklist. SOURCE:
Developed by Jean Pyfer as part of
practicum course P.Ed. for Women,
Indiana University.

Student's Name:_____

Please respond to the following categories by recording the month and year under the appropriate headings to the right.

	Can do	Can't do
Coordinated creeping pattern		
Coordinated crawling pattern		
Walk forward on a straight line on floor — 10 steps		
Walk forward on a 4" low balance beam from end to end		
Walk forward on a 2" low balance beam from end to end		
Walk backward on a straight line on floor — 10 steps		
Walk backward on a 4" low beam from end to end		
Walk backward on a 2" low beam from end to end		
Run on a 4" low balance beam		
Run on a 2" low balance beam		
Hop forward 5 times with eyes open:		
Right foot		
Left foot		
Hop forward 5 times with eyes closed:		
Right foot		
Left foot		
Hop backward 5 times with eyes closed:		
Right foot		
Left foot		
Jump, ¼ turn in air, keep balance when landing		
Jump, ½ turn in air, keep balance when landing		
Jump, ¾ turn in air, keep balance when landing		
Jump, full turn in air, keep balance when landing		
Jumping (record distance):		
Long jump		
Vertical jump		
Stork stand, eyes open, hold 10 seconds		
Stork stand, eyes closed, hold 10 seconds		

	Can do	Can't do
Front scale on floor		
Front scale on 4″ low beam		
Front scale on 2″ low beam		
Rope jumping		
Swagger walk for 20 feet		
Inch worm for 20 feet		
Mule kick, 3 in succession		
Turk stand		
Through the Stick		
Chinese Getup, 5 in succession		
Wring the Dishrag, 5 in succession		
Rocker (dual stunt)		
Leap Frog		
Log Roll, 5 in succession staying on mat		
Human Ball, 3 in succession		
Single forward roll		
Series of 3 forward rolls		
Single backward roll		
Series of 3 backward rolls		
Forward roll followed by backward roll		
Shoulder rest for 5 seconds		
Forearm stand for 5 seconds		
Tripod held for 5 seconds		
Tie-up for 5 seconds		
Trampoline Work:		
Sitting bounce		
Standing bounce		
Seat Drop		
Knee Drop		
Knee Slap in air (tuck position)		
Tuck in air		
Pike in air		
Pike with toe touch in air		
½ twist in seat drop position		
Swivel Hips (series of ½ twists)		

Figure 8–22. Rhythm skills checklist. SOURCE: Developed by Jean Pyfer as part of practicum course P.Ed. for Women, Indiana University.

Student's Name:_____

Please respond to the following categories by recording the month and year under the appropriate headings to the right:

	Rhythms			
Keeping time:	2/4	3/4	4/4	6/8
Clapping				
Tapping				
Moving feet (no weight)				
Moving hands and feet (no weight)				

Movements to music:	Can do		Can't do	
Marching (M)				
Walking (W)				
Running (R)				
Jumping (J)				
Hop (H)				
Leap (L)				
Skip (Sk)				
Slide (Sl)				
Gallop (G)				

Spatial perception — suggested movements for use with each category follow in parentheses:

Limited use of space (W,R,H,Sl,G)

Unlimited use of space (M,R,L,Sk,G)

Levels — high, medium, low (L,J)

Concepts — suggested movements: W,R,J,L

Fast-medium-slow speeds

Pushing-pulling efforts

Swinging-lifting efforts

Happiness-sadness-anger emotions

Strong-weak-tired-peppy states

Heavy-light qualities

Tall-short qualities

	Can do	Can't do
Laterality and directions — suggested movements: M,W,R,J,H		
Forward-backward		
Sideways: left-right		
Turns:		
Left-right		
About face		
Straight line		
Circle		
Square		
Triangle		
Parallel Lines		
Movement combinations:		
Hop-step		
Step-close		
Schottische		
Rhythm unit		
Suggested singing games:		
Go In and Out the Window		
Looby Loo		
Did You Ever See a Lassie		
The Muffin Man		
The Farmer in the Dell		
Down Yonder in the Paw Paw Patch		
Hokey Pokey		
Others:		
Suggested square and folk dances:		
Green Sleeves		
Troika		
Danish Dance of Greeting		
Children's Polka (Kinderpolka)		
Gustaf's Skoal		
I See You		
Seven-Jumps		

Figure 8-22. (continued)

	Can do	Can't do
Seven-Steps		
Noble Duke of York		
Red River Valley		
Take a Little Peek		
Duck for the Oyster		
Right Hand Star		
Others:		
Miscellaneous:		
Exercise to music		
Conscious relaxation		
Ball bouncing to music		
Flag swinging		
Wand routines		
Lumme sticks		

Figure 8-23. Four test items from the Adapted Physical Education Assessment Scale: ocular control test (top, left); vertical jump test (top, right); posture screening test (bottom, left); and alternate hopping test (bottom, right).

BIBLIOGRAPHY

American Alliance for Health, Physical Education, Recreation, and Dance. *Youth Fitness Test.* Washington, D.C.: American Alliance for Health, Physical Education, Recreation, and Dance, 1975.

American Alliance for Health, Physical Education, Recreation, and Dance. *Lifetime Health Related Physical Fitness.* Reston, Virginia: American Alliance for Health, Physical Education, Recreation, and Dance, 1980.

Banus, B. S., et al. *The Developmental Therapist.* Thorofare, New Jersey: Charles B. Slack, Inc., 1971.

Bobath, B. *Abnormal Postural Reflex Activity Caused by Brain Lesions.* London: William Heinemann Medical Books, Ltd., 1965.

Bobath, B., and Bobath, K. *Motor Development in the Different Types of Cerebral Palsy.* London: International Ideas, 1975.

Cooper, K. H. *The Aerobics Way.* New York: M. Evans (Bantam Edition), 1978.

Fiorentino, M. R. *Reflex Testing Methods for Evaluating C.N.S. Development.* Springfield, Illinois: Charles E. Merrill, 1963.

Fiorentino, M. R. *Reflex Testing Methods for Evaluating C.N.S. Development.* 2d ed. Springfield, Illinois: Charles C. Thomas, 1972.

Geddes, D., and Seaman, J. A. *Competencies of Adapted Physical Educators in Special Education.* Washington, D.C.: Information and Research Utilization Center, AAHPER, 1978.

Heath, B. H., and Carter, J. E. L. "A Modified Somatotype Method." *American Journal of Physical Anthropology* 27 (1967): 57–74.

Leighton, J. "An Instrument and Technique for the Measurement of Range of Joint Motion." *Archives of Physical Medicine* 36 (1955): 571–578.

McCloy, C. H. "A Preliminary Study of Factors in Motor Educability." *The Research Quarterly* 11 (1940): 2.

Mathews, D. K. *Measurement in Physical Education.* 5th ed. Philadelphia: W. B. Saunders Co., 1978.

Metheny, E. "Breathing Capacity and Grip Strength of Preschool Children." *University of Iowa Studies in Child Welfare* 18 (1940): 114–115.

Seaman, J. A. *Adapted Physical Education Assessment Scale.* Los Angeles: Los Angeles Unified School District, 1979.

Sharkey, B. J. *Physiology of Fitness.* Champaign, Illinois: Human Kinetics, 1979.

Weiss, C. E., and Lillywhite, H. S. *Communicative Disorders.* St. Louis: C. V. Mosby, 1976.

Wells, K. F., and Dillon, E. K. "The Sit and Reach — A Test of Back and Leg Flexibility." *The Research Quarterly* 23 (1952): 115–118.

Sport skills tests are commonly available in physical education measurement texts. Resources are provided here for the reader's convenience:

Barrow, H. M., and McGee, R. *A Practical Approach to Measurement in Physical Education.* 3d ed. Philadelphia: Lea and Febiger, 1979.

Baumgartner, T. A., and Jackson, A. S. *Measurement for Evaluation in Physical Education.* 2d ed. Boston: Houghton Mifflin, 1981.

Hodges, P. B. *A Comprehensive Guide to Sport Skills Tests and Measurements.* Springfield, Illinois: Charles C. Thomas, 1978.

Johnson, B. L., and Nelson, J. K. *Practical Measurements for Evaluation in Physical Education.* 3d ed. Minneapolis: Burgess, 1979.

Safrit, M. J. *Evaluation in Physical Education: Assessing Motor Behavior.* 2d ed. Englewood Cliffs, New Jersey: Prentice-Hall, 1980.

9 Data Collection: Self-Reporting and Unobtrusive Measures

Guiding Questions

1. What are the advantages of self-reporting, and with what types of students can it be used?
2. What are three self-reporting techniques?
3. What are the advantages of using unobtrusive measures?
4. What are the uses of rating scales, case studies, and anecdotal records?

The adapted physical educator may find it helpful to supplement the data gathered through observation, formal testing, and direct measures with two other techniques: self-reporting and unobtrusive measures. Students are often the best sources of information about their own attitudes toward physical education, which activities they like or dislike, and with whom they prefer to interact. Too often, professionals overlook the student's own wants and feelings. Students can provide rich insight that will help the physical educator design a program that is both appropriate, and workable — *because* the student has been included in the planning process.

Data may also be gathered unobtrusively — that is, without the student being aware of the data-gathering. Data gathered in this way complements the self-report, because it reveals what students actually *do* in a given situation rather than what they *say* they do. Rat-

ing scales and case studies can be effectively used with students who would not be considered reliable reporters of their own behavior, as well as with students for whom additional data is desirable.

SELF-REPORTING

Self-reporting — in which students are asked to tell how they feel or what they think about a particular object, person, or experience — requires that students be able to express themselves well enough to make their desires understood, and that they be considered as reliable sources of information about their own feelings, activities, and wishes. Three forms of self-reporting tools will be discussed here: (1) attitude inventories, (2) rating scales, and (3) sociometric techniques.

Attitude Inventories

Attitude inventories measure a person's feelings toward an attitude object — usually a situation, experience, process, group, or value. Attitude objects of interest to the adapted physical educator may include the experience of physical education, particular sports, members of a team, or the process of choosing teams in class. For students who are capable of reading and responding to written statements, two methods of measurement have found common usage: the Thurstone-Chave Method (1929) and the Likert Method (1932). Reported correlations between the two methods range from .77 to .92. Each method requires the development of statements by the physical educator about the particular attitude object of interest. If an appropriate tool is not already available to the physical educator, one must be modified or developed. It is wise to try out modifications with a few students of the same age and achievement level as the students to be measured in order to assure that the statements are clear and the words are easily understood.

The Thurstone-Chave Method requires that a group of people (called "judges") arrange the statements into eleven piles in order of their favorability toward the attitude object. (The judges may be other teachers or students capable of doing this arranging.) That is, pile one contains the most favorable statements; and pile eleven the least favorable; with the others distributed along the continuum and the neutral items in pile six. Through a series of simple calculations (Mathews, 1978:373), each item is weighted, using a number value according to its favorability or unfavorability, between one and eleven. These values normally do not appear on the inventory. Students have the choice of agreeing or disagreeing with each statement. The score is then determined by the weighted values of the "agree" items only, with a total score determined by adding the weighted values and

dividing by the number marked "agree" (i.e., the mean). Total (mean) scores between one and six would indicate a more favorable attitude, whereas scores between six and eleven would indicate a less favorable attitude toward the attitude object.

The Adams Scale (1963) was found to have a correlation coefficient for validity of 0.61 and 0.69 for two forms of the inventory relative to a self-rating scale. A split-half reliability coefficient* of 0.84 was obtained for the two forms combined (see Figure 9–1).

The Likert Method is similar in terms of generating the statements, but does not require judges. It is necessary, however, to determine the favorability or unfavorability of each statement in order to facilitate scoring. Rather than using a dichotomous (i.e., agree or disagree) system, as in the Thurstone-Chave Method, the Likert Method allows the student to indicate degree of agreement by responding on the following scale: "strongly agree," "agree," "undecided (neutral)," "disagree," and "strongly disagree." Scoring involves assigning a point value of 5 to favorable statements and a point value of 1 to unfavorable statements. Thus a "strongly agree" response to a favorable statement is scored as 5 points, and a "strongly disagree" response to an unfavorable statement is also scored as 5 points. The total score is the sum of all assigned points resulting in a high score (i.e., 5 points × number of items) indicating a more favorable attitude, and a low score (i.e., 1 point × number of items) indicating a less favorable attitude.

One example of the Likert Method is the Seaman Attitude Inventory (1970). It has a validity of .76 with self-rating and a split-half reliability coefficient of .96 when the odd-numbered items were correlated with the even-numbered items. Reading level required is

---

* Statistical terms such as "reliability" and "validity" are discussed in Chapters 7 and 10.

Figure 9-1. The Adams Scale for measuring attitude toward physical education. SOURCE: R. S. Adams, ''Two Scales for Measuring Attitude Toward Physical Education,'' in *The Research Quarterly* (March 1961): 91.

1. Physical education gets very monotonous.
2. I only feel like doing physical education now and then.
3. Physical education should be disposed of.
4. Physical education is particularly limited in its value.
5. I suppose physical education is all right but I don't much care for it.
6. Physical education is the most hateful subject of all.
7. I do not want to give up physical education.
8. On the whole I think physical education is a good thing.
9. People who like physical education are nearly always good to know.
10. Anyone who likes physical education is silly.
11. Physical education has some usefulness.
12. Physical education is the ideal subject.
13. Physical education develops good character.
14. (School) College would be better without physical education.
15. Physical education has little to offer.
16. Physical education is my favorite subject.
17. Physical education gives lasting satisfaction.
18. Physical education's good and bad points balance out each other.
19. Physical education is a pleasant break.
20. Physical education seems useless to me.
21. Physical education only serves the interests of a few people.
22. Physical education encourages moral improvement.
23. There is no subject as good as physical education.
24. Sometimes I think physical education is good and sometimes I think it is useless.
25. In physical education we learn many things of no use.
26. There is little to be said for or against physical education.
27. Physical education is quite good.
28. It is a pity we have to do physical education.
29. Physical education should be a main part of a child's education.
30. Physical education is fundamentally unsound.
31. I think physical education is very good.
32. Physical education is one of the best subjects I have ever taken.
33. Physical education has not yet proved itself indispensable in education.
34. Physical education is a deplorable waste of time.
35. Physical education has something to commend it.
36. I don't like physical education.
37. I hate physical education more than anything else.
38. I think physical education is good.
39. I enjoy physical education if I can do it.
40. Physical education is decreasing in value to society.

sixth grade, and the instrument was designed specifically for use with students in adapted physical education (see Figure 9-2).

Attitude inventories for nonreaders have not yet been developed for use by physical educators, but could be based on several good models currently available for sampling attitudes toward other attitude objects (Guthrie, 1964; Werner and Carrison, 1942; Ziller, 1969; Meyrowitz, 1962). These instruments use pictures, three-dimensional forms, and diagrams to sample attitudes of the retarded, emotionally disturbed, and other nonreaders toward such attitude

Figure 9-2. The Seaman Attitude Inventory.

The attitude inventory consists of forty items for which 1 to 5 responses may be given. The scale, using the Likert technique, allows subjects to indicate not only direction but also intensity of a given attitude. Each statement can be responded to in terms of: strongly agree; agree, but not strongly; neutral; disagree, but not strongly; and strongly disagree. These five choices are scored 5-4-3-2-1 respectively, according to the subject's preference or liking. Subjects receive a score of 5 on a favorable item if they reply strongly agree, or a score of 1 if they reply strongly disagree to the same item. If subjects respond strongly agree to an unfavorable statement, scoring would be reversed and they would receive only 1 point. With 40 statements and a possible range of replies valued 1 to 5 points, the total scores could range from 40 being the least favorable to 200 being the most favorable.

Item Scoring

Positive Items (receiving a score of 5 points if strongly agree is indicated):			Negative Items (receiving a score of 1 point if strongly disagree is indicated):	
1	14	28	4	30
2	15	29	7	33
3	16	31	19	35
5	17	32	22	36
6	18	34	23	37
8	20	38	34	39
9	21	40		
10	25			
11	26			
12	27			
13				

The items in the attitude scale sampled various aspects influencing attitudes toward physical education. Items were labeled on the basis of which aspect it measured, as judged by a panel of five professionals in the field of physical education. The five aspects measured are given below with the items in each cluster itemized.

Social aspects	Psychological aspects	Administrative aspects	Physical aspects
1	5	4	2
8	6	7	3
9	17	11	10
13	18	12	15
14	23	22	19
16	25	29	24
20	26	30	27
21	28	32	31
	33	38	34
	36		35
			37
			39
			40

ATTITUDE INVENTORY

Directions: Below you will find some statements about physical education. I would like to know how you feel about each statement. Please consider physical education only as you know it as an activity course taught during a regular class period. No reference is intended to varsity or intramural sports.

On the separate answer sheet, record your reaction to each statement in terms of:

A	B	C
Strongly agree	Agree, but not strongly	Neutral

E	E
Disagree, but not strongly	Strongly disagree

After reading each statement carefully, go to the answer sheet and opposite the number of the statement, blacken in the area which best expresses your feeling about the statement. For example: if you agree with a statement, decide whether you simply agree or strongly agree, then blacken in the area in the proper column opposite the number of that statement. If you are undecided (or neutral) concerning your feeling about the statement, then blacken in the area in the column marked "C," but try to avoid marking "C" or "neutral" too often.

Remember — this is NOT a test — there are no right or wrong answers. I am interested in knowing how you *feel* toward physical education. Your answers will not affect your grade in any course so please BE TRUTHFUL AND ANSWER EVERY STATEMENT.

1. Physical education provides leadership opportunities for everyone.
2. Physical education contributes to the physical development of the students.
3. One who participates in physical education feels healthy.
4. I dislike dressing and undressing for physical education class.
5. It is not possible for everyone to be good at every game, but it is fun to try.
6. Physical education helps to work off emotional tensions.
7. I am afraid of not succeeding in physical education.
8. Playing with others in physical education class is fun.
9. I like to participate in competition between teams.
10. Physical education provides an outlet for extra energy.
11. Teachers of physical education take into consideration the physical needs of the students.
12. Physical education should be required for graduation from high school.
13. I enjoy keeping score for a game, but would rather play.
14. Learning to play in a group is a major contribution of physical education to one's personality.
15. One should take physical education even if it were not a required course.
16. Physical education class provides a relaxed atmosphere in which to make friends.
17. Physical education contributes to the mental development of the students.
18. I like physical education.
19. A physical education class does not improve health.
20. I like being with others in a physical education class.
21. Skills learned in physical education classes are useful in social life.
22. I don't like my body to be exposed in a gym uniform.
23. I like competition among students in a physical education class.
24. I get all the physical exercise I need in just taking care of my daily needs
25. I look forward to physical education classes with enthusiasm.
26. Through physical education one learns how to be a good sport.

Figure 9-2. (continued)

27. I would advise anyone to take physical education if he/she were physically able.
28. If a sport skill is within the limits of a person's physical abilities, he/she should try to do it.
29. I would rather play than watch a game.
30. I feel uncomfortable in a physical education class.
31. One who participates in physical education looks healthy.
32. Physical education helps develop self-confidence.
33. It is not easy to relax in a physical education class.
34. If physical education were an elective, I would choose to take it.
35. I feel awkward in a physical education class.
36. Physical education class upsets a person emotionally.
37. Physical education does not help one to control his/her bodily movements.
38. In a physical education class, everyone should be allowed to participate.
39. I do not want to be in good physical condition.
40. Participation in physical education makes for a more wholesome outlook on school life.

objects as self, groups, and authority. A great deal of information can be gleaned from using such a technique. Although more teacher time is required to gather data on attitudes, it can provide a useful key to individual program planning.

Rating Scales

Rating scales may be completed by either the student (self-reporting) or the teacher (unobtrusive measures), according to the capabilities of the student being assessed. A self-reporting rating scale may be used by the adapted physical educator to determine students' interests in terms of class activities. For example, the students may be asked to rate a number of activities on a 5-point scale: 5 = my favorite; 4 = I like it a lot; 3 = it's okay; 2 = I don't like it; 1 = I don't like it at all. This scale is useful (especially at the secondary level) in determining activity units through which individualized goals and objectives can be achieved. Another form of rating scale is to have students rank-order their preferences. For example, a number of different ways of forming teams for class participation is listed: using skill test results to balance the teams, teacher chooses, team captains choose, and so on. The students are then asked to place a "1" on the list in front of the method they like best, a "2" in front of the method they like next best, and so on. The

method preferred by the majority of students is the one that will be used.

Sociometric Techniques

Sociometric tools are used to measure the amount of organization shown by social groups (Moreno, 1934). These tools may be used by the adapted physical educator to determine who students know in the class, or who students would like to participate with in physical education activities. For example, in planning large or small group activities, the teacher can use these techniques unobtrusively to determine which students interact and how many are interacting at one time in a play situation.

Todd (1953) suggests two types of sociometric tests that are particularly useful in physical education: (1) acquaintance volume test and (2) functional choice test. The functional choice test, which is thought to be the most useful to the adapted physical educator, will be the only one discussed here.

The *functional choice test* measures who desires to be with whom. Class members are asked to indicate whom they would like to be with in various contexts (including being on a team, going on a picnic, or being in the same class), as well as whom they would reject. Degrees of proximity to another classmate can be determined by including activities that

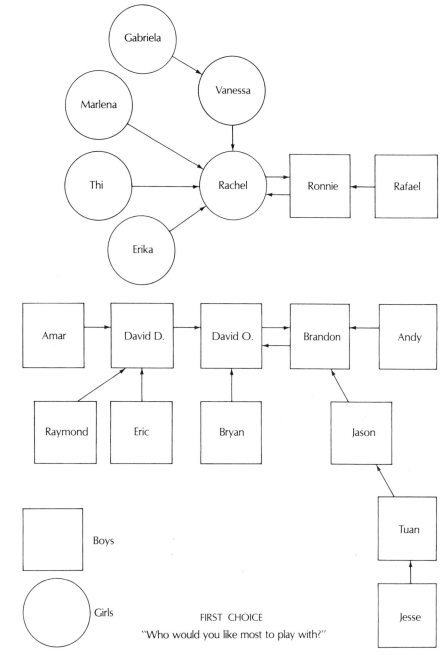

Figure 9-3. The sociogram is a diagrammatic representation of social interactions. SOURCE: Rozanne La Russo, CSULA class assignment.

FIRST CHOICE

"Who would you like most to play with?"

require only one other person, a small group, a larger group, and a very large group. Nonverbal students may be asked to "point to" or "show me the person," and may respond by walking over to them and touching them.

This technique may be used as an unobtrusive measure by observing what children play or in other ways interact with the other children in the group. The number of "contacts" can be tallied on a sociometric tally sheet (Kozman, 1951:200) or on a sociogram (see

Figure 9-4. These children have selected their playmates, as indicated by the sociogram shown in Figure 9-3.

Figure 9-3) — a diagrammatic representation of the various contacts (Jennings, 1948). (See Figure 9-4.) The types of contacts can also be recorded on the sociogram by color coding or number coding the contacts to represent parameters of interest (e.g., sharing a toy, verbal request, aggressive behavior).

UNOBTRUSIVE MEASURES

Unobtrusive measures generally require less teacher-pupil contact time, because they can take place without the physical presence of the student. "Unobtrusive," as used in measurement, refers to the indirect collection of data — that is, without the student being aware of it (Webb, 1966). In adapted physical education, unobtrusive measures provide ways of collecting data in a time efficient manner that cannot be obtained by observing, testing, or asking the student; they may also validate or substitute for self-reporting. The three types of unobtrusive measures discussed in this section are (1) rating scales; (2) case studies; and (3) anecdotal records.

Rating Scales

Rating scales can be used in lieu of self-reporting for students who are incapable of self-reporting, or who are not considered reliable reporters of their own behavior, feelings, and attitudes. For the adapted physical educator, the greatest value in using a rating scale unobtrusively is that data can be gathered on what the student actually *does* in a physical activity context. Rating scales are more useful than developmental profiles and observational techniques in measuring play behavior and indirectly measuring social development and self-esteem when the degree of performance is preferred over dichotomous scores. Items of interest in measuring self-esteem may include "plays cooperatively with others" (a clue to the appropriateness of group activities); "initiates _____" (a particular activity defined on the individual education plan); and "is willing to try something new" (a clue to potentially needed teaching strategies). The score is commonly placed on a 5-point scale that includes "always," "almost always," "sometimes," "seldom," and "never" to reflect the frequency with which the stated behav-

Figure 9-5. Self-esteem questionnaire.

Name_____   Observer_____

Below are some statements about situations involving games and number tasks. These statements have nothing whatsoever to do with the student's competence or functioning level, but rather with his or her tendency to approach or avoid these two types of situations. Please put an "X" in the column that best describes the behavior of the student named above, in relation to each of the statements.

The person whose name appears above . . .	Almost always	Often	Sometimes	Seldom	Almost never	Behavior not emitted
1. continues work involving numbers, even though the use of numbers is difficult for him/her.	____	____	____	____	____	_____
2. has indicated that he/she dislikes tasks involving numbers.	____	____	____	____	____	_____
3. plays noncompetitive games with his/her peers.	____	____	____	____	____	_____
4. works with numbers whenever it is necessary.	____	____	____	____	____	_____
5. plays competitive games or sports with his/her peers.	____	____	____	____	____	_____
6. initiates playing games or sports by inviting others to join in.	____	____	____	____	____	_____
7. shows signs of frustration when unsuccessful in a game or sport.	____	____	____	____	____	_____
8. quits playing games or sports when he/she is unsuccessful.	____	____	____	____	____	_____
9. has indicated that he/she enjoys tasks involving numbers.	____	____	____	____	____	_____
10. has indicated that he/she is good in games or sports.	____	____	____	____	____	_____

ior is demonstrated. Negative behaviors can also be included, with the scoring reversed. The total score then represents the positive or negative self-esteem relative to physical activity.

The Self-Esteem Questionnaire is an example of this type of tool. Because it was designed to measure approach and avoidance behaviors relative to specific activities (Seaman, 1972), any activity can be entered in the statements. Unlike an attitude inventory, this too directly measures what a student is actually doing relative to an attitude object, and indirectly (unobtrusively) measures self-esteem (see Figure 9-5).

Case Studies

While case studies have enjoyed greater use in medicine and business than in education, they have great potential for use by the adapted physical educator. Two types of case studies have particular relevance to the physical education setting: (1) the diagnostic case study, and (2) the incidence report (Willings, 1968), sometimes referred to in physical education literature as the anecdotal record. As used in business, the case method refers to the use of cases for decision making, usually in management training (Leenders and Erskine, 1973). Because decision making is part of the assessment process, this method of data collection should not be excluded from consideration. As outlined by Leenders and Erskine, steps involved in the case study include personal analysis, discussion with others, definition of the problem, identification of alternatives, statement of objectives, establishing decision criteria, selecting a course of action, and planning for implementation.

The case study has five notable features: (1) it is a bit of history (accurately reported); (2) it indicates relationships between people and events; (3) it depicts motion (the chronology of a story); (4) it is a picture (for our purposes, of a special child); and (5) it has integrity, because it is not biased by the reporter (Pigors and Pigors, 1961:18–19). The advantage of the diagnostic case study over the use of data sheets (which are used to report formal performance testing or direct measures) is that it allows the teacher to record not only the results of measurement, but also such results of observations of behavior as reactions to the examiner, to required tasks, and to other children. Thus a complete picture may be drawn of the child about whom a decision will be made by the interdisciplinary team. At its 1979 meeting, the International Congress of Health, Physical Education, and Recreation cited greater development and use of the case study as a tool for better serving handicapped individuals in health, physical education, and recreation. The following diagnostic case studies are offered as examples.

SAMPLE CASE STUDY 1

Identifying Information

Name: Sunny
Birthdate: 1/15/60
Father: Carl   *Occupation:* Chef
Mother: Susan   *Occupation:* Housewife
Siblings: Sister, 22; sister, 24

Birth History

Pregnancy: 9 months.
Birth conditions: 14 hours labor; birthweight — 4 lbs., 7 oz.; complications — difficulty breathing (anoxia), cord wrapped around neck twice, color — pasty.
Conditions following birth: incubator, oxygen, hospitalized for two weeks after birth.

Physical and Developmental Data

Health history: History of seizures from age 1, at which time she contracted pneumonia and ran fever of 105 degrees.

— Diagnosed as having neurological dysfunction (petit mal) at 3 yrs.; given dilantin and mebarol.

— Second convulsion 1965 — generalized seizure.

— At age 6, grand mal; EEG disclosed Minor Convulsive Disorder. EEG was abnormal, the bilateral occipital lobe showed spikes, slowing, and slow waves; placed on anticonvulsants (dilantin, phenobarbital, and zarontin); later placed on mysoline because EEG found temporal lobe abnormality; at age 6, behavior included hyperactivity to the point that mother kept her home from school on rainy days so she would not upset the class.

— After this, major and minor seizures at 6, 10-13 years characterized by brief episodes of staring.

Present health: Cranial nerves within normal limits, deep tendon reflexes — hypoactive; but present bilaterally; no pathological reflexes; seizures during sleep.

Developmental history: Walk — 12 months.

— Toilet trained at 2 years.

— Began talking at 2 years.

— Glasses since 8 years.

— Perceptual problems.

— Occasionally lapses into bizarre sentence structure or irrelevant discussion; usually quiet.

— Clumsy child due to perceptual problems.

Social and Personal Factors

Friends: Never made friends during elementary school, played by herself on the playground, was observed standing and staring at the sun frequently, which she readily admitted doing. At Interim Classroom, NPI [Neuropsychiatric Institute], 10/73 peer interaction was inappropriate, related more readily to adults than peers; was required to approach another pupil at least one time to play a game at each recess or she would lose a behavior point. This approach worked satisfactorily; in fact, she seemed relieved to be forced into interaction.

Sibling relationships: Normal. When rebellious or angry, older sister is only one who can calm her down.

Hobbies, interests, recreational activities: Enjoys discussing and learning about her Italian and Puerto Rican heritage; writing love stories involving movie or singing idols; much infatuated with rock group Tony Orlando and Dawn (Tony is Puerto Rican).

Home and parent attitude: Short temper, noncompliance, rebellious and aggressive behavior. Note: parents had no response to question, "What pleases you most about your child?"

Personal: Psychological work-up suggests psychological disorder is present. Behavior: going into trances, short attention span, imaginary playmates, irrelevant and disorganized behavior, problems with hyperactivity. Individual and family therapy since 1974. Does not express herself; inability to deal adaptively with angry feelings.

Educational Factors

School experiences: Had attended EH [i.e., educationally handicapped] classes since kindergarten; never diagnosed as MR [i.e., mentally retarded]. From 1968, placed in EH classes except for PE and electives.

10/73: Enrolled in Neuropsychiatric Institute School—Interim classroom for behavioral and academic assessment. Referral to NPI because of increasing rebellious and aggressive behavior; program is two hours per day with individualized program; made progress in all areas, especially social.

1/75: Enrolled in Almansor Education Center for the Learning Disabled—junior high classroom

Achievement scores: Diagnosed as mildly retarded at UCLA; full scale test performance (WISC)—borderline of intellectual function; Verbal Scale functioning at top of retarded range; tests revealed problems of lack of organization, poor short-term memory.

1/75 WRAT: reading 5.2; spelling 5.5; arithmetic 5.7

3/76 WRAT: reading 7.5; spelling 5.8; arithmetic 6.3

Teachers' reports:

Sunny has made gains in academic areas and is working diligently and independently.

She has a good attitude toward her learning problem and is able to explain to aides and practicum students not to get angry with her because she is a slow learner. When first entering Almansor, she retreated to her desk in the corner and refused to acknowledge anyone. She still uses the bathroom as a haven from frustrating tasks, although this is lessening.

She now takes part in conversation with three people and functions well during the lunch-hour card games.

Daily living tasks are age adequate; she is mindful of her appearance.

Progress Reports

April 22, 1976

Slaps ball rather than dribbling; when moving and dribbling, can keep control of ball but must bend at knees and hips (crouching low to ball) in order to keep up with ball. In this position she has a difficult time changing directions; can make 5 out of 10 baskets but requires a long time before actually shooting. She catches well stationary, misses when running and catching, (i.e., uses protective actions rather than catching). Throwing form is stiff and reduces accuracy of aim. Unable to pass towards side when moving.

Works well with other students; talks continuously rather than doing task, talking ceases as soon as she begins activity.

April 29, 1976

No real changes, works well with others though and gets very excited after successful passing and moving drills. She informed me that it is hard for her to keep her eye on the ball and she does tend to look sideways at the ball or target.

May 13, 1976

A good day! Sunny put glasses on during middle of class, which seemed to improve performance slightly; catching and throwing were much better. She appears more comfortable with the ball and is catching more often rather than protecting herself from being hit. Aim is much better. She is anticipating consequences of her throw and partner's running pattern very well. Changes focus from dribbling ball to partner with more ease and consequent pass is made more quickly than previously. Dribbling is still in crouched position although a little less flexed. Pivoting and passing is good, but can not pass towards side of body while facing forwards; instead she will turn and use front pass. Talking in between tasks has decreased as she is more excited about playing, but still requires long time before shooting.

June 3, 1976

Dribbling — no longer slaps ball with preferred hand (left), dribbling while moving has improved. She still bends at hips and knees but flexion is less. Changing directions is much easier for her now. Most improvement can be seen in catching when running, she attempts to reach for the ball and protective actions are rarely seen. Throwing actions are less stiff. I tried blocking drills for the first time today, and she did very well, especially with bounce pass under opponent's arm, although she had to stop and hesitated before passing ball. She talks much less and plays more. In man-to-man defense, she keeps right with assigned player and constantly looks behind her for that player! Put glasses on before we started game as if signaling she meant action.

I just noticed today that she jumps up and down more when facing the windows in the gym. Locomotion is smoother with her back to the sun. I remember in her file it said that she used to enjoy standing and staring at the sun; I wonder how the two are related. I wish that I had noticed this sooner. It would have been interesting to "play around" with lighting and see if any beneficial trends in motor patterns could have emerged.

SOURCE: Bonnie Thomson, California State University at Los Angeles, class assignment.

SAMPLE CASE STUDY 2

Identifying Information

Name: Alice
Birthdate: August 6, 1961
School grade: 7th, Almansor Educational Center
Parents: Placed at 3 years of age in present foster home, was in two homes before this.
Father: Bob *Occupation:* Salesman
Mother: Jane *Occupation:* Secretary
Sibling: Foster sister, 10 years
Referral: to Almansor from General Pediatric Clinic, July, 1974, John Morgan, M.D. To General Pediatric Clinic, November, 1973, from elementary school, because of long history of school, and behavior problems.

Birth History

Pregnancy: No information available.
Birth conditions: No information available.

Other: Mother in mental institution when born; put up for adoption but determined ''unsuitable for adoption'' and placed in two foster homes before present placement.

Physical and Developmental Data

Health history: German measles, measles, chicken pox, mumps, normal amount of colds.

Present health: A healthy child but rounded shoulders, severe kyphosis; pubertal changes but flat chest; reflexes — normal; gross coordination — normal; cerebellar (balance) — normal; sensory systems — failed two-point discrimination 20% of the time; appears tired or depressed; is sullen in speech and attitude.

Developmental History

— No information available for birth to 3 years.
— Could not walk properly at age 3 when placed in present foster home.
— Clumsy child, nervous child.
— Toilet trained — 4 years.
— Talked in sentences — 5 years.
— Stares a lot ever since 3 years, as though in world of her own.
— Glasses — 12 years
— Right-handed, right-eyed, right-footed.
— Unable to hop rhythmically accurately after three trials.
— Unable to copy examiner in rhythmic clapping.

Social and Personal Factors

Friends: Has always had difficulty making friends because of explosive and violent temper; at present can function with two or three peers at a low frustration task for approximately twenty minutes.

Siblings: Always fighting with other foster children as a child and preferred to be by herself; much difficulty with present foster sister.

Hobbies, interests, recreational activities: Enjoys crafts, especially building with scrap materials; likes athletics, especially basketball, but is reluctant to play basketball with boys in the class.

Home and parent attitude: Does not obey, argues a lot, stubborn, moody, loses temper easily, especially when provoked, can be nice when she wants to be.

Personal: Diagnosed as schizoid personality and depressive reaction in 1972; long history of school and behavior problems, which got worse when she discovered she was a foster child (1/74); self-destructive behavior, beginning 1/74 (i.e., swallowing pins in class and poking veins with needle); laughs inappropriately.

School Experiences

Kindergarten: Regular class
1st–3rd (1968–71): EMR [i.e., educable mentally retarded] class.
4th–6th (1971–73): Regular class.
Expelled from school November, 1973 (two months after starting 6th grade), and has been seeing a psychiatrist ever since.
No school from November, 1973, to September, 1974.
Entered Almansor Educational Center for the Learning Handicapped, September, 1974—junior high class.
Achievement Scores:
3/76 WRAT: spelling 4.3; reading 4.6; arithmetic 4.9
9/74 WRAT: spelling 3.0; reading 3.2; arithmetic 2.0; difficulty recognizing cut-up pictures of familiar objects.
4/74 WISC: 57 I.Q.; mild mental retardation; greatest impairments in perceptual organization and spatial visualization.

Teachers' Reports

When Alice first entered Almansor, all she did was scream and throw violent temper tantrums (throwing chairs and other objects across the room). The students in her class quickly learned to avoid her and/or not provoke her. At the end of this school year (1976), she has become very conscientious about her schoolwork, consistent in completion of academic assignments, and is making a great deal of progress academically.

Daily living tasks are age-adequate. She is mindful of her appearance and able to travel by bus to and from school (10 miles).

Interpersonal relations are still somewhat delicate, but emotional status is far more stable.

Progress Reports

April 22, 1976

Good stationary and moving dribbling skills, both hands; passing and catching are good; can make basket from free-throw line, 4 out of 10 times—uses one handed push shot, but frustration increases each time she misses, which ruins form and concentration (i.e., she misses more often); running and changing direction is very good.

Expressed disinterest for about one-third of class period, although participated during this time, after coaxing; dislikes working with others, especially Starr; once she is involved in playing, is genuinely enthusiastic, hamming it up; low tolerance for mistakes in others and rarely converses with other two girls.

April 29, 1976

Expressed disinterest and needed some coaxing in order to play; worked with others in pairs without complaining, but made difficult passes for others to catch; seemed unchallenged by dribbling and passing drills (probably justifiably so, as she is well skilled in these areas), and began wandering off when I would not comply with her requests to shoot baskets. Finally, I made shooting contingent upon completion of two more drills and she worked, although hurriedly, making it harder for the other girls to keep up with her in drills of running, dribbling, and passing.

The girls played "Around the World" and she did very well close to the basket – 7 to 10 feet (no more than 2 tries per station), the further out she got, the more frustrated she became because of her misses and consequently began shooting haphazardly. It was a real blow to her when Starr, the least skilled of the group, made a shot she had missed repeatedly.

May 13, 1976

Expressed disinterest but did not need coaxing to participate; got really enthused about pivoting and passing drill and started joking and talking to other girls. What a great change! But, I should have remembered her frustration with shooting at last week's class. She began missing and shooting haphazardly, walked to other side of gym, came back, missed a few more, then stormed out of the gym. Thank heavens for May, who followed her and calmed her down. I will be more attentive to Alice's signs of frustration and next time introduce a new activity, change to something previously successful, or sit girls down and talk about basketball or feeling frustrated – depending upon the situation.

May 27, 1976

Alice alone did not express usual disinterest until we entered the gym and saw one man playing basketball alone. But, this was more embarrassment than disinterest and was only momentary. Good passing while moving — could place the ball in front of and behind me, above and below my waist upon request very well and seemed to enjoy my trying to fake her out (she was successful here); turns quickly and easily when dribbling if I approach her from the side to take the ball, indecision of action if approached head-on; shooting for baskets is still frustrating — but less so today because other girls were absent and probably because she did not have any image to maintain. I began asking her what kind of a shot she made (i.e., too short, hard, etc.), and what she could do to improve it. She responded well to this (i.e., frustration at missing was less and I could tell she was compensating for mechanics of previous shot). After a while, she was consistently hitting the rim and concentrating more on target just prior to shooting.

Alice was very receptive today and readily accepted my changes from shooting to dribbling, which was a problem in the past; while we rested she really opened up and began talking about her likes and dislikes. I will be interested to see if this receptivity carries over with the other girls since she usually does well on a one-to-one basis anyway.

NOTE: The last day I was there, Alice missed PE with me because during that time, the school administrator was telling her she would be removed from her present foster home. Her next move, either to a new home or residential school, is unknown.

SOURCE: Bonnie Thomson, California State University at Los Angeles, class assignment.

SAMPLE CASE STUDY 3

Purpose of Report

To show the physiological and psychological changes of a C5 quadraplegic within a ten-year span, and the resulting development of a secondary rehabilitation program.

Hospital History

2/7/67–2/18/67 San Gabriel Hospital
2/18/67–4/18/67 Kaiser Foundation Hospital, Hollywood
4/18/67–11/17/67 Rancho Los Amigos Hospital

Patient History

On February 7, 1967, Vincent, a sixteen-year-old white male, sustained a traumatic compression injury of the spinal column at level C5-C6 in a high jump accident. From the onset of the injury to 48 hours he was only able to move his head and neck, and shrug his shoulders. He was transferred to Kaiser approximately ten days later, when his condition stabilized, and remained in traction for another seven weeks. At this time he was fitted with a leather brace from chin to navel for support.

On April 18, 1967, Vincent was transferred to Rancho Los Amigos Hospital for initial rehabilitation. He had several complications to his condition upon admission (i.e., thrombophlebitis of the lower extremities, diabetes mellitus, pressure sore on the left heel, and a urinary tract infection). His initial examination showed the pattern of a complete quadraplegic below C6 level, with sensation along the thumb, index finger, and radial side of forearm. His muscle picture was: deltoid — good minus; clavicular pectoralis — trace; elbow flexion — good; elbow extension — negative; radial wrist extension — trace to poor.

On May 9, 1967, the myelogram revealed minimal wedging of C6 and no evidence of total obstruction from L2 to the basiocciput.

On May 11, 1967, he had a posterior fusion operation of C4-C6. The surgical report stated that there were bilateral lamina fractures at C5. The spinal cord was inspected beneath the fracture site and ''there was no evidence of pressure on the cord and the nerve roots appeared to be free.''

May 17, 1967, the updated muscle picture was: bilateral deltoids — fair; biceps — fair plus; upper and middle trapezius — good; internal rotators — fair; radial wrist extensors — poor; and all other muscles were zero. He was then placed on a two-hour a day treatment program for muscle strengthening and range of motion exercises. On May 18, 1967, he was fitted with hand splints.

Upon discharge on November 17, 1967, Vincent had lost 35 pounds, and has had slow increase in strength. He is independent in brushing his teeth, shaving, propelling his wheelchair, but needs assistance in dressing and putting on the hand splints. It was recommended that he continue the strengthening program, his typing and writing skills, daily skin inspections, and changing his posture every two hours to prevent pressure sores.

There is no information on the patient's history until nine years later. On November 4, 1976, Vincent was evaluated by another technique known as the ''monopolar needle electrode'' method, by which the electrical potentials of the nerves are tested through electromyography (EMG). The results of this test showed that on voluntary contraction, up to 80% of the normal number of units was observed firing in the supraspinatus, rhomboids, and up to 40%

of normal in the left deltoid, 20% of normal in the right deltoid and 20% of the biceps bilaterally. The triceps were firing 10% of normal on the left and 5% of normal on the right. The brachioradialis was firing 20% of normal bilaterally. Voluntary control was also seen in the cervical paraspinal muscles in the C5, 6, 7 regions with a small amount of voluntary control in the upper thoracic area.

The comments given by the physician were as follows: "The patient clearly shows normal innervation of C5 innervated muscles, partial innervation of C6, 7, 8, and T1 innervated muscles of the upper extremities.... On the left side the degree of remaining innervation is greater than on the right. Large complex units indicate peripheral sprouting and reinnervation has followed in some instances the denervation.... The long complex units which indicate reinnervation are not as large as often observed and probably indicate a considerable degree of disuse atrophy...."

The sharp peaks for the left brachioradialis muscle which is C6 innervated shows the existence of voluntary muscle control below the lesion level. With such encouraging results, Vincent became aware that a higher level of physical functioning could be achieved, so he developed a secondary rehabilitation program.

Secondary Rehabilitation Routine

His routine consisted of gross and fine motor activities.

Gross motor activities:

A. Those activities done at home
   1. Torso-twisting: From the sitting position in the wheelchair, the subject had a 25-pound bar placed across the shoulders and rotated his torso back and forth. Vincent had increased his endurance from 5 minutes to 25 minutes, increased range of motion 35 degrees, and also gained strength in the upper trunk muscles.
   2. Standing: Performed in a mechanical standing frame to help reduce the incidence of colitis and spasticity of the trunk and lower extremity. Vincent tries to stand for about 45 minutes at a time.

B. Those activities performed at Adapted Physical Education
   1. Pull Down Exercising: Done at the pull down station of the Universal weight machine. Strap wrists to the bar; then, from the sitting position, pull arms down and into chest. Vincent began this exercise

with 3 sets of 10 repetitions at 10 pounds and improved to 3 sets of 10 repetitions at 30 pounds.

2. Upper Extremity Exercising: 2½-pound plates were attached to the arm by wrist braces and the following was performed:
   a. 3 sets of 15 repetitions of arm abduction.
   b. 3 sets of 15 repetitions of arm flexion.
   c. 3 sets of 15 repetitions of horizontal abduction. These exercises were to be performed bilaterally; however, due to the instability and weakness of Vincent's trunk, these exercises were done one arm at a time. By the end of 10 weeks, he was doing 3 sets of these repetitions with a 5 pound plate on his left arm.
   d. After the sixth week, Vincent added 3 sets of 15 repetitions of biceps curls.
      These exercises not only resulted in an increase in strength, but also in more fluid and coordinated movement.

3. Wheelchair Pushing: A wheelchair with peg extensions was used by Vincent to propel himself through the locker room hallway. He began by pushing approximately 150 feet per session. After 10 weeks, he was propelling himself 100 yards in 50 minutes.

Fine Motor Activities:

Neuromuscular re-education was being attempted at Lyn Taylor R.P.T. Clinic through EMG and biofeedback approximately 40 minutes twice a week. Some of the muscles being re-educated included abdominals, back extensors, wrist and finger extensors and flexors, triceps, and thumb flexors and extensors. Although some of the muscle power exhibited by these muscles is only 1% of normal, there is an indication that voluntary control is slowly improving.

As of December 16, 1980, Vincent has become even more independent of other people. He can now drive a car, performs self-range of motion, increased trunk stability, and performs a looping depression transfer to and from bed. Psychologically, he states that he has regained psychological freedom, has increased his self-image, and now is able to act as a whole entity again after becoming physically active. He has returned to school as a graduate student.

SOURCE: Adapted from a self-report by Jeanette Kaichi, California State University at Los Angeles, class assignment.

Anecdotal Records

The incidence report or anecdotal record has been used for years in physical education (Wikman, 1928), but has particular value for the adapted physical educator in collecting data on attitudes, self-esteem, behavioral disorders, progress, and the like. An anecdote, as used in general literature, is a brief account or story of a specific happening, usually personal or biographical. In adapted physical education, it can help the teacher to maintain current data that can later be used in case studies, program planning, and annual reviews. The anecdotal record focuses on a specific parameter or behavior, such as a temper tantrum. Four elements should be included if the anecdotal record is to have continued usefulness: (1) a description of the antecedent conditions of the happening, including activity being conducted at the time, other children involved, and time of day; (2) a description of the happening or event itself, including movements, crying (if any), and language used; (3) a description of the conditions following the episode to include how the child reacted, how other students reacted, and how you as the teacher acted and reacted; and (4) conclusions and recommendations regarding what precipitated the happening and how it might be avoided in the future.

The anecdote or incident should be recorded as soon after it happens as feasible, in order to assure a clear, accurate report. Recording on index cards is helpful, because it allows easy access and filing by student name so new entries can be added without leafing through a lot of other papers. The record could also include baseline data on target behaviors used to develop a behavior modification program. The frequency of the undesirable target behavior should be recorded during specified time periods daily for one or two weeks. The anecdotal record card can then be pulled from the file and studied before developing the behavior management plan. The anecdotal record shown in Figure 9–6 is offered as an example.

RECOMMENDATIONS FOR DATA COLLECTION

To use the developmental approach effectively, as much information as possible must be brought to bear on the decision-making process. Granted, it is not possible to sample performance in all of the areas discussed in this chapter. The adapted physical educator, therefore, must make some decisions regarding the assessment process. By answering the following questions, the physical education specialist will be able to narrow the focus of the assessment plan for each student, based upon that student's unique characteristics.

1. Do I (the adapted physical educator) have access to an occupational or physical therapist's report of reflex testing?
2. Is there a medical report of a neurological examination, including sensory system function, or any reason to suspect that one might be needed?
3. Do I have a history of developmental milestones or can I get one from other records or the parent?
4. If this student was referred by another professional, what were the reasons for referral?
5. What other special services, if any, is the student receiving (e.g., psychological services; speech, occupational, or physical therapy)?
6. What are the sociological characteristics of the student? (E.g., how does the student feel about himself or herself? About others? About physical activity?)

There are a number of different ways of collecting data for assessment: observation, formal performance testing, direct measures, self-reporting, and unobtrusive measurement. There is no one best method for all teachers in all situations. Many formal testing tools are available on the market, some of which are based on use with normal populations and others on exceptional students. Whether the purpose for testing is placement into a regular or separate class, or whether

Name _Ronnie_

Date	THERAPY LOG
10/29	Scooter board down ramp onto mat with tactile stimulators — very good with board turning. Doesn't fully extend body when rolling on mat. "Simon Says" on balance board very good, except slight problem with left & right side distinction on command. Problems with responding to command discipline.
10/31	Spun 3 turns — 7 rotations, 7 rotations and 10 rotations. Walked the lines with little difficulty — ½ turn onto mat - hit suspended ball w/colored stick while on balance board.
11/7	Seemingly more hyper today. Copied 1-7 w/difficulty. ½ turn & roll onto ramp.
11/21	One-half and full turns onto mat. Excellent in net - calmed - tolerated more large circles, etc. Only once showed dizzy (scared) reaction.

Figure 9-6. Anecdotal record.

the intent is to measure progress toward goals of an individualized educational program, the method or tool selected may vary.

For placement purposes, tools that are normed on the normal school population should serve as the criteria against which students with special needs should be compared. The Perceptual-Motor Survey* appears to be most practical for school use, since it can be administered to a group and samples a broad spectrum of sensory and perceptual motor functions. The Denver Developmental Screening Test is a useful tool for measuring motor development, and administration time is reduced by allowing some data collection by report of the parent. Motor ability and motor skills as well as information gathered indirectly on sensory and perceptual-motor function and fitness can be obtained through use of the Bruninks-Oseretsky Motor Proficiency Test. Although individually administered, this tool has a short form and contains norms on youngsters from four to fourteen years of age. Mr. Peanut's Guide to Physical Fitness, used in conjunction with the AAHPERD Lifetime Health-Related Fitness Test, can give a comprehensive picture of fitness with a minimum amount of teacher time. Posture screening using the CSULA Group Screening Form (or similar instrument) can be used to screen large numbers of students efficiently, with direct measures following as needed. Sport skills are easily measured using the series of sports skills tests published by the AAHPERD.

Somewhat different recommendations are offered for the purpose of measuring progress toward educational goals among students in separate adapted physical education classes and for severely handicapped and very young children. Criterion-referenced rather than norm-referenced tools may be more appropriate in some instances, particularly if change in performance takes place over a long period of time. The Koontz Child Development Program may provide

*See Chapter 8 for more detailed descriptions of these tests.

more useful information when used with young children (0 to forty-eight months) or very low functioning students, since it contains a sequence of developmental activities that can be used to develop performance objectives. The California State University Motor Development Checklist, although giving a general picture of development of motor patterns and skills, covers the range of development from five months to seven years and can be administered, for the most part, in an unstructured play environment. Fitness progress for the blind or retarded could be measured using one of the tools listed in Chapter 8 as appropriate for use with specific disability groups.

The most desirable solution to the assessment process is the development of an instrument such as the Adapted Physical Education Assessment Scale (APEAS) currently being developed by Los Angeles Unified School District. APEAS meets most of the criteria for test selection, and measures a broad spectrum of motor performance. Once completely normed, APEAS will be appropriate for all students from five to eighteen years, and the norming sample will include representative samples of students with special needs. Another solution, for tests measuring a more narrow spectrum of parameters, would be to include students who have special needs in the norming sample. Including exceptional students in the norming sample would then net a set of norms that would be truly representative of the general population.

SUMMARY

In addition to performance testing, taking direct measures, and gathering data through observation, the adapted physical educator has available tools and procedures for self-reporting and unobtrusive measures. Self-reporting instruments include attitude inventories, rating scales used by the teacher, and sociometric techniques. Unobtrusive measures include rating scales used by the student, case studies, and anecdotal records. These tools and procedures can be used to bring other than performance measures into consideration in the decision-making process. Gathering data about how a student thinks, feels, and interacts with others provides relevant information for planning appropriate physical education programs.

BIBLIOGRAPHY

Guthrie, G. M. "Non-Verbal Expression of Self-Attitudes of Retardates." *American Journal of Mental Deficiency* 69 (July 1964): 42–49.

Jennings, H. *Sociometry in Group Relations.* New York: American Council of Education, 1948.

Kozman, H. C., ed. *Group Processes in Physical Education.* New York: Harper and Brothers, 1951.

Leenders, M. R., and Erskine, J. A. *Case Research: The Case Writing Process.* Canada: Research and Publications Division, School of Business Administration, The University of Western Ontario, London, 1973.

Likert, R. "A Technique for the Measurement of Attitudes." In *Archives of Psychology*, vol. 22, edited by R. S. Woodworth. New York: Columbia University Press, 1932–1933, pp. 140–146.

Meyrowitz, J. H. "Self-derogation in Young Retardates and Special Class Placement." *Child Development* 33 (1962): 443–51.

Moreno, J. L. *Who Shall Survive? A New Approach to the Problem of Human Relationships.* Washington, D.C.: Nervous and Mental Disease Publishing, 1934.

Pigors, P., and Pigors, F. *Case Method in Human Relations: The Incident Process.* New York: McGraw-Hill, 1961.

Posavac, E. J., and Carey, R. G. *Program Evaluation: Methods and Case Studies.* Englewood Cliffs, New Jersey: Prentice-Hall, 1980.

Seaman, J. A. *The Effects of a Bowling Program on Number Concepts and Social Self-Esteem of Mentally Retarded Children.* Bloomington, Indiana: unpublished doctoral thesis, 1972.

Thurstone, L. L., and Chave, E. J. *The Measurement of Attitude.* Chicago: University of Chicago Press, 1929.

Todd, F. "Sociometry in Physical Education." *Journal of Health, Physical Education and Recreation* 24 (May 1953).

Webb, E. J., et al. *Unobtrusive Measures: Nonreactive Research in the Social Sciences.* Chicago: Rand McNally, 1966.

Werner, H., and Carrison, C. "Measurement and Development of Finger Schema in Mentally Retarded Children." *Journal of Educational Psychology* 33 (April 1942): 252–264.

Wickman, E. K. *Children's Behavior and Teachers' Attitudes.* New York: Commonwealth Fund, 1928.

Willings, D. R. *How to Use the Case Study in Training for Decision Making.* London: Business Publications Limited, 1968.

Ziller, R. C., et al. "Self-esteem: A Self-Social Construct." *Journal of Consulting and Clinical Psychology* 33 (February 1969): 84–95.

10   Interpretation

Guiding Questions

1. When should (1) norm-referenced and (2) criterion-referenced tests be used in the assessment process?
2. Define performance sampling, test validity, reliability, and specificity.
3. How can test results be used as indicators and to find relationships?
4. What are the six procedural steps for interpretation?
5. What are the relationships for interpretation among reflex behavior, sensorimotor function, motor development, motor ability, motor skills, and physical fitness?
6. How is the model for interpretation of test results used?
7. What three types of statements should be made in the interpretation of test results?

COMPLETING THE ASSESSMENT PROCESS

Interpretation is the point in the assessment process at which analysis of measurements is done in order to make decisions about a student's educational program. It is probably the most challenging aspect of adapted physical education, since it requires skills that most physical educators have not been taught nor previously been required to demonstrate.

In many instances, the adapted physical educator must adopt a model for interpretation in order to "make sense out of" a student's performance, since many useful tools do not provide such a model. Although tests that have been factor analyzed do provide a model of item relationships, most available tests have not been factor analyzed. Furthermore, a combination of tools may have to be used in order to get a broad picture of a student's performance. Thus it is even more important to use a comprehensive model that allows the adapted physical educator to determine the relationship among poor performances measured by items within a test as well as across tests.

Assessment is required of adapted physical educators for (1) determination of appropriate placement for a student in the least restrictive physical education environment; and (2) individualized program planning. Using measurements to determine appropriate placement is not really new to physical educators; testing for the purpose of classification is commonly used and mentioned by most measurement textbook authors

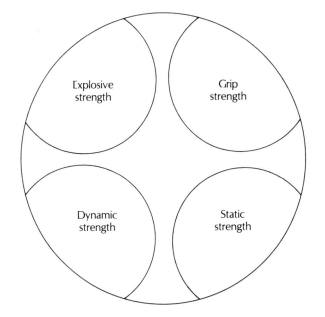

Figure 10-1. Factors used to describe strength.

(e.g., Barrow and McGee, 1979, Baumgartner and Jackson, 1981). These authors, however, are referring to the process of classification or placement of students into homogeneous ability groups or grading categories, or partitioning out students to meet a group need or the instructor's needs. Herein lies a major difference between general and adapted physical education: placement of students into or out of adapted physical education groupings or programs should be based on the student's needs rather than on any external criteria.

Evaluation — referring to the use of norm-referenced tests — should be used in making placement decisions, since consideration must be given to what constitutes the least restrictive environment for a given student. If the student is being assessed for placement into a self-contained adapted physical education class, measurements from norm-referenced tests will demonstrate how the student's performance compares with that of others of the same age and sex. If performance is poor, separate class placement can be justified. Similarly, if a student is being considered for placement from a self-contained adapted physical education class back into the regular physical education

class, the probability of success can best be projected by comparing that student's performance with performance of others in the mainstream.

When assessment is being carried out for the purpose of program planning or continued programming, criterion-referenced tools may — and perhaps should — be used. Even a student's annual goal and short-term performance objectives, if written in measurable terms, can serve as the criterion against which a given performance can be compared. Additionally, if programming in adapted physical education is going to be continued, criterion-referenced tools often provide more useful information regarding program content and sequencing of learning experiences than the typical norm-referenced instrument.

CONCEPTS NEEDED FOR INTERPRETATION

There are six general concepts regarding interpretation of measurements: (1) performance sampling; (2) test validity; (3) test reliability; (4) test specificity; (5) tests as indicators; and (6) test relationships.

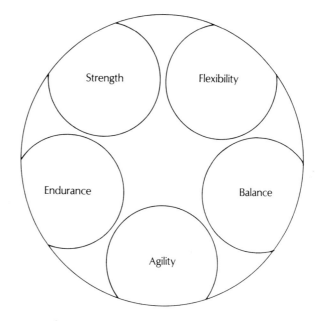

Figure 10–2. Factors used to describe physical fitness.

Performance Sampling

All human qualities are composed of many intricately woven factors, and motor performance is no exception. Because each factor contributes uniquely or in combination to comprise a given quality, it is virtually impossible to measure all of them. Thus the typical approach to measurement is to sample the factors in order to draw conclusions about the integrity of the quality.

Let us take as an example the parameter known as "strength" (the word "parameter" here refers to one of the qualities of motor performance; in this case, strength). Some of the strength factors that can be readily measured make unique or collective contributions to the quality (see Figure 10–1).

As can be seen, the entire area within the circle defining strength is not covered or sampled by the factors indicated. There are some contributions to strength that cannot be reasonably measured in an educational setting (e.g., oxygen transport, the subject's motivation to perform). Furthermore, there are some factors that contribute to strength that are either not

yet fully understood or are so variable that they cannot be consistently measured (e.g., the contributions of hormones and adrenalin). Therefore the aspects of strength that can be reasonably measured are used as a sample of strength to draw conclusions about the overall strength of the performer.

Likewise, the larger parameter of physical fitness is measured by sampling some of the contributing factors. As in the previous example, all of the factors cannot be reasonably measured, nor are all the contributing factors truly known, understood, or agreed upon. Furthermore, all factors do not make equal contributions, nor do they make contributions of the same importance in all situations. Therefore most physical fitness tests sample the larger parameter of physical fitness by measuring performances that are known to contribute to physical fitness, so a conclusion can be made regarding the integrity or level of physical fitness of a given individual. All items on a given fitness test must be administered in order to have an adequate sampling of the overall quality or parameter known as fitness. This process of sampling performance plays a major role in interpretation (see Figure 10–2).

Test Validity

The physical educator must know what the test is intended to measure, and must analyze each test item to validate that it does indeed measure that quality. For example, the APEAS (1979:14) test of static balance gives this instruction:

> Student folds arms (with hands grasping opposite elbows) and holds them close against the chest. Examiner touches the student's right leg and says: "Raise this foot and balance until I tell you to stop, like this." Examiner demonstrates the standing posture. . . .

Another test of static balance, however, may give a somewhat different instruction:

> Examiner stands facing the student and says: "Fold your arms, raise your right leg, and balance as long as you can."

The physical educator who is comparing these two tests for validity should choose the first example as providing the most valid measurement of balance. This instruction allows the student to understand the task by watching the examiner perform, thus eliminating the need to process language concepts. It also has a definite beginning — "RAISE THIS LEG" — and a definite ending — "STOP" — which further eliminates the need to process such information as "Which is the right leg? How long is 'as long as I can'? How many things do I have to do and in what order?" In contrast, a test like the second example can be considered as valid a measure of language and cognition as it is of balance.

Analyzing a test in this way will yield *face or content validity* because, unless there are some subtle forces at work, the test does or does not clearly measure what it claims to measure. Sometimes test makers will report *external validity*. External validity shows what the relationship is between performance on a particular test and some external criterion. The external criterion may be another test that is widely accepted as a valid measure of the same parameter, or it may be a direct measure, rating of the parameter in a game, teacher's or coach's ratings of the level of quality of this parameter in overall performance, and so on.

As an example of validity, let us take a basketball dribble skill test that requires the student to dribble a basketball the length of the court, around three traffic cones, and back. It seems to have face validity in that it does require dribbling the basketball. A criterion for external validity might be the number of turnovers while dribbling that occurred during a game. The relationship between the two scores can be found using a *correlation coefficient*, and that value becomes the *coefficient of external validity*. Unfortunately, test makers in physical education are not particularly consistent in establishing and reporting validity, so it is up to the adapted physical educator to at least establish face validity by analyzing each task. If other factors, such as language and cognition, impinge on the validity of the performance, this must be considered and reported when interpreting the results of measurement.

Test Reliability

The reliability or consistency with which a test measures performance — as well as the magnitude of the measurement error — is crucial. If the inconsistency is great, it could mean the difference between recommending a student for placement in adapted physical education based on testing one day, and *not* recommending placement based on testing a different day. Tests that require multiple trials or practice trials to negate learning, or tests that include several items sampling a given parameter, tend to be more reliable than tests that do not have these features. Even test items that are known to be fairly reliable will result in students obtaining slightly different scores each time they take the test. Because younger children and students who have special needs tend to be less

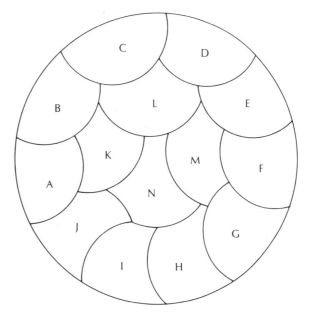

Figure 10-3. All factors of motor performance.

consistent in performance, the factors that affect validity will also influence reliability. Of course it must be remembered that the variance in some performances is inherent in the performer and not due to the measurement device. Thus the adapted physical educator must be alert to the mood and nonverbal cues from the student in order to ascertain both validity and reliability of the performance (Montoye, 1970:82).

The examiner must watch for signs of boredom, lack of motivation, or such statements as, "Can I go back to my room now?" and "How many more do I have to do?" Obviously, a student who cries through the entire testing session, throws a tantrum, or hides under the table is likely to perform better under different conditions on another day. When these situations occur, it is best to report them when interpreting results, and perhaps even recommend retesting once a better rapport is established between the student and examiner.

Test Specificity

Because test items are fairly specific, three or four item tests have obvious limitations. The more samples

of motor performance that can be obtained on a student, the more accurate a picture of "true ability" (see Figure 10-3).

If it were possible to obtain scores on factors A through N, an absolute picture of true ability could be drawn. However, such a task would require an enormous series of tests that would be neither practical nor possible. Thus it can be seen that an unnecessarily lengthy test may be as inappropriate as too short a test. An appropriate test should have enough items to yield valid information for interpretation, yet it should be short enough so as not to interfere with the reliability of performance due to fatigue and boredom. Generally, the expected attention span for the age and disability of the students being tested should be the guide as to the length of the test. A test that exceeds this time span can be partially administered on one day and continued on another day. This break in test administration should also be considered during interpretation.

Some tests are developed in such a way that an *order effect* is present; that is, all the normative data is gathered at one time, with test items given in a specified order. Thus performance on item 2 is influenced by the student's having taken item 1 just before, and item 2 may influence performance on item 3. This order effect is reflected in the norms. Therefore if the teacher stops testing a child after item 8 and begins fresh with item 9 on another day, the child's performance is likely to be different — probably better — than it would have been had it occurred after eight other items. This break in administration should be reported and, if the fresh testing session yields considerably different scores than were expected, the measurements should be interpreted accordingly. Some tests are developed in such a way as to avoid an order effect. Look for this information in the test manual before testing.

Tests as Indicators

Test items indicate areas of weakness for programming (Montoye, 1970:83). Thus a student who does poorly on the flexed arm hang can be described at least as having poor upper arm strength, and possibly poor overall body strength. Physical fitness tests generally have been factor analyzed, and the few items included in the test tend to be the best indicators of a specific parameter. Although other items on the fitness test or other tests are not intended to measure strength specifically, look at the performances on items in which strength is a factor. If the student does poorly on the flexed arm hang, it is possible to find support for the conclusion that the student lacks overall body strength. The interpretation should take into account the source of the student's disability. If the youngster has Duchenne muscular dystrophy, for example, not only will the conclusion be unrevealing, but recommendations for programming are likely to be different than if the student did not have muscular dystrophy.

More often than not, it will be necessary for the adapted physical educator to discover the commonalities among test items in order to find the clusters or areas of weakness indicated by poor performance. For example, balancing on one foot, vertical jump, and curl-ups are common performances used in physical education tests. Balancing on one foot is often found on perceptual-motor, motor ability, or fitness tests; vertical jump is usually seen as a motor ability, fitness, or developmental item; and curl-ups are usually found on fitness tests. It is impossible to generalize on the basis of the category of the test, or draw any specific interpretation or conclusion, since it is very likely that these data were obtained through the use of more than one tool. Therefore the physical educator must find the commonality or commonalities among these three items in order to interpret the measurements — especially if the data have come from three different sources. If left to the examiner, this becomes a question of face or content validity. The question must be asked, "Besides balance, the jumping pattern or jumping ability, and muscular endurance, what other element, parameter, or entity is entering into these performances?" This is determined by logically examining the three performances and finding the common element that, when absent, has caused these three items to cluster together. The conclusion reveals a factor that persists in all three test items, without which performance on all items will be poor (see Figure 10-4).

Test Relationships

Although part of the interpretation process involves finding commonalities to explain a cluster of poor performances, some variables simply have nothing in common with one another. Relationships found in such cases are true relationships. For example, the amount of education and income, age and hair style, and gender and clothing styles are all relationships that tend to exist at a fairly predictable level. Thus information that is available for one variable could be used to in-

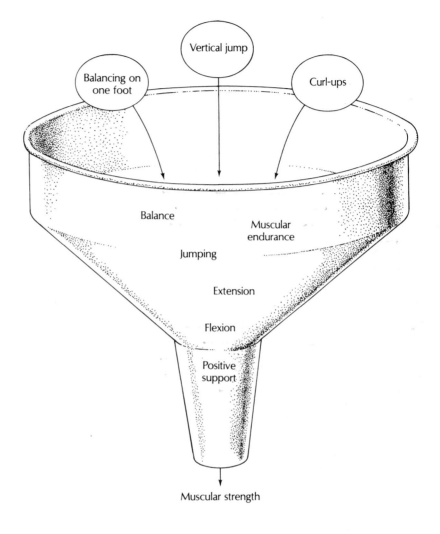

Figure 10-4. Determining commonalities in test item performance.

terpret or explain scores on the other variable, even though they seem to lack a common entity.

If this were to be done <u>statistically</u>, the *coefficient of determination* would be used. This is computed by squaring the correlation coefficient expressing the relationship between the two variables. The resulting value is the shared variance, or the percentage of variance that the two variables share. For example, let us say the relationship between body weight and pull-up score is -.70. The coefficient of determination — $(-.70)^2 = .49$ — tells us that 49 percent of the vari-

ability is due to body weight. In other words, in the case of a heavy boy who does poorly on pull-ups, 49 percent of the cause of his poor performance is the fact that he is so heavy! The other 51 percent of the relationship between the performances is due to other factors. Thus it is necessary to look at clusters of data and poor performances to determine if some parameters are fundamental to and therefore interfere with other performances. A classic example of this concept is the child with asymmetrical tonic neck reflex who also cannot perform a log roll.

PROCEDURES FOR INTERPRETATION

Once these general concepts for interpretation are well in mind, six procedural steps should be followed in order to identify the underlying sources of movement deficiencies: (1) analyze the demands; (2) order developmentally; (3) determine the commonalities; (4) cluster by commonalities; (5) describe performance; and (6) interpret. These must be done in sequence in order to draw valid conclusions and make confident recommendations.

Analyze the Demands

Analyze the sensory, cognitive, language, and motor demands of the task(s) within each test item. Using the developmental model (Figure 2-1), determine which reflexes have to be present or inhibited, which sensory systems have to be functioning normally (or, upon which sensory systems the task places demands), and which motor responses, patterns, or skills are required for the student to successfully complete the task.

This analysis will help the examiner identify commonalities and elements of the task needed in the interpretation process. For example, the shuttle run is commonly used as a measure of speed and agility. Without proprioception, vestibular function (i.e., balance), equilibrium responses, or visual perception, the performance will be poor. In the log roll—a commonly used developmental item—interference from the asymmetrical tonic neck reflex, inability to isolate body segments due to poor proprioception, and inability to keep the body extended due to overriding flexor tone will certainly result in poor performance, if not in an unsuccessful attempt.

The language demands of the test and the concepts represented in the language must also be analyzed. Did the test require the student to sequence several commands before performing? Did the administration procedure allow the student to get visual cues in addition to language cues from the examiner?

Did the performance require good auditory discrimination? (E.g., when the child was asked to touch his toes, did he touch his nose? Did the student seem to understand the meaning of the words that were used?) Did the test require an understanding of time, space, and directional relationships? These and other language and cognitive demands must be identified in the analysis to determine the underlying source(s) of motor deficits before any logical course can be taken toward interpretation.

The 6- or 12-minute walk-run (*California Physical Performance Test, AAHPERD Lifetime Health-Related Fitness Test,* 1980) is used to measure cardiorespiratory endurance, but the limitations imposed by mental retardation, for example, may preclude a valid performance. If students are not motivated, do not understand the concept of an "all-out effort," or lack the proprioceptive and tactile feedback to "pace" the rate at which they run, this test item may be a better measure of cognitive or intellectual function than of cardiorespiratory endurance.

Many physically handicapped students are obviously limited in their ability to meet the motor demands of a task. For example, while a paraplegic girl in a wheelchair will assuredly be limited in meeting the motor demand of standing on one foot as a measure of balance, this does not mean that she does not have normal or adequate balance—within the limits of her disability. Youngsters with poor proprioception, vestibular, or tactile function may also be unable to perform this task, and it is the physical educator's challenge in interpretation to identify which source or combination of sources is contributing to poor performance on the standing balance task.

Order Developmentally

The items should be developmentally ordered according to the model in Figure 2-1. Since each level of function in the developmental model relies on adequate function at the lower levels, programming and interpretation should address the basic or lower-level functions first. This is not to say the sensory systems, responses, or patterns at higher levels will not be involved in a given test item; but the purpose for selecting a given activity for the individual educational program should be based on the most fundamental source that can be identified through data collection.

For example, a smooth, efficient running pattern is at least partially influenced by vestibular function and balance mechanisms. Therefore balance should be addressed before working on running technique; proprioception and body image — knowing where one's body parts are in space — should precede tumbling skills; integrating the two body sides — a motor response — should precede softball batting; and so on. The ultimate goal in adapted physical education is to give each student the functions, responses, and patterns necessary for learning the activities inherent in a physical education program. Analysis of the task and developmental ordering can help the teacher to better identify the basis of successful motor performance and plan appropriate programs for each individual.

Determine the Commonalities

Once the demands of each task have been analyzed and developmentally ordered, the factors of performance common to the low items should be evident. Items that share no common factor with the other items should be separated out and checked for true relationships. Do these seemingly unrelated items share some other factor, such as language or cognition? Do they involve variables upon which the desired performance depends, such as body weight, body type, or even cultural factors? (For example, some native American tribes have no cultural concept for competition.)

Some relationships will be found in this way, and clusters will be formed among these items. If there are still items for which no mutual factors can be found, they should be set aside. Such items may represent totally independent parameters that require a separate interpretation.

Cluster by Commonalities

Poor performances should be grouped according to clusters of common factors, and kept in order developmentally. At this point, the profile of the child's performance should begin to take shape, and the factors underlying poor performance should begin to emerge. The developmentally lowest factor or problem area should be the first priority for program planning. The remaining factors should be ordered developmentally, and according to the frequency with which they appear in poor performance. Since each level of function depends on adequate functioning at lower levels, this hierarchy should be adhered to in interpretation and subsequent program planning.*

Describe Performance

This is where the actual articulation of the interpretation begins, either in written or verbal form (reporting results will be discussed more thoroughly later in this chapter). The report should begin with a description of the positive attributes of the student's performance — what the student was able to do and how the performance was executed. Among moderately and severely handicapped students, dysfunctions will be evidenced even among the performances a student was able to do. Thus reporting how a performance

---

*It should be noted that most children develop higher level skills for which they truly have inadequate underlying functions. These are what Kephart (1971) has called "splinter skills." These skills, however, have no utilitarian value for general motor performance and hence are counterproductive to the goal of equipping each student with the tools necessary to successfully participate in a physical education program.

was executed will often reveal poor quality that may be explained by the dysfunctions identified later in the report.

Next, the report should describe what the student was not able to do, and how the student approximated the desired performance. These should be discussed in clusters according to the common factors of performance identified earlier. The commonalities should *not* be revealed at this point. These are the conclusions, and should be reported later, after all the data have been presented. Instead, only what can be seen at this point should be described. Scores, percentile ranks, or other information that will orient the listener or reader to the relative quality of the performance should be reported along with the description (e.g., "Joe scored at the tenth percentile" and "Susie scored four points out of twenty").

Interpret

If the test maker has already factor analyzed the test items, this step will be much easier. The language of the test maker should be used to define the areas of dysfunction. For example, if the test maker calls an area of performance "balance and posture," then poor performances in that section of the test should be interpreted as a dysfunction in balance and posture. Ultimately, the physical educator will relate these performances to the levels of the developmental model once the interpretation is fully reported.

Unfortunately, few test makers will have factor analyzed the test. In this case, the physical educator should go to the basic clusters of common factors in order to label the areas of weakness. Be specific without drawing conclusions that cannot be supported by observed performance. If the interpretation is reported verbally in a school appraisal team meeting, the data will frequently be supported or verified by data gathered by other professionals. Speculation should not go beyond the limits of the data. The adapted

specialist should interpret only what is certain, and maintain a policy of silence as matters get further away from documentable information. Very often, in a team meeting, another professional will bring up something that can be speculated on. This is the time to raise questions, opinions, or inferences — "I wonder if Johnny should be given a reflex test" or "I, too, noted that he had some problems with tasks requiring visual figure-ground discrimination" or "His performance suggested that he was not hearing everything I said to him." The cross-validation implied here may also help to make sense out of those seemingly unrelated performances mentioned earlier. It is hoped that all the necessary information needed can be gathered before the final conclusion is drawn. Sometimes this is not possible, since other professionals may be gathering data during the same time period. Therefore the physical educator must be alert and ready to compute and interpret new information as it is added.

RELATIONSHIPS FOR TEST INTERPRETATION

When a student is referred to the adapted physical educator for assessment, the data-gathering process has already begun. A child who is continually falling and skinning his chin, a youngster who misses the ball every time it is thrown, or a student who completes the 6-minute walk-run in seven minutes is bringing to the testing situation data that lends itself to and requires interpretation. Each of these pieces of information not only suggests some specific areas of dysfunction that can be used to plan the testing program, but provides added information to the formal test results that can validate and support the measurement derived, and vice versa. For example, a student who is referred for testing on the basis of poor vitality and low fitness should be tested on parameters measured by a fitness test, such as strength, flexibility, or endurance. A test of motor ability is not only likely to miss identification of the sources of poor vitality, but it also may not generate data that can be validated or serve to validate the initial referral information. The child who falls often and skins his chin should be tested for protective extension reflex, balance, and equilibrium responses as well as proprioception, vestibular function, and body image. Formal test results, then, can be combined with this observational and referral information for interpretation. The relationships among the various levels of the model, as well as with the ''real life'' manifestations of dysfunction at each level of the model, must be clearly understood in order for the adapted physical educator to make maximum use of the information available.

Reflex Behavior

If a child referred for testing is known to have brain damage, abnormal reflex behavior should always be suspected. If a child referred for testing is not thought to have brain damage, abnormal reflex behavior should not be ruled out. In other words, the adapted physical educator should start looking for deficits at the lowest possible level. Even if a therapist is available to do reflex testing, the specialist should watch for abnormal reflex behavior as it manifests itself in motor performance which can be further validated through formal testing by a therapist (see Table 10-1 for a list of observable signs of abnormal reflex behavior and corresponding reflexes to suspect).

Although this list is not exhaustive, it should give some idea of how the relationship between referral information and observed behavior can be used not only to plan the testing program, but also to interpret and validate measurements.

Sensorimotor Measurements

Sensorimotor instruments have historically focused upon the later-maturing systems and their interaction with movement. A child's development however, does not begin with visual and auditory function and the motor responses of eye-hand interaction, bilateral use of the body, or reaching and grasping. Thus interpretation of sensorimotor measurements should also include analysis of the processing and integration of all sensory input, regardless of whether or not the test is purported to measure it directly. Sensorimotor functioning is inherent in all motor performance. Although novel tasks are often used to measure sensorimotor elements, their influence cannot be truly separated from all other elements or parameters of motor performance any more than the influence of muscular strength can be separated from an endurance run.

Three principles for interpretation of sensorimotor measurements will be discussed in this section: (1) hierarchical sequence of influence; (2) intrasensory influence; and (3) structural interdependence. Like the parameters they deal with, these principles cannot be considered apart from the previous discussion of reflexes, nor the following discussion of other types of measurements.

Hierarchical Sequence of Influence

Because there is a hierarchical sequence of influence upward through the developmental model, systems and functions that mature later are related to and interdependent upon earlier-maturing systems and functions. The motor response of balance, for example, is often used as an indirect measure of vestibular function. In addition, the ability to stand on one foot relies heavily upon righting responses as well as on the motor response of contralateral body side use. Body awareness is measured by several sensorimotor tools. Tasks used to measure this parameter usually require postural and equilibrium responses to remain upright, proprioception in order to know where the body parts are in space, and, in some instances, auditory perception to understand the instructions of the task. Tasks

Table 10-1. Signs of abnormal reflex behavior

Observed performance	Suspected reflex
1. The child's arms collapse when going through obstacle course on hands and knees.	1. Residual symmetrical or asymmetrical tonic neck reflex.
2. The child stops crawling toward an object when he/she looks up to see where it is.	2. Residual symmetrical tonic neck reflex.
3. The arm on the face side extends when the child is doing a log roll.	3. Residual asymmetrical tonic neck reflex.
4. The child cannot throw accurately toward a target.	4. Residual asymmetrical tonic neck reflex.
5. The child's body extends when doing a forward roll.	5. Residual tonic labyrinthine reflex.
6. The child does not remain tucked when attempting a backward roll.	6. Residual tonic labyrinthine reflex.
7. The child rolls over on his/her side to get up from a back-lying position.	7. Residual tonic labyrinthine reflex.
8. The child often falls and skins elbows and chin.	8. Undeveloped protective extension and/or poor equilibrium responses.
9. The child avoids vigorous activity, running, climbing, jumping, etc.	9. Same as above.
10. The child expresses fear of heights.	10. Same as above.
11. The child falls off chairs or out of desk in classroom.	11. Same as above and/or poor righting reactions.

measuring spatial orientation, directionality, and spatial awareness typically rely on vestibulo-ocular interaction to process and plan movement of the body through space, righting reactions, proprioception, and patterns such as walking, running, stepping, hopping, and jumping. Therefore interpretation of inadequate performance on tasks measuring each of these param-

eters should be based on the hierarchical sequence of influence inherent in human development.

Intrasensory Influence

Intrasensory influence means that one sensory system influences the functioning of another. For example, because vestibular stimuli has a profound influence on visual and auditory processing, performance on visual tasks that involve movement is likely to be enhanced by the vestibular influence derived from the movement. Moving through an obstacle course requires visual processing and planning as well as the motor output demands relative to body awareness. Mere movement may assist with the solution of the visual problem in the obstacle course, which may not have seemed possible based upon a given student's performance on strict visual tasks. Proprioceptive influence from the muscles of the neck, along with the vestibular influence from head position, enhances visual function. Tilting the head forward to write at a desk sends continuous bombarding proprioceptive and vestibular stimuli to the central nervous system and enhances visual function. Writing on a chalkboard allows righting responses to control the head position automatically, thus providing less proprioceptive influence and negligible vestibular activity. Thus performance on visual perception tasks is likely to be better when the tasks are performed at a desk or table as opposed to on the chalkboard.

Structural Interdependence

Structural interdependence within the central nervous system enhances or deters motor performance. The following example demonstrates the *vertical structural interdependence* of the central nervous system. When the brain stem—the master control area for muscular activity—is performing its function adequately, performance on such tasks as moving through an obstacle course is controlled automatically and the attention of the cortex can be directed to the planning, processing, and adapting required to complete the obstacle course successfully. If the brain stem is not doing its job, then the cortex or the conscious attention must be focused on the muscular activity rather than on planning how to get through the obstacle

course, thus deterring or interfering with motor performance.

There is also a *lateral interdependence* between the hemispheres of the brain and the related structures, which is significant in motor performance. On a bilateral, contralateral, or ipsilateral task found in many tests (e.g., Purdue Perceptual Motor Survey, Six-Category Gross Motor Test, Southern California Sensory Integration Tests) the global meaning of the task must be interpreted and processed in one hemisphere of the brain, and that information communicated to the other hemisphere of the brain for control of the motor output. For example, a task such as "Angels-in-the-Snow" found in the Purdue test requires the examiner to point to the right arm and say, "Move that arm." The auditory and visual stimuli enters both ears and eyes at the same time. While the left hemisphere is discriminating the sounds of the words, the right hemisphere is interpreting the meaning of the words. This information is passed through the corpus callosum and brain stem to the left hemisphere, which integrates, plans, and then controls the motor output or movement of the right limb. Simultaneously and similarly the visual stimuli (pointing) is being interpreted and associated with the language (auditory). Without this interhemispheric communication, neither the global concept of the task nor the meaning of the command could be brought to bear on the motor output. (When the left limb is moved, the problems of executing the movement are reversed.)

Observational data, too, can lend insight into the way a student processes sensorimotor information. A student who pulls away from your touch or touches everything and everyone in sight may be displaying a disorder in the tactile system. Avoiding swings and slides, or constantly running to these pieces of equipment, may indicate a vestibular disorder. Constantly jumping, pushing, or pulling may be proprioceptive-seeking behavior and these observations should be considered along with formal measurements. A behav-

Table 10–2. Behavioral checklist

Behavior	Example	Possible Cause
Hyperkinesis	Student is constantly up out of seat, cannot attend to task, fidgets when required to sit or stand in one place, learning does not take place.	Poor postural muscle tone, poor cocontraction.
Problems in peer interaction	Starting fights, shoving in line, refusing to participate with peers.	Poor proprioception, seeking input tactually or is tactually defensive; inability to motor plan.
Immature emotional behavior	Does not react emotionally as others of same age do, may cry, whine. Can't accept losing a game. Exhibits jealousy of peers.	General nervous system immaturity.
General incoordination	Can't throw a ball, play common playground games, hit a ball with fist or implement.	Not receiving good tactile or proprioceptive input.
Doesn't follow directions	"Forgets" what he/she was supposed to be doing, appears to not be listening to directions during an activity.	Dyspraxia (inability to motor plan).
Constantly injuring self (accidently)	Scrapes on knees, bruises on arms.	Does not have protective extension; possible proprioceptive dysfunction.
Self-stimulating behavior	Slight rocking when sitting or standing, bouncing against back of chair.	Seeking vestibular input.
Self-abusive (purposefully)	Biting hand or arm, banging head, hitting own body.	Seeking tactile input.
Abnormal ambulation	Plodding, seemingly just to make noise. Has to "run" everywhere.	Seeking more proprioceptive input. Seeking more vestibular input.
Sloppy work	Handwriting is messy, bears too hard or too soft with the pencil or crayon when writing or drawing.	Does not have normal tactile discriminative ability.

SOURCE: Lou Stewart, California State University at Los Angeles, class project.

ioral checklist can be used to gather observational data on suspicious sensory system function (see Table 10–2).

Measurement of Motor Development

Tools designed to gather data on motor development often include other aspects of human development as well. Since movement is the primary manifestation of cognitive, social, and language development, at least during the first two years of life, motor tasks are commonly used to measure these parameters. The developmental schedule in Appendix A could be used to separate out (as much as is possible) the expected motor output from the other parameters at any given level of development.

Measurements of motor development on norm-referenced instruments are usually expressed in months or years of developmental lag, or at the age of actual functioning. A nine-month old infant who cannot sit upright unsupported is said to be developmentally at the six-month old level or showing a three-month lag in motor development, since that milestone should be accomplished within the sixth month of life. Understanding and applying the principles discussed in the previous section is also important here, since the interference of undeveloped head, neck, and optical righting reflexes may be contributing to this lack of "performance" on the independent sitting task. Development, although sequential, may often have gaps, and youngsters may be capable of performing some tasks at one level and incapable of performing tasks at an earlier level. Many parents of exceptional children have reported their children missing the crawling stage, while other children cannot jump. Understanding the principles involved in motor control of the central nervous system will assist in making sense out of these gaps or apparent voids in development.

Any physical impairment will interfere with the accomplishment of some developmental milestones.

Cerebral palsy, clubfoot, and other lower limb involvements will obviously interfere with weight bearing and upright posture. Motor development measurements should be reported in terms of these physical restrictions.

Data gathered through observation can help piece together the developmental puzzle for some children. Children who are dyspraxic (i.e., who have difficulty with motor planning or sequencing, sometimes referred to as apraxic) will sometimes demonstrate performances in play that the examiner was not able to elicit in a formal testing situation. The good examiner, who is also a keen observer, will store this information away for use when it comes time to interpret formal test results.

Measurement of Motor Ability

Motor ability tests tend to measure novel tasks that have some predictive ability to infer success in game and sport skills. Historically, they make the assumption that there are basic, innate abilities that cut across many different physical activities. Relative to the developmental model, motor ability tests tend to measure at the motor-sensory responses and motor patterns levels. Common motor ability items such as high jump, broad jump, dashes, and basketball throws measure patterns and learned skills more or less directly. Other parameters measured by these tests include timing, rhythm, and coordination, which are described in the developmental model as motor responses. Interpretation of scores on these tests relies heavily on the ability of the examiner to analyze tasks required on the test. Thus reflexes that can interfere with performance of each of the tasks should be identified, and sensory systems that are involved (or systems upon which demands are being placed) should be analyzed.

For example, to throw a baseball accurately, a child must have an integrated asymmetrical tonic neck reflex and adequate tactile, proprioceptive, and visual system functions, as well as the motor responses of contrasting body side use and the pattern of throwing. If the asymmetrical tonic neck reflex is present, the head position will interfere with full extension of the throwing arm; poor tactile discrimination will diminish the ability to know where the ball is in the hand; lack of accurate proprioceptive information will decrease the ability to know where the body parts are in space; and the visual system is the key to discriminating the target from other things in the visual field. Obviously, without the ability to use the two body sides in contrast, the task will be hopeless.

Together, these support systems generate a coordinated performance. Without them, the result is motor inability. Once analyzed, motor ability test items will tend to cluster together based upon deficits in the supporting systems or functions.

Measurement of Motor Skills

Motor skills tests tend to measure specific applications of motor patterns and combinations of motor patterns. Many instruments in this category also include motor responses and fine-motor control. Since tasks required in these tests tend to rely heavily upon learning and experience, a child's innate neural capacity, cognition, and educational opportunities will weigh heavily on the ability to perform reliably. Poor performances on test items should be reported in terms of the skill or cluster of skills, with an accompanying analysis of the commonalities among developmental parameters (i.e., reflexes interfering, sensory system disorders, inadequacies in motor responses and patterns). Again, disorders should be approached developmentally, with programming beginning at the level of dysfunction rather than working on the specific skills.

For example, a highly skilled long jumper will work on leg strength, explosive power and running speed (at least in the off-season). This program tends to improve jumping ability even though the athlete may go for weeks without taking a single jump. The individualized program for a student with asymmetrical tonic neck reflex who has done poorly on a throwing skills test should involve participation in activities that will inhibit the reflex. Once this is accomplished, it is more than likely that the throwing skill will also improve.

Measurement of Physical Fitness

Fitness tests are probably the easiest tools for physical educators to interpret. Not only have the tests usually been factor analyzed for the teacher, but they represent a category of tests most physical educators have learned to administer as part of their professional preparation. The challenge to the adapted physical educator is to differentiate between deficits in the parameters that the fitness test is measuring and deficits in the numerous other parameters that support the fitness performance. For example, the flexed arm hang is used in some fitness tests normed on the exceptional population as a measure of arm and shoulder girdle strength and muscular endurance. When a child fails to perform well on this item, the interpretation is typically that the student is weak in upper body strength. The examiner must be aware that tactile identification (for contact with the bar), proprioception (for discrimination of muscles to contract), head and ocular righting reflexes, and the concept of a sustained effort must *precede* the performance of a flexed arm hang. Many parameters measured by a fitness test can be further validated by direct measures or other performance measures in order to separate these functions out.

A MODEL FOR INTERPRETATION

A generic developmental model for interpretation of measurements can, at the most, be a stimulus for ideas

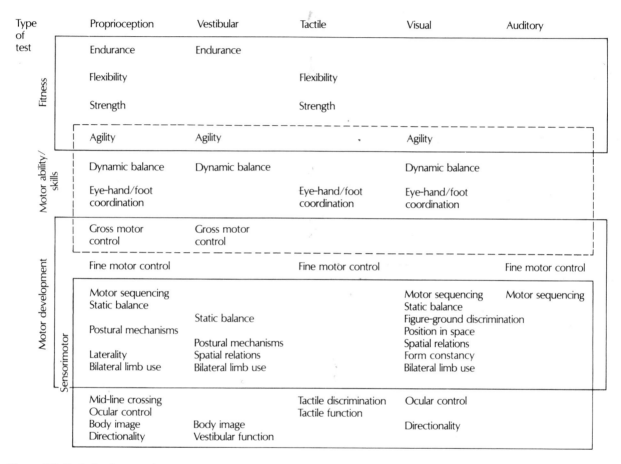

Figure 10–5. A developmental model for test interpretation.

and a guideline for analyzing test performances from a developmental point of view. Some test makers, such as Kephart, Frostig, and Ayres, include information for use in interpretation of measurements gathered using their instruments. As has been stated repeatedly in this chapter, however, most tests available to the adapted physical educator are not factor analyzed, nor are guidelines provided for use in their interpretation (see Figure 10–5 for an analysis of the sensory de-

mands of many parameters commonly used in the types of tests discussed in Chapter 8).

The test items or tasks used to sample each of the parameters in Figure 10–5 require the functioning of or place demands on the sensory system(s) indicated at the top of the column(s) in which the parameter appears. The type of test and the variety of parameters each type usually measures is framed in the corresponding box. For example, since static balance is commonly found in sensorimotor and motor development tests, it is framed by those two boxes. Tasks usually used to measure static balance include standing on one foot with eyes open or closed; it may also be measured in developmental profiles in the form of balancing while sitting independently or standing on two feet. Static balance requires proprioception and vestibular function; if the eyes are open, the visual system is also used. Therefore this parameter appears in the three columns headed by each of those three sensory systems. Of course, static balance also requires some normal reflex activity such as positive support, equilibrium, and righting reactions, which do not appear in the model.

Although this model is presented as a springboard for thought, it does graphically describe how the task used by the test maker can be "factored out" to identify the underlying sensory system commonalities. If, for example, the motor skill of forward roll is measured and the examiner determines that body image, bilateral body side use, balance, spatial relations, and postural mechanisms are some of the functions required in order to successfully complete the forward roll, the single commonality found among these functions is adequate function of the vestibular system. Vestibular system function can more directly be measured through a test of postrotary nystagmus or a caloric test to further validate these findings. On the other hand, other performance tests requiring vestibular system function can be administered. Further information can be gathered from the student or the student's parents, classroom teacher, and others to determine whether the child has ever had the opportunity to learn the skill or whether there are interfering postural reflexes, language, or cognitive disorders that would preclude the student from performing the skill.

Let us take another example. A fourth-grade student is referred for testing. She continuously bumps into people and things, swings a bat long after the ball has gone by, and even when she does hit the ball hesitates before running and sometimes runs toward the wrong base. The Purdue Perceptual Motor Survey is administered, and the student does poorly on the following: identification of body parts, imitation of postures, obstacle course, ocular tracking, chalkboard (drawing double circles and horizontal lines), and visual achievement forms. The examiner who is familiar with this test will find that these items, in terms of Figure 10–5, require directionality, body image, ocular control, midline crossing, bilateral limb use, laterality, postural mechanisms, motor sequencing, and fine motor control. The support system common to all of these parameters is proprioception. Vision certainly is a factor, but is reliant on proprioception and the vestibular system for optimal function. The dysfunction, therefore, should be considered grounded in the proprioceptive system and activities designed to enhance proprioception should be planned for her program.

REPORTING ASSESSMENT RESULTS

Within the mandates of PL 94–142, assessment-reporting must take place in a formal meeting of interdisciplinary personnel comprising the Evaluation and Assessment Service, Evaluation and Planning Team or the School Appraisal (Review) Team. Reporting results requires not only a good understanding of the assessment process, but also well-practiced interdisciplinary communication skills. In addition, the parent will often be present, thus requiring the teacher to have the ability to communicate technical information in nontechnical language.

There are three levels of reporting assessment findings that the adapted physical educator must keep in mind in order to assure credibility, communicate clearly, and remain in compliance with current legislation: (1) factual, (2) probable, and (3) inferential.

A *factual* statement must be based on something that is known, that can be observed, and that comes as close as possible to certainty. Thus a statement of fact can only come after an observed performance. For example, "Sam has contractures and 30 degrees of extension in the right arm" is a statement of fact. It is observable, it is being made after testing, and is as close to certainty as anyone can come. "The student cannot throw a ball" is not a statement of fact, because it goes beyond what can be observed.

Statements of *probability,* on the other hand, go beyond what can be observed. They describe performances that are very likely, based on what has been observed and on theoretical foundations established as part of the specialized training of the adapted physical educator. They should include such phrases as, "It is likely," "It is very possible," or "It is highly probable," in order to differentiate them from statements of fact. To use the example given above, "Sam has contractures and 30 degrees of extension in the right arm, and it is very possible that he cannot throw a ball," would be a valid use of a statement of probability because it is supported by a statement of fact.

The final level of assessment reporting is *inferential*. As with statements of probability, inferences go beyond what can be observed. They actually are degrees of probability and, when possible, should be supported by statements of fact. They can be made at any time relative to the performance, and are often characterized by the use of such terms as "theoretically," "presumably," "possibly," "wondering," "assuming," and "thought." Statements of inference are assumptions or projections made based on previous, similar circumstances. To elaborate on the ball throwing example, we will add the information that Sam — the student with limited range of motion who probably cannot throw a ball — is a fifteen-year-old, cerebral-palsied adolescent. An appropriate inferential statement, added to the factual and probability state-

ments already made, might be, "I assume he will not ever be able to gain enough extension in the elbow to throw a ball." Based on the teacher's experience, what he or she knows about cerebral palsy, and the fact that this adolescent has gone so many years with limited extension in the arm, it is very unlikely it can be developed at this late date and the inference is probably quite valid. (This is not to imply that the teacher should stop working with Sam to maintain whatever range of motion that he has, nor should his use of an approximation of a throwing pattern be excluded. The teacher has simply stated that the mechanics of an efficient throwing pattern are probably beyond the realm of possibility for this student.)

SUMMARY

Interpretation of measurements is one of the most challenging of all aspects of teaching adapted physical education. Understanding the significance of test results requires an analysis of parameters measured by a given tool or procedure, as well as an analysis of the demands of each task. Ordering items developmentally, determining commonalities among inadequate performances, and describing the deficits identified will assist in interpretation. Distinguishing between statements of fact and inferences made based on the described deficits is an important skill to cultivate when reporting the interpretation of measurements. The multidisciplinary team meeting provides an invaluable forum for validating and piecing together bits of information that may seem nonsensical. The adapted physical educator should utilize the team's rich resources as much as possible in order to get the full picture of each student's motor performance profile.

BIBLIOGRAPHY

AAHPERD. *Lifetime Health Related Fitness Test.* Washington, D.C.: American Alliance for Health, Physical Education, Recreation, and Dance, 1980.

Ayres, A. J. *Southern California Sensory Integration Tests.* Los Angeles: Western Psychological Services, 1972.

Barrow, H. M., and McGee, R. *A Practical Approach to Measurement in Physical Education.* 3d ed. Philadelphia: Lea and Febiger, 1979.

Baumgartner, T. A., and Jackson, A. S. *Measurement for Evaluation in Physical Education.* 2d ed. Boston: Houghton Mifflin, 1981.

California Department of Education. *California Physical Performance Test.* Sacramento: State Department of Education, 1973.

Frostig, M., and Maslow, P. *Movement Education: Theory and Practice.* Chicago: Follett, 1970.

Kephart, N. C. *The Slow Learner in the Classroom.* 2d ed. Columbus, Ohio: Charles E. Merrill, 1971.

Kirkendall, D. R., Gruber, J. J., and Johnson, R. *Measurement and Evaluation for Physical Educators.* Dubuque: Wm. C. Brown, 1980.

Los Angeles Unified School District. *Adapted Physical Education Assessment Scale.* Los Angeles: Field draft, 1979.

Montoye, H. J., ed. *An Introduction to Measurement in Physical Education,* vol. 1. Indianapolis: Phi Epsilon Kappa Fraternity, 1970.

Roach, E. G., and Kephart, N. C. *The Purdue Perceptual Motor Survey.* Columbus, Ohio: Charles E. Merrill, 1966.

University of Colorado. *Denver Developmental Screening Test.* Denver: University of Colorado Medical Center, n.d.

11 Determining the Individualized Educational Program

Guiding Questions

1. What are some of the elements of an individualized educational program (IEP)?
2. What are some procedural elements in the assessment process that are identified in the law and are important to the physical educator?
3. What are the three necessary components of a performance objective?
4. What are some ways in which realistic criteria for annual goals may be set?

The professional's goal and purpose for assessment is to plan an individualized educational program (IEP) for each student who has special needs. Assessment involves gathering data through testing, taking direct measurements, and observing a student's performance; and interpreting that data for the purpose of program planning. This is what PL 94–142 refers to as *determining the current level of performance*. The physical educator should be familiar with some of the procedural elements set down in the law in order to carry out this mandate.

LEGAL REQUIREMENTS

Before an assessment is conducted, the parents or guardians must be fully informed of and give consent to the selective testing and measurement of their child. If a student is singled out for testing, this process — known as *informed consent* — must be carried out. Since one of the primary functions of testing in physi-

cal education has always been to measure achievement, many schools carry on a regular program of skills and fitness testing throughout the year. Thus, if a student's poor performance is first identified through a mass testing program that is normally carried out as part of the physical education curriculum, informed consent is not necessary. Through regular testing, however, many students are identified for further testing and possible special services such as adapted physical education. In these cases, further testing requires informed consent (see Figure 11-1).

A second element set down by the law requires that the assessment procedure be completed *within thirty-five school days* after receiving the written consent. In addition, a meeting date must be set in order to discuss the results of assessment and determine the need and scope of an IEP. Thirty-five school days may seem like an adequate length of time to complete the assessment procedure; however, consideration must be given to the time lost to the child's absences from school, school assemblies, and other demands on the

Figure 11-1. Example of an assessment plan requiring parental consent.

ASSESSMENT PLAN

Pupil Name _____ Birthdate _____ Date _____

Assessment will be done by appropriately qualified staff members in the areas checked below. The assessment may include pupil observation in a group setting and may include an interview with you and a review of any reports you have authorized us to request or that already exist in current school records. The purpose of this evaluation is to determine individual educational needs and may result in a recommendation for special education placement or services.

_____ ACADEMIC/PREACADEMIC ACHIEVEMENT

Purpose: These tests measure current reading, spelling and arithmetic skills or skills such as matching or sorting. Tests may include, but are not limited to: Peabody Individual Achievement Test, KeyMath Diagnostic Test, Spache Diagnostic Reading Scales, Developmental Scales, Wide Range Achievement Test.

_____ SOCIAL/ADAPTIVE BEHAVIOR

Purpose: These scales of development help to tell what an individual can do for himself and how he gets along with other people. They may include, but are not limited to: Adaptive Behavior Scale, Fairview Self-Help Scale, Vineland Test of Social Maturity, Pre-School Attainment Record, Burk's Behavior Rating Scales.

_____ PSYCHO-MOTOR DEVELOPMENT

Purpose: Instruments in this area measure how well an individual coordinates body movements in both small and large muscle activities. They may also measure vital perceptual skills. Assessment tools may include, but are not limited to: Frostig Developmental Test of Visual Perception, Bender-Gestalt Visual Motor Integration Test, Developmental Scales, Purdue Perceptual Motor Inventory.

_____ LANGUAGE/SPEECH/COMMUNICATION DEVELOPMENT

Purpose: These tests measure the individual's ability to understand, relate to and use language and speech clearly and appropriately. They may include, but are not limited to: Illinois Test of Psycholinguistic Ability, Peabody Picture Vocabulary Test, Northwestern Syntax Screening Test, Language Samples, Fisher Logemann Articulatoon Test, Language Developmental Scales.

_____ INTELLECTUAL DEVELOPMENT

Purpose: These tests measure how well an individual remembers what he has seen and heard around him, how well he can use that information and how he solves problems. They also reflect learning rate and assist in predicting how well (s)he will do in school. Verbal and performance instruments are used, as are appropriate. Tests may include, but are not limited to: Cattell Intelligence Scale, Stanford Binet Intelligence Scale, Wechsler Tests of Intelligence, Leiter International Performance Scale, Merrill-Palmer Scale.

____ AUDIOLOGICAL ASSESSMENT

Purpose: These instruments measure the nature and degree of possible hearing loss. Tests may include measures of how well an individual hears, understands and listens to speech. On-going assessment of adequacy of hearing aids and monitoring of hearing levels is indicated for some individuals. Tests may include, but are not limited to: Air and bone conduction pure-tone audiometry, speech awareness, reception, discrimination tests, impedance audiometry, and visual inspection of the external ear.

____ OTHER: (Include Vocational or Medical Assessment Here)

The following professional(s) will be involved in the Individual Assessment outlined above:

____Adapted Physical Education Teacher ____Psychologist
____Program Specialist ____Counselor
____Resource Specialist ____Audiologist
____Language/Speech Specialist ____Nurse
____Teacher

PARENTAL CONSENT FOR PUPIL ASSESSMENT

If pupil speaks other than English at home, please indicate language_____

I authorize the use of a suitable interpreter or pre-recorded tests in individual's primary language as appropriate.

I have received a Notice of Intent to conduct pupil assessment and proposed Assessment Plan, and understand its purpose. The box checked below indicates my decision.

____Yes, I give permission to conduct the assessment as described.
____No, permission is denied.

Parent/Legal Guardian/Adult Pupil/Acting Parent (Specify)   Date

PLEASE SIGN AND RETURN SECOND COPY TO SCHOOL

child's time such as speech therapy, physical therapy, and special reading groups. Demands on the physical educator's time for instruction, attending meetings, and assessment of other students must also be considered. It is a good policy to schedule time periods during which testing can be carried out. This will serve to avoid some of the last-minute pressure often created by circumstances beyond the physical educator's control.

The third element requires that testing and measurement materials and procedures be presented either in English, in the *native language* of the pupil, or in the child's usual mode of communication. In addition, as with all educational materials, the assessment procedure should not in other ways be racially or culturally discriminatory. This also means that, if a child has a sensory, physical, mental, or language impairment, the test must accurately reflect motor performance rather than a manifestation of this impairment. Therefore it is vitally important that the physical educator be able to analyze the measurement tool being used for its possible discriminatory effect on motor performance.

A fourth element mandates that assessment procedures shall be *valid* for the specific purpose for which they are being used. Furthermore, the procedures must be designed to measure *performance specific to the pupil's educational needs.* Two parts of this element require discussion. First, the question of validity. As discussed in the previous paragraph, one part of the validity question can be answered by whether or not the tool being used does in fact measure motor performance rather than language, mental ability, or some other interfering impairment. Only the physical educator's analysis of the tool relative to each child can provide the answer to this question. The statistical question of validity may have already been answered by the test maker, and some test makers have used additional, commonly accepted measures against which to compare performances on their tests (i.e., external validity). Although different than the first question of validity, this information can serve to instill confidence in the tool and the results the tool generates.

The second part of this element refers to the measurement of performance specific to the pupil's educational needs. This particular issue has been under discussion for many years, and continues to be subject to interpretation. Because the early physical educators were medical doctors, the philosophy and rationale underlying the contribution of physical education to the growth and development of handicapped students has historically been based on the medical model. The medical model typically suggests that one

would diagnose, treat the ailment, and evaluate the results, which are expected to show some form of cure or remediation. Under PL 94–142 and modern educational philosophy, however, the goal of professional educators is to identify and address a child's educational, not medical, needs. Furthermore, PL 94–142 mandates services for youngsters whose disabilities are not the result of a pathological condition that can be treated medically. Therefore, unless a pathological condition interferes with a child's benefiting from educational services, it should be left in the hands of medical personnel to treat. For example, a boy who is diagnosed and is being treated medically for epilepsy may or may not have special educational needs. If his seizures are under control through medication, there is usually no reason to separate this youngster from his peers for physical education. In contrast, a student who is diagnosed as having moderate scoliosis and who, in addition, has a limited range of motion and poor performance on other physical measures, is a very likely candidate for adapted physical education services. Thus a pathological condition *alone* is not reason enough to separate students from their peers for physical education. Medical data may be — and, when available, should be — brought to bear on the decision-making process. The effect of any existing pathology on motor performance, and hence on the educational needs of the student, must be the prime focus in the assessment process.

The fifth element set down in the law is that the decision for *placement* and planning the IEP must be made by the multidisciplinary team and *based on evaluation*. A statement of clarification and interpretation published early in 1980 by the U.S. Office of Education (1980) identified four levels of physical education for students with special needs: (1) a regular physical education class; (2) a regular physical education class with modifications; (3) a separate class, such as adapted physical education; and (4) a physical education class in a separate facility, such as a school for the handicapped. Usually, placement in either a regular school or a special school will have been made prior to the physical educator's involvement. Placement in a separate adapted physical education class, however, has often mistakenly been based on a child's placement in a separate special education classroom. This decision for placement is often invalid and in direct violation of current legislation. Placement into a separate adapted physical education class must be based on assessment of *motor performance,* not on the educational classification of the child. For a student placed in a regular physical education class, an IEP is not required. If a student in a regular class requires modifications, only the modifications must be described. Students in a separate class or a separate facility must have an IEP for physical education (U.S. OE, 1980).

A sixth element is that the parents or guardians have a right to obtain an *independent evaluation* of their child by a qualified examiner who is not employed by the educational agency. This mandate alone could have grave impact on professionals who are not thorough in their assessment. Thus it is imperative that the physical educator follow the procedures outlined in Chapters 8, 9 and 10 in order to identify all of the possible sources of motor dysfunction. This is where the developmental model has special significance. Although physical educators in private practice are not plentiful, there are other qualified examiners who measure parameters that impinge on motor performance, including psychologists, educational and movement therapists, physical and occupational therapists, and medical personnel. Thus it is incumbent upon the physical educator to identify possible sources of dysfunction using the developmental model and interpret those or make referrals for further assessment to professionals in related areas. This concept will be discussed more fully later in this chapter.

The final procedural element is that *parent or guardian consent* is needed prior to any change in the identification, assessment, or placement of a pupil.

Once the assessment process is concluded by the multidisciplinary team meeting, which includes the parent, the agreement to either write an IEP and place the child in a separate adapted physical education class or to retain the child in a regular physical education class with modifications must have the parents' or guardians' written consent (see Figure 11–2).

Although these procedures may seem cumbersome at first, they truly provide guidelines for educators and assurances for parents and children that each child's educational needs will be addressed. Further discussion of the significance of these procedures and the IEP for the child, the parent, and the educator will appear later in this chapter.

WRITING THE INDIVIDUALIZED EDUCATIONAL PROGRAM

The legal mandates of PL 94–142 require that at least five components be included in the IEP: (1) annual goal(s), (2) short-term performance objectives, (3) dates for when the objectives will be achieved, (4) strategies or materials to be used to achieve goals, and (5) related services needed for the student to benefit from special education services.

Writing Annual Goals

Goals are statements that indicate the broad, general outcomes desired for the student. Since goals, by definition, are to be achieved in the future, some exceptional children may not attain a stated goal within the year for which it has been written.

Typical goals used in physical education include (1) to improve physical fitness, (2) to improve eye-hand coordination, and (3) to improve the ability to play cooperatively with peers. These are rather traditionally stated goals, and most school districts would accept them in this form. Some school districts, however,

Figure 11-2. Example of an IEP.

LOS ANGELES UNIFIED SCHOOL DISTRICT
DIVISION OF SPECIAL EDUCATION

PAGE 1 OF 3

INDIVIDUALIZED EDUCATION PROGRAM

`7 | 2 | 7 | 5 | 0 | 3 | 9 | 4 | 4 | 0 | 4`
STUDENT I.D. NUMBER

A. DATES
1. Present meeting __2_/ _10_/ _82_
2. Anticipated Annual Review __2_/ _83_
3. Anticipated 3-yr. Reassessment __2_/ _85_
   (IF APPROPRIATE)

B. TEAM MEETING INFORMATION
Team: SAT ☑ EAS ☐ Location: __LINCOLN SCHOOL__

__3__
ADMINISTRATIVE AREA

Type of Meeting: Initial ☐ Review ☑
Review based on 3-yr. Reassessment ☐
Amendment of IEP dated ___/___/___ to add ☐ or delete ☐ a DIS. Specify DIS.: ____

C. PUPIL-PARENT INFORMATION
Pupil Language: __ENGLISH__ Home Language: __ENGLISH__ BINL: ☐ (if appropriate)

Pupil: __SMITH__ __CAROL__ __JEAN__
       (LAST)   (FIRST)   (MIDDLE)

B/D: _11_/ _9_/ _75_ Sex: M __ F _✓_ Ethnic Code: _5_ Grade: _2_
     MO   DA   YR

Address: __4404 DUARTE ROAD__ · __ARCADIA__
         (STREET)   (CITY)

Parent/Guardian: __SMITH__ __WILLIAM & JANICE__
                 (LAST)   (FIRST)

Home phone: _343-6731_ Work phone(s) _254-4490_/ _224-3216_ ☐ Foster Home ☐ Licensed Children's Institution:

School of Attendance: __LINCOLN__ Loc. Code: _8041_ School of Residence: __EMPEROR__ Loc. Code: _8037_

D. PRESENT LEVEL OF PERFORMANCE

Check if assessed. Use same numbers to identify statements.

☑ 1. health/vision/hearing
☑ 2. cognitive/general ability
☑ 3. academic achievement
☑ 4. social/emotional status
☑ 5. speech/language
☑ 6. motor abilities
☐ 7. other; specify: _____

Based on a multidisciplinary assessment, summarize present levels of performance in all appropriate areas. Include/identify outside assessment information. Indicate strengths and weaknesses. The summary shall be descriptive of the pupil's exceptionality.

1. MEDICAL RECORDS SHOW RIGHT HEMI-CP MILD

2. SLOW TO GRASP CONCEPTS/ROUTINE IN CLASS PROCEDURES.
   FUNCTIONS BEST IN SMALL GROUPS OF 10-12 SS

3. W.R.A.T.: READ-6, SPELL -9, ARITH.-2. FLAT PROFILE @ 4 YEARS
   RECOGNIZES 6 LETTERS AND 4 NUMBERS

4. IMMATURE SOCIALLY (VERY), EAGER CHILD BUT WORKS BEST IN
   SMALL GROUPS

5. I.T.P.A.: A.E.-I-4.0, II-3.6, III-3.6, II-39, I-36

6. HAS ACQUIRED DEVELOPMENTAL MILESTONES FOR 3.9 YEARS; PM FUNC:<5P
   ON BAL, IPOC; MOTOR DEVEL:<5P; MOTOR ACHIEVEMENT:<5P; PHY FIT:10-15P;
   POSTURE: 50P.

E. ELIGIBILITY AS AN INDIVIDUAL WITH EXCEPTIONAL NEEDS:
1. ☑ Meets eligibility criteria as indicated: _TMR_: _MH_ ____; (use handicap code(s)).
2. ☐ Meets eligibility criteria for special education services in the Assessment Program ☐ or the Non-Categorical Program ☐
3. ☐ Specific eligibility undetermined; recommend: ____
4. ☐ Does not meet eligibility for handicap(s) considered: ____; ____; ____; (use handicap code(s)).

F. CULMINATION GOAL/DIFFERENTIAL STANDARDS
1. Working toward ☐ diploma or ☐ letter of recommendation.
2. Regular proficiency standards ☐ or differential proficiency standards ☐.
3. If differential standards are required, specify alternate mode(s) of assessment: ____
4. Demonstrates sufficient progress toward mastery of the 3 basic skills: Gr. 4 ☐; Gr. 6 ☐; All 3 tests passed: Jr. High ☐; Sr. High ☐.
5. ☐ Alternate culmination goal is acquisition of vocational training/independent living skills.

FORM 27.808-1 (Rev. 6/81) P.O. 12D-242240-0

SERVICE COPY

280

INDIVIDUALIZED EDUCATION PROGRAM (Page 2)

PUPIL NAME: _SMITH CAROL JEAN_   B/D: _11 / 9 / 75_   Date of Meeting: _2 / 10 / 82_

G. ANNUAL GOALS AND SHORT TERM OBJECTIVES

(Use of a number/code system for writing of goals/objectives must first be approved by the Division of Special Education and, if approved, explanatory material shall be attached to the IEP for parent and service provider.)

Goals/Responsible Personnel	Short Term Objectives	Evaluation Criteria For Objectives
1. ☑Instruc. Area: _SPEC. CLASS_ ☐ DIS Area: ____ Goal: _CAROL WILL IMPROVE IN LETTER AND NUMBER RECOGNITION_ Responsible Personnel: _CLASSROOM TEACHER_ Beginning date: _2 / 82_ Ending date: _2 / 83_ If RSP☐ or DIS☐ indicate frequency and total minutes per week: _/_	a. _CAROL WILL RECOGNIZE AND NAME 12 LETTERS_ b. _..... 8 NUMBERS_	**Objectives** a b Expected date of achievement _10.82 10.82_ Observation ☐ ☑ Informal Assess. ☐ ☐ Formal Test ☐ ☐ Other ☐ ☐ Date achieved _✓_ Not achieved ☐ Comment: ____
2. ☑Instruc. Area: _SPEC. CLASS_ ☐ DIS Area: ____ Goal: _CAROL WILL LEARN TO SHARE MATERIALS WITH OTHERS_ Responsible Personnel: _CLASSROOM TEACHER_ Beginning date: _2 / 82_ Ending date: _2 / 83_ If RSP☐ or DIS☐ indicate frequency and total minutes per week: _/_	a. _CAROL WILL NOT FIGHT WHEN ANOTHER STUDENT TAKES A TOY FROM HER_ b. _..... WILL OFFER ONE OF HER TOYS TO ANOTHER STUDENT(S)_	**Objectives** a b Expected date of achievement _10.82 2.83_ Observation ☑ ☑ Informal Assess. ☐ ☐ Formal Test ☐ ☐ Other ☐ ☐ Date achieved _✓_ Not achieved ☐ Comment: ____
3. ☐ Instruc. Area: ____ ☑ DIS Area: _Speech_ Goal: _Improve articulation of selected sounds_ Responsible Personnel: _Speech Pathologist_ Beginning date: _2 / 82_ Ending date: _2 / 83_ If RSP☐ or DIS☑ indicate frequency and total minutes per week: _2 / 40_	a. _Articulate;_ _S_ _th_ _in medial and final positions_ _J_ b. _Pronounce:_ _ye_ _yes_ _but_ _and similar with_ _thank you_ _greater clarity_	**Objectives** a b Expected date of achievement _12.82 2.83_ Observation ☐ ☐ Informal Assess. ☐ ☐ Formal Test ☑ ☑ Other ☐ ☐ Date achieved _✓_ Not achieved ☐ Comment: ____
4. ☐ Instruc. Area: ____ ☒ DIS Area: _APE_ Goal: _TO IMPROVE PERFORMANCE IN MOTOR DEVELOPMENT AND PERCEPTUAL MOTOR FUNCTION_ Responsible Personnel: ____ Beginning date: _2 / 82_ Ending date: _2 / 83_ If RSP☐ or DIS☒ indicate frequency and total minutes per week: _DAILY / ROOM_	a. _SCORE AT 10% OF AREAS FOR THROWING AND CATCHING_ b. _BALANCE ON ONE FOOT FOR AT LEAST 15 SECONDS_	**Objectives** a b Expected date of achievement _2/83 10/82_ Observation ☐ ☐ Informal Assess. ☐ ☐ Formal Test ☒ ☒ Other ☐ ☐ Date achieved ____ Not achieved ☐ Comment: ____

FORM 27.808-2 (Rev. 6/81) P.O. 12D-24240-0

SERVICE COPY

281

Figure 11–2. (continued)

INDIVIDUALIZED EDUCATION PROGRAM (Page 3)

PUPIL NAME: _SMITH CAROL JEAN_   B/D: _11 / 9 / 75_   Date of Meeting: _8 10 82_

H. VOCATIONAL EDUCATION/ PHYSICAL EDUCATION

When appropriate, indicate any necessary modifications in the regular vocational and/or physical education program.

_____

_____

_____

I. EXTENDED SCHOOL YEAR (For EAS Team use only)

Eligibility is based on state law.
☐ Pupil is eligible. ☐ Pupil is ineligible.

Based on current district policy the pupil, if eligible, may receive:

_____ / _____
DAYS   # HRS./DAY

Note any parent requests/comments:

_____

J. PROVISION FOR TRANSITION TO REGULAR CLASS PROGRAM

When appropriate, indicate provisions for transition to regular class program for any part of the school day.

_____

_____

For EAS Team use only: Indicate total amount of time per week to be spent in regular program. Use hours and/or minutes or number of periods, as appropriate:

_____ _____ _____
PERIODS   HOURS   MINUTES

K. RECOMMENDATION FOR INSTRUCTIONAL SETTING (check as appropriate)

☐ Regular School
(also check if return from NPS☐)

☑ Special School
(also check if return from NPS☐)

☐ Nonpublic School
(also check if initial NPS placement☐)

☐ Other: _____

☐ Resource Specialist Program

or

☑ Special Day Class

☑ Designated Instruction/Services

Transportation per LAUSD policy ☐ Yes ☐ No

L. PARENT DECISION/SIGNATURES OF INDIVIDUALIZED EDUCATION PROGRAM PARTICIPANTS

Parent Decision

☑ I have attended the IEP meeting and participated as a member of the team; I consent to the IEP.

☐ I was notified of the IEP meeting and was unable to attend; I have reviewed the IEP and consent to it.

☐ I disagree with the:
  a. ☐ assessment
  b. ☐ eligibility
  c. ☐ specific instruction/services
  d. ☐ instructional setting

☐ I agree to referral to the Educational Assessment Service, if appropriate.

☐ I wish to schedule an informal meeting to attempt to resolve a due process issue.

☐ I wish to initiate a due process hearing. (Use form SE-17.)

Signature(s): _William T. Smith_ Date: _8 / 10 / 82_
Janice W. Smith Date: _2 / 10 / 82_

Signatures of Other Participants

Administrator/Designee: _LAWRENCE R. PETERSON_ Date: _2/10/82_
Teachers: _LAWRENCE R. PETERSON_ Date: _2/10/82_
Mary Jane Parker Date: _2/6/82_
Pupil: _____ Date: _____

Others   Title   Date
Erin Matthews   _Speech_   _2/10/82_
Roger Dulson   _A.P.E._   _2/10/82_

Parent comments, if any, (e.g., agree with IEP but want child in regular program):

_____

M.
(This space is provided for recording any other information, follow-up actions, etc., as may be required by legislative/district actions.)

_____
_____
_____

FORM 27.808 3 (Rev. 6/81) P.C. 12D 242400

SERVICE COPY

require that the annual goals stated in the IEP be measurable — that is, a specific, observable behavior that can be used to measure whether or not the goal has been met must be included in the statement. Given this criterion, the statements would become: (1) to improve in physical fitness by scoring at least at the tenth percentile on (the test used by the school district); (2) to improve eye-hand coordination by catching the ball at least half the time in a softball game; and (3) to improve in the ability to play cooperatively with peers by participating in kickball daily, without fighting with classmates.

Areas in which reasonable goals might be pursued are indicated in federal legislation in the definition of physical education: physical and motor fitness, activities for motor development, game and sport skills, skills in aquatics, dance, and so on. Specific activities, patterns, or skills to be performed could be stated in the performance objectives used to achieve these goals.

Writing Short-Term Performance Objectives

Performance or behavioral objectives serve several purposes besides those leading to compliance with the law. First, a performance objective communicates to the teacher what it is that must be taught. Second, performance objectives that are written in line with annual goals communicate in what order or sequence material must be taught. Finally, a performance objective communicates information to its reader, who can determine — from observing a class — that the students have learned. Well-written performance objectives are stated in terms of student behavior and should always begin with the student's name or, when referring to a group, should begin "The students will. . . ."

The following terms may be used in writing goals, and are usually used in writing performance objectives. *Behavior* refers to any visible activity displayed by the student (Mager, 1962). Thus the word or words used in either goals or objectives must describe behaviors that can be seen. *Terminal behavior* refers to the behavior the student should demonstrate at the end of the period specified by the IEP. *Criteria* are standards of judgment by which behavior is evaluated. Thus "goals" traditionally refer to terminal behaviors, which may or may not include criteria, depending upon the requirements of any given school district. Today the word *performance* is commonly substituted for behavior and is used interchangeably in this text.

Objectives include three components that, when present, achieve the purposes stated above (Mager, 1962): (1) performance, (2) conditions, and (3) criteria. The *performance* stated in the objective is the behavior that can be observed as evidence that the student has achieved the objective and learned what was being taught. Physical education should be the easiest area of instruction for writing performance objectives. Even in a regular physical education class, the vast majority of material taught results in the students' demonstration of learned responses, patterns, or skills. A list of typical, observable behaviors or performances commonly sought in physical education instruction might include the following: run, jump, leap, skip, hop, somersault, throw, swim, skate, ski, dive, pitch. These observable performances describe behaviors that might be sought in any physical education curriculum. An additional list of uniquely appropriate performances for adapted physical education classes includes terms that describe motor responses and patterns that are often the focus for lower-functioning individuals: reach, grasp, roll, bend, push, pull, float, walk, stand, stretch, climb, kick.

The second component found in well-written performance objectives is the *conditions* under which the performance is to take place. For example, the performance of running can be done under any number of conditions such as: with help, on the track, without stopping, and so on. The conditions for running would be determined by a number of different factors, including the child's needs; the physical environment in which the child is being taught; the child's limitations as a result of a handicapping condition; or movement elements such as speed, force, or direction. For example, the performance objective "Johnny will be able to run . . ." could be completed by the following conditions: ". . . without verbal coaxing" (child's needs); ". . . on the grass" (physical environment); ". . . with the use of canes" (child's limitations); and ". . . toward the teacher's voice" (movement element). Thus it can be seen that performances vary based on what is to be learned, and the conditions under which the performance is to occur can be changed according to various considerations.

The third element in a well-written performance objective is the *criteria* to be used to determine whether or not the student has performed at an acceptable level. This element describes the extent or accuracy of the performance, and assists the teacher in knowing whether the learner has learned a sufficient amount to go on to the next learning task. To use a rather high-level example, a teacher may have as a student's goal, "Olivia will have improved cardiovascular efficiency sufficient for competition in Special Olympics." The teacher finds that, for Olivia's age group, unless she can run 400 meters on the track in 90 seconds or less, she will not have an adequate opportunity for success. Thus the performance objective of running — the conditions of 400 meters on the track — must meet the criterion of 90 seconds or less before the teacher and the student can go on to the next step of entering and competing in Special Olympics. The criteria, like performance and conditions, can be varied to place greater and greater demands on the student. Such variance in criteria for this particular objective might include reducing the amount of time in which the performance is to be completed. Thus a series of performance objectives can be used to direct the learning process closer and closer to normal peer performance and move the student toward achieving the goal of improved cardiovascular efficiency.

A decision for placing a student into the mainstream of physical education could be based on setting the criteria for performance at a level that represents the mainstream. For example, the average number of bent-knee curl-ups for twelve-year-old boys is 18 (APEAS, 1979). The goal statement for a twelve-year-old boy might be: "To improve abdominal strength to the level of average performance for Michael's age" (e.g., fiftieth percentile = 18 curl-ups). Michael's current level of performance indicates that he is able to do 8 curl-ups, which puts him below the fifth percentile for his age. A series of performance objectives could be written to point the direction of instruction for the coming year:

1. Johnny will be able to do 10 bent-knee curl-ups in 30 seconds with his feet held.
2. Johnny will be able to do 14 bent-knee curl-ups in 30 seconds with his feet held.
3. Johnny will be able to do 16 bent-knee curl-ups in 30 seconds with his feet held.
4. Johnny will be able to do 18 bent-knee curl-ups in 30 seconds with his feet held.

Table 11–1 shows some of the goal areas that have been defined in PL 94–142, and some sample performance objectives.

Progress may be slow with some students, and change may be difficult to assess. According to Mager (1962:18), "The more objectives you include, the more successfully you will communicate your intent." Thus by writing several incremental objectives, change can be more easily seen. For example, the following broad objective might be written for a child who is just learning to balance on one foot: "Mario will balance on one foot for five seconds when asked to do so." Since Mario is a five-year-old Down's syndrome child, however, it may be months before this objective can be achieved. A more appropriate series of objectives would be:

Table 11–1. Examples of goal areas and performance objectives

Goal	Performance	Conditions	Criteria
Physical fitness	■ will be able to run ■ will be able to jump ■ will be able to do sit-ups	■ 300 yards on the track ■ vertically ■ in hook-lie position	■ under 70 seconds ■ 10 inches in 3 trials ■ 20 times in 30 seconds
Development of ambulation	■ will be able to stand ■ will walk ■ will walk	■ without support ■ with support ■ toward teacher's voice	■ for 10 seconds ■ 10 steps/2 out of 3 trials ■ using 5 steps
Game and sport skills	■ will throw ■ will catch ■ will long jump	■ a softball ■ a playground ball ■ into a sand pit	■ 30 feet ■ 80% of the time ■ at least 12 feet
Aquatics skills	■ will float and recover ■ will roll from prone to supine float ■ will dive	■ prone with hands on steps ■ unassisted ■ from crouched position	■ 3 out of 5 trials ■ 100% of the time ■ 2 out of 3 trials
Dance and rhythms skills	■ will walk and clap ■ will step-close-step ■ will dance the Schottische	■ to march music ■ to music with 4/4 rhythm ■ to music	■ with 80% accuracy ■ 2 out of 3 trials ■ with less than 5 errors

1. Mario will shift his weight to one foot when he is asked to do so, three out of five times.
2. Mario will raise one foot off the ground three out of five times after shifting his weight to the opposite foot.
3. Mario will raise one foot off the ground and balance on the opposite foot for one second, three out of five times, when asked to do so.
4. Mario will balance on one foot for three seconds when asked to do so.
5. Mario will balance on one foot for five seconds when asked to do so.

Physical performance is probably the easiest area for which to write objectives, because the behavior is almost always observable. Writing performance objectives for something that is seemingly not observable — for example, understanding, appreciating, knowing, enjoying, and believing — is a bit more challenging. In these instances, students must demonstrate knowledge or appreciation by *doing* something. They may write, recite, identify, explain, construct, list, compare, or contrast. These are observable behaviors that can then be compared against the objective. For example, to teach students to appreciate the game of soccer, the following objective can be written: "The students will demonstrate an appreciation of soccer by attending at least two soccer games during Fall semester."

The three components necessary for a performance objective can be identified as follows: The performance is "attending . . . soccer games," an activity that can be observed. They will attend under the conditions of "during Fall semester," and the level at which this performance or behavior is to be demonstrated is "two" times. One can only assume, of course, based upon psychological and educational research, that appreciation is acquired through experience, and that the more the students "experience" the game of soccer, the greater their appreciation will be.

The following observable performances or behaviors can be considered as manifestations of less observable learnings: defines, describes, identifies, labels, lists, names, selects, explains, writes, tells. Remember that effecting cognitive learning can only be measured by observing behavior. The following terms should be avoided in writing objectives: understanding, knowing, appreciating, enjoying, grasp the significance of, believe, have faith in, feel. Unless terms can be associated with these words that describe observable behaviors that demonstrate that these qualities have been acquired, there is virtually no way of measuring their acquisition.

Writing Achievement Dates

Performance objectives must include an achievement date. Many school districts interpret this to mean that the date associated with each objective should show progress throughout the school year — that is, the objectives are written in a sequence such that one or more can be achieved every two to three months. To take the example given earlier — entering Olivia in Special Olympics competition — each two months, the objective to be achieved should show the criteria re-

duced by how many seconds are shaved off the 400-meter running time:

1. Olivia will run 400 meters on the track in 120 seconds or less by November 1.
2. Olivia will run 400 meters on the track in 110 seconds or less by January 15.
3. Olivia will run 400 meters on the track in 100 seconds or less by March 1.
4. Olivia will run 400 meters on the track in 90 seconds or less by June 1.

Timelines for the achievement of objectives are very difficult for the beginning teacher to determine. The experienced teacher, who has taught many students similar to the student currently being assessed, has a point of reference from which to decide approximately how rapidly a particular student will progress. For the beginning teacher, however, a little more effort may be required to realistically determine the amount of progress to expect from a student in any given period of time. It may be necessary to locate test norms, preferably norms based on the population that includes this student. If, for example, Olivia is moderately retarded, her current level of performance could be found on a table of norms based on the moderately retarded population. The teacher can use the norms by finding Olivia's current raw score and then moving upward in the table of raw scores to determine what the next realistic raw score would be.

The teacher must remember that learning and development do not always progress at a steady rate. Usually, when dealing with physical parameters that require a strictly physiological response to conditioning, the changes in observable performance will appear to be more steady. But where learning is involved, research conclusively indicates that observable performance shows rapid gains early in an instructional program, followed by a leveling off or plateau with little or no observable change; later in the program, an increase in performance is again observable. Thus it is important for the adapted physical educator to be a good observer of the way a student approaches a new learning task to try to determine whether or not progress is likely to be rapid or slow at the onset of instruction.

Another technique for projecting performance within given timelines is to calculate the ratio between the current level of performance and the student's chronological age, using developmental milestones. For example, Billy, an autistic child, is chronologically eight years of age, but performs on a developmental profile at six years of age. He is functioning motorically at 6/8, or approximately three-quarters his chronological age. While a nonhandicapped child would be expected to develop at a rate commensurate with his chronological age, Billy would only be expected to develop at three-quarters that rate. Thus a year from now, at his annual review, he will be nine years old, and will be expected to perform equivalent to a youngster six years nine months of age (i.e., at a level equivalent to three-quarters his chronological age). A realistic criterion for performance, then, could be obtained from a table of norms for boys six years nine months of age. (These techniques for systematically quantifying performance should not be construed as an intent to limit a child's development by placing a ceiling on behavior through teacher expectations. Rather, they are offered as a means for physical educators to establish a realistic projection of performance when writing goals and objectives.)

The intelligence quotient (IQ) is more significant to the physical educator when considered as an indication of the rate of learning rather than the amount learned. A third technique used in the case of youngsters having below-average intellectual functioning is to use the IQ to indicate the rate of expected progress. A moderately retarded youngster who has an IQ of 50 could be expected to learn at about half the rate of a mentally normal child of the same age. Thus, if one would expect a mentally normal child to progress to a

given point in two months, one would expect the moderately retarded child to require four months to accomplish the same.

Strategies and Materials to Be Used to Achieve Goals

Once the annual goals, performance objectives, and dates for achieving these have been established, physical activities must be identified that will be used to accomplish the goals and objectives. Effective programming, selection of activities, and program planning will be dealt with at length in Part III. A few basic concepts, however, are appropriate to include here.

Objectives have been written so as to lead toward the achievement of annual goals. The objectives describe the performances that must be taught, but the activities used to achieve those objectives must also be sequenced according to some logical considerations. First, at the secondary and upper elementary levels, some consideration must be given to appropriate *seasonal activities*. This should be considered in order to keep the adapted physical education class as much like the regular physical education classes as possible. Not only are there social and emotional values to consider; motorically, it is appropriate (where possible) to teach patterns and skills that can be applied to participation in the mainstream. For example, if soccer is a typical seasonal activity in the regular physical education classes in the fall, it would be appropriate to facilitate achieving individualized performance objectives through soccer and soccer-like activities. These activities may include relays while dribbling the ball with the feet, running, kicking a rolling ball, kicking a stationary ball, and running and kicking a rolling or stationary ball. Each of these represents skills used in soccer that could serve as part of the lead-up sequence for mainstreaming students into regular physical education classes.

As in the examples above, a second consideration

in sequencing activities is the complexity of the ac-tivities to be used. The teacher should start with the simple and progress to the compound and complex motor activities. A child whose current level of per-formance in kicking a stationary ball is at the fifth percentile is certainly not ready to run, intercept, and kick a rolling ball, as would be required in a game of soccer. However, a sequence of activities that could be used to shape appropriate behaviors would be:

1. Kick a stationary ball while standing.
2. Run up to and kick a stationary ball.
3. Kick a rolling ball while standing.
4. Run up to and kick a rolling ball.
5. Run up to, trap, and kick a soccer ball.

In this example, activities are sequenced from the most simple to the most complex.

The third consideration fundamental to the other two is the developmental sequence of activities to be used. For example, a youngster for whom a goal is "To improve eye-hand and eye-foot coordination" should have developmentally sequenced tasks leading from simple to complex within a seasonally appropriate con-text. Thus a twelve-year-old who cannot catch an 8-inch ball could not be expected to catch and kick a football, even though the seasonal setting may be ap-propriate. Catching and drop-kicking a soccer ball are not only just as seasonally appropriate, but require de-velopmentally lower level skills because the ball is larger and round and therefore simpler to handle.

Determining Related Services

The fifth and final piece of information the physical educator may contribute to the IEP is to help deter-mine related services. The physical educator usually sees students in a different context than many of the other professionals who work with them. Furthermore, the physical educator sees the student perform in more of a total body effort than most other profes-sionals. It is possible, then, that the student will display behaviors not observed by other members of the multidisciplinary team. Therefore it is extremely impor-tant that the physical educator be a good observer — of motor performance in particular — in order to recog-nize significant deviations that may require related services.

The physical educator must have not only a good understanding of the various roles of other members on the multidisciplinary team, it is also important to know which of those potential team members are available to deliver services to the student. Remember that related services are defined by law as those ser-vices necessary for the child to benefit from special education. Observations of or questions about behav-ior should be discussed with the parent before recommending even an evaluation for related services. A discussion with the parent may also clarify observa-tions made during the data-gathering phase of assessment. Most school districts have related service personnel available for evaluations, and can identify which professional services are available for referrals.

SIGNIFICANCE OF THE IEP

Once the individualized educational program plan is completed, it serves as a blueprint for the child's edu-cation for the year. For the child, this means that a clear and specific direction has been set by those who have the most intimate knowledge of his or her edu-cational needs. For the very low functioning multihandicapped child who needs work on a variety of behaviors, the IEP brings into focus the specific di-rection and priorities for instruction that will be pursued. For the higher functioning students, the IEP represents a scope of instruction that educators are committed to deliver.

For the parent, the IEP provides some assurance that a specific curriculum and set of behaviors will be pursued. It has only been in recent years that parents have initiated litigation against school districts for not having taught their children to read, write, or calculate. Although the IEP is not a binding contract, it does provide the child and the parent with some level of commitment that specified behaviors will be the center of program focus.

A parent once said to an adapted specialist, "My son needs so much, no matter what you do, it has to help him." Sadly, there are many children in adapted physical education about whom one could make this statement. Thus the IEP assists the physical educator in maintaining focus on the behaviors that are considered of greatest importance at any given point in time. The dedicated professionals, especially when working with the severely or multihandicapped, often feel that there are many things that should be done to enhance growth and development. The IEP helps to narrow the scope of behaviors being addressed within a realistic framework. Thus the individualized educational program not only sets direction for the educator and assurances for the parent, but also facilitates the most important goal: learning for the child.

SUMMARY

The chief purpose for a systematic assessment process is to plan an appropriate physical education program for each student who has special needs. Understanding the legislative mandates and the procedures for appropriately placing students so they can receive service is the responsibility of the adapted physical educator. Once a student with special needs is appropriately placed, annual goals, performance objectives, teaching strategies, and related services must be identified to complete each student's individualized program. Writing appropriate and realistic goals and objectives requires a systematic procedure that the adapted physical education specialist learns to do with ease. Parents and teachers as well as students benefit from outlining the goals required by the IEP.

BIBLIOGRAPHY

Education of All Handicapped Children Act, PL 94–142. Washington, D.C.: *Federal Register* (August 23, 1977).

Los Angeles Unified School District. *Adapted Physical Education Assessment Scale (APEAS).* Los Angeles: Field draft, 1979.

Mager, R. F. *Preparing Instructional Objectives.* Belmont, California: Fearon, 1962.

U.S. Education Department. *Individualized Education Programs (IEPs) OSE Policy Paper.* Washington, D.C.: U.S. Education Department, Assistant Secretary for Special Education and Rehabilitation Services (May 23, 1980).

Vort Corporation. *Action Words Directory: An Index to Verbs for Setting Objectives.* Palo Alto, California: Vort Corporation, 1979.

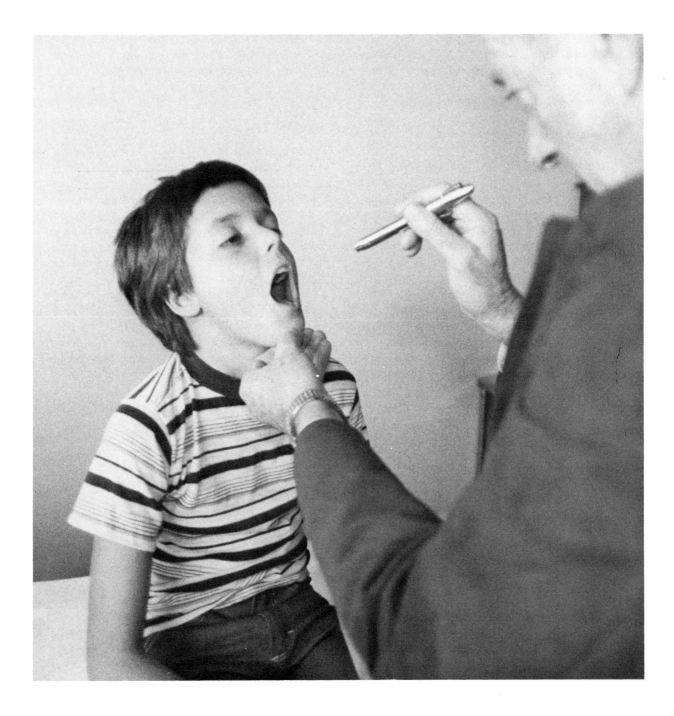

12 Additional Factors That Influence Motor Performance

Guiding Questions

1. What factors, in addition to sensory and motor development, directly or indirectly influence motor performance?
2. How can the use of medication for seizure or behavior control influence motor performance?
3. How do nutritional and environmental factors adversely affect motor performance?

Sensory and motor development are not the only influences on motor performance. Other areas of human development — such as intellectual or cognitive, language, and social development — and other factors — such as medical pathology and environmental influences — have an indirect but significant effect on a student's motor performance. The adapted physical educator should have at least a working knowledge of these influences in order to successfully serve as a member of an interdisciplinary team.

INTELLECTUAL TESTING

Wechsler Intelligence Scale for Children — Revised (WISC — R). The Wechsler Intelligence Scale for Children (WISC — R) has been used for over twenty years in the public schools. The most recent revision yields a verbal intelligence quotient (IQ), a performance IQ, and a full scale score. It is normed on individuals from six years to sixteen years eleven months of age, and is quite popular in the public schools. Performance tests of particular interest to the physical educator include picture completion, picture arrangement or sequencing, making block designs by rearranging blocks, assembling picture puzzles, coding, and a paper and pencil maze drawing. Investigators who have used the WISC — R (Clements, et al., 1964; Bannatyne, 1968) have found that children who score significantly higher on the verbal IQ than on their performance score have difficulty in perceptual-motor areas. Very often, youngsters who have difficulty arranging pictures in sequence, seeing relationships among parts of a puzzle to the whole, and rearranging blocks to create a specified design also have difficulty sequencing, arranging, and rearranging their body parts to replicate a motor task.

Wide Range Achievement Test (WRAT). The Wide Range Achievement Test (WRAT) is more an estimate of general ability than it is a test of intelligence. It is normed on individuals ranging in age from five years to adulthood, and it generates scores in the areas of spelling, arithmetic, and reading. Of particular interest to the adapted physical education specialist are the performances required on the spelling subscale. This subscale requires copying marks resembling letters, writing one's name, and writing single words. Here, the child is asked to give a fine motor performance as an indication of mental ability. When control of small muscles is poor, use of those muscle groups in catching, throwing and ocular control is often poor. The WRAT does, however, provide an oral section for retarded and very young children that does not require fine motor output.

Leiter International Performance Scale. The Leiter is a nonverbal intelligence test used with individuals who are speech or auditorily handicapped, illiterate, foreign born, and culturally or educationally deprived. This test is normed on individuals two years to adult, and generates both a mental age and IQ. The student is presented with a set of blocks that must be arranged in a specified order. Again, the subject is required to give a motor performance as an indication of intellectual functioning. Low scores on the Leiter often suggest below-age motor performance as well as low intellectual function.

Detroit Tests of Learning Aptitude. The Detroit consists of nineteen subtests normed on individuals from three to nineteen years of age. It provides a wide range of information for educators, and yields a general mental age, a mental age for each subtest, and IQ. Of particular interest to adapted physical educators are subtests for motor speed and precision, visual attention span for objects, social adjustment, oral differences, and verbal likenesses and differences. The relationship between motor speed, visual attention and motor performance should be clear to the physical educator. Poor motor speed, visual attention, and motor performance on the Detroit will usually verify similar findings on motor performance tests.

Goodenough-Harris Draw-A-Man Test. This test, originally designed by F. L. Goodenough in 1926, was

intended to measure intelligence. However, D. B. Harris (1963) revised it to emphasize the developmental aspect of drawing a figure. This test is normed on children from five to fifteen years, and is used as an indication of intellectual maturity rather than a measure of intelligence. Harris also added a draw-a-woman component, and added to the scoring a system for measuring the accuracy of a child's observation and the development of conceptual thinking. This test correlates modestly with the Stanford-Binet Test of Intelligence (this modest relationship should come as no surprise to the astute physical educator, who sees the limitations of using a motor performance such as drawing as an indicator of intellectual function).

Other Tests. Other tools that might be reported by a member of the school appraisal team (usually the psychologist) might include The Pre-School Attainment Record (PAR), the Raven Coloured Progressive Matrices, or one or more of the subtests of the Brigance Inventory for Early Development. These tests (as do the achievement tests noted above) tend to go beyond the limits of strict intelligence testing. Just as in the area of measuring motor performance, test makers have found it difficult to separate intelligence from other aspects of parameters of human development. Thus some of these tools include the measurement of language, social, and motor development in addition to the development of cognitive functioning. This discussion should further serve to point out the intricate interaction among all aspects of human development, and the influence of each on the others.

The reports of intelligence testing should provide the adapted physical educator with valuable information regarding the likelihood of a student's ability to understand concepts involved in selected learning sequences. A child's IQ should be considered an indication of the rate of learning rather than the amount learned. Thus a ten-year-old with a 50 IQ would be expected to understand concepts at about the same level as a five-year-old. For example, although many mentally normal ten-year-olds understand some of the concepts involved in baseball and football strategy, mentally normal five-year-olds do not. Therefore a trainable mentally retarded youngster ten years of age with an IQ of 50 should not be expected to grasp the concepts of those sports. Concepts represented in those sports that could be understood by a mentally normal five-year-old should be taught, or should at least serve as a starting point for instruction.

SPEECH, LANGUAGE, AND AUDITION TESTING

Speech, language development, and audition fall under the general rubric of language development. In some states, these three areas are addressed by a single professional—the Speech, Language, and Hearing Pathologist or therapist. In other parts of the country, audiologists are licensed or certificated separately from the speech therapist.

Articulation Testing

Goldman-Fristoe Test of Articulation. The Goldman-Fristoe measures articulation of consonant sounds in initial, medial, and final positions in a word. Because it is a quick test to administer and is normed on children aged six to sixteen years, it enjoys wide popularity. Of interest to the physical educator in this and other articulation tests is the demand on the student to sequence the motor components with finite discrimination, in order to create the sounds of consonants and vowels in specific positions in a word. A child who is unable to sequence movements of the speech mechanisms is said to be dyspraxic, or without the ability to sequence purposeful movements for creating speech. Children with articulation problems often have more global indications of dyspraxia—that is, in gross motor

performance they often are also unable to carry out a sequence of purposeful movements, demonstrating the same lack of articulation or sharpness of gross movements as they do in speech.

Fisher-Logemann Test of Articulation Competence. This test is primarily used with kindergarteners to measure language sounds or phonemes according to distinctive features or commonalities in speech production. The adapted physical educator should take particular notice when the results of these or other articulation tests are reported. These tests generate data describing the ability to sequence movements that can be used to validate the results of motor performance testing. This is especially true if the physical educator has observed, measured, or suspected a motor sequencing difficulty.

Language Testing

The Illinois Test of Psycholinguistic Abilities (ITPA). The Illinois Test of Psycholinguistic Abilities (ITPA), which is among the best known and most widely used language tests, measures expressive and receptive language in ten areas. The test is normed on children two to ten years of age, and yields both a linguistic age and an estimate of the Stanford-Binet mental age. Of particular interest to the adapted physical educator are subtests measuring verbal and manual expression, auditory and visual sequential memory, auditory and visual reception, and auditory and visual association. Again, the performances on this test require a motor output based on either visual or auditory input. If visual or auditory processing is poor, then the resultant motor performance is likely to be poor.

Peabody Picture Vocabulary Test. The Peabody, normed on individuals one year nine months to eighteen years of age, is used to measure listening, mental abilities, and mental processes. The test yields a mental age, an IQ, and percentile ranks. The child is required to process single words in order to identify pictures of things that the examiner labels. Although scoring on this test does not rely as heavily on motor output as the earlier mentioned tests in this subsection, the ability of a child to understand single words can be revealed through this test and should be a clue to the physical educator as to whether or not items such as "ball," "bat," or "beam" can be identified by the student.

Utah Test of Language Development. The Utah test measures expressive and receptive language. Normed on children from one year six months to fourteen years five months of age, it generates a language age, and is used to study growth or change in language development. It has particular use in identifying individual differences and exaggerated differences, as found in the communicatively gifted or handicapped student. Because it measures both expressive and receptive language, its scores can serve the physical educator by revealing the difference between what a student is able to understand in contrast to how much a student is able verbally to express.

Northwestern Syntax Screening Test. The Northwestern Syntax Screening Test is a quick test that measures expressive and receptive use of syntactic forms. That is, it measures how a child understands strings of words and puts words together for use. It is normed on children three years to seven years eleven months of age, and reveals how much a physical educator should give a child to process at one time.

Auditory Testing

Auditory testing may be carried out through two methods: (1) audiological examination or (2) testing of auditory processing. The audiological examination (performed by an audiologist), which serves to determine an individual's ability to hear, measures the loudness or softness of sounds heard and the frequency or pitch of sounds measured in cycles per second. Normal conversational speech occurs at a rate of approximately

300 to 3,000 cycles per second. A student who has difficulty hearing sounds in that range will have difficulty learning in the normal educational environment without modifications. Similarly, students who have a hearing loss of approximately 60 decibels or greater will also have difficulty learning without amplification and possible modifications in the learning environment.

Part of the process in determining why a child is not performing as requested should include an audiological examination to identify or rule out a possible hearing loss.

Kindergarten Auditory Screening Test (KAST). The Kindergarten Auditory Screening Test (KAST) tests kindergarteners and beginning first graders on auditory skills important to learning. These skills are auditory figure-ground, sound-blending, and auditory discrimination. Auditory figure-ground, like visual figure-ground perception, requires that the child distinguish the important sounds (e.g., the teacher's voice) from the unimportant sounds (e.g., the noise outside on the playground). Sound-blending, also measured by the ITPA, measures the child's ability to synthesize phonemes or word sounds into words. Auditory discrimination measures whether or not the child is able to tell whether word pairs are the same or different (e.g., mat and bat). A child's ability to discriminate the teacher's voice, especially in a physical education class, is important to the ability to pay attention to instruction. Telling whether words sound the same or different can be significant when requesting a child to perform. If Billy is told to pick up the bat, and he is not able to tell the difference between bat and mat, he is likely to be confused or in error. These pieces of auditory information can be used by the adapted physical education specialist to make sense out of a child's motor behavior or to lend support to earlier suspicions.

Other Tests. Other tests that might be used in this area include The Denver Articulation Test, a companion to the Denver Developmental Screening Test; The Sequenced Inventory of Communication Development; the Goldman, Fristoe, Woodcock; or the Boehm Test of Basic Concepts. Like the tests previously discussed, these tools measure various aspects of speech, language, audition, and intellectual development.

The processes of language sampling and phonological assessment are receiving increased attention. In addition to formal testing, speech pathologists find that *language sampling* can give them a better picture of the language development of a given child. Talking with children and listening to the way they form sentences, the length and order of words in sentences, and the grammar used is often found to be more useful than formal language testing. *Phonological assessment,* or the assessment of how a child makes sounds in various contexts, is thought by some speech pathologists to be more practical than formal testing. Because there is wide variance in how children make sounds at any given age, the adapted physical educator using the developmental model may find more value in discussing with the speech therapist or pathologist the results of language sampling and phonological assessment as it relates to motor performance.

The relationship between speech as a motor act and the more global movement concerns of the physical educator cannot be overemphasized. Far too often, youngsters who have articulation difficulties have other motor performance deficits as well. Furthermore, children who have language or auditory dysfunction tend not to demonstrate valid motor responses, as a result of these deficits. It is incumbent upon the adapted physical educator to analyze motor performance tools to be certain they do not discriminate against the language- or hearing-impaired student.

SOCIAL DEVELOPMENT TESTING

Many tests, such as the Detroit and the Brigance, measure components of social development, either as a subtest or as inferences drawn from subtests in previously mentioned tools. Data on social development or maturity can contribute much to the physical educator's total picture of the student.

The Vineland Social Maturity Scale. This is perhaps the best-known single tool. Standardized on individuals from birth to maturity, this test generates a social age. It measures eight areas of development, most of which have direct implications for motor performance. These areas include self-help skills in dressing, eating, directions, and general; communication; socialization, locomotion, and occupation. A student's ability to dress for class, put on or tie shoes, or perform cooperatively with others in group activities has significant implications for the organization of an adapted physical education class. For example, a sixteen-year-old who is unable to relate to more than one person at a time will have grave difficulties in curricular activities typically planned for sixteen-year-olds. The adapted physical educator may not have the opportunity to observe a student acting or interacting with peers. Therefore particular attention should be given to information relating to a student's social age. One obvious implication is that the ability of a youngster to function in a group will significantly affect the physical educator's recommendation for placement.

MEDICAL EVALUATION AND INFORMATION

The medical evaluation, including a neurological examination, can provide important information for the educator, especially when considering placement into a special class. The medical examination usually has as its foundation a family history; details of pregnancy, birth and neonatal development; illness, injury, and infections; motor behavior; and social and school behavior (Lerner, 1976). In addition, students who have special needs should have a record of a neurological examination. This examination should include the following:

1. Physical measures: height, head circumference, weight.
2. Examination of cranial nerves: vision, hearing, facial expression, taste, chewing, swallowing, vestibular function, speaking.
3. Posture and equilibrium responses: muscle tonus in static and dynamic situations.
4. Components controlling motor functions: reflexes (deep and superficial), locomotion, taxias (coordination), praxis (series of purposeful movements), oculomotor praxis (visual tracking or control).
5. Electroencephalography (EEG) measures electrical activity of brain.
6. X-rays of skull and blood vessels of brain.
7. Biochemical studies.
8. Endocrinological studies.
9. Genetic examination.

Unless a physician is particularly accustomed to dealing with children who have neurological impairment, only some of the tests listed above will be carried out. As Schain (1972) points out, the most definitive indicator of neurological dysfunction among children who are otherwise pathologically sound is that they are not learning. Even the electroencephalogram (EEG) is not a very reliable test in separating learners from nonlearners (Freeman, 1971). Also, many times, the physician is not looking for so-called soft neurological signs. A few of these signs in isolation found in children who are learning adequately are not considered to be significant. But a child who is not learning, and who also demonstrates these soft neurological signs, should be evaluated for minimal brain dysfunction (see Figure 12–1).

The following is a list of soft neurological signs in children, adapted from Schain (1972):

1. Clumsiness in fine motor tasks.
2. Mild dysphasias (language disturbances).
3. Choreiform (jerky) movements.
4. Finger agnosia (inability to attach meaning to tactile input).
5. Borderline hyperreflexia (overactive reflexes).
6. Associated movements (neurological overflow).
7. Dysgraphesthesias (incorrect tracing shapes, sizes, etc.).
8. Pupilary inequalities.
9. Avoidance of outstretched hands.
10. Unilateral winking defect.
11. Reflex asymmetries.
12. Tremor.
13. Ocular apraxia.
14. Endpoint nystagmus.
15. Dysdiadochokinesia (inability to perform opposite movements).
16. Whirling.
17. Mixed laterality and disturbed right/left discrimination.
18. Extinction to double tactile stimulation.
19. Awkward gait.

These soft neurological signs should have obvious significant implications for the adapted physical educator, because most of them are observed through overt motor performance. A child with choreiform movements, associated movements, tremor, ocular apraxia, and dysdiadochokinesia is going to have difficulties performing motor tasks. This medical information can further validate data or explain observations made during the data gathering phase of assessment.

Medication

Another factor that influences motor performance is the ingestion of drugs. Many students who have special needs maintain a regimen of medication for the management of their conditions. If youngsters are medicated during the physical education class, their

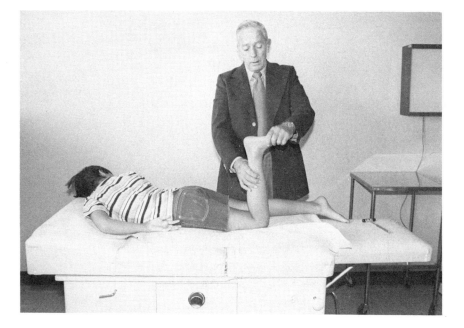

Figure 12-1. A pediatric neurologist giving a child a neurological examination.

performances may be significantly different than the performances of similar children who are not receiving medication or their own performances when the medication has worn off. For example, students receiving amphetamines for the control of hyperkinetic behavior will also experience constricted blood vessels; increased heart rate; constriction of the pupils and gastrointestinal sphincters; and some effects on muscles of the bladder, uterus, sweat glands, and hair erector muscles of the skin and intestines (Noback, 1975). Some psychotropic drugs used to manage behavior tend to lower the seizure threshold. Thus seizure-prone children who are taking anticonvulsants for their control, and who are also taking psychotropics, may have more frequent seizures due to the reversing effects of psychotropic drugs taken for behavior control. The interaction between physical activity and the pharmacologic effects of medication should be established between a student's physician and physical educator before an IEP is written.

The adapted physical educator should know which students are receiving medication, the purpose of the medication, and when in the cycle of administration the student participates in physical education.

Through the school nurse or directly from the child's physician, the physical educator should determine what adverse or heightening effects physical activity might have on the child when combined with the medication (Table 12-1 presents some commonly used drugs and their trade names, treatment, uses, and possible side-effects).

Drug research has resulted in progressively and consistently more effective medications during the four decades over which drugs have been used for psychological and electrochemical disorders. Research continues at such a rate that drugs that are available today may not have been in use at the time this textbook was written. Thus it is the responsibility of the educator to learn as much as possible about the medications used in order to better understand and teach their students.

Many other medications are used for treatment of other conditions. Antihistamines and related drugs are used routinely to control allergies among school-age children. The physical educator should be aware of the pollens, dust, grasses, and other allergens commonly found in the physical activity environment, and help students to avoid them. Youngsters with asthma may

Table 12-1. Drugs commonly used in pediatric psychopharmacology

Category: Chemical name (trade name)	Treatment uses	Side-effects
NEUROANALEPTICS		
1. Methylphenidate (Ritalin, Ciba)	■ hyperkinesis ■ distractibility ■ hypermotor activity ■ learning disorders	■ nausea ■ increased heart rate and blood pressure
2. Dextroamphetamine (Dexedrine, Benzedrine)	■ same as above	■ stimulates some autonomic functions ■ weight loss
3. Pemoline (Cylert)	■ hyperkinesis	
4. Imipramine (Tofranil)	■ hyperkinesis ■ sleep disorders ■ depression ■ impulsiveness ■ refusing to go to school ■ nonpsychotic aggression	■ lowers seizure threshold ■ dizziness ■ blurred vision
NEUROLEPTICS (major tranquilizers)		
1. Chlorpromazine (Thorazine)	■ severe anxiety ■ motor agitation ■ nonpsychotic aggression ■ impulsiveness	■ dizziness ■ nasal stuffiness ■ blurred vision
2. Trifluoperazine (Stelazine)	■ withdrawal (psychotic) ■ agitation (psychotic) ■ adolescent schizophrenia	■ same as above
3. Thioridazine (Melaril)	■ hyperactivity ■ impulsiveness ■ refusing to go to school ■ agitation (psychotic) ■ nonpsychotic aggression ■ nonpsychotic anxiety ■ adolescent schizophrenia	■ same as above but less severe

Table 12-1. (continued)

Category: Chemical name (trade name)	Treatment uses	Side-effects
4. Thiothixene (Navane)	■ agitation (psychotic) ■ adolescent schizophrenia	■ very minor
5. Haloperidol (Haldol)	■ same as above	■ lowers seizure threshold
MINOR TRANQUILIZERS (sedatives) 1. Diphenhydramine (Benedryl)	■ hyperkinesis ■ sleep disorders ■ refusing to go to school ■ nonpsychotic anxiety ■ sedation	■ occasional dizziness ■ mild oversedation
2. Hydroxyzine (Atarax, Vistaril)	■ hyperkinesis ■ nonpsychotic anxiety ■ sedation	■ very minor
3. Diazepam (Valium)	■ sleep disorders	■ drug dependence
4. Chlordiazepoxide (Librium)	■ sleep disorders ■ nonpsychotic anxiety	■ excitation paradox ■ drowsiness ■ ataxia ■ hostility
5. Promethazine (Phenergan)	■ hyperkinesis ■ nonpsychotic anxiety	■ blurred vision ■ dry mucus membranes
SEDATIVE-HYPNOTICS 1. Paraldehyde	■ anticonvulsant ■ sedation	■ drug dependence
2. Flurazepam (Delmane)	■ same as above	■ excitation paradox
3. Chloral Hydrate	■ same as above	■ nausea ■ nightmares ■ ataxia

Table 12–1. (continued)

Category: Chemical name (trade name)	Treatment uses	Side-effects
4. Barbiturates (Phenobarbital, Mebaral, Mysolin)	■ anticonvulsant ■ sleep disorders	■ increases hyperkinesis ■ drowsiness ■ skin rash ■ high fever
5. Hydantoin derivatives (Dilantin, Mysantoin)	■ anticonvulsant	■ nausea, vomiting ■ nystagmus ■ ataxia ■ skin rash
6. Succinimide derivatives (Zarontin, Milontin, Celontin)	■ anticonvulsant	■ headache ■ dizziness ■ drowsiness ■ skin rash
SUBSTITUTED PROPANEDIOLS 1. Meprobamate (Miltown, Equinil)	■ transient anxiety ■ sleep disorders ■ anticonvulsant	■ drowsiness ■ ataxia ■ allergic reactions

SOURCE: Adapted from James H. White, *Pediatric Psychopharmacology* (Baltimore: Williams and Wilkins, 1977); and Michael J. Cohen, *Drugs and the Special Child* (New York: Gardner Press, 1979).

need to take bronchial tree relaxants during an acute attack, and the physical educator may be needed to assist in administering the drug. Allergic and asthmatic reactions may also occur in the presence of excitement, stress, overexertion, and temperature changes. The educator must be alert to these conditions and be prepared to modify activities for youngsters who seem to have a low allergic threshold in situations that give rise to a reaction.

Sulpha drugs have many uses for infections such as trachoma (a viral infection of the cornea and eyelid) and rheumatic fever. Students who have had rheu-matic fever may routinely take sulpha drugs, penicillin, or other antibiotics, to prevent recurrence of the infection (Mullins, 1979). Other medications may be used on a short-term or long-term basis, and the adapted physical educator is encouraged to become familiar with their use as the need arises.

Nutrition

The basic elements of nutrition are often taken for granted by educators, unless they teach in an especially impoverished community. Most educators have themselves come from a background of sound nutritional practices, and have learned through their formal education that eating the right foods, getting enough rest, and exercising regularly contribute to a healthy, wholesome life. What many educators do not realize is that the chubby, lethargic child may be just as victimized by under-nutrition as the skinny, apathetic youngster. Willgoose (1979:58) defines malnutrition as "a state of impaired health resulting from an inadequate or imbalanced intake of nutrients." Thus children whose diet consists primarily of bread, noodles, grits, corn meal, rice, or tortillas may appear as though they are getting plenty to eat even though they are not getting enough of the right foods.

The National Dairy Council (1964) and the United States Department of Agriculture (1973) have recommended that foods be consumed from each of the four basic food groups: dairy foods, meats, fruits and vegetables, and breads and cereals. Students who are not receiving enough foods from *each* of these groups will show signs of nutritional deprivation. Since the most observable effects are on the body and its growth, the physical educator will observe depressed vitality and productivity; learning and behavior disorders; deficits in speed, coordination, and stamina; general listlessness, muscular atrophy, and failure to grow (Willgoose, 1979). A more complete checklist follows listing the observable signs of the main conditions of malnutrition: protein-calorie deficiency, Vitamin A deficiency, anemia and Vitamin B complex deficiency. Whether the child is suffering from a primary deficiency, that is a direct deprivation of essential nutrients, or a deficiency secondary to another condition, which prevents the absorption or utilization of nutrients, the school nurse or physician should be consulted (see Table 12–2).

Allergist Benjamin F. Feingold created a flurry of discussion throughout special education in the mid-seventies with his discoveries of the effects of food additives on children's (and adults') behavior. Over a period of ten years, Feingold developed the K-P Diet. This diet is based on research and clinical findings that certain substances found commonly in foods create an adverse reaction or intolerance in the human organism — child or adult. Some of the reaction may be manifested through a true allergic response with accompanying skin rashes, hives, redness, and other skin disorders. The adverse reaction for which the diet is most commonly used with children (not a true allergy) is hyperactivity (Feingold, 1975).

The K-P Diet eliminates two groups of foods: (1) all foods containing artificial flavoring and coloring, plus two preservatives (BHT and BHA); and artificial salicylates and many fruits and vegetables containing natural salicylates. Feingold discovered that nearly all pediatric medications contain some form of artificial color or flavor to make them more palatable. Furthermore, many so-called "convenience foods" and "junk" foods contain these preservatives and artificial sweeteners. Thus, besides eliminating bakery goods, ice cream, chewing gum, potato chips, soft drinks, and the like, Feingold also recommends the elimination of almonds, apples, apricots, peaches, tomatoes, cough drops, and many other foods containing salicylates. In collaboration with his wife, Feingold published a cookbook for hyperactive children (1979), which includes many useable foods not containing the eliminated substances and a collection of recipes for their preparation. Although Feingold's work has been criticized by some, many parents have sought dietary control with a great deal of success as an alternative to the use of medication.

Other children may also require dietary control to avoid aggravation of their conditions. For example, foods such as eggs and wheat may be controlled in asthmatics, and children with cystic fibrosis may have a diet modified by limited fat and starch intake. Diabetes, by definition, implies the control of sugar intake; yet most foods contain some natural sugars.

Table 12-2. ABCs of nutritional deprivation in children

Observation (check when observed)	Indicators of possible nutritional difficulty	Nutrients implicated
APPEARANCE		
_____ Growth	■ failure to grow within expected growth curve norms ■ maturation lag	■ deficiency of protein, calories, generally poor diet
_____ Height		■ deficiency of calories, protein, generally poor diet
_____ Weight	■ failure to meet expected weight norm ■ overweight for age, height	■ overweight caused by excess calories, diet may be generally good or inadequate in other nutrients
_____ Posture	■ fatigue posture, rounded shoulders, winged shoulder blades	■ generally poor diet ■ protein, calorie deficiency
_____ Hair	■ lacking in luster, brittle, sparse	■ deficiency of Vitamin A ■ protein deficiency
_____ Eyes		
_____ Eyelids	■ crusting and inflammation at margins	■ deficiency of Vitamin A, riboflavin ■ excess intake of carbohydrates
_____ Corners of eyes	■ cracks at corners where eyelids meet	■ deficiency of riboflavin
_____ Conjunctiva/ sclera (white)	■ dryness, thickening, ``smoky'' appearance ■ redness (engorged capillaries) extending through conjunctiva	■ deficiency of Vitamin A ■ deficiency of niacin, riboflavin
_____ Skin under eyes	■ dark circles under eyes	■ unknown specifically ■ general poor diet or health
_____ Lips	■ inflammation of line of closure	■ deficiency of niacin, protein, riboflavin, B-complex
_____ Corners of mouth	■ fissures and/or heaping of greyish-white epithelium to appear radiating out from mouth	■ deficiency of riboflavin, niacin, B-complex
_____ Tongue	■ swollen, beefy red or magenta color, fissured, abnormally smooth or rough	■ deficiency of niacin, B-complex
_____ Gums	■ swollen, bleeding, spongy	■ deficiency of ascorbic acid
_____ Teeth	■ cavities	■ over-use of refined carbohydrates and sugar
_____ Skin	■ easy bruising	■ deficiency of ascorbic acid

Table 12–2. (continued)

Observation (check when observed)	Indicators of possible nutritional difficulty	Nutrients implicated
_____ Color	■ pallor	■ deficiency of iron, B-complex
_____ Texture	■ small nodules (permanent "goose flesh")	■ deficiency of Vitamin A
_____ Complexion	■ acne	■ deficiency of riboflavin, B-complex, Vitamin A ■ overuse of refined carbohydrates and sugars
_____ Fingernails	■ spoon-shaped ■ symmetrical (both hands) opaque, white hands	■ deficiency of iron
_____ Bones	■ Pigeon-chested, knock-kneed, bow-legged, flat-footed	■ deficiency of calcium, Vitamin D
BEHAVIOR		
_____ Activity level	■ hyperactivity — restlessness; listlessness, sluggishness, apathy ■ inability to fall asleep, restless sleep, awakening with fright	■ general poor nutrition; deficiency of iron, protein, calories, B-complex vitamins ■ overuse of refined carbohydrates and sugars ■ food allergies may result in hyperactivity ■ hypoglycemia, a disturbance in glucose metabolism, may also result in symptoms. Although hypoglycemia may not result from diet deficiencies, it may be diet-controlled.
_____ Emotionality	■ hyper-irritability, inability to tolerate correction or criticism	■ general poor nutrition ■ deficiency of thiamine, riboflavin, niacin, B-complex
COMPLAINTS		
_____ Fatigue	■ lack of stamina, lack of ambition, weakness	■ general poor nutrition, deficiency of iron, calories, B-complex vitamin, ascorbic acid
_____ Eyes	■ irritated by light ■ night blindness	■ deficiency of riboflavin, Vitamin A ■ deficiency of Vitamin A
_____ Digestion	■ abdominal discomfort, constipation	■ diet lacking in bulk, fiber
_____ Vague pains	■ tenderness in calf of leg, numbness of legs ■ frequent headaches	■ deficiency of Thiamine ■ long period without food (e.g., no breakfast)
_____ Infection	■ delayed healing of wounds	■ deficiency of Vitamin C, Vitamin K, Vitamin A

SOURCE: Subhash N. Jani and Linda A. Jani, "Nutrition Tools for LD Teachers," in _Academic Therapy_ 14 (2) (November 1978), pp. 165–177. Used with permission of the authors and Academic Therapy Publications.

Besides the obvious control of sweets, the student may need to weigh the food consumed at each meal or select foods on an exchange or substitution basis from a list prepared by the American Diabetes Association. It is important for physical educators to be conversant with the special dietary needs of students in order to plan appropriately for athletic trips, outings, holiday parties, or any other occasion in which foods may be served to students during a physical education, athletic, or recreational event. This planning should be done in consultation with the nurse, physician and parent.

ENVIRONMENTAL FACTORS

Factors in the environment probably do not positively or adversely affect handicapped children any differ-

ently than the nonhandicapped. However, specific environmental factors can amplify, worsen, or bring to the fore previously existing handicapping conditions. Children are generally affected by three environments: home, school, and community; a few of the factors which tend to adversely affect the child in each environment will be highlighted in this section.

Housing conditions and living space in the urban regions of our country are deteriorating daily. More than half of all Americans live in three major areas: the East Coast (Boston through Washington, D.C.); the Great Lakes Region (New York through Chicago); and the West Coast (San Francisco through Los Angeles) (Willgoose, 1979). Long-term exposure to the stress created by overcrowding and close living quarters disturbs people's physiological and psychological balance (see Figure 12–2).

Figure 12-2. Crowded living conditions contribute to the physiological and psychological stress on children.

Children who are emotionally disturbed or hyper-kinetic are likely to be adversely affected in a more dramatic way than other children. Homes in which there is little interaction between parent and child or siblings of a handicapped youngster may contribute to worsening certain conditions. Ott (1968) reported lethargy in subjects tested who spent all their leisure time in front of the television set. This "tired child syndrome," he claims, is attributed to radiation from the television. Add this possibility to the characteristics of Down's syndrome, obesity, and some respiratory conditions, and the result is an inactive child. Besides the child's not getting the activity needed, there may be radiation risk or aggravation of the existing condition. Animal studies reveal that UHF waves create more motor activity than was evident when the animals were not exposed to radiation (Korbel-Eaton and Thompson, 1965).

Another factor in the home, which may even lead to handicapping conditions, is child abuse. Child abuse, as a source of retardation, physical disabilities, and adversity for the child, is on the increase. Physical and other educators have a responsibility as advocates for the child to report any suspicion of child abuse to the school nurse or other school official who can report it to the authorities. Bruises, cuts, and scratches that show impressions of a striking implement or that in other ways seem unnatural, should at least be discussed with another professional.

The school environment is normally thought of as a safe, secure place that is most conducive to learning. However, one common element that has received a lot of adverse attention is fluorescent lighting. Installed in nearly every classroom in the country because of their intensity and economy, conventional cool-white fluorescent lights have been found to increase hyper-active behavior by as much as 35 percent. When full-spectrum lighting was used with radiation shielding, hyperactivity and dental caries (cavities) were reduced (Mayron, 1975). In addition, Russian scientists found

subnormal EEG activity in a group of 120 people exposed to fluorescent lighting (Kevork'ian, 1948). These individuals also showed signs of nervous exhaustion, irritability, and slowed heartrate. These findings have significance for all children, not just those prone to hyperactivity.

In the community, many factors have a broad range of influence. The conditions of overcrowding in the cities give rise to infestations of rodents and other disease-carrying agents. Any pollutant can be an allergen and, of course, cities produce the greatest amount of harmful pollutants — especially for individuals with asthma and other known allergies. Willgoose (1979) reports that children who live in heavily polluted communities all their lives have an increased risk of acute respiratory disease, with the lifelong effect equal to moderate smoking. Other con-

Figure 12–3. Airborne pollutants cause eye, nose, and throat irritation as well as long-term effects on health.

taminants, such as mercury consumed through fish and fowl, ozone in the atmosphere (Zelac, 1971), and lead and residuals from toxic chemical wastes all have devastating effects on chromosome structures and central nervous system integrity, and contribute to the overall discomfort of all who have the slightest exposure (see Figure 12-3).

Other environmental factors affecting all children — not just those with special needs — include upset at home; death in the family; excitement because of good news, a gift, or a new baby in the home; changes in weather conditions; lack of attention; teacher or favorite friend absent from school; lack of sleep; and so forth. The physical educator must realize that the inevitability of these events is not as obvious to children as to an adult, and children have much more difficulty understanding and adjusting to new events. A warm and caring approach to changes in a student's behavior is usually tbe best approach to take.

The teacher's expectations of a student's performance can also be an influencing factor. For example, if the teacher does not expect much from a particular student, based solely on the student's educational clas-sification, then a lower expectation is set and not as much is demanded. If the student then performs only to the level of expectation, it is a classic example of the self-fulfilling prophecy. This phenomenon demonstrates why the developmental approach tends to be more helpful: expectations are determined by the student's functioning level, *not* by an educational label that may or may not be related to motor performance.

SUMMARY

Many factors influence the motor performance of students with special needs. Intellectual, language, and social development; medical pathology; medication; nutrition; and environmental influences all determine the quality of motor performance. Certainly each of these will have more or less significance to the adapted physical educator, depending on the geographical location and the population being served. The adapted physical educator should take into account all factors that might affect a child's motor performance.

BIBLIOGRAPHY

American Diabetes Association. *A Cookbook for Diabetics: Meal Planning with Exchange Lists.* New York: American Diabetes Association, n.d.

Baker, H. J., and LeLane, B. *Detroit Tests of Learning Aptitudes.* Indianapolis: Bobbs Merrill, n.d.

Bannatyne, A. "Diagnosing Learning Disabilities and Writing Remedial Prescriptions." *Journal of Learning Disabilities* 1 (April 1968): 28–34.

Boehm, A. E. *Boehm Test of Basic Concepts.* San Francisco: The Psychological Corporation, n.d.

Brigance, A. H. *Inventory for Early Development.* Woburn, Massachusetts: Curriculum Associates, n.d.

Butter, H. A., and Lapierre, W. D. "The Effect of Methylphenidate on Sensory Perception in Varying Degrees of Hyperkinetic Behavior." *Disfunctioning Nervous System* 36 (1975): 286–288.

Clements, S. D., Lehtinen, L. E., and Lukens, J. *Children with Minimal Brain Injury.* Chicago: National Society for Crippled Children and Adults, 1964.

Cohen, M. J. *Drugs and the Special Child.* New York: Gardner Press, 1979.

Doll, E. A. *Pre-School Attainment Record.* Circle Pines, Minnesota: American Guidance Service, n.d.

Doll, E. A. *Vineland Social Maturity Scale.* Circle Pines, Minnesota: American Guidance Service, n.d.

Dunn, L. M. *Peabody Picture Vocabulary Test.* Circle Pines, Minnesota: American Guidance Service, n.d.

Feingold, B. F. *Why Your Child Is Hyperactive.* New York: Random House, 1975.

Fisher, H., and Logemann, J. *Fisher-Logemann Test of Articulation Competence.* Boston: Houghton Mifflin, n.d.

Freeman, R. D. "Special Education and the Electroencephalogram: A Marriage of Convenience." In *Educational Perspectives in Learning Disabilities,* edited by D. Hammill and N. Bartel. New York: Wiley, 1971, pp. 41–58.

Harris, D. B. *A Revision and Extension of the Goodenough Draw-A-Man Test.* New York: Harcourt Brace Jovanovich, 1963.

Hedrick, D., Prather, E., and Tobin, A. *Sequenced Inventory of Communication Development (SICD).* Seattle: University of Washington Press, n.d.

Jani, S. N., and Jani, L. A. "Nutrition Tools for LD Teachers." *Academic Therapy* 14 (November 1978): 165–177.

Jastak, J. F., and Jastak, S. R. *Wide Range Achievement Test, Revised.* Los Angeles: Western Psychological Services, 1976.

Katz, J. *Kindergarten Auditory Screening Test.* Chicago: Follett, n.d.

Kevork'ian, A. A. *Work with Ultrahigh Frequency Generators from the Point of View of Work Hygiene.* Moscow: Academy of Medical Sciences, USSR, 1948.

Kirk, S. A., McCarthy, J. P., and Kirk, W. D. *The Illinois Test of Psycholinguistic Abilities,* rev. ed. Urbana: University of Illinois Press, 1968.

Korbel-Eaton, S., and Thompson, W. D. "Behavioral Effects of Stimulation by UHF Radio Fields." *Psychological Reports* 17 (1965): 595–602.

Lee, L. L. *Northwestern Syntax Screening Test.* Evanston, Illinois: Northwestern University Press, n.d.

Leiter, R. G. *Leiter International Performance Scale.* Los Angeles: Western Psychological Services, n.d.

Lerner, J. W. *Children with Learning Disabilities.* 2d ed. Boston: Houghton Mifflin, 1976.

Mayron, L. W., et al. "Light, Radiation and Academic Achievement: Second Year Data." *Academic Therapy* 11 (Summer 1976): 397–407.

Mecham, M. J., Jex, L. J., and Jones, J. D. *Utah Test of Language Development.* Salt Lake City: Communication Research Associates, n.d.

Millichap, J. G. "Drugs in Management of Minimal Brain Dysfunction." *International Journal of Child Psychotherapy* 1 (1972): 65–81.

Mullins, J. B. *A Teacher's Guide to Management of Physically Handicapped Students.* Springfield, Illinois: Charles C. Thomas, 1979.

National Dairy Council. *Basic Four — A Guide to Good Eating.* Chicago: National Dairy Council, 1964.

Noback, C. R. *The Human Nervous System.* 2d ed. New York: McGraw-Hill, 1975.

Ott, J. N. "Responses of Psychological and Physiological Functions to Environmental Stress — Part II." *Journal of Learning Disabilities* 1 (1968): 348–354.

deQuiros, J. B., and Schrager, O. L. *Neuropsychological Fundamentals in Learning Disabilities.* San Rafael, California: Academic Therapy, 1978.

Raven, J. C. *Raven Coloured Progressive Matrices.* New York: The Psychological Corp., n.d.

Schain, J. J. *Neurology of Childhood Learning Disorders.* Baltimore: Williams and Wilkins, 1972.

Spring, C., et al. "Reaction Time and Effects of Ritalin on Children with Learning Problems." *Journal of Perceptual Motor Skills* 36 (1973): 75–82.

Taylor, R. L., and Perez, F. I. "Neurological and Environmental Variables in Learning Disabilities." *Academic Therapy* 15 (1980): 339–345.

U.S. Department of Agriculture (FDA). *Food for Fitness — A Daily Food Guide.* Washington, D.C.: Agriculture Research Service, Leaflet No. 24, 1973.

Vuckovich, D. M. "Pediatric Neurology and Learning Disabilities." In *Progress in Learning Disabilities*, vol. 1, edited by H. Mykelbust. New York: Grune and Stratton, 1968, pp. 16–38.

Wechsler, D. *Wechsler Intelligence Scale for Children, Revised.* New York: The Psychological Corp., 1974.

White, J. H. *Pediatric Psychopharmacology.* Baltimore: Williams and Wilkins, 1977.

Willgoose, C. E. *Environmental Health.* Philadelphia: W. B. Saunders, 1979.

Zelac, R. E., et al. "Inhaled Ozone as a Mutagen." *Environmental Research* 4 (1971): 262–282.

Part Three

Application of the Developmental Approach

13 Strategies for Meeting Individual Needs

Guiding Questions

1. What are the factors that affect learning, and how do these apply to handicapped students?
2. What are some of the methods of individualized instruction?
3. What are the three main modification techniques, and how are these applied in either the generalist or specialist settings?
4. What is the purpose of task analysis?
5. Why must and how can behavior management be successfully used in physical education?

In order to effectively plan, implement, and evaluate physical education programs for exceptional children, it is necessary to have mastery of a variety of teaching strategies. The physical educator must understand (1) the process of learning; (2) the factors that affect learning; (3) the meaning of individualized instruction; and (4) the development of appropriate strategies for meeting individual needs.

THE PROCESS OF LEARNING

Learning – a relatively permanent change in behavior as a result of experience and training – takes place as a result of the interaction between the individual and the environment. It is a process of adaptation to the environment and a progression from simple to complex adjustments (Lawther, 1978).

E. L. Thorndike (Thorndike et al., 1928), a pioneer in learning theory, stated three laws of learning: (1) the law of effect; (2) the law of frequency; and (3) the law of readiness. The *law of readiness* means that, for optimal learning to take place, the learner must be ready to learn the material presented. Very little learning occurs without a sense of receptivity and interest. The *law of frequency* refers to how often time is spent in learning. Repetition is necessary for the attainment of given levels of learning. The *law of effect* refers to the sense of accomplishment and feelings of satisfaction that facilitate the learning process. Knowing that one has learned and has made progress enhances subsequent learning.

FACTORS THAT AFFECT LEARNING

Both the teacher and the learner bring factors affecting learning to the learning situation. Mental conditions (e.g., preconceived ideas, distractions, shyness, boredom, mental block, and fear) and physical conditions (e.g., fatigue, illness, and discomfort) on the part of teacher or student can negatively or positively influence learning. The teaching approach, physical mannerisms, speech quality, patience, relationship to class, and levels of expectation are examples of conditions that the teacher can control to positively influence the learning process. Awareness of the presence and effect of these conditions is the first step in meeting students' individual needs and selecting appropriate strategies.

The literature in motor learning contains other factors affecting learning, from which the following list has been compiled:

1. *Amount and type of practice*: practice that is concentrated into one large unit (massed) or done at intervals (distributed). Motor activities are generally learned more readily if practice (exposure or experience) is distributed.
2. *Methods of learning*: whether the material to be learned can be learned as a whole or whether it must be broken down into parts. The part method is better for learning and practicing unfamiliar motor activities. The whole method is better utilized with familiar activities, and is more effective for the more intelligent learner.
3. *Meaningfulness of activity*: how meaningful the material is to the learner. That which is familiar tends to be more meaningful; teaching from the known activities to the unknown enhances the learning process.
4. *Activity versus passivity*: the level of involvement with the material by the learner. Learners who are more actively involved in the process will learn more rapidly.
5. *Knowledge of results*: when the learners actually know what they have done. Knowledge of results refers to verbal or nonverbal feedback.
6. *Transfer of learning*: the effect that previous learning or experience has upon the learning of a subsequent task. *Positive* transfer means that the previous experience (usually of a similar nature) has enhanced learning of subsequent tasks; *negative* transfer means that previous experience has interfered with the subsequent learning.
7. *Plateaus in learning*: the "leveling off" or the temporary stoppage of learning at a given ability level. Plateaus tend to occur normally in the process of learning.
8. *Retention*: the degree of persistence of learning over periods of no practice (Lawther, 1978). Retention, or memory, is better with meaningful, active learning in which the learners have knowledge of their progress. Overlearning can contribute to better retention.
9. *Motivation*: being aroused to action. Psychological alertness and interest in a given task tend to enhance learning.
10. *Feedback*: information that arrives constantly during activity and is a consequence of one's own response; or it arrives as new information input from external sources (Robb, 1972). It is used to compare present behavior to a reference response. Feedback is necessary to motor function, and is associated with information fed back into the central nervous system via the sensory systems.

These factors underlie the learning process for both normal and handicapped individuals. It is additionally important to become aware of these factors because they relate to and affect the learning of the handicapped in unique ways.

Generally speaking, practice over time done at intervals (i.e., distributed) is better for the handicapped. Daily physical education and continuous practice of a given motor activity will enhance the progress and ability levels of students. If the child is distractible, hyperactive, or has a short attention span, shorter periods of practice with breaks are definitely more beneficial.

The whole and part methods will be discussed as instructional techniques in the following section. The range of whole and part methods should be considered as viable options for instruction to the handicapped, depending on the nature of the material and the conditions impinging on the learning process.

As with normal individuals, although the meaningfulness of the activity is important to learning for the handicapped student, it may not be readily understood by the learner. Some exceptional individuals, such as the seriously emotionally disturbed, severely mentally retarded, and multihandicapped, may find no meaning in the activity except that imposed by the teacher. Instruction of children who have no mental impairment should include meaningful learning experiences.

It is vitally important that, whenever possible, the handicapped child be as actively involved in the learning process as possible. Knowledge of results is also extremely important. Students with limited cognitive ability should be given reinforcement as a form of knowledge of results, and should be told verbally and nonverbally — with hugs, pats on the back, and so forth — when they've done well.

Transfer of learning is quite variable among the handicapped. Generally speaking, the type of transfer of learning (positive or negative) is directly proportional to innate neural capacity and intellectual capabilities. It should not be assumed with the severely handicapped that any transfer has taken place.

Plateaus in learning are more common among the handicapped than the general population. More and longer duration plateaus are noted with the handicapped. There is very little predictability in the relationship between plateaus and handicapping condition.

Retention, or memory, is also quite variable among the handicapped. Those with retardation or processing dysfunction (i.e., lack of integration) usually do not re-tain a given level of motor ability over a period of time without practice. Allowing time and experience for overlearning for the mentally retarded, severely or multihandicapped, or learning-disabled is considered appropriate programming.

Some handicapped individuals will never become truly motivated to learn, just as some normal students never become motivated to learn. Often, exceptional children within the categories of autistic, mentally retarded, severely handicapped, and learning-disabled require extrinsic sources of motivation (i.e., rewards), while other exceptional children can be and are highly motivated. The principle remains the same as with normal students — the greater the motivation, the better the chances for improved learning and performance.

Feedback is of utmost importance for exceptional individuals. Since many handicapped children are neurologically disordered or have some neurological impairment, appropriate and quality sensory feedback is necessary to enhance learning. Those handicapped who are mentally, physically, or health-impaired rely heavily upon information received from their bodies to assist with appropriate motor responses.

INDIVIDUALIZED INSTRUCTION

Instruction intended to meet individual needs seems like an awesome task to the physical education teacher. Individualized instruction is not synonymous with one-to-one instruction, although that would be considered one of the appropriate contexts. Designing instruction to meet individual needs involves an understanding of the individual; the individual's needs, limitations, and capacities; and the development of appropriate strategies for working with them. An entire class may be engaged in one activity, but the levels of expectation, the quality and type of language used, and the particular performances emphasized may differ for each student.

Styles of teaching, techniques, and methods of instruction are many and varied. Although each teacher usually develops a personal teaching style, it is important to be aware of and be able to use a variety of methods and techniques. The term "strategy" is used to refer to the myriad styles, techniques, and methods used in concert at any given time by any given teacher. The strategies used may vary from one activity to another and from one student to another. The variability among the handicapped makes it imperative that the physical educator have a variety of strategies available. Four specific instructional methods can assist the physical educator in developing strategies for programming for the handicapped: (1) part and whole methods; (2) explanation/demonstration; (3) guided discovery; and (4) movement exploration.

Part and Whole Methods

In the true *part method,* the parts of an activity are learned and practiced as parts. After all the parts have been learned, they are put together into the whole activity. An example of use of the part method would be to teach the skills of dribbling, shooting, and passing before presenting the experience of the entire basketball game. In teaching a gymnastics routine, the part method of instruction would include learning and practicing each of the stunts independently, adding transitions between each stunt, and then putting them together into the whole routine.

The true *whole method* refers to practicing only the whole activity. This method involves practice of the entire task with as many repetitions as needed to reach criteria. This method has value for instruction to the handicapped, depending on the size of the task and the severity of the handicapping condition. The smaller the whole and the greater the degree of impairment, the better the approach will work. Autistic children, or the severely retarded, often need to learn and practice a given task (e.g., throwing) as a whole.

Breaking the pattern into parts would serve no purpose for children who have severe processing deficits and mental retardation. The whole method may also be beneficial to those handicapped who have normal or above normal intelligence. The whole method allows the handicapped to make their own modifications and adaptations.

The *"whole to part to whole" method* is a commonly used variation of the part and whole methods. Generally speaking, the whole task is presented, then the parts are taught and put back into the whole. Often, the parts are practiced in conjunction with the entire task. Teaching the javelin throw by this method would involve presenting the entire skill and having the student attempt it; teaching the approach, release, and follow-through or a combination of these; allowing practice of each part separately; and then practicing the whole skill again. In another example, the motor pattern of jumping would be experienced as a whole; then the arm swing, forward body lean, two-footed take off, and landing would be taught and practiced; and finally jumping as a whole would be practiced. Most handicapped individuals could benefit from this or a slightly modified whole-part-whole approach. The smaller the steps, the greater are the chances that the severely handicapped can attain success. The rate of instruction and the amount of repetition and reinforcement are inversely related in determining the progress made by the handicapped. The slower the pace of instruction and the greater the repetition, the better the progress of the handicapped person.

In the *progressive part method,* the parts are taught sequentially and then put together progressively. For example, part one and part two are taught separately and then combined and refined; part three is taught and subsequently combined with the previously learned parts one and two. This pattern continues until the whole skill or task is taught. The progressive part method is commonly used in teaching

Figure 13-1. This child is learning to jump at different heights through the guided discovery method. SOURCE: Photo by Ben Esparza.

the steps in a folk dance. This technique is especially good for those handicapped children who have difficulty processing, sequencing, or integrating information (e.g., the mentally retarded, learning-disabled, and emotionally disturbed). A mentally retarded child could be taught the appropriate stance for jumping and the proper arm swing in combination; then the two-footed take off and landing. By progressing at the child's own rate and teaching the parts along the way, the jumping pattern can be learned by children who have not developed it naturally.

Explanation and Demonstration

These methods are commonly used in most physical education programs. The key for use is the combination of and focus on explanation (verbal, written, or manual communication) and actual demonstration. For example, an overhand throw can be described (orally or in written form) and then demonstrated by the teacher or another student. A slight variation includes an explanation during the demonstration. Explanation and demonstration can serve to reinforce learning, and most handicapped children can profit from this technique of instruction. For some individuals, such as the language-disabled, deaf, or mentally retarded, the ex-

planation might be somewhat meaningless; but the demonstration could help put the missing pieces together. On the other hand, visually handicapped children or those with visual perception disorders may derive more meaning from the explanation than the demonstration. There are still others, such as the severely emotionally disturbed, deaf/blind, severely mentally retarded, and multihandicapped, who may need additional assistance or adaptation of instruction.

Guided Discovery

In this approach to teaching, the learner is guided through small, sequential discoveries until the ultimate focus or selected goal is reached (Mosston, 1972). Guided discovery can be utilized effectively in the mainstream where the entire class, including the handicapped, determines the best way to modify a game for fair and equal participation. Because guided discovery involves cognitive processing, it can be used both as an approach to instruction, and as a means of encouraging the processing of information. Those who are handicapped but not mentally impaired might find this approach most interesting for discovering the best methods of moving or adapting within their physical environment (see Figure 13-1).

Movement Exploration

Movement exploration is a specific method that allows students the freedom to investigate various ways of moving and using their bodies. It is based on the problem-solving approach to the teaching of movement skills. The students are told "what" to do but not "how" to do it. The "how" of the activity is the invention of the student. For example, the students are told to balance on five different body parts. Each student then discovers how many different ways he or she can balance on five body parts. In another example, a student is told to throw the basketball to a classmate in as many ways as possible, thus exploring the multitude of choices. (See Figure 13-2.)

Movement exploration can be tried with most handicapped children. The more severely handicapped the child is, the less creativity and hence success will be found in using this approach. Those who can benefit the most include those with perceptual-motor deficits, short attention spans, poor body images, low retention, poor self-esteem and self-identity, low tolerance for competitive activities, slight emotional or behavioral disorders, and learning problems. Movement exploration provides the opportunity for success-oriented, failure-free motor activity, and can be used to reinforce or help develop cognitive or perceptual processing ability.

DEVELOPMENT OF APPROPRIATE STRATEGIES

To develop appropriate strategies to meet the needs of individual students, the physical educator must consider modifying methods of instruction and the learning environment.

Techniques for Modifying Instruction

To meet the needs of exceptional children in physical education, it is often necessary to modify or adapt the

Figure 13-2. This boy is responding to the command, "Balance on two body parts," as part of a movement exploration exercise. SOURCE: Photo by Ben Esparza.

specific behaviors of the instructor. The degree and type of modification varies with the needs, limitations, and capacities of the handicapped child and with the educational setting. The ability to adapt and modify any of the aforementioned methods of instruction, along with the careful selection of the following techniques, will prove to be valuable assets.

Although closely related to methods previously discussed, techniques for the modification of instruction often escape notice. When performed skillfully, the use of these techniques does not require additional effort on the part of the teacher and does enhance learning. The following are associated with the instructor and, when modified, increase communication to the learner: (1) using language, (2) making concepts concrete, (3) sequencing tasks, (4) allowing time for learning, and (5) utilizing multisenses.

Using Language

Language provides the basis for communication. Before learning can occur, understanding on the part of the student must take place. This understanding is founded in communication between the instructor and the learner. Therefore, modification of language used may be necessary.

Language-impaired individuals are not the only ones for whom the modification of language is necessary. Exceptional children who are very young, functioning at a young age level, have processing or behavioral disorders, mental or sensory impairments, or minor language impairments all require that attention be given to the language used by the instructor.

The seemingly simple sentence, "I want you to run to the fence and run back," can cause a great deal of confusion to children who have some language difficulty. Some can process only the first three words, and the first part of the command blocks out the last part (retroactive inhibition). Others can only process the last three words, and the last part of the command blocks out the first (proactive inhibition). Many students may follow what the rest of the class does without understanding the task, or simply may not respond at all.

Some students will hear and understand "run" or "run to the fence"; they will probably run somewhere, but they might not run back. Fortunately, many of the students will process the entire sentence or at least pick up the key words ("run," "fence," and "run back") and complete the task appropriately.

There are many ways in which to modify one's language, but the first step is to be aware of the language used and to observe the responses to language

from the students. It may be necessary to make appropriate language adjustments, such as shortening the length of sentences used or statements made. A sentence such as the one mentioned earlier could be easily shortened to "run to the fence and run back." Severely language-impaired (this is not intended as a category but a descriptor of exceptional individuals in any category) children may benefit most from the abbreviated phrase "run fence . . . run back." Other modifications might include the following:

1. Simplify the words used (e.g., "next to" rather than "beside"; "in back of" rather than "behind"; "same or not same" rather than "alike or different").
2. Use single-meaning words, especially action words (e.g., "run to first base" rather than "go to first base"; "step back" rather than "get back").
3. Give only one command at a time, or as many pieces of information as the child can process at once.
4. Say the command and demonstrate the task, unless the demonstration inhibits (blocks out) the command.
5. Give the command and participate with students in the task.
6. Ask the student to repeat the command before performing. This serves as a check of what the child has processed, reinforcement for language development, and encouragement of language use.

Making Concepts Concrete

Making concepts concrete goes hand in hand with the appropriate use of language. The focus is on making the task or activity as clear and meaningful as possible. For example, the teacher might ask, "How many ways can you make a circle? You can *draw* one on paper, *form* one with your hands, *bend* your body into the shape of a circle, *join hands* with the rest of the class in the shape of a circle, and so on.'' Depending on the situation, each of the above would be the appropriate response. Each requires action, yet there is no specific action word in the command (see Figure 13–3).

The physical education teacher can communicate precisely what is desired by choosing the most appropriate action words. Then the concept of ''circle'' can be taught through demonstration and cues. Using lines painted or drawn on the ground would be an example of a cue for ''lining up'' and ''making a circle.'' For children who have limited mental ability or those in need of structure and routine (e.g., autistic, severely emotionally disturbed, severely mentally retarded), using the same words to denote an activity or convey a specific meaning is often necessary.

Sequencing Tasks

The first aspect of sequencing assumes the learner has the ability to understand and sequence movements that are prerequisite to the task. The command ''walk to the door,'' given to a seated individual, requires many steps to be taken prior to actually walking to the door: the child must hear, process, and prepare to respond; adjust bodily position in preparation for standing; stand up; and walk. If a child is having difficulty with a sequence of events, getting to the task may be a major challenge. The teacher must be aware of this and assist either verbally or manually at any given step in the sequence. For example, a mentally retarded child is asked to do a forward roll. It may be necessary to instruct the child in each step of the forward roll: ''Stand on the mat, bend your knees (squat down), place your hands on the mat, lean forward, put your head down . . .'' and so on. With many exceptional children, the assumption must not be made that the child has fully processed and understood the steps to be taken in order to complete the task.

The second aspect of sequencing tasks refers to

Figure 13–3. These children are learning the concepts ''circle'' and ''square'' by holding cutouts of the shapes.

sequential memory — the ability of the learner to process and respond to a series of commands in sequence. Awareness of the level of sequencing ability of a child will assist the physical educator in knowing the number of tasks or directions that can be given in sequence and understood. This information can be obtained from the classroom teacher, speech therapist, or psychologist. The physical education teacher should start with simple commands, directions, or tasks, and progress through compound to complex tasks.

Allowing Time for Learning

Allowing enough time for learning or even processing of certain information is necessary in working with the

Figure 13-4. By touching the child's limbs during angels-in-the-snow, the teacher is giving tactile information to reinforce the position. SOURCE: Photo by Ben Esparza.

handicapped. Many exceptional children require only the average amount of time for learning, but others need more time to process information and to learn a given motor activity. Overlearning is sometimes necessary for the more severely handicapped. Providing practice time for known skills not only results in overlearning, but serves as its own reward for children who seldom experience success while moving.

Using Multisenses

Physical educators often use techniques that stimulate more than one sensory system at a time, but not always systematically. Many children learn more easily when one sensory system is used as a cue or reinforcement for another: this is a multisensory approach. A few examples might include the following:

1. Verbally describe and demonstrate the performance.
2. Touch the body part to be moved and describe the movement.
3. Have the child describe or give verbal cues at the same time he or she is performing.
4. Point out to the learner how the performance "feels."

It may be that a given individual needs the combined sensory stimulation in order to process what another child can get through stimulation of only one sense. On the other hand, it is important to keep in mind that some exceptional children (e.g., hyperactive, distractible, short attention span, learning-disabled) may become confused with too much stimulation from either one or more sensory systems. If the child is not learning with multisensory stimuli, reduce the input to just one modality and use that to teach. Then gradually introduce another form, using the first to reinforce it (see Figure 13-4).

The key to this approach, and any of the other techniques discussed, lies in the ability to observe the behaviors and motor responses of the students. If the desired performance is not occurring, then the physical educator must analyze the problem and adjust the technique spontaneously. There is great variation in abilities among the handicapped, and each individual's lack of consistency of performance demands much of the physical educator.

Techniques for Modifying the Learning Environment

At the very basis of educational deficit for some children is their inability to learn in the regular class setting (e.g., learning-disabled, distractible, short attention span, mentally retarded). To enhance learning in physical education, it becomes necessary to change the setting or learning environment to better meet the educational needs of these children.

These are techniques for modifying the environment of each student to achieve the setting that is most conducive to learning, and can be used as the students' needs demand and the educational environment permits: (1) modifying the facilities; (2) using space creatively; (3) eliminating distractions; (4) providing structure and routine; (5) varying class format; and (6) individualizing instruction.

Modifying the Facilities

Structural modifications of existing facilities or providing new facilities might be necessary for adequate physical education programming for exceptional children. The physical education teacher should be aware of architectural standards for accessibility, barrier-free construction, and help aids, and make suggestions for appropriate modifications.

Until, and even after, modifications of facilities occur, the physical educator may need to make some minor alterations. Since facilities are discussed in a subsequent chapter, the discussion here addresses modifications the teacher can implement. Modifications of facilities that can be done by the physical educator include:

1. Painting, chalking, or taping lines and boundaries.
2. Devising "temporary" ramps for wheelchair accessibility.
3. Painting or taping a trailing path for the visually handicapped.
4. Constructing movable basketball goals.
5. Devising creative ways for storage.
6. Using existing playground equipment creatively.

Creative Use of Space

If at all possible, both indoor and outdoor space should be obtained for use in physical education. Too small or too large a space can be a deterrent to a good physical education program. There are ways of working with almost any space available to make it an appropriate learning environment.

Indoors or outdoors, it is good to use any existing markings or landmarks as boundaries or dividers. A large fenced playground can be made smaller simply by using one corner of it. For control of hyperactive, distractible students, it is best to place the students' backs toward the corner of the playground and stand in front of the class (see Figure 13–5).

This use of space provides the teacher with the ability to stop any student who is inclined to run away from the group. This format may not allow for de-

Figure 13–5. Modification of play space. The students stand with their backs toward the corner of the playground, and the teacher stands in front of the class.

Figure 13-6. By defining spatial limits, carpet squares help children learn to stay in their own space. SOURCE: Photo by Lyonel Avance.

creasing the distractibility of the students, if there is a lot of activity on the playground.

Hula hoops and carpet squares make excellent space dividers. They can be used to locate each child's own personal space while sitting, standing, or moving. These can be used initially for class organization and warm-up exercises as well as for activities using movement exploration and guided discovery methods. It is necessary to keep the space as free as possible of obstacles and other hazards (see Figure 13-6).

Eliminating Distractions and Focusing Attention

Distractions should be eliminated or at least reduced as much as possible. Possible distractions can include any of the following:

1. Extraneous noises and sounds.
2. Other people within the visual field.
3. Obstacles and objects in close proximity to the working area.
4. Busy environment (e.g., too much stimuli on bulletin boards).
5. Too much talking by the teacher.

6. Extraneous movement or gestures by the teacher.

Especially for those individuals who are distractible, hyperactive, or who have a short attention span, the above should be viewed as potential distractors; the same factors may not be distractions to other exceptional students. It may be necessary to remove or eliminate any and all of the above in order to focus attention upon the task. Redirecting or focusing attention on the task can be assisted by the following:

1. Organized, smooth-running, and adequately paced instruction.
2. Appropriate management of behavior.
3. Class organization format appropriate to students' needs.
4. Teacher enthusiasm.
5. More time spent in active participation.

Providing Necessary Structure and Routine

Young children and most handicapped students are in need of some sort of structure and routine. Those exceptional children who do not have processing,

Figure 13–7. Working in small groups is a good way to vary the class format, especially for children who can't tolerate large groups. SOURCE: Photo by Ben Esparza.

cognitive, or emotional impairment can usually function within the usual class structure and routine modifications may even be minimal. Children who do have processing, cognitive, sensory, or emotional involvement usually require more structure than nonhandicapped students and a more regular routine. Keep in mind that cognitive, mental, social, and emotional impairments can cut across all categories of handicapping conditions.

Children who have only sensory impairments (e.g., deaf, hard-of-hearing, visual impairment) need some structure and routine to assist in coping with the environment. Inconsistency and lack of continuity of class structure and routine can be completely upsetting and confusing to the emotionally disturbed or behaviorally disordered, the autistic, the learning-disabled, and some mentally retarded individuals. More severely handicapped students need more structure and routine for learning to take place and to lessen frustration and confusion. As the end of the severity continuum is reached, the need for increased structure and routine is less noticeable.

Modifications in structure and routine should not

be overused. Adaptation to change for handicapped persons is part of learning and is necessary, but should be introduced gradually. Boredom should not be allowed to occur. Structure and routine can afford handicapped children the opportunity to enhance learning and development, but should not be used to the detriment of learning.

Innovative Class Formats

Often, formats used for class organization in adapted physical education are unique. They may vary from seemingly no organization at all to a highly structured organizational format. The following are typically used types of class organizational formats, ranging from highly structured to least structured:

1. *One-to-one* instruction: a ratio of one teacher to one student. Teaching aides, assistants, or classroom teachers could also be utilized to work one-to-one with additional children during physical education.

2. *Small group:* three to four students working together with the teacher or aide. The entire class

may consist of only these three or four students, or may be comprised of several small groups (see Figure 13-7).

3. *Large group:* the entire class participating together as one large unit.

4. *Mixed groups:* utilizing varying group organizations within a class period. Possibilities include starting with the large group then going to small group activity and then returning to the large group at the end of the period. This order, of course, could be reversed.

5. *Peer teaching:* utilizing nonhandicapped classmates or students from other classes for teaching and assisting the handicapped (see Figure 13-8).

6. *Teaching stations:* setting up several locations around the activity area and requiring different performances at each. In this manner, practice in or exposure to several skills or abilities during one physical education instructional period can be accomplished (see Figure 13-9).

7. *Self-paced independent work:* individually planned instruction pursued by each student at the student's own pace. Students may work on each aspect of their program at random and have the teacher check them against criterion-referenced performances when they are ready.

These various class formats can be used in almost any educational setting, from the mainstream to the special class. Depending on the handicapped individuals involved and the specific goals and objectives to be met, any of the formats can be used. These general comments should help guide the decision-making process in choosing an appropriate class format:

1. One-to-one instruction is not synonymous with individualized instruction. It can be used in conjunction with any other class format, and may be necessary for maximum development of severely involved children.

Figure 13-8. Peers often have special insight into learning new skills, and serve as good teachers.

Figure 13-9. Using stations for different activities—such as this sit-up station—allows students to progress at their own pace. SOURCE: Photo by Lyonel Avance.

2. Small groups are more beneficial to the students in adapted physical education and more commonly found.

3. Teaching stations, peer teaching, and self-paced independent instruction can be used effectively to assist the teacher in individualizing instruction.

4. Varying the group organization is good for variety and assists in holding interest and attention. It should not be used so much that it distracts or confuses students.

Innovative Teaching Techniques

The following six categories of teaching techniques comprise the 6-P program developed by Seaman (1973): (1) patterning; (2) positioning; (3) progression; (4) perception; (5) prompting; and (6) principles. The techniques of patterning, positioning, perception, and prompting can be construed as modifying the environment, and thus will be the only ones discussed here. Although originally implemented with the mentally retarded, the applicability of these techniques to individual needs should be evident.

Patterning, sometimes called "motoring," refers to manipulation of a body part through a range of motion. This process provides the student with kinesthetic and proprioceptive feedback. The information received through this manual assistance helps guide the movement later, when attempted unassisted. Having "felt" the correct motor response, the information can be stored in memory for retrieval at a later time.

Body positioning and limb positioning are often necessary in order to provide accurate proprioceptive feedback. The simple command "bend your knees" may not be understood, but by positioning the child in the bent knee position, the association between the command and the feedback can be made. Again, storage of this information for later use is more likely to occur since the internal environment (feedback) has been enhanced in quality through positioning.

Perception refers to the reception and integration of sensory stimulation, which adds to the student's pool of information, and which in turn enhances learning. Using sensory stimuli in the environment can and does assist the child in processing information.

Prompting, not normally thought of as a teaching technique, is the final technique for modifying the environment. Prompting, through verbal or manual assistance, aids the child in retrieving the task or sequence from memory. Short cue-words should be used to remind the child. Prompting eventually can be eliminated once the student is able to make the associations without it.

Techniques for Modifying the Activity

Any physical activity can be modified. The modifications should be made for the purposes of inclusion and equal participation by the handicapped in the mainstreamed setting, but not to the exclusion or limitations on participation by nonhandicapped students. Modifications of the activity in physical education should be done with the participation and learning experience of all students in mind. Following are six techniques for modifying physical education activities: (1) placement of the individual in the activity, (2) modification of the time of participation, (3) adaptation of the skill, (4) use of substitutions, (5) modification of equipment, and (6) modification of the rules. Examples of each include those for the mainstreamed and the adapted physical education settings.

Placement

Most team sports include active and less active positions. Placing a student with limited mobility into a less active role may be the only modification needed. In a softball game, for example, a wheelchair-bound student could probably play almost any less active position with other modifications (e.g., rules, equip-

Figure 13–10. Playing in the front row of a volleyball game requires less movement, so these students in wheelchairs can participate easily with the group. SOURCE: Photo by Lyonel Avance.

ment). Consideration of safety factors as well as equality for the handicapped and normal individuals should be given. Right field, first base, pitcher, or catcher could probably be played quite successfully by a student in a wheelchair, with other minimum adjustments. In most cases, there are no "right" or "wrong" modifications, only degrees of appropriateness. Placing a visually impaired or hearing-impaired child close to the teacher during instruction and near other students during activity would be most appropriate. Hyperactive or distractible children should probably be located near the teacher for behavior control and on-task monitoring. (See Figure 13–10.)

Time of Participation

Limiting or altering the amount of time a student participates may be needed for those who have health impairments either as their sole handicapping condition or coexisting with other conditions. Limiting the time (i.e., shortening the time) would also be recommended for the very young and those with short attention spans. The student's level of endurance and strength must also be considered in determining the time of participation. Students who have prostheses and assistive devices, as well as sedentary or obese students, usually tend to fatigue more quickly and may have

limited strength, flexibility, and endurance. Cardiac, asthmatic, hemophiliac, and other health-impaired children may need their time of participation limited, depending on the severity of the condition. Spacing rest intervals or varying the pace of the activity (e.g., vigorous activity with quiet activity) would be examples of modifying the time of participation.

Substitution

Rotating one person with another or using two players to make one would qualify as examples of substitution. Alternating a cardiac individual with an asthmatic during a vigorous game or sport is a viable solution in meeting their individual needs for limited participation time, for meeting the demands of the game, and for fair treatment of the others in the class. Substitution can also be used between the normal and the handicapped.

Adapting Skills

It may be necessary to change the skill or motor requirements of an activity to fit within the limitations of the student. In some cases, adapting the skill would also require modifying the rules. A post-polio individual with atrophied upper arm muscles may be allowed to "palm" the ball or bounce and catch the ball in basketball; a paraplegic individual may be allowed to hit or dribble (soccer style) the ball with a crutch; a young severely mentally retarded child may be allowed to catch the ball after one bounce instead of catching the ball in flight. In working developmentally with handicapped children, many modifications of the motor requirements may be necessary in progressing to attainable skill or ability levels (see Figure 13–11).

It is important in all cases to strive for the development of the most efficient movement patterns and motor skills possible. A hemiplegic cerebral palsied child, paraplegic post-polio victim, or student with a lower leg amputation may never be able to successfully execute a motorically perfect jump, but should be expected to become proficient within their limitations. A mentally retarded youngster who is not physically limited should be encouraged and able to develop a near-perfect jumping technique.

Equipment

At some time, the equipment used in physical education programming will need modification or special equipment will be needed (detailed modification of equipment is presented in a subsequent chapter). Equipment modification should be considered as a means of meeting the needs of the handicapped for participation in physical activity. Some general ideas for modifying equipment include (1) use of brightly colored objects for the visually impaired; (2) use of auditory cues, such as a bell inside a ball, for the blind; (3) use of longer or shorter striking implements, as necessary, for the physically impaired; (4) lowered nets; (5) use of suspended or stationary objects for striking or kicking; (6) use of lightweight objects, such as balloons instead of balls; (7) use of assistive devices, such as ramps, rails, and supports; (8) side barriers attached to table games for the wheelchair bound; and so on.

Figure 13–11. Innovations, such as allowing this student to use his crutch while kicking the ball, can help integrate handicapped students into general physical education classes.

Rule Modification

In modifying activities for the inclusion of the handicapped, the saying that "rules are made to be broken" applies. Rules should not be modified or changed so much that the purpose of the game is lost; however, rule changes should be considered as part of the learning process. Simple rule changes might include (1) one bounce instead of an inflight catch; (2) ten players on a baseball team instead of the usual nine; (3) two steps allowed after catching a basketball pass; (4) baserunners must walk when the ball is fielded by a handicapped person; (5) four strikes and you're out; (6) each team's turn at bat consists of every person on the team batting once; and so on.

TASK ANALYSIS

Task analysis is a method whereby the components of a given task (skill or ability) and the prerequisite behaviors can be determined. It is extremely important in the determination of the level of the child's ability, the appropriate level to begin instruction, the most natural and meaningful progression (i.e., sequence of events), and for establishing written performance objectives.

An example of a written analysis begins on page

Table 13-1. Task analysis of jumping

Starting position	Preparation for jump	Take-off	Landing
■ standing	■ foot placement	■ start momentum	■ feet spread
	■ leg position	■ elevation of body	■ toes first
	■ body position	■ final force	■ relaxed knees
	■ head position		■ arms assist
	■ arm position		

328. The detail is excellent and offers precise information. It is not always necessary to write such an in-depth analysis, but a skilled physical educator goes through these steps mentally. It is of major importance to know what the prerequisite skills or abilities are, to break the task into its component parts, and to order the steps. If the student does not have the prerequisite skills, he or she is not *ready* to learn the task. Through these thought processes, the physical educator can analyze performance systematically, thus providing the foundation upon which good physical education programs for exceptional individuals can take place. (Table 13-1 breaks the task of jumping as outlined in the task analysis into time-sequence related subtasks. Figure 13-12 divides the task of throwing into specific motor components.)

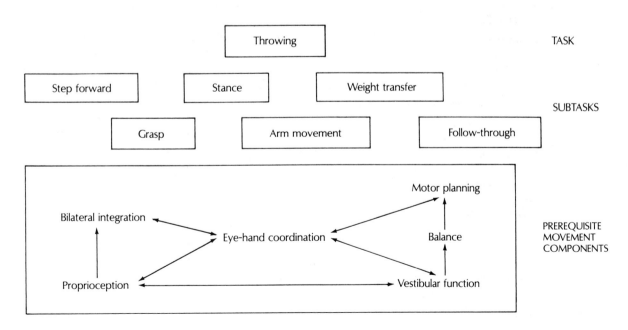

Figure 13-12. A diagrammatic task analysis of throwing.

TASK ANALYSIS

Task: The Jump — Two-footed take-off and two-footed landing
1. Starting position
   A. Standing
      1. Feet 3 inches apart and parallel.
      2. Toes pointing forward.
      3. Body erect.
      4. Arms at sides of body (arms straight and relaxed).
2. Preparation for the jump
   A. Feet
      1. Firm on ground.
      2. Pointing forward.
   B. Legs
      1. Ankles flexed.
      2. Knees flexed.
         a. Knees bend straight forward over toes so force exerted on extension can pass straight through the joint and not at an angle.
   C. Body
      1. Hips flexed.
      2. Trunk slightly leaning forward (about 3 degrees).
   D. Head
      1. Slightly tilted forward (about 3 to 5 degrees).
   E. Arms
      1. Elbows.
      2. Wrist relaxed with equal contraction between flexors and extensors.
         3. Fingers flexed in easy fisted position.
3. Take-off
   A. Start momentum
      1. Head tilted forward.
      2. Body leaning forward.
      3. Arms swing forward then backward.
         a. Elevation can be effected by increasing forcefulness of upward swing of the arms.
   B. Elevation of body
      1. A forceful contraction of all extensor muscles to forcefully extend all joint flexed.
         a. Wave summation of all joints in action.
      2. Arms thrust upward, head thrusts up.
         a. The momentum of the arm swing is transferred to the upper body and, if timed with leg extension, adds force to the jump.
         b. Center of gravity is lower when arms are down, so swinging them upward raises the center of gravity and causes the body to rise higher.
      3. Final force applied by ankles and toes being forcefully extended.
         a. The more force produced against the floor the greater the counter-pressure that projects the body (deeper the crouch) the

more force obtained. However, the body must be lifted through the distance that it is lowered, more work is done when a low crouch is used. Optimal depth of the crouch should depend on the strength of the leg muscles.

4. Landing
   A. Before touching the ground spread feet to about shoulder width for better balance.
   B. Toes first, then heels touch the ground.
   C. Relax knee and hip joints enough to help absorb landing shock.
   D. Arms slowly come down to aid in balancing.
   E. Body extensors slowly contract to stabilize body to standing position.
      1. The forceful extension of legs in jump for height leaves them in position directly below the center of gravity of the body so that equilibrium on landing is no problem and being extended they are in position to flex at all joints on contact with the floor in order to reduce the downward momentum gradually and absorb the force of landing without injuring the body.

SOURCE: Irma Pack
Class assignment
California State University,
Los Angeles.

BEHAVIOR MANAGEMENT

Behavior management refers to handling, controlling, directing, or guiding behavior. The term is broad in scope and includes commonly used techniques of behavior modification, contingency management, and motivation to produce favorable conditions for learning.

Behavior management requires analysis of the interaction between the individual and the group forces that act on the individual. The physical educator must consider the developmental level of the individual, and the intellectual and language development of the student in order to adjust expectations of behavior. For "acting out," aggressive, or emotionally disturbed children, the environment must impose some structure and limits on behavior. When the limits are surpassed, intervention becomes necessary to maintain classroom control.

The following guidelines for intervention for behavior management were adapted from the Bulletin of the School of Education at Indiana University (1961):

1. *Reality dangers:* intervention by the teacher when the activity places the individual in physical danger.
2. *Psychological protection:* intervention when the child is being picked on or psychologically abused.
3. *Protection of property:* intervention when school property, equipment, or facilities are in danger of being destroyed or damaged.
4. *Protection of the ongoing program:* intervention when one child is disrupting and threatens the motivation and cohesiveness of the group.
5. *Protection against negative contagion:* intervention when one child with high social power is contributing negatively to the activity.
6. *Highlighting a value area:* intervention by the teacher to present a value point (e.g., sportsmanship, courtesy).

Figure 13-13. Signal interference is being used by this teacher to quiet the class.

7. *Avoiding conflicts with outside world:* intervention when the public or persons other than the class members view the class.

Managing behavior or emotional disorders of children in physical education does require specific techniques. Redl (1965) has listed various techniques and methods of controlling inappropriate behaviors:

1. *Planned ignoring:* ignoring noncontagious behavior.

2. *Signal interference:* the use of cues (nonverbal, such as hand clapping, eye contact, facial expression, and body postures) to transmit to the child the feeling of disapproval and control (see Figure 13-13).

3. *Proximity control:* the teacher moving into the immediate vicinity of the child to control behavior.

4. *Interest boosting:* involving the child more directly in the activity as a means of eliciting more interest and attention.

5. *Reduction of tension through humor:* using humor or making light of a tense situation.

6. *Hurdle lesson:* restructuring the activity or task to lessen frustration and disruption and to enhance the possibility of success.

7. *Restructure the classroom program:* a change in the program as being beneficial to behavior management.

8. *Support from routine:* the need for routine and structure that enhances the feeling of security.

9. *Remove seductive objects:* the removal of objects that have potential disruptive, distractive, or destructive influence upon the children.

10. *Verbal removal:* telling the child verbally to leave the room or the area in an effort to get the child temporarily out of the area, but not necessarily for punishment.

11. *Physical restraint:* physically controlling an individual who is violent and out of control.

Behavior Modification

Behavior modification is considered an educational approach that applies theories of learning to the teaching of selected behaviors. Reinforcement is the key in behavior modification, which has as its ultimate goal bringing about behavior that is controlled, constructive, predictive, and orderly.

According to Rushall and Siedentop (1972:5), "Reinforcement is the operation of presenting a reinforcer

Table 13–2. Positive and negative reinforcers

	Positive	Negative
Social	■ signs of approval, attention, praise, hugs, hand shakes, encouragement, recognition	■ disapproval, chiding, sarcasm, ridicule in front of peers
Material	■ candy, money, awards, tokens, badges, prizes	■ booby prizes, criminal record, demerits, low grades, tickets
Primary	■ activity, air, food, love, affection, novelty, sex, sleep, warmth, water	■ shock, drugs, physical pain, intense stimulation, spanking, physical punishment
Internal	■ self-control, self-generated reinforcement, consciousness, imitation of famous athletes	■ self-control, consciousness regarding observation of a negatively reinforcing behavior (e.g., damage done by fire)
Performance information	■ intrinsic or artificial feedback of a positive nature	■ distorted feedback, unsuccessful response or motor skill

upon the performance of a behavior." Stimuli that occur after the performance or behavior, and serve to change the probability of the same behavior occurring again are called reinforcers.

There are two classes of reinforcement: positive and negative. A reinforcer that follows a behavior and has the effect of increasing the probability of recurrence of that behavior is a *positive reinforcer*. A reinforcer that has the effect of decreasing the recurrence of a given behavior is a *negative reinforcer*. Reinforcers are classified as social, material, primary, internal, and performance information. The classification system includes both positive and negative reinforcers (see Table 13–2).

Other aspects of reinforcement include: (1) the amount of reinforcement, (2) the delay of reinforcement, and (3) the schedule of reinforcement (continuous or intermittent). As the amount and quality of reinforcement increase, the effect is increased. Delaying the reinforcement often causes slippage in the modification of behavior or in the learning process.

Reinforcement is most effective when given immediately after the expected behavior. It is more efficient to provide continuous reinforcement at first until the response is well-established, and then gradually change to intermittent reinforcement. Behavior learned in this way is highly resistant to extinction.

There are two identifiable situations in which behavior modification is utilized: (1) teaching new behaviors; and (2) eliminating behaviors that are interfering with learning. The teaching of new behaviors has four formal stages: (1) shaping; (2) transfer; (3) modeling; and (4) guidance. *Shaping* is the reinforcement of successful approximations of the desired behavior. The child is reinforced for even the smallest attempts at the behavior, which serves to continue the process of behavior modification. *Transfer* is the occurrence of one behavior learned in one setting and the same behavior occurring appropriately in another setting. *Modeling* is the learning of behavior through observation and imitation of another person's behavior. *Guidance* is manual assistance in the learning of a

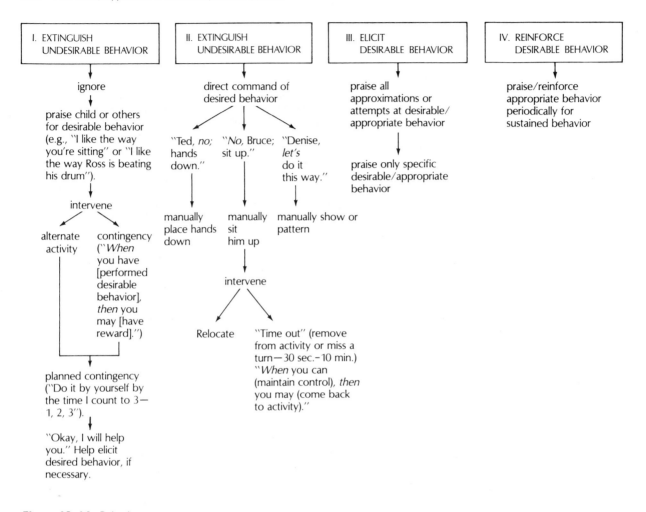

Figure 13-14. Behavior management flow chart. Objective: to extinguish undesirable behavior, to elicit desirable behavior, to reinforce desirable behavior.

behavior. It is important to remember that a negative reinforcer *decreases* the occurrence of undesirable behavior. If the negative reinforcers in Table 13-2 are used and the undesired behavior still persists, then it has become a positive reinforcer and another technique should be used. (Figure 13-14 presents possible courses of action to be taken in controlling behavior. The chart includes three major aspects: extinguishing undesirable behavior, eliciting desirable behavior, and reinforcing desirable behavior. The chart does not re-

fer strictly to any specific type of behavior management, but tends to include aspects of both behavior modification and contingency management.)

Contingency Management

Contingency management is a behavior control system that specifies the relationships between tasks and reinforcements. This technique controls and alters be-

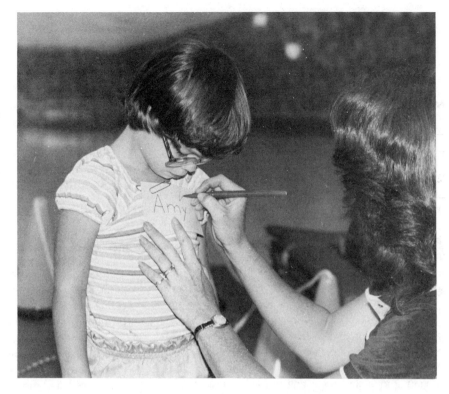

Figure 13–15. A special mark on a child's name tag can help reinforce positive behavior, and is an example of contingency management.

havior while focusing upon tasks. Seven guidelines are important to contingency management (Rushall and Siedentop, 1972):

1. Behaviors must be defined in observable and measurable terms.
2. Terminal behaviors must be clearly stated.
3. Continuous measurement is necessary.
4. Target behavior must be the one that is reinforced.
5. Contingencies must be clearly stated.
6. Contingencies must be fair.
7. Tasks should be small and reinforcement frequent at the beginning.

Contingency management systems are classified into three categories: (1) simple task-reward systems; (2) token systems; and (3) contract systems. The simple *task-reward system* refers to immediate reinforcement after the completion of the task. Examples include reaching a skill level and thereupon entering the game, ten minutes of instruction followed by five minutes of free practice, or completing a task and being dismissed (see Figure 13–15).

The second form of contingency management is the *token system*. Poker chips, points, task cards, and marks are given token status. They then act as powerful reinforcers, because they can be exchanged for rewards that give more reinforcement (our economy runs on this system, with money as the token). Earning points to achieve a certain grade in the course, or passing specified skill level tests in three sports and then not having to take a general skill test at the end of the year are examples of this token system.

The most sophisticated form is the *contract system.* The contract is the agreement between student and teacher that determines the reinforcement after completion of a specified task. Setting up the specific objectives or tasks to be completed is the first step in the contract system. Contracting to attain a certain weight loss, or to be at a given level of physical fitness at the end of a given time and as a result pass the course are examples of the contract system.

Motivation

Motivation refers to the state of being roused into action. It is the urge to push toward a specific goal. Three general sources of motivation are (1) factors within the task; (2) factors within the individual; and (3) factors external to the task and to the individual (Waggoner, 1973).

There are at least two factors of motivation within the task. The first is the *novelty* of the task, which might include a new task, a unique task, a new teacher, or a change in the old familiar activity. Doing something familiar in an unfamiliar way can also be quite motivating. The second factor is the *complexity of the task*. Tasks that are too complex will probably lead to frustration in a child who has emotional, learning, or behavioral disorders. Some exceptional children with normal cognitive functioning will probably find complexity an exciting challenge. Tasks that are too simple bore most people, handicapped or not. The complexity of the task should vary with the child's ability to be motivated by it and to handle such.

Intrinsic motivators — motivational factors within the individual — include internal satisfaction from successful achievement, level of aspiration set by the individual, and knowledge of results. Many handicapped individuals do not get internal satisfaction from success. To assist with establishing intrinsic motivation, reinforcement and knowledge of results should be given to exceptional individuals. Aspiration levels do affect motivation, and handicapped individuals frequently have difficulty in setting appropriate levels of aspiration for themselves.

The factors external to the task and to the individual are known as *extrinsic motivators*. Social reinforcers and material reinforcers are two examples of extrinsic motivators. The learner is more apt to perform effectively when there is positive reinforcement in the form of praise, acknowledgment, material rewards, or other payoff.

SUMMARY

In order to individualize instruction, it is necessary to understand the process of learning and the factors affecting learning, and to develop strategies appropriate for meeting individual needs.

The motor learning literature contains ten factors affecting learning — amount and type of practice, methods of learning, meaningfulness of activity, activity versus passivity, knowledge of results, transfer of learning, plateaus, retention, motivation, and feedback. These factors tend to affect the learning of the handicapped in unique ways and should be well understood in order to individualize instruction.

Styles of teaching and techniques and methods of instruction are many and varied. A teacher may employ one or more of the following instructional methods — part and whole method, explanation and demonstration, guided discovery, and movement exploration. Individualizing instruction may be accomplished through modification of instruction, learning environment, and activity. These strategies should be used along with task analysis and behavior management techniques in physical education programs for handicapped individuals.

BIBLIOGRAPHY

Arnheim, D. D., Auxter, D., and Crowe, W. C. *Principles and Methods of Adapted Physical Education and Recreation.* St. Louis: C. V. Mosby, 1977.

"Guidelines for Intervention." *Bulletin of the School of Education.* Bloomington, Indiana: Indiana University, 1961.

Lawther, J. D. *The Learning and Performance of Physical Skills*. Englewood Cliffs, New Jersey: Prentice-Hall, 1978.

McClenaghan, B. A., and Gallahue, D. L. *Fundamental Movement: A Developmental and Remedial Approach*. Philadelphia: W. B. Saunders, 1978.

Mosston, M. *Teaching: From Command to Discovery*. Belmont, California: Wadsworth, 1972.

Redl, F. ''Managing Surface Behavior of Children in School.'' In *Conflict in the Classroom*, edited by H. J. Long. Belmont, California: Wadsworth, 1965.

Robb, M. D. *The Dynamics of Motor Skill Acquisition*. Englewood Cliffs, New Jersey: Prentice-Hall, 1972.

Rushall, B. S., and Siedentop, D. *The Development and Control of Behavior in Sport and Physical Education*. Philadelphia: Lea and Febiger, 1972.

Seaman, J. A. ''Right Up Their Alley.'' *Teaching Exceptional Children* (Summer 1973).

Thorndike, E. L., et al. *Adult Learning*. New York: Macmillan Co., 1928.

Waggoner, B. E. ''Motivation in Physical Education and Recreation for Emotionally Handicapped Children.'' *Journal of Health, Physical Education, and Recreation* 44 (1973): 73–76.

14 Effective Programming: Developmental Activities for the Whole Child

Guiding Questions

1. What sort of information about a handicapped child should one have in order to determine a program plan? To determine the actual level of physical education programming?
2. How can teaching suggestions offered for various handicapping conditions be utilized in a successfully integrated physical education program?
3. How can a physical educator appropriately select activities for the ability of a given child and for a given group of individuals?

The adapted physical educator who intends to plan and implement effective physical education programs for the handicapped should remember the following:

1. Focus on ability not disability.
2. Provide challenges for the handicapped.
3. Ensure safety but do not overprotect the handicapped.

DETERMINING A PROGRAM PLAN

Based on the results of assessment and the contents of the individualized education plan (IEP), an appropriate physical education program plan can be designed. The IEP must include the current level of performance, individualized goals, and specific behavioral objectives. In addition, the following information is often available on the IEP forms, or can be ascertained through the team approach:

1. Preferred modality for learning.
2. Level of cognitive development.
3. Level of language development.
4. Level of social development.
5. Behavior management techniques.

The above information is vital to the individually planned, well-organized, effective physical education program. By knowing the levels of cognitive, language, and social development, those components can be adjusted within the physical education program. Knowing the child's preferred modality for learning is also important so that the teacher can make the necessary adjustment of instruction. Knowing techniques for managing behavior assists the teacher in maintaining classroom control and providing the best environment for learning.

Using the developmental model as a guide, one can determine the appropriate level at which to begin programming. In general, the younger or more se-

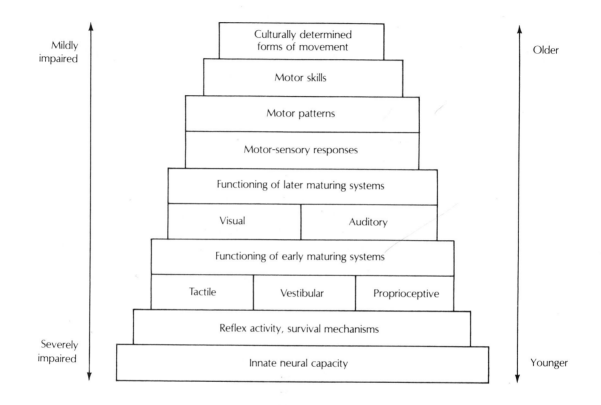

Figure 14-1. Developmental levels at which to begin physical education programming according to age of child and severity of handicap.

verely handicapped the children, the more appropriate are the lower levels of the model for initiation of programming. The older or mildly impaired individuals benefit from and can achieve success in the activities at the higher levels of the model. As a general rule of thumb, the older the student, the more that student should be involved in age-appropriate activities. Figure 14-1 graphically illustrates this point, and also identifies the levels of greatest attention for the various handicapping conditions.

As shown, the level of physical education programming for the mentally retarded and orthopedically impaired runs the gamut, depending on the age of the individual and the severity of the condition. In general, the physical education program for the multi-handicapped, deaf/blind, and severely handicapped should include the middle and lower levels of the model. This is not to say that these children could not achieve or benefit from activities at the upper levels; when appropriate, activities found at the upper levels should be provided. The major focus of physical education programming for the deaf or hard-of-hearing, visually impaired, seriously emotionally disturbed, other health-impaired, and learning-disabled should be placed on the middle and upper levels. Again, whenever necessary, programming should include activities at the reflex or basic sensory stimulation levels. These comments are offered as general programming tips.

More specifically, the factors necessary for determining the level of programming include (1) results of assessment, (2) goals and objectives, (3) chronological age (CA), (4) mental age (MA), and (5) developmental age (DA).

The CA is the actual age of the individual in years and months. The MA refers to the level at which the individual is functioning cognitively or intellectually. The DA, as used in this text, is a composite of the CA, the MA, and the developmental profiles for each child. Each profile includes the level of cognitive, social, language, and motor ability. The DA is not determined by years and months; rather, it tends to describe a composite age range as a basis for programming. The results of assessment, long-range goals, and specific objectives should assist in the determination of DA and in planning the physical education instructional or program plan, including specific activities.

Activity analysis serves a dual purpose here. (Figures 14–2 through 14–5 present examples of activity analysis.) The analysis of any given activity yields the

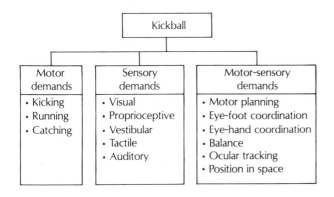

Figure 14–2. Activity analysis 1.

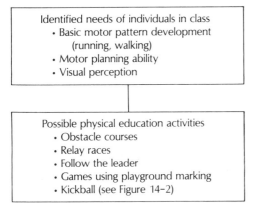

Figure 14–3. Activity analysis 2.

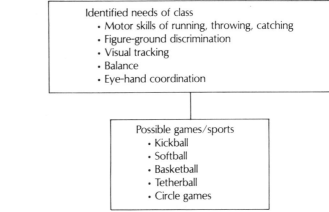

Figure 14–4. Activity analysis 3.

Figure 14–5. Activity analysis 4.

Example #4

Pasadena Unified School District Secondary Schools

Program Planning Worksheet

School ______________________

Period ______________________

Tally the number of students in each class scoring 0 or 1 point on each of the ten test items below. Identify areas of greatest need by the number of students scoring low on any given item. Using two or more areas of need, follow those lines across until an "x" is found in both need areas under an activity area. The activity area at the top of the column is suggested for meeting the identified individual and group needs.

Tally the number of students in each class scoring 0 or 1 point on each of the ten test items below. Identify areas of greatest need by the number of students scoring low on any given item. Using two or more areas of need, follow those lines across until an "x" is found in both need areas under an activity area. The activity area at the top of the column is suggested for meeting the identified individual and group needs.

# Students	Performance area / Activity area	Swimming	Rhythms	Stunts & tumbling	Dance	Archery	Four-square	Golf	Tennis	Basketball	Volleyball	Softball	Track & field	Weight lifting	Soccer	Football (modified)	Bowling	Batacas	Obstacle course	Table tennis	Table games
	Strength (Sit-ups)	x		x	x	x		x	x			x	x	x	x	x	x	x			
	Eye-implement coordination					x		x	x			x						x		x	
	Agility (Side-step)		x	x	x		x		x	x	x	x	x		x	x		x	x	x	
	Bilateral control	x	x	x	x	x	x	x	x	x	x	x	x	x	x	x	x	x	x	x	
	Eye-hand coordination					x	x	x	x	x	x	x				x	x			x	
	Balance (Beam)		x	x	x			x	x	x	x		x		x		x	x	x		
	Limb lower flexibility	x		x	x						x		x	x			x				
	Upper limb flexibility	x		x	x						x		x	x			x				
	Eye-foot coordination														x	x					
	Endurance	x			x				x	x			x	x		x		x			

motor, sensory, and motor-sensory response demands of that activity. This information can be used in the following ways:

1. To find the aspect(s) of the activity with which the individual is having difficulty and provide specific remediation (developmental) activities.
2. To determine appropriate activities that can be

employed to the benefit of the individuals in the class as well as to the class itself.

The examples shown become broader and broader, from determining the demands of a specific activity to applying those demands to the needs of an entire class. Figure 14-5 parallels the demands of a particular school district's assessment tool with move-

Table 14-1. Physical education program for the very young, multihandicapped, or severely handicapped

Category	Activities
Developmental activities	■ sensory stimulation activities ■ localizing sensory stimulation ■ identifying body parts on self and others ■ obstacle courses ■ influencing muscle tone through vestibular and resistive activities ■ passive range of motion ■ body positioning ■ fundamental locomotor skills, nonlocomotor skills ■ basic balance activities ■ visual tracking ■ hand usage ■ grasping activities (palmar and pincer) ■ releasing objects
Physical and motor fitness	■ maintenance of position, sustaining movement (endurance) ■ basic strength activities (head control, sitting, pulling up, standing)
Games and sports	■ ball skills — rolling, catching, throwing ■ obstacle courses

Table 14-2. Physical education program for moderately and mildly impaired children through adolescence

Category	Activities
Developmental activities	■ locomotor activities ■ balance/equilibrium responses ■ nonlocomotor activities ■ perceptual-motor developmental activities
Games and sports	■ circle games ■ recreational and lifetime games/sports ■ team games ■ gymnastic activities, including trampoline ■ aquatics or water play ■ dance and rhythm activities ■ table games
Physical and motor fitness	■ strength activities ■ flexibility activities ■ endurance activities ■ agility activities ■ speed activities

ment components within the district's curricular activities.

The program plan for physical education includes the general areas of concentration in the physical education program for the class as a whole, as well as the necessary individualization for each handicapped person in the class. By legal definition, a physical education program includes physical and motor fitness, developmental activities, and games and sports. Wherever appropriate, activities from each of these aspects should be included in the physical education program for all children. The developmental model identifies (in greater detail but in a somewhat different manner) aspects or levels of activities appropriate in physical education programming (see Tables 14-1 and 14-2 for examples of program plans).

In each of the examples, the areas and activities listed are representative of the overall physical education program for a school year. Each individual should be worked with on an individualized basis, as needed, to achieve the specific goal or objectives. As much as possible, the class should be taught as a whole, with one-to-one instruction as the exception rather than the rule (see Figure 14-6).

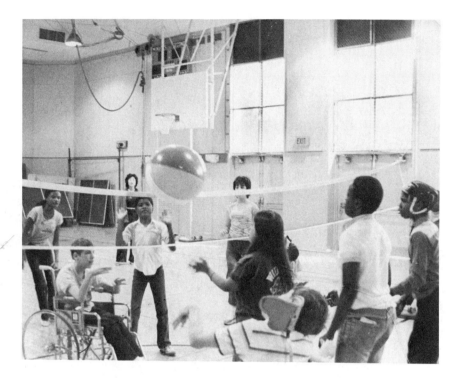

Figure 14-6. This class is playing together as a group. A balloon or beach ball may be used to accommodate weaker students to allow them to play volleyball with the group.

TEACHING SUGGESTIONS

The following teaching suggestions have been adapted from a suggested list developed by AAHPERD (1976). These techniques should prove helpful to the regular physical education teacher instructing handicapped individuals in an integrated setting, as well as to the adapted physical education specialist.

1. Progress slowly, offering familiar activities first.
2. Introduce new or unfamiliar activities early in the physical education period.
3. Give clear directions.
4. Use concrete examples.
5. Use a firm but positive approach.
6. Show enthusiasm.
7. Be aware of attention and interest level of students.
8. Give students goals to which they can aspire.
9. Use praise often.
10. Ensure enjoyment as a part of the physical education program.
11. Maintain a balance between vigorous and less demanding activities.
12. Base new experiences on previously learned movements.

Figure 14-7. Because each student has his own ball, all can participate in the activity. They also get more participation time, because they do not have to wait for a ball. SOURCE: Photo by Lyonel Avance.

13. Present ideas slowly and a few at a time.
14. Provide experiences that allow each individual to participate (see Figure 14-7).

Of course, differences among the various handicapping conditions will affect how an activity may be taught. Following are specific teaching hints in relation to the type of handicap, adapted from AAHPERD (1976a), AAHPERD (1976), and Bundschuh (1979).

Orthopedically Impaired or Physically Handicapped

Orthopedically impaired students can participate in most physical education activities with appropriate modification. The following are suggestions for physical education teachers:

1. Obtain periodic medical approval of the student's program and plan accordingly.

2. Obtain medical recommendations after a student is absent due to illness or surgery.

3. Plan so that every student has the opportunity to participate as much as possible.

4. Be aware that the handicapped student requires more individual and hazard-free space for activity than the non-handicapped student (see Thompson, 1976, for space specifications).

5. Provide frequent periods of rest for those who have limited endurance.

6. Be aware of the dangers of twisting, bending, falling, and lifting.

7. Teach the orthopedically handicapped to fall correctly from crutches, wheelchairs, or unsupported positions.

8. Substitute sitting or lying positions for standing positions when necessary.

9. Use lighter-weight equipment when necessary.

Specific Learning Disabilities

The learning-disabled student may have difficulties processing verbal instruction, remembering the sequence of instruction, interpreting visual signs and markings, and relating to the activity space. Short attention span, tension, and sometimes inappropriate social behavior result in a need for a structured environment.

1. Give instructions one at a time.

2. Use short, simple sentences and face the student when giving instructions.

3. Eliminate as many extraneous auditory and visual stimuli as possible (see Figure 14–8).

4. Use multisensory cues when possible, if not confusing.

5. Set limits of acceptable behavior individually with the hyperactive or impulsive student.

Figure 14–8. Covering equipment when it is not in use helps keep students from being distracted.

6. Provide the time before class to review with the student the written materials that are to be used.
7. Plan so that the student has many successful experiences, especially at the beginning of each instructional unit.

Speech- or Language-Impaired

Students with speech or language impairments should be able to participate in regular physical education activities. The following are teaching suggestions:

1. Use familiar words when giving instructions.
2. Break down instructions into smaller steps, as necessary.
3. As speech improves, encourage students to use newly acquired language skills.
4. Give instructions one at a time, or whatever number the student can process, then increase.
5. Use short sentences containing only the essential information (e.g., prompting).

Deaf and Hearing-Impaired

Communication and balance are two areas of concern for deaf and hearing-impaired individuals. Only a few modifications of activities or equipment will be necessary for this group.

1. Place student where the teacher's face is visible.
2. Establish eye contact when introducing an activity.
3. Use hand signals or manual language along with verbal commands (see Figure 14–9).
4. Use many visual aids and demonstrations (see Figure 14–10).
5. Encourage the student to follow the example of classmates.
6. Be aware that deaf and hard-of-hearing children may have balance difficulties.
7. Post safety rules for use of facilities and equipment at eye-level and in appropriate locations.

Figure 14–9. A young adult is using total communication to communicate with her classmate.

Figure 14–10. Demonstration, as traditionally used in athletics, is also appropriate for use with the deaf and hearing-impaired. SOURCE: Photo courtesy of CSULA *University Times.*

Mentally Retarded

Mental retardation refers to a condition in which the student functions significantly below average in intellectual and adaptive behavior. Due to their lower level of intellectual functioning, mentally retarded students are not able to assimilate information at the same rate as average students. Therefore, adaptations in instruction are needed.

Mildly or Moderately Mentally Retarded

1. Use simplified and sequential instructions.
2. Reinforce terminology of the activities.
3. Praise attempts and reinforce performance.
4. Include structure and routine.
5. Find ways to provide opportunities for decision-making and independent action.

6. Provide opportunities for increasing emotional adaptability by systematically and slowly changing the structure.
7. Use demonstrations by teachers and other students.

Moderately or Severely Mentally Retarded

1. Allow more time for learning to take place.
2. Use fewer game terms and frequently reinforce terms.
3. Simplify sequence and repeat instructions (see Figure 14-11).
4. Shorten sentences.
5. Teach one skill at a time.
6. Praise attempts and performance.
7. Use color-coding and concrete prompts when necessary.

Figure 14-11. Holding up fingers to sequence the parts of a task helps students to understand instructions.

Figure 14-12. Using a student to demonstrate to the class is rewarding to the student, helps the class to see what they are expected to do, and allows the teacher to observe or give individual help.

8. Teach and stress safety rules.
9. Use demonstrations by teacher and other students (see Figure 14-12).

Seriously Emotionally Disturbed or Behaviorally Disordered

While the behaviorally disordered student can participate in most physical education activities, the teacher should be aware of and plan for the rapid changes in mood and attitude that these students often exhibit. Since surprises may upset the student, the teacher should plan the procedures to be followed in the physical education class.

1. Plan arrival and departure procedures and follow them carefully and consistently.
2. Minimize the waiting time for activity to begin.
3. Avoid unsupervised periods of time.
4. Minimize "lining up" and "staying in line."
5. Give ample warning before making changes in routine. Avoid sudden changes of program.
6. Offer a choice of activities on occasion.
7. Include many noncompetitive games and activities. Minimize competition and foster the idea of fun and participation.
8. Praise attempts and performance.

Autistic

1. Before all else, get and maintain eye contact (see Figure 14-13).
2. Use simple, concrete language.
3. Use manual assistance (patterning and positioning) whenever necessary.
4. Use positive reinforcement.
5. Provide definite structure and routine.
6. Be consistent.
7. Encourage imitation, using words such as "do this," "watch me," "you do it."
8. Progress from simple to complex tasks.
9. Plan activities initially in a confined area.

Visually Impaired

A physical education program that includes visually impaired students often needs modification. Some changes will be necessary, however, to accommodate students with eye conditions that do not allow participation without restriction in regular physical education.

1. Be aware of potentially dangerous situations that might cause additional eye damage.
2. Enlarge target objects (see Figure 14-14).

3. Use brightly colored equipment and materials.
4. Provide appropriate lighting.
5. Be aware of possible need to modify activities that require students to change direction.
6. Be aware of the use of space and unnecessary clutter in the space.
7. Be consistent.
8. Provide structure and routine.

Other Health-Impaired

A physical education program that includes health-impaired individuals (e.g., diabetics, epileptics, cardiacs) often needs little additional modification other than what is dictated by the specific health conditions.

Figure 14–13. Securing eye contact with a young autistic boy is not always easily accomplished but must be done before instructions are given.

SUCCESSFUL INTEGRATION IN REGULAR PHYSICAL EDUCATION: MAINSTREAMING

Since the passage of PL 94–142, "mainstreaming" has become a commonly used term. Although not mandated by law, mainstreaming does represent one level in the continuum of services required by the least restrictive environment mandate contained in the law.

Integrating into regular physical education those handicapped children who can safely and successfully participate without undue interference with the nonhandicapped students can be successful. Due to the impact of recent legislation, a brief discussion of mainstreaming and tips for successful mainstreaming are presented here.

Although currently a major process in education, mainstreaming is often misunderstood and misused. The Council for Exceptional Children (CEC) has described mainstreaming as an educational procedure and process for exceptional children, based upon the conviction that each child should be educated in the least restrictive environment in which the child's educa-

Figure 14–14. For the visually impaired, using a large ball can assist in developing eye-hand coordination.

Figure 14–15. Relaxing, being enthusiastic, and having fun are fundamental qualities for teachers of adapted physical education.

tion and related needs can be satisfactorily provided (CEC, 1974). The Council continues to further define mainstreaming as:

1. Providing the most appropriate education for each child in the least restrictive environment.
2. Looking at the educational needs of children, not clinical or diagnostic labels.
3. Looking for and creating alternatives that will help general educators with learning or adjustment problems in the regular setting.
4. Uniting the skills of general education and special education so that all children have equal educational opportunity.

The Council further delimits mainstreaming as *not* being:

1. Wholesale return of all exceptional children to regular classes.
2. Permitting children with special needs to remain in regular classes without the needed support services.
3. Ignoring the needs of some children for the needs of others.
4. Less costly than serving children in self-contained classes.

Some general guidelines for successful mainstream-

ing have been offered by Moran and Kalakian (1977). They have stated that all decisions to mainstream should be accompanied by provisions for instructional support, in which the physical educator has input regarding the amount and type of support services needed. All personnel who will work with the handicapped, including the physical education generalist and specialist in adapted physical education, should be involved in planning and evaluating the program. More specifically, the physical educator must obtain data at least yearly to evaluate the child's progress and the total program. The annual evaluation should be shared with those involved in the process of planning, implementing, and evaluating the education program for a handicapped individual for the continuation or improvement of such services.

Every person involved in the mainstreaming process contributes to its success. The following are tips specific to the physical education teacher:

1. Learn about the handicapping conditions and associated characteristics.
2. Prepare the nonhandicapped students for the inclusion of the handicapped in regular physical education.
3. Provide fellow students as companion guides initially and as necessary.

4. Constantly reevaluate the effectiveness of the program.
5. Do not compromise nor offer a reduction in quality of the physical education program.
6. Relax, have fun, be yourself in teaching and interacting with the handicapped. Help the students to do the same (see Figure 14–15).
7. Keep your perspective on the handicapping condition. Keep in sight the whole person, not just the handicap.
8. Ask the handicapped person his or her strengths, weaknesses, needs, and so on.
9. Let common sense and consideration be your guide.

SELECTING APPROPRIATE ACTIVITIES FOR DEVELOPMENTAL NEEDS

Reflex Development and Inhibition

The material in this section is presented to acquaint the reader with activities for reflex development, reflex inhibition, and contraindications for activity. The physical educator is advised to attempt these activities with the utmost caution and sound experiential base. With the inclusion of severely handicapped individuals into adapted physical education classes, it becomes necessary for specialists to include activities for reflex development or inhibition. This should be done only after proper training and, whenever possible, consultation with medical personnel, or physical or occupational therapists.

A brief description of the various reflexes is presented, followed by a listing of appropriate activities and contraindications (the lists are not meant to be all-inclusive). Activities mentioned in the reviews, such as animal walks, angels-in-the-snow, and balance board activities, are discussed in a subsequent section of this chapter.

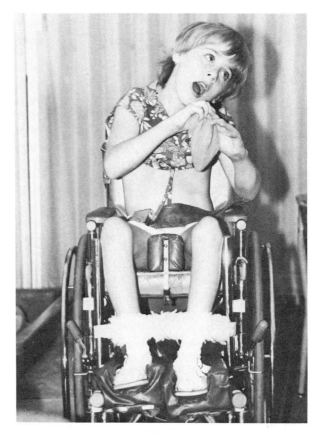

Figure 14–16. This cerebral palsied child is working on grasp and release by changing the bean bag from one hand to the other.

Grasp Reflex: Automatic grip upon stimulation of the palm, difficulty with voluntary release

1. Offer a variety of tactile experiences for the hands, play with textures, and in sand box.
2. Place objects (e.g., blocks, ball) in the hand in such a way that the hand is kept partially open.
3. Place objects in front of the child and encourage the grasp reflex.
4. Have the child build towers or stack objects.
5. Use progressively weighted objects for grasping.
6. Use a variety of sizes of objects.
7. Have the child use one or both hands to grasp and hold objects (see Figure 14–16).

Figure 14-17. Rolling in a texture-lined barrel will help this child inhibit his asymmetrical tonic neck reflex (ATNR).

Contraindications/Precautions

1. Do not force the child's hands open.
2. Do not pull on the child's fingers to straighten them.

Startle Reflex: Automatic abduction, then adduction of limbs in response to sudden noise, movement, or change in environment

1. Stimulate the child auditorily through a variety of sounds (e.g., clap, bell, rattle, voice), increasing in intensity.
2. Slowly move the child and place limbs in a variety of body positions.
3. While the child is positioned over a bolster (e.g., sitting position), place objects in front of the child to encourage voluntary movement.
4. Gradually introduce noises, changes, and movements when the child is unaware.

Contraindications/Precautions

1. Avoid quick movement or sounds without the child being aware at first.
2. Ensure safety when the child is known to have the presence of the startle reflex. Don't leave such a child unattended.

Crossed Extension Reflex: Supine; one leg flexed, opposite leg extended

1. Slowly and passively flex both of the child's legs at the same time.
2. Slowly and passively extend both of the child's legs at the same time.
3. Have the child roll up in a variety of textured materials.

Contraindications/Precautions

1. Avoid activities early that stimulate only one side of the body.
2. Avoid sudden quick changes in leg positions.

Asymmetrical Tonic Neck Reflex (ATNR): Fencing position: extension of arm on face side and flexion of arm on skull side after rotation of head

1. In either prone or supine position, the child rotates the head from side to side and looks at objects; arms remain at sides.
2. While supine, child brings arms to midline of the body.
3. While supine, child reaches for objects above body but at midline of body.
4. Child rolls with arms at sides and above head.
5. Child rolls in barrel (see Figure 14-17).

Figure 14-18. Elephant wrestling helps to integrate the symmetrical tonic neck reflex (STNR), and to promote balance and equilibrium responses. SOURCE: Photo by Ben Esparza.

6. Child crawls and creeps forward, focusing on object directly ahead.
7. In hands and knees position, child maintains balance while turning head only.
8. Child creeps with head turned sideways.
9. Child maintains three-point balance position while turning the head toward the side or a raised extremity.
10. While standing with weight supported by extended arms against the wall, child rotates head, keeping elbows straight.
11. Child stands with arms outstretched and rotates head from side to side, with no movement of arms.

Contraindications

1. When ATNR is known to be present, avoid activities that allow flexion and extension on opposite sides of body.
2. Do not allow the child to remain in the ATNR position; reposition whenever possible.

Symmetrical Tonic Neck Reflex (STNR): Flexion of head; upper limbs flex, lower limbs extend; extension of head, upper limbs extend, lower limbs flex

1. Child assumes and maintains creeping position, flexes and extends head. Position the child correctly.
2. Child creeps forward, maintaining the proper position with head flexed or extended.
3. With the body supported by extended arms on wall, child flexes and extends head.
4. Standing with arms outstretched in front, child moves head up and down with no change in arm position.
5. Child may perform most animal walks and wrestling games (see Figure 14-18).

Contraindications

1. Child should avoid prolonged "bunny-scooting."
2. Child should avoid rocking forward and backward while in creep position.

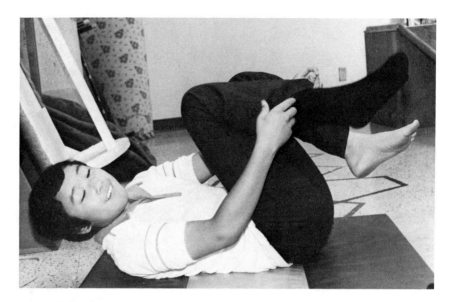

Figure 14–19. While supine, lifting one's head and feet off the floor to put on socks and shoes helps to integrate the tonic labyrinthine reflex (TLR).

Tonic Labyrinthine Reflex: Prone (TLR:P) and Supine (TLR:S): Increased trunk flexion when prone, increased trunk extension when supine

Tonic Labyrinthine Reflex: Prone

1. Child rolls with arms over head or at sides.
2. Child rolls in a barrel.
3. Prone, child raises head only and looks at ceiling.
4. Prone, child raises chest, head, arms and legs off the floor and holds the position.
5. Prone with extended arms, child pushes head and chest off the floor.
6. Child performs prone "egg roll" — grasps ankles and rolls sideways.
7. Prone, child lifts legs only, then arms only.
8. Prone on scooterboard, child propels forward.
9. Child pulls self forward, using rope, while prone on scooterboard.

Tonic Labyrinthine Reflex: Supine

1. Child rolls with arms over head or at sides.
2. Child rolls in a barrel.
3. Supine, child lifts head off floor and looks at toes (see Figure 14–19).
4. Child rolls in a ball from supine position.
5. Supine, child holds large soft objects with arms and legs.
6. While supine, child lifts arms and legs simultaneously, then lowers them.
7. While sitting on a scooterboard, child propels forward with arms.
8. While supine on scooterboard, child pulls self along suspended rope.

Contraindications/Precautions

1. When TLR is known to be present, avoid teaching the forward or backward roll; proceed slowly when teaching any roll.
2. Avoid prolonged prone-lying or supine-lying positions.

Positive Support: In standing, extension of legs and plantar-flexion of feet; *negative support* (lack of weight bearing); *stepping reflex* (automatic high stereotypic walking when placed in standing position)

1. Place the child in standing position, encourage proper stance, position if necessary.
2. Increase amount of weight bearing in the standing position by having the child stand longer.
3. Provide proprioceptive stimulation (i.e., pressure) to the bottom of feet while the child is supine, ensuring dorsiflexion of feet and extension of both legs.

Figure 14–20. Maintaining vertical head position while balancing on a tilt board elicits righting reactions.

Contraindications/Precautions

1. Do not leave the child unattended in standing position.
2. Avoid "walking" without weight bearing.

Righting Reactions: *Neck righting* (trunk rotates with head); *body righting* (log rolls); *optical righting* (head orients to midline of body in either vertical or horizontal position)

1. Child rolls with arms over head or at sides.

2. Child rolls in a barrel.
3. Child rolls up and down an incline.
4. Child creeps forward and backward, keeping eyes fixed on an object in front of the child.
5. Child maintains balance and vertical head position while on a tilt board (see Figure 14–20).

Contraindications/Precautions

1. Avoid reinforcing or practicing log rolls, substitute with segmental rolling.
2. Ensure safety while in balancing activities.

Protective Extension: Extension of arms, abduction and extension of fingers in response to falling

1. Prone with arms extended, child pushes chest and head off floor.
2. Child supports weight on arms while tilted forward over bolster (see Figure 14-21).
3. Child extends arms while rolled forward and downward on cage ball.
4. Child extends arms and supports self while suddenly pushed forward from kneeling, sitting positions.
5. Teacher rocks child slowly forward, backward, and sideways while in prone or sitting position on large bolster or cage ball.
6. Child maintains extension of arms while prone over bolster.

Contraindications/Precautions

1. Protect child from precarious positions that could cause loss of balance and falling.
2. When protective extension reflex is not present, do not leave the child unattended on balance apparatus.
3. Remove obstacles to prevent tripping and falling.
4. Protect child's head from injury.

Activities for Sensory Stimulation and Discrimination

The need for sensory stimulation is well documented in the literature. For growth and development, the child is in need of sensory stimulating activities coupled

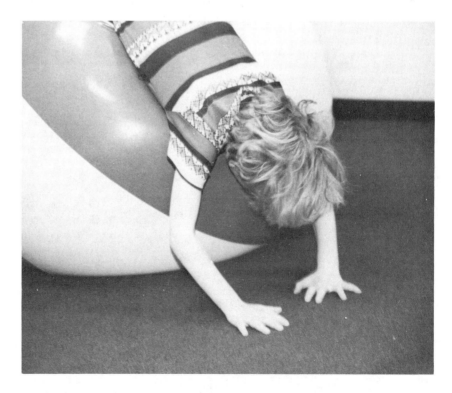

Figure 14-21. Supporting weight on the arms while tilted forward over a cage ball helps to develop protective extension.

with motor response. Each sensory system has a developmental sequence that progresses from gross sensation to discrimination. In the following sections, activities presented for each sensory system are designed to provide sensory stimulation and, later on, to require discrimination and refined use of sensory input.

Tactile System

The tactile system utilizes touch receptors of the skin. It has both an arousal and calming effect upon the central nervous system, and has a profound effect upon the sensorimotor process. The following activities are included initially to provide stimulation, and then to require use of that tactile information for discrimination.

Tactile Stimulation

1. Tactile play with sponges, soaps, washing cloths, tactile toys.
2. Water play in a small wading pool, sprinkler, or commercially available "Slip 'N Slide."
3. Water play in search of objects.
4. Sandbox play: child looks for hidden objects; buries objects; covers hands, feet; builds castles (see Figure 14–22).
5. Mud play; styrofoam pellets play.
6. Tactile play for hands in a container of edible items (e.g., oatmeal, rice, beans). This is a very good substitution for the sandbox for young children or children who put everything in their mouths.
7. Modeling clay.

Figure 14–22. Searching for objects in a sandbox stimulates the tactile system and helps develop tactile discrimination. SOURCE: Photo by Ben Esparza.

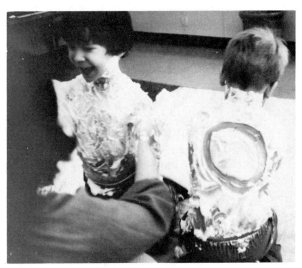

Figure 14-23. Tactile stimulation. The older students (left) enjoy painting themselves and each other. By drawing designs in shaving cream on each other's backs, younger children can learn shapes and derive tactile stimulation at the same time (above).

8. Hand, foot, or body painting (see Figure 14-23).
9. "Dry off" or roll up in blankets, assorted cloths, various textures (e.g., silk, net, burlap).
10. Shaving cream play: child paints body, plays with hands and feet, and slides and rolls in shaving cream (see Figure 14-23).
11. Cornstarch images drawn on child's arms or back after spreading powder on body.

Tactile Discrimination

1. Draw shapes, numbers, or letters on child's back and ask child to identify.
2. While blindfolded, child must locate the teacher's touch, either single or two simultaneous touches.
3. Feeley bag: objects are concealed in a bag or box, and child must identify each by touch.
4. Tactile box with textures, shapes, or letters; match them only by feel.
5. Blindfolded, child identifies shapes cut out of paper (see Figure 14-24).

6. Carpet squares: use for sitting, standing, kneeling, lying on, rolling over, etc.
7. Rope route: child follows a rope maze or obstacle course purely by touch. Child can use hands, feet, or move on scooterboards.

Vestibular System

Vestibular input is an extremely powerful source of sensory stimulation. Once received and organized, vestibular stimulation can be used to enhance balance and equilibrium responses. Although there is an element of vestibular stimulation in almost everything we do, the following activities are suggested for their high content of vestibular input.

1. Child swings in a playground swing, hammock, net, tire, or swing. This can be done sitting, prone, kneeling, and so forth.
2. Prone sliding down an incline.
3. Scooterboards, skateboards, skates, bicycles, etc.

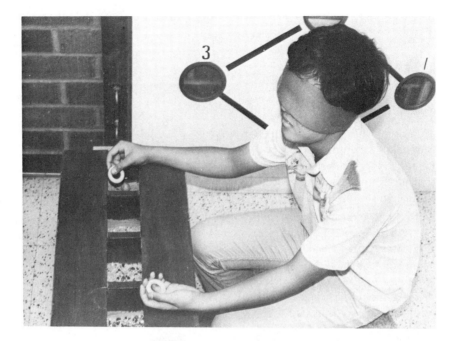

Figure 14-24. This boy is trying to match two wooden shapes by using only the tactile system.

provide a great deal of vestibular stimulation (see Figure 14-25).

4. Rolling, somersaulting, and trampolining.
5. Riding down an incline on a scooterboard.

Proprioceptive System

Proprioceptive input provides stimulation that helps utilize information about where one's body is in space, and also serves to enhance balance. Proprioceptive stimulation is also included in almost all activities found in physical education. Only a few examples are cited here.

1. Reaching and stretching activities.
2. Pushing and pulling objects, with hands and feet.
3. All animal walks and wrestling games.
4. Tug of war.
5. Climbing ropes, ladders, and jungle gyms.
6. Tumbling and trampolining activities.
7. Pressure applied directly to child's legs, arms, body parts to increase the amount of proprioception received: pushing down on upward extended legs while supine, pushing on extended arms, pushing against person in sitting position to elicit resistance.

Figure 14-25. Riding a scooterboard in prone position provides this boy with a great deal of vestibular stimulation.

Auditory System

Much of the information from the environment comes in the form of sounds through the auditory channel. Additional experiences in discrimination and listening skills will assist in the processing of auditory information.

1. Naming various sounds while blindfolded (e.g., bell, ball bouncing, whistle, clap, stomp).
2. Identifying the direction of the sound; child hears and must point in the direction of the sound.
3. Blind man's bluff or blind tag: object is to play the game relying solely on auditory input.
4. Identifying words or directions spoken over background noise (auditory figure-ground).
5. Performing a motor activity when given an auditory cue (e.g., clap means jump, whistle means stop).

Visual System

Visual input is utilized in most physical education activities. It is advisable to include activities specific to the visual system to enhance processing.

Ocular Training Activities

1. Following a swinging or moving ball with just the eyes.
2. Hitting a swinging ball with a stick using both hands; one hand; alternating hands.
3. Hitting a suspended ball toward a given target (see Figure 14–26).
4. Following the flashlight beam in a darkened room with eyes and with body.

Space and Form Perception

1. Making one's body into various shapes (e.g., circle, triangle, letters). Playing individually or in groups.
2. Navigating through a maze on the ground (see Figure 14–27).

Figure 14–26. Ocular tracking activities can be provided by having the child hit a suspended ball—in this case, using a paddle.

3. Moving through an obstacle course involving small and large spaces (see Figure 14–28).
4. Moving through large containers (e.g., old refrigerator boxes) cut into various shapes (e.g., crawl through the square, go backwards out the diamond).
5. Distinguishing a given letter or shape from a maze of lines on the ground.
6. Using jump ropes to make letters, shapes, numbers.
7. Moving through hula hoop(s) suspended in the air.
8. Playing follow-the-leader.
9. Making mirror images (two children, facing one another, perform identical movements).

Figure 14-27. A scooterboard can be used to help a child navigate through a maze of lines on the ground, thereby enhancing figure-ground discrimination. SOURCE: Photo by Karen DePauw.

Figure 14-28. Finding one's way through an obstacle course can teach space and form perception. SOURCE: Photo by Lyonel Avance.

Activities for Enhancing Motor-Sensory Responses

The child must be able to organize and utilize sensory information for motor action. This process involves integration resulting in motor-sensory responses, which include the following:

1. Praxis (motor planning ability).
2. Integration of both sides of the body.
3. Balance/equilibrium responses.
4. Eye-hand/eye-foot interaction and coordination.
5. Crossing the midline of the body.
6. Body awareness.

Praxis (Motor Planning)

Motor planning—the ability to plan and execute purposeful nonhabitual movement—is required in most activities found in a physical education program. The following activities are presented for their relative content to demands on motor planning.

1. Rolling, crawling, creeping, walking, running up and down an incline, over and under objects, forward and backwards, and so on.
2. Performing any or all locomotor movements in a sequence, moving quickly from one to the other.
3. Moving through an obstacle course blindfolded.
4. Following a rope maze blindfolded.
5. Performing angels-in-the-snow.
6. Performing animal walks and wrestling games.
7. Following a serpentine rope.
8. Playing "tag" games.
9. Imitating postures and positions quickly and slowly.
10. Playing follow-the-leader.
11. Moving to different beats of drum or music.
12. Performing balance tasks or stunts. (see Balance, Stunts).
13. Performing novel movement tasks.
14. Performing mirror images with partner.
15. Stringing beads.
16. Duplicating peg board or rubber band board patterns.

17. Dropping clothespins into containers.
18. Participating in puppet play.
19. Putting one's body into various shapes.
20. Following a specified line in a maze.
21. Following a rhythm using rhythm sticks.

Integration of Both Sides of the Body

It is important for the body sides to work together efficiently as well as to work independently. The following activities enhance both bilateral and reciprocal action of the body sides.

1. Jumping through hula hoops.
2. Jumping on trampolines, inner tubes, tires, and so on.
3. Prone, propelling oneself forward on scooter-board, using arms.
4. Pushing cage ball with both feet together or both arms together.
5. Catching a ball with two hands.
6. Clapping hands together.
7. Catching bean bags or yarn balls with scoops.
8. Bilateral play with ribbon sticks.
9. Pulling oneself up an incline by rope, hand over hand.
10. Alternate hopping.
11. Riding a tricycle.
12. Hitting a suspended ball, alternating hands (e.g., tetherball).
13. Hitting a suspended ball with a stick held horizontally (hands at ends and hands together in the middle).
14. Performing animal walks.
15. Performing wrestling games.
16. Participating in balance activities.
17. Playing wheelbarrow.
18. Moving specified limb (specified by touch or name of part) without moving any other body part.

Figure 14–29. In lieu of using a regulation-size trampoline, a mini-trampoline can be used to accomplish the same objectives.

19. Hitting balloons with two hands together, then alternating hands.
20. Playing tug of war.
21. Climbing ropes, ladders, jungle gyms.
22. Using "Play-Buoy."
23. Performing parachute activities.

Balance and Equilibrium Responses

1. Maintaining balance in side-lying, sitting, kneeling, hand and knee, and standing positions.
2. Maintaining balance while sitting on a T-stool.
3. Maintaining a variety of body positions on a tilt board or balance board.
4. Rolling in an inner-tube barrel or texture-lined barrel.
5. Maintaining body positions while gently being pushed by teacher.
6. Participating in trampoline activities (see Figure 14–29).
7. Playing Twister, playing Funny Bones.

8. Balancing various body parts identified by name and/or number.
9. Roller skating.
10. Skateboard activities.
11. Scooterboard activities.
12. Balance beam activities.
13. Participating in animal walks and wrestling games.
14. Sliding down an incline on a carpet square.
15. Following footsteps painted or placed on floor.
16. Walking on a specified line.
17. Stepping on newspapers (or hula hoops, carpet squares, etc.) placed throughout room.
18. Walking on tin can stilts or blocks of wood, traveling across the room.
19. Participating in tumbling activities.
20. Climbing on playground apparatus.
21. Balancing in various positions with eyes closed.
22. Forming pyramids with several children.
23. Locomoting on an uneven surface.
24. Balancing bean bags on various body parts (e.g., head, shoulder, knee, back of hand, elbow).
25. Balancing bean bags and moving around the room.
26. Moving oneself through self-held hula hoop.

Eye-Hand or Eye-Foot Interaction/Coordination

1. Reaching for object with hand.
2. Stacking objects.
3. Building towers.
4. Nesting objects.
5. Hitting suspended ball with hands.
6. Hitting suspended ball with feet.
7. Pushing objects with one foot; with two feet together.
8. Participating in kicking, catching, bouncing, striking, and throwing activities.
9. Keeping balloons in the air as long as possible.
10. While sitting or supine, keeping balloons in the air with feet.

11. Clapping hands to music.
12. Beating drum to a rhythm.
13. Using rhythm sticks.
14. Rolling ball up and down and around body.
15. Walking through a ladder (or tires) placed on the ground.
16. Forming shapes (e.g., letters, numbers) with rope.
17. Tracing letters, numbers, shapes, and so on.
18. Throwing bean bags onto letter grids.
19. Kicking or rolling ball around room or space.
20. Playing Pat-a-cake.
21. Catching and blowing soap bubbles (see Figure 14–30).
22. Sorting and matching small objects (e.g., nails, clips, tacks, screws).

Figure 14–30. Blowing and catching soap bubbles helps promote eye-hand coordination. SOURCE: Photo by Ben Esparza.

Crossing Midline of Body

1. Child imitates postures, positions, or movements that require a body part on one side to cross midline of the body:
   a. hand on opposite ear, eye;
   b. hands on opposite knees, thighs, feet;
   c. cross-over walking pattern.
2. Hitting a suspended object using hand contralaterally, forcing hand across midline.
3. Rolling segmentally up and down incline.
4. Rolling in a barrel.
5. Catching small objects two-handed (e.g., bean bags, balls) thrown at side of body.
6. Reaching with both hands to left foot then to right foot.
7. Stacking objects on one side of the body.
8. Keeping suspended ball in motion, alternating hands for striking.

Body Awareness

1. Identifying the body planes (front, back, side, top, bottom) and body parts:
   a. back of body;
   b. back of hand;
   c. side of head;
   d. top of foot;
   e. front of leg.
2. Identifying planes in relation to objects:
   a. place back on ground;
   b. top of head against wall;
   c. bottom of hand on ball.
3. Touching specified body parts on self.
4. Touching specified body parts on others.
5. Identifying body parts and their movements:
   a. lift arm above head;
   b. point toe toward ground;
   c. wiggle nose.

Figure 14–31. Playing Twister helps to promote body awareness, balance, and equilibrium responses.

6. Identifying right and left on self and others.
7. Moving toward the right and left of self and objects.
8. Painting parts of one's body with liquid soap and tempera.
9. Assuming basic body positions (e.g., supine, prone, long-leg sit, crossed-leg sit, kneel, squat, hand and knees) upon command.
10. Performing angels-in-the-snow.
11. Moving body in specified pattern:
    a. walk in a circle;
    b. make triangle with elbow;
    c. draw a figure eight with hand.
12. Moving body in relation to object:
    a. both feet in hula hoop;
    b. hands on carpet squares;
    c. total body over hula hoop.
13. Playing Simon Says.
14. Playing Hokey Pokey.
15. Play Twister, Funny Bones (see Figure 14–31).
16. Tracing entire body on paper, then coloring and cutting out.

Figure 14-32. This severely handicapped child is beginning to learn head control by raising his head to look at a favorite toy.

Activities for Enhancing Motor Patterns and Motor Skills

Activities at this level of the model include those which are either passive or active in an attempt to provide the individual with a repertoire of movement experiences. For those who are not so severely handicapped, range of motion activities or basic body movements occur in conjunction with normal motor development and other basic motor experiences; thus they need not be isolated. For the severely or very young handicapped children, range of motion (ROM), body positioning, and early motor experiences may occur neither naturally nor sequentially. Some of the activities listed here are intended to help these children.

Early Motor Experiences and Motor Patterns

Range of Motion. Since the child is primarily incapable of voluntary movement, these activities should be done for the child by the teacher.

1. Flex both legs up; lower one leg slowly, then the other.

2. Move one leg out to the side, then the other.
3. Flex legs, turn knees in, then out; return to straight leg position.
4. Move feet in a circular pattern around ankle.
5. Flex legs, rotate both knees and lower legs to each side.
6. Raise one arm overhead, then the other.
7. Raise arm out to side, then arm over head; repeat with other arm.
8. With arm flexed and held at shoulder height, move hand and lower arm above shoulder and then below; repeat with other arm.
9. Extend arm.
10. Rotate extended arm inward and outward; repeat with other arm.
11. Extend wrist through entire range of motion.
12. Move hand in circular pattern around wrist.

Head Control. In order to foster head control, the following activities can be utilized.

1. With child prone over bolster, visually stimulate child to lift head by holding colorful object in front of child (see Figure 14-32).

2. With child prone over bolster, stimulate back of neck to assist in head raising.
3. In sitting position, visually stimulate child to raise head.
4. Pull child from supine position to sitting slowly to initiate head control.
5. While supine, place head in correct alignment for back-lying position.
6. When correct head position is achieved, hold shoulders to help child maintain head position.

Rolling over. In each of the following activities, place objects within the reach of the child or stimulate auditorily to elicit the rolling-over pattern.

1. Child rolls from side-lying position to supine with and without assistance (see Figure 14–33).
2. Child rolls from side-lying to prone position with and without assistance.
3. Child rolls from prone to supine position with and without assistance.
4. Child rolls from supine to side-lying to prone position with and without assistance.

5. Child rolls from supine to prone position with and without assistance.
6. Totally manually assisted, roll child from prone to supine and supine to prone with arms extended over head.
7. Roll child in textured lined barrel.
8. Roll child in inner tube barrel.
9. Roll child up in textured materials.
10. Roll child up and down an incline.

Crawling (on stomach, reciprocal action of limbs). It is advisable to place objects or position the teacher directly in front of the child to encourage crawling.

1. Crawling, both arms pull together, legs still.
2. Crawling, both arms pull together, legs use reciprocal action.
3. Crawling, both arms use reciprocal action, legs still.
4. Crawling, both arms use reciprocal action, legs use reciprocal action.
5. Crawling over, under, around objects.
6. Crawling up and down an incline.

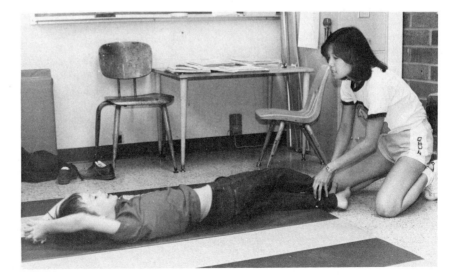

Figure 14–33. This teacher is helping the boy roll from supine to side-lying position (log roll). SOURCE: Photo by Ben Esparza.

Creeping (on hands and knees). The creep is the four-point position for locomotion. It consists of moving forward on hands and knees.

1. Placing child over bolster in creep position, child bears weight on arms.
2. Placing child over bolster in creep position, child bears weight on legs.
3. While over bolster in creep position, child bears weight on arms and legs.
4. In creep position, child bears weight on arms and legs with and without support from teacher.
5. Creeping forward.
6. Creeping over, under, around, through, and so on (see Figure 14–34).
7. Creeping through tunnels.
8. Creeping up and down an incline.
9. Creeping in or on a specified pattern.

Sitting.

1. Placing child in crossed-leg sit, hands at sides; child maintains position with and without support (see Figure 14–35).
2. While child is in crossed-leg sit, place child's hands in lap and maintain position with and without support.
3. While child is sitting, place objects within reach of child in front and encourage reach and grasp while returning to upright sitting position.
4. Sitting on bolster, child bears weight on legs without and with support.
5. Sitting (straddling) bolster, weight is equally distributed between legs; child maintains position.
6. Sitting in chair, child plays with objects in front.

Figure 14–34. Creeping through objects, such as a hula hoop, helps to develop the creeping pattern and teach the concept "through."
SOURCE: Photo by Ben Esparza.

Figure 14–35. Maintaining balance in a cross-legged sit (tailor position) affords the child an initial opportunity to develop sitting.

Kneeling.

1. Child kneels in upright position using arms on object (table, bolster) for support; maintains position and reaches for toys.
2. Child kneels in upright position with one-arm support.
3. Child kneels in upright position without assistance.
4. Child walks forward on knees.
5. Child walks up and down incline, through obstacle course, and so on.

Standing/Walking.

1. Child stands in upright position, leaning or with arms supporting body.
2. Child stands with one-arm support.
3. Child stands without support.
4. Child walks along objects (cruising).
5. Child walks from object to person.
6. Child walks from person to person.

7. Child walks forward and backward with and without assistance.

Stairclimbing.

1. On hands and knees, child creeps up stairs.
2. Child sits on top step and descends by sitting on each step on the way down.
3. Child creeps up forward and creeps down backwards.
4. Using one step, child steps up on platform, turns around, and steps down with and without support; repeats with other foot (see Figure 14–36).
5. While holding handrail, child ascends each step one at a time with both feet placed on each landing, same lead foot.
6. Child descends, both feet on each step.
7. With support, child ascends each step alternating lead foot; descends with same lead foot.
8. Child ascends each step alternating lead foot; descends with alternate feet with and without support.

9. Vary height and width of steps used for stairclimbing.

Hand/Arm Usage.

1. Putting objects in child's hands.
2. Placing child's hands in tactile box for play.
3. Placing objects in front of child; encourage reach and grasp (palmar then pincer grasp).
4. Playing Pat-a-Cake.
5. Imitating hand movements.
6. Stacking blocks.
7. Nesting blocks.
8. Hitting suspended ball, balloons.
9. Stringing beads.
10. Picking up tiny objects.
11. Opening and closing clothespins.
12. Placing pegs in holes.

13. Stretching, reaching, bending arms.
14. Pushing and pulling large cage ball, large beach ball.
15. Pulling objects (e.g., pull-toys).
16. Pushing small carts while walking.
17. Pushing oneself up incline using rope.

Activities for Motor Pattern Development: Locomotor

Walking: Progressive alternate leg action and continuous contact with supporting surface; one foot moves ahead of the other with heel of forward foot touching ground before toe of opposite foot pushed off, and the arms and legs move synchronously in opposition. (Wickstrom, 1977)

1. Walking forward from one point to another.
2. Walking backward from one point to another.

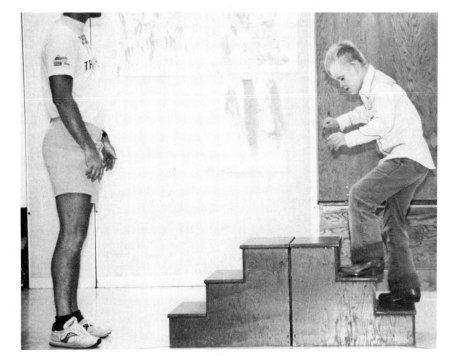

Figure 14–36. Developing stair-climbing ability. Although this child is able to ascend stairs without support by alternating his feet, the awkward position of his arms indicates that the pattern is not well established.

Figure 14-37. Not only does running around cones require motor planning, it also requires refinement of the basic motor pattern.

3. Walking between parallel lines drawn on floor.
4. Walking on single line on floor.
5. Walking, following curved line, figure eight, or any specified pattern.
6. Walking up and down incline.
7. Walking through a ladder or tires on ground.
8. Walking quickly or slowly.
9. Walking on tiptoes.
10. Walking through obstacle course.
11. Walking on footprints, following a specified pattern.

Running: A natural extension of walking in which each leg goes through a support phase and a recovery phase, and the full sequence produces two periods of nonsupport; forward trunk lean with arm swing in opposition to leg action.

1. Running forward or backward.
2. Running quickly, slowly.
3. Running up and down an incline.

4. Running along a straight line, or zigzag course.
5. Running through traffic cones (see Figure 14-37).
6. Running for distance.
7. Running and showing ability to change directions quickly.
8. Running, and stopping and going on command.

Jumping: Forward, explosive propulsion of the body off the ground with both legs; in crouch position, body weight forward, arms swing forward and upward; flexion and extension of hips, legs, and ankles at takeoff; knees bent at landing; body weight forward and downward at landing.

1. Jumping forward.
2. Jumping over line, over rope.
3. Jumping forward and backward over rope raised slightly off the ground, gradually increasing height.
4. Performing a series of forward and backwards jumps.
5. Jumping down from step, increasing the height of take-off platform.
6. Jumping into a designated space (e.g., hula hoop, carpet square) (see Figure 14-38).
7. Jumping up to reach object over head with one hand, then both hands.
8. Jumping sideways over line or rope.
9. Jumping over moving rope.
10. Jumping quickly, slowly.
11. Jumping with feet together; with feet apart.
12. Straddle jumping.
13. Teaching jump rope:
   a. step over rope;
   b. jump over rope moving forward and backwards;
   c. with rope passing over head, step over rope;
   d. with rope passing over head, jump over rope;
   e. jump over rope twice in a row;
   f. increase number and tempo of rope.
14. Use long rope jump and follow similar progression as in item 13.

Figure 14–38. Hula hoops can be used to provide additional challenges for jumping.

Hopping: Slight body lean forward; weight supported on one foot; nonsupport leg bent at knee; arms move upward; landing on toes, transfer weight to ball of foot, then to heel; maintain upright balance.

1. Initiating hop of the preferred foot with and without support (see Figure 14–39).
2. Hopping forward one step.
3. Performing a series of hops.
4. Hopping on the nonpreferred foot.
5. Alternating feet for hopping.
6. Hopping in a variety of directions.
7. Hopping forward and backward.
8. Hopping through an obstacle course.

Sliding: Sideways locomotion; one foot brought sideways close to contact with other foot, which then moves sideways away from the body; weight shifts from side to side in one direction.

1. Stepping sideways on line (i.e., step together, step together) (see Figure 14–40).
2. Stepping sideways in one direction, then other.

Figure 14–39. This child is learning to hop with support from the teacher.

Figure 14-40. Stepping sideways on a line can be used to teach the sliding pattern. SOURCE: Photo by Lyonel Avance.

3. Increasing speed of slide, with more weight on balls of feet.

4. Sliding to a rhythm.

5. Alternating direction and lead foot of slide.

Activities for Motor Pattern Development: Manipulative

Rolling ball.

1. While seated, rolling ball away from self with both hands together (e.g., hands under ball, hands on top, hands on side).

2. Rolling ball toward object or person.

3. While kneeling or squatting, rolling ball underhand with one and both hands, away from self.

4. Rolling ball toward object, person, or specified direction.

5. Varying the distance of the roll.

6. Varying the size and weight of the ball to be rolled.

Throwing. Movement sequence that involves thrusting an object into space; initiated by forward step with contralateral leg, followed by hip and trunk rotation; whipping action of propelling arm, follow through after release of ball.

1. Hurling small objects (e.g., paper balls, yarn balls, rubber balls, tennis balls).

2. Throwing small objects underhand without specified speed, force, direction, and so on (see Figure 14–41).

3. Underhand throwing, specify direction of (to knock down objects).

4. Throwing, specify speed.

5. Teaching child the backswing, step forward, and followthrough for underhand throw.

6. Varying the size, weight, and shape of the object to be thrown (e.g., bean bag, ball, balloon, medicine ball, bowling ball).

7. Throwing toward moving target (e.g., rolling hula hoop).

8. Throwing while moving.

9. Rolling hula hoop toward object using underhand pattern; vary speed, direction, force, quality, and so on.

10. Repeat items 1 through 9 using overhand throw.

11. Throwing various objects (e.g., bean bags, baseball, small balls, football) using overhand pattern.

12. Throwing objects sidearm, varying factors as appropriate.

13. Throwing a Frisbee.

Figure 14-41. Initial learning of either the underhand or overhand throw can be done in a seated position to eliminate balance problems.

Bouncing Ball.

1. Grasping rubber playground ball with two hands, dropping and catching with two hands.
2. Varying size of ball for drop-catch.
3. Pushing ball downward (bounce) with two hands and catching with two hands.
4. Varying size and weight of ball.
5. Using one hand to bounce ball and catching two-handed.
6. Performing continuous bounce (stationary).
7. Walking forward while bouncing ball (dribbling).
8. Varying the locomotor pattern while dribbling.
9. Dribbling around cones, in figure eight patterns.
10. Varying size, weight, speed, and force while dribbling.
11. Bouncing a ball two-handed toward a person or object.
12. Varying the height of the bounce.
13. Varying the direction of the bounce.
14. Varying the length and speed of the bounce.
15. Two-handed chest pass or bounce pass to moving or stationary object, person, or target.

Catching. Use of hands to stop and control aerial ball; arms raised in front of body; hands raised and/or cupped; hips and knees flexed; hands contact and grasp ball; body gives in direction of trajectory.

1. Trapping a rolled ball with two hands while sitting in long straddle position.
2. Catching a ball after dropping it (drop-catch).
3. Catching a bounced ball at chest height with two hands (see Figure 14-42).
4. Varying type of ball (e.g., rubber ball, beach ball, basketball).
5. Varying speed, direction, force of bounced ball.
6. Catching tossed ball by trapping it.
7. Catching tossed ball with arms, then two hands.
8. Playing catch with another student in class, varying the size of the ball, length of throw, speed.
9. Catching balls thrown over objects.
10. Catching objects with one hand (e.g., bean bags, frisbees, balls).
11. Catching while moving through space.
12. Playing Hot Potato.

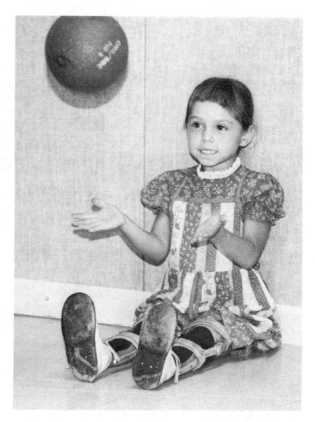

Figure 14–42. Catching can be learned and practiced in both an upright (left) and seated position (right).

Striking. Contact with an object (ball) by an implement (bat, hand, foot); body weight shifted (step) in direction of intended hit; hips and trunk rotation (turn); arms swing around and forward (swing) (Wickstrom, 1977).

1. Hitting suspended object (e.g., ball, balloon) while kneeling or standing (see Figure 14–43).
2. Trying to keep a balloon in the air with hand.
3. Varying the height of the object to be struck.
4. Hitting object toward a target.
5. Hitting object hard-easy, fast-slow.
6. With striking implement (e.g., baton, bat, stick), hitting object suspended above head, at head height, chest, waist, or knee height, and on ground; using one or both hands on implement.

7. Holding stick horizontally with two hands, hit suspended ball.
8. Specifying direction, speed, force of strike.
9. Varying size of implement and object to be hit (large-large, large-small, small-large, medium-medium).
10. Striking appropriate (stationary) objects with baseball bat, hockey stick, racquet, and so on.
11. Striking appropriate object (moving) with implement (e.g., baseball bat, hockey stick, tennis racquet, badminton racquet).

Kicking. Contact with an object by the foot; step forward on support leg; forward swing of kicking leg; extension of lower leg into object; forward swing of opposite arm in reaction.

Figure 14-43. Striking a ball suspended slightly overhead helps develop the overhand pattern.

1. Pushing ball away from the body with preferred, then nonpreferred foot.
2. Kicking ball away from the body with preferred, nonpreferred foot.
3. Kicking stationary ball toward target, in specified direction, or back and forth between partners.
4. Varying speed, distance, and height of kick.
5. Varying the size and weight of ball.
6. Kicking a stationary ball with side of foot (soccer style).

7. Running to stationary ball and kicking.
8. Dribbling (i.e., continuous kicking of ball) forward, in specified direction and/or through obstacle course.
9. Dribbling between partners.
10. Kicking a variety of stationary balls (e.g., football, kickball, soccer, playground) in appropriate manner.
11. Kicking a moving ball.

Activities for Motor Pattern Development: Nonlocomotor

Bending.

1. Bending the body forward.
2. Bending the body backward.
3. Bending the body sideways (see Figure 14-44).
4. Bending (flexing) the body parts — one leg, both legs, one arm, knees, both arms, arms and legs, hands, and so on.
5. Bending quickly, slowly.

Reaching/Stretching.

1. Reaching with one and two hands to touch object overhead, while standing.
2. Touching toe and/or floor with one and two hands from standing position.
3. Reaching (stretching) forward, backward, and to each side from standing position.
4. Stretching forward to touch toes with both hands from long-sitting position.
5. Bending from long-sitting straddle position and touching each foot with one and two hands.
6. In supine position: pointing toes and extending legs as far as possible; extending arms over head.

Turning/Twisting.

1. Rotating each body part around axis (e.g., foot, arm circles, leg circles, hand circles).
2. In upright position: turning entire body in a small circle.

Figure 14-44. The nonlocomotor pattern of bending can be developed as part of class warm-up exercises. SOURCE: Photo by Lyonel Avance.

3. In upright position: twisting upper body in one direction; then in opposite direction (see Figure 14-45).

4. In supine position: bending knees and rotating to one side, then the other.

5. Jumping and turning body one-quarter, one-half, three-quarters, and full turn in both directions.

6. From side-lying position: rotating upper and lower body in opposite directions.

Pushing/Pulling.

1. In sitting position: pushing large cage ball away with one and two hands, or one and two feet.

2. In supine position: pushing cage ball with hands or feet or both.

3. In prone position: pushing body off floor.

4. In upright position: pushing against heavy or light object; against stationary or movable object.

5. Walking forward pushing object (e.g., cage ball, cart, box).

6. In hand and knee position: pushing another person with entire body (e.g., wrestling games).

7. Prone on scooterboard: propelling forward and backward using feet or hands on wall or floor.

8. Prone or supine on scooterboard: pulling oneself along suspended rope.

9. Pulling oneself prone up incline.

10. In upright position: pulling objects on string toward oneself using reciprocal arm actions.

11. Walking forward and pulling objects along behind.

Activities for Motor Skill Development

Motor skills emanate from motor patterns; that is, skills are the more accurate and specific uses of motor patterns and combinations of patterns. Each of the motor experiences and motor patterns discussed in the previous section included activity suggestions for the development of skill, although not specified as such. A few further examples are presented here.

Generally speaking, as variables are manipulated in an attempt to refine motor ability, the activities are said to be for enhancing motor skills. Varying the speed, rhythm, quality, direction, surface, or area within which the activity is performed requires that the pattern be refined into skill. Examples include

1. Walking, running, hopping, and so on, forward in a straight line as fast as possible.

2. Walking backward blindfolded on a balance beam.

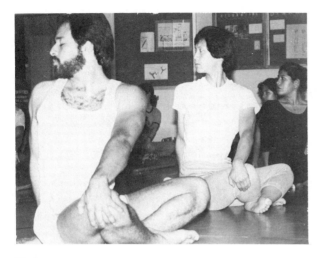

Figure 14–45. Trunk twisting ability for yoga, as shown here, is based upon initial development of the turning/twisting pattern.

3. Jumping over an object and landing on one foot, or jumping into a specified area.
4. Throwing at a target.
5. Running through an obstacle course.
6. Hopping, under control, downhill.

Combinations of motor patterns result in motor skills. A gallop is a combination of a step and slide; a skip is a step-hop; and a leap is an airborne giant step (initial part of hop with landing on opposite foot).

Gallop. Forward motion of the body in which the same foot leads on each stride, opposite foot is brought adjacent and parallel; step-hop action.

1. Walking forward on a line with same foot in front.
2. Speeding up the "lead leg walk" into a gallop.
3. Walking forward with the nonpreferred foot in front.
4. Galloping with the nonpreferred foot forward.
5. Galloping along a path (e.g., circle, line, shape).
6. Alternating the lead leg for gallop.

Skipping. Alternate step and hop action with each foot; weight shifting forward with step; arms move in opposition.

Figure 14–46. Slipping must first be taught through developing the step-hop combination. SOURCE: Photo by Lyonel Avance.

1. Following footsteps for teaching step-hop.
2. Performing a step-hop with one foot, repeat (see Figure 14–46).
3. Performing a step-hop with other foot and repeat.
4. Performing step-hop with one foot, then with other foot, repeating pattern.
5. Increasing the number of alternating patterns; step-hop right, step-hop left, and so on.
6. Increasing the speed of repetition.
7. Skipping quickly and slowly.
8. Skipping in a circle or along a path.
9. Skipping to music.

Leaping. Push forward with support leg and catch with opposite leg; alternate arm action during leap; weight shifted forward and upward on takeoff; downward and forward on landing.

Figure 14–47. The difficult pattern of running and leaping involves a combination of patterns in addition to the alternate use of body sides. SOURCE: Photo by Stan Carstensen, Instructional Media Services, California State University, Los Angeles.

1. Taking a very large step forward with the preferred foot forward.
2. Taking a large step quickly.
3. One foot take-off into air, taking large step quickly.
4. Performing leap: one foot take-off, above ground flight, land on opposite foot.
5. Repeating items 1 through 4 with nonpreferred foot.
6. Alternating lead foot; alternate leaping.
7. Leaping over low object such as line, rope, shoes.
8. Leaping as high as possible.
9. Leaping as long as possible.
10. Running and leaping to music or rhythm (see Figure 14–47).

SPECIAL ACTIVITIES AND SPECIAL EQUIPMENT

Besides the variations possible for obstacle courses, relay races, and elementary games, special activities and special equipment assist in the development and refinement of motor patterns and motor skills. The following are offered as suggestions for activities, and are not intended to be all-inclusive. Many of them have been suggested for use in the previous sections of this chapter.

Angels-in-the-Snow (adapted from Kephart, 1971)

For all activities, the child lies supine.

1. Imitate bilateral movements:
   a. move both arms along the floor until they touch above head simultaneously and return to side of body;
   b. move both legs apart and then together, arms stationary;
   c. move all four limbs apart and together;

d. move any three limbs apart and together while the other remains stationary;

e. move arms quickly or slowly, legs stationary;

f. move legs quickly or slowly, arms stationary;

g. move both arms and legs quickly or slowly.

2. Imitate unilateral movements:

a. move the right arm and right leg simultaneously, left limbs remain stationary;

b. move the left arm and leg simultaneously, right remain stationary;

c. alternate right and left limbs moving;

d. move quickly or slowly.

3. Imitate cross lateral movements:

a. move right arm and left leg apart and together, while other limbs are stationary;

b. move right leg and left arm apart and together;

c. move opposite limbs quickly or slowly.

The above activities can also be done in the prone position. The commands can be given verbally, in printed form, and by touching the specified limb(s). Initially, it may be valuable to move the child passively through the positions.

Animal Walks (adapted from Seaman and DePauw, 1979; Huettig, 1980)

1. *Snail:* move any way one wishes but very slowly.

2. *Busy Bee:* move any way one wishes but very fast.

3. *Snake:* slither along the ground both prone and supine.

4. *Elephant:* stand on feet, bend at the waist with hands together hanging down. Move slowly around room, letting arms sway like the trunk of an elephant (see Figure 14–48).

5. *Lion:* on hands and feet, walk around room with head held high.

6. *Bear:* on hands and feet, move around room with the right hand and right foot moving to-

Figure 14–48. The elephant walk (top) and the crab walk (below) are two of many types of animal walks that place great sensory and motor demands on the child. They are also fun.

gether; left hand and left foot move together.

7. *Seal:* in semi-push-up position, weight supported on hands, legs straight and dragging behind (toes pointed), move forward alternating hands and dragging legs behind.

8. *Crab:* hands and feet on ground with front side of body toward the ceiling and back side of body toward the floor, move forward, back, and sideways keeping buttocks off the floor.

9. *Inchworm:* hands and feet on ground almost touching each other (legs and arms extended in toe-touch position), keep feet stationary while hands "walk" forward until person is in push-up position, then "walk" feet forward to starting position, continue across room.

10. *Kangaroo Hop:* hold object between knees, jump with feet together.

11. *Chicken:* while balancing on knees, hold feet off the ground with hands, walk around the room without letting go of feet.

12. *Rabbit:* in crouch position, knees bent, hands and feet close together, lean forward, stretch arms out in front on ground and quickly push off with feet together and "hop" feet back to starting position.

13. *Alligator:* move in a prone position, with body completely in contact with floor. Pull body along with arms, leaving the tail (that is, the legs) to drag along behind.

14. *Dog:* move on all fours.

15. *Three-legged Dog:* move using only three limbs.

16. *Crazy Dog:* move in a four-point walk, but with arms crossed in front of body.

17. *Frog:* assume a semi-squat position and spring forward to another semi-squat position.

Balance Beam (Walking Board) Activities

1. Walk forward across board heel to toe with eyes on target.

2. Walk forward across board and carry a weight in the left hand.

3. Repeat item 2 with a weight in the right hand.

4. Walk forward across board and change the weight from hand to hand.

5. Walk backward across board.

6. Walk forward across board with a chalkboard eraser balanced on the head.

7. Walk backward across board with a chalkboard eraser balanced on the head.

8. Walk forward across board with a chalkboard eraser balanced on the head and carry a weight in the hand.

9. Walk across board and throw a beanbag at a target on command.

10. Walk across board and catch a beanbag and throw it back.

11. Walk across board and bounce and catch a ball (see Figure 14–49).

12. Walk sideways across board — lead with right foot.

13. Walk sideways across board — lead with left foot.

14. Walk sideways across board and carry a weight in both hands.

15. Walk sideways across board and change weight from hand to hand.

16. Walk sideways across board with a chalkboard eraser on top of the head and carry weight in the hand.

17. Walk sideways down board with weight in hands; in middle of board, turn around and continue backward to end of board.

18. Walk across board with arms extended to sides; then to the front, back, both to one side; then both to other side.

19. Walk across board with arms extended in front; to back; to opposite sides; both to one side; both to the other side.

20. Walk forward with left foot always in front of

right; combine activities covered in items 1 through 19.

21. Repeat item 20 with right foot always in front of left.

22. Walk backward with right foot always in back of left.

23. Walk backward with left foot always in back of right.

24. Walk forward and pick up a chalkboard eraser from the middle of the beam

25. Walk backward and pick up a chalkboard eraser from the middle of the beam.

26. Walk sideways leading with left side and pick up a chalkboard eraser from the center of beam.

27. Walk sideways leading with right side and pick up a chalkboard eraser from the center of the beam.

28. Repeat items 24, 25, 26, and 27, but this time pick up a chalkboard eraser and place it on top of the head and continue to end of beam.

29. Have partner hold a wand 12 inches over center of beam. Walk to center, step over the wand, and continue to end of beam.

30. Repeat items randomly from 1 through 28, using a wand. Increase height of step necessary to clear the wand, *but only high enough*. Be sure to tell the child if he or she steps *too high*.

31. Walk across beam in various ways. Teacher stands at end of board with target; child keeps eyes on target while moving across the board.

32. Repeat item 31, with child keeping eyes on target as target is moved. Call to the child's attention the fact that he or she has lost the target or looked away.

33. Repeat items randomly from 1 through 32 — include the task of going over and under the wand.

34. Walk beam forward with arms out, palms down, with a chalkboard eraser on the back of each hand.

35. Repeat item 34, but walk backwards.

Figure 14–49. This young man is demonstrating his ability to walk the balance beam while bouncing and catching a ball.

36. Walk board in various directions, with weight on the balls of the feet.

37. Walking on the balls of the feet, carry various weights across board and change weight from hand to hand while walking. Be sure child is looking at a definite target while walking.

38. Walk to center of board, kneel on one knee, straighten other leg forward until heel is on board

Figure 14-50. The balance board can be used to foster both sitting (left) and quadraped (four-point) position (right).

and knee is straight. Stand and walk to end of board.

39. Child walks to center of board and stops. Teacher goes to end of board, facing the child. Teacher moves arms and legs in various positions and child does same thing. If position is not correct, call the child's attention to the fact.

40. Child walks to center of board. Teacher throws the child a bean bag and child throws it back to teacher and at a target. Upon direction, child moves to various positions on the board while teacher stays in one place. Child throws the bean bag to the target and to teacher.

41. Walk board, keeping time to beat of drum or clapping of hands.

42. Child walks length of board, keeping eyes closed.

43. Partners join hands, with one person walking forward and one walking backward the length of the board.

44. Partners start at opposite ends of the board, walk slowly forward to center of board, pass each other, and continue walking to ends of board.

45. Partners start walking slowly forward on two separate boards; they pass a ball back and forth while continuing to walk.

46. Partners start at opposite ends of two separate walking boards and walk toward each other on their respective boards attempting to toss and catch a bean bag back and forth.

Balance Board

Each of the following activities can be done on any size balance board, starting with the largest base and largest platform and progressing to the board with the smallest base and platform (see Figure 14-50).

1. Sit on balance board and maintain balance.

Figure 14–51. Standing behind, next to, or in front of carpet squares can be used to teach the relationship of the body to other objects.

2. Balance on hands and knees on board:

    a. lift one leg, then the opposite leg;

    b. lift one arm, then the opposite arm;

    c. lift one arm and the opposite leg;

    d. lift arm and leg on same side of body.

3. Maintain kneeling balance.

4. Maintain standing balance.

5. While balanced in any of the above positions, keep bean bag positioned on various body parts (e.g., head, shoulder, back of hand).

6. While balanced, throw and catch bean bag or ball.

7. Vary direction, speed, height and thrown object to individual on balance board.

8. While balanced in any position, hit suspended ball with and without stick, two hands together, or each hand alternately.

Hula Hoops/Carpet Squares

The following activities can also be performed with newspaper sections, areas designated on the ground, jump ropes formed into shapes, and so on. One of the initial purposes for using hula hoops or carpet squares is to help children identify their own personal space.

1. Stand, sit, kneel, lie down, and so on, on carpet square or hula hoop (see Figure 14–51).

2. Move around space on command and return to hula hoop or carpet square.

3. Use locomotor patterns and skills in conjunction with hula hoop:

    a. jump over, jump in, jump around;

    b. run around;

    c. straddle hoop;

    d. stand in front of hoop;

    e. crawl or climb through hoop.

4. Place hula hoop/carpet square in front, behind, to the side of the body.

5. Move around space carrying hula hoop/carpet square; when signaled to stop, quickly sit (or jump, lie down, kneel, etc.) on or in space.

6. Move through an upright hula hoop.

7. Use hula hoop as jump rope.

8. Climb through a maze of hula hoops held upright.

9. With hula hoops/carpet squares placed in a specific pattern, locomote through course.

Parachute

The parachute is an exciting catalyst for movement. It can be used successfully for all grade levels. An entire class can be continuously and vigorously involved in parachute activities and all students, regardless of handicapping conditions, can participate (adapted from DePauw, 1978).

Group Stunts

1. *Inflation* — Hands are at waist level holding canopy. On signal to begin, students squat and seal chute on ground. On command "one-two-stretch," the arms are thrust overhead. The object is to get as much air as possible under the canopy. When the center of the canopy comes down and touches the floor, repeat the stunt trying to get an even better inflation. This stunt is the basic pattern for other stunts listed below.

2. *Tenting* — The students inflate the chute as listed in No. 1, and then walk forward three steps toward the center. (Teacher may wish to cue the students by saying, "In! 1-2-3.") Students hold onto the parachute and as it starts to descend the teacher can give the command "Out! 1-2-3."

3. *Mushroom* — The idea of this group stunt is to inflate the parachute and then quickly pull the edges down to the floor (or ground), sealing off the rapid escape of air. The class should continue to hold the edges down tight until the center of the canopy descends to the floor. You may wish to have a contest between two teams to see which one can keep the mushroom inflated the longest. The name "Mushroom" comes from the shape of the canopy when sealed with air inside. Have the class try it from both a stationary position and walking three steps in before sealing it.

4. *Hide-A-Way* — In this stunt, the participants seal themselves inside of the canopy. The parachute is inflated and the students walk three steps forward. They quickly turn and re-grasp the chute on the inside edge, and then kneel down holding the edge against the ground. The students remain sealed inside the chute until it begins to descend, whereupon they stand holding the chute and duck under to the outside. You may wish to try numbering the students by twos, with one group sealing themselves inside and one group sealing themselves outside.

5. *Sunflower* — The parachute is inflated and the students take three steps forward. They quickly bring the parachute down and kneel on the outside edge. (The chute should be sealed in the shape of a mushroom.) All students should now join hands, and on the commands "In" and "Out," they lean forward and back to represent a sunflower opening and closing.

6. *Fly Away* — The parachute is inflated and the participants take one step forward. On the command, "Release!" they let go of the canopy, which should remain suspended in air for a few seconds before floating to the ground.

7. *Grecian Flurry* — Eight students grasp a designated front arc (side) of the parachute using the right hand only, and hold it high in the air. On command, "Forward, run!" they travel a designated distance, keeping the right arm up high. A new group of eight students should be waiting at the finish line to repeat the stunt. You may wish to use eight squads in shuttle formation so that each person gets a turn in order.

Conditioning

1. *Bicep Builder* — With one leg forward, students plant their feet firmly and lean back, using palms-up grip, with arms almost fully extended. On a signal to begin, students pull the chute toward themselves without moving their feet or jerking

the chute. The pulling should continue as hard as possible for six seconds. Teacher should count aloud and offer encouragement for holding it. Use palms-down grip for variation.

2. *Wild Horse Pull*—Students turn with back to the chute and grasp the edge of the canopy with a palms-down grip. With one foot forward and one back, they plant their feet firmly on the ground and lean forward. On a signal (e.g., whistle), they should pull as hard as they can. Teacher may wish to make team competition out of this exercise by seeing if one half of the parachute can pull the other half in their direction.

3. *Ocean Waves*—Participants hold the parachute at waist level and, on a signal, slowly begin shaking the chute up and down. The tempo should gradually be increased. Have the participants pull back on the chute as they shake it. A variation for greater arm action is to have the students kneel and then shake it up and down.

4. *Sky High Pull*—Participants start with the parachute held at waist level using a palms-down grip. They should spread the feet for balance and on signal slowly lift the parachute up until the arms are fully extended overhead. Using just the arms and shoulders (feet, waist, and back do not move), all pull back and hold firmly for six seconds. Use the palms up grip for variation.

5. *Wrist Roll*—The parachute is held at waist level (arms extended) with a palms-down grip. On a signal to begin, all participants begin slowly rolling the edge of the canopy toward the center. Stress that the group stays together, and at the same time the canopy must be kept tight by pulling a little before each roll of the wrists.

6. *Straight Arm Pullover*—Starting position is with the parachute held at waist level using a palms-down grip. Feet are shoulder distance apart and on a signal to begin, the arms are extended slowly overhead. Participants should breathe in slowly in rhythm with the arm lift. At the point of full extension, the arms are slowly lowered to starting position and participants should exhale. This complete action is repeated at an even tempo for a given number of repetitions.

7. *Bend and Stretch*—Students hold chute at waist level with palms-down grip. On a signal to begin, they bend forward touching the edge of the canopy to their toes (count 1). On a count of 2, they extend arms overhead stretching as far as possible. On count 3, the students bend forward at the waist and again touch toes. They return to overhead extended arm position on count 4. This represents one completed repetition of the exercise.

8. *Push-Ups*—Students inflate chute and form a mushroom by sealing the edges to the ground. They take push-up position with hands holding the edges tight on the ground. Students perform push-ups by command from the teacher with the chute inflated in the shape of a mushroom.

9. *Modified Squat Thrusts*—Performed in same manner as item 8 (Push-Ups), except that students extend legs straight back from squat position on the count of 1 and return to squat position on the count of 2. Count 3, legs are again extended straight back, and count 4 return to squat position. This is one complete four-count repetition. Students do not come to a standing position as in a regular squat thrust.

10. *Tug-of-War*—The parachute is first of all rolled into one long unit similar to a rope. Two teams are selected, and one team lines up along each half of the parachute. The activity is then conducted as a regular tug-of-war with the students pulling on a given signal to begin. The nylon chute is extremely strong and can be used safely for this activity.

Figure 14-52. A small group of children plays "Ball Shake" with a parachute.

Games

1. *Ball Shake* — The class is divided into two equal teams with one team gripping each half of the canopy at the edges. A number of light balls are placed on top of the canopy (e.g., rubber balls, volleyballs, beach balls). On a signal to begin, each team attempts to shake the balls off on the other team's side of the chute. Participants may not use their hands to keep the balls from leaving the canopy. One point is awarded each time a ball leaves the chute and touches the ground (see Figure 14-52).

2. *Numbers Exchange* — The students are numbered by fives or sixes, depending on the size of the class. The chute is inflated and, as it reaches the maximum height, a number is called out. Everyone with that number must leave their places on the chute and change places with another student having the same number. All exchanging takes place under the canopy. Students must get to another place before the chute descends and touches their body. Penalties may or may not be imposed. Children in lower grades will probably have difficulty getting the chute high enough to run under. For extremely large groups, it is better to use more numbers so that fewer students are moving about under the parachute. Running, skipping, hopping, jumping, and other locomotor movements can be incorporated into this game.

3. *Numbers Race* — The class is divided into two equal teams. Each team counts off consecutively. The parachute is inflated and the teacher calls a number. The person on each team whose number is called must travel around the outside of the parachute and return to his or her place before the center of the chute touches the ground. The teacher should vary the type of locomotor skill used in moving around the chute. Teacher may wish to award one point to first player returning to his or her own position.

4. *Steal the Bacon* — A bean bag or other small object is placed under the chute at approximately the middle or center of the canopy. The class is divided into two equal teams and each player has a team number. The parachute is inflated and, at its highest point, the teacher calls a number or numbers. The players who have the number called must attempt to secure the bean bag and get back to their position without being tagged by the opponent. Also, if the chute descends on them while under the canopy, no points are awarded. A player who successfully gets back to his or her team position without being tagged or touched by the descending chute scores one point for the team.

Figure 14-53. These two boys are learning to use their bodies in new ways by trying to replicate the shape formed by the rope. SOURCE: Photo by Ben Esparza.

Basic Locomotor Movements

1. *General Approach* — Children grasp the edge of the parachute at a seam and use one hand (right or left) designated by the teacher. The teacher has many options in regard to direction that may be used. These options include: (1) circle forward in the line of direction; (b) circle backward; (c) circle forward, on a signal, change gripping hands and reverse the line of direction; (d) circle forward and on a signal move backward; (e) move in toward the center of the chute and back out; and (f) other combinations using the above listed directions.
2. *Locomotor Skills to Be Stressed* — (a) walking, (b) running, (c) hopping, (d) jumping, (e) leaping, (f) skipping, (g) galloping, and (h) sliding.

Special Activities

1. *Tumbling Activities* — Mats are placed under the parachute. Members of the class hold the chute in the inflated position while other pupils perform forward rolls, backward rolls, animal stunts, and so on.
2. *Pyramids* — Class is divided into teams of six. Each team tries to build a pyramid under the parachute before it comes down from an inflated position and touches them. Mats are placed under the chute for the students to perform on. Teams must be allowed time to practice their pyramids without the parachute so that each member of the team knows exactly what to do.
3. *Self-Testing Activities* — Students can be given the challenge of ball bouncing, rope jumping, and so on under the inflated chute.
4. *Long Jump Rope* — The parachute can be rolled up in the form of a long jump rope. As a long rope, children can run and jump over it, and then crawl under it coming back. They can also hop and jump back and forth over the chute when it is lying on the ground like an extended rope. Many other movement patterns can be presented using the chute in this manner.
5. *Dance Steps* — Basic dance steps such as the schottische, step-hop, two-step, polka, and mazurka can be practiced using the parachute as a stimulus for movement. Music will add greatly to this activity.

Ropes

1. Use jump ropes to make different shapes.
2. Form jump ropes into letters, numbers, and so on.
3. Use ropes formed in items 1 and 2 for activities suggested under hula hoops and carpet squares.
4. Make shapes with ropes and place body in same shape inside rope (see Figure 14-53).

Figure 14-54. By pulling himself along the rope while supine on a scooterboard, this child is receiving vestibular stimulation and tonic labyrinthine reflex (TLR) inhibition.

5. Use rope at different heights for jumping over or for going under.
6. Jump over serpentine or swinging rope.
7. Follow rope maze with and without vision.
8. Follow rope maze walking, or on scooterboard.

Scooterboard

1. Ride prone down ramp.
2. Ride prone down incline, hit or grab suspended object.
3. Ride prone down incline, pick up objects.
4. Ride prone down incline, pick up bean bags and place in containers.
5. Ride prone down incline, turn and roll onto mat.
6. Prone, follow line (rope) maze.
7. Prone, follow rope maze blindfolded.
8. Prone, follow maze by memory.
9. Prone or supine, push off wall and glide.
10. Prone or supine, pull self along suspended rope (see Figure 14-54).
11. In sitting position (prone, supine, kneeling), maintain balance while being pulled by teacher with an inner tube strip or old bicycle tire.
12. In sitting, kneeling, prone position propel self in a given direction using plumber's helper.

13. Play relay races on scooterboard.
14. Play scooterboard soccer, volleyball, basketball.

T-Stool (One-legged stool with varying width base)

1. Sit and maintain balance with and without vision.
2. Imitate postures while seated.
3. Life one leg, then other while seated.
4. Balance bean bag on body parts while maintaining balance (see Figure 14-55).
5. Kick ball while sitting on T-stool.
6. Throw and catch ball while balanced.
7. Play handball while seated on T-stool.
8. Play T-stool foursquare.

Tin Can Stilts (Stilts made out of tin cans or small wooden blocks (see Figure 14-56)

1. Stand and maintain balance on stilts.
2. Walk forward on stilts.
3. Walk backward.
4. Walk sideways.
5. Walk along a specified pattern.
6. Step over objects.
7. Play relay or foot races.

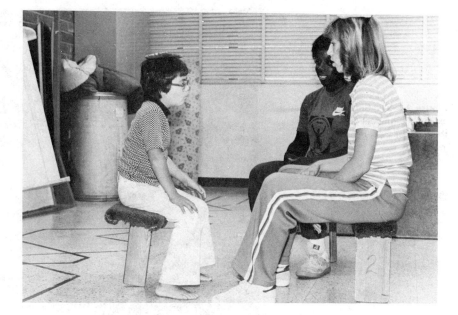

Figure 14–55. It is a challenge to maintain balance on a T-stool while keeping a bean bag on one's head.

Figure 14–56. Tin can stilts are fun to walk on and easy to make.

Tin cans

1. Cans varying in size from small and low (tuna fish cans) to tall and wide (juice or coffee cans) can be used.
2. Two holes are punched in opposite sides near the closed end.
3. Rope or heavy cord is strung through the holes and tied together inside the can. The length of the rope depends on the length of the child's arms.
4. The child stands on the cans and pulls on the rope, keeping it taut.

Trampoline

1. Lie prone or supine, be passively bounced (see Figure 14–57).
2. Roll over, sit up while being bounced.
3. Roll along the bed of trampoline.
4. Crawl, creep, walk on trampoline.
5. Jump in center of trampoline.
6. Jump as high as possible.
7. Jump as long as possible without losing control.
8. Alternate jumping with feet together, feet apart.
9. Jump and touch toes.
10. Perform knee drop, return to standing.
11. Perform seat drop, then return to standing.
12. Perform front drop, then return to standing.
13. Perform back drop, then return to standing.
14. Jump with one-quarter, one-half, and full turn.
15. Perform swivel hips with as many repetitions as possible.
16. Perform two tasks in a sequence (seat drop to knee drop).
17. Perform three-task sequence (knees to seat to knees).
18. Perform multi-task sequence.
19. Perform specified task upon verbal or written command.

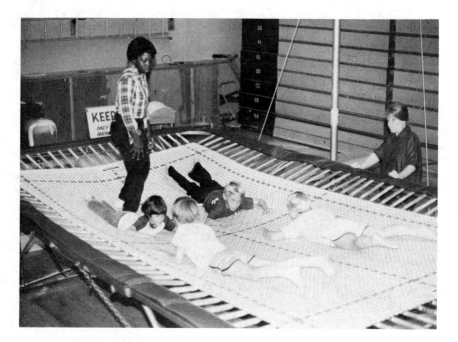

Figure 14-57. Small children can experience the feel of the trampoline through passive bouncing by the instructor.

20. Read letters (or numbers, words, actions) while jumping.
21. Read command and perform task.

Wrestling Games (adapted from Seaman and DePauw, 1978)

The following activities are meant to be fun and not highly competitive. Choose appropriate activities according to the child's ability.

1. *Elephant Wrestle:* on hands and knees, two children put shoulders or sides together (not heads) and attempt to push the other off the mat, rug, or out of prescribed area.
2. *Alligator Wrestle:* in push-up position, two children face each other and attempt to pull the other's hand out from under the body until one falls to the ground.
3. *Arm Wrestle:* opponents face each other across a table, one with elbows on the table and forearms straight up. Clasping hands, each tries to push the other's arm down onto the table.
4. *Indian Wrestle:* with the outside of the same foot touching and same hands grasping each other,

two children attempt to cause each other to lose balance or to move feet.
5. *Slap Hands:* two children stand facing each other at arm's length. Each pushes (not holds) and lightly slaps the other's hands until the opponent moves feet or loses balance.
6. *Leg Wrestle:* two children lie on their backs with waists together and heads at opposite ends. They hook elbows, and lay hands on their own stomach. Raise inside leg three times and touch opponent's foot; on third raise, hook legs at the knees and try to pull leg to the ground, thus forcing opponent to go over backward.
7. *Thumb Wrestle:* opponents grasp each other's right hand with thumbs extended upward (only curled fingers), and try to "pin" the opponent's thumb down.

APPROPRIATE LEVELS OF INTERVENTION

Not all of the activities included in Chapters 14 and 15 are appropriate for all handicaps. Each handicapped individual has unique needs and capacities. Table 14-3 is included as a guide for the physical education in-

Table 14–3. Appropriate levels of intervention 391

Category of exercise	Multihandicapped/ severely handicapped	Seriously emotionally disturbed	Deaf/blind	Mentally retarded	Other health-impaired	Orthopedically impaired	Deaf/hard-of-hearing	Blind/visually impaired	Speech-/language-disabled	Learning disabled
Reflex development/inhibition	A	A	A	A		A				A
Sensory stimulation/discrimination	A	A	A	A	A	A	A	A	A	A
MOTOR SENSORY RESPONSES										
Praxis	A	A	A	A	A	A	A	A	A	A
Integration of body sides	A	A	A	A	A	A	A	A	A	A
Balance	M	A	A	A	M	A	A	A	A	A
Eye-hand/eye-foot	A	A	A	A	A	A	A	A	A	A
Crossing midline	A	A	A	A	A	A	A	A	A	A
Body awareness	A	A	A	A	A	A	A	A	A	A
MOTOR PATTERNS/MOTOR SKILLS										
Early motor experiences	A	A	A	A	A	A	A	A	A	A
Motor patterns	A	A	A	A	A	A	A	A	A	A
Motor skills		A	M	M	M	M	M	M	A	A
Special activities/equipment	M	A	M	A	M	M	M	M	A	A
FORMS OF MOVEMENT FOR APPLYING SKILLS										
Aquatics	M	A	M	A	M	M	A	M	A	A
Conditioning	M	A	M	A	C	C	M	M	A	A
Dance/rhythms	M	A	M	M	M	M	M	M	A	A
Fitness	M	A	M	M	C	M	M	M	A	A
Games and sports	M	M	M	M	C	M	M	M	A	A
Stunts		M	M	M	C	C	M	M	A	A
Therapeutic activities/exercises		A	M	M	C	C	A	M	A	A
Weight training		M	M	M	C	C	A	M	A	A

Key: A = appropriate level of intervention
M = modifications needed, but level of intervention is appropriate
C = specific contraindications for some, but otherwise appropriate; possible modification

structor in the selection of appropriate activities for various handicapping conditions.

SUMMARY

Effective programming is contingent upon a thorough understanding of the needs, limitations, abilities, and interests of handicapped children. When teaching physical education to handicapped children, not only must the needs of the class as a whole be considered, but also the unique needs of each child. Activities must be chosen from the reflex level to the motor skills level of the developmental model, according to each child's needs. A number of enjoyable games and activities can be included in the program in order to stimulate children to develop the necessary motor-sensory responses, motor abilities, and motor skills.

BIBLIOGRAPHY

Adams, R. C., Daniel, A. N., and Rullman, L. *Games, Sports, and Exercises for the Physically Handicapped.* Philadelphia: Lea and Febiger, 1975.

American Alliance for Health, Physical Education, Recreation, and Dance. *Physical Activities for Impaired, Disabled, and Handicapped Individuals.* Washington, D.C.: AAHPERD, 1976.

American Alliance for Health, Physical Education, Recreation, and Dance. *Physical Education, Recreation, and Related Programs for Autistic and Emotionally Disturbed Children.* Washington, D.C.: AAHPERD, 1976a.

American Red Cross. *Adapted Aquatics.* Garden City, New York: Doubleday, 1977.

Bundschuh, E., et al. *Adapting Physical Education Activities.* Project D.A.R.T. Athens, Georgia: University of Georgia, 1979.

Council on Exceptional Citizens. *Exceptional Children* 7 (1974): 8.

Cratty, B. J. *Learning and Playing.* Freeport, New York: Educational Activities, 1968.

DePauw, K. P. *Adapted Aquatic Checklist,* mimeographed, 1977.

DePauw, K. P. *Parachute Activities,* mimeographed, 1978.

Dunn, J. M. *Adaptive Physical Education.* Salem, Oregon: Mental Health Division, 1980.

Frostig, M. *Move, Grow, Learn.* Chicago: Follett, 1969.

Huettig, C. *Adapted Physical Education Curriculum.* Denton, Texas: Denton County Special Education Cooperative, 1980.

Jacobson, E. *Young Must Relax.* New York: McGraw-Hill, 1962.

Kephart, N. C. *Slow Learner in the Classroom.* 2d ed. Columbus, Ohio: Charles E. Merrill, 1971.

Kuizinga, J., and Wilbarger, P. *Activities for the Remediation of Sensorimotor Dysfunction in Primary School Children.* Goleta, California: Title III ESEA Project, Goleta Union School District, n.d.

Lawrence, C., and Hackett, H. *Water Learning.* Palo Alto, California: Peek Publications, 1975.

Meisels, S. J. *First Steps in Mainstreaming: Some Questions and Answers.* Boston: Media Resource Center, Massachusetts Department of Mental Health, March 1977.

Montgomery, P., and Richter, E. *Sensorimotor Integration for Developmentally Disabled Children: A Handbook.* Los Angeles: Western Psychological Services, 1978.

Moran, J., and Kalakian, L. *Movement Experiences for the Mentally Retarded or Emotionally Disturbed.* Minneapolis: Burgess, 1977.

Richardson, H. A. *Games for Elementary School Grades.* Minneapolis: Burgess, 1969.

Seaman, J. A., and DePauw, K. P. *Sensory Motor Experiences for the Home: A Manual for Parents.* Los Angeles: Trident Shop, 1978.

Thompson, D. "Space Utilization: Criteria for the Selection of Playground Equipment for Children." *Research Quarterly* 47 (October 1976): 472–481.

Wickstrom, R. L. *Fundamental Motor Patterns.* Philadelphia: Lea and Febiger, 1977.

15

Applying Motor Skills in Culturally Determined Forms of Movement

Guiding Questions

1. What are some examples of games and sports in which handicapped individuals can participate?
2. How can relaxation techniques be used effectively in physical education programs?
3. What are some activities used for therapeutic exercises and weight training?
4. In general, what activities would have contraindications for individuals with certain handicapping conditions?

Many books, card files, and articles describe activities for handicapped individuals at the skill level, including games, sports, athletics, dance, and so on. A number of these are included in the bibliography at the end of this chapter and in Appendix E. The following section includes listings of activities in aquatics, dance, conditioning, fitness, games and sports, relaxation, weight training, and therapeutic exercise. The listings are not intended to be all-inclusive, but to illustrate appropriate activities.

AQUATICS

The water is a wonderful <u>medium for movement,</u> especially for the handicapped. Almost every handi-

capped individual can participate in water learning activities, and many can learn to swim. The American Red Cross (1977) has identified five safety skills to be taught each handicapped person:

1. Turning over from prone to supine.
2. Changing directions.
3. Prone float.
4. Supine float.
5. Breath control.

As soon as possible, these skills should be taught the handicapped for their own safety and the safety of others. Keep in mind that there are many water activities in which the handicapped can participate that may not lead to the acquisition of swimming skills (adapted from DePauw, 1977).

Figure 15-1. Water-play is fun for handicapped and nonhandicapped swimmers (left); a handicapped swimmer successfully completes one lap of the back stroke (right).

Water Adjustment

On deck – wading pool:

1. Sit in water.
2. Splash water.
3. Wash face with water.
4. Water play: pour water with bucket, squeeze sponges (see Figure 15-1).
5. Retrieve objects (e.g., chips) from water.

In water – swimming pool:

1. Sit on step.
2. Splash water on body and face.
3. Move down steps into water.
4. Wade in waist-deep, assisted.
5. Wade in waist-deep, unassisted.
6. Wade in chest-deep, assisted.
7. Wade in chest-deep, unassisted.
8. Move forward, backward, and sideways, unassisted.
9. Bend knees and submerge to chin.
10. Put parts of head (i.e., chin, ears, cheeks, forehead, nose, mouth, eyes) into water.
11. Quickly place nose and mouth into water.
12. Place whole face into water.
13. Submerge body to ears.
14. Submerge with head under water.

Breath Control

1. Out of water: inhale, exhale.
2. With body in chest-deep water: *easy* inhale, slow exhale.
3. Blow ping pong ball across pool.
4. With mouth in water: *slowly exhale* into water, making bubbles.
5. With face in water, blow bubbles.
6. Submerge and blow bubbles.
7. Rhythmic bobbing 3- or 4-second intervals.
8. Exhale through nose into water.

Body Control

1. Walk slowly through water.
2. Walk fast through water.
3. Jump while in water.
4. Squat under water.
5. Sit on bottom of pool.

6. Kneel on bottom of pool.
7. Lie prone on bottom of pool.
8. Lie supine on bottom of pool.
9. Roll over while on bottom of pool.
10. Combination of movements (e.g., knees to sitting, sitting to prone) while on bottom of pool.
11. With hands on steps, bring legs up to floating position, unassisted recovery.
12. With hands on steps, prone float position, unassisted recovery.
13. With hands on steps, prone float position, kick with legs.
14. With hands on steps, kick quickly.
15. With hands on steps, kick slowly.
16. While held in prone position in chest-deep water, recover to standing, with assistance.
17. While held in prone position, recover without assistance.
18. While held in supine position in chest-deep water, recover to standing, with assistance.
19. While held in supine, recover to standing, without assistance.
20. While being pulled in prone position, maintain relaxed body position.
21. Retrieve objects (e.g., diving rings, chips) from 2 to 3 feet of water.
22. Jellyfish float: arms and legs hang and float.
23. Turtle float: grab legs, feet off bottom and float.
24. Prone float and recovery.
25. Supine float (knees bent and recovery).
26. Roll over from prone float to supine float.
27. Roll from supine float to prone float.

Basic Skills

1. Steamboat: kicking while being pulled through water.
2. Prone glide with assistance.
3. Prone glide to steps and recover.

4. Prone glide to instructor (3 feet away from steps), assisted recovery.
5. Prone glide to instructor (3 or 4 feet from steps), unassisted recovery.
6. Prone glide width of pool (6 to 10 feet).
7. Kick glide to steps (3 feet).
8. Kick glide to instructor (3 or 4 feet), assisted recovery.
9. Kick glide (3 or 4 feet), unassisted recovery.
10. Kick glide the width of pool (6 or 10 feet).
11. While in supine position, finning and sculling* with hands.
12. Beginning armstroke with underwater recovery of arms.
13. Armstroke: hand over hand.
14. Beginner's stroke with kick.
15. Front crawl without breathing.
16. Change directions while swimming.
17. Swim two widths of pool (15 to 20 feet).
18. Jump into chest-deep water.
19. Jump into head-deep water and swim 15 to 20 feet.

Swimming Skills

1. Front crawl with breathing.
2. Swim under water (5 to 8 feet).
3. Jump into deep water and swim 30 feet.
4. Tread water with arms and legs.
5. Dive into pool from sitting position.
6. Dive into pool from one knee.
7. Dive into pool from crouch position.
8. Dive from standing position.
9. Elementary backstroke.

*Finning and sculling use only hands for movement. Finning is done supine with hands at sides moving in finning motion; body moves head first. Sculling is done supine with arms over head; body moves feet first.

10. Breaststroke.
11. Back crawl.
12. Side stroke.
13. Dive from low board.

Creative Movement

1. Somersaults forward in water.
2. Somersaults backward in water.
3. Log rolls in water.
4. Egg rolls in water.
5. Handstands in shallow water.
6. Elbow stands in shallow water.
7. Walk on hands in shallow water.
8. Corkscrew swimming.
9. Shark swim (swim in circle with one hand on hip — elbow out of water).
10. Swim without arms, legs only.
11. Swim without legs, arms only.
12. Swim without legs or arms.
13. Swim through hula hoops.
14. Retrieve objects from bottom.
15. Rhythmic bobbing in deep water.

Group Activities

1. Inner tube tag.
2. Inner tube relay races.
3. Kickboard relays and races.
4. Marco Polo.
5. Water volleyball.
6. Water polo.
7. Water basketball.
8. "Jump-Dive."
9. Jump and Catch.
10. Water ballet.
11. Synchronized swimming.
12. Academic/Language games.

CONDITIONING

The activities listed below have been selected to provide physical education teachers with some basic physical conditioning activities (adapted from Adams, Daniel, and Rullman, 1975). For conditioning exercises that can be done in the water, the reader is referred to Conrad (1975).

1. Push-ups from kneeling position.
2. Push-ups from full position.
3. Pull-ups, overhead grip, with feet on floor.
4. Pull-ups, feet off floor from start.
5. Pull-ups, underhand grip, feet on floor.
6. Pull-ups, underhand grip, feet off floor.
7. Moving forward and backward on horizontal ladder from arm-hanging position.
8. Hanging as long as possible from overhead bar.
9. Arm support with forward and backward movement on parallel bars.
10. Medicine ball activities, throwing and catching (see Figure 15-2).
11. Sit-ups with knees and hips flexed.
12. Jumping jacks.
13. Trunk bending forward, sideways, and backward.
14. Toe-touching from sitting position.
15. Toe-touching from standing position.
16. Trunk twister.
17. Run in place.
18. Rope climbing with legs wrapped around ropes.
19. Run through tires and/or obstacle course.

DANCE/RHYTHMS

1. Clap to music.
2. Keep time to music with instruments.
3. Walk (move) to drum beat (fast, slow, loud, soft, and so on).
4. Walk to music.

Figure 15-2. Passing the medicine ball from one child to another can be used as a conditioning exercise, and to provide additional balance challenges.

5. March to a specified beat.
6. Play London Bridge, Hokey Pokey, I'm a Little Teapot, Farmer in the Dell, and so on.
7. Use Dance-A-Story records.
8. Hap Palmer records.
9. Line dances (Hora, Bunny Hop, Cotton-Eye Joe).
10. Circle dances (Circasian Circle, Teton Mountain Stomp).
11. Square dance (Virginia Reel).
12. Run and leap to music.
13. Imitate partner in time to music.
14. Slow mirroring of partner in time with slow music.
15. Interpretative dance.
16. Dance with ribbons, sticks, flags, clubs, scarves.
17. Orff Schulwerk chants.
18. Exercise to music.
19. Jump rope to music.
20. Combine exercises to make a routine set to music.
21. Aerobic dance.
22. Swedish gymnastics.
23. Disco dancing.

FITNESS ACTIVITIES

An important objective of any physical education program should be to improve the physical fitness of those participating. This applies also to handicapped children in both regular physical education and adapted physical education. The following activities should be included as an integral part of the physical education program.

1. Warm-up exercises:
   a. slow stretching;
   b. running in place.

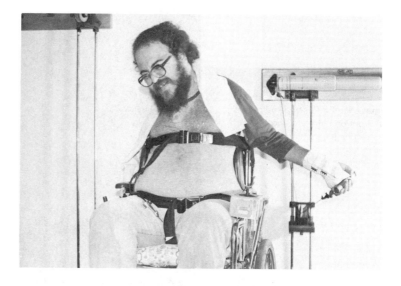

Figure 15-3. Using weights for conditioning. A quadraplegic uses wall pulleys to develop arm strength (right). The double-leg amputee (below, left) has attained national recognition by developing extraordinary upper body strength. The young man whose legs have atrophied because of polio (below, right) is doing pull-downs to maintain the upper body strength he needs for using crutches.

2. Strength: weights used can be free weights, a weight machine, or homemade weights (see Figure 15–3):

a. bench pull on stomach and back;

b. pull-ups;

c. push-ups;

d. wall pushing;

e. sit-ups;

f. rope climbing;

g. pole climbing.

3. Isometric exercises.

4. Ride bicycle ergometers.

5. Jumping rope for fitness.

6. Roller skating for endurance and fitness.

7. Long distance running for endurance.

8. Jogging.

9. Sprints, short distance runs for speed.

10. Par courses:

a. sit-ups;

b. run through tires;

c. balance beam;

d. pull-ups;

e. step-ups;

f. tennis ball squeeze;

g. hurdles;

h. push-ups;

i. jump ropes;

j. sprints;

k. and so on.

11. Weight training.

12. Interval training.

13. Exercises with inner tube strips:

a. pull with arms above head, across chest, like bow and arrow;

b. pull with legs apart;

c. one arm with one leg pull;

d. while sitting, place inner tube strip over feet and pull with two hands;

e. pull between partners;

f. pull with forearms only.

14. Flexibility exercises:

a. reach and stretch every body part;

b. touch toes, floor;

c. egg rock;

d. circles with arms, hands, head, legs, feet, and so on;

e. sit and spread legs;

f. while sitting, touch toes, knees;

g. body twists.

GAMES AND SPORTS

Low organization:

1. Table tennis.

2. Shuffleboard.

3. Tabletop croquet.

4. Miniature tetherball.

5. Tetherball.

6. Prisoner.

7. Foursquare.

8. Tag.

9. Duck Duck Goose.

10. Dodge ball.

11. Handball.

12. Drop the handkerchief.

13. Box hockey

14. Chess, checkers, Ping-Pong.

15. Statues.

High organization:

1. Adapted table tennis.

2. Air riflery.

3. Angling.

4. Archery.

5. Badminton.

6. Bowling.

7. Cross-country running.

Figure 15-4. A wheelchair-bound student practices hitting drills in tennis.

8. Fencing.
9. Gymnastics.
10. Horseback riding.
11. Ice skating.
12. Paracanoeing (boating).
13. Camping.
14. Golf (miniature and regulation).
15. Skiing.
16. Tennis (see Figure 15-4).
17. Wrestling.
18. Softball/baseball.
19. Volleyball.
20. Soccer.
21. Football.
22. Hockey.
23. Track and field.
24. Basketball.
25. Self-defense.
26. Cycling.
27. Hiking/backpacking.

28. Roller skating.
29. Sport shooting.

RELAXATION ACTIVITIES

Many children are in need of assistance in calming themselves or just relaxing. It is recommended that each physical education session include some form of relaxation. For the overly active, relaxation activities might be beneficial at the beginning of the class; for all students, the relaxation activities are beneficial at the end. In general, any activity that involves deep pressure, slow stretching, or a slow rocking motion tends to be relaxing. Eliminating extraneous stimuli such as sounds or light may provide assistance in the process of relaxation training (see Figure 15-5).

1. Deep breathing exercises (in comfortable sitting or supine position):

   a. count the number of times one breathes;

b. feel the rise and fall of the chest during breathing;

c. actively attempt to slow down one's breathing pattern;

d. inhale and exhale slowly and completely;

e. continue slow deep breathing for several minutes.

2. Stretch and let go:

a. stretch entire body and then release and sink to the floor;

b. alternate pulling of right leg-left arm, left leg-right arm, out away from the body simultaneously;

c. clasp hands, pull them toward feet then stretch over head and pull;

d. arch back, then curl;

e. hold knees to chest, rock from side to side.

3. Limp rag:

a. child makes total body as limp as possible in whatever position;

b. teacher lifts child's head and lets it fall into hands;

c. child lifts each arm and leg, one at a time and shakes out all tensions;

d. child lifts each limb and allows to drop into hands of teacher.

4. Listening/imagery:

a. focus attention on a single stimulus.

b. watch a flickering candle;

c. listen to a small stream of water;

d. listen to soft music;

e. imagine being in a favorite spot;

f. imagine being very sleepy;

g. imagine being a puppy or kitten asleep.

5. Progressive relaxation (Jacobson, 1962):

a. assume supine position;

b. tighten face and relax;

c. tighten neck and relax;

d. tighten muscles in shoulder, and arms, then relax;

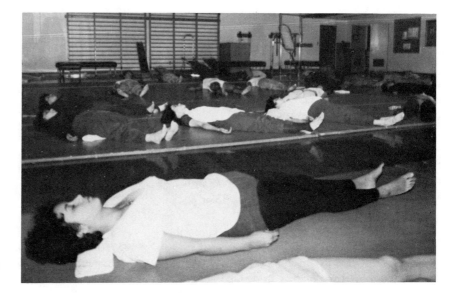

Figure 15-5. Deep breathing exercises, progressive relaxation, and yoga, as shown here, are examples of relaxation activities that can be used to calm children down.

Figure 15-6. Incredible stunts, such as this handstand performed by a double-leg amputee, can be accomplished through perseverance and practice.

e. tighten stomach and relax;
f. tighten legs and relax;
g. tighten lower legs, relax;
h. tighten muscles in hands and relax;
i. tighten muscles in feet and relax;
j. and so on, throughout the body.

STUNTS

1. *Knee Scale:* support body on one knee and lower leg, raise head and arms, point nonsupport leg backward.
2. *Front Scale:* support body weight on one foot and balance in arches position over that foot.
3. *Side Scale:* support weight on hand and foot on the same side, keeping body rigid.
4. *Shoulder Stand:* support weight on back of shoulders and arms, extend legs into air.
5. *V-set:* balance weight on buttocks while extending legs and trunk in air, body resembles a V.
6. *Angel Balance:* one child in fully extended prone position balances on upward extended legs of supine child.
7. *Head Stand:* balance upside down on head using the hands, forming a triangle with the head, for support.
8. *Hand Stand:* balance upside down on hands only (see Figure 15-6).
9. *Forward Somersault:* complete a forward roll from crouched position over the head and hands.

10. *Backward Somersault:* roll over backward from crouched position.
11. *Egg Roll:* in prone position, grasp feet with hands and perform sideways roll in crouched position.
12. *Tip-up:* balance on hands only, with elbows tucked inside knees for support.
13. *Dive-N-Roll:* dive over an object or another child (or children) and dive a forward roll.
14. *Pyramid Building:* several children in hand and knee position side by side form the base for the next layers of children in hand and knee position (one leg and arm on the back of one child, the other arm and leg on the adjacent child), forming a pyramid.
15. *Body Surfing:* several children lie prone next to each other in a row; one child lies across the lower backs of the children in a row; the children in the row roll over simultaneously and the child on top "rides across the surf."
16. *Back-to-Back Stand:* two children, back to back with elbows entwined, rise to standing from sitting position.
17. *Turk Stand:* sit in crossed-leg fashion with arms folded on chest, rise to standing keeping arms folded.
18. *Stork Stand:* one-legged stand.
19. *Statues:* move around room, then freeze to form a statue.

THERAPEUTIC ACTIVITIES

Exercises for Arthritis (Stafford and Kelly, 1965)

1. *Deep Breathing:* stand or lie on back, with hands spread beneath lower ribs; inhale and contract abdominal muscles, spreading ribs outward with fingers; hold ribs in extended position and exhale as abdomen is drawn in and up; repeat.
2. *Finger Exercise:* sit with back of hand resting on table or other support; oppose each finger to thumb; extend each finger after each contact with thumb; repeat with each hand.
3. *Finger Spread:* any position where hand is unobstructed; spread fingers as far apart as possible; relax and repeat.
4. *Foot Exercise:* lie on back with legs straight or sitting on a stool; dorsiflex the feet; plantarflex the feet; make a circle with foot, stressing inward movement; repeat with other foot.
5. *Leg Exercise:* lie on back, feet dorsiflexed and inverted; toes in plantarflexion; "pedal" with legs but do not raise higher than ten inches off floor.
6. *Abdominal Exercise:* lie on back, hands above head, knees bent; swing hands up and toward knees; slowly lower back to floor; repeat.
7. *Bridging:* lie on face with ankles support, hands at side; lift head and shoulders off floor; return to starting position; repeat.
8. *Shoulder Exercise:* sit in an erect position with hands clasped behind head; keeping elbows at shoulder height, thrust them backward as far as possible; hold; relax and repeat.

Asthmatic Exercise Program

1. *Abdominal Breathing Exercise:* start in hook-lying position with hands on upper abdomen; contract abdominal muscles and exhale as hands sink in toward spine; relax abdominal muscles while taking short breath.
2. *Trunk bending* and rotation to mobilize spine.
3. *Relaxation* exercises and activities.
4. *Blowing* bits of paper or a ping pong ball across a table.
5. *Side-Expansion Exercise:* sit with hands on lower ribs, feet apart; breathe out through mouth slowly, sinking chest and lower ribs; squeeze

ribs to expel all air; breathe in, expanding lower ribs; relax.

6. *Forward-Bend Exercise:* sit with legs apart; exhale and bend trunk forward; take a quick breath and raise trunk; exhale slowly and let head drop downward and chest sink inward; take a quick breath and return to erect position.

7. *Sidebend Exercise:* stand with feet apart; exhale slowly, bending trunk to one side; inhale and raise trunk; repeat 4 to 6 times; repeat on opposite side.

8. *Wave Exercise:* start in supine position with paper or cardboard placed on abdomen; breathe in and out, making paper go up and down.

Deep Breathing Exercises

1. Supine position with hips and knees flexed, feet on floor; inhale through nose to maximum; hold briefly; exhale through mouth with hissing sound.

2. Supine position, hips and knees flexed, feet flat on floor; place one hand on chest, other on abdomen; inhale through nose, elevate chest only; hold briefly; exhale through mouth.

3. Supine position, hips and knees flexed, feet flat on floor; place one hand on each side of ribs; inhale through nose; elevate chest only; hold briefly; exhale through mouth; push hands together during expiration.

4. Supine position, hips and knees flexed, feet flat on floor; place folded towel around chest; grasp ends of towel; inhale through nose, elevate chest only; hold briefly; pull towel tight during expiration.

5. Sitting in chair, arms at sides; slowly flex at waist; exhale through mouth as flexing toward floor; hold briefly; slowly sit up; inhale through nose; hold at sitting position.

6. Divide chest into three parts—upper, middle, lower; inhale deeply and then exhale completely in each part.

Miscellaneous Activities

Various activities can be used specifically as therapeutic exercise. Aquatic activities and bicycling are in themselves therapeutic. Other examples include:

1. Volleyball setting for round shoulders.
2. Backstroke for round shoulders.
3. Soccer kicking for pigeon-toed.
4. Swimming for scoliosis.

THERAPEUTIC EXERCISES

Detailed descriptions of these exercises can be found in books such as Adams, Daniel, and Rullman (1975), Stafford and Kelly (1965) and many others.

1. *Abdominal Curls.*
   Primary purpose: ptosis (protruding abdomen), lordosis.
   Secondary benefit: forward pelvic tilt.
   Description: lie on back with elbows flexed (90 degrees) at side of body and with knees flexed, feet flat on floor; keep the lower back flat on mat with elbows at sides while starting with the head, curl slowly forward and up to a 45 degree angle, lifting vertebra by vertebra off the mat; uncurl slowly and under control.

2. *Advanced Abdominal.*
   Primary purpose: abdominals, coordination.
   Secondary benefit: lordosis.
   Description: lie on back with arms extended over head; exhale, lift heels just off the mat and draw them to the buttocks while simultaneously raising the upper body in an abdominal curl, bringing the outstretched arms past knees; balance on buttocks; inhale while slowly returning to mat.

3. *Advanced Push-Up.*

Primary purpose: pectoral, triceps, hip extensors.

Secondary benefit: general development.

Description: lie prone with palms down on mat directly beneath the shoulders; do regular push-up, but raise alternate legs so weight is supported by hands and one leg.

4. *Advanced Sit-Ups*

Primary purpose: ptosis, abdominals.

Secondary benefit: lordosis, general muscle tone, chest condition.

Description: lie on the back with arms extended sideward at shoulder level, toes hooked under stall bar for support with knees bent at 45 degrees; sit up, keeping the chin in and head back, with chest high and arms well back; from sitting position, straighten the back, flex arms; inhale, re-lax, and straighten legs; curl down slowly.

5. *Ankle Stretch.*

Primary purpose: stretching anterior tibial and gastrocnemius, heel cord stretch.

Secondary benefit: weak longitudinal and meta-tarsal arches, fractures of ankles, postoperative repair, after removing of cast.

Description: stand on lower rung of stall bar, feet slightly pigeon-toed with weight on balls of feet; grasp upper rung for sup-port; rise on toes; lower body to stretch heel cords as heels are slowly lowered below level of support; return to starting position.

6. *Back Stoop Fall.*

Primary purpose: development of spinal and hip joint extensors, shoulder strengthening.

Secondary benefits: none.

Description: sit on mat with legs extended and hands (palms down) on mat; extend arms and straighten body keeping head back, chin in, and back flat so that weight is supported on hands and heels; exhale while returning to starting position.

7. *Back Stoop Falling with Alternate Leg Lift.*

Primary purpose: shoulder strength, hip flexion.

Secondary purpose: none.

Description: sit on mat with legs extended and hands on mat; extend arms and straighten body as in Back Stoop Fall: hold position and alternately raise the right and left leg keeping the knees extended, first pointing the toes and then the heels; return to starting position.

8. *Bicycle.*

Primary purpose: general warm-up, foot and leg stretch.

Secondary benefit: knee flexion (after injury) (avoid in cases of round circles).

Description: lie on back with elbow flexed (90 degrees) at side of body, bring knees to chest and roll up so that weight of the body rests on the shoulders and neck; place hands under hips for support and pedal an imaginary bicycle, stressing full motion in hip, knee, and ankle.

9. *Breaking Chains.*

Primary purpose: round shoulders.

Secondary benefit: kyphosis, forward head, flat chest, lordosis.

Description: stand with feet together; place fists together in front of chest with elbows at shoulder level; ``break chains'' by stren-uously pulling fists apart keeping elbows at shoulder level and pinching shoulder blades together; inhale; hold; relax and exhale.

10. *Building Mounds.*

Primary Purpose: metatarsal arch.

Secondary benefit: flexibility of feet, Morton's Toe.

Description: sit on bench with towel folded lengthwise (with weight on one end), the left foot directly under the knees with toes placed at one end of towel; grip towel with toes and ball of left foot and pull toward body, "building a mound"; heel remains on floor with pull of towel done by toe flexion; repeat movements until weight is reached; repeat movements with opposite foot.

11. *Cardiac Exercises: Lying Position.*
Primary purpose: exercise for cardiac individuals.
Secondary benefit: none.
Description: lie on back, hands at sides; inhale and stretch; hold for three counts; relax; raise arms up over head and to floor; repeat five times; raise arms sideward to overhead position; spread feet apart, return to start; flex knees, slide heels along floor to buttocks, return to start, repeat three times; pull alternate knees to chest, three times.

12. *Cardiac Exercises: Sitting Position.*
Primary purpose: exercise for cardiac individuals.
Secondary benefit: none.
Description: sit, knees extended, fingers laced on top of head; inhale and stretch upward, hold; relax; repeat three times; sit, knees extended, feet apart, arms horizontal; twist trunk to alternate sides slowly; repeat alternate toe touching, repeat three times; arm forward circles, five counts; then backward circles, five counts.

13. *Cardiac Exercises: Standing Position.*
Primary purpose: exercise for cardiac individuals.
Secondary benefit: none.
Description: stand, rise on toes and stretch as tall as possible; hold three counts, repeat; stride stand position, bend trunk left, right, forward three times; trunk circumduction, three times; half knee bends, three times; backstroke movement of arms, repeat five cycles.

14. *Crab Walk.*
Primary purpose: shoulder strength.
Secondary benefit: shoulder conditions, hip extensors, body coordination.
Description: sit on mat with knees bent and hands on mat just behind buttocks; lift buttocks off mat; walk forward and backward on hands and feet.

15. *Dorsal Flat Back.*
Primary purpose: stretch for dorsal region, flat back.
Secondary benefit: none.
Description: kneel on mat; slowly lower trunk and sit on heels; slowly bend forward rounding the back, slowly raise hips pushing upward in dorsal region; return to starting position.

16. *Elbow Side Falling.*
Primary purpose: scoliosis.
Secondary benefit: body lean or torsion.
Description: rest on side toward which the back curves, extend the opposite arm shoulder height to side and left hip off floor; lower hip, assume sitting position; repeat.

17. *Elephant Walk.*
Primary purpose: foot.
Secondary benefit: heel and stretch, tight hamstrings, lordosis.
Description: crouch on hands and feet; straighten knees and back, toeing in with heels on floor; bring left hand and foot forward simultaneously, keeping heel on floor and curling arch while straightening right knee; repeat with right hand and foot; continue to walk forward.

18. *Foot Circling.*
Primary purpose: metatarsal arch.

Secondary benefit: foot flexibility, foot and ankle strength, longitudinal arch.

Description: sit on bench with knees and feet fully extended with heels resting on floor; with toes flexed, circle foot in; circle foot up; circle foot out; circle foot down; repeat movements several times achieving full range of motion.

19. *Foot Curling.*

Primary purpose: longitudinal arch.

Secondary benefit: pronated ankles, tibial torsion.

Description: sit erect on bench with thigh horizontal to floor; place left heel forward of knee about six inches; bring toes of right foot to rear and outside of extended heel to serve as a brace; fold towel lengthwise and place next to outside of left foot; lift and turn foot to left, then press ball of foot forcibly on the towel and rotate lower leg and foot to the right pulling towel inward; repeat until towel is completely pulled across; repeat with other foot; add weight on towel for resistance.

20. *Foot Drag.*

Primary purpose: stabilizing knee joint, improvement of muscle tone of whole leg and thigh.

Secondary benefit: pronated ankles, weak longitudinal arches, tibial torsion.

Description: stand erect with feet pointed straight forward, knees slightly flexed, weight mostly on right foot; push left foot forward and backward, left and right and diagonally to form an "X," circle foot clockwise and counterclockwise; repeat with other foot.

21. *Foot Supinator.*

Primary purpose: foot pronation, longitudinal arch.

Secondary benefit: metatarsal arch, foot flexibility.

Description: sit tall, cross leg so the ankle of right foot rests across left knee, keeping the foot at right angles to the right leg and turning the sole of the foot upward; grasp the sole of the foot with left hand; push up on the seaphoid bone of right foot with left thumb, simultaneously grasp the toes of right foot with right hand and rotate foot, knee, and hip clockwise and counterclockwise; repeat with left foot; repeat without use of hands.

22. *Frog Kick.*

Primary purpose: foot pronation, longitudinal arch.

Secondary benefit: knee.

Description: sit on floor with legs extended; place hands on mat behind buttocks with fingers pointed forward; fully flex knees and place soles of feet together; with heels on floor and feet perpendicular to the floor, extend legs keeping soles of feet together; hold and stretch.

23. *Gripper.*

Primary purpose: strengthening hand, wrist, and forearm.

Secondary benefit: improving muscle tone.

Description: grasp rubber or tennis ball; squeeze hard while tensing upper arms; rotate wrist one direction, then the other; flex and extend wrist; relax; repeat.

24. *Heel Cord Stretch.*

Primary purpose: stretch heel cord and back of leg.

Secondary benefit: none.

Description: stand at arm's length from wall, body inclined slightly forward, back flat, feet toed in slightly; place hands on wall at shoulder height; bend arms until chest nearly touches wall with body held erect and heels on the floor; return to starting position; move feet progressively farther away from wall; repeat exercise.

25. *Hip Roll.*

Primary purpose: abdominals.

Secondary benefit: lordosis, passive buttocks massage.

Description: sit on mat with knees drawn up; raise feet and hands off the mat and roll from side to side on buttocks or progress by shifting weight from side to side.

26. *Horizontal Ladder.*

Primary purpose: functional scoliosis curves in spine, total body stretch, kyphosis, forward head, low shoulders.

Secondary benefit: arm and shoulder girdle strength.

Description: child grasps rung of the horizontal ladder with hands, body held erect and completes one of the following variations: (1) hang and stretch; (2) pendulum swing; (3) side hanging on one side; (4) climbing horizontal ladder.

27. *Knee-Chest Curl.*

Primary purpose: abdominal strength, ptosis, lordosis.

Secondary benefit: hip flexors, stretch spinal extensors.

Description: lie on back with knees bent at right angles, feet flat on floor, arms out from shoulders; bring knees to chest curling spine; hold; uncurl; repeat.

28. *Knee Raises.*

Primary purpose: abdominals, hip flexors.

Secondary benefit: shoulder girdle, arms.

Description: hang from top rung of stall bars (back to bars) or from horizontal bar; bend right knee and raise it to chest, and

return; repeat with both knees; keep lower back flat and pelvis rotated upward.

29. *Knee Rotator.*

Primary purpose: knock knees, tibial torsion.

Secondary benefit: pronated ankles, longitudinal arch, weak knees.

Description: stand with stall bars for hand support, heels 3 inches apart, toes together, with weight toward outside of foot; flex knees slightly and rotate outward vigorously trying to bring heels together against the friction of floor, but don't let them move; relax; repeat.

30. *Knee Tensor.*

Primary purpose: stabilizing the knee anteriorly.

Secondary benefit: none.

Description: stand with feet pointed straight ahead and the knees locked; gradually increase amount of weight on foot; extend knee well backward; tense knee cap or raise it; relax muscles allowing knee cap to drop to regular position.

31. *Leg Cross-Overs.*

Primary purpose: general stretch, hip flexors, abdominals, low back stretch.

Secondary benefit: warm-up, post-knee injury.

Description: lie on back with arms extended at shoulder level, palms up, and heels pointed; flex the left leg at the hip to lift heel to rest on right toes; twist body to right, bringing the left foot across to the floor; with knee straight, slide foot toward right hand; stretch; return to starting position; repeat in other direction.

32. *Leg Extensor.*

Primary purpose: hip extensors, iliopsoas stretch.

Secondary benefit: general conditioning.

Description: push-up position lying face-down with hands palm down on mat; raise right leg to horizontal position; point toe; point heel; lower right leg; repeat with left leg.

33. *Mad Cat.*

Primary purpose: lordosis, abdominals.

Secondary benefit: dysmenorrhea.

Description: kneel on all fours (hands and knees); hump up the back by tightening the abdominal and buttock muscle; lean forward by bending arms until the forehead touches the floor; exhale; return to starting position.

34. *Marble Grip.*

Primary purpose: knock knees.

Secondary benefit: tibial torsion, metatarsal and longitudinal arches, pronated ankles, knee.

Description: sit on bench with feet on the floor; place two marbles in front of each foot; grip marble in toes of left foot and bring the ankle to rest on right knee; force left knee downward with left hand; lift left foot from right knee and lower to the floor; rest foot and release marbles; repeat exercise with right foot.

35. *Neck And Back Flattener.*

Primary purpose: forward head, cervical lordosis, kyphosis, lordosis, forward shoulders.

Secondary benefit: abdominal strength, pelvic tilt.

Description: lie on back with knees drawn up and with arms at sides, palms down; inhale and expand the chest as the nape of neck is forced to mat by stretching tall and pulling chin toward chest; flatten the small of the back to mat by tightening the abdominal and buttock muscle; check to see if back is flat; exhale; relax; repeat.

36. *Pelvic Tilt.*

Primary purpose: lordosis, pelvic tilt.

Secondary benefit: abdominal strength.

Description: lie on back, knees flexed, feet flat on floor with toes touching and heels 1 inch apart; arms at sides with palms flat on floor; hold knees forcibly together while tucking buttock muscles and drawing in on abdominals; slowly rotate pelvis upward raising hips slightly off floor; gradually curl pelvis up raising buttocks off floor; lower, vertebra by vertebra to starting position.

37. *Pelvic Tilt: Sit-Up.*

Primary purpose: scoliosis.

Secondary benefit: none.

Description: lie supine, with knees flexed; tilt pelvis and hold; with elbows straight, roll up to touch knees with fingers; roll down to supine position; relax tilt.

38. *Pelvic Tilt: Supine.*

Primary purpose: scoliosis.

Secondary benefit: none.

Description: lie supine with knees flexed; keep shoulders flat on floor; tighten buttocks muscle; force small of the back into floor; relax, repeat.

39. *Pendulum Swing.*

Primary purpose: spine, back muscles, shoulder girdle.

Secondary benefit: strengthening muscles and ligaments of spine, strengthening arms and shoulder girdle muscles.

Description: hang from horizontal bar, hands shoulder width apart with feet together; lift body slightly; swing both feet, thighs, and legs to left; lower legs; swing to right; repeat

40. *Pigeon-Toe Walk.*

Primary purpose: pronated ankles and feet, tibial torsion, knock knees, longitudinal arch.

Secondary benefit: knee movement.

Description: stand; walk pigeon-toed with a deliberate toeing in, while placing one foot directly in front of the other; keep sole of foot parallel to floor with weight on outer border.

41. *Pull-Ups.*
Primary purpose: biceps, latissimus.
Secondary benefit: shoulder girdle.
Description: hang from bar in over-bar grip; keep body straight while flexing arms to raise chin over the bar; return to hanging position; repeat.

42. *Push-Up.*
Primary purpose: shoulder girdle, triceps, pectoral strength.
Secondary benefit: general strength, conditioning, abdominals.
Description: lie prone with palms of hands down on mat directly beneath the shoulders; push body up off ground by extending the arms so that weight is supported on hands and toes; lower body enough so that chest touches mat and push up again; repeat.

43. *Round Back.*
Primary purpose: total round back, round back without lordosis.
Secondary benefit: none.
Description: lie prone with arms horizontally at side; inhale as shoulder blades are pinched together; raise trunk, arms, chin, and face 3 inches from floor; hold shoulder blade position; relax while returning to starting position.

44. *Round Hollow Back.*
Primary purpose: kyphosis, lordosis.
Secondary benefit: none.
Description: lie on back, hands on neck, soles of feet together, knees spread and bent; raise legs to chest, raise head forward.

45. *Rowing Machine.*
Primary purpose: anterior and posterior alignment; shoulder divergencies.
Secondary benefit: general conditioning.
Description: sit on rowing machine with hands grasping oars; flex arms and pull elbows back as far as possible, keeping elbows at shoulder level as knees are straightened; inhale; extend arms and "feather" oars (rotate blade of oars by flexing wrists), bend knees; exhale.

46. *Shoulder Blade Tightener.*
Primary purpose: kyphosis, forward shoulders.
Secondary benefit: forward head, lordosis.
Description: lie on back with knees flexed and feet flat on floor; place elbows out at shoulder level with forearms parallel to head with palms up; press elbows into mat, causing shoulder blades to be drawn together; inhale; exhale and relax.

47. *Spine Extension.*
Primary purpose: scoliosis.
Secondary benefit: none.
Description: lie in prone position, with knees held down; tilt pelvis; raise shoulders about 6 inches against firm resistance between the shoulder blades; return to prone position; relax.

48. *Stall Bar Stretch.*
Primary purpose: kyphosis, round shoulders.
Secondary benefit: tight pectorals, development of shoulder muscles.
Description: lie forward on bench with hands on bar at shoulder height; raise elbows, tuck chin in and lift head; lower elbows and relax.

49. *Streamliner.*
Primary purpose: forward head.
Secondary benefit: round shoulders, kyphosis, flat chest.

Description: stand with feet together, ends of fingers touching lightly on back of neck; bend forward at hips, keeping trunk straight; extend arms sideways at shoulder level with palms up; return to standing position holding arms in extended position; flex wrists and elbows while inhaling; hold; relax.

50. *Supine Stretch.*

Primary purpose: general loosening and stretching of body, relaxation.

Secondary benefits: lateral curvatures of spine, kyphosis, forward shoulders, low shoulders.

Description: lie on back on a mat with legs extended; extend arms overhead and reach as far as possible; stretch heels as far away from hands as possible with back flat on mat; relax right leg and left arm and stretch crossways; repeat with opposite arm and leg; relax after each stretch; repeat.

51. *Toe Lifts.*

Primary purpose: ankle extensors (gastrocnemius, soleus).

Secondary benefit: heel cord stretch.

Description: stand with weight at neck rest position, place toes and balls of feet on a block of wood; stretch lower leg and heel cord; rise up on forefoot until heels are higher than support; hold; lower and repeat.

52. *Towel Wringing.*

Primary purpose: tension of entire arms and shoulder.

Secondary benefit: strengthening entire arm and upper back, developing rotation of forearm.

Description: hold elbows close to sides and grasp the center of folded towel with both hands; twist towel as if wringing water from it; repeat.

53. *Wall Stretch.*

Primary purpose: kyphosis, forward head.

Secondary benefit: flat chest, round shoulders.

Description: stride standing position; place both hands against wall or stall bars at shoulder height bending forward until back is horizontal at hip height; extend head back, and hold for four counts; return to starting position.

54. *Windmill.*

Primary purpose: back stretch, hamstring stretch, warm-up.

Secondary benefit: abdominals, shoulder girdle.

Description: sit on mat with arms extended out to the side at shoulder level and legs spread wide apart; twist to the right and bend forward so that fingers of the left hand touch the toes of the right foot; stretch and hold, keeping legs straight; return to starting position; twist to the left and return; repeat.

55. *Windmill Lying.*

Primary purpose: abdominals and thigh flexors.

Secondary benefit: lower back and hamstring stretch.

Description: lie on back with arms at side; rise to sitting position, spread legs and raise extended arms to shoulder level; twist body and bend trunk to touch right hand to left toes; twist body and bend trunk to touch left hand to right toes, return to starting position.

56. *Windmill Standing.*

Primary purpose: ptosis, hamstring stretch.

Secondary benefit: strengthening muscles of neck, back, arms, and shoulders.

Description: stand with feet apart, arms extended sideward at shoulder level; twist and bend trunk so that the left hand touches right foot; return to starting position; twist and bend trunk to left foot; return to starting position.

WEIGHT TRAINING

1. *Two-Arm Curl.*

   Description: stand, body erect, with feet about 12 inches apart; arms at sides; grasp bar with undergrip palms up, shoulder width apart; keeping elbows at hips, slowly lift weights by flexing elbow and bringing weights toward shoulders; hold; lower to starting position; repeat.

2. *Two-Arm Press.*

   Description: stand with feet about 12 inches apart, bar on floor in front of feet; bend knees, grasp bar with overgrip, shoulder width apart; bring bar and weights to chest in one motion by flexing elbows and straightening knees; hold weight at chest level; slowly push bar and weights overhead; hold; lower slowly to chest; repeat overhead repetitions; lower to starting position.

3. *Two-Arm Reverse Curl.*

   Description: stand with body erect with feet 12 inches apart, arms at sides; grasp bar at thigh height with overgrip, extend wrist to maximum; flex elbows, lifting bar to chest; hold bar at chest level, lower bar to thighs; hold; repeat; return to starting position.

4. *Supine Press.*

   Description: supine position, shoulders comfortable on floor or bench with bar and weights resting behind head; grasp bar; lift bar upward; straighten elbows, arms

should be perpendicular to floor; slowly lower bar and weights to chest; slowly push bar and weights upward until elbows are straight; repeat; return to starting position.

5. *Rise on Toes.*

   Description: stand with heels together, toes turned out; place bar behind the neck; grasp bar with hands at shoulder width; slowly rise up on toes as high as possible; hold; lower slowly; repeat; return to starting position.

6. *Sit-ups.*

   Description: supine position with feet slightly higher than head, ankles supported; place bar and weights behind neck, grasp bar at shoulder width; slowly come to sitting position; hold; return; repeat.

7. *Rowing.*

   Description: stand with feet 12 inches apart, bar and weights resting on floor in front; flex trunk at waist, grasp bar with overgrip; flex elbows bringing bar and weights to chest; hold; lower to straight elbow position; repeat.

8. *Quadriceps Lift.*

   Description: sit on table; hands grasp front of table, small rolled towel under knee, knee flexed 10 to 20 degrees, foot resting on stool; attach weight device on foot; extend knee to left weight; hold at full extension; return to starting position; repeat.

9. *Forward Raise.*

   Description: stand with feet 12 inches apart, bar with weight in middle; grasp bar with overgrip, bring bar to thigh level; lift bar and weights forward and overhead keeping elbows extended; lower weight; repeat.

10. *Shoulder Shrugging.*

Description: stand with feet 12 inches apart, arms at sides; grasp bar with overgrip, bar at thigh level with elbows extended; shrug shoulders; lower shoulders to starting position; repeat.

11. *Regular Dead Lift.*

Description: stand with feet 12 inches apart; flex hips and knees; grasp bar with overgrip; with back flat, slowly straighten knees until body is straight; return weights to floor; repeat.

12. *Straddle Lift.*

Description: stand with feet straddling bar; flex knees, keeping back straight; grasp bar with front hand overgrip, rear hand undergrip; slowly stand upright lifting weights off ground; hold; flex knees, return to starting position.

13. *Straight Arm Pullovers.*

Description: supine position with hips and knees straight, arms extended overhead; grasp bar resting on floor behind head; raise bar slowly above head; hold; return bar to floor.

14. *Triceps Press.*

Description: supine with hips and knees straight, arms straight, elbows extended toward ceiling; bar is placed in hands; grasp with overgrip; lower bar to bridge of nose keeping elbows pointed to ceiling; slowly straighten elbows; repeat.

15. *Triceps Press (Standing).*

Description: stand with feet 12 inches apart; hold bar above head with arms extended; slowly lower bar behind head keeping elbows pointed toward ceiling; extend arms slowly until weight is directly overhead; repeat.

16. *Back Lift.*

Description: stand with feet 12 inches apart with bar behind heels; flex hips and knees; grasp bar with overgrip; slowly return to standing position; repeat.

17. *Lateral Raise.*

Description: stand with feet 12 inches apart, arms at sides; grasp one dumbbell in each hand; slowly raise dumbbells to shoulder level, keeping elbows extended; hold; lower weights; repeat.

18. *Forward Raise.*

Description: stand with feet 12 inches apart, arms at sides; grasp one dumbbell in each hand, dumbbells resting on thighs; raise dumbbells directly overhead, keeping elbows straight; hold; lower weights; repeat.

19. *Alternate Curl.*

Description: stand with feet 12 inches apart, arms at sides; grasp one dumbbell in each hand; slowly flex right elbow and supinate hand; bring dumbbell to right shoulder; slowly extend right elbow and pronate hand returning to starting position; as right is lowered, left dumbbell begins curl; repeat; alternate.

CHILDBIRTH TRAINING TECHNIQUES

Prenatal Techniques

1. *Sitting Tailor Fashion:* sit on a hard surface, knees bent and widely separated, dropped as close to floor as possible; ankles crossed; chest is lifted, back straight; ribs open and reaching forward; hands rest easily on legs; sit often in this fashion.

2. *Pelvis Rock on Hands and Knees:* on hands and

knees, hands directly under shoulders, back flat; rock pelvis (tuck buttocks under), back rounds; tighten abdominal muscles; gradually relax back and abdomen; breathe naturally during exercise.

3. *Costal (Rib) Breathing:* sit tailor fashion or use supine position, knees bent, feet slightly separated; place one hand on abdomen and other on ribs; inhale, spreading ribs; exhale, feeling rib cage shrink; breathe in through nose and out through mouth; repeat five times.

4. *Kegel (Vaginal Contraction):* supine position, knees flexed; or sitting position; tighten muscles used to hold urine back; hold; repeat often throughout day.

5. *Rocking the Pelvis on Back;* supine on floor with knees flexed and apart, soles of feet on floor, head resting on pillow; tuck buttocks under, flattening lumbar spine against floor; tighten abdominal muscles; return to starting position; relax.

6. *Assume Side Relaxation Position:* torso prone and legs on side; place one arm behind with elbow bent 90 degrees; place pillow under head with shoulder on floor; one leg above and slightly forward, both knees bent; relax completely.

7. *Flexing and Extending the Leg, Seated:* sit on floor with legs extended diagonally; lift knee slightly, flex ankle and increase knee flexion; extend both knee and ankle, pointing toes pushing back of knee into floor; repeat with other leg; alternate legs 5 times.

8. *Tension and Relaxation on Back:* supine with knees flexed and apart; rock pelvis; inhale deeply and hold breath; tense entire body; exhale quickly, loosen all muscles completely relaxing; repeat four times.

9. *Abdominal Strengthening:* supine, shoulders on floor, head resting on pillow, knees flexed, feet flat on floor, arms at sides; lift head off pillow, moving chin toward chest; raise right arm and extend toward left knee; only right shoulder and head are lifted; return to starting position; repeat with other side.

10. *Spine Stretching:* sit on floor, soles of feet together, knees apart, hands grasp knees; rock pelvis slowly; gradually straighten elbows; lift chest and return to sitting tall; repeat.

11. *Rock the Pelvis Standing:* stand arm's length away from counter, hands grasp edge, elbows straight; lean body forward, lumbar spine arched; rock pelvis, tucking buttocks under; return to starting position.

12. *Sitting in Chair and Rising:* stand in front of chair; lower hips, keeping them under shoulders; reach down to feel chair with hands; transfer weight to front edge of chair; rise to standing.

13. *Sit and Stretch Position:* sit with soles of feet together, as close as possible to body; push knees down on hands placed on floor; repeat several times.

14. *Knee to Chest:* supine with legs straight with pillow under head; pull one knee up to chest; stretch and slowly bring leg straight down; alternate with other leg; repeat.

15. *Blow out the Candle:* supine with knees bent, feet flat on floor and pillow under head; take a deep breath and let it out naturally; purse lips and continue blowing until there is no more air to blow; repeat.

Postnatal Techniques

1. *Kegel (Vaginal Contraction):* see item 4 under Prenatal Techniques.

2. *Pelvis Rock on Back:* see item 5 under Prenatal Techniques.
3. *Prone Rest with Pillows under Pelvis:* prone with abdomen on pillow; can be used for sleeping or resting.
4. *Abdominal Strengthening:* see item 9 under Prenatal Techniques.
5. *Torso Stretch:* stand with chin lifted, looking at ceiling; extend both arms up from shoulders; rock pelvis; stretch one arm fully, simultaneously elevate opposite heel so that it raises the left hip; repeat on opposite side.
6. *Flexing and Extending the Legs, Seated:* see item 7 under Prenatal Techniques.
7. *Upper Hip Roll:* supine, flex knees and hips until knees are close to nose; spread arms out at shoulder level, resting on floor; drop both knees together to right, then to left, touching the floor on each side; repeat.
8. *Rock the Pelvis, Standing:* see item 11 under Prenatal Techniques.

SUMMARY

When programming for handicapped individuals in physical education, the full range of physical activities can and should be utilized. The activities presented in this chapter — aquatics, dance, conditioning, fitness, games and sports, stunts, therapeutic activities and exercises (including childbirth techniques), and weight training — can be further modified to meet the unique needs of the handicapped individual(s) and the physical education class.

BIBLIOGRAPHY

Adams, R. C., Daniel, A. N., and Rullman, L. *Games, Sports, and Exercises for the Physically Handicapped.* Philadelphia: Lea and Febiger, 1975.

American Red Cross. *Adapted Aquatics.* Garden City, New York: Doubleday, 1977.

Conrad, C. C. *Physical Conditioning Through Water Exercises.* Washington, D.C.: President's Council on Physical Fitness, 1975.

DePauw, K. P. *Adapted Aquatic Checklist.* Mimeographed, 1977.

Jacobson, E. *Young Must Relax.* New York: McGraw-Hill, 1962.

San Diego City Schools. *Teaching Adapted Physical Education in the Secondary School.* San Diego, California: San Diego City Schools, 1971.

Stafford, G. T., and Kelly, E. D. *Adapted and Corrective Physical Education.* 4th ed. New York: Ronald Press, 1965.

16   Program Organization

Guiding Questions

1. What steps should be taken in preparing a list for acquiring equipment?
2. What are some qualities or considerations to be made when selecting equipment or when modifying or constructing equipment?
3. What are some modifications in existing facilities that you are aware of that would make them accessible or more easily used by the handicapped population?

To facilitate learning in adapted physical education, it is often necessary for the teacher to modify the learning environment. This can be done in two areas: (1) the purchase, modification, and acquisition of equipment; or (2) the construction, modification, and use of facilities and other play spaces. Although physical educators infrequently have the opportunity to influence the construction of new facilities, they always have the opportunity to influence the acquisition of equipment. Educators are encouraged to be as frugal and as clever as possible in the acquisition of materials and resources.

PLANNING

The physical educator must make some projections into the future in order to acquire and develop material resources that will serve the school over an extended period of time. This can be done by reviewing the current levels of performance of students in the school over the last two to three years. The average expected lifespan for a piece of equipment, being used in the public schools on a daily basis, is only three to five years. Thus it is hardly necessary to reflect back more than that period of time. Of course, it would be desirable to maintain a list of equipment and facility needs as the program progresses and the teacher wants to do something for which the facilities and equipment are unavailable. From that list, or on the basis of current needs, two "wish lists" could be made for equipment and facilities. On each list, itemize everything that is thought to be needed (see Table 16-1).

Set the lists aside and make up an inventory of all the equipment and facilities currently available. Do not ignore equipment available through the classroom teachers, therapists, nurse, and other personnel. Also include community facilities that have been or could be used for the physical education program. If equipment needed for the physical education program is already available, there is no reason why the physical educator cannot use that equipment. Sometimes there is a restriction on the use of equipment, or it is being used so often by other professionals that it is unavailable at the times needed for physical education.

Table 16-1. Example of a wish list

Facilities	Equipment
■ paint colored lines on courts	■ standing frame
■ 4' "warning path" around field	■ 20' X 20' mat 1" thick
■ lower one mirror in locker room	■ physician's scale
■ lower one shower head in locker room	■ 2 Exergenies
■ install grab bars/widen one toilet stall	■ 15 individual mats (replacement)
■ install mirrors (20' X 8') on one side of exercise room	■ portable stairs with handrails
	■ 2 10' benches — 17" high
	■ 2 skinfold calipers
	■ posture screen
	■ 2 incline boards
	■ large bulletin board (10' X 4')

SOURCE: I. J. Pack, San Fernando Jr. High School, Los Angeles Unified School District. Used with permission.

Examples of restricted equipment would include modalities used by physical therapists for which only they are licensed; or certain tests requiring special training, which the physical educator may not be trained to use (e.g., S.C.S.I.T., Bayley Scales, Denver Developmental Scales). Otherwise, equipment owned by a school district should be made available for use by any certificated personnel.

Physical educators using the developmental approach should have available to them equipment and facilities that provide experience and opportunities for learning along the entire developmental continuum. The exact type of equipment or facilities may vary depending upon the student population and their needs. For example, a secondary school for physically handicapped students probably would require different equipment for providing tactile experiences than would an elementary school for the severely handicapped. Yet equipment for providing opportunities for tactile experience and learning should be available in both contexts. Next, compare the inventory list against

the developmental model. Are equipment and facilities available for providing experiences at each level? Remember, particularly when evaluating equipment relative to the sensory systems, that certain sensory systems have demands placed upon them simply on the basis of the way in which the equipment is used. Therefore it is necessary to evaluate the inventory list on the basis of the primary intended use or actual use of the items on the list. For example, a softball places demands on the tactile and proprioceptive systems; yet a softball is not intended nor is it primarily used to provide a tactile experience or enhance tactile development. It is, of course, primarily used for activities at the top of the developmental model in the area of culturally determined forms of movement—that is, the sport of softball. The use of varying weights of softballs can enhance proprioception. Therefore the creative use of common equipment is encouraged. Once the inventory is evaluated in terms of the developmental model and a tally made of needs met by existing resources at each level of the model, go back to the "wish lists." Compare the wish lists with the levels of the model for which few resources are available. If the wish list contains items to provide experiences at levels of the model for which there are few resources, these items should be prioritized at the top of your "final request list." Follow this procedure, prioritizing items according to the scarcity of materials available (see Table 16-2). These, then, should be requested according to the prioritized request list. The following examples show this same process for a program for the severely handicapped. Where school district funds are depleted as items are purchased from the list, this point on the list marks the beginning point for seeking supplemental funding and support (see Table 16-3).

EQUIPMENT

Selecting equipment can be both enjoyable and frustrating. Sometimes the equipment the physical educator has in mind is not available, has not been invented or constructed, or is so obscure that identifying a distributor or source of the equipment is very difficult. In such an instance, the teacher should make use of colleagues to brainstorm with on equipment ideas. Do not be hesitant to ask the physical and occupational therapists, speech therapist, or classroom teachers if they have seen or heard of such a piece. Professional conferences and conventions in physical education and special education are good places to learn about available equipment. The exhibitors usually supply literature and are eager to discuss newly marketed educational supplies and equipment (see Figure 16-1).

Selecting Equipment

Several considerations should be brought to bear on equipment selection: (1) portability; (2) washability; (3) durability; (4) economy; (5) size; and (6) diversity.

Table 16-2. Example of final request list

Facilities	Equipment
■ 4' "warning path" around field	■ 2 Exergenies
■ paint colored lines on courts	■ standing frame
	■ 2 incline boards
■ install grab bars/widen one toilet stall	■ 2 skinfold calipers
■ lower one mirror in locker room	■ 20' × 20' mat 1" thick
	■ physician's scale
■ lower one shower head in locker room	■ portable stairs with handrails
■ install mirrors (20' × 8') on one side of exercise room	■ 2 10' benches — 17" high
	■ 15 individual mats (replacement)
	■ posture screen
	■ large bulletin board (10' × 4')

Portability

The portability of a piece of equipment is most important, of course, in itinerant programs in which the teacher travels from school to school. It may also be significant for use within a school, depending on the ambulation of the students, space available for the program, and climatic conditions.

If a room or gymnasium is available for the physical education program, it may not be necessary to have equipment that is easily transported, since the students can be brought to the activity room. The amount of space available for storing large, unportable equipment, and the possibility of masking equipment as distractors when the equipment is not in use, are also factors. If the population is not ambulatory and the physical educator must deliver service in the classroom, then the ease with which the equipment can be transported will need consideration. If weather con-

Table 16-3. Wish list and final request list for severely handicapped students

a. Example of wish list		b. Example of final request list	
Facilities	*Equipment*	*Facilities*	*Equipment*
■ install mirrors (20′ × 8′) on one wall of activity room	■ portable tunnel	■ install 4″ × 6″ beam in ceiling with screw-eyes	■ portable tunnel
■ install one set of stall bars	■ balance beam	■ install mirrors (20′ × 8′) on one wall of activity room	■ ramp for scooterboards
■ install 4″ × 6″ beam in ceiling with screw-eyes	■ cargo net	■ install one set of stall bars	■ slide
	■ suspended tires		■ suspended tires
	■ suspended platforms		■ swings
	■ ramp for scooterboards		■ cargo net
	■ sandbox		■ suspended platforms
	■ sliding pole		■ sandbox
	■ walkways		■ sliding pole
	■ 4 balance boards		■ balance beam
	■ Jumpin' Jiminey		■ walkways
	■ swings		■ 4 balance boards
	■ slide		■ Jumpin' Jiminey

SOURCE: D. Dillon, *Adaptations and Modifications of Playground Equipment for the Severely Handicapped* (Los Angeles: California State University, unpublished paper, 1980), p. 4.

ditions are such that outdoor space can be used a great deal of the time during the school year, this may be a deciding factor in choosing between a portable and unportable piece of equipment.

Washability

The washability, or the ability to keep a piece of equipment clean and hygienic, may also be important to consider. Youngsters who drool or are likely to have bowel or bladder movements during activity will be utilizing equipment on which they lie or sit, and should also be protected from the spread of germs and bacteria through the equipment. A great deal of this type of equipment is available with plastic, vinyl, or

other washable coverings. Existing equipment, or equipment that has been handmade, should be maintained for its washability with regular sanding and lacquering of surfaces.

Durability

The durability of a piece of equipment is important if the equipment is to be useful. Significant considerations in judging how durable a piece of equipment needs to be include the age and size of the students using it; the frequency of use; how it is to be used; and whether or not it will be used in structured, supervised, or unsupervised activity. Although children may have been taught the safe and careful use of

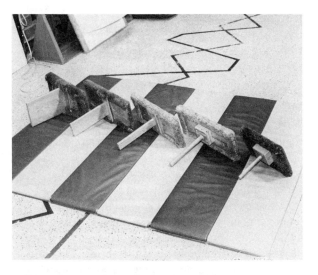

Figure 16-1. Unique equipment having a variety of uses in adapted physical education includes T-stools with different sized bases (top left); cage balls (top right); various sizes of bolsters (above); and air-flow mattresses (above right). SOURCE: Photo (top right) by Greg Fulton.

equipment and other materials, vigorous play and carelessness will inevitably contribute to the destruction of some pieces.

Economy

The actual cost of construction, purchase, and maintenance of equipment may also be an important consideration. Economy is important, but "economical" does not always mean "cheap." In the case of a piece of equipment available through several manufacturers, the least expensive of the choices may not be the most economical. If a piece of equipment is likely to be used frequently by several teachers, there will be more wear and tear on that piece than if it were to be used infrequently, and its use controlled by only one person. The durability of the piece can certainly contribute to its economy.

The maintenance required for a piece of equipment may also detract from the economical values of a lesser price. If there are moving parts, or mechanical or electrical components that can malfunction, the availability of service needed in the district or through a maintenance agreement with the manufacturer should also be computed into the price. A sign once seen in a fine china shop read, "The bitterness of poor quality remains long after the memory of a cheap price." When purchasing equipment for use with children, remember that they deserve the best.

Size

The size of the equipment purchased should be determined by the space in which it is used, and the physical body size and developmental levels of the stu-

dents using it. The available activity space as well as the space available for storage of large pieces of equipment may dictate both the size and the number of pieces that can realistically be obtained. The students' size, of course, is important in terms of the appropriateness and durability of a piece of equipment. In addition, the developmental level of the students is going to play an important role. For example, older cerebral palsied students who are developmentally young may need a larger ball (10 or 12 inches) than would ordinarily be used with this age group. The durability of the ball, however, may also be a factor if motor control is so poor that the force applied in catching, kicking or throwing the ball cannot be controlled. Ordinarily, a small beach ball might be appropriate for this population, especially if ocular tracking and catching abilities are poor. If the beach ball is smashed every time it is caught, however, a more durable, lightweight ball of the same size might be more appropriate. Although the more durable ball may initially be more expensive, it may be more economical to purchase one that will endure than to have to replace a beach ball every week (see Figure 16–2).

Figure 16–2. A variety of ball sizes should be kept on hand to accommodate differences in body sizes and developmental levels (below); scooterboards may be stacked for easy storage (right). SOURCE: Photo by Ben Esparza (left).

Figure 16-3. Wrist cuffs have limited application to quadraplegics, but may be essential in some programs.

Diversity

The diversity or range of use may be a major consideration when working with a school population having very diverse needs. If a piece of equipment can be used to achieve a variety of goals and objectives, it is probably more practical than a similar piece having a limited application (see Figure 16-3). An air-flow mattress, for example, may provide a variety of experiences and serve to accomplish numerous objectives in the areas of relaxation, vestibular stimulation, tactile experiences, locomotor, and equilibrium activities. Although this piece of equipment would be considered somewhat expensive, its purchase would be economical because of its diversity, durability, and washability. It could be used in place of several other pieces of equipment. Table 16-4, on the following page, lists a variety of materials and equipment that have been used successfully to achieve goals and objectives at each level of the developmental model. A list of distributors and manufacturers begins on page 431.

Modifying Equipment

Although there is a great deal of good, appropriate equipment available in the marketplace, a given piece may not be quite right for the physical educator's context, the population to be served in general, or any given child. Therefore modifications of existing equipment, or newly acquired equipment, may be necessary. Some of the features discussed in the previous section may be obtained or enhanced through equipment modification. Nonportable items can be made portable by attaching removable wheels or constructing or having constructed a transport dollie. As an example, most companies making trampolines also manufacture removable wheels made of tubular steel, which can easily be attached to the frame of the trampoline in order to move it from one place to another or into storage. A large piece of equipment such as a vestibular board, a Bobath ball or mushroom, or even a softball backstop can be transported by building a dollie upon which the equipment is placed, or having a dollie attached to the equipment in such a way that it can be easily used. The washability of a piece of equipment may be improved without affecting its function by fashioning a vinyl or fabric cover that can be removed and washed. The durability of some pieces of equipment can be improved by reinforcing the supporting members, especially pieces like tables, standing frames, and other pieces upon which students are going to rely for weight support. These should be carefully inspected for their durability, with the idea of possible reinforcement.

In practice, the size of most pieces of equipment can more easily be reduced than expanded. Of course, this possibility may vary with each individual piece. Equipment that is intended to hold a student in place—such as a standing table, swing, or wagon—can easily be modified by filling the space not filled by the student's body with foam rubber, styrofoam, or some similar material. This material, then, may be removed

Table 16–4. Basic equipment useful for each developmental level

Developmental level	Equipment	
Reflex development and inhibition	■ pans of sand, beans, styrofoam pellets, wood beads, sponges ■ small balls, blocks, rods, sponges ■ small bright objects, rattles, noisemakers ■ 35 mm film cans with varying weight inside ■ stuffed animals, dolls, hand puppets ■ mats or body-sized carpet pieces — 1 per student ■ bolsters, large cushions, padded barrel ■ large pieces of fabric of varying textures	■ large cardboard boxes for crawling through ■ scooterboards — 1 per student ■ rope — ½ inch × 15 feet ■ balloons — 4 per student ■ standing frame ■ parallel bars for walking ■ tilt board ■ 36-inch cage ball
Sensory stimulation and discrimination	■ water hose with nozzle, "Slip 'n' Slide," sprinkler ■ wading pools — 1 per 3 students ■ wading pool filled with sand ■ pans of oatmeal, cereal, rice, other edibles ■ modeling clay ■ tempera paint, liquid detergent, shaving cream, cornstarch ■ blindfolds — 1 per student ■ tactile box with armholes and various objects inside ■ swings, slides, swinging tire, net, hammock, incline ramp	■ tricycles, skateboards, bicycles ■ mini-trampoline, "Jumpin' Jiminey" ■ climbing equipment — stall bars, ladder, jungle gym ■ rhythm instruments — tambourine, bell, ratchet, rhythm sticks, drum, blocks — 1 per student ■ parachute ■ suspended balls — 1 or 2 ■ flashlight ■ hula hoops — 1 per student ■ wall mirrors — 6 × 10 feet
Enhancing motor-sensory responses	■ record player, records ■ beads and string — 1 set per student ■ peg board, pegs, rubber bands — 1 set per student ■ clothespins, container ■ bean bags, yarn balls, sponge balls, scoops — 1 per student ■ "Play-Buoy" — 2 per class ■ T-stools — 1 per student ■ balance boards — 1 per 2 students ■ inner-tube barrel, lined (padded) barrel ■ commercial games — Twister, Funny Bones, Simon (electronic game)	■ roller skates — 1 pair per student ■ tapered balance beam, 4-inch balance beam (low) ■ tin can stilts — 1 pair per student ■ tumbling mats ■ rubber balls — 1 per student, various sizes ■ grids on roll plastic with letters, numbers, shapes, colors ■ soap bubbles — 1 bottle per student ■ small objects for sorting — nails, clips, screws, nuts ■ butcher paper — 1 body-sized piece for each student
Enhancing motor patterns and skills	■ set of stairs with hand rail ■ 2 or 3 pull toys, wagon ■ 2 dozen boundary markers (traffic cones) ■ 2 dozen milk cartons, candlesticks, plastic bowling pins ■ medicine ball	■ tennis balls, baseballs, softballs, soccer balls, footballs — 1 per 2 students ■ frisbees — 1 per 2 students ■ batons, bats, sticks, racquets — 1 per student ■ inner tube strips

Table 16–4. (continued)

427

Developmental level	Equipment
Culturally determined forms of movement	
Aquatics	■ buckets, sponges, washcloths ■ flotation devices — floaties, life jackets, belts, inner tubes ■ kickboards ■ hydraulic lift for pool
Conditioning	■ individual jump ropes ■ chinning bar ■ free weights, bars
Dance/Rhythms	■ ribbons, flags, scarves ■ disco records, rock, and other dance music
Fitness	■ universal gym, wall weights, weighted boots, suspended ropes ■ bicycle ergometer
Games and Sports	■ equipment for table tennis, shuffleboard, croquet, tetherball, chess, checkers, box hockey ■ equipment for air rifling, angling, archery, badminton, indoor bowling, fencing, golf, tennis ■ volleyballs, basketballs

depending on the needs of each child. An example of modifying a piece of equipment to make it larger would include wrapping foam rubber or threading a tubular sleeve onto the handle of a bat or racket for use by students whose grip strength is only adequate in the wider ranges of finger extension. The diversity of a piece of equipment may be enhanced by adding features or qualities to the existing piece. A typical example of enhancing the diversity of a wheelchair is to add a counting and letter board or an eating board by attaching it to the arms of the chair (see Figure 16–4 for examples of modifications).

In modifying equipment, often a first consideration should be a given student's unique needs relative to the use of that equipment. Adding a weighted ring to the end of a baseball bat as used by athletes for warm-up would enhance proprioception and would add to a student's awareness of where the bat is in space. Other modifications commonly used to increase the useability of a piece of equipment by all students would be the addition of straps, weights, textured ma-

terials, bright colors or other visual cues. Straps of velcro attached to the equipment or wrist cuffs worn by the student can be used to substitute for grip strength on equipment such as archery bows, wall pulleys, racquet and paddle handles or cue sticks. Youngsters with minimal hand strength and control may be able to guide a pool or shuffleboard cue if given the opportunity to maintain contact with the equipment. Commercially available gloves with a flap wrapping around the stick and attaching back onto the glove could also be used. These commercially made items can often be substituted with velcro, canvas and other materials plus a little creativity. Weights attached to striking implements or sewn into cuffs worn on the wrists or ankles can enhance proprioception in students with little to no kinesthetic awareness. A very few ounces are needed for this purpose. Items such as large washers or drapery weights provide just enough stimulation to help students become more aware of where the implement or their body parts are in space. The goal, of course, is to gradually reduce

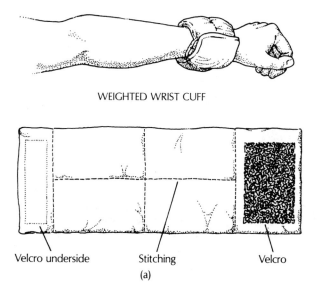

WEIGHTED WRIST CUFF

Velcro underside   Stitching   Velcro
(a)

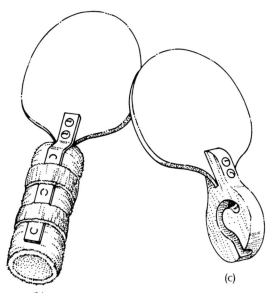

(b)

(c)

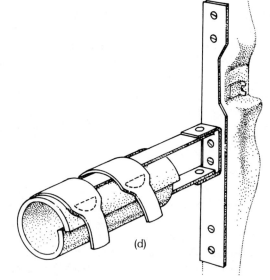

(d)

(e)

Figure 16–4. Examples of equipment modification include a weighted wrist cuff for a student who is unable to grip a weight (a); an adapted table tennis racket for a student with a sensitive skin condition (b); an adapted table tennis racket for a prosthetic hook (c); an adapted archery bow for a student with a paralyzed hand (d); and an adapted archery release mechanism for a prosthetic hook (e). SOURCE: Jim Cowart, *Instructional Aids for Adaptive Physical Education* (Hayward, Calif.: Alameda County School Department, 1977), used with permission.

the amount of weight as awareness and skill increase.

Wrist and ankle cuffs are commonly used in the rehabilitation setting, but have had only limited use in the physical education program. These items, usually made of leather with a metal ring firmly riveted to the midpoint, provide access for the quadraplegic to resistive exercises and activities. The equipment to be moved, such as a wall pulley, is then clipped to the metal ring so the student can use the upper or lower limb movement available to exercise active muscle groups. The texture of a piece of equipment with which a student has contact may be altered to enhance the tactile awareness. For youngsters with tactile imperception, a football may be altered with a handprint (applied with a rubberized silicone substance) outlining the position of the hand required to effectively pass the ball. This works quite successfully in teaching the youngsters the hand position, while at the same time avoiding their use of visual cues to verify that they are, in fact, holding the ball in the correct position. Covering a balance beam with a different texture provides added information for the tactile learner whose proprioception and balance may not be equal to the task. As the student improves in ability to walk the beam or even do tricks, the texture can be changed and the amount of abrasiveness reduced so the student must further rely on proprioceptive and vestibular information. This procedure should be followed, as in the case of enhancing proprioception through the use of weights, until the added texture is no longer needed. The visual stimuli provided by a piece of equipment can easily be modified by painting or applying bright colors. Yellow playground balls are commercially available; however, in the absence of such balls, the existing supply can be modified by spray-painting the balls with yellow or white paint. This serves the needs both of the visually impaired and the visually imperceptive child, who may have difficulty with ocular tracking, visual discrimination, or visual attending. Applications can be made by cutting out

pieces of brightly colored vinyl or contact paper. Circles of this material of yellow or red can be applied, for example, to a basketball backboard indicating the spot where the ball must hit for a lay-up in order for it to go into the basket. As we use the trademark on a softball bat to indicate the correct and safest position of the bat, a brightly colored circle out of contact paper can be put on the bat to mark the place where the ball should make contact. This again can serve the purpose of demanding visual attention to the point of contact.

Minimal Equipment

Although there has been much discussion of the acquisition and modification of equipment, an elaborate inventory of equipment is not necessary for the delivery of appropriate services. Certainly there are minimal basic pieces that are needed for providing a variety of movement experiences, just as there is a minimal amount of space required in order for children to move. Having no equipment or minimal equipment, however, is no excuse for an inappropriate program. The very least a physical educator brings to the teaching situation are hands and legs. Therefore, resistive exercises at the very least can be provided through manual resistance. Beyond that, only the physical educator's creativity limits the scope of the adapted physical education program (see Table 16–5).

Making Equipment

Raw materials with which to construct equipment must be obtained through any means available. If local merchants can be patronized through purchasing raw materials with school district or community funds, that source should be exhausted first. When funds run out, alternative means should be explored. One such means is the use of discarded items. Merchants, com-

Table 16–5. Equipment and aids commonly available

Category	Equipment and aids	
Daily living aids	■ plastic bowls and dishes with suction cups ■ utensils with built-up handles (bamboo, plastic, wood, foam) ■ utensils with extended handles, angled handles, or handles curving around the hand ■ plastic squeeze bottle ■ cup with straw holder or built-in straw (Sippit) ■ thermal tumbler or cup with double-wall insulation, or with built-in straw (Thermo-Sip) ■ flexible straw ■ toothbrush with hand strap ■ bath rails ■ shower chair ■ shower and bathtub safety treads and mats ■ elevated toilet seat ■ toilet safety rails	■ zippers with ring instead of tab ■ socks, shorts, and pants pull-on (long dowel with cup hook at one end) ■ wraparound skirt, dress, blouse, with simple closure (velcro, large button, hook, etc) ■ short wheelchair coat ■ wheelchair cape ■ loafers, or shoes with elastic shoelaces ■ lightweight battery shaver ■ electric shaver with hand strap or metal extension arm attached to table ■ lipstick with built-up handle or extension arm ■ long-handled comb and brush ■ comb and brush with handcuffs ■ around-the-neck mirror
Sitting, standing, and mobility aids	■ propping devices (sandbags, pillows, rubber tire, bolsters, wooden support, carton open at top) ■ seatbelts for chair, wheelchair, or car ■ barrel or beachball ■ creeper on wheels ■ crawler on wheels	■ Scoot-a-bout propelled by arms, prone-stander ■ sit-in table (for one or two children) ■ adult stand-in table ■ vertically positioned tiltboard or Stryker frame with body belts ■ stand-up desk
Canes	■ hardwood ■ aluminum (adjustable, nonadjustable) ■ variations: special handles (curved, T-grip, spade, offset); cane-seat combination; quad cane (four legs, adjustable, with or without two wheels); tripod (crab cane); cane glider (two wheels, two tips)	■ special tips (for ice, etc) ■ special handgrips (molded plastic, padded) ■ long white canes for the blind
Crutches	■ hardwood or aluminum, double-upright, axillary (underarm), in various sizes and usually adjustable ■ single-upright, adjustable	■ forearm, with arm cuff or trough forearm ■ underarm offset
Walkers	■ aluminum, with four legs (adjustable, nonadjustable) ■ folding, nonfolding ■ with two or four wheels ■ stair walker, walker-chair combination	■ infant and child models ■ training walker with body support ■ one-sided walkette ■ child walker with brakes

Table 16-5. (continued)   **431**

Category	Equipment and aids	
Wheelchairs	■ standard chair with fixed armrests, stationary or swinging footrests, with or without elevating legrests, upholstered or nonupholstered seat and back ■ folding ■ amputee chair ■ semi- and full-reclining chair ■ economy model ■ lightweight model ■ tiny tot and "growing" chair	■ junior chair ■ institutional model ■ light- and heavy-duty clinical models ■ motorized chairs (folding, nonfolding; guided by adapted hand control, chin, head, or breath) ■ stair-climbing chair ■ accessories: tray; lapboard; worktable; arm slings; heel strap, headrest and head wings; pneumatic tires; knobs attached to wheel rims for propelling, width reducer for narrow spaces

SOURCE: Robert M. Goldenson (ed.), *Disability and Rehabilitation Handbook* (New York: McGraw-Hill, 1978).

munity groups, and parents will be willing to save castoffs once the needs of the adapted physical education program are made known to them. Items such as carpet samples, cardboard tubes used in holding roll carpeting or linoleum, bleach bottles, milk cartons, cans, and scraps of wood are all items that are readily available at no charge. Specific materials that may not fit into the category of discarded items may be donated by local merchants either through direct contact or through service clubs in which they hold membership. As related to the "wish list" discussed earlier, the list should be carefully evaluated in terms of what pieces of equipment can be made and what must be purchased.

A variety of equipment can easily be made. The "homemade" equipment should meet the same criteria as commercially made equipment — that is, considerations should be made for portability, washability, durability, economy, size, and diversity. When making equipment, it is important that it be safe and practical. Edges should be smoothly sanded, wood should be sealed with varnish or lacquer, and the metal edges should be carefully masked to avoid any injury or harm to the student. Any equipment made according to printed instructions should follow specifications to the letter to avoid problems with liability (see Figure 16-5).

Resources

The following list of resources is intended to provide the physical educator with the names of some companies that make equipment appropriate for use in the adapted physical education program. This is not to imply that the list is complete, by any means, nor should distributors and manufacturers on this list be considered in lieu of physical education, sport, and athletic suppliers already being used for the regular program. This list is provided as a supplement to other sources of physical education and athletic equipment, especially for those unique items used to enhance development below the top level of the developmental model. Also included on this resource list are distributors and manufacturers of equipment that has been exclusively designed for use by the handicapped. This list is *not* an endorsement of products.

1. AFW of North America
   Bank of North America
   Bank of New York Building, Suite 311
   North Union Street
   Olean, NY 14760

2. Adaptive Therapeutic System, Inc.
   965 Dixwell Avenue
   Hamden, CT 06514

PURPOSE: TACTILE EXPERIENCES

Barrel Roller

Barrel of any size with carpet, burlap, sheep skin, or other fabrics attached inside and out. Stitch pieces together to cover and line the barrel; then punch holes near top and bottom rims and sew to barrel using nylon cord and overhand stitch.

SAMPLE OBJECTIVE

Child will roll in barrel a distance of 10 feet.

Innertube "tube"

Inflate 4 or 5 innertubes and tie together in twos.

Child will roll in innertube in both directions a distance of 10 feet.

Incline mat

Wedge-shaped construction with 3/4" plywood top and sides. Top should be padded or carpeted. Supporting ribs of 1 × 2s should be equally spaced inside for durability.

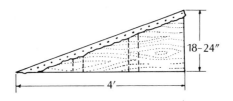

Child will roll up and down incline in 3 pieces of textured fabric.

PURPOSE: VESTIBULAR EXPERIENCES

Balance beam

2" × 8" × 10' of hardwood board can be used flat on the floor or on supports made from same material. Notches in supports are 2" and 4" to hold beam flat or on edge for variations in balance challenges. A third support may be used in the center for heavier, older children.

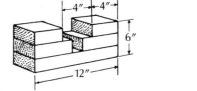

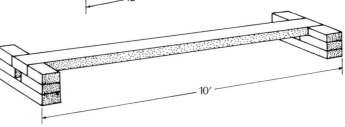

Child will walk length of beam unassisted 3 out of 5 trials.

Figure 16–5. Equipment that can be made. SOURCE: Janet Seaman and Karen DePauw, *Sensory Motor Experiences for the Home* (Los Angeles: Trident Shop, 1979).

3. American Guidance Service
Circle Pines, MN 55104

4. Baffle Products
P.O. Box 1601
Salt Lake City, UT 84110

5. Bell, Inc.
12 South Main Street
Homer, NY 13077

6. Bomar Records, Inc.
10515 Burbank Blvd.
North Hollywood, CA 91601

7. CEC Publications Sales
1920 Association Drive
Reston, VA 22091

8. Childcraft Playthings, Inc.
155 East 23rd Street
New York, NY 10010

9. Creative Playthings, Inc.
5757 W. Century Blvd.
Los Angeles, CA 90045

10. Crow River Industries, Inc.
Skyway Plaza Office Building
Suite 1
1415 East Wayzata Blvd.
Wayzata, MN 55391

11. Developmental Design
P.O. Box 55
Carpinteria, CA 93013

12. Educational Activities
P.O. Box 392
Freeport, NY 11520

13. Elementary Gym Closet, Inc.
2511 Leach Road
Auburn Heights, MI 48057

14. Exceptional Play, Inc.
P.O. Box 1015
Lawrence, KS 66044

15. Flaghouse, Inc.
18 W. 18th Street
New York, NY 10011

16. Gym Master Co.
3200 Zuni St.
Englewood, CO 80110

17. Gymnastic Supply Co.
247 W. 6th Street
San Pedro, CA 90733

18. Gould Athletic Supply Co.
8156 North 96 Street
Milwaukee, WI 53222

19. Gym-Thing
5550 Newberry Street
Baltimore, MD 21209

20. Handicapped Children's
Technological Services
RFD 2, Box 60B
Woster, RI 02825

21. Hanover House
Hanover, PA 17331

22. Hubbard Scientific
1946 Raymond Drive
Northbrook, IL 60062

23. J. A. Preston, Corp.
71 Fifth Avenue
New York, NY 10003

24. Jamison, Inc.
P.O. Box 1685
San Pedro, CA 90733

25. J. L. Hammett Company
U.S. Route 29 South
Lynchburg, VA 24502

26. Jayfro Corporation
P.O. Box 400
Waterford, CT 06385

27. Kaye Products, Inc.
202 South Elm Street
Durham, NC 27701

28. Kimbo Educational
P.O. Box 477
Long Branch, NJ 07740

29. Laerdal Medical Corp.
Box 190
Armonk, NY 10504

30. Lind Climber Co.
807 Reba Place
Evanston, IL 60202

31. Montgomery Ward Co.
(Nationwide)

32. Mosier Materials
P.O. Box 3036
San Bernardino, CA 92413

33. Oregon Worsted Co.
8300 So. East McLoughlin Blvd.
Portland, OR 97202

34. Peek Publications
4067 Transport Street
Palo Alto, CA 94301

35. Play Gate Co.
P.O. Box 14587
Phoenix, AZ 85063

36. Premier Athletic Products
25 East Union Avenue
East Rutherford, NJ 07073

37. Prentke Romich Co.
Electronics Center
RD 2, Box 191
Shreve, Ohio 44676

38. Program Aids Company Inc.
No. 1 Physical Fitness Drive
Garden, NY 11530

39. Reedco, Inc.
54 East Genesee Street
Auburn, NY 13021

40. School Yard Big Toys
Donald Much
General Recreation, Inc.
P.O. Box 263
Narberth, PA 19072

41. Sears Roebuck and Co.
(Nationwide)

42. Shield Manufacturing, Inc.
425 Fillmore Avenue
Tonowanda, NY 14150

43. Snitz Manufacturing Co.
2096 Church Street
East Troy, WI 53120

44. Special Olympics, Inc.
1701 K Street, N.W., Suite 203
Washington, D.C. 20006

45. U.S. Games, Inc.
P.O. Box 874 EG
Melbourne, FL 32935

46. United Canvas and Sling
155 State Street
Hackensack, NJ 07601

47. The Vital Years
Educational Teaching Aids
159 W. Kinzie Street
Chicago, IL 60610

48. The Wheelchair Travel
Ball Hill Road
Milford, NH 83055

49. Widen Tool and Stamping, Inc.
1206 South Front Street
St. Peter, MN 56082

50. Wolverine Sports
745 State Circle
Ann Arbor, MI 48104

51. Young People Records
100 Sixth Avenue
New York, NY 10003

FACILITIES

The physical educator may have the opportunity to offer suggestions for the modification of facilities. Factors to keep in mind include accessibility, outdoor facilities, indoor facilities, and available space.

Accessibility

Numerous pieces of legislation have addressed the problem of making facilities and programs accessible to the handicapped. We have become acutely aware over the past five to ten years of the efforts made in both the public and private sectors for modifying existing facilities and providing in new facilities mechanisms for accessibility. Some of these mechanisms include ramps; handrails; wider bathroom stalls with grab bars; the lowering of telephones, sinks, and drinking fountains; automatic door openers; and braille characters on a variety of directional and informational signs. Two pieces of legislation, in particular, are being addressed when these kinds of physical changes become evident in the community. The first is the Architectural Barriers Act of 1967 and the second — The Rehabilitation Act of 1973. The minimum standards for accessibility to educational facilities that these laws set can be summarized as follows:

1. Determine the size, shape, and location of spaces within or adjacent to a building, such as parking and stairs.
2. Control the size, shape and location of objects, such as door handles, rest rooms, toilets, water fountains, and control knobs.
3. Indirectly place a limit on both personal energy output by the handicapped person — by limiting the angles of ramps, etc. — and on the degree of hazard to be encountered by modifying door hardware design to alert blind people when doors lead to hazardous spaces.

4. Specify the size and nature of signs and signals that guide a handicapped person in entering and using a building.

Although a specific administrator within an educational agency ordinarily would be designated to head up an evaluation of facilities for their accessibility and initiate modifications in facilities in order to bring the agency into compliance, the physical educator may be called upon to give some input when alternatives are available. Thus physical educators should not only be alert to some of the architectural barriers within the physical education plant, they should also be aware of modifications that could be made (but are not necessarily required to be made) that would make accessibility much easier (see Table 16–6).

Table 16–6. Examples of facility modifications for the handicapped

- changing tables in dressing rooms
- eliminate thresholds into shower and bathroom stalls
- lower mirrors to height of wheelchair users
- provide shower chairs for wheelchair users
- slanted mirrors over wash basins
- texture cement floors to avoid slipping
- raise toilet seats for transfer and enlarge toilet stalls
- raise lavatories, install long-handled faucets, insulate hot water pipes
- lower towel and soap dispensers
- lower light switches, fire alarms, drinking fountains for people in wheelchairs
- install flashing lights in addition to audible bell alarms for deaf
- light directional markings and exit signs for partially sighted
- provide removable row of bleachers for wheelchair "seating"
- reduce excessive pressure needed to operate doors

Outdoor Facilities

Outdoor facilities basically fit into one of two categories: space and structures. The size of the space available for use can seldom be altered unless there is undeveloped property that belongs to the school district. Thompson (1976) recommends 60 square feet per child, but this is often not available on the school grounds. Adjoining or nearby property such as parks and open fields may provide additional needed space. Many communities have worked jointly with the local school district in developing park property immediately adjacent to the school grounds.

This arrangement not only provides a satisfactory means of expanding use for both agencies, but also assures that both facilities will be used for greater amounts of time. The community recreation program, for example, that has as its peak service delivery periods school vacations, can use school property during times when it would ordinarily sit idle. This joint arrangement also allows, at least in the development period, the opportunity to avoid duplication of equipment and use features. For example, the school

playground may appropriately contain swinging and climbing equipment and the adjacent park may provide equipment offering supplemental experiences for exploring, crawling, and imaginative play (see Figure 16–6). Outdoor structures that may require modification include pools; stadiums; playing courts such as tennis, basketball, volleyball, handball, and racquetball; tracks; softball, baseball, and multipurpose playing fields. One major modification that might be desirable would be the added construction or acquisition of an enclosure over some of these structures. Portable, air-filled enclosures are available and in use in many parts of the country to extend the months of use of structures such as pools and playing courts. These are relatively inexpensive in contrast to a permanent enclosure, and may possibly be within the realm of acquiring through a federally or privately funded project or as a major project for local community groups.

Minor modifications of outdoor structures include adding a ramp or lift, handrails, and grab bars in and around the edge of the swimming pool. The physical educator and the responsible administrator should also

Figure 16-6. These creative play areas provide opportunities for children to practice all the movement patterns.

be aware of such minor barriers as thresholds or steps leading onto playing courts, fields, and asphalt-surfaced play areas. Attention should also be given to the width of gates to play areas for accessibility by a wheelchair. The grass on play fields should be kept short-cropped and, where possible (depending on the growing conditions) should be a hard-surfaced grass that does not retain nor require a great deal of water (e.g., zoysia, St. Augustine, Bermuda, or Fescus). This kind of surface is much easier for moving wheelchairs and walkers.

Outdoor asphalt playing surfaces are often marked for regulation volleyball and basketball, or (in the elementary schools) for games of low organization such as circle games, four-square, and obstacle courses. Often, there are so many lines painted on the playing surface that children without visual problems have difficulty distinguishing one set of game lines from another. For children with visual figure-ground perception difficulties, a premarked playing surface presents an insurmountable visual task. If space permits, it is desirable to not have overlapping lines at all. If this is not possible, as is often the case in small and inter-city schools, the lines for each game or sport should be painted in different colors. This will help, at least in a small way, with the visual figure-ground problems.

Indoor Facilities

Some suggestions for modifying existing indoor facilities have already been made in an earlier section of this chapter. In a separate special education school, of course, it is desirable to have a room or gymnasium especially designated for physical education. Where this is possible, certain permanent equipment should be installed. Such equipment includes mirrors (that can be covered); stall bars; wall-pulley weights; a scale for measuring body weight and height; hanging and chinning bars; and, depending on the population of the

school, special equipment such as a ramp for riding scooterboards, large crash pads, swinging apparatus, parallel bars for gait training, an oscillating bed, and perhaps a bicycle ergometer. In a regular school serving students in separate adapted physical education classes, a separate room or facility should not be designated specifically for adapted physical education. The class should provide as many normalizing experiences as possible with the full range of equipment and facility modifications made at each teaching station within the physical education plant. Thus the dance studio, weight room, gymnasium, multipurpose room, and swimming pool should be used by all students, with each facility being accessible and containing equipment needed for students having a diverse set of needs. Providing students with the experience of using the entire physical education facility also will assist in the transition to mainstreaming since students transferred into regular classes will have had previous experience with the facility and use of equipment and will have learned the appropriate behaviors for that context (see Figures 16-7 and 16-8).

Using Available Space

Knowing what are desirable and ideal facilities and conditions and actually having them are often two different matters. The adapted physical educator at the elementary school level (whether permanent or itinerant) and the adapted physical educator at the secondary school level often find themselves in a situation in which the space they use for instruction is that space left over after everyone else takes their share. At the elementary level, the adapted physical educator—especially the itinerant teacher—is often vying for space with the music teacher, art teacher, psychologist, nurse, speech therapist, special assemblies, and many other itinerant and intermittent programs. At the secondary level, the adapted physical educator's claim on space may present slightly different problems, not

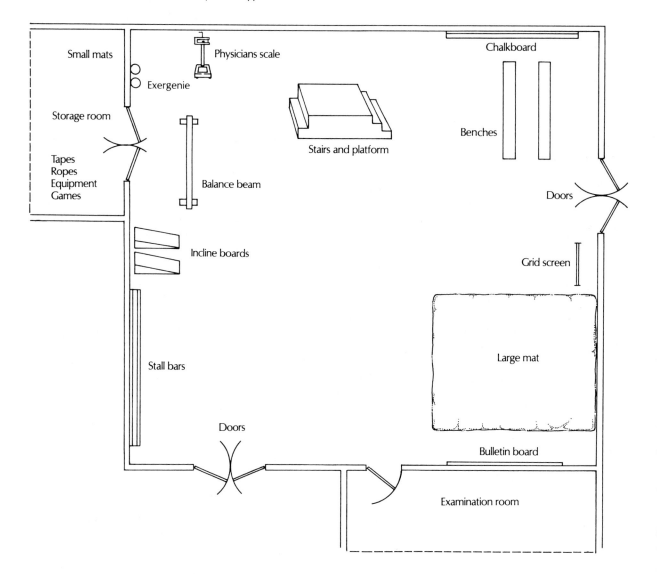

Figure 16–7. Sample junior high school activity room. SOURCE: Irma J. Pack, CSULA class assignment, 1974.

Figure 16–8. Sample elementary school activity room. SOURCE: Janet Seaman and J. Grzymko, unpublished paper, 1971.

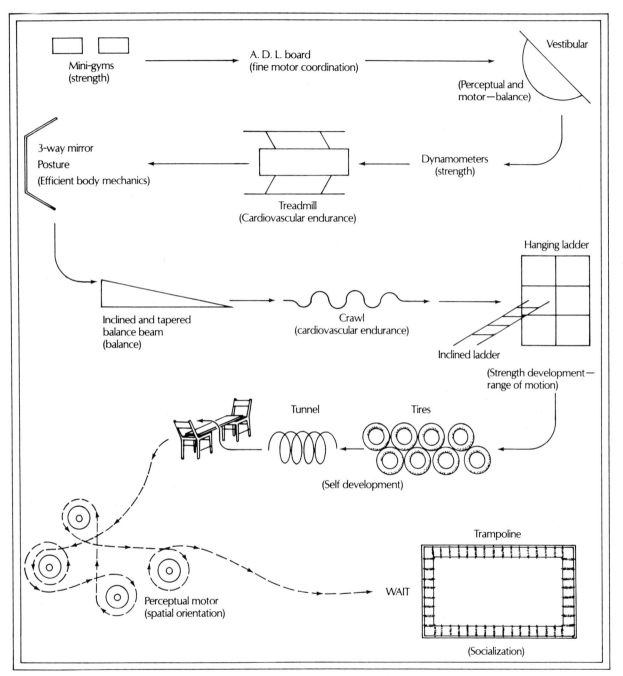

Mini-gyms
(strength)

A. D. L. board
(fine motor coordination)

Vestibular

(Perceptual and
motor—balance)

3-way mirror
Posture
(Efficient body mechanics)

Dynamometers
(strength)

Treadmill
(Cardiovascular endurance)

Inclined and tapered
balance beam
(balance)

Crawl
(cardiovascular endurance)

Hanging ladder

Inclined ladder

(Strength development—
range of motion)

Tunnel

Tires

(Self development)

Trampoline

WAIT

Perceptual motor
(spatial orientation)

(Socialization)

Colorcode system for specific children to be determined by previous testing and/or observations.

Due to differences, varied activities may be used: bean bag, quoits, etc.

necessarily problems of less magnitude. At least at the secondary level there should be clearly identified teaching stations for which all staff members put in their bid. If instructional units for adapted physical education can be designed to coincide with the instructional unit timeframe of the regular physical education program, then the rotation of facilities could be made at the same time in the school year.

When considering alternate locations for holding class, consider the space needs of all children in each class. Sometimes the leftover space is truly more appropriate and functional than the space originally preferred by the physical educator. Children who are distractible may function far better in a barren hallway or small room than they would in the open space of the gymnasium or playing field. Some autistic, emotionally disturbed, behaviorally disordered, and other children tend to "freak out" and lose their orientation in larger open spaces. Children with a history of running away from the group may also attend better to the task and be less inclined to stray from the group if the limits of their play area are clearly defined by the walls of a room. Even locker rooms have provided certain novel opportunities for activities and experimentation. Three- or five-minute step tests for measuring cardiovascular response to activity, crawling, and balancing tasks have been known to be successful when done on locker room benches. The stage in an elementary school provides a well-defined activity area with a certain muting effect on noise and hence behavior, because of the surrounding draperies. Small classes could meet on the school stage on a regular basis; for some groups, that would be the most desir-

able area of the entire school facility. A young teacher at a special education school recently reported using a portion of a very wide hallway in which to conduct her adapted physical education classes with trainable mentally retarded children. To avoid distractions and frequent interruptions, she uses gymnastics mats standing on edge to mask off the activity area from the portion of the hallway used for traffic. Except for the noise created when another class goes by, this seems to be a fairly reasonable solution to a situation in which space is limited. As mentioned in an earlier chapter, class organization and equipment modifications can be made in order to get the greatest use out of the space available.

SUMMARY

As with other aspects of the adapted physical education program, the acquisition, modification, and use of equipment and facilities should be approached systematically and creatively. The needs of the population to be served should provide the foundation for this process in order to make the best use of available resources. Securing sources of funding outside the educational context will be an important step in maintaining quality services in a tightening economy. Even with little or no resources, the adapted physical educator has the responsibility to provide appropriate educational experiences. Thus imagination and creativity can pave the way for new and different solutions to old problems.

BIBLIOGRAPHY

Aitken, M. H. *Play Environment for Children: Play Space, Improved Equipment and Facilities.* Bellingham, Washington: Educational Designs and Consultants, 1972.

Bayes, K. *Designing for the Handicapped.* London: Godwin Ltd., 1971.

Cook, W. B. "Picking Playground Equipment." *American School and University* 44 (August 1972): 38.

Dillon, D. *Adaptations and Modifications of Playground Equipment for the Severely Handicapped.* Los Angeles: California State University, unpublished paper, 1980.

Goldenson, R. M., et al. (eds.). *Disability and Rehabilitation Handbook.* New York: McGraw-Hill, 1978.

Gordon, R. "Playgrounds Can Be Experience Equalizers." *American School and University* 45 (October 1973): 37–38, 40–41.

Harms, T. "Evaluating Settings for Learning." *Young Child* 25 (May 1970): 304–308.

New York State Construction Fund. *Making Facilities Accessible to the Physically Handicapped.* New York: New York State Construction Fund, 1967.

O'Meara, J. "A Total Fitness Program in a Special School Program." *California Association for Health, Physical Education, Recreation, and Dance Journal* (November 1980): 11–12.

Orange County Board of Public Instruction. *An Adaptive Playground for Physically Disabled Children with Perceptual Deficits.* Orlando, Florida: Orange County Board of Public Instruction, 1969.

Pack, I. J. *Adapted Physical Education at San Fernando Junior High School.* Los Angeles: California State University, unpublished paper, 1974.

Seaman, J. A., and Grzymko, J. L. *To Teach Adapted Physical Education: A Resource Manual for Physical Educators and Classroom Teachers.* Bloomington, Indiana, unpublished, 1971, 50 pp.

Thompson, D. "Space Utilization: Criteria for the Selection of Playground Equipment for Children." *Research Quarterly* 47 (October 1976): 472–481.

17   Education Through Physical Activity

Guiding Questions

1. How are cognitive learning and language development related through physical education?
2. How can the physical education teacher encourage language use and development through physical education activities?
3. What are the ways through which socialization and affective growth can be enhanced through physical activities?

Learning can and does take place through the medium of movement. Thus, while learning in the motor domain must be the primary concern of physical educators, it must not exclude other learning experiences. Educational experiences in the following areas can be incorporated into physical education programs: (1) cognition; (2) language; (3) socialization; and (4) affective learning.

Learning through movement is not a new idea to the physical educator. Jessie Fahring Williams coined the phrase "education through the physical" in the early twentieth century. More recently, Mosston, Kiphard, Cratty, and Humphrey have utilized this concept in physical education programming. Although diverse in content and approach, the programs have all yielded positive results when physical activity and cognition were combined.

COGNITIVE LEARNING

Movement provides a natural medium through which children discover and explore their environment and learn about the world. Movement allows the opportunity for physical growth and social interaction, it is enjoyable, and it provides for release of tension. It is no wonder that philosophers from Plato to Rousseau, and educators from Itard to Montessori, have argued for the inseparability of sensorimotor and educational experiences, postulating that movement experiences enhance and enrich intellectual attainment.

Teaching Cognitive Skills

Simple recognition skills can be taught through physical activities. Letter, number, color, and shape recognition activities can be easily incorporated into a physical education program. For example, the teacher can ask the students to perform the following activities:

1. Stand on the letter "a" or "A."
2. Jump on the number "1."
3. Walk on the lines that form a triangle.
4. Sit on the "blue" carpet square.

5. Put their bodies into the shape of a circle.

6. Hop "two" times.

7. Make an "I" with their bodies.

8. Find the diamond shape.

Letter or number grids, painted or taped on the ground or floor, can be used for these activities. Other equipment and supplies might include flashcards of numbers, letters, colors, and shapes; colored carpet squares and hula hoops; jump ropes for making shapes; and blocks of various colors, shapes, letters, and so on.

Depending on the ability of the child, recognition skills can be expanded to include spelling, reading, counting, and simple arithmetic activities. For example, the teacher can ask the children to perform the following activities:

1. Spell their names by stepping on each letter in sequence.

2. Use a locomotor skill and spell its name.

3. Tell their age by jumping on the number(s).

4. Add, subtract, multiply, or divide using the number grid.

5. Play word scramble: with word cards placed between two teams, one member from each team scrambles to find a specified letter or word, to complete a sentence, or to answer a question.

Almost any academic subject can be brought into the physical education program. In addition to reading, spelling, and math, activities might include telling time, or learning a lesson in history by participating in the sports of the time such as jousting, cricket, running, and so on.

Figure 17-1. This child is first of all seeing the obstacle course (right), and then using memory and motor planning to go through it blindfolded (facing page). SOURCE: Photos by Ben Esparza.

Teaching Concepts

Concepts such as small, large, over, under, on, around, through, flat, round, right, left, and so on, can be taught or reinforced through movement experiences and physical activities. Group and individual exploration of such concepts are made concrete through physical movement.

Distinct concepts are easier to teach and reinforce through physical education than subtle concepts. Thus distinct concepts should be taught first, with instruction in subtle concepts following. Some distinct concepts include big/little, large/small, fast/slow, up/down, top/bottom, and high/low. Some subtle concepts include round, flat, right/left, wide/narrow, around/through, and in/out. Concepts can be taught through (1) movement activities specific to the concept, (2) movement exploration activities, and (3) obstacle courses involving the concepts (see Figure 17–1).

Movement activities specific to the concept will vary with the concept being taught. For example, to teach the concepts of big/little, the physical educator can ask students to perform the following activities:

1. Make their bodies as big as possible.
2. Make their bodies as little as possible.
3. Bounce a big ball (little ball).
4. Make a big movement (little movement) of the arm.
5. Take a big step (little step).

The same concepts taught by movement exploration approach include the following question-performance activities:

Figure 17–2. Through the movement exploration method, children can experience making their bodies as ''big'' as possible (right) and as ''little'' as possible (below). SOURCE: Photos by Ben Esparza.

1. How big (little) can you make your body (see Figure 17-2)?
2. Show me two or three big parts (little parts).
3. How many ways can you move a big (little) part of your body?
4. Show me how you can make a big movement (little movement).
5. Show me how you can run in a big space (little space).

Obstacle courses can be designed to provide the experience of several stations for the concept of big and little. The following are examples:

1. Climb big steps (little steps) (or stairs).
2. Make a big circle (little circle) with a jump rope.
3. Crawl through a big tunnel and then through a little tunnel.

4. Bounce a big ball (little ball).

Activities can be designed that are specific to the concept. Initially, it is advisable to work on or include only one concept or its opposite in the physical education program (this will vary with age and ability level). Other concepts can be added periodically throughout the program and reinforced singularly or in combination by the aforementioned methods. For example, specific activities could include:

1. Bounce a large (small) ball quickly (slowly).
2. Make your body large and flat (see Figure 17-3).

or movement exploration activities:

3. How quickly (slowly) can you move in a circle?
4. Show me how you can be round and wide.

Figure 17-3. Older children, too, can respond well to the movement exploration method as part of the class warm-up exercises. SOURCE: Photo by Lyonel Avance.

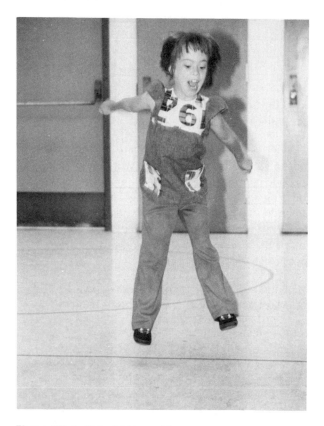

Figure 17–4. This child is working on the jumping pattern and learning the concept "over" by jumping over a line.

Obviously, obstacle courses can be planned to reinforce or introduce any number of concepts. Varying the type of movement with concept affords the opportunity to teach a variety of motor patterns and skills as well as a variety of concepts. Examples in one obstacle course include:

1. *Walking around* a *triangle*.
2. *Jumping over* a *small* object (see Figure 17–4).
3. *Crawling under* an object.
4. *Climbing on* a *large* box.

Problem Solving

The ability to solve problems can be included in physical education programs for exceptional children.

As with other aspects of cognitive learning, problem-solving ability can be made more concrete through actual experience. There are at least five types of activities through which to encourage problem solving: (1) task-specific activities, (2) movement exploration activities, (3) group problem-solving activities, (4) individual problem-solving activities, and (5) guided discovery activities.

The spectrum of simple to complex problem solving activities can be included in physical education programs, varying as appropriate for age and ability. Examples of problem-solving activities include:

1. Finding the fastest way to get from "A" to "B."
2. Finding the most direct route from "A" to "B."
3. Finding the most efficient way of moving.
4. Determining the best way to modify a game or piece of equipment so handicapped students can participate in the activity.

Task-specific activities are ones in which the teacher determines the problem to be solved and directs the activity toward that end. For example, the task is to solve the problem in terms of speed: the fastest way to get from "A" to "B," the fastest way to move around a given area, and the fastest way to complete a game. The movement exploration approach would allow the group or individual to solve given problems in a variety of ways:

1. Show me one way in which you can move quickly from A to B; another way; which was (is) faster?
2. Show me ways in which one can move around a given space.
3. What are possible ways of finishing (or completing) a game?

Any or all of these methods can be incorporated into physical education programs, depending on teaching style and the age and ability of the handicapped students.

Memory Activities

Memory plays an important role in cognitive learning. It is necessary that learning be retained and thereby provide a base for further learning. Memory, or retention, is just as important for learning in the motor domain; and motor experiences can assist in enhancing memory. Activities repeated quite frequently can provide the opportunity for overlearning, which tends to increase retention.

Introducing memory into the physical education program can take two basic avenues: general memory or specific memory tasks.

General memory in physical education refers to the ability to remember learned motor skills and physical activities (including games, sports, dance, and play). Memory can also include the ability to remember rules of games, parts of dances, warm-up exercises, and the like. Memory ability may often be impaired in the handicapped person, especially the mentally retarded, multihandicapped, and learning-disabled. Thus it becomes important for teachers (1) to be aware of this possible impaired ability and (2) to include time for reinforcing learning (i.e., overlearning) in an effort to increase memory.

Specific memory activities can be included in the physical education program. These can be of three types: (1) symbolic memory, (2) sequencing ability, and (3) serial memory activities. Serial memory activities are by far the easiest to understand and implement. Examples include the following instructions:

1. Give two directions (e.g., *run* to the fence and *run* back) with the same motor demand (run).
2. Give three or more directions with the single motor demand.
3. Give two directions with multiple motor demands (e.g., *run* to the tree and *walk* to the fence).
4. Give three or more directions and increase the number of motor demands.

Symbolic memory is coined phraseology representing the ability to respond to stimuli of a coded nature. For example, if children are asked to jump whenever they hear the sound of a bell and walk at the sound of a whistle, they must respond motorically based on a preset, memorized coding system. For example:

1. Children perform a different motor task to a specified auditory cue (e.g., jump: bell sound; walk: whistle).
2. Children perform a different motor task to each specified visual cue (e.g., walk: hands held up).
3. Children perform the appropriate motor task based on the visual or auditory cue presented randomly by the teacher.
4. Children are required to memorize the sequence of cues and then perform the motor tasks.

Encouraging Creativity

Human creative ability often lies dormant, and this is frequently the case with handicapped students. Whenever possible, physical education teachers should incorporate creativity into their programs. Ways of encouraging creativity include (1) movement exploration, (2) creative rhythms and dance, and (3) inventing new games and activities.

The key to encouraging creativity is to involve the child in the learning process. The teacher should encourage the child to find a new way of moving, or to do something different or unique. Encouraging creativity often requires initial guidance or structure by the teacher through environmental manipulation and class discussions. Some specific ways of stimulating creativity include the following:

1. How many ways can you make yourself large (small, flat, round, and so on)?
2. How many different body parts can you balance on? Balance on two parts, two different parts; three, four, or more parts?

3. Given a topic, plan and execute an expressive movement or series of movements. This can be done individually or in a group. Topics might include anger, joy, windy day, silence, slow moving animals, busy city, washing machine, calculator, snow, the ocean, and so on.

4. Move body parts or total body to music. Music can be varied from loud/soft, heavy/light, fast/slow, and so on. This can be done individually or in a group.

5. Given a type of music, move individually or as a part of a group to the music according to personal feeling (see Figure 17–5).

6. Tell a story through movement with or without music.

7. Create a new activity or new game: this can be done by the teacher initially setting some guidelines — one person only, with no equipment, using a locomotor pattern; more than one person, two types of locomotion; a ball and bean bag as equipment, no other stipulations; a balloon and two teams of children who must not use their

hands. Manipulation of any or all of the variables are possible.

LANGUAGE DEVELOPMENT

Language development can be fostered by a language-enriched physical education environment. A language approach to teaching physical activity is a method whereby concepts, words, meanings, and utilization of language are incorporated with actual physical education instruction. At times, it is important to place special emphasis on language acquisition and use in physical education. All children, handicapped and nonhandicapped, can benefit from a language-enriched learning environment. This emphasis, however, is most beneficial to the speech- or language-impaired child, and to the autistic, learning-disabled, and mentally retarded.

A language-enriched atmosphere requires a conscious effort by teachers to adjust their language to the level of the child, to monitor the amount and quality of language used, and to encourage language use by

Figure 17–5. This creative use of rhythms included the performance of ethnic dances from around the world before an audience of parents and invited guests. SOURCE: Photo by Lyonel Avance.

Figure 17-6. Gesturing, in addition to repeating the instructions, helps to emphasize what is to be done.

the student. Initially, the development of a language-enriched physical education program may not be easy; ultimately, it can become an integral part of the physical education program and a natural part of the teacher's repertoire. Language development can be stimulated through (1) verbalization by students, (2) identification and naming, (3) reinforcement of language concepts through movement, (4) use of sensory channels, and (5) use of language games. (See Figure 17-6.)

Verbalization/Vocalization by Students

The handicapped, especially the speech- and language-impaired, should be encouraged to speak during physical education. Even those who are severely involved can be required at least to vocalize or approximate the sound or word. This vocalization requirement is especially applicable to autistic, severely handicapped, and moderately mentally retarded children. As an integral part of the physical education program, aphasic and autistic students should be required to speak or vocalize whenever possible.

A relatively easy way for a teacher to encourage and require language verbalization is direct inquiry:

Teacher asks:	Student answers:
1. What are you going to do?	1. Run tree; run back; go outside; line up; find ball.
2. What did you do?	2. Ran tree; ran back; stood on line; got ball.
3. Where did you go?	3. Tree; outside.
4. How did you move?	4. Ran; walked; rolled.
5. What did Sally do?	5. Ran; walked; she ran; she walked.
6. What color is the ball?	6. Blue; red.

A similar method is to have the handicapped children repeat the directions as best they can. Initially, simple directions can be repeated, progressing toward verbal repetition of several directions or complex tasks. The children can be encouraged to greet the teacher and other students, lead the warm-up exercises, and interact verbally with others.

The quality of the verbalization must also be considered. Consultation with the speech or language pathologist or classroom teacher will reveal the quality of language production appropriate for each child that should be expected during language use in physical education. When working with handicapped students on a strict language-based program, the physical educator should work closely with the classroom teacher and other specialists for consistency of language utilization, quality of language production, behavior management, and reinforcement of language.

Identification and Naming

A specific way in which language utilization can be encouraged is through the identification and naming of objects, body parts, directions, actions, sizes, shapes, colors, and so on. The list is actually endless. Parts of speech such as nouns, verbs, prepositions, adverbs, articles, and adjectives can all be used in this fashion. Initially, it is best to have the students understand and use nouns, verbs, and some adjectives. All of the above-mentioned parts of speech, especially prepositions, adverbs, articles, and adjectives, are those whose concept or meaning can be reinforced or made concrete through movement. Suggestions of activities for language development include the following:

1. Name body parts.
2. Name objects in the physical education environment.
3. Name actions or movements (e.g., run, walk, roll, hop).
4. Name contrasting qualities of objects or movements (e.g., fast/slow, big/little, long/short).
5. Identify directions, shapes, colors and so on.
6. Name combinations of the above (e.g., red ball, big step, fast run, little finger).

Reinforcement of Language Concepts Through Movement

Words from every part of speech, and their concept or meaning, can be reinforced or made concrete through movement experiences. Prepositions such as over, under, around, through, on, into, and out can be demonstrated through movement. Adjectives and adverbs can best be understood through action (e.g., quick(ly), slow(ly), strong(ly), weak(ly), thin, flat, round). Some of the more complex nouns (e.g., game, circle, space, area) and verbs (e.g., fling, toss, rotate, twist, flex, extend), when put into movement, are more easily understood than without the kinesthetically felt motor performance.

Through the student's verbalization, speech and language production and utilization can be encouraged. Thus the student might be asked to describe the action before, during, and after the actual motor performance. Emphasis can be placed on the correct usage of the parts of speech in relation to the motor performance: *ran quickly, moved around* the *large space, jumped on top* of the *round* object, and so on.

Use of Sensory Channels

Much of the previous discussion has naturally centered around auditory input. But language acquisition, production, and use can and should be encouraged through other sensory channels, including multisensory input. Visual input is a valuable channel utilized in language development, and all of the previously mentioned activities can be easily modified to include visual input. Examples of visual input include the following:

1. Letter grids.
2. Number grids.
3. Flashcards of letters, words, numbers, and so on.
4. Pictures, photographs, or drawings of objects, animals, and so on.

Many activities using this type of input were included in the discussion of teaching cognitive skills and teaching concepts, all of which can also be used to increase language acquisition and utilization.

Learning grids and other types of activities involving children moving appropriately in marked areas of

Figure 17-7. Playing tug-of-war promotes cooperative behavior and contributes to the development of strength. SOURCE: Photo by Lyonel Avance.

the playground or floor can be used to facilitate language with children. Such activities as asking children to spell words with which they are having trouble by jumping into the various squares, or answering questions asked by other students, allow students to become more involved in the learning process. Games of this type can be created by the students themselves, with myriad variations available.

Auditory coding has excellent application for children at higher cognitive levels. Students assign an auditory cue (e.g., a clap, whistle, or spoken word) to a motor activity (e.g., one hop, two jumps, or somersault). One student can give the series of auditory cues, while the other student must decode them into physical movement.

Using Language Games

Although games that stimulate language do exist, most language-oriented games are found in the creative minds of both the children and teachers in our schools today. Games and activities such as Simon Says, Mother May I, Red Rover, Orff-Schulwerk activities, and even Duck, Duck, Goose, can be used successfully in facilitating language in children. Commercially available records are also excellent tools for creating a language-rich atmosphere.

SOCIALIZATION

Physical education provides one of the best means whereby socialization is encouraged and developed. Physical education, by its very nature, allows the opportunity for individuals to experience a variety of social experiences and social interactions. The intent of this section is merely to discuss socialization as it can occur in physical education, and not to make a case for great advances of the socialization of handicapped individuals due to physical education. Physical education instructors are advised to vary social situations and to provide opportunities for handicapped students to experience various aspects of human interaction.

Handicapped children often lack the ability to relate to others or to respond appropriately to a given social situation; this may be due, at least in part, to the lack of opportunity. Thus the physical educator must provide social situations and guide those needing assistance through the variety of social experiences available in physical education. Handicapped children must learn to interact appropriately and be able to handle a variety of social situations. Examples of appropriate interaction include the following:

1. Demonstrating cooperative behavior (e.g., as a team member in tug of war) (see Figure 17-7).
2. Not withdrawing from the situation, nor exhibit-

Figure 17-8. Participation in modified athletic events, such as this shot-put, is a rewarding culmination of a good physical education program.

ing acting-out behavior (e.g., by staying with the team or activity).

3. Exercising self-control (e.g., by not losing one's temper or acting out).

4. Showing the ability to follow as well as lead (e.g., be captain, team member, lead warm-up activities).

5. Demonstrating social awareness of others (e.g., looking out for another's safety, success).

6. Abiding by the rules.

7. Taking turns.

8. Being a gracious winner and loser (e.g., shaking hands with the other team).

9. Showing good sporting behavior.

As much as possible, handicapped students should be provided the opportunity to participate in one-to-one situations, as well as in partners or pairs, small groups, and large groups. If appropriate, the individual team competitive experiences can be valuable to the handicapped person. Opportunities for socialization include the following activities and experiences:

1. Experience winning and losing.

2. Participation as a member of a team.

3. Function in various leadership roles — captain, co-captain, leader of exercises or warm-up.

4. Participation in dance activities.

5. Participation in specific activities of taking turns, obeying rules, social confrontations, exercising self-control, social awareness of others, and so on.

6. Participation in class discussions of appropriate and inappropriate social behavior.

7. Nonparticipation in withdrawal, antisocial, or aggressive behavior.

AFFECTIVE LEARNING

Affective learning refers to changes or development in the child's emotional response to situations. This affective learning usually occurs in conjunction with changes in other areas of development, and increases in appropriate social behavior are often concomitant with affective development.

Often, the first noticeable changes in the behavior of handicapped students occur in the affective domain. Increased mental and physical ability often lead to increased confidence, more assertive behavior, and increased feeling of self-worth. Although the primary goal of physical education for the handicapped is not to increase affective development, it is frequently a by-product. It is important to note that changes in a student's confidence, self-concept, and self-worth can and do occur often, and are influenced by the physical education experience.

The old adage "nothing succeeds like success" is applicable here: success in physical education activities breeds emotional growth (increased self concept, confidence, and self-worth) as well as fostering development in the motor domain. Handicapped children, in general, fail more often than they succeed. Thus care must be taken to ensure some measure of daily success. It must not be done at the expense of growth or challenge, however; there is much to be learned in and by failure, even for the handicapped.

The handicapped child needs a modicum of structure and routine that allows for a feeling of security and success. Eventually, structure and routine must give way to change, challenge, and additional demands. The handicapped child must be able to adapt to change and to accept challenges, for it is in this process that development and learning take place.

One of the greatest results of physical education programming is the handicapped student who wants to, can and will actively participate in physical activity, who seeks out and accepts challenges, and who feels confident and worthwhile as an individual. A positive physical education experience tends to increase the chances of this occurrence and to enhance growth in the affective domain (see Figure 17–8).

SUMMARY

Educational experiences in other than the motor domain can be provided through physical activity. Utilizing movement as the medium, cognitive learning can be reinforced, language development encouraged, socialization experienced, and opportunities for affective learning created. For effectively planning programs for the whole child, cognitive, social, language, and affective developmental experiences should be and can be easily incorporated into the physical education setting.

BIBLIOGRAPHY

Cratty, B. J. *Active Learning.* Englewood Cliffs, New Jersey: Prentice-Hall, 1971.

Cratty, B. J. *Coding Games.* Denver, Colorado: Dove, 1980.

Cratty, B. J. *Physical Expressions of Intelligence.* Englewood Cliffs, New Jersey: Prentice-Hall, 1972.

Graham, G., Holt/Hale, S. A., McEwen, T., and Parker, M. *Children Moving: A Reflective Approach to Teaching Physical Education.* Palo Alto, California: Mayfield, 1980.

Hackett, L. C. *Movement Exploration and Games for the Mentally Retarded.* Palo Alto, California: Peek Publications, 1970.

Hackett, L. C., and Jensen, R. G. *A Guide to Movement Exploration.* Palo Alto, California: Peek Publications, 1967.

Humphrey, J. H., and Sullivan, D. D. *Teaching Slow Learners Through Active Games.* Springfield, Illinois: Charles C. Thomas, 1970.

Kiphard, E. J. ``Behavioral Integration of Problem Children Through Remedial Physical Education.'' *JOHPER* 41(4) (1970): 45–47.

Learning to Move – Moving to Learn. Los Angeles: Los Angeles City Schools, Division of Instructional Planning and Services. Publication No. EC–260, 1968.

Mosston, M. *Teaching Physical Education.* Columbus, Ohio: Charles E. Merrill, 1966.

Part Four

Toward Fruition of the Developmental Approach

18

The Team Approach: Working with Educational Personnel

Guiding Questions

1. What are some differences between multidisciplinary, interdisciplinary, and cross-disciplinary approaches to serving the handicapped?
2. According to PL 94-142, who *must* serve on the multidisciplinary team?
3. What are some communication skills important to the success of multidisciplinary interaction?
4. What are some human qualities important for effectively providing service to the handicapped?
5. What are some emerging roles for the adapted physical educator?

THE TEAM APPROACH

Professionals involved in implementation of the Education for All Handicapped Children Act, PL 94-142, are well aware of the demands in this law for interdisciplinary interaction. Not only are new structures for professional interaction mandated by this legislation, new concepts for the intermeshing of professional services are also having to be considered. The team approach is not new to the larger arena of service delivery to handicapped individuals. Teams have been dealing with the special needs of handicapped individuals for many years. These teams have emanated from the medical model, such as the acute-care treatment team of doctor, nurse, and medical-social worker. In education, however, the team approach is relatively new, at least in its present form. In regard to this approach, various and often confusing terms have been used: cross-disciplinary, interdisciplinary, and multidisciplinary have frequently been used in educational contexts without clear distinction.

Cross-disciplinary is often used to refer to the "mixing" of job roles, and frequently refers to the style with which services are delivered in a specific context. For example, the physical therapist may be primarily responsible for moving the student's limbs through various ranges of motion (called ROM). The therapist may teach the techniques to the classroom teacher or physical educator, thus enabling the student to have opportunities to be moved through a range of motion more frequently than the one or two times per week physical therapy services are delivered. This does not mean that the classroom teacher or the physical educator are delivering physical therapy, but that they have helped to extend the services and objectives of the therapist. Similarly, the classroom teacher may teach the physical therapist techniques for soliciting language from the child. In this way, while receiving physical therapy, the youngster is continuing to get the same kind of stimulus and feedback for initiating language as is received in the classroom. As a further example, the adapted physical educator may teach the generalist to "pattern" a student through a throwing pattern in a regular physical education class. This does not mean the generalist is teaching adapted physical education, but that he or she is using a technique not commonly used in the regular class.

Interdisciplinary is a term usually used to refer to the interaction and meshing of ideas among professionals and between disciplines. It usually does not imply that the professionals teach one another specific techniques used primarily in their own discipline; rather, it means that they interact in such a way as to be aware of the goals and objectives each has for the child so that they can mesh their own efforts, goals, and objectives to provide a package of services that complement each other. If the classroom teacher is using a secondary reinforcer such as stars for reinforcing desirable behavior, the physical educator should be using the same system in reinforcing the same behaviors in the physical education class. The goal of the interdisciplinary approach is to strive for all professionals to work in concert with one another and not seek goals for the student that are contrary to those of another professional.

Multidisciplinary means that there are many disciplines involved in the service delivery process. This broader term may apply to those specific contexts in which a cross-disciplinary style is being used, and certainly suggests that interdisciplinary interaction would be important. From the onset of the service delivery process, PL 94–142 requires that, "The evaluation . . . [be] made by a multidisciplinary team . . ." (U.S. Office of Education: Federal Register 1977: Section 121a.532[e]), and then suggests areas for evaluation having implications for the inclusion of myriad professionals. The regulations further imply the interaction of groups of personnel at least yearly for the purpose of reviewing and revising each child's individualized

education program (Section 121a.343[d]); and at least every three years for reevaluation (Section 121a.543[b]).

Thus the law *requires* that many professionals give input into the plan designed for each student's education, yet does not require that all professionals involved cooperate with one another in carrying out that plan. Certainly, there are many contexts in which the cross-disciplinary style would be desirable and most appropriate for delivering services; but, at the very least, interdisciplinary interaction must take place. Thus a section of this chapter is devoted to the discussion of skills needed for this successful interaction.

THE MULTIDISCIPLINARY TEAM

Although the cross-disciplinary style and interdisciplinary interaction imply a rather informal series of contacts among professionals, the multidisciplinary team, as defined by law, must formally hold meetings at times specified in the earlier cited regulations. These meetings, though often including many more professionals, must by law include the following participants (see Figure 18–1):

1. A representative of the public agency, other than the child's teacher, who is qualified to provide, or supervise the provision of, special education.
2. The child's teacher.
3. One or both of the child's parents.
4. The child, where appropriate.
5. Other individuals at the discretion of the parent or agency (U.S. Office of Education: Federal Register 1977: Section 121a.344[a]).

If the student has only motor deficits and would be referred from a regular class, the physical education generalist or classroom teacher would be the child's teacher and the adapted specialist should be the "representative . . . qualified to provide . . . special ed-

Figure 18-1. The multidisciplinary team must include at least a special educator, the student's teacher, one or both parents, and sometimes the child. Here, the physical educator is providing the special education service.

ucation." The physical educator and/or the adapted physical educator would be one of those "other individuals" included on the team as a part of the evaluation process in instances in which the child is to be assessed in all areas related to the suspected disability, which includes motor abilities (U.S. Office of Education: Federal Register 1977: Section 121a.532[e]). Once the child has been placed in adapted physical education, then the adapted physical educator would continue to be a part of the multidisciplinary team through the reevaluation and review process. One of the major challenges for the adapted physical educator is to make the contributions of physical education to the growth and development of students who have special needs well known to the other professionals on the multidisciplinary team, and to have a thorough enough understanding of the roles of other professionals on the team so that physical education's contribution can be articulated in a meaningful way to the parents and other professionals involved. The physical educator knows better than any other person on the team, the scope of contributions made to the growth and development of children by a well-planned physical education program.

Probable Team Members

Of the mandated members of the multidisciplinary team, the special educator and the child's regular classroom teacher, or counselor at the secondary level, are the only services to consistently be delivered. Since physical education is a direct service under PL 94–142, the adapted physical educator should be one of the special educators and a regular member of the team. Those "other individuals at the discretion of the parent or agency" will vary, depending on each student's disability and educational needs. The following section includes discussion of those professionals most commonly employed in the schools and, hence, most likely to be included on the multidisciplinary team. These professionals include the nurse, occupational therapist, physical therapist, psychologist, special educator, and speech-language pathologist.

Nurse

The field of nursing provides a wide range of services, and includes many individuals delivering nursing services who have a variety of training and credentials. A professional nurse or RN is a graduate of a four-year college program and is registered (licensed) in at least one state. Technical nurses have completed a two-year training program, and practical nurses have completed a one-year program. Although they are seldom seen in schools, hospitals and extended care facilities also have nurse aides or assistants on staff. These paraprofessionals are not licensed, and their training is usually provided at the facility at which they are working or some similar facility. The level of training and licensing of nurses dictates what services they can deliver. Most nurses found in the schools are RNs, and an increasing number are receiving additional training to become Nurse Practitioners. Nurse Practitioners are licensed to give medical examinations, and to order diagnostic tests and medications. The level of training and licensing for practicing nursing in the public schools is determined by each state's Board of Education.

Occupational Therapist

Occupational therapy is an applied health service concerned with the quality of daily living from birth to death. Its primary mode of treatment is based on the belief that one can influence one's own state of health through a balance of work, play, education, self-care, and home management (Reilly, 1962). Many occupational therapists (OTs) have also received additional training in sensory integration therapy. All modes of treatment delivered by the OT are based on the interdisciplinary study of the biological, behavioral, social, and medical sciences and services. The primary function of OTs in the schools is to work with the student, family, medical, and educational personnel to achieve the goals of remediation or rehabilitation of deficits impairing daily activities; prevention of the deterioration and/or loss of function; and the development and maintenance of functions and skills necessary for age-appropriate activities. Often, the OT is called upon to assist with fitting students with wheelchairs and other orthotic aids, based upon needs identified in the performance of daily work, play, education, and self-care activities.

Physical Therapist

Physical therapy is the treatment of the sick and disabled by using physical modalities such as heat, cold, light, water, electricity, massage, ultrasound, exercise, and functional training on the prescription of a physician. The physical therapist (PT) primarily treats individuals who have neuromuscular, muscoloskeletal, cardiovascular, and respiratory disorders that contribute to deficits in strength, endurance, balance, coordination, sensation, and joint range of motion. Measurements taken by the PT include muscle function and strength of individual muscles (muscle testing); posture and gait analysis; goniometry (range of motion); electrophysiological testing (electrical stimulation of nerve and muscle tissue); electromyography (measurement of muscle action potential); presence of abnormal muscle tone and action; and vital signs. Physical therapists are licensed by examination in each state and the American Physical Therapy Association.

Either the occupational therapist or physical therapist may also measure extremity girth and length, sensory perception, sensorimotor ability, abnormal motor patterns and reflexes, and general or specific body function. The physical educator should find out which of the above mentioned services the PT and OT are equipped to perform for students in each local educational agency.

Psychologist

Psychology is rooted in the behavioral sciences, and the psychologist is a scientist practitioner whose services are used in nearly every human service context and school program imaginable. The programs requiring the presence of a psychologist vary from state to state, as do the licensing or certification requirements. The field of psychology has grown in scope and acceptance over the last thirty years to include services such as psychotherapy, behavior modification (management), diagnostic evaluation, teaching, research, and career counseling. The psychologist is often a good resource for the physical educator in substantiating suspicion of neurological soft signs, perceptual-motor, and sensory system dysfunctions.

Special Educator

The special educator, like the physical educator, tends to focus on the acquisition of strategies of learning, problem-solving, attitudes, values, intelligent and active citizenship, lifelong competence, human awareness, health, and recreational habits. The special educator, however, like the regular classroom teacher, uses different materials and modes for achieving these shared goals. The physical educator can obtain a great deal of information and help from the special educator, since the special educator often spends three to five hours per day with a youngster (in contrast to the thirty to sixty minutes spent by the physical educator). Information such as effect of the learning environment on learning, attention span, appropriate group size, adaptive behavior, interaction styles, learning mode preferred, cognitive level, effective reinforcement, and unique factors affecting a student at any point in time can be obtained through effective communication with the special educator.

Speech-Language Pathologist

It is estimated that one in twenty children reach school with hearing handicaps, one in ten have speech handicaps, and one in twenty have handicaps in language structure, grammar, and vocabulary (Weiss and Lillywhite, 1976). It is therefore quite common to find speech-language pathologists on the staff of nearly every school district in the nation. The speech-language pathologist deals with disorders of language comprehension, language expression, speech production, rhythm, voice quality, and hearing. These professionals may carry different titles in various districts, including speech correctionists, speech pathologists, communication therapists, and communicalogists. The Legislative Council of the American Speech and Hearing Association (ASHA) has officially adopted speech-language pathologist as the official title for these professionals (Healy and Dublinske, 1977). ASHA grants certification of clinical competence (CCC) for delivering clinical services, which specifies different requirements for speech pathology than audiology; however, each state sets its own requirements for delivering services in the public schools.

REQUIREMENTS FOR INTERDISCIPLINARY INTERACTION

As stated earlier, current legislation requires that many professionals be involved in determining the educational program for students who have special needs, and serve as contributing members of the multidisciplinary team. In order to serve effectively in the best interests of the student, it is necessary that the physical educator not only understand the needs of the whole child, but be able to interact effectively across disciplinary boundaries. Interaction skills are not commonly stressed in teacher preparation programs. Thus the following section is devoted to identifying some of the skills and qualities needed in order to interact effectively in the interdisciplinary arena and on the multidisciplinary team.

To anyone who has worked with individuals who have special needs, it is clear that serious learning problems transcend the knowledge of any one individual or profession. As pointed out by Landreth, ``A multi-faceted disability presents a complexity which must be matched with nothing less than multi-faceted remediation, the kind of remediation that only a team approach can provide'' (Landreth, 1969:83). Under PL 94–142, in which the intent is to provide the most appropriate education in the least restrictive environment, the collective opinion of a team should be far more prudent than the opinion of any single professional working in isolation.

Other advantages of the interdisciplinary approach are reaped by the team members themselves. Creative approaches and professional commitment tend to be enhanced by the team interaction (Christoplos and Valletutti, 1977:6). Vital information for the efficacy of adapted physical education, such as attending behavior, effective reinforcers, desirable practices for the use of orthotic devices, and much more, can come from quality interdisciplinary interaction. Furthermore, the responsibility for decisions having ethical implications is shared by team members, bringing professionals closer together in the kindred commitment that disabilities do not occur in isolation (Landreth, 1969:83).

Communication: The Prerequisite

As stated by Valletutti and Christoplos (1977:1):

Interdisciplinary communication is prerequisite to the interdisciplinary cooperation needed to identify goals for [students] and to prescribe treatment priorities, sequences, strategies, implementation processes, materials, and evaluative procedures. Sharing interdisciplinary information is an initial step toward providing a mechanism through which the collective wisdom of individual interdisciplinary team members may be marshalled for the purpose of arriving at the most logical, productive, and efficient means to remediate the difficulties that [students] experience.

Although these and other authors agree that interaction skills among team members are critical, they are rarely incorporated into the training skills of profes-

sionals who participate on multidisciplinary teams. The development of awareness, knowledge, and skill in group dynamics should be prerequisite for participation on a team. If the needed skills are not possessed by school personnel serving on the multidisciplinary team, the acquisition of needed skills should be made possible through inservice training sessions provided by the educational agency. Funds for the purpose of providing personnel development are made available through Public Law 94–142.

Communication implies shared meaning. Communication skills that are most critical in interdisciplinary interaction include (1) reflective listening, (2) observing nonverbal communication, (3) congruent message sending, and (4) resolving the angle of a dilemma.

Reflective Listening

Reflective listening is an important skill to develop, because it allows the speaker to get feedback from the listener indicating that the meaning of what was said is clear. A reflective listener summarizes and restates the concepts presented by the speaker to assure the speaker of having been heard. This technique further encourages the speaker to add information to the basic statements, because the restatement or paraphrase tells the speaker that the meaning is being shared. Reflective listening will not be used all the time in a team meeting, but is invaluable when any speaker feels the message is not being heard and understood.

If skills for reflective listening are common among team members, a typical interaction may sound like this:

(Speaker):	''Anytime we try to have a group game, Michael fights and gets angry and wants to quit the game.''
(Listener):	''Michael doesn't function well in a group.''
(Speaker):	''That's right, but when we play games

such as foursquare or handball he performs well and his skills are about the same as the other children's."

(Listener): "He functions better in small groups."

(Speaker): "Yes. He also does very well when I help him at his desk in the classroom, but when he gets into the reading group he starts acting silly."

(Listener): "He seems to lose control of his behavior when he's in a group."

(Speaker): "Yes. I think he should be placed in a smaller class. We should implement a behavior modification program until he can function more consistently in a regular-sized class."

(Listener): "I agree."

It is not uncommon for professionals using this technique to ask to be "reflected" or have their ideas restated, if they believe the listener is not hearing the meaning of their message (Cornish et al., 1977). A typical statement would be, "I think I understand what you are saying (after reflectively listening), now I need to be sure that you understand my position on the kind of context in which I think Michael could learn best. Would you reflect my ideas?" If all team members are competent in the use of this technique, far more communication can take place in considerably less time than is usually required for team meetings.

Observing Nonverbal Communication

A second skill needed by team members is the ability to observe and respond to the nonverbal elements of communication. Kinesics, or the body language of the speaker, enhances the verbal part of the message considerably. A speaker who leans forward, gestures strongly, or has very animated facial expressions, communicates differently than one who leans back with arms folded and is expressionless (Birdwhistle, 1970).

The physical distance between members of the team can also enhance or stifle group communication. In our culture, physical closeness during communication represents trust and commonality. Team members who are not willing to sit next to one another, or who pull their chairs away from the group, may be demonstrating a lack of trust or feeling of cohesiveness with the group. Individuals with a larger personal space may consistently move away in any context, but this pattern can easily be distinguished from a lack of trust. Even the location in the group represents various positions of power and either encourages or suppresses communication. At a rectangular table, the ends and the middle of the sides of the table are stronger positions and most conducive to communication, because they allow for full eye contact with all members present. These are also the positions of power. This is why the chairman of the board of corporate directors sits at the end of the table and is in a position to have the full, undivided attention of all board members present. The corner positions tend to be the weakest, because people in those positions are closer than the accepted range of comfortable interpersonal communication with individuals in the stronger positions; hence, their ability to take the leadership may be limited. Knowing where one feels most comfortable in a group structure and what position will most enhance one's ability to communicate is something professionals in adapted physical education should plan before going into a multidisciplinary team meeting.

Vocal intonation used by the speaker is another aspect of nonverbal communication that should be understood by team members. The volume of speech is a quality with nearly universal meaning; but the inflections implying certainty, commitment, and competence must be understood as well. Communication is far more likely to take place when a team member states, "My assessment is really not conclusive," than it is if the member implies the same message by presenting scores in a faltering voice.

Congruent Message Sending

A third competency needed for interdisciplinary functioning is congruent message sending (Cornish, 1977). This refers to the agreement between the verbal and nonverbal aspects of the message. For example, we may be greeted by an acquaintance with the familiar question, "How are you today?" while it is obvious from nonverbal clues that the speaker does not really want to know! Jargon or technical language should never be used unless clearly defined. "Specialized language must not be an indirect way of saying, 'Stay out of my domain!'" (Valletutti and Christoplos, 1977:5), but often is. The adapted physical educator should be aware that this form of communication is a real possibility, and should not be afraid to ask to have words defined. Likewise, in communicating information relative to motor performance, terms should be defined as much as possible and the professional integrity shown by professionals and others who ask for other terms to be clarified should be respected. There is nothing more frustrating than to give an entire assessment report and have a parent say, "I didn't understand a word you said."

Team members must be sensitive to the congruence between the verbal and nonverbal aspects of their messages in order to be credible parts of a multidisciplinary team. Such factors as being organized for the meeting and having each student's performance levels clearly in mind lend credibility and foster communication.

Resolving the Angle of a Dilemma

The angle of a dilemma is reached when team members have differing opinions on the solution to a problem. Resolving the angle of a dilemma (Cornish, 1977) incorporates all the skills just discussed. Reflective listening is needed to allow each speaker to totally explain his or her point of view and rationale for suggested solutions. Then an objectively determined list of possible solutions to the problem can be made, with each team member making a contribution. The group can prioritize the list into the most desirable, practical, or feasible solutions, until a decision is reached to which all team members can agree. If this is not possible, any team member, including the parent, can sign the IEP form in disagreement with the team decision and the rationale for dissent can be stated. Under PL 94–142, however, there are so many alternatives available for meeting the needs of handicapped students that, with effective communication, almost all problems can be resolved.

Multidisciplinary team members should be viewed as individuals who have insights and skills that are necessary to the team's functioning, rather than as representatives of a given profession. To infer that all physical therapists respond in some particular way makes no more sense than to imply that all physical educators are obsessed with competition. "Interdisciplinary intervention demands a rare virtue in human interaction—the ability to cooperate among individuals who represent different professional orientations and training experiences" (Peters, 1977:149). It should be realized that the skills for effective interdisciplinary interaction must be based on some definable human qualities; but "To fail to communicate . . . information that is pertinent and jargon-free is to fail the purposes of [a multi-disciplinary] team" (Peters, 1977:149). Thus each of these skills previously discussed should be built upon the fundamental human qualities each professional brings to the learning environment.

Human Qualities

Several authors have listed "human qualities" or "behavioral characteristics" that purport to be descriptive of either effective communicators or ineffective communicators. *Effective communicators* have been characterized by openness and security, good will, a sense of humor and freedom from status bias, a substantial degree of self-confidence, and minimal defensiveness (Landreth et al., 1969:87; Valletutti and Christoplos, 1977:3–5), and "an accepting and understanding attitude toward members on a staff conference team" (Fitzsimmons, 1977:282). Bass (1970) indicated that effective communicators show solidarity, make comments that raise the self-esteem of others, give help and reward, help relieve tension by laughing and joking, and nonverbally demonstrate agreement, acceptance, concurrence, and satisfaction. In general, an effective communicator has human qualities of openness, supportiveness, sincerity and security.

In contrast, *ineffective communicators* have been characterized as defensive, manipulative, nonempathetic, nonaccepting, disagreeable, rejecting, withholding help, withdrawing, showing antagonism, discounting others, derisive, hypocritical, and insecure (Gibb, 1970; Fitzsimmons, 1977; Bass, 1970). Interaction in which these elements are present usually results in a lack of meaningful input and, often, a decision in which the child's best interests are not the focal point of discussion.

In learning skills for effective interdisciplinary interaction, the physical educator must consider what natural, human qualities are brought to the communication setting. Important questions to ask include: What kind of communicator am I? Am I open or defensive, supportive or derisive, sincere or hypocritical, secure or insecure? Most people are somewhere in the middle of these continuums. Based on this introspection, the physical educator would do well to begin working on improving in those areas which are weakest.

Additional desirable human qualities that contribute less directly to effective team membership go much deeper in the educator's personality than those mentioned above. These include love of children, kindness, gentleness, sensitivity to others, tolerance, flexibility, empathy (not sympathy), enthusiasm, consid-

eration, thoughtfulness, and patience. Whether these qualities can be acquired or not is debatable. Through self-evaluation, honesty, and a concerted effort to demonstrate behaviors that indicate the above qualities are present, they can be developed to some extent. Future physical educators who have none of these qualities would do well to reevaluate their career goals.

THE ADAPTED PHYSICAL EDUCATOR AS A RESOURCE PERSON

The role of the adapted physical educator is changing from being a direct service provider to delivering services indirectly by consulting or serving as a resource to other teachers or a combination of these roles. It is one matter to have the skills for teaching children skillfully, and another matter to be able to instruct, guide, and consult with other professionals who may themselves be providing the physical activity experiences for children. Many states have implemented the so-called "consultant model" or have cast adapted physical educators in roles as "resource teachers or specialists" (see Figure 18–2). As more children are appropriately placed in the mainstream of physical education, adapted physical educators may find themselves delivering service to only the most severely handicapped students in the school and advising classroom teachers or generalists in physical education on appropriate programming for mildly handicapped students in their classes.

Functioning as a resource person requires near mastery of the knowledge base known as adapted physical education. This does not mean that such people have all the knowledge stored away in their heads, but that they have a high level of understanding of the field and know where to go to get the rest. A good library, or the knowledge of what materials and resources are available in the school district or commu-

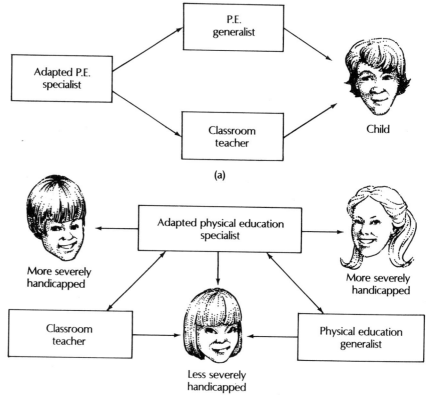

Figure 18-2. The consultant model: the adapted physical education specialist as a resource person (a); the adapted physical education specialist delivering direct and indirect services (b).

nity is a necessity. Having a good personal library, appropriate to the population to be served, is very helpful. A good set of human resources is invaluable, and includes what journalists call a "tickler file" of names, phone numbers, and addresses of people who can be called upon to answer specific questions within the purview of their job roles. Usually these human resources will be found within the local educational agency, but professionals at the regional or state levels as well as in public and private agencies should not be overlooked. Professional organizations such as the American Association for Health, Physical Education, Recreation, and Dance (AAHPERD) as well as many other agencies and organizations (see Chapter 19) should be surveyed for materials, resource lists, bibliographies and other useful suggestions. Professional conferences and conventions often provide opportunities for gathering resources. Speakers at such meetings often can be added to a systematic file of

names and addresses of those whose expertise may be needed in the future.

Having the interpersonal skills for communication that were discussed earlier in this chapter is indeed a necessity for success as a resource person. Reflective listening is an especially good tool to use to allow the classroom teacher or generalist the opportunity to add any information deemed necessary to obtain the help needed on a given student or problem. The resource person should reflect, paraphrase, or summarize the information before giving an opinion or suggestion. The following is an example of an interaction between a generalist in physical education (G) and an adapted physical education resource specialist (A):

G: "Patty is cerebral palsied and is in my swimming class. Although she can stand on the bottom of the pool, she doesn't seem to have enough muscle control and total body control to get her hips up to float in supine."

A: "She can support her weight standing but she can't float."

G: "That's right. When she tries to float in supine, her hips and legs sink so she's almost floating in an L-shaped position."

A: "Her legs and hips sink, then."

G: "Yes."

A: "Have you tried tying any floatation devices to her ankles?"

G: "No. Do you mean inflatable cuffs?"

A: "Yes, or styrofoam cylinders."

G: "No, I haven't, but we have them so I'll try that."

With a large repertoire of experience, creative ideas, and resources, the adapted specialist could be threatening to other professionals and very easily could fall into a series of "why don't you; yes, buts" by suggesting a technique or procedure before all the information has been gathered. Example:

G: "Patty, the cerebral palsied student in my swimming class, can't float in prone."

A: "*Why don't you* have her try it from a supine float first?"

G: "*Yes, but* she can't float in supine either."

A: "Well, then, *why don't you* put a life vest on her for a while until she learns to relax."

G: "*Yes, but* her trunk is no problem, it's her legs that sink."

A: "Oh, then, have you tried floatation devices on her legs?"

G: "No, but I can."

Although this discourse may not seem to be any more time consuming than the prior interchange, eventually this type of interaction can become very frustrating and irritating. Once a relationship between two professionals becomes strained, it is very difficult to recover a positive communication setting for future contacts. Skillful communicators are not only more productive and efficient, they are also more comfort-

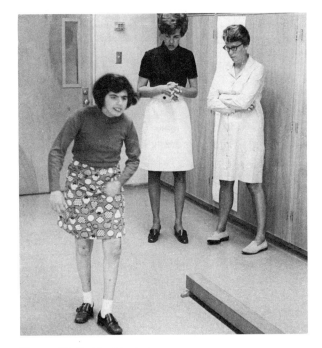

Figure 18-3. The physical educator consults with the classroom teacher about a student's progress. SOURCE: Photo by Lyonel Avance.

able in their working relationships with other professionals (see Figure 18-3).

Asking questions in order to get more information is another technique for gathering information for making suggestions. Sometimes a very vague introduction to a child is given the adapted physical education specialist, such as "I have this child in my class who can't . . . ." The adapted specialist may need the teacher presenting this case to report some *observable* behaviors before any suggestions can be made, and should ask questions such as:

1. What *does* the child *do* when he can't . . . ?
2. What does the child *look* like when he runs (walks, hops, and so on)?
3. How old is he (or she)?
4. Is there any diagnosed disability?
5. Can you characterize the child's language? social skills? intellectual functioning?

By asking questions, the specialist can get a more

global picture of the child, and can fill in information about the child's performance that will help in solving the problem. Here is an example:

G: "I have a girl in one of my classes who can't skip."

A: "How old is she?"

G: "Ten."

A: "What class is she in? Does she have a known disability?"

G: "Yes. She comes in with the first graders, but she's from the TMR class."

A: "Then she's probably functioning between five and six years old and, developmentally, even mentally normal children would only be learning to skip at that age."

G: "Oh. But all the other children can skip."

A: "Can she hop?"

G: "No."

A: "Can she balance on one foot?"

G: "No."

A: "It sounds to me like she needs to learn to balance on one foot and to hop first. Some games like 'Statues' or stunts such as the 'Stork Stand' could be used to work on balancing. Then get her into some activities requiring hopping, such as relays or obstacle courses, where you can build hopping into the game and give her and the other children a chance to practice the loco-motor patterns they have trouble with."

G: "Okay, I'll try that."

Obviously, this kind of interaction between specialist (resource person) and generalist (regular class teacher) is much more professional and productive than starting with a phrase like, "Well, anyone knows that children have to be able to hop before they can skip!" Emphasizing the role of *resource* over specialist will result in the adapted physical educator being consulted over and over again — as it should be.

Each professional should also be given the chance to "save face" if they don't know or perhaps have forgotten basic information. The specialist deals with information such as this every day; the generalist often does not. If all educators had the same store of knowledge as the specialist, then there would be no need for a specialist. By definition, the specialist is a person who has knowledge and skills that are different from and go beyond the knowledge and skills of the generalist. Sharing that knowledge and skill when the need arises simply fulfills the job role.

INSERVICE TRAINING

PL 94–142 not only requires that a plan of personnel development be approved at each level of educational administration annually, it also makes available federal money for this purpose. Adapted physical education specialists are being asked to participate in this program both by their supervisors and by other professionals with whom they work. This is a very important responsibility to be assumed by the adapted physical education specialist, since most professionals with whom they work rely on their own experience with physical education as it was "when they went to school" and very few, if any, were ever in an adapted physical education class. Therefore specialists should not expect their professional colleagues to somehow "intuitively know" what they are trying to accomplish in the adapted physical education program, why they are planning certain activities, and how they view their roles relative to others in the program. A well-analyzed, well-planned, well-rehearsed, and well-executed inservice training program in adapted physical education is all-important. The responsibility of the adapted specialist is to drive home the values of physical education to the growth and development of the students that are of mutual concern to the specialist and the inservice training audience (see Figure 18–4).

Figure 18-4. Using a student to demonstrate a traditional technique used in physical education classes is also effective in an adapted class.

Usually, a request for participation in inservice training will be specific. A topic may be precipitated by such questions as: "How do we know what students should be referred for testing for adapted physical education? How can I modify sports activities to include the students I have who are in wheelchairs? How do I go about planning activities to achieve the objectives I have written? How can I meet the needs of the three handicapped students I have when there are fifty others in the same class?" These sorts of questions will suggest very specific topics to be addressed in the inservice training meetings. Most school districts allow only one to three hours periodically for such meetings, so it is important to narrow the topic considerably. It would take a series of meetings to adequately cover all of the above questions. Such sessions usually come at the end of a school day and, like children, professionals can only absorb so much when they are tired. Also, it is a good idea to follow the old adage, "Tell them what you are going to tell them. Tell them. Then, tell them what you told them." In other words, time must be allowed to introduce the topic, cover it and summarize it. It is also a good idea to allow time for questions. Approximately 20 percent of the total time allowed is generally sufficient, and allows any specific

problems or questions relative to the topic to be answered without undue rush. Thus if one hour and fifteen minutes are allowed for the meeting, prepare about one hour of material and allow fifteen minutes for questions.

Audience Analysis

Most requests for inservice training by the adapted physical education specialist will pertain to professional performance. Each of the questions listed above asks "How do I *do* something?" relative to delivering physical education services to students who have special needs. Usually, questions dealing with legislative compliance, policies and procedures will be addressed by administrators or other district personnel.

For the first step in planning how to teach the audience how to *do* something relative to adapted physical education, the model of analyzing performance problems developed by Robert Mager and Peter Pipe (1970) helps to delimit or narrow the scope of choices. Although Mager and Pipe's problem-solving model is designed for industry, its application is thought to be relevant in education as well (see Figures 18-5 and 18-6).

Figure 18–5. Analyzing performance problems: a model for audience analysis. SOURCE: Robert Mager and Peter Pipe, *Analyzing Performance Problems, or, "You Really Oughta Wanna"* (Belmont, California: Fearon, 1970). Used by permission of Pitman Learning, Inc.

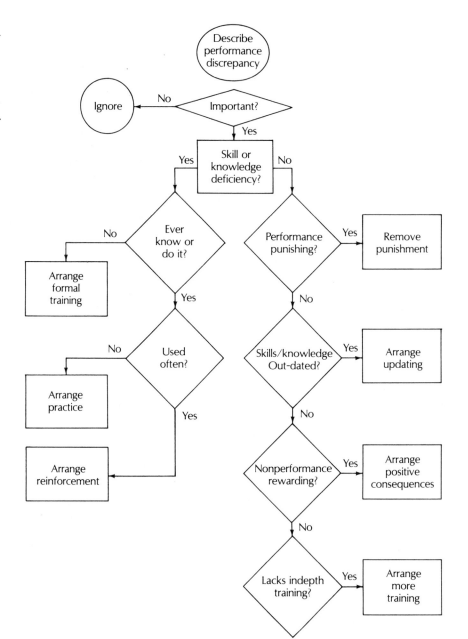

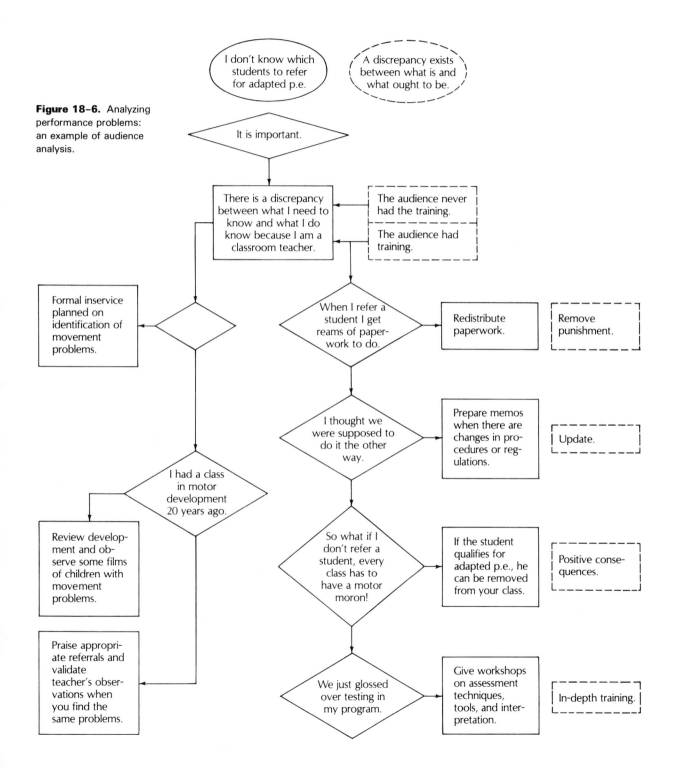

Figure 18-6. Analyzing performance problems: an example of audience analysis.

First, a clear dichotomy can be made in analyzing the audience using this model in determining whether or not the audience ever knew the material or had the skills. An audience of classroom teachers would not be expected to have had the same background as an audience of physical educators. It would be preferable to inservice these two groups separately on most topics. If the audience would not be expected to have ever had the skills to begin with, this would suggest a different approach than if they had had the skills and for some reason are not demonstrating them.

Usually, this situation would require that some foundational background be given in addition to the "how to's" of concern. For example: following the topic of "Identifying and Referring Students for Adapted Physical Education" may require some background on the significance of specific motor behaviors before the teachers can grasp the meaning of the behaviors they are observing. A child who lies on his arm to write at his desk, trips and falls often in the classroom, sometimes falls out of his desk, and is up out of his seat and moving around the classroom a lot may be viewed as incorrigible. If, on the playground, this same youngster heads for the swings and spends the entire recess time on them, but avoids other activity (especially with large groups), he may be manifesting a disorder of vestibular function. His constant swinging or avoiding, however, may not seem significant to a classroom teacher who does not understand a bit about how the functioning of this system underlies all motor behavior. Thus a brief background of the systems and mechanisms underlying motor performance would be needed in order for this audience to understand the meaning of the specific behaviors they would be asked to look for in making a referral.

In contrast, some physical educators who have had at least a brief introduction to the mechanisms of the inner ear as they affect balance may not use that information often and may need updating or a more in-depth coverage of the material, or perhaps they have not been reinforced for using it. The physical ed-

ucation generalist is also going to see the child described above in a different context than the classroom teacher, and thus would require different identifiable behaviors suggestive of vestibular system dysfunction. The adapted physical education specialist may need to ask some questions relative to the background and desired goals of the audience in order to be able to plan the most meaningful inservice, especially if the specialist is not particularly familiar with the personnel. Questions such as "How many people will be in the audience? What do they want to do with the information? What are their job roles? Backgrounds?" and so on are important pieces of information to have before planning the meeting.

Once the audience analysis has been completed, the topic should be narrowed to the three or four points (depending on the amount of time allotted) to be made in the presentation. In a one hour inservice session, it is difficult to adequately cover more than three or four skills or concepts. Just as in planning a physical education program for handicapped students, the specialist should identify the objectives to be accomplished; what should the audience be able to do or to know when they finish the session? Then, as in a task analysis, the specialist should determine what foundation is needed before they can grasp the skills or concepts to be taught. More than one session may be necessary. If this is not possible, the next best thing is to provide graphics such as diagrams, slides, film, video tapes, or articles for them to read after the presentation to help fill in the material not covered in the time allotted. The background material should be cut to the bare bones, if necessary, to allow ample time for the "how to's," which is really what they wanted in the first place.

Motivation

The next major step in planning the inservice meeting is to organize the material to be presented in a logical, interesting, and motivating sequence. The following five-step sequence for persuasion has worked successfully: (1) attention; (2) problem; (3) dissonance; (4) solution; and (5) action.

The first step requires the speaker to *get the audience's attention*. Without this, all will be lost. Telling a joke or humorous story is a favorite used by public speakers for centuries. "A funny thing happened to me on the way to school today" sounds a little stilted, but humor of some sort often relaxes the audience, establishes a feeling of warmth for the speaker, and sometimes helps to establish the credibility of the speaker as someone worth listening to. A shocking story, a sad story, or some other appropriate attention-getter would also be effective.

Stating the problem is to describe the discrepancy in performance. This is the reason for the presentation — the audience does not have some information or skills that they should have. Each person in the audience must be able to relate to the problem as "their" problem. Thus it is important for the speaker to be familiar with the context in which the members of the audience work. Are they classroom teachers? Do they teach special education classes? Do they have students in the mainstream? Are their handicapped students physically, mentally, emotionally, or language handicapped? Are they elementary, junior high, or high school students? These and many more questions need to be answered before the problem can be stated and examples given that are appropriate and meaningful to each person in the audience.

Once the speaker has the audience's attention and has made the problem "their" problem, the next step is to *create cognitive dissonance*. Dissonance refers to a lack of harmony, and this step creates in the audience a feeling of discomfort. To motivate the audience to do something about the problem, it is necessary to make them say to themselves, "This is not right," or "This problem should not be allowed to continue." For example: "If students do not get referred for testing and consideration for adapted physical education placement, it is possible that this service will not be made available for even the most severely handicapped students. It is not fiscally sound to keep a teacher to serve just a few students. Soon the district will find another way to deliver the service." Or: "Many students who are unsuccessful in regular physical education classes may have definite motor learning deficits. I cannot see all eight thousand students in the district, and therefore I need your help to identify them. Without your help, many youngsters who need special services will go on failing and hating physical education when perhaps a special program or a modified program can help them be successful."

Once the audience feels uncomfortable with the situation as it is, they will agree that a *solution to the problem* is in order and will be receptive to the points the speaker wants to make. The solution should be presented in a conceptual form first, in order to have a broad appeal and application to all situations in which the audience is working. For example: "In order to expedite referrals, we need to have a systematic way for each of you to gather data on your students, a standard form on which to record the information, and a designated way to route the referral form to me so I can get parental consent for testing."

The final step (and, in an inservice meeting, probably the step on which the most time is spent) is the *action* step — those "how to's" that the audience has been wanting all along. What kinds of motor behavior should they look for? In what context? At the beginning of each semester? When a student first enters their class? Monthly? These are all suggestions that will have to be addressed at this point. Perhaps the standard form, mentioned in the solution step, could take the form of a checklist (see Figure 18-7). As in Figure 18-7, listed behaviors can be checked or described. If the audience is fairly homogeneous — that is, teaching approximately the same type and age of student — the behaviors listed could be somewhat specific. If the audience is diverse, then perhaps a list of more global behaviors or more than one checklist for different educational levels will be necessary.

Figure 18–7. A checklist for identifying students who have special needs.

Name of student_____ Home room_____

Dear Teacher:

Below are some behaviors that, when present, may indicate that the student named above should be considered for Adapted P.E. Please check all that apply.

	Most of the time	Often	Some of the time
Cannot perform age-appropriate motor skills	_____	_____	_____
Has low fitness scores	_____	_____	_____
Has poor basic motor patterns	_____	_____	_____
Awkward and clumsy when moving	_____	_____	_____
Participates in group activities voluntarily	_____	_____	_____
Easily distracted	_____	_____	_____
Distracts others	_____	_____	_____
Accepts change of activity	_____	_____	_____
Follows directions	_____	_____	_____
Dresses for P.E. class	_____	_____	_____
Tires more easily than other students	_____	_____	_____
Uses free time for active play	_____	_____	_____
Performs tasks more slowly than others	_____	_____	_____
Prefers solo play	_____	_____	_____
Has indicated dislike for physical education	_____	_____	_____
Complains about well-being	_____	_____	_____
Has messy handwriting	_____	_____	_____
Pokes or hits classmates	_____	_____	_____

Please return this completed form to the adapted physical education teacher at your school.

Thank you.

Using Visual Media

The use of slides, film, video tape, diagrams, posters, and other such representations of concepts or procedures cannot be overvalued. Surely, it is possible to inundate the audience with meaningless, dissociated graphics; but a well-planned, tastefully executed media production can be dynamic. Educators tend to be good visual learners, and use of visual stimuli to demonstrate a point, underscore an idea, or clarify a procedure can be far more effective than an elaborate description. Visual images tend to last longer than do verbal images.

Media can be used, as mentioned earlier, to encapsulate material which the speaker may not have enough time to present verbally. "A picture is worth a thousand words" may not be totally true, but it certainly takes less time! Film, video tape, or slides of children falling, swinging and missing the ball, or standing by the corner of the school building alone, tell much more about the agony experienced by students who fail in motor activity than many speakers could ever describe. These media serve to involve the audience and can be used effectively throughout the inservice presentation.

When planning the use of media, it is helpful to map out a "story-board" — that is, to plan out what is to be said and which illustration will best represent that point. This should be done for every slide, diagram, or film footage to be used. A picture or descriptor of what will be seen by the audience should be included (see Table 18-1).

This method of planning the visual to accompany the narration, lecture, or comments should be used for every presentation that includes visual media. The visual should never go unsupported or unaccompanied by either narration or background music, unless there is a specific reason for doing so. People feel uncomfortable watching something without guidance as to what to look for, what they should be seeing, or what it is they are to get out of the visual experience.

Table 18-1. Story-board for a media presentation

Audio	Visual (slides)
Have you ever wondered about the challenges of the playground?	Long shot of playground with many children.
What do children face when trying to meet their needs to be part of the social structure known to us as free play?	Medium close-up of small group of children huddled together.
This jungle gym looks like part of Marine Corps training from the level of a five-year-old.	Close-up looking up at jungle gym from 3 feet above ground.
And to catch a ball under these conditions could drive a child back to the sandbox.	Long shot of airborne ball with children, etc. in background.

The audience should be exposed to each visual cue for at least four seconds in order for them to see the entire stimulus. Depending on the effect to be created, rapidly moving slides can create excitation and anxiety if advanced more than five every twenty seconds. Other illustrations such as posters or diagrams may need to be before the audience for several minutes, again depending upon what it is the audience is to get from them. Sometimes it is helpful to reproduce graphs, diagrams, and the like so each member of the audience can have a copy. In a lighted room, the members of the audience may feel more comfortable looking at their own copy and perhaps making notes on it during the lecture, rather than looking up at a screen and then down to a note pad. Anything with elaborate descriptions, such as an article, should not be distributed until the end of the session. Invariably, some of the audience will try to read it during the presentation—and there is nothing more disconcerting to a speaker than to be looking at the tops of everyone's heads!

Only one concept or fact should be presented in each illustration. This will keep the points of the presentation clear and easy to follow. If an illustration such as a slide of a group of students in activity demonstrates more than one point, a duplicate should be made and used at a different time. This should be done very carefully, by neutralizing the projector and rotating the carrousel to the specific slide to be used a second time. Avoid flipping back and forth between several slides. This is very amateurish, gives the appearance of disorganization, and—as a result of the intense, rapid visual stimuli—may actually create enough vestibular upset within the audience as to cause nausea.

INTEGRATING STUDENTS INTO REGULAR PROGRAMS

Once the unique needs of each student have been identified through the assessment process, it is a rather routine matter to match children on the basis of needs in order to form subgroups within a class for program planning. The following worksheet, used by one school district, shows how the various needs or weaknesses can be prioritized according to their frequency within a given class (see Figure 18–8).

Those two or three areas having the most frequency suggest the areas that should be the focus of the program. For example, if twenty out of thirty students in a regular physical education class have weaknesses in eye-implement coordination, bilateral control, and eye-hand coordination (as measured by this district's test), then possible activities in this secondary program could include archery, softball, golf, tennis, and table tennis. These are activities included in this district's state-approved curriculum, but other ac-

tivities could include racquet ball, handball, badminton, and the like. If these were the priority areas or areas of need within an elementary class, some sample activities would include foursquare, kickball, softball, steal the bacon, and similar games. Granted, the physical educator including students with special needs in the regular class may need to vary the environment, the activity, or teaching strategies. With practice, however, this can be easily done.

Analyzing the classroom teacher's or physical educator's need may require some observation of classes in addition to what the educator is able to verbalize. Earlier in this section, much discussion focused on getting the other professionals to reveal what they feel least comfortable doing—what they feel unprepared for. This may not be possible. In conducting an integrated program with students who have special needs, the teacher may not know what is going wrong, and may not be able to identify what it is that is causing the breakdown in a lesson. Adapted physical educators as resource persons must interact diplomatically, sensitively, and gently in order to make themselves available to teachers who need their help. Physical educators who come on strong can not only threaten the very people they intend to help, but can alienate them from receiving any services at all.

Providing follow-up to the teachers served in inservice training, consulting, or acting as a resource person is very important. As included in the model for audience analysis, continued performance of high quality is not likely to occur without at least one of the following elements: practice of skills/knowledges learned, reinforcement, updating, positive consequences for performance, and more training when needed. As Mager and Pipe (1970) discuss, many work settings actually reward nonperformance. Without the feedback and reward from a smile on a child's face, a successful wheelchair slalom, or a loving hug from a grateful Down's syndrome child, education could be nonrewarding as well.

Figure 18-8. Program planning worksheet.

Example #4

Pasadena Unified School District Secondary Schools

Program Planning Worksheet

School _____

Period _____

Tally the number of students in each class scoring 0 or 1 point on each of the ten test items below. Identify areas of greatest need by the number of students scoring low on any given item. Using two or more areas of need, follow those lines across until an "x" is found in both need areas under an activity area. The activity area at the top of the column is suggested for meeting the identified individual and group needs.

Tally the number of students in each class scoring 0 or 1 point on each of the ten test items below. Identify areas of greatest need by the number of students scoring low on any given item. Using two or more areas of need, follow those lines across until an "x" is found in both need areas under an activity area. The activity area at the top of the column is suggested for meeting the identified individual and group needs.

# Students	Performance area	Swimming	Rhythms	Stunts & tumbling	Dance	Archery	Four-square	Golf	Tennis	Basketball	Volleyball	Softball	Track & field	Weight lifting	Soccer	Football (modified)	Bowling	Batacas	Obstacle course	Table tennis	Table games
	Strength (Sit-ups)	X		X	X	X		X	X			X	X	X	X	X	X	X			
	Eye-implement coordination					X		X	X			X						X		X		
	Agility (Side-step)		X	X	X		X		X	X	X	X	X			X	X		X	X	X
	Bilateral control	X	X	X	X	X	X	X	X	X	X	X	X	X	X	X	X	X	X	X	X
	Eye-hand coordination					X	X	X	X	X	X	X				X	X			X	
	Balance (Beam)		X	X	X			X	X	X	X		X		X		X	X	X		
	Limb lower flexibility	X		X	X						X		X	X			X				
	Upper limb flexibility	X		X	X						X		X	X			X				
	Eye-foot coordination														X	X					
	Endurance	X			X			X	X			X	X		X		X				

SUMMARY

The multidisciplinary team provides for a pooling of information so that students can be given the most appropriate education for their needs. A core of individuals (including the special educator, the student's teacher, the parent, and the student) serves consistently on the team, with professionals representing special services as needed. Specific skills and a clear understanding of the role of each team member are needed to communicate in the multidisciplinary arena.

New roles are emerging for adapted physical educators as well as for other professionals. These new roles include: consulting, inservice training, and serving as a resource person. As these roles emerge, especially as implemented locally, the adapted physical educator must sense the responsibility for developing the needed skills to assure the best quality physical education programs for students who have special needs.

BIBLIOGRAPHY

Bass, B. "Group Effectiveness." In *Small Group Communication*, edited by R. S. Cathcart and L. A. Samoua. Dubuque: Wm. C. Brown, 1970.

Birdwhistle, R. L. *Kinesics and Context*. Philadelphia: University of Pennsylvania Press, 1970.

Christoplos, F., and Valletutti, P. J. "Education." In *Interdisciplinary Approaches to Human Services*, edited by F. Christoplos and P. J. Valletutti. Balitmore: University Park Press, 1977, pp. 81-92.

Cornish, R., et al. *Communication, Trust and Other Important Things — Pulling the Pieces Together*. San Jose, California: Office of the Santa Clara County Superintendent of Schools, 1977.

Davis, K. G., and Strasser, J. "Nursing." In Christoplos and Valletutti, *Interdisciplinary Approaches*, pp. 155-171.

Fitzsimmons, R. M. "Fostering Productive Interdisciplinary Staff Conferences." *Academic Therapy* 12(3) (Spring 1977): 281-287.

Gibb, J. R. "Defensive Communication." In *Small Group Communication*, edited by R. S. Cathcart, and L. A. Samoua. Dubuque: Wm. C. Brown, 1970.

Healey, W. C., and Dublinske, S. "Notes from the School Services Program." *Language, Speech and Hearing Services in Schools* 8 (1977): 67-71.

Hoffnung, A. S. "Speech, Hearing and Language Pathology." In Christoplos and Valletutti, *Interdisciplinary Approaches*, pp. 387-413.

Landreth, G. L., et al. "A Team Approach to Learning Disabilities." *Journal of Learning Disabilities* 2(2) (1969): 82-87.

Lansing, S. G., and Carlsen, P. N. "Occupational Therapy." In Christoplos and Valletutti, *Interdisciplinary Approaches*, pp. 211-236.

Latimer, R. M. "Physical Therapy." In Christoplos and Valletutti, *Interdisciplinary Approaches*, pp. 279-305.

Mager, R. F., and Pipe, P. *Analyzing Performance Problems, or 'You Really Oughta Wanna.'* Belmont, California: Fearon, 1970.

Peters, N. A. ''An Interdisciplinary Approach to the Assessment and Management of Severe Language-Learning Problems.'' In *Reading Problems: An Interdisciplinary Perspective*, edited by W. Otto, N. A. P, and C. W. Peters. Reading, Massachusetts: Addison-Wesley, 1977.

Reilly, M. ''Occupational Therapy Can Be One of the Great Ideas in Twentieth Century Medicine.'' *American Journal of Occupational Therapy* 16 (1962): 1–9.

United States Office of Education, *Federal Register* (42)163 (1977): 42474–42518.

Weiss, C. A., and Lillywhite, H. S. *Communicative Disorders*. St. Louis: C. V. Mosby, 1976.

Wellner, A. M. ''Psychology.'' In Christoplos and Valletutti, *Interdisciplinary Approaches*, pp. 337–355.

19   Beyond the Schoolyard Fence

Guiding Questions

1. Who are some of the professionals adapted physical educators are likely to encounter in the community, and what are their roles?
2. What are some local service organizations that could be approached for sharing their resources with the handicapped?
3. What are some private organizations that have emerged as a response to specific needs of the handicapped?
4. What are some sports organizations that provide opportunities for athletic competition for the handicapped?
5. What are some ways that communication about physical education can be maintained with the home?
6. How can volunteers be successfully used in the adapted physical education program?

The adapted physical educator is often called to reach beyond the educational environment for services that will enhance the education and growth of handicapped students. Services available in the school and various services in the community may be indicated for inclusion as related services on the IEP. Still other services, which may not qualify as related services, are available to complement the educational program. Related services, as defined in PL 94–142, Section 121a.13, are those "supportive services . . . required to assist a handicapped child to benefit from special education. . . ."

Regardless of whether specific services are indicated as related services, the adapted physical educator often has the occasion to interact with professionals delivering services to students outside the educational context, and with parents providing home activities. A brief overview is provided in this chapter of those disciplines that often impinge on the lives of handicapped students. They are presented here to give a representative sampling of the variety of services available, and to clarify the role of professionals involved in order to avoid duplication of services.

PROFESSIONAL SERVICES

Professional services may be available through government-supported agencies such as city, county, or state facilities, or by private agencies. Although often available at residential care facilities, this chapter will focus on those most commonly available to indi-

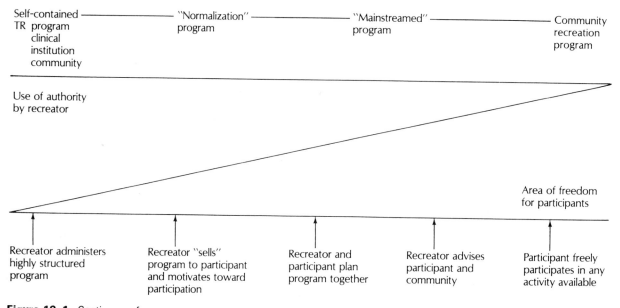

Self-contained ──────────────── "Normalization" ──────────────── "Mainstreamed" ──────────────── Community
TR program   program   program   recreation
clinical   program
institution
community

Use of authority
by recreator

Area of freedom
for participants

Recreator administers   Recreator "sells"   Recreator and   Recreator advises   Participant freely
highly structured   program to participant participant plan   participant and   participates in any
program   and motivates toward   program together   community   activity available
                         participation

Figure 19-1. Continuum of therapeutic recreation service. SOURCE: Cynthia Bertholf et al., "Therapeutic Recreation—A Continuum." In *Therapeutic Recreation, Its Theory and Practice,* edited by V. Frye and M. Peters (Harrisburg, Pennsylvania: Stackpole, 1972).

viduals with special needs who live in their own natural or foster homes and attend school in the public sector.

Therapeutic Recreation

Therapeutic recreation is a special service within the broad area of recreational services. It is a "process which utilizes recreation services for purposive intervention in some physical, emotional and/or social behavior to bring about a desired change in that behavior and to promote the growth and development of the individual" (Frye and Peters 1972).* Therapeutic

*Statement formulated at Ninth Southern Region Institute of Therapeutic Recreation, University of North Carolina, 1969. In Virginia Frye and Martha Peters, *Therapeutic Recreation: Its Theory, Philosophy, and Practice.* Harrisburg, Pennsylvania, Stackpole Books, 1972, p. 41.

recreation may take place anywhere along a continuum of service environments (see Figure 19-1). Thus therapeutic recreation programs may be found along the continuum from residential institutions and correctional facilities through and including the community environment. The goals of therapeutic recreation are the same as the habilitative or rehabilitative goals of the agency or institution in which the program takes place. Like adapted physical education, therapeutic recreation is a process that meets individuals at their levels of functioning and helps them gain greater independence and growth. All people with disabling conditions do not need therapeutic recreation; however, anyone needing habilitative or rehabilitative activities, whether on a permanent or temporary basis, can profit from therapeutic recreation. Thus programs are often provided for the aging, socially disadvantaged, mentally ill, and delinquent as well as for individuals typically found in categorical programs in the schools.

The commonality between adapted physical education and therapeutic recreation lies primarily in the medium of physical activities and the use of techniques of evaluation, goal planning, and activity analysis. In addition to physical activities, therapeutic recreation provides program activities that go beyond those typically included in physical education: creative arts, camping and outdoor recreation, hobbies, excursions, horticultural activities, social recreation, and table games. The variety of leisure services available to the recreation therapist includes diversional recreation — that which provides pleasure and satisfaction; adapted or modified activities — activity changes making it possible for the disabled person to participate; transitional programming, skill development, normalization, trips into the community and ''half-way'' programs; leisure education; increase in self-awareness; development of leisure attitudes, values, beliefs, knowledge, and skills; leisure counseling — a ''helping process that utilizes specific verbal facilitation techniques to promote awareness, understanding, and clarification of the individual's self . . .'' (Park and Annand, 1977:422). (See Figure 19-2.)

Regular communication with the recreation therapist in the community or residential facility can serve to complement or supplement the skills taught in the educational context. It may, however, become the responsibility of the adapted physical educator to make the initial contact with the recreation therapist or recreation program director in order to open lines of communication. Once this has occurred, a relationship may develop that will serve to meet the needs of individual students.

Dance Therapy

Dance therapy ''is a form of psychotherapy that makes use of movement and movement interaction as

Figure 19-2. Therapeutic recreation includes arts and crafts and other normalizing activities. SOURCE: Photo courtesy of City of Anaheim, Public Information Office.

Figure 19–3. This line dance is one of the more structured activities used in dance therapy. SOURCE: Photo courtesy of City of Anaheim, Public Information Office.

the bases for intervention" (Bunney, 1977:49). Dance therapists are often found in residential facilities and some private agencies; they are infrequently found in the schools. Their medium of human movement is closely related to at least one instructional element used in physical education: therapists encourage clients to move in their own way as an expression of inner feelings. This process is in contrast to the dance educator, who teaches skills and techniques.

Dance therapy capitalizes on the interrelatedness of mind and body and is often used to provide participants the opportunity to express themselves through movement rather than through verbalization. Emerging in the 1940s from the impact of World War II, dance therapy seeks to change one's self-concept, self-awareness, behavior, and interpersonal interactions, in addition to changing the body itself and providing opportunities for the release of tension and anxiety. In this process, the therapist serves as a catalyst and facilitator.

Dance therapy sessions, like physical education, begin with warm-up activities. During this time, the therapist assesses the group needs and rhythm. Unlike education, the activity portion of each session usually consists of movement experiences based on themes and the group's interaction and needs at that point in time. Often, the final part of each session strives toward resolution of conflict and restoration of the self-concept for each individual. Although dance, like recreation, can have therapeutic value for all people, dance therapy is primarily used in conjunction with psychotherapy for individuals who have emotional, social, or cognitive problems (see Figure 19–3).

Dentistry

Modern dentistry is moving toward the holistic approach, with greater emphasis on the interrelationships that exist between professionals, clients, families and the community. In addition to the traditional roles of restoration and prevention, students of dentistry are now being exposed to the handicapped during their training. Through the efforts of the American Fund for Dental Health, Academy of Dentistry for the Handicapped, National Foundation of Dentistry for the Handicapped, and the American Academy of Pedodontics, a closer relationship has developed among therapists, educators, and dentists. Dentists or dental hygienists often serve as part of a team in residential facilities. These professionals may also serve in a consultant role, educating parents and teachers on how to clean the oral cavity of physically handicapped children on a daily basis. They may also serve as resource personnel for teaching dental self-help skills. Although adapted physical educators may not be involved in teaching this skill progression, they are often involved in helping to develop requisite skills such as grasping, range of motion in the limbs to be used, and reinforcement of skills being taught by other professionals.

Pediatrics

Pediatrics is "that medical specialty which provides a broad scope of health care services to children from birth through adolescence" (Johnson, 1977:253). Numerous subspecialties in the area of children's medicine have emerged recently, and physical educators are likely to have contact with pediatric neurologists, developmentalists, cardiologists, and allergists. The main thrust in pediatrics is the prevention, diagnosis, and therapeutic threatment of childhood conditions. Pediatricians are becoming much more aware of the psychological and emotional impact on the educational functioning of children who have special needs. Thus communication between the adapted physical educator and the pediatrician is essential in understanding the impact of the child's condition on planned movement experiences.

Psychiatry

Modern clinical psychiatry is "that branch of medicine which is concerned with the genesis, dynamics, management and treatment of such disorders as undesirable functioning of the personality, as to distort either the subjective life of the individual, his relationships with others or with society" (Noyes and Kolb, 1958:1). The role of the psychiatrist has described an

ever-widening circle of influence in recent years. It has been projected that as many as 8 percent of the school-age population have a need at one time or another for psychiatric services. In addition to the traditional role of dealing with immaturity, disorganization, disintegration of personality, and psychopathology among the mentally ill, severely emotionally disturbed, and childhood psychotics and their families, psychiatrists are often called upon to intervene in other less classical circumstances: delinquency, aggressiveness, violence, child abuse, and teenage alcoholism and suicide, to name but a few. It is imperative that the adapted physical educator communicate with a child's psychiatrist and parents regarding methods of management and any mood-altering medication that may influence a student's motor performance.

OTHER SERVICES AVAILABLE IN THE COMMUNITY

Besides the medical services and therapies already mentioned in this chapter, other services encountered less frequently are also available in the community. These services are social work, rehabilitation counseling, art therapy, and music therapy. Because of the infrequency with which adapted physical educators come in contact with these professionals, their roles shall be discussed briefly. Physical educators who find themselves having more contact with these professionals are encouraged to seek further information regarding the role of each and their impact on the students with whom they work.

Social Work

Social workers assist people to enhance the quality of their lives in their social relationships. The social worker may be encountered as a regular staff member in the public schools, but more frequently serves in an as-

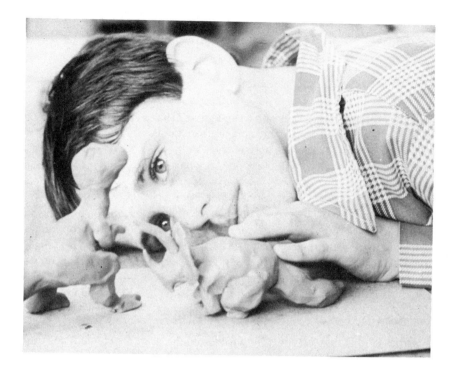

Figure 19-4. Clay is an excellent medium for use in art therapy.

sistive role in residential facilities and public agencies. The professional scope of the social worker's services ranges from providing substitute parental care, as in adoption or foster home placement, through intervention in child abuse, and psychiatric institute placement. Social workers are primarily advocates for the population they serve. Therefore, in serving children, the social worker may provide a variety of evaluative, brokerage, and intervention services.

Rehabilitation Counseling

Rehabilitation counseling was born in the late 1920s, following enactment of the Vocational Rehabilitation Act. It was evident, in the emerging milieu of therapeutic services, that a professional was needed to evaluate the needs of the client and coordinate the rehabilitation program. The rehabilitation counselor facilitates the rehabilitation process by purchasing services for the client, ranging from physical restoration to training and employment. Maintenance during rehabilitation, transportation, services to families, and learning aides

are also part of the rehabilitation counselor's role. For eligible clients, rehabilitation counselors provide follow-along contact to be certain that clients have, in fact, completed the rehabilitation program and are functioning adequately within the limits of their disabilities. Normally, these services would be available to older physically and mentally traumatized individuals.

Art Therapy

Art therapy, which emerged in the 1940s as a means of using art as a form of psychotherapy, is "the purposeful use of art to meet psychological needs . . ." (Ulman, et al., 1977:13). This form of therapy uses free association, and capitalizes on using "images produced [to] constitute symbolic speech" (Naumburg, 1958). As a complement to psychotherapy, art therapy provides an extension of psychoanalytic and interpretive techniques for allowing clients to reveal their inner feelings. Like imaginative play, it allows reality to be temporarily suspended; yet play is transient, and art produces a permanent product for the whole world to see. Thus art conveys, in a concrete way, the individual's relationship to fantasy (see Figure 19–4).

Music Therapy

Music has long been recognized for its curative potential and its effects on social, emotional, and physical behavior. An example of its passive effect is found in modern cinema, in background music carefully selected to influence the mood of the audience. Since the expansion of therapeutic services in the 1920s, music has enjoyed systematic, purposeful use as a therapeutic tool. Music may be used to affect mood and physical and physiological function, to provide a vehicle for expression, and to elicit behavioral changes. The music therapist may use such activities as passive listening (i.e., to calming or excitatory background music), active listening, dancing, singing, playing instruments, and song writing as vehicles for eliciting desired changes (see Figure 19–5).

COMMUNITY ORGANIZATIONS

In addition to the assessments and input provided the adapted physical educator from parents and other professionals, a vast set of resources is available among laypersons in the community. Such sources in-

Figure 19–5. Singing games that incorporate gestures are used in music therapy and also contribute to the development of fine motor control. SOURCE: Photo courtesy of City of Anaheim, Public Information Office.

clude service clubs, youth groups, sports, and private organizations. Adapted physical educators should tap these resources as much as possible in order to provide the greatest range of alternatives for their students. Using community organizations to provide human and monetary benefits can only serve to enhance the quality of the physical education program; taking advantage of sport and private organizational offerings can only serve to enhance the variety of the physical activity experiences.

Some of the following service clubs meet in nearly every community in the United States. Men's clubs include local chambers of commerce, Jaycees, Kiwanis, Knights of Columbus, Optimists, Lions, Rotary International, 20-30 Clubs, and YMCAs. Women's clubs include Altrusa, Soroptimists, Lady Jaycees, women's chambers of commerce, YWCAs, and local women's organizations. Youth groups include Assisteens, Boy Scouts and Girl Scouts, college and university sororities and fraternities, Kiwanettes, Letterman's clubs, and Rotary Annes.

These organizations may be sought out to provide a variety of services. Some clubs will endorse or sponsor a specific project on a regular basis. For example, the Lions have been noted for their sight-saving program. Historically, in every community in which they are located, they will provide services and funding for visually impaired children. Services may range from providing eye examinations and transportation through purchasing corrective lenses for students in need. Other clubs, if approached with a specific project such as sponsoring a Special Olympics team, may be encouraged to do this on a continuing basis. Women's groups also may provide the same range of services, from providing financial assistance for specific projects, through sponsoring and holding an annual event such as a Christmas party for the benefit of all youngsters in a given school. The youth groups tend to provide human resources more often than financial resources. The vigor and enthusiasm that can be brought to your

program by high school- and college-aged service-oriented individuals cannot be matched. Specific fund-raising projects are often within the purview of youth organizations. Raising money through a jog-a-thon, rope-jumping-a-thon, or bike-a-thon is tackled with enthusiasm by youth organizations. Utilizing any service club member as a volunteer in your adapted physical education program can also provide enrichment for your students. Using volunteers of any age, however, requires some concerted effort on the part of the adapted physical educator; some of the skills involved in utilizing volunteers are discussed at the end of this chapter.

PRIVATE ORGANIZATIONS

A number of organizations have cropped up in the past thirty years to provide services where there were none, and to supplement educational and community services. Some of these organizations grew out of parental and community concern; others emerged as a result of a need felt by professionals to pool their resources. Some organizations have as their distinct role that of advocacy for a specific population. One such organization that began this way is the National Association for Retarded Citizens (formerly the National Association for Retarded Children). This organization, like many others, has gone to bat for the rights of the disabled (see National Association for Retarded Children vs. The Commonwealth of Pennsylvania 1971 litigation in Abeson, n.d.). Since Public Law 94–142 was enacted and more services are available in the schools, many of these organizations have shifted their focus and expanded their service to be supplemental to school programs. In many areas of the country, there is still a need for some of these organizations to provide educational services. Adapted physical educators should become aware of organizations beyond the educational agency that can serve as resources that can be utilized for providing a fuller, more enriching experience for children who have special needs. Some of these organizations at the local level provide supplemental therapy, recreation, and summer and year-round camping opportunities, and should be explored. The following list is not complete by any means. An attempt has been made, however, to provide a resource list that shows the scope of organizations in existence and perhaps serve as a springboard to the physical educator to seek other local resources.

1. American Academy of Pediatrics
   1801 Hinman Avenue
   Evanston, Illinois 60204

2. American Association for Health, Physical
   Education, Recreation, and Dance
   1900 Association Drive
   Reston, Virginia 22091

3. American Art Therapy Association
   P.O. Box 11604
   Pittsburgh, Pennsylvania 15228

4. American Association for the Education of
   Severely and Profoundly Handicapped
   1600 W. Armory Way, Garden View Suite
   Seattle, Washington 98119

5. American Association on Mental Deficiency
   5201 Connecticut Avenue, N.W.
   Washington, D.C. 20015

6. American Occupational Therapy Association
   6000 Executive Boulevard
   Rockville, Maryland 20852

7. American Physical Therapy Association
   1156 15th Street, N.W.
   Washington, D.C. 20005

8. American Rehabilitation Counseling Association
   1607 New Hampshire Avenue, N.W.
   Washington, D.C. 20009

9. American Speech and Hearing Association
   10801 Rockville Pike
   Rockville, Maryland 20852

10. Association for Children with Learning Disabilities
    5225 Grace Street
    Pittsburgh, Pennsylvania 15236

11. Council for Exceptional Children
    1920 Association Drive
    Reston, Virginia 22091

12. Epilepsy Foundation of America
    1828 L Street, N.W., Suite 406
    Washington, D.C. 20036

13. Mainstream
    1200 15th Street, N.W.
    Washington, D.C. 20005

14. National Association for Gifted Children
    1920 Association Drive
    Reston, Virginia 22091

15. National Association for Music Therapy, Inc.
    P.O. Box 610
    Lawrence, Kansas 66044

16. National Association of the Physically Handicapped
    76 Elm Street
    London, Ohio 43140

17. National Association for Retarded Citizens
    2709 Avenue E, East
    Arlington, Texas 76011

18. National Association of Social Workers
    1425 H Street, N.W.
    Washington, D.C. 20005

19. National Braille Association
    85 Godwin Avenue
    Midland Park, New Jersey 07432

20. National Easter Seal Society
    2023 W. Ogden Avenue
    Chicago, Illinois 60612

21. National Foundation of Dentistry for the
    Handicapped
    1121 Broadway, Suite 5
    Boulder, Colorado 80302

22. National Foundation – March of Dimes
    1275 Mamaroneck Avenue
    White Plains, New York 10605

23. National Society for Autistic Children
    169 Tampa Avenue
    Albany, New York 12208

24. National Therapeutic Recreation Society
    1601 North Kent Street
    Arlington, Virginia 22209

25. United Cerebral Palsy Association
    66 E. 34th Street
    New York, New York 10016

SPORTS ORGANIZATIONS

As a result of changing social and economic conditions, sports organizations have been emerging in this
country since the end of World War II. Some of the

key elements that have provided the appropriate climate for this movement include a changing educational philosophy over the last thirty-five years, an increased receptivity on the part of our society to seeing the disabled appear and compete in public, and an increase in political accountability requiring the political system to be responsive and responsible to all its constituents. Adapted physical educators should be well-versed in the availability of sports participation and competitive athletic programs in their communities for individuals who have special needs. Section 504 of PL 93–112 provides that equal extracurricular activity programs must be made available to handicapped students. In cases in which the regular extracurricular programs are not accessible to otherwise qualified handicapped students, educational agencies receiving federal funds for any reason must provide a similar program for handicapped students. If an existing program is appropriate, it is the physical educator's responsibility to be aware that it exists, and to refer students to that program in order to comply with federal legislation (see Figure 19–6).

Figure 19–6. Sports organizations such as Special Olympics (facing page, top), National Wheelchair Athletic Association (facing page, bottom); United States Association for Blind Athletes (above, right), and the National Handicapped Sports and Recreation Association (right) provide opportunities for competitive and recreational participation in sports. SOURCE: Photos by Charles Buell (above, right) and by courtesy of the Handicapped Sportsperson's Association of Sacramento (right).

Only a few of these organizations will be discussed in this chapter. These have been selected as representative samples of the numerous organizations in existence in order to give the reader insight into the variety of programs available to a broad range of disability groups. A comprehensive listing of sports organizations for the handicapped and their addresses appears in Appendix F.

American Athletic Association for the Deaf

This organization was founded in 1945 in Akron, Ohio. It fosters and regulates athletic competition for the deaf, and is affiliated with the Amateur Athletic Union (AAU), the American Softball Association through the National Beep Baseball Association, and (on an international level) with the Comite International des Sports Silencieux. The AAAD sanctions and promotes state, regional, and national basketball and softball competition. It promotes participation and strives to send deaf and hard of hearing athletes to the World Games for the Deaf.

The National Association for Sports for Cerebral Palsy

The National Association for Sports for Cerebral Palsy (NASCP), founded in 1978, recognizes the importance of competitive sports in the social and physical development of the cerebral palsied person. Because it emerged to fill a gap for sports participation among the cerebral palsied population who did not qualify for National Wheelchair Athletic Association participation nor Special Olympics, one of its primary goals is to provide competitive sports activities for athletes who have cerebral palsy and other multiple disabling conditions. NASCP provides competition for minimally and maximally disabled people. Events that have been included in NASCP competition in the past include archery, table tennis, weightlifting, swimming, billiards, bowling, wheelchair soccer, track and field, horseback riding, and rifle shooting.

National Wheelchair Athletic Association

Probably the oldest form of organized athletics for the handicapped exists today in the form of events sponsored by the National Wheelchair Athletic Association (NWAA). World War II, with all its horrors, ironically brought to disabled individuals something better than they had previously known. The tens of thousands of veterans who returned home paraplegics, amputees, or otherwise disabled were heroes in their own right; yet they faced a new and entirely different lifestyle than they had known before their injury. With new impetus in the fields of medicine and rehabilitation, sports were seen from the beginning as an integral part of rehabilitation programs. In the United States, an interest arose in wheelchair basketball, which adapted the rules and regulations of regular basketball to the specific needs of wheelchair competitors. Thus, in 1946, the National Wheelchair Basketball Association was formed to govern basketball and promote public awareness of wheelchair sports. By 1948, Europe's first organized wheelchair sports program was introduced by the well-known neurosurgeon Dr. Ludwig Guttman, founder of the Spinal Injury Center in Stoke-Mandeville, England. Thus annual international Stoke-Mandeville Games continue to be the site of international competition for American athletes in wheelchairs.

Other activities being taught by physical educators in veterans hospitals during this post-war era included ping-pong, billiards, bowling, volleyball, water polo, softball, and touch football. These early physical educators, working in hospitals, brought their expertise in sport to the rehabilitation team. They were the forerunners to the modern day corrective therapists. Through the NWAA, numerous other opportunities for competition have evolved, including the International Paralympics, the Olympic Winter Games for the Disabled, and the Pan-American Games, as well as state, regional, and national wheelchair games competition.

Special Olympics

Special Olympics, founded in 1968 by the Joseph P. Kennedy, Jr. Foundation, is an international program of physical fitness, sports training, and athletic competition for mentally retarded children and adults. Nearly one million mentally retarded individuals take part in Special Olympics competition, making it the largest program of its type in the world. A key feature of Special Olympics is a series of olympic-type events held annually at the local, state, and regional levels. Every three years, an international games is held in the United States. In 1979, the international games housed 3,500 competitors from all fifty states and more than twenty foreign countries. Special Olympics offers fourteen official sports: track and field, swimming, diving, gymnastics, ice skating, basketball, volleyball, soccer, floor hockey, poly hockey, bowling, Frisbee-disc, Alpine and Nordic skiing, and wheelchair events.

United States Association for Blind Athletes

The USABA was founded in 1976 to develop sports programs for blind and visually impaired people in the United States, and programs are offered to interested people who have been classified as legally blind. Although participation is the major objective, many athletes strive for the utlimate goal of competing in regional, national, and international championships. Where possible, competitions are also held with sighted athletes. Championships hosted by USABA include track and field, swimming, Alpine skiing, cross-country skiing, wrestling, rowing, goal ball, gymnastics, sailing, and cycling (tandem).

THE HOME

Communication with the significant people in the home environment can be of value to the physical ed-

ucator, especially the specialist in adapted physical education. Although there is less occasion and time for the generalist to interact with the parents, guardians, and families of students with special needs, the information provided in this section may prove useful as resource material.

Since the IEP process initiates communication between the home and school, these channels should be kept open. In the past, much of the communication with the home has been of a negative nature, and educators have clearly communicated to parents "stay out of my domain." It is hoped that this trend has begun to change, and that change can be facilitated by the individual efforts of teachers. This communication and interaction between the home and school is a two-way street, and teachers must make it clear to parents that their contact is welcomed.

Values

Communication and interaction with people in the child's home environment can be most informative and enlightening. Such people include parents, guardians, foster parents, siblings, surrogate families, and others living or interacting in the home environment. An initial positive experience will greatly enhance the interaction.

The following are the values and benefits of home-school interaction:

1. Provides supplemental information about the child, which will enhance appropriateness of physical education programming.
2. Allows for consistency, continuity, and reinforcement of skills and behaviors between the home and school programs.
3. Stimulates interest and participation in physical activities for the family and instills the value of motor activity for exceptional individuals.

4. Creates situations for family/child interaction (see Figure 19–7).

5. Provides for implementation of home programs with specific benefits to the child.

The whole child must be considered in physical education programming, and information obtained from the family can be valuable in creating a total picture of the child. Often, parents know their child's capabilities and limitations better than can be ascertained through assessment. Those individuals in the home environment can be queried specifically about the child's hidden abilities, likes and dislikes, preferred mode of communication, means of motivation, and so on. Gathering all possible information provides the means whereby the most appropriate and individualized program can be designed.

Consistency is vital in the educational process. With communication between the home and school environments, the opportunity exists for continuity and consistency in all aspects of educational programming. For example, specific techniques of behavior management can be shared and utilized in both en-

vironments. Reinforcement for learning skills that have been taught at school can be provided by those in the home environment, and vice versa. Thus increased awareness of the child's performance is fostered. This consistency and continuity can also be carried through to after-school programs. Communication with outside individuals providing services (such as the recreation therapist) fosters enhanced programming, and the family can play a key role in the transference of information.

Handicapped children, especially the more severely involved, often do not participate in nor know how to play or enjoy leisure activities outside of school-sponsored activities. Often, the handicapped person cannot play independently, and requires the assistance or supervision of someone else in the home. The parent or family member may be ill-equipped to help or intervene with the child, unless there has been communication and interaction for sharing methods and techniques found to be successful. The family members can be instructed on strategies and techniques of movement intervention and play at home, and some may volunteer at school or in related ser-

Figure 19–7. This handicapped adolescent is regularly included in family play. SOURCE: Photo courtesy of City of Anaheim, Public Information Office.

Figure 19-8. Through family programs, parents can learn techniques for helping their handicapped child achieve success. Patterning for throwing (right) and batting (below) helps to teach skills important to the mainstream. SOURCE: Photos by Greg Fulton (below) and by courtesy of City of Anaheim, Public Information Office (right).

vices; they can also be informed of community and organizational resources and opportunities of which they may not be aware.

With information shared specifically about the physical education program, interest and participation in general physical activities in the after-school hours can be stimulated. The value of movement to the handicapped child can be instilled in parents and family members. Information on community activities, available motor programs, special workshops, and the like can be provided to families, which may in turn encourage the whole family to participate.

Situations can be created to foster increased family/child interaction. Casual or more general opportunities would include family outings, family games, playtime, leisure time activities, trips to the playground, park, swimming pool, bowling alley, or even watching selected television shows together. Other opportunities include participation in organized movement and physical activity programs (e.g., Special Olympics, Let's-Play-To-Grow, Scouting programs, Therapeutic Recreation programs, church groups, camps). Both the child and the family benefit from participation in any of the above (see Figure 19-8).

A specified home program of physical and move-ment experiences can be designed and implemented, from which the child can derive great benefit. Areas of weakness can be strengthened and development en-hanced. Through involvement in a home program, family members can learn the basic play movements for the handicapped — what to do and how to do it. The limitations and capacities of the handicapped child become more apparent, and a deeper understanding of the individual's physical and motor needs is pro-moted. The success of the home program is related to the level of communication between the physical ed-ucation teacher and those in the home environment.

Methods of Communication

The following suggestions are offered for initiating and fostering communication with those in the child's home. Once the channels are open, the physical edu-cator should strive to keep them open. Parental support and interest in the physical education program can be a valuable asset.

1. Send letters home about the general physical ed-ucation program (see Figure 19–9).
2. Provide, in written form, how the specific goals of the IEP for each individual will be met through physical activity.
3. Provide parent/family workshops, inservices, play nights.
4. Hold parent conferences on a regular basis.
5. Sponsor and hold play days, festivals, demon-strations.
6. Provide "homework" — activities to practice at home or an activity of the week, designed to meet specific goals.
7. Send any special notes home whenever appro-priate — "good job" note, completion of objective note, certificates of award.
8. Provide a list of community organizations, books,

sport programs, related services, resource people for parents.
9. Use a photo display to explain program.
10. Develop a home program for any interested family, which would include home visitations and parent-at-school visitations.
11. Use parents as volunteer aides for the physical education program.

Home Programs

In designing a home program or offering suggestions of activities, the ability level of the child must serve as a foundation. The child's ability level can be deter-mined relative to the levels of the developmental model and assessment results. Based on the level of functioning, suggestions for activities can be offered to the family. Many of the activities discussed in chap-ters 15 and 16 as appropriate to each ability level may be modified, if necessary, and implemented at home.

In addition to or in place of a specified program of motor activities offered by the physical educator, the family/parents can be directed to available resources. Published program ideas such as *Let's-Play-to-Grow* and *Sensory-Motor Experiences for the Home* are ex-amples of materials that can be made available. Existing programs in the community such as Special Olympics, Very Special Arts Festival, Therapeutic Recreation, Scouting, and other sports programs also allow for some parent/family involvement. Examples of activities taken from *Let's-Play-to-Grow* and *Sensory-Motor Experiences for the Home*, as well as a bibliography of resources for parents, are included in Appendix G.

Let's-Play-to-Grow is a program of play designed primarily to help families with their special child. It con-tains a manual for parents and teachers and twelve Play Guides on topics such as bowling, swimming, ball skills, severely handicapped, and others. *Sensory-Motor Experiences for the Home* is a manual for par-ents that lists many activities and experiences adapted

Figure 19-9. Newsletters can help keep parents informed and interested in the adapted physical education activities at their child's school.

NEWS AND MUSE

February 1982   Volume 3   Number 6

Dear Parents,

The year started with a bang in the physical education, Let's-Play-to Grow, and Special Olympics programs. We had ten families participate in the doubles bowling tournament on Saturday, January 9. All had a wonderful time. The division winners were:

Division A
Fred and Brad Ball — 899

Division B
Laurie and Amy Fause — 768

Division C
Leslie and Tim Raber — 679

Congratulations to them all!

Special Olympics News

Our swimming instruction in physical education is paying off on Sundays, when the Special Olympics practice is held at the YMCA. Billy Barber has improved his time in the 50 m freestyle by three seconds and Susie Morgan has trimmed five seconds off her time! For parents who have not yet entered their children in Special Olympics and would like to, call the school office for registration forms.

Physical Education

After finishing our bowling unit in December, the results became evident at the January Let's-Play-to-Grow Tournament. We are now in a six-week unit of instruction in swimming at the YMCA. Our goal is to make all students water-safe, and those who are swimming have individual goals to accomplish. Contact the P.E. office at school for specific goals of your child, or refer to the IEP form written for this school year.

— Jodi, Kathy and Al
The P.E. Staff

or designed specifically for the home environment to enhance the sensorimotor development of special children.

THE COMMUNITY: NORMALIZATION AND MAINSTREAMING

The success with which a student who has special needs functions in the community depends a great deal on previous experiences and opportunities pro- vided in the contexts discussed earlier. Whether a child has had a broad expanse of services in the schools, outside the schools, and at home, or opportunities for athletic and recreational experiences, the investment of those services is clearly on the line when that child meets nonhandicapped peers for the first time. To help the child, the adapted physical educator must under- stand two concepts that have been part of school and community services in recent years: normalization and mainstreaming.

Normalization is the process of providing as near equal opportunities and experiences in all of life's aspects as possible within the limits of a child's disability. Adapted physical education, recreation, dance, and art and music therapy all tend to provide experiences that are at least in part identical to those experiences provided the nonhandicapped population, but they take place primarily in a segregated setting. Various experiences provided by private and sports organizations also tend to be much like those experiences provided for the nonhandicapped population. Without these normalizing opportunities, many students who have special needs would never have the opportunity to develop the necessary physical, mental, and social skills for functioning in the community. These skills learned through normalizing activities tend to be skills also needed in the mainstream.

The concept of *mainstreaming* is that of maximum integration in the regular class combined with minimal concrete assistance from the regular (physical education) class teacher. The role of adapted physical education specialists is changing to include consulting and assisting regular physical educators who have students with special needs integrated into their classes. It should be noted that neither PL 94–142 nor its regulations include the word "mainstreaming." It *does* say that each student who has special needs must be educated in the "least restrictive environment." For some students, maximum integration in the regular class with minimal assistance from the teacher is, for them, the least restrictive environment. In contrast to the categorical approach to delivering educational services, the mainstream may provide the most appropriate, least restrictive environment for some students carrying a particular categorical label, while it may be inappropriate for others in the same classification. It should be further noted that the mainstream may not be the most appropriate, least restrictive environment for a given child right now; but with normalization and opportunities to learn, the mainstream might be the most appropriate placement for that same child in the future.

The extent to which a student with special needs can be successfully integrated into a regular class depends on several factors. The first factor is the extent to which the teacher accepts the student as a valuable and contributing member of the class (Gearheart and Weishahn, 1980). The attitude of the generalist in physical education toward a student with special needs will serve as a model for the behavior and interaction of other students with the handicapped student (Bandura, 1965). If the physical educator consistently uses the handicapped student to pass out towels, referee, scorekeep, and serve in other roles not consistent with the goals of physical education, that student will be devalued by other students in class. On the other hand, if the physical educator clearly strives to modify the environment, the activity, and the teaching methods used in order to integrate the student who has special needs, that student's value as a contributing class member will be enhanced.

The second factor upon which mainstreaming relies is the interaction between students who have special needs and their peers (Peterson, et al., 1977; Bricker and Bricker, 1976). It has been clearly documented that the opportunities afforded handicapped students for observing and modeling the behavior of their peers contributes greatly to each student's ability to integrate successfully into the mainstream. Here again, normalization activities provide opportunities for the handicapped to interact in the larger community. If the only models for imitating behavior are disabled or retarded, then the student never has the opportunity to learn other styles of behavior.

The third factor is the attitude and value systems of the nonhandicapped students (Wolfensberger, 1972). As previously mentioned, our attitudes and value systems are learned from those around us. In the educational context, particularly in the early years, the significant adults in a child's environment foster the attitudes and value systems that follow that individual through life. If the physical educator and other adults directing programs for children clearly demonstrate that they value the contribution and presence of students who have special needs, then these attitudes and values will likely be embraced by the nonhandicapped students as well.

The fourth factor contributing to successful mainstreaming is the extent to which systematic efforts provide nonhandicapped students with specific information, experiences, and opportunities to discuss handicapping conditions (Lilly, 1971; Chennault, 1967; Rucker and Vincezo, 1970). This systematic effort may take the form of using a buddy system, peer teaching (PEOPEL Project), rap sessions, mini-inservice sessions, and working with other educators to incorporate reading, writing, and film viewing of materials about handicapped children into their curriculum. People tend to be hesitant and at times fearful of situations and conditions they do not understand. When the adapted physical educator provides opportunities for interaction between handicapped and nonhandicapped students, and makes available information on the disabilities, appliances, or procedures used by the handicapped students, the nonhandicapped can come to realize that such people are simply classmates who coincidentally have handicapping conditions.

Numerous opportunities for mainstreaming are available outside the school environment. Where physical activity and motor performance is involved in such programs as Scouting, community recreation, Little League, or sports clubs, the adapted or regular physical educator may need to take the initiative to contact program organizers. This contact could be made to offer services for consulting, if needed. For example, calling the program organizers, discussing briefly that you understand that Johnny is starting in the gymnastics program at their YMCA, that you have worked with Johnny who is a student who has special needs, and that you are willing to give them any

information or assistance they may desire, and leaving your telephone number, does not take more than a few minutes. The investment of that small amount of time may result in an understanding that will allow Johnny to reap years of benefits from a successful experience in this new program. Ray Barsch once said, "What you know, is what you owe."* It is because of the great magnitude of rewards from such a small investment that most of us are in education to begin with.

USING VOLUNTEERS

The use of volunteers may require some concerted effort on the part of the adapted physical educator, but can serve only to enhance the adapted physical education program. Volunteers are special human beings who must be cared for and nurtured; except for classroom teachers, aides and parents are usually volunteering because they have a need to contribute something to others less fortunate than they. Each must be handled with respect and care as though they were a rare gem. Many organizations need people who can give their time for free, and agencies are craving for their services. Therefore, unless the adapted physical educator makes volunteers feel as though what they are doing is important, they will take their services elsewhere (see Figure 19–10).

The Successful Use of Volunteers

The following seven principles for the use of volunteers have been found to be important considerations in implementing a volunteer program.

First, *use volunteers for important, significant tasks.* People who volunteer want to feel as though what

---

*Luncheon speech at the Eighth International Conference on Physical Activity for the Exceptional Individual, Los Angeles, 1978.

Figure 19–10. These volunteers at Exceptional Games (right), Special Olympics (below), and Wheelchair Games (facing page) give hundreds of hours of their time to make these programs successful. SOURCE: Photo (right) by Cheryl Hitchings.

they are doing is important. Thus it is inadvisable to use a volunteer to be first base, to pass out towels, or to serve as the target for accuracy throwing if these are the only tasks they are assigned. There are other, more meaningful ways of using volunteers. Volunteers should be asked to do things only human beings can do. Certainly there are tasks that are not the most desirable chores including assisting students in the bathroom, taking roll, and transporting equipment to and from the activity area. The important key in utilizing volunteers for these sorts of tasks is that the adapted physical educator should also be seen doing the same tasks. Adapted specialists should ask themselves, "Would I be willing to do the job I have asked the volunteer to do?" If the answer is "yes," more than likely the specialists are assigning appropriate, needed, and meaningful tasks that will keep volunteers coming back day after day.

Second, *do not assume the volunteers know anything about students who have special needs, or about adapted physical education.* Obviously, if you have volunteers who have had previous experience with the handicapped, formal training, or some other related experience, this is a bonus. Do not assume, however, that volunteers truly understand instructions,

even though they may nod their heads. Just as in evaluating performance objectives, the true sign of understanding is whether or not volunteers can demonstrate the performances requested.

Third, *provide regular inservice education.* Providing opportunities for volunteers to learn more about students with special needs and adapted physical education could be an added bonus for the volunteers.

Depending upon the needs and interests of the volunteers, these inservice education meetings may take a variety of formats. For example, students in high school or college who are studying or planning to study in the fields of adapted physical education or special education may be interested in inservice education workshops that are rather sophisticated and theoretical in nature. On the other hand, community volunteers who do not have career goals related to working with the handicapped, such as men and women's service club members, may be primarily interested in understanding and carrying out the specific tasks or activities for which their help is needed. Thus sessions held at the beginning of each semester, school year, or instructional unit may include information on program and class procedures, general goals, and assignment of specific tasks. As the instructor and director of the

program, whether it is the instructional program or an extracurricular activity such as Special Olympics, it is the adapted physical educator's responsibility to analyze what the volunteers need to know, what knowledge they bring to the experience, and what they want to do with the information that is given them. Then the inservice education program can be planned accordingly.

Fourth, *have a special means of designating volunteers.* Using a special badge, shirt, arm band, or other designation serves several purposes in your volunteer program. First of all, a badge or some other designation creates the aura of officiality. Children learn to recognize badges, uniforms, and the like as relating to authority and the official capacity in which the person is serving. Second, a special designation is important in working with students with special needs in order to clearly distinguish the volunteer from a group with which they are working. Sometimes a responsible person is needed in a hurry, such as when there is a seizure, an injury, or a runaway. Having a means of identifying the teacher, aide, or volunteer quickly may save the time needed in an emergency. Young people from the community or local college or university often look as young as the students. With a special designation, someone who is not familiar with the students in the class can easily identify the volunteer. Finally, the special designation is an indication to the volunteers themselves that they are, in fact, official and special. The badge, or whatever is used, carries with it an aura of responsibility and gives the volunteers status associated with their responsibilities.

Fifth, *assign specific tasks.* As mentioned earlier, tasks assigned must be important and meaningful if the volunteer is to stay with the program. Assigning a specific task, such as, ``Line up the class in two lines, have them practice the bounce-pass back and forth in partners for five minutes, then divide them into four groups and run the bounce-pass relay that we did last week,'' is an example of a specific task. Previous experience with the volunteer will give the adapted physical educator an idea of what the volunteer knows, yet this example is far more clear to any volunteer than telling them, ``Drill the students on the bounce-pass.'' Obviously, the second, more general request assumes that the volunteer knows what a drill is and how to set one up. Providing even more specific information for the volunteer is even better. For example, the physical educator might have added to the assigned task for the bounce pass drill, ``Remind Johnny to step forward with his left foot, and keep trying to get Susie to use her stump to support the ball.''

Sixth, *state clearly the expected student performance.* The adapted physical educator must make clear to the volunteer what performance should be expected from the students. This level of expectation,

of course, is based on the performance objectives in the students' IEPs and the current level of performance observed in the pervious class period. To continue our example, the physical educator may have noted in the previous class period that Johnny could step forward with his left foot, but needed to be reminded in order to do it consistently. So that Johnny does not regress while the volunteer is directing the drill, the volunteer must be given information as to what should be expected from each student. Clearly, some volunteers are more capable, observant, and better trained than others. Therefore the amount and type of input from the adapted physical educator must be based on information about the volunteer.

Finally, *keep records of each volunteer's work.* It is always best to document the work of volunteers just as one would document the progress of students. There are numerous reasons why this should be done, the most important of which is so that the adapted physical educator can give periodic and appropriate recognition and awards to the people who give so unselfishly of their time. A further reason, depending on the goals of the volunteers, is to provide colleges, universities, potential employers, or other agencies with information about the nature and quality of the service delivered by the volunteer. Volunteer service is often requested on applications for entrance into courses of study, jobs, and other volunteer experiences. Having the information on record so that a valid recommendation and report can be made provides further service to the requesting party. This is also the kind of information the educator should receive when seeking new volunteers. The kind of information that should be kept should include a running record of the number of hours donated to the program, a log of the type and quality of the work being done by the volunteer, and a note on reliability and dependability. Clearly, volunteers come in all sizes, shapes, colors, and backgrounds. The skillful educator can utilize volunteers to enhance the quality of the program. Professionals who find they have difficulty keeping volunteers involved should review these seven principles and reevaluate their use of these people who so generously give of their time.

Helping Volunteers to Help the Adapted Physical Educator

In order to have the most satisfying results from volunteers in the program or parents involved in home play, useful guidance from the physical educator is needed. The professional in physical education has the theoretical and practical background and experience, but transmitting that knowledge and competence to others is important. The following pointers can be passed on to volunteers in order to help them to be more effective in assisting students with special needs in physical activity: (1) think about how the body works; (2) break the skill into parts; (3) teach movement parts in order; (4) be the model; (5) move with the child; (6) use cues; (7) keep the instructional periods short; (8) make it fun; (9) use make-believe; and (10) provide as much success as possible. The adapted physical educator might explain these points to the volunteer as follows.

Think about how the body works. To help students learn a new skill or pattern, it is important to know how the body works. Think about how the limbs and trunk move; better yet, go through the movement yourself and pay particular attention to what your body does. Then assist the student by moving the body parts in the same order and through the same motion.

Break the skill into parts. Most of us do not learn an entire skill all at one time. Teach each small segment of the skill in order and, as they are learned, do segments together. This is very much like learning the words to a new song. You learn the first verse, then the chorus; then you practice those two parts together before going on to the second verse.

Teach movement parts in order. The sequence of movement parts can be very critical in some activities. For example, a child cannot do the hopping part of a skip before stepping and shifting the body weight to one foot. In other activities, one component can be learned before others that ordinarily would come in a different order in the game. For example, a child can learn to shoot the basketball at the hoop before learning to dribble or pass the ball. Teaching these skills in this order would also serve to keep the student interested and motivated to learn.

Be the model. Let the student imitate the movements of another student or yourself. Some children learn best in this way, and there is no need to confuse the issue with a lot of directions. Start by saying, "Watch me." Demonstrate, then say, "Now you do it."

Move with the child. Many concepts of movement can be taught by moving with students while they are learning. The concept of running "fast," for example, may be "felt" only if someone runs with the student, holding onto his or her hand and moving along at a fast pace. Exaggerate arm movements and facial expressions, if necessary to get the point across.

Use cues. Often single-word cues can be used to remind the student what to do. This technique is used in coaching all the time. Words like *back, down,* and *up,* as well as phrases such as *hands up, thumbs up,* and *roll over* can give the volunteer, parent, or teacher a means of assisting a student while a movement sequence is being learned.

Keep the instructional periods short. Look for signs of fatigue and boredom. All of us get tired of doing the same thing eventually, no matter how motivated we might have been at the beginning. Students with special needs are no different. In about fifteen to twenty minutes most young children will tire of a structured activity. Thirty to forty-five minutes is about enough, even for older students. If instructional periods are controlled by the school schedule, break up the time available into two or three activities. At home it is always possible to come back to an activity and practice in two or three shorter time segments rather than fatiguing or boring the child by giving one long instructional period.

Make it fun. At first, learning a new skill may not seem like fun. Make the instructional time as much fun as possible, and reinforce the notion that being successful is fun even though the effort was a repetitious drill. Reward the student for every attempt, even if unsuccessful, with a "Nice try," or "You are really doing a good job!" Eventually, students will develop their own measures of success and the external rewards will not be necessary.

Use make-believe. Use mimetics to vary the pace and style of instruction. Teaching a student to use his or her arms while running might best be done by having the student imitate a favorite football star. Watch television or sports films, then have the student imitate the players.

Provide as much success as possible. Do everything you can to help the student feel successful. This is especially important during the early stages of learning new skills. The student should, however, have periodic opportunities to fail, for what other way is

there to measure success? Put the student in places where success is most likely—near the net in volleyball, right in front of the basket in basketball, or shorten the basepaths in softball and kickball. Once skills are learned and success is fairly common, change these variables so these children are playing more like other children.

SUMMARY

With the increasing visibility of the handicapped and the responsivity of the community to the needs of the handicapped comes a greater circle of resources for enhancing the quality of life for this population. Adapted physical educators often become the pivot point for coordinating movement experiences for students in their charge, and thus must be familiar with resources and opportunities outside the educational context. Whether working closely with professionals in related services, parents, or volunteers, the constant driving energy should be the desire to provide appropriate, satisfying movement experiences for students with special needs.

BIBLIOGRAPHY

Abeson, A. *A Continuing Summary of Pending and Completed Litigation Regarding the Handicapped.* Reston, Virginia: Council for Exceptional Children, n.d.

Bandura, A., and Rosenthal, T. "Vicarious Classical Conditioning as a Function of Arousal Level." *Journal of Personality and Social Psychology* 3 (1965): 54–62.

Bricker, W., and Bricker, D. "The Infant, Toddler, and Preschool Intervention Project." In *Intervention Strategies for High-risk Infants and Young Children,* edited by P. D. Tjossem. Baltimore: University Park Press, 1976.

Bunney, J. B. "Dance Therapy." In *Interdisciplinary Approaches to Human Services,* edited by F. Christoplos and P. J. Valletutti. Baltimore: University Park Press, 1977, pp. 49–60.

Chennault, M. "Improving the Social Acceptance of Unpopular Educable Mentally Retarded Pupils in Special Classes." *American Journal of Mental Deficiency* 72 (1967): 455–458.

Cliff, S., Gray, J., and Nymann, C. *Mothers Can Help.* El Paso, Texas: El Paso Rehabilitation Center, 1974.

Connaughton, J. P. "Psychiatry." In Christoplos and Valletutti, *Interdisciplinary Approaches,* pp. 307–336.

Davis, W. E. *Educator's Resource Guide to Special Education: Terms-Laws-Tests-Organizations.* Boston: Allyn and Bacon, 1980.

Fox, L. A. "Dentistry." In Christoplos and Valletutti, *Interdisciplinary Approaches,* pp. 61–79.

Frye, V., and Peters, M. *Therapeutic Recreation: Its Theory, Philosophy, and Practice.* Harrisburg, Pennsylvania: Stackpole, 1972.

Gearheart, B. R., and Weishahn, M. W. *The Handicapped Student in the Regular Classroom.* 2d ed. St. Louis: C. V. Mosby, 1980.

Hersey, W. J., Jr. "Social Work." In Christoplos and Valletutti, *Interdisciplinary Approaches,* pp. 373–386.

Johnson, R. B. "Pediatrics." In Christoplos and Valletutti, *Interdisciplinary Approaches,* pp. 253–266.

Kennedy, The Joseph P., Jr. Foundation. *Let's-Play-to-Grow.* Washington, D.C.: The Joseph P. Kennedy Jr. Foundation, 1978.

Lilly, S. "Improving Social Acceptance of Low Socioeconomic Status, Low Achieving Students." *Exceptional Children* 37 (1971): 341–347.

Ludwig, A. J. "Music Therapy." In Christoplos and Valletutti, *Interdisciplinary Approaches,* pp. 135–154.

Naumburg, M. "Art Therapy: Its Scope and Function." In *The Clinical Applications of Projective Drawings,* edited by E. F. Hammer. Springfield, Illinois: Charles C. Thomas, 1958, pp. 511–517.

Noyes, A. P., and Kolb, L. C. *Modern Clinical Psychiatry. Philadelphia: W. B. Saunders, 1958.*

Park, D. C., and Annand, V. S. "Therapeutic Recreation." In Christoplos and Valletutti, *Interdisciplinary Approaches,* pp. 415–432.

Peterson, C., Peterson, J., and Scriven, G. "Peer Imitation by Nonhandicapped and Handicapped Preschoolers." *Exceptional Children* 43(4) (1977): 223–224.

Rucker, C., and Vincenzo, F. "Maintaining Social Acceptance Gains Made by Mentally Retarded Children." *Exceptional Children,* 36 (1970): 679–680.

Schumacher, B. "Rehabilitation Counseling." In Christoplos and Valletutti, *Interdisciplinary Approaches,* pp. 357–372.

Seaman,., and DePauw, K. P. *Sensory-Motor Experiences for the Home.* Los Angeles: Trident Shop, 1979.

Ulman, E., et al. "Art Therapy." In Christoplos and Valletutti, *Interdisciplinary Approaches,* pp. 13–48.

Wolfensberger, W. *Normalization: The Principles of Normalization in Human Services.* Toronto: National Institute on Mental Retardation, 1972.

Appendix A
Adapted Physical Education Guidelines

In response to a growing need for direction in the preparation of personnel to provide physical education services to the disabled, three structures within the alliance have developed guidelines in adapted physical education. These guidelines, in the form of competencies, were developed by the following AAHPERD structures: Adapted Academy, NASPE, Therapeutics Council, ARAPCS, and the Unit on Programs for the Handicapped. Initially drafted in July 1979, the guidelines have been subjected to internal and external review, including a national dissemination in the January 1980 *IRUC Briefings*. Data gathered from this publication, from interested individuals, and from state associations have been compiled into the final guidelines.

It should be noted that these guidelines identify competencies but do not address the areas of learning activities, evaluation techniques, or performance criteria. The committee (Task Force) felt these areas are the responsibility of those using the guidelines.

Based on continued input and suggestions from adapted physical education professionals, the committee (Task Force) makes the following suggestions for additional study in the area of personnel preparation in adapted physical education.

The guidelines are limited to competencies necessary for the regular physical education generalist and the adapted physical education specialist. The generalist will be increasingly responsible for meeting physical and motor needs of students with disabilities in regular physical education classes. Competencies identified are, for the most part, limited to those with direct relationship to dealing with individuals with disabilities in regular physical education classes, or those which would serve as the basic foundation for the more specialized competencies of the adapted physical education specialist. The adapted physical education specialist should possess the competencies identified for the generalist as well as specialist. The adapted physical education specialist is an individual who is capable of teaching not only students with various disabilities who are integrated into regular physical education classes, but also the more disabled students requiring a special physical education program.

Physical education generalist | *Adapted physical education specialist*

1.0 BIOLOGICAL FOUNDATIONS

1.1 Kinesiology

1.1.1 Demonstrate understanding of functional anatomy as it applies to analyses of motor skills.

1.1.2 Demonstrate understanding of the organization and function of the nervous system including implications of neuromuscular relationships and functioning.

1.1.1 Demonstrate ability to apply understanding of motor dysfunctions and their implications to adapted physical education programs.

1.1.2 Demonstrate ability to apply understanding of neurological disorders and their implications to motor functioning.

SOURCE: *IRUC Briefings,* January 1980. Washington D.C.: AAHPERD, 1980.

Physical education generalist	*Adapted physical education specialist*

1.1 Kinesiology (continued)

1.1.3   Demonstrate understanding of deviations from normal physical growth and development, including musculoskeletal deviations, neurological disorders, and neuromuscular deficiencies.

1.1.4   Demonstrate understanding of influences which the human structure exerts on motor capabilities of individuals with or without disabilities.

1.1.5   Demonstrate proficiency in evaluating and analyzing motor performances and motor dysfunctions in terms of biomechanical principles and laws.

1.1.3   Demonstrate ability to apply understanding of deviations from normal physical growth and development to analyses of motor skills.

1.1.4   Demonstrate proficiency in evaluating and analyzing motor performances in terms of motor dysfunctions.

1.1.5   Demonstrate ability to apply understanding of unique structures of individuals with disabilities to individualized instruction in adapted physical education.

1.1.6   Demonstrate ability to apply biomechanical principles which affect motor functioning to wheelchair, crutch, braces, and artificial limb use.

1.1.7   Demonstrate ability to apply biomechanical principles which affect motor functioning to posture, and neurological, muscular, and other specific physical health needs.

1.2 Physiology of Exercise

1.2.1   Demonstrate understanding of immediate as well as long term physiological response of the human body to exercise.

1.2.2   Demonstrate ability to design instructional physical education programs in accordance with essential physiological considerations and principles.

1.2.3   Demonstrate proficiency in conducting instructional physical education programs in accordance with essential physiological considerations and principles.

1.2.4   Demonstrate proficiency in communicating physiological benefits of regular physical activity for program participants.

1.2.5   Demonstrate ability to apply research findings from exercise physiology to instructional physical education programs.

1.2.1   Demonstrate knowledge of how dysfunctions affect physiological responses to exercise.

1.2.2   Demonstrate ability to design instructional physical education programs in accordance with essential physiological considerations and principles specific to individuals with disabilities.

1.2.3   Demonstrate proficiency in conducting instructional physical education programs in accordance with essential physiological considerations and principles specific to individuals with disabilities.

1.2.4   Demonstrate ability to apply research findings in the area of exercise physiology specific to individuals with disabilities.

1.3 Physiological and Motor Functioning

1.3.1   Demonstrate understanding of the components of physiological and motor functioning.

1.3.2   Demonstrate understanding of functional capacity, complexity, and adaptability of the human organism as bases for skillful motor performances.

1.3.3   Demonstrate understanding of anatomical and physiological deviations in the human organism and effect such deviations have on motor performances.

1.3.1   Demonstrate ability to apply an understanding of physiological functioning of individuals with physical, mental, sensory, neurological and other specific health needs to programs designed to improve motor performances of these individuals with disabilities.

1.3.2   Demonstrate ability to apply an understanding of physiological motor characteristics for individuals with physical, mental, sensory, neurological and other specific health needs to programs designed to improve motor performances of these individuals with disabilities.

Physical education generalist	*Adapted physical education specialist*
1.3.4 Demonstrate understanding of specific basis for preventing and caring for injuries common to physical education, sport, dance, and play activities.	1.3.3 Demonstrate ability to apply techniques for the prevention and care of injuries specific to individuals with specific disabilities.

2.0 SOCIOLOGICAL FOUNDATIONS

2.1 Sport, Dance, and Play

2.1.1 Demonstrate understanding of roles and importance of sports, dance, and play activities to individuals living in contemporary American society, including their significance for individuals with disabilities.	2.1.1 Demonstrate ability to analyze the role and significance of sports, dance, and play in the lives of individuals with disabilities.
2.1.2 Demonstrate understanding of ethnic, social, and cultural aspects of sports, dance, and play.	2.1.2 Demonstrate understanding of roles and significance of lifetime physical activities for individuals with disabilities.
2.1.3 Demonstrate knowledge of roles and importance of sports, dance, and play for individuals in the community, including such opportunities for individuals with disabilities.	2.1.3 Demonstrate understanding of influences of community social agencies on sports, dance, and play in lives of individuals with disabilities.
2.1.4 Demonstrate awareness of community opportunities in sports, dance, and play for individuals with disabilities.	
2.1.5 Demonstrate understanding of values of lifetime physical activities to all individuals, including those with disabilities.	

2.2 Cooperative/Competitive Activities

2.2.1 Demonstrate understanding of the potential of cooperative/competitive activities for human interaction and social behavior.	2.2.1 Demonstrate ability to apply understanding of the potential for human interaction and social behavior occurring in cooperative/competitive activities for individuals with disabilities.
2.2.2 Demonstrate knowledge of organizations which conduct adapted sport, dance and play programs and activities for individuals with disabilities.	2.2.2 Demonstrate ability to work and cooperate with organizations which conduct adapted sport, dance, and play programs and activities for individuals with disabilities.

2.3 Social Developmemt

2.3.1 Demonstrate understanding of social learnings involved in experiencing human movement and its effects on perception, motivation, and personality.	2.3.1 Demonstrate ability to apply understanding of the potential that sport, dance, and play provides for social interaction among individuals with and without disabilities.
2.3.2 Demonstrate understanding of the potential that sport, dance, and play provides for social interactions among individuals with and without disabilities.	

Physical education generalist	Adapted physical education specialist

3.0 PSYCHOLOGICAL FOUNDATIONS

3.1 Human Growth and Development

3.1.1 Demonstrate understanding of human growth and development.

3.1.2 Demonstrate understanding of how deviations in normal human growth and development can result in disabilities.

3.1.3 Demonstrate knowledge of normal and atypical motor development.

3.1.1 Demonstrate ability to apply understanding of deviations in normal human growth and development of individuals with physical, mental, sensory, neurological, and other specific health needs.

3.1.2 Demonstrate ability to apply understanding of atypical motor development to individuals with disabilities.

3.2 Motor Learning

3.2.1 Demonstrate proficiency in applying principles of motor learning to teaching and learning of motor skills.

3.2.2 Demonstrate ability to apply principles of motivation, including to individuals with disabilities, on learning of motor skills.

3.2.1 Demonstrate ability to apply principles of learning to individuals with specific physical and motor needs.

3.2.2 Demonstrate ability to apply principles of motivation on development of motor skills by individuals with disabilities.

3.3 Self-Concept and Personality Development

3.3.1 Demonstrate understanding of relationships among positive and negative movement experiences and self concept.

3.3.2 Demonstrate ability to help students with and without disabilities develop self-concepts.

3.3.3 Demonstrate ability to apply skills and techniques to assist individuals with and without disabilities overcome attitudinal barriers which can affect interpersonal relationships and development of positive self-concepts.

3.3.4 Demonstrate understanding of relationships between an individual's personality development and participation in physical education, sport, dance, and play programs.

3.3.1 Demonstrate understanding of how participating in physical and motor activities contributes to positive self-concepts of individuals with disabilities.

3.3.2 Demonstrate ability to apply understanding of how interpersonal relationships are effected by participation in physical and motor activities.

3.3.3 Demonstrate ability to apply skills and techniques to assist individuals with disabilities overcome additional barriers which can effect interpersonal relationships and development of positive self-concepts.

3.4 Management of Behavior

3.4.1 Demonstrate ability to apply various methods for developing appropriate student behavior.

3.4.2 Demonstrate an understanding of principles of motivation as they affect human behavior and promote motor performance.

3.4.1 Demonstrate ability to apply appropriate techniques for managing behavior (i.e., Behaviorism, Existentialism, Humanism).

3.4.2 Demonstrate ability to apply techniques of motivation to enhance acceptable behavior and promote motor performance.

Physical education generalist	*Adapted physical education specialist*

4.0 HISTORICAL-PHILOSOPHICAL FOUNDATIONS

4.1 Historical Development

4.1.1 Demonstrate understanding of the historical development of physical education.

4.1.2 Demonstrate understanding of roles and significance of physical education professional organizations on development of professional standards, ethics, and programs related to physical education.

4.1.1 Demonstrate understanding of the historical development of adapted physical education.

4.1.2 Demonstrate understanding of roles and significance of professional and voluntary organizations on development of professional standards, ethics, and programs related to adapted physical education.

4.2 Philosophical Development

4.2.1 Demonstrate understanding of the philosophies of physical education.

4.2.2 Demonstrate ability to apply a personal/professional philosophy of physical education.

4.2.3 Demonstrate understanding of current issues and emerging trends in physical education and their philosophical significances.

4.2.4 Demonstrate ability to identify ways that individuals realize and express their individualities and uniquenesses through physical education, sport, dance, and play programs.

4.2.1 Demonstrate understanding of philosophies of adapted physical education.

4.2.2 Demonstrate ability to apply a personal/professional philosophy of adapted physical education.

4.2.3 Demonstrate understanding of current issues and emerging trends in adapted physical education and their philosophical significances.

4.2.4 Demonstrate understanding of ways individuals with disabilities realize and express their individualities and uniquenesses through physical education, sport, dance, and play programs.

5.0 ASSESSMENT AND EVALUATION

5.1 Program Goals and Objectives

5.1.1 Demonstrate understanding of goals and objectives of physical education, including programs and activities for individuals with disabilities.

5.1.2 Demonstrate ability to identify performance or instructional objectives leading to fulfillment of physical education goals in psychomotor, affective, and cognitive domains.

5.1.1 Demonstrate ability to apply goals and objectives of adapted physical education.

5.1.2 Demonstrate ability to develop instructional objectives which lead to fulfillment of physical education goals in psychomotor, affective, and cognitive domains by individuals with disabilities.

5.2 Screening and Assessment

5.2.1 Demonstrate proficiency in using appropriate instruments i.e., screening devices through standardized test—and procedures to measure physiological, biomechanical, and psychomotor functions.

5.2.2 Demonstrate ability to select various assessment instruments for measuring physical and motor performance.

5.2.1 Demonstrate proficiency in applying appropriate instruments and procedures for measuring levels of physiological, biomechanical, and psychomotor functioning of individuals with disabilities.

5.2.2 Demonstrate proficiency in applying appropriate criteria in constructing assessment instruments for measuring physical and motor performances of students with disabilities.

Physical education generalist	*Adapted physical education specialist*

5.2 Screening and Assessment (continued)

5.2.3 Demonstrate ability to construct various assessment instruments for measuring physical and motor performance.	5.2.3 Demonstrate proficiency to interpret assessment results of students with disabilities in terms of physical education goals and objectives.

5.3 Evaluation

5.3.1 Demonstrate proficiency in using appropriate instruments to evaluate physical and motor needs of individual students. 5.3.2 Demonstrate ability to apply basic evaluation principles in determining student progress in physical education. 5.3.3 Demonstrate ability to interpret evaluation results as they apply to physical education goals, and activities. 5.3.4 Demonstrate proficiency in applying evaluation results to appropriate physical education goals, objectives, and activities.	5.3.1 Demonstrate proficiency in applying appropriate instruments in determining physical and motor needs of individuals with disabilities. 5.3.2 Demonstrate proficiency in applying principles of evaluation in determining student progress in adapted physical education.

6.0 CURRICULUM PLANNING, ORGANIZATION, AND IMPLEMENTATION

6.1 Program Planning

6.1.1   Demonstrate ability to plan instructional programs emphasizing the following areas . . .
  . . . physical and motor fitness
  . . . fundamental motor skills and patterns
  . . . skills in aquatics, dance, individual and group games and sports, including lifetime sports and leisure skills.
	6.1.1 Demonstrate proficiency in planning instructional programs to meet needs of students with disabilities emphasizing the following areas . . .
	  . . . physical and motor fitness
	  . . . fundamental motor skills and patterns
	  . . . skills in aquatics, dance, individual and group games and sports, including lifetime sports and leisure skills.
	
	6.1.2 Demonstrate ability to plan individual physical education programs based on goals and objectives established by an interdisciplinary team.
	
	6.1.3 Demonstrate ability to adapt physical and motor fitness activities, fundamental motor skills and patterns, aquatics and dance, and individual and group games and sports, including lifetime sports and leisure skills, to accommodate needs of individuals with disabilities.
	
	6.1.4 Demonstrate understanding of organizations that govern adapted sports and games.

| *Physical education generalist* | *Adapted physical education specialist* |

6.2 Individual Instruction

6.2.1 Demonstrate understanding of the principles of individualized instruction.

6.2.2 Demonstrate ability to plan physical education programs based on student's current levels of performance.

6.2.3 Develop ability to apply strategies for individualizing instruction in regular physical education settings.

6.2.1 Demonstrate ability to apply strategies for individualizing instruction for students with disabilities in a variety of instructional settings.

6.2.2 Demonstrate ability to apply task analysis techniques in the process of individualizing instruction.

6.2.3 Demonstrate ability to implement appropriate physical education programs for individuals with disabilities based on each student's current level of performance.

6.3 Program Implementation

6.3.1 Demonstrate understanding of relationships among supportive factors (i.e., administrative policies, facilities, equipment, faculty, community) and effective implementation of physical education curricula.

6.3.2 Demonstrate understanding of role and significance of physical educators as members of interdisciplinary teams.

6.3.1 Demonstrate ability to implement appropriate physical education curricula for individuals with disabilities based upon adequate supportive factors (i.e., administrative policies, facilities, equipment, faculty, and community).

6.3.2 Demonstrate ability to function effectively as a member of an interdisciplinary team.

6.3.3 Demonstrate ability to apply appropriate techniques for facilitating interdisciplinary communication among all persons working with individuals with disabilities.

6.4 Safety Considerations

6.4.1 Demonstrate understanding of safety principles related to physical and motor activities.

6.4.2 Demonstrate knowledge of specific safety considerations for individuals with disabilities when they participate in physical education, sport, dance, and play program activities.

6.4.1 Demonstrate ability to apply principles of safety to wheelchair transfers, lifts, and assists needed when individuals with disabilities participate in physical activities.

6.4.2 Demonstrate understanding of scientific bases for specifically contraindicated exercises and activities for individuals with disabilities.

6.5 Health Considerations

6.5.1 Demonstrate understanding of appropriate health principles and practices related to physical and motor activities.

6.5.2 Demonstrate knowledge of special health considerations when individuals with disabilities participate in physical education, sport, dance, and play programs.

6.5.1 Demonstrate ability to apply principles of appropriate health practices to participation in physical and motor activities by individuals with disabilities.

6.5.2 Demonstrate understanding of effects of medication, fatigue, and illness on mental, physical, and motor performances of individuals with disabilities.

6.5.3 Demonstrate understanding of implications of personal hygiene, posture, and nutrition for individuals with disabilities.

Appendix B
Developmental Schedule

AT BIRTH

I. Reflex activity

   A. Asymmetrical tonic neck reflex—elicited by rotation of the head to one side—increases extensor tone on the face side and flexor tone on the skull side; one limb flexes, the other extends (deQuiros and Schrager, 1978).

   B. Moro reflex (deQuiros and Schrager, 1978), startle reaction (Bobath and Bobath, 1971)—abduction and extension of arms resulting from loud noise, sudden movement or unsupported head tipping backward.

   C. Rooting reflex—in response to stimulus at corner of mouth—the lower lip drops, tongue moves toward stimulus, and head turns to follow it (Fiorentino, 1972).

   D. Sucking reflex—in response to finger placed on lips— immediate sucking motion of lips; jaw drops and lifts rhythmically (Fiorentino, 1972).

   E. Crossed extension reflex—one leg held in extension and stimulation to the foot results in flexion and extension of the opposite leg and fanning of toes (Fiorentino, 1972).

   F. Withdrawal reflex—with both legs extended and soles of feet stimulated—the result is extension of the toes and dorsiflexion of the feet, followed by flexion of legs (Fiorentino, 1972).

   G. Labyrinthine righting reflex—with vision occluded, held in prong, supine, and vertical tilt, head moves to normal position (Fiorentino, 1972).

   H. Primary walking—automatic walking (sometimes called step reflex)—when held upright (Fiorentino, 1972).

   I. Grasp reflex—pressure in palm of hand results in flexion of the fingers (Fiorentino, 1972).

   J. Placing reaction—infant held up, dorsum of hand brushed against under edge of table results in the infant flexing the arm and bringing clenched fist down on table top (Fiorentino, 1972).

   K. Tonic labyrinthine reflex—results in maximal extensor tone when head is about 45 degrees above horizontal in supine and maximal flexor tone when head is about 45 degrees below horizontal in prone (Bobath and Bobath, 1971).

II. Head and trunk postures

   A. Head usually turned to side.

   B. When pulled to sitting, head sags backward then falls forward onto chest.

III. Upper extremities

   A. Hands fisted most of the time (Banus, 1971).

   B. Crude circular movements of arms as reaction to stimuli.

IV. Lower extremities

   Legs flexed, externally rotated, and alternately flexing and extending as response to stimuli.

V. Play behavior
   None.

BIRTH TO SIX WEEKS

I. Reflex activity

    A. Inhibition of crossed extension reflex (Fiorentino, 1972).

    B. Neck righting reflex—turning of the head results in a turning of thorax and torso (Bobath and Bobath, 1971).

II. Head and trunk postures

    A. Lifting of head and chin when prone (Jersild, 1954). This is the beginning of formation of the cervical curve.

    B. Head erect but bobbing when held in sitting position (Covert, 1965).

    C. Uniformly rounded back (Gesell, 1940).

    D. Control of oculomotor muscles (Gesell, 1940).

III. Upper extremities

    A. Ring retained when placed in hand (Halverson, 1933).

    B. Flexion and extension of arms (Gesell, 1940).

    C. Circular arm movements.

IV. Lower extremities

    A. Reflexive creeping motion when prone (Gesell, 1954).

    B. Unilateral flexion of knee (Gesell, 1945).

V. Play behavior

    A. Leg thrusting (Shirley, 1933). This is seemingly a response to pleasurable stimuli.

    B. Plays with hands.

    C. Brings objects in hands to mouth.

SIX WEEKS TO THREE MONTHS

Average height: 22 in. (54 cm.)
Average weight: 10 lbs. (4.6 kg.)

I. Reflex activity

    A. Asymmetrical tonic neck reflex begins to become inhibited (deQuiros, 1978).

    B. Withdrawal reflex inhibited (Fiorentino, 1972).

    C. Primary walking reflex inhibited (Fiorentino, 1972).

    D. Placing reaction begins to become inhibited (deQuiros and Schrager, 1978).

II. Head and trunk postures

    A. Trunk strongly dominated by flexor tone (Fiorentino, 1972).

    B. Head held erect (Ilg and Ames, 1960).

    C. Chest held up when in prone position (Jersild, 1954).

    D. Eyes follow object past 90 degrees (Banus, 1971).

    E. Eyes fixate on object (Ilg and Ames, 1960).

III. Upper extremities

    A. First directed arm movements in response to objects (Gesell, 1940).

    B. Reaches and touches from lying or sitting position (Ilg and Ames, 1960).

IV. Lower extremities

    A. Extended legs and alternate kicking (Gesell, 1954).

    B. Supports a fraction of body weight when held erect (Gesell, 1954).

V. Play behavior

    A. Holds rattle and glances at it (Gesell, 1940).

    B. Pulls at other's clothing (Gesell, 1940).

    C. Learns by seeing and putting objects in mouth.

THREE MONTHS TO SIX MONTHS

Average height: 24 in. (60 cm.)
Average weight: 14 lbs. (6.4 kg.)

I. Reflex activity

    A. Inhibition of asymmetrical tonic neck reflex (deQuiros and Schrager, 1978).

    B. Inhibition of moro reflex (deQuiros and Schrager, 1978).

    C. Inhibition of rooting reflex (Fiorentino, 1972).

    D. Inhibition of sucking reflex (Fiorentino, 1972).

    E. Grasp reflex inhibited (Fiorentino, 1972).

    F. Landau reaction (Fiorentino, 1972)—increased extensor tone in prone. This is stimulating deep postural muscles of the back and neck required for standing.

    G. Appearance and inhibition of symmetrical tonic neck reflex (deQuiros and Schrager, 1978)—extension of the head causes extension of the arms and flexion of the hips; flexion of the head causes flexion of the arms and extension of the hips.

(Inhibition of Asymmetrical Tonic Neck Reflex)

II. Head and trunk postures

    A. Complete head control (Shirley, 1933).

    B. Sits with minimal support (Gesell, 1940). This posture begins the development of the lumbar curve.

    C. Lifts abdomen from floor (Ilg and Ames, 1960).

    D. Rolls from supine to side or to prone position (Shirley, 1933).

    E. Tenses for lifting, when on back (Ilg and Ames, 1960).

    F. Ocular pursuit in a sitting position (Covert, 1965).

III. Upper extremities

    A. Both bilateral and unilateral reaching for dangling objects (Gesell, 1954); bilateral activities at midline (Fiorentino, 1972).

    B. Supports self on extended arms (Gesell, 1940).

    C. Simultaneous flexion and thumb opposition (Shirley, 1933).

    D. Releases against resistance or drops (Jersild, 1954).

IV. Lower extremities

    A. Momentarily supports large part of body weight (Gesell, 1940).

    B. Extends and lifts legs symmetrically when in supine (Gesell, 1954).

    C. Holds knees straight (Gesell, 1940).

V. Play behavior

    A. Visually pursues lost toys (Banus, 1971).

    B. Grasps feet (Banus, 1971).

    C. Rescues toy dropped within reach (Banus, 1971).

SIX MONTHS TO NINE MONTHS

Average height: 26 in. (65 cm.)
Average weight: 17 lbs. (7.6 kg.)

I. Reflex activity

    A. Tonic labyrinthine reflex inhibited.

    B. Protective extensor reaction (parachute) appears (Fiorentino, 1972)—forward movement in the upside-down vertical position results in what helps "break one's fall" when losing one's balance.

(Inhibition of Tonic Labyrinthine Reflex)

II. Head and trunk postures

    A. Sits alone without support (Ilg and Ames, 1940).

    B. Leans forward from a sitting position without losing balance (Ilg and Ames, 1960). This is assisted by protective extensor reaction for support when leaning forward.

    C. Maintains balance when turning from side to side (Gesell, 1940).

    D. Creeps on stomach with reciprocal rather than bilateral action of limbs (Banus, 1971; Fiorentino, 1972).

III. Upper extremities

    A. Props self up on one arm flexed, when in prone position (Gesell, 1940).

    B. Has independent use of hands (Gesell, 1940).

    C. Complete thumb opposition, partial finger prehension (Jersild, 1954).

    D. Rotates wrist in manipulation of object (Jersild, 1954).

    E. Drops for release (Gesell, 1940).

IV. Lower extremities

    A. Pulls to knees for standing position (Gesell, 1940).

    B. Draws up knees into crawling position (Gesell, 1940).

    C. Stands with support.

    D. Begins to crawl (on all fours) (Jersild, 1954).

V. Play behavior

    A. Manipulates string of dangling rings (Gesell, 1954).

    B. Reaches for toys out of reach (Banus, 1971).

    C. Holds one object, regards and grasps another (Banus, 1971).

NINE MONTHS TO TWELVE MONTHS

Average height: 27 in. (67 cm.)
Average weight: 19 lbs. (8.6 kg.)

I. Reflex activity

Landau reaction very strong (Bobath and Bobath, 1971).

II. Head and trunk postures

    A. Sits indefinitely (Gesell, 1940).

    B. Changes from sitting to prone position (Ilg and Ames, 1960).

    C. Does not tolerate supine position (Gesell, 1940).

III. Upper extremities

    A. Grasps with neat pincer grasp (Banus, 1971).

    B. Turns leaves of a magazine (Shirley, 1933).

    C. Holds cup with assistance (Gesell, 1940).

    D. Drops voluntarily (Gesell, 1940).

    E. Precise poking with extended forefinger (Ilg and Ames, 1960).

IV. Lower extremities

    A. Synchronous movement of arms and legs in crawling position (Gesell, 1954).

    B. Alternate flexion and extension when arm and leg on opposite body sides move (Gesell, 1954). This action is preparatory to balanced upright locomotion.

    C. Stands with support and takes steps (Shirley, 1933).

    D. Walks when led (Jersild, 1954). Although beginning to walk, the infant will revert to crawling when efficient locomotion is needed.

    E. Supports entire weight on soles of feet (Gesell, 1940).

V. Play behavior

    A. Plays pat-a-cake (Shirley, 1933).

    B. Retains ball and attempts to throw or roll it (Gesell, 1940).

    C. Stands and moves around furniture.

TWELVE MONTHS TO EIGHTEEN MONTHS

Average height: 28 in. (70 cm.)
Average weight: 20 lbs. (9.2 kg.)

I. Reflex activity

Continued labyrinthine righting, parachute, and Landau reactions (deQuiros and Schrager, 1978).

II. Head and trunk positions

Good balance (Gesell, 1940).

III. Upper extremities

    A. Grasping with wide-open hand primitive (Shirley, 1933).

B. Exaggerated finger extension in throwing (Gesell, 1940).

C. Walking before and after casting (Gesell, 1940).

D. Primitive grasp in writing (Shirley, 1933).

E. Use of butt end of crayon; uses shoulder movement in writing (Gesell, 1940).

F. Poor but improved release (Gesell, 1940).

IV. Lower extremities

A. Secure in walking (Gesell, 1940).

B. Stands on one foot when held (Jersild, 1954).

C. Steps before and after throwing (Gesell, 1954).

D. Walks a 1.6 in. (4 cm.) board for 12 in. (30 cm.) (Gesell, 1954).

E. Begins to run (Gesell, 1954).

F. Climbs and stands on chair (Gesell, 1954).

G. Descends from stool 10 in. (25.5 cm.) high (Gesell, 1954).

H. Creeps up flight of six steps and descends by creeping, sitting bumps, and later marking time (Gesell, 1954).

I. Jumps a distance of 12 in. (30 cm.) (Gesell, 1954).

J. Attempts to kick a ball (Gesell, 1954).

V. Play behavior

A. Builds five-block tower (Shirley, 1933).

B. Inserts key in lock (Gesell, 1954).

C. Puts pellets in bottle (Gesell, 1954).

D. Nests four boxes (Shirley, 1933).

E. Marks with pencil (Shirley, 1933).

F. Hugs doll (Banus, 1971).

G. Walks into a ball; tries to kick later in this stage (Banus, 1971).

TWO YEARS TO THREE YEARS

Average height: 32 in. (80 cm.)
Average weight: 28 lb. (13 kg.)

I. Reflex activity

No change.

II. Head and trunk postures

Secure in balance and movement.

III. Upper extremities

A. Reaches for object without supporting self or twisting trunk (Gesell, 1940).

B. Holds spoon by thumb and radial fingers (Fokes, 1971).

C. Folds paper, pulls off socks, finds armholes, strings beads, turns doorknob, holds glass with one hand, builds six-block tower (Gesell, 1940).

D. Holds crayons with fingers (Gesell and Armatruda, 1941).

IV. Lower extremities

A. Stands alone either foot (Jersild, 1954).

B. Stands on walking board with both feet (Jersild, 1954).

C. Stands with heels together when shown (Gesell, 1940).

D. Walks in the direction of a line (Gesell, 1940).

E. Walks between parallel lines (Gesell, 1940).

F. Carries large object while walking (Gesell, 1940).

G. Walks on tiptoe (Gesell, 1940).

H. Walks backward 9.9 ft. (3 m.) (Gesell, 1940).

I. Runs on toes (Gesell, 1940).

J. Kicks a ball (Fokes, 1971).

K. Jumps distance of 12 in. (30 cm.) with one foot leading (Gesell, 1940).

L. Jumps from ground with both feet (Gesell, 1940).

M. Ascends a few steps on alternating feet (Gesell, 1940).

N. Ascends and descends steps by marking time (Jersild, 1954).

V. Play behavior

A. See those suggested in III and IV above.

B. Strings beads with needle (Gesell, 1940).

C. Folds paper when shown (Gesell, 1940).

D. Turns pages in book (Gesell, 1940).

E. Draws vertical and circular strokes (Gesell, 1940).,

F. Imitates simple actions of others (Gesell, 1940).

THREE YEARS TO FOUR YEARS

Average height: 38 in. (96 cm.)
Average weight: 33 lbs. (15.5 kg.)

I. Reflex activity

No change.

II. Head and trunk postures

A. Shoulders erect (Gesell, 1940).

B. Abdomen less protruding (Gesell, 1940).

C. Upright posture characterized by extreme lumbar curve.

III. Upper extremities

A. Leans, extends arms, and twists easily while reaching (Gesell, 1940).

B. Picks up small objects without fingers touching table top (Gesell, 1940).

C. Unbuttons but cannot button clothing (Gesell, 1940).

D. Drives nails and pegs (Strang, 1959).

E. Uses both hands to steady block tower (Gesell, 1940).

F. Begins to use scissors (Strang, 1959).

G. Uses shoulders and elbows to throw; guides course of ball with fingers (Gesell, 1940).

H. Rests shaft at juncture of thumb and index finger when writing; extends medius on shaft (Gesell, 1940).

I. Releasing, free and easy (Gesell, 1940).

IV. Lower extremities

A. Uniform walking pattern using heel to toe progression (Jersild, 1954).

B. Walks backward a long distance (Gesell, 1940).

C. Walks 20 to 28 ft (6 to 8 m.) on walking board in 15 seconds with three errors (Gesell, 1940).

D. Walks in circular path of circle 4.5 ft. (14 cm.) in diameter (Jersild, 1954).

E. Walks on tiptoes 9.9 ft. (3 m.) (Jersild, 1954).

F. Runs easily and smoothly with moderate speed (Gesell, 1940).

G. Hops up to seven steps on one foot (Gesell, 1940).

H. Skips on one foot (Jersild, 1954).

I. Uses alternate feet in ascending up to three steps (Jersild, 1954).

J. Rides tricycle (Gesell, 1940).

V. Play behavior

A. Holds pen between thumb and index finger (Gesell, 1954).

B. Copies circle (Covert, 1955).

C. Traces a square (Gesell, 1940).

D. Builds tower with nine to ten blocks (Gesell, 1940).

E. Catches a large ball with arms fully extended (Gesell, 1940).

F. Feeds self without spilling food, laces shoes, and removes clothing (Gesell, 1940).

FOUR YEARS TO FIVE YEARS

Average height: 42 in. (1.3 meters)
Average weight: 39 lbs. (18 kg.)

I. Reflex activity

No change.

II. Head and trunk postures

Balanced and steady (Gesell, 1940).

III. Upper extremities

A. Reaching lacks poise; uses arms rather than hands (Gesell, 1940).

B. Picks up small objects with thumb and index finger (Gesell, 1940).

C. Puts toys away, washes face and hands (Strang, 1959).

D. Brushes teeth, undresses with assistance (Gesell, 1940).

E. Uses preferred hand for throwing; throws forward without regard for height; throws overhand (Gesell, 1940).

F. Catches a large ball, one out of three trials (Gesell, 1940).

G. Good precision and timing on release; releases without pressure (Gesell, 1940).

IV. Lower extremities

    A. Walks and runs long distances (Strang, 1959).

    B. Stops and goes quickly in running (Gesell, 1940).

    C. Balances on toes (Gesell, 1940).

    D. Hops on either foot seven or eight times (Gesell, 1940).

    E. Descends stairs on alternate feet (Jersild, 1954).

    F. Jumps skillfully (Strang, 1959).

G. Shifts weight in throwing.

H. Slides (Gutteridge, 1939).

V. Play behavior

    A. Uses play apparatus, will play with others to some degree if guided.

    B. Fantasy play with others.

    C. Gives life to playthings, talks to them.

FIVE YEARS TO SIX YEARS

Average height: 43.5 in. (1.3 meters)
Average weight: 42.5 lbs. (19.5 kg)

I. Reflex activity

  No change.

II. Head and trunk postures

  No change.

III. Upper extremities

    A. Precision in use of tools (Gesell, 1940).

    B. Throws skillfully at shoulder level (Gesell, 1940).

    C. Catches ball with hands (Gesell, 1940).

    D. Precise release (Gesell, 1940).

IV. Lower extremities

    A. Walks long distances on tiptoe (Gesell, 1940).

    B. Balances on toes for several seconds; stands on one foot indefinitely (Gesell, 1940).

    C. Skips on alternating feet (Gutteridge, 1939); skips to music (Strang, 1959).

    D. Climbs easily (Gutteridge, 1939).

    E. Descends long staircase with alternate feet (Gesell, 1940).

    F. Roller skates and rides bicycle (Strang, 1959).

    G. Kicks ball 8 to 10 ft. (2.5 to 3.3 meters) with accuracy (Gesell, 1940).

    H. Broad jumps 28 to 30 in. (70 to 78 cm.) (Gesell, 1940).

V. Play behavior

    A. See those suggested in III and IV above.

    B. Interested in stunts and trapeze type play (Marx, n.d.).

    C. Ice skates (Marx, n.d.).

SIX YEARS TO SEVEN YEARS

Average height: 46 in. (1.5 meters)
Average weight: 48 lbs. (23 kg.)

I. Reflex activity

  No change.

II. Head and trunk postures

  No change.

III. Upper extremities

    A. Uses elbows and wrists in throwing: guides path of ball (Gesell and Armatruda, 1941).

    B. Catches tossed ball chest high from a distance of 3.3 ft. (1 m.) two out of three trials (Gesell and Armatruda, 1941).

IV. Lower extremities

    A. Uses walk, run, jump in strenuous activities (Gesell and Armatruda, 1941).

B. Stands on each foot alternately with eyes closed (Gesell and Armatruda, 1941).

C. Hops 50 ft. (15.5 m.) in nine seconds (Gesell and Armatruda, 1941).

D. Jumps 12 in. (21 cm.) and lands on toes (Gesell and Armatruda, 1941).

E. High jumps 8 in. (21 cm.) (Gesell and Armatruda, 1941).

F. Kicks soccer ball with accuracy 10 to 18 ft. (3.5 m.) (Gesell and Armatruda, 1941).

V. Play behavior

A. Likes wrestling, tumbling, crawling, climbing, swinging (Banus, 1971).

B. Enjoys small group games.

BEYOND SEVEN YEARS

Beyond seven years of age, motor patterns already developed evolve into motor skills and eventually become refined game and sport skills.

BIBLIOGRAPHY

Banus, B. S., et al. *The Developmental Therapist*. Thorofare, New Jersey: Charles B. Slack, Inc., 1971.

Bobath, B., and Bobath, K. *Abnormal Postural Reflex Activity Caused by Brain Lesions*. London: William Heinemann Medical Books, Ltd., 1971.

Covert, C. *Mental Retardation*. Chicago: American Medical Association, 1965.

Fiorentino, M. R. *Normal and Abnormal Development*. Springfield, Illinois: Charles C. Thomas, 1972.

Fokes, J. "Developmental Scales of Motor Abilities." In *Training the Developmentally Young*, edited by Beth Stephens. New York: John Day Company, 1971.

Gesell, A. *The First Five Years of Life*. New York: Harper and Row, 1940.

Gesell, A. "The Ontogenesis of Infant Behavior." In *Manual of Child Psychology*, edited by L. Carmichael. New York: Wiley, 1954.

Gesell, A., and Armatruda, C. S. *Developmental Diagnosis*. New York: Harper and Bros., 1941.

Gutteridge, M. "A Study of Motor Achievements in Young Children," *Archives of Psychology* 244 (1939): 5–178.

Halverson, H. M. "The Acquisition of Skill in Infancy." *Journal of Genetic Psychology* 43 (1933): 3–48.

Ilg, F., and Ames, L. *Child Behavior*. New York: Dell Publishing Company, 1960.

Jersild, A. *Child Psychology*. New York: Prentice-Hall, 1954.

Marx, Orrin. *Motor Activities: Newborn to Six Years of Age*. Washington, D.C.: American Alliance for Health, Physical Education, Recreation, and Dance, n.d.

deQuiros, J. B., and Schrager, O. L. *Neuropsychological Fundamentals in Learning Disabilities*. San Rafael, California: Academic Therapy Publications, 1978.

Shirley, M. "The First Two Years: A Study of 25 Babies." *Institute of Child Welfare Monograph Series* 7 (1933): 2.

Strang, R. *An Introduction to Child Study*. New York: Macmillan Company, 1959.

Appendix C
Annotated Bibliography of Selected Perceptual-Motor Theorists and General Perceptual-Motor Books

A. JEAN AYRES

Ayres has published articles over the past twenty years in journals such as *American Journal of Occupational Therapy, Physical Therapy Journal, Perceptual and Motor Skills, Journal of Learning Disabilities,* and *Academic Therapy.* Articles have also appeared in J. Helmuth's *Learning Disorders* and *Claremont Reading Conference Yearbook.* In addition Ayres has developed the Southern California Sensory Integration Test battery, Southern California Post-rotary Nystagmus Test, and clinical observations. Her books include the following:

Sensory Integration and Learning Disorders. Los Angeles: Western Psychological Services, 1975.

This book describes the neuro-behavioral theory of sensory integrative therapy to assist children with learning deficits. References are made to basic brain research as well as to the author's behavioral research. Treatment rationale and techniques are presented.

The Development of Sensory Integrative Theory and Practice. Dubuque: Kendall/Hunt, 1974.

A comprehensive monograph including twenty-eight articles and reports on the theoretical formulation, concepts of remediation, factor analytic studies, and research in sensory integration by Ayres through 1972.

RAY BARSCH

Barsch has published articles in the *Journal of Genetic Psychology, Exceptional Children, American Journal of Occupational Therapy,* and the *Journal of Learning Disabilities.*

One of his papers is included in the book *Learning Disorders,* and several articles have been published in the journal *Rehabilitation Literature.* His books include the following:

Achieving Perceptual Motor Efficiency. Seattle: Special Child Publications, 1967.

Presentation and detailed description of Barsch's theory and methodology for all handicapped individuals. Practical suggestions based upon various principles of learning are offered to help the child achieve perceptual-motor integration. This book is volume I of a series.

A Movigenics Curriculum: An Experimental Approach to Children with Special Learning Disabilities Conducted at the Longfellow School, Madison, Wisconsin during the 1964–1965 School Year. Madison, Wisconsin: State Department of Public Instruction, 1965.

Detailed presentation of the movigenic curriculum: rationale, planning dimensions, classroom organization, theoretical constructs, and positive and negative aspects of the program.

Enriching Perception and Cognition. Seattle: Special Child Publications, 1968.

This book is the second volume written by Barsch regarding his perceptual-motor theory and curriculum. This volume focuses upon the basic patterns of movement as being a dominant theme in his movigenics theory.

MARIANNE FROSTIG

Articles by Frostig and her coworkers have appeared in such journals as *Reading Teacher, Journal of Special Education,*

American Journal of Orthopsychiatry, Journal of Education Research, and the *Journal of Learning Disabilities.* In addition, her articles have appeared in H. Myklebust's *Progress in Learning Disorders,* and J. Helmuth's *Learning Disorders.* She has developed the Frostig Test of Visual Perception and a Move-Grow-Learn curriculum. Her books include the following:

Move-Grow-Learn. Chicago: Follett, 1969.

The card file contains several hundred illustrated exercises and recommended activities for perceptual-motor development. The activities focus on movement and learning experiences simultaneously.

Movement Education—Theory and Practice. Chicago: Follett, 1970.

This book describes Frostig's eclectic approach to human development, which isolates and emphasizes remediation of visual perception. The book also presents the motor aspects of her program, which include agility, coordination, balance, strength, speed, flexibility, endurance, and body awareness.

ROBERT DOMAN and CARL DELACATO

Articles by these two men have appeared in the *American Medical Association Journal, McCall's,* and *The Claremont Reading Conference Yearbook.*
Books by Robert Doman include the following:

What to Do About Your Brain-Injured Child. Garden City, New York: Doubleday, 1974.

This book discusses the Doman-Delacato theory and treatment techniques for use with brain-injured children. It provides an in depth analysis of the development of the system and intervention techniques.

Books by Carl Delacato include the following:

The Diagnosis and Treatment of Speech and Reading Problems. Springfield, Illinois: Charles C. Thomas, 1963.

Presentation, discussion, and update (from 1954) of Delacato's theory of neurological organizations and treatment procedures for the brain-injured.

Neurological Organization and Reading. Springfield, Illinois: Charles C. Thomas, 1966.

Overview and general discussion of Delacato's theory of neurological organization. The application to brain-injured children is discussed along with descriptions of scientific experiments supporting the theory.

The Treatment and Prevention of Reading Problems. Springfield, Illinois: Charles C. Thomas, 1954.

The first book in which Delacato presents his theory of neurological organization, its application to and treatment procedures for the brain-injured child.

The Ultimate Stranger. Garden City, New York: Doubleday, 1974.

This book specifically deals with the autistic child. The book is a record of Delacato's search for answers regarding the behavior of autistic children. Delacato applies his theory of neurological organization to autistic children.

GERALD N. GETMAN

Getman, an optometrist, published primarily in the 1960s but continued to give conference presentations during the next twenty years on his visual-motor theory and its interaction with learning. Books by Gerald N. Getman include the following:

(With E. R. Kane, M. R. Halgren, and G. W. McKee.) *Developing Learning Readiness.* Manchester, Missouri: Webster Division, McGraw-Hill, 1968.

This book presents the visual training approach to learning readiness. The reader is presented with methodology and aspects of visual-motor training specifically designed to enhance learning.

How to Develop Your Child's Intelligence. Luverne, Minnesota: Self-published, 1962.

A paper published by the author, which presents his methodology based upon the theory that visual training will remediate educational difficulties.

The Physiology of Readiness. Minneapolis: Programs to Accelerate School Success, 1964.

A manual for training visual-motor skills of children.

D. O. HEBB

Although not widely published, Hebb adopted a neuro-psychological focus in which he stressed the importance of early motor learnings as an integral part of neurological growth. Books by D. O. Hebb include the following:

The Organization of Behavior. New York: Wiley, 1949.

In this book, Hebb attempts to bridge the gap between neurophysiology and psychology. Included are discussions of the problems of learning, perception, levels of processing, motivation, and intelligence. The book presents a theory of behavior based upon the physiology of the nervous system.

JEAN MARC ITARD

Itard is considered to be the first to attempt work with the retarded rather than locking them up. Seguin studied with him, and together they worked with Victor, the wild boy.

The Wild Boy of Aveyron. New York: Appleton-Century-Crofts, 1962.

This book, which describes Itard's work with a young boy found living in the woods, is simply a case study through which Itard presents and elaborates upon his principles and techniques of educational strategies. It is the first book to deal with sensory education, and was originally published in 1801.

NEWELL C. KEPHART

Newell C. Kephart collaborated with several other authors on articles and books, which have appeared in *Academic Therapy, Exceptional Children Journal,* and J. Helmuth's *Learning Disorders.* Kephart, along with Eugene Roach, developed the Purdue Perceptual-Motor Survey.

(With C. M. Chaney.) *Motoric Aids to Perceptual Training.* Columbus: Charles E. Merrill, 1968.

Description of Kephart's perceptual-motor theory, including the following: motor system, motor generalization, ocular-motor coordination, differentiation of body parts, cognition, and speech readiness.

(With B. Godrey.) *Movement Patterns and Motor Education.* New York: Appleton-Century-Crofts, 1969.

Presentation of Kephart's theory and its application to physical education and movement education.

Slow Learner in the Classroom. Columbus: Charles E. Merrill, 1960.

This book contains Kephart's perceptual-motor theory in its entirety. Regarded as a basic reference, it includes diagnostic methods and techniques of remediation.

The Brain-Injured Child in the Classroom. Chicago: National Society for Crippled Children and Adults, 1963.

This book presents an overview and brief description of the author's theory and approach to brain-injured children.

(With D. H. Radler.) *Success Through Play.* New York: Harper and Row, 1960.

This book is a popularized treatment of Kephart's theory and training methods designed for easy reading by parents and lay persons.

(With A. A. Strauss.) *Psycho-pathology and Education of the Brain-Injured Child.* New York: Grune & Stratton, 1947.

Kephart's earliest work presenting the theory espoused by the authors regarding the problems, assessment, and education of the brain-injured child.

MARIA M. MONTESSORI

Montessori herself has authored at least fifteen books during her lifespan, and over thirty books have been written about the woman and her approach to education.

The Absorbent Mind. New York: Holt, Rinehart and Winston, 1967.

This is Montessori's classic work, which presents an analysis of the physical and psychological aspects of a child's growth. The first six years of a child's life are highlighted as being the most significant period of human life.

The Advanced Montessori Method. Cambridge, Massachusetts: Robert Bentley, 1964.

This book expands and further delineates the method of teaching developed by Montessori. It describes the advanced methodology and techniques.

The Montessori Method. New York: Fredric A. Stokes, 1912.

A basic text on the Montessori approach to education. Presented in this book are the details of her pedagogy. Sensory education, the concept of "help me to help myself," and the education of children three to six years are stressed.

The Secret of Childhood. Notre Dame, Indiana: Fides Publishers, 1966.

This book focuses on children and their emergence as human beings oriented to their environment. The origins of the methods, the child as a whole person, and the environment-individual interaction are topics covered throughout the text.

Spontaneous Activity in Education. New York: Schocken Books, 1965.

In this book, Montessori describes children's reaction to and interaction with the environment as a valuable experience in education.

(By R. C. Oren.) *Montessori and the Special Child.* New York: G. P. Putnam's Sons, 1969.

The Montessori method and its application to exceptional individuals is well presented in this book. Background information, Montessori's principles of education, and practical examples of programs are provided.

JEAN PIAGET

Well over one hundred books have been written either about Piaget or his approach to child development and learning. Piaget has authored many texts, some of which have been translated into English.

Behavior and Evolution. New York: Pantheon Books, 1978.

This book presents Piaget's views on behavior and evolution. After much theoretical discussion, Piaget concludes that there is an organizing and a variational evolution, and that behavior is its motor.

The Origins of Intelligence in the Child. New York: Penguin Books, 1936.

This book presents the framework and underlying foundation of Piaget's work. Included are the biological problem of intelligence and an in depth discussion of the stages of sensorimotor development.

Science of Education and the Psychology of the Child. New York: Orion Press, 1970.

This book presents two of Piaget's contributions to the understanding of genetic psychology and child development. Specifically included are a summary of Piaget's education and teaching since 1935, and the psychological foundations of Piaget's newer methods of education.

(With B. Inhelder.) *The Psychology of the Child.* New York: Basic Books, 1969.

Presentation of a useful introduction and a synthesis of the work done in child psychology. The book deals specifically with mental growth and the development of behavior patterns up to adolescence in sensorimotor, cognitive, and affective domains.

JULIO B. DeQUIROS

DeQuiros' work has been ongoing for the past twenty years, although it has just recently gained exposure in the United States. Articles by deQuiros and his colleagues have appeared in the *Journal of Learning Disabilities, Academic Therapy,* and many journals in South America. His books include the following:

(With O. L. Schrager.) *Neuropsychological Fundamentals in Learning Disabilities.* San Rafael, California: Academic Therapy Publications, 1978.

This book presents the neuropsychological approach utilized by deQuiros in understanding the learning-disabled. Discussed are the sensory systems, the perceptual processes, motor activity and learning, assessment, and therapeutic techniques.

EDOUARD SEGUIN

On the basis of his early training with Itard, Seguin, a French physician, developed the neurophysiological approach to teaching retarded individuals. Not only is he considered to be the founder of perceptual-motor theory, he is also considered to be the founder of the American Association of Mental Deficiency.

Idiocy and Its Treatment by the Physiological Method. New York: Columbia University, 1907.

In this book, Seguin translates his educational philosophy into a developmental program. He discusses his neurophysiological approach and presents a flexibly evolved, multifaceted strategy of intervention.

PERCEPTUAL-MOTOR BOOKS

Annotated Bibliography on Perceptual-Motor Development. Washington, D.C.: American Association of Health, Physical Education, Recreation, and Dance, 1973.

Annotated bibliographic references dating through 1972 in the following areas: (1) general reading; (2) works of Ayres, Barsch, Doman and Delacata, Frostig, Kephart; (3) specific areas of perceptual-motor learning; and (4) perceptual-motor programs.

Ball, T. S. *Itard, Seguin, and Kephart.* Columbus: Charles E. Merrill, 1971.

An excellent book that reviews the literature on sensory education and specifically interrelates Itard's, Seguin's and

Kephart's theories. Identified are the roots of current thinking in the area of perceptual-motor theory.

Foundations and Practice in Perceptual-Motor Learning—A Quest for Understanding. Washington, D.C.: American Association for Health, Physical Education, Recreation, and Dance, 1971.

Contains speeches and discussions presented at the Perceptual-Motor Development: Action with Interaction Conference held in 1970. Also lists resources for tests, films, and programs of perceptual-motor development.

Hallahan, D. P., and Cruickshank, W. M. *Psychoeducational Foundations of Learning Disabilities.* Englewood Cliffs, New Jersey: Prentice-Hall, 1973.

Contains several chapters on perceptual-motor theorists within the field of learning disabilities, perceptual-motor development, and the efficacy of perceptual-motor training.

Lerch, H. A., Becker, J. E., Ward, B. M., and Nelson, J. A. *Perceptual-Motor Learning—Theory and Practice.* Palo Alto, California: Peek Publications, 1974.

A book designed to acquaint the reader with the theoretical and practical viewpoints of perceptual-motor development. Included are discussion of perceptual-motor theorists and research, screening instruments, designing programs including suggested activities, and resource materials.

Perceptual-Motor Foundations: A Multidisciplinary Concern. Washington, D.C.: American Association for Health, Physical Education, Recreation, and Dance, 1969.

Contains the proceedings of the Perceptual-Motor Symposium held in 1968. Also included is a series of addresses and articles by noted authorities.

Appendix D
Testing Procedures

LOS ANGELES UNIFIED SCHOOL DISTRICT
ADAPTED PHYSICAL EDUCATION
ASSESSMENT SCALE

Introduction and Norming

The Los Angeles Unified School District Adapted Physical Education Assessment Scale is an 18-item test of motor performance. Its primary purpose is to determine appropriate placement of students in physical education. The Adapted Physical Education Assessment Scale (A.P.E.A.S.) is designed to measure five areas of motor performance: motor development, motor achievement, perceptual motor function, posture, and physical fitness. The 1980 revision is normed on children from five to twelve years eleven months of age and includes 1 percent moderately retarded (TMR) and 1 percent severe language-delayed children. Scores for over 2,100 children randomly selected from the Los Angeles City Schools and the Santa Clara County Special Education Division are included in the norms, which are divided into six-month intervals for ages 5.0 to 7.11 years, with boys' and girls' scores combined. For ages 8.0 to 12.11, ages are divided into one-year intervals, with boys' and girls' norms separated.

General Procedures

The test is designed for item-independence so that the performance on one item will not influence the performance on the next item. The items are arranged so that all items (nos. 1–8) that must be administered outdoors are together. The remainder of the items (nos. 9–18) are to be administered either indoors or outdoors. The outdoor space required includes a 4' × 18" wall target with at least 15' × 16' of free space in front for throwing, running, and kicking, and a 50-yard rectangular running course. Equipment needed includes: 8½" rubber ball, 18" ruler, five 6" × 6" bean bags, stopwatch, test manual and score sheets, chalk, clipboard, pencil with eraser. The time required for an experienced examiner to test one student is approximately 20 minutes. As many as five students can be tested at once in about 75 minutes.

Test Items

1. *Agility Run*—run between two lines 16 feet apart as many times as possible in 20 seconds as an indicator of agility and speed.
2. *Throwing Accuracy*—throw the bean bag into the target as many times as possible in 5 trials.
3. *Hand Preference*—determines hand preference for item 2.
4. *Kick Stationary Ball*—kick the ball into the target as many times as possible out of 5 trials as an indication of eye-foot accuracy.
5. *Foot Preference*—determines foot preference on item 4.
6. *Catching*—catch the ball as many times as possible out of 5 trials.
7. *Kicking Rolling Ball*—kick the ball as many times as possible out of 5 trials.
8. *Running*—determines the quality of the running pattern.
9. *Posture*—determines the quality of body alignment.
10. *Vertical Jump*—jump as high as possible as an indication of leg strength and power.
11. *Jumping Form*—determines the quality of the jumping pattern.
12. *Ocular Control*—follow a moving object with the eyes.
13. *Bent-Knee Curl-Up*—complete as many curl-ups as possible in 30 seconds as an indication of abdominal strength.
14. *Imitation of Postures*—imitate as many postures as possible as an indication of kinesthetic awareness, bilateral control, and motor planning.
15. *Standing Balance*—stand as long as possible on each foot as an indication of static balance.

16. *Alternate Hopping*—hop as many 2-2, 2-2 patterns as possible in 10 seconds, as an indication of dynamic balance and motor planning.
17. *Arrhythmical Hopping*—hop as many 2-1 patterns as possible in 10 seconds as an indication of dynamic balance, bilateral motor control, and motor planning.
18. *Endurance*—complete as many 50-yard segments around the handball court as possible in 6 minutes.

Data Analysis

Factor analysis revealed five factors were measured by the A.P.E.A.S. as projected. Discriminant analysis resulted in the conclusion that A.P.E.A.S. correctly classifies 89 percent of the time; thus placement decisions can be made using A.P.E.A.S. with 89 percent confidence. In order to obtain the test manual and norms, contact:

Adapted Physical Education Consultant
Los Angeles Unified School District
450 North Grand Avenue–Building G
Los Angeles, California

APPENDIX D.2
THE CSULA MOTOR DEVELOPMENT CHECKLIST

The CSULA Motor Development Checklist is a screening device to be used by classroom teachers and physical educators for identifying students with potential movement problems. It is intended for use only in a minimally structured play situation, using observational techniques, for identifying students who need further testing.

The checklist is divided into seven parts, each of which suggests a game or lesson in which the target behaviors can be observed (see pages D-3 and D-4). The criterion for performance for each item can be found in the literature on motor development.

I. Obstacle Course. Set up an obstacle course in an activity room or classroom having designated locations and obstacles requiring the indicated movements. The patterns or skills required can be demonstrated and then the entire class can go through the course at once with the teacher scoring each child or a few children at a time.
II. Warm-ups. Warm-ups consist of activities that can be done in squad-formation. Wig-wag (imitating various limb positions of the teacher's choice), angels-in-the-snow (moving specified limbs), and the Kraus-Weber (chest and thigh lift from prone) are used to identify the students' ability to identify and discriminate specific body parts and

muscle groups for use. Single leg-lifts, sit-ups and toe touches sample the strength and flexibility parameters for which these items are typically used. The teacher may demonstrate and/or do these performances with the class.
III. Rhythms. This section samples the students' general coordination with an auditory stimulus. The music can be of any type appropriate to the class.
IV. Hokey Pokey. The standard Hokey Pokey tune and activity is used to help the teacher identify students who have not yet discriminated right from left body sides. Gross body part identification can also be evaluated. The teacher should watch for those students who look around at their peers for cues as to what to do.
V. Ball Handling/VI. Kick Ball. These two sections can be sampled in the same activity—Kick Ball or some variation thereof. If each child is given the chance to be the pitcher, rolling the ball can be observed easily. The other skills will be demonstrated as the game proceeds.
VII. Gunny Sack Relay. A simple relay race with both feet in a gunny sack can be used to observe jumping ability. Perhaps a practice run would be needed to determine the quality of jumping ability, before the "pressure" is on to jump fast.

APPENDIX D.3
USING THE "QUICK REFERENCE TO TESTS ON THE MARKET" CHART

The parameters or movement elements measured by the tests covered in Chapter 6 are listed across the top of the chart, which begins on page D-6. An "X" is marked in the column for each parameter measured by any given test. Movement elements have been clustered into eighteen parameters so you can quickly identify a test or tests that show promise of meeting your needs. Examine each test on the basis of parameters measured rather than title of the test, since some test names are not fully descriptive of all the parameters they measure. Once you have narrowed your choices, you can look at the individual instruments and make a selection. Here is a set of criteria recommended for your process of elimination.

1. Does the test measure the movement elements you need to measure for your population or program?
2. Is the test appropriate for the chronological age or developmental age of your students?
3. Is the test appropriate for the disability of your students?
4. Is the test appropriate for the purpose for which you plan to test (i.e., placement or program review)?
5. Is the test easy to administer?

MOTOR DEVELOPMENT CHECKLIST

	Name													Age norms
I. Obstacle Course														
1. Roll														5 months
2. Creep														9 months
3. Crawl (hands and knees)														12 months
4. Walk														12 months
5. Walk beam forward														3 years
6. Walk beam backward														
7. Walk beam right														
8. Walk beam left														
9. Run														4 years
10. Hop														4 years
11. Climb (stairs with alternate feet)														4–5 years
12. Skip														4–6 years
13. Walk over, under, between														5 years
14. Footsteps with crossover														5 years
a. Both feet														5 years
b. One foot														7 years
II. Warm-ups														
15. Wig-Wag														3 years
16. Angels-in-the-snow														4 years
17. Single leg lifts														6–7 years
18. Hook lie sit-up														6–7 years
19. Toe Touch														6–7 years
20. Kraus-Weber														6–7 years
III. Rhythms														
21. Jump rope with music														7 years
22. Clap and walk with music														

MOTOR DEVELOPMENT CHECKLIST
continued

	Name														Age norms
IV. Hokey Pokey															
23. R-L discrimination															7 years
24. Identification of body parts (head, arms, hands, legs, feet)															2 years
V. Ball Handling															
25. Roll															3–4 years
26. Bounce on target															3–7 years
27. Bounce and catch															5 years
28. Overhand throw															
29. Catch bounced ball															6 years
VI. Kick Ball															
30. Kick stationary ball															3 years
31. Kick rolled ball															7 years
VII. Gunny Sack Relay															
32. Jumping (2 feet)															3 years

Scoring: 1 = Cannot do   2 = Inadequate   3 = Adequate

SOURCE: Developed by Janet A. Seaman, P.E.D.

6. Does the test provide norms?
7. Does the test require individual or group administration?
8. Does the test's administration require special training?
9. Is the test economical in terms of cost, materials required, and personnel needed?
10. Is the test objective, valid, and reliable?

The chart also gives additional information on each test, which is coded below:

A. Recommended use

P = Placement: If a student is being considered for placement into an adapted physical education program or transfer out of the program into the mainstream, it is recommended that tests normed on the normal population be used.

PR = Program Review: For students who are going to be retained in adapted physical education, it is recommended that criterion-referenced tests or tests normed on special populations be used; tests standardized on normal populations having a .80 test-retest reliability coefficient are also recommended for this purpose.

B. Special training?

N = No special training is needed to administer this test.

Y = Yes, special training is required by the test maker or publisher.

NS = No special training is required, but extensive standardized administration procedures demand considerable practice for consistent administration; therefore, special training and/or practice is recommended.

? = It is unknown to these authors whether special training is required.

C. Norms? Ages

N = No, there are no norms available at this time.

numbers = The ages for which the norms were determined are given in years, unless otherwise noted.

CR = Criterion-referenced: The test maker has expressed the norms in terms of levels of performance relative to the criterion performances.

B = At birth

M = Males: this test is normed for males only.

L = The literature on posture describes the criterion.

D. I or G Administration

I = Test can or must be administered individually to one child at a time.

G = Test is written so it can be administered to groups.

number = The approximate time of administration according to the test maker is given in minutes.

UN = The amount of time needed to administer the test is undeterminable.

Ob = The data is gathered through observation, and the time to administer the test is often variable.

E. Norming sample

Norm = The reported norms are based on performances of unselected individuals or individuals having no known mental, physical, or emotional handicap.

EMR = Norms are based on educable (mildly) retarded individuals.

TMR = Norms are based on trainable (moderately) retarded individuals.

PH = Norms are based on physically (orthopedically) handicapped individuals.

Blind = Norms are based on blind and partially sighted individuals.

CH = Norms are based on the communicatively handicapped; aphasic, autistic language delayed, severe oral language handicapped.

NI = Norms are based on the neurologically impaired.

ED = Norms are based on the emotionally disturbed (also indicated SED).

LD = Norms are based on the learning-disabled.

AUT = Norms are based on the autistic.

BI = Norms are based on the behaviorally impaired.

Gen Sch Pop = Norms are based on the General School Population stratified by disability group according to incidence in the schools.

QUICK REFERENCE TO TESTS ON THE MARKET

TEST NAME / PARAMETERS	Strength	Flexibility	Endurance	Agility	Power	Balance	Speed	Visual skills	Eye-foot/hand coordination	Throwing	Kinesthetic awareness	Bilateral control	Tactile discrimination	Gross motor patterns	Rhythm	Fine motor control	Language development	Emotional/social development	Recommended use	Special training?	Norms?	Ages	I or G administration	Norming sample
Sensory Motor Testing																								
Perceptual-Motor Survey						X					X								PR	?	N		I G	Norm
Purdue PMS						X		X	X		X								P PR		NS	6–9	I / 45	Norm
QNST								X			X		X	X		X			P PR		NS	6–18	I / 20	Norm LD UN
VMI									X										P PR		N	2–15	I G / 20	Norm
Frostig DTVP								X	X										P		NS	4–8	I G / 45	Norm
SCSIT						X		X	X		X	X	X						P PR		Y	4–11	I / 90	Norm
MVPT								X			X								P PR		N	5–7	I / 10	Norm
Caloric Test						X													P		Y	B	I	Norm
Direct Pressure													X						P		N	2–5	I	Norm
Motor Development Profiles																								
Denver														X		X	X	X	P PR		NS	0–5	I	Norm

TEST NAME	Strength	Flexibility	Endurance	Agility	Power	Balance	Speed	Visual skills	Eye-foot/hand coordination	Throwing	Kinesthetic awareness	Bilateral control	Tactile discrimination	Gross motor patterns	Rhythm	Fine motor control	Language development	Emotional/social development	Recommended use	Special training?	Norms? Ages	I or G administration	Norming sample
Peabody														X		X			P	NS	0-7	I	Norm
CSULA Checklist									X		X	X		X					P	N	½-7	I G	Norm
Koontz														X		X	X	X	P PR	N	0-4	I	Norm
Bayley								X						X		X			P	Y	2-30 mo	I 45-90	Norm

Motor Ability

TEST NAME	Strength	Flexibility	Endurance	Agility	Power	Balance	Speed	Visual skills	Eye-foot/hand coordination	Throwing	Kinesthetic awareness	Bilateral control	Tactile discrimination	Gross motor patterns	Rhythm	Fine motor control	Language development	Emotional/social development	Recommended use	Special training?	Norms? Ages	I or G administration	Norming sample
Six Category				X		X			X	X	X								P PR	NS	5-24	I 30	Norm TMR EMR
Lincoln-Oseretsky						X	X							X		X			P	NS	6-14	I 45	Norm
Active	X		X			X			X					X					P PR	NS	5-17	I 20	Norm CH, NI, ED, EMR
Trampoline Screening						X								X		X			PR	?	N	I	ID, EMR, SED, AUT
GPI						X	X	X	X	X	X		X	X		X			PR	N	N	I 30-45	Norm LD, MR, AUT
Stott						X	X		X	X		X		X		X			P PR	N	5-16	I 20-45	Norm
O.S.U. Sigma											X			X					PR	N	CR	UN	Norm

QUICK REFERENCE TO TESTS ON THE MARKET
continued

TEST NAME	Strength	Flexibility	Endurance	Agility	Power	Balance	Speed	Visual skills	Eye-foot/hand coordination	Throwing	Kinesthetic awareness	Bilateral control	Tactile discrimination	Gross motor patterns	Rhythm	Fine motor control	Language development	Emotional/social development	Recommended use	Special training?	Norms? Ages	I or G administration	Norming sample
Motor Ability (continued)																							
Preschool Battery				X	X	X	X		X					X					P	?	3–6	I 45	Norm
Bruninks-Oseretsky	X		X	X	X				X			X				X			P PR	NS	4½–14	I 20–60	Norm
BMAT		X		X					X					X	X				P	N	4–12	I G 15–40	Norm
BCTC				X		X						X		X					P PR	N	5–14	I G 15	Norm
Motor Skills																							
Phys. Ability Rating Scale						X			X	X				X					PR	?	0–6	I Ob	Norm
Psychoed. Inv. Basic Learn								X	X	X	X		X	X				X	PR	?	CR	I Ob	Norm
Move-Grow-Learn	X	X	X	X		X		X	X		X			X	X	X				N	N	I Ob	
Physical Fitness																							
Battery for MR			X	X	X	X													PR	N	9–20	I G 60	EMR TMR
Mr. Peanut's Guide	X	X	X		X	X							X						P	N	7–9	I G 60	Norm
Phys. Fit. for MR	X	X	X		X														PR	N	8–17	I G 120	TMR

TEST NAME	Strength	Flexibility	Endurance	Agility	Power	Balance	Speed	Visual skills	Eye-foot/hand coordination	Throwing	Kinesthetic awareness	Bilateral control	Tactile discrimination	Gross motor patterns	Rhythm	Fine motor control	Language development	Emotional/social development	Recommended use	Special training?	Norms? Ages	I or G administration	Norming sample
Elementary Test for Boys and Girls	X		X		X		X												P	N	6–12	I G 60	Norm
Special Test for MR	X		X	X	X		X							X					PR	N	5–18	I G 120	EMR
Motor Fit. Test for Moderate MR		X	X		X		X			X				X					PR	N	6–20	I G 120	TMR
AAHPERD for Blind			X	X	X		X												PR	N	6–20	I G 120	Blind
Skinfold																			P PR	Y	18+	I 5	Norm
12 Min./1.5 mi.			X																P PR	N	13+	G 20	Norm
Flexometer		X																	P PR	Y	16	M	Norm
Strength Index	X																		P PR	NS	8–18	I 20	Norm
Somatotyping																			P PR	Y	17–23	I	Norm

Screening Tests

TEST NAME	Strength	Flexibility	Endurance	Agility	Power	Balance	Speed	Visual skills	Eye-foot/hand coordination	Throwing	Kinesthetic awareness	Bilateral control	Tactile discrimination	Gross motor patterns	Rhythm	Fine motor control	Language development	Emotional/social development	Recommended use	Special training?	Norms? Ages	I or G administration	Norming sample
Group Posture																			P PR	Y	L	G	Norm
Plumb Line (Posture)																			P PR	Y	L	I	Norm

QUICK REFERENCE TO TESTS ON THE MARKET
continued

TEST NAME	Strength	Flexibility	Endurance	Agility	Power	Balance	Speed	Visual skills	Eye-foot/hand coordination	Throwing	Kinesthetic awareness	Bilateral control	Tactile discrimination	Gross motor patterns	Rhythm	Fine motor control	Language development	Emotional/social development	Recommended use	Special training?	Norms? Ages	I or G administration	Norming sample
Screening Tests (continued)																							
Posture Screen																			P PR	Y	L	G	Norm
Pedioscope																			P PR	Y	L	I	Norm
Conformateur																			P PR	Y	L	G	Norm
Comprehensive Motor Performance																							
APEAS	X		X	X	X		X	X	X	X	X		X		X				P PR G	NS	5–18	I 20 G	Gen Sch Pop
Basic Mot. Fit.	X	X	X	X	X	X	X							X		X			PR	?	4–18	I	ED BI MR

Appendix E
Articles on Physical Education and Recreation for the Handicapped from *Journal of Physical Education and Recreation*

Following is an index of the *Journal of Physical Education and Recreation (JOPER,* formerly *JOPHER)* containing articles dealing with physical education and recreation for the handicapped from 1950 to 1980. This index lists the articles under the following headings:

ADAPTED PHYSICAL EDUCATION

A Developmental Physical Education Program, 1978, Vol. 49, No. 9, Pg. 36.
Adapted Games in the Body Mechanics Program, 1956, Vol. 26, No. 9, Pg. 10.
Adapted Physical Education, 1969, Vol. 40, No. 5, Pg. 45.
Adapted Sports and Recreation for the Handicapped Child, 1972, Vol. 43, No. 9, Pg. 53.
Adapted Table Tennis for the Physically Handicapped, 1968, Vol. 39, No. 9, Pg. 79.

Games Teaching: Adaptable Skills, 1977, Vol. 48, No. 1, Pg. 17.
Guiding Principles for Adapted Physical Education, 1952, Vol. 23, No. 4, Pg. 15.
Let the Doctors Recommend Adapted Physical Education, 1958, Vol. 29, No. 5, Pg. 28.
Physical Education Adapts to the Visually Handicapped, 1964, Vol. 35, No. 3, Pg. 25.
Sports Adaptations for a Student Without Fingers, 1976, Vol. 47, No. 1, Pg. 46.
Therapeutic and Adapted Physical Education and Recreation, 1977, Vol. 48, No. 3,
        Pg. 36.
Adapted Table Tennis—Wheelchair Multi-Handicapped, 1974, Vol. 45, No. 1, Pg. 81.
The Nature of P.E. Programming for the Mentally Retarded and Physically Handicapped,
        1974, Vol. 45, No. 2, Pg. 89.
Competitive Athletics for the Handicapped, 1973, Vol. 44, No. 1, Pg. 89.
Handicapped Swim Clinic, 1970, Vol. 41, No. 8, Pg. 66.
Indoor Target Golf (Programs for the Handicapped), 1971, Vol. 42, No. 1, Pg. 73.
Outward Bound for the Handicapped, 1976, Vol. 47, No. 5, Pg. 54.
Physically Handicapped Children Use the Stegel (Versatile Climbing Equipment), 1972,
        Vol. 43, No. 6, Pg. 71.
Putt-Putt Golf (Programs for the Handicapped), 1971, Vol. 42, No. 1, Pg. 73.
Special Olympics (Programs for the Handicapped), 1972, Vol. 43, No. 2, Pg. 49.
Swimming Activity for the Handicapped, 1953, Vol. 24, No. 4, Pg. 14.
Tournament Bowling: An Activity for the Handicapped, 1972, Vol. 43, No. 9, Pg. 56.
Wheel Chair Karate, 1972, Vol. 43, No. 2, Pg. 49.
Fencing for the Quadraplegic, 1974, Vol. 45, No. 1, Pg. 79.
Celebrating Adapted Physical Education and Therapeutic Recreation, 1980, Vol. 51, No. 8,
        Pg. 65.
Dance Therapy, 1980, Vol. 51, No. 7, Pg. 33.
Ice Skating, 1980, Vol. 51, No. 1, Pg. 32.
Integrating the Physically Handicapped Child Into Physical Education Classroom, 1980,
        Vol. 51, No. 4, Pg. 17.
PEOPEL, 1980, Vol. 51, No. 7, Pg. 28.
Physical Education Facilities for the Handicapped, 1980, Vol. 51, No. 6, Pg. 50.
Problems of Accessibility, 1980, Vol. 51, No. 6, Pg. 36.
Put Independence and Dignity into Your Pool, 1980, Vol. 51, No. 6, Pg. 35.
Sports and the Deaf: A Quest for Meaningful Experiences, 1980, Vol. 51, No. 3, Pg. 35.
Teaching the Handicapped Child in the Regular Physical Education Class, 1980, Vol. 51,
        No. 2, Pg. 32.
What Is It Like to Be Handicapped?, 1980, Vol. 51, No. 3, Pg. 36.
Camp Swim for the Handicapped, 1979, Vol. 50, No. 7, Pg. 82.
Direction or Misdirection in Physical Education for Mentally Retarded Students, 1979,
        Vol. 50, No. 7, Pg. 22.
Independent Study in Physical Education for Exceptional Students, 1979, Vol. 50, No. 9,
        Pg. 24.
Integrating the Disabled into Aquatics Programs, 1979, Vol. 50, No. 2, Pg. 57.
Model Staff Development Program for Implementing PL 94–142 in Physical Education,
        1979, Vol. 50, No. 3, Pg. 35.
Participation for the Handicapped, 1979, Vol. 50, No. 8, Pg. 81.
Sport, Myth, and the Handicapped Athlete, 1979, Vol. 50, No. 3, Pg. 33.
Coming Out Ahead on the Long Run, 1978, Vol. 49, No. 7, Pg. 24.
Handicapped Can Dance Too!, 1978, Vol. 49, No. 5, Pg. 52.

AGING

AQUATICS FOR THE HANDICAPPED

Laboratory Training in Underwater Exercises (for the Physically Handicapped), 1956,
Vol. 27, No. 5, Pg. 14.
Overcoming the Fears of Swimming, 1968, Vol. 39, No. 5, Pg. 75.
Swimming Activity for the Handicapped, 1953, Vol. 24, No. 4, Pg. 14.
Swimming for the Child With Multiple Birth Defects, 1971, Vol. 42, No. 4, Pg. 64.
Swimming for the Deaf, 1956, Vol. 26, No. 5, Pg. 12.
Swimming for the Physically Handicapped, 1954, Vol. 25, No. 4, Pg. 12.
Swimming for the Spina Bifida, 1970, Vol. 41, No. 8, Pg. 67.
Teaching Non-Swimmers, 1954, Vol. 25, No. 2, Pg. 11.
Using Movement Exploration in the Swimming Pool with Mentally Retarded, 1971, Vol. 42,
October, Pg. 65.
Camp Swim for the Handicapped, 1979, Vol. 50, No. 7, Pg. 82.
Integrating the Disabled into Aquatics Programs, 1979, Vol. 50, No. 2, Pg. 57.

ASTHMATICS AND RESPIRATORY CONDITIONS

Blowing Games for Asthmatic Children, 1972, Vol. 43, No. 7, Pg. 77.
New Dimensions in Physical Activity for Children with Asthma and Other Respiratory
Conditions, 1972, Vol. 43, No. 7, Pg. 75.
Putt-Putt Golf (Programs for the Handicapped), 1971, Vol. 42, No. 3, Pg. 48.
Resources for Asthma and Activity Programs for Asthmatics, 1972, Vol. 43, No. 7, Pg. 79.
Trampoline Tumbling for Children with Chronic Lung Disease, 1973, Vol. 44, No. 4,
Pg. 86.

CARDIOVASCULAR

Are We Gaining on Heart Disease?, 1953, Vol. 24, No. 2, Pg. 16.
Cardiovascular Health, 1968, Vol. 39, No. 9, Pg. 36.
Physical Activity for the Child with Cystic Fibrosis, 1977, Vol. 48, No. 1, Pg. 50.
Physical Educators Need to Know About Heart Disease, 1960, Vol. 31, No. 3, Pg. 26.
Putt-Putt Golf (Programs for the Handicapped), 1971, Vol. 42, No. 3, Pg. 48.
The Cardiovascular System: What You Should Know About It, 1950, Vol. 21, No. 7,
Pg. 41.
Exercise Stress Testing: Potential Heart Disease, 1974, Vol. 45, No. 6, Pg. 35.

CEREBRAL PALSY

Putt-Putt Golf (Programs for the Handicapped), 1971, Vol. 42, No. 3, Pg. 48.
Swimming for the Physically Handicapped, 1954, Vol. 25, No. 4, Pg. 12.

DEAF

Dance for the Deaf, 1969, Vol. 40, No. 3, Pg. 81.
Dance for the Deaf Child, 1959, Vol. 30, No. 6, Pg. 46.
Is There a Deaf Child on Your Team?, 1976, Vol. 47, No. 2, Pg. 63.
Swimming for the Deaf, 1956, Vol. 26, No. 5, Pg. 12.
Teaching Games Skills Theory Sight and Sound (Using Visual Aids), 1952, Vol. 23, No. 6,
Pg. 12.

Teaching Physical Education in Schools for the Deaf, 1972, Vol. 43, No. 4, Pg. 81.
The Deaf Student in Physical Education, 1969, Vol. 40, No. 3, Pg. 69.
Sports and the Deaf: A Quest for Meaningful Experiences, 1980, Vol. 51, No. 3, Pg. 35.
Signing. Communicating with Hearing Impaired Individuals in Physical Education, 1978, Vol. 49, No. 5, Pg. 19.

DIABETIC

Let the Diabetic Play, 1975, Vol. 46, No. 5.
The Diabetic in Physical Education, 1977, Vol. 48, No. 3, Pg. 88.

EPILEPTIC

Children with Epilepsy, 1952, Vol. 23, No. 6, Pg. 39.
The Child with Epilepsy, 1973, Vol. 44, No. 4, Pg. 83.

HANDICAPPED INDIVIDUAL

Can People with Impairments Overcome Society's Handicaps? 1977, Vol. 48, No. 6, Pg. 60.
Integrating Education and Recreation for the Handicapped, 1973, Vol. 44, No. 8, Pg. 66.
A Philosophical Perspective on Leisure Services for the Disabled, 1975, Vol. 46, No. 5, Pg. 26.
Programs for the Handicapped, 1968, Vol. 39, No. 8, Pg. 83.
Programs for the Inconvenienced, 1972, Vol. 43, No. 4, Pg. 83.
Sense and Nonsense About Mainstreaming, 1976, Vol. 47, No. 1, Pg. 43.
The Need for Leisure Education for Handicapped Children and Youth, 1976, Vol. 47, No. 3, Pg. 53.
We Can Serve the Student with Disabilities, 1959, Vol. 30, No. 3, Pg. 45.
What Is It Like to be Handicapped? 1980, Vol. 51, No. 3, Pg. 36.

HEMOPHILIAC

The Role of Athletics in the Total Care of the Hemophiliac, 1972, Vol. 43, No. 2, Pg. 53.

HIP DISORDERS

Physical Activity Guidelines for Children with Developmental Hip Disorders, 1975, Vol. 46, No. 2, Pg. 69.

HOSPITAL RECREATION

Camping: Transition Between Hospital and Home for the Mentally Ill, 1961, Vol. 32, No. 5, Pg. 24.
Coping with Hospitalization Through Play, 1975, Vol. 46, No. 5, Pg. 35.
Hospital Management Looks at Hospital Recreation, 1954, Vol. 25, No. 4, Pg. 8.
Hospital Recreation: Therapy or Fun? 1958, Vol. 29, No. 8, Pg. 25.
Hospital Recreation (The Veterans Administration Program), 1951, Vol. 52, No. 5, Pg. 24.

Hospital Recreation Is Unique, 1952, Vol. 23, No. 5, Pg. 29.
Recreation: A Needed Hospital Service, 1955, Vol. 26, No. 1, Pg. 21.

KINESIOLOGY

A Functional Motor Endplate, 1977, Vol. 48, No. 7, Pg. 50.
A Kinesmatic Interpretation of Running and Its Relationship to Hamstring Injury, 1970,
    Vol. 41, No. 8, Pg. 83.
Kinesiology and the Profession, 1965, Vol. 36, No. 7, Pg. 69.
Kinesiological Review of Muscle Function for Physical Education Majors, 1977, Vol. 48,
    No. 5, Pg. 60.
Physical Therapy Suggestions for Gross Motor Activities, 1972, Vol. 43, No. 9, Pg. 54.

Exercise—Kinesiology

Applied Physiology of Exercise: A Biological Awareness Concept, 1973, Vol. 44, No. 8,
    Pg. 30.
Exercises: Good, Bad, and Indifferent, 1953, Vol. 24, No. 1, Pg. 14.
Excerises for Abdominal Muscles, 1966, Vol. 37, No. 7, Pg. 67.
Injury Control Through Isometrics and Isotonics, 1967, Vol. 38, No. 2, Pg. 26.
Isokinetic Energy and the Mechanical Energy Potentials of Muscle, 1968, Vol. 39, No. 5,
    Pg. 40.
Physiology of Exercise, Part I, 1956, Vol. 26, No. 3, Pg. 16.
Physiology of Exercise, Part II, 1956, Vol. 26, No. 4, Pg. 28.
Advances in Physiology of Exercise, Part III, 1956, Vol. 26, No. 8, Pg. 22.
Potential Hazards of Abdominal Exercises, 1971, Vol. 42, No. 1, Pg. 73.
Strengthening Muscles and Preventing Injury with a Controlled Program of Isometric
    Exercises, 1964, Vol. 35, No. 1, Pg. 57.
More on Applied Physiology of Exercise, 1974, Vol. 45, No. 2, Pg. 18.

Movement—Kinesiology

Analyzing Muscles in Action, 1967, Vol. 38, No. 3, Pg. 79.
Formation and Organization of Human Motion, 1970, Vol. 41, No. 5, Pg. 73.
G. B. Duchenne's Physiology of Motion, 1967, Vol. 38, No. 2, Pg. 67.
Physics Applied to Human Motion, 1977, Vol. 48, No. 1, Pg. 42.
The Neuromuscular Base of Human Motion: Feedback, 1965, Vol. 36, No. 8, Pg. 61.
The Structural Base of Human Movement, 1965, Vol. 36, No. 8, Pg. 59.
Toward a Science and Discipline of Human Movement, 1966, Vol. 37, No. 8, Pg. 65.
Your Muscles See More Than Your Eyes, 1966, Vol. 37, No. 7, Pg. 38.

MAINSTREAMING/INTEGRATION

Integrating the Disabled into Aquatics Program, 1979, Vol. 50, No. 2, Pg. 57.
Integrating the Physically Handicapped Child into the Physical Education Classroom, 1980,
    Vol. 51, No. 4, Pg. 17.
PEOPEL, 1980, Vol. 51, No. 7, Pg. 28.

MENTALLY RETARDED

MULTIPLE SCLEROSIS

MUSCULAR DYSTROPHY

PHYSICALLY HANDICAPPED/ORTHOPEDICALLY HANDICAPPED

Recreation for the Orthopedically Handicapped, 1954, Vol. 25, No. 3, Pg. 45.
Swimming for the Child With Multiple Birth Defects, 1971, Vol. 42, No. 4, Pg. 68.
Integrating the Physically Handicapped Child into the Physical Education Classroom, 1980,
        Vol. 51, No. 4, Pg. 17.

POSTURE

Faulty Posture in Relation to Performance, 1958, Vol. 29, No. 4, Pg. 14.
Let's Do Something About Posture Education, 1963, Vol. 34, No. 1, Pg. 14.
Photo Metric Posture Pictures, 1954, Vol. 25, No. 2, Pg. 11.
Poor Posture Among Children, 1950, Vol. 21, No. 7, Pg. 60.
Posture Education, 1963, Vol. 35, No. 2, Pg. 28.
What We Don't Know About Posture, 1958, Vol. 29, No. 5, Pg. 31.

PSYCHOLOGICAL ASPECTS

Helping to Solve the Social and Psychological Adjustment Problems of the Handicapped,
        1960, Vol. 31, No. 3, Pg. 35.
Mental Health for Children, 1951, Vol. 21, No. 1, Pg. 9.

RECREATION FOR THE HANDICAPPED

An Adapted Surfing Device, 1975, Vol. 46, No. 7, Pg. 57.
Adapted Sports and Recreation for the Handicapped Child, 1972, Vol. 43, No. 9, Pg. 53.
Archery for the Handicapped, 1951, Vol. 22, No. 5, Pg. 28.
Aquatics for the Handicapped, 1976, Vol. 47, No. 2, Pg. 42.
Camping for the Severely Disabled Adults, 1958, Vol. 29, No. 3, Pg. 22.
Camping for the Handicapped, 1950, Vol. 21, No. 5, Pg. 312.
Celebrating Adapted Physical Education and Therapeutic Recreation, 1980, Vol. 51, No. 8,
        Pg. 65.
Disabled and Recreational Opportunities on Campus, 1980, Vol. 51, No. 4, Pg. 43.
Higher Levels of Therapeutic Play with Children, 1980, Vol. 51, No. 9, Pg. 21.
Therapeutic Play for Beginners, 1980, Vol. 51, No. 2, Pg. 30.
Recreation Services for Students with Handicapping Conditions, 1980, Vol. 51, No. 4,
        Pg. 41.
Role of Evaluation in Therapeutic Recreation Service, 1980, Vol. 51, No. 8, Pg. 48.
Equality in Recreation for Special Needs Children, 1978, Vol. 49, No. 3, Pg. 50.
Resort Model, 1978, Vol. 49, No. 9, Pg. 42.
Therapeutic Implications of Ice Skating, 1979, Vol. 49, No. 9, Pg. 42.
Designing Parks for the Handicapped, 1978, Vol. 49, No. 6, Pg. 24.
Mainstreaming at Dae Valley Camp, 1978, Vol. 49, No. 5, Pg. 28.

REHABILITATION

New Horizons in Physical Rehabilitation, 1950, Vol. 21, No. 6, Pg. 335.
Rehabilitation of the Handicapped Child, 1951, Vol. 22, No. 6, Pg. 19.
Teamwork: Prescription for Rehabilitation, 1960, Vol. 31, No. 8, Pg. 42.

RHEUMATIC FEVER

Rheumatic Fever, 1951, Vol. 22, No. 9, Pg. 39.

TUBERCULOSIS

Controlling Tuberculosis in the High School, 1955, Vol. 26, No. 2, Pg. 14.
Recreation Helps the Tuberculous Child, 1953, Vol. 24, No. 9, Pg. 18.

VISUALLY HANDICAPPED

Blind Bowling, 1971, Vol. 42, No. 4, Pg. 59.
Blind Skiing. Cross Country/Blind Skiing Downhill, 1976, Vol. 47, No. 2, Pg. 63.
The Blind "See" the World of Nature on the Braille Trail, 1972, Vol. 43, No. 1, Pg. 85.
Children with Impaired Vision Are "Seeing" Through Touch, 1969, Vol. 40, No. 2, Pg. 95.
Dance for the Blind, 1968, Vol. 39, No. 5, Pg. 28.
Development of Aerobics Conditioning Program for the Visually Handicapped, 1975,
        Vol. 46, No. 5, Pg. 39.
Integrating Visually Handicapped Children into a Public Elementary School Physical
        Education Program, 1971, Vol. 42, No. 4, Pg. 61.
Is Vigorous Activity Feasible for Blind Children in Public Schools? 1969, Vol. 40, No. 2,
        Pg. 97.
Physical Education Adapts to the Visually Handicapped, 1964, Vol. 35, No. 3, Pg. 25.
Physical Education for the Visually Handicapped, 1970, Vol. 41, No. 6, Pg. 37.
Physically They See, 1959, Vol. 30, No. 3, Pg. 45.
Recreation's Role in Rehabilitating Blind People, 1958, Vol. 59, No. 1, Pg. 21.
Teaching the Blind Student Archery Skills, 1969, Vol. 40, No. 4, Pg. 85.
Teaching Game Skills Through Sight and Sound, 1952, Vol. 23, No. 6, Pg. 12.
Therapeutic and Adapted P.E. and Rec., 1977, Vol. 48, No. 3, Pg. 36.
The Unseen Target, 1953, Vol. 24, No. 6, Pg. 15.
Tin Cans and Blind Kids, 1971, Vol. 42, No. 4, Pg. 64.
Leisure Time Activities for the Visually Impaired, 1974, Vol. 45, No. 8, Pg. 69.

Appendix F
Sports Organizations
for the Handicapped

American Athletic Association for the Deaf, Inc.
3916 Lantern Drive
Silver Springs, Maryland 20902

American Blind Bowler's Association
150 North Bellaire
Louisville, Kentucky 40206

Amputees in Motion
14248 Burbank Boulevard, Suite C
Van Nuys, California 91401

Blind Outdoor Leisure Development, Inc.
B.O.L.D.
533 Main
Aspen, Colorado 81611

Braille Sports Foundation
Room 301
730 Hennepin Avenue
Minneapolis, Minnesota 55402

British Paraplegic Sports Society
International Sports Organization for the Disabled
International Stoke-Mandeville Games Federation
Stoke-Mandeville Spinal Injury Center
Aylesbury, England

Coordinating Committee/Sport for the Physically Disabled
333 River Road
Ottawa, Ontario K1L 8B9
Canada

Exceptional Games
Los Angeles County Parks and Recreation Department and
California State University
155 West Washington Boulevard
Los Angeles, California 90015

Handicapped Sportsperson's Association of Sacramento
(formerly National Amputee Skiers Association)
3738 Walnut Avenue
Carmichael, California 95608

International Council on Therapeutic Ice Skating
Box 13
State College, Pennsylvania 16801

The National Association of Sports for Cerebral Palsy
1 State Street
New Haven, Connecticut 06511

National Beep Baseball Association
3212 Tomahawk
Lawrence, Kansas 66044

National Foundation of Wheelchair Tennis
3857 Birch Street, Box 411
Newport Beach, California 92660

National Handicapped Sports and Recreation Association
10 Mutual Building
4105 East Florida
Denver, Colorado 80222

National Wheelchair Athletic Association
4024 62nd Street
Woodside, New York 11377

National Wheelchair Basketball Association
110 Seaton Building
University of Kentucky
Lexington, Kentucky 40506

North American Riding for the Handicapped Association
Box 100
Ashburn, Virginia 22011

Ski for Light, Inc.
1455 West Lake Street
Minneapolis, Minnesota 55408

Southern California Inconvenienced Sportsman's Association
11023 Ocean Drive
Culver City, California 90230

Special Olympics, Inc.
Suite 203
1701 K Street, N.W.
Washington, D.C. 20006

United States Association for Blind Athletes
55 West California Avenue
Beach Haven Park, New Jersey 08008

United States Blind Golfer's Association
c/o Patrick Browne, Jr.
28th Floor
225 Baronne Street
New Orleans, Louisiana 70112

Appendix G
Examples of Materials Available to Parents for Home Use

LET'S PLAY TO GROW

The following material from *Let's-Play-to-Grow*, published in 1977 by the Joseph P. Kennedy, Jr., Foundation in Washington, D.C., is reproduced by permission of the Foundation.

Let's-Play-to-Grow
For the Special Child who is Very Young or Severely Handicapped

Guide 1

Even when they are very young or severely handicapped, special children can enjoy and benefit from physical activity. You can help these children learn to control their movements and discover what fun it is to play. Even with the child who is not severely impaired, you may want to start out with the basic movements suggested in these pages. They will give you a clearer idea of what your child can do, and they will give him pleasure.

Gaining Skills-Warm-Ups

Whenever you play with your child, it's a good idea to start with a few simple exercises that get the body ready for sports and games. Three to five minutes will do it. Done correctly these activities stretch the body and get the blood going. They're fun because everyone does them together. Five of each of the following kinds of activity will get you off to a good start.

"Locomotive"
Raise knees as high as possible and pump arms back and forth. Start slowly, run fast as you can and taper off. Do this for at least 2 minutes.

"Jumping Jacks"
Stand at attention. Then jump and clap hands over head ending up with legs spread. Jump back to attention. Repeat at least ten times.

8

Learning Soccer

To Start

Let's-Play-to-Grow Guide 7 outlines and breaks down basic ball-handling skills.

Kicking

Soccer is a particularly good Let's-Play-to-Grow sport because it combines kicking, running, dribbling, and teamwork.

Soccer skill starts with kicking. Fortunately, you don't need a lot of room to practice kicking, and it can be done in or out of doors.

Use a soft, lightweight ball so that your child will not hurt himself or damage anything. (A light beach ball, a partially deflated volleyball or soccer ball is ideal.) Choose a target. If possible have the child kick against the wall so he can kick his own rebound. Start kicking short distances; then, increase the distance as your child improves. Set up two poles or chairs to form a "goal" and practice kicking the ball

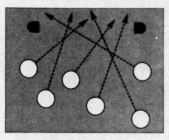

into the goal from various angles and distances. Start with a stationary ball. As skill improves, work on kicking a moving ball.

2. Dribbling

Dribbling the ball in soccer is kicking it along the ground while walking or running. The player tries to keep control of the ball by tapping it gently with the inside or outside of the foot and keeping it no more than about twelve inches ahead of the dribbler.

DRIBBLE BALL WITH OUTSIDE OF FOOT...

...INSIDE OF FOOT

Your child will enjoy games in which he must dribble through a course, which you set up with chairs, poles, cushions, or other objects. Or, stand between your child and the goal and challenge him to dribble past you to the goal. Don't forget — praise and reward for effort and success.

3. Ball Control

In soccer, it's no hands on the ball, except when it goes out of bounds. Only the goalie is allowed to use his hands. The player must learn to stop the ball with his feet, body, even his head and then control it with his feet.

BOUNCE BALL OFF CHEST...

BOUNCE BALL OFF HEAD

Start with your child standing about two feet away from you. Throw the ball gently at his chest to show that the ball does not hurt and

1

Let's Begin

Learning About the World Through the Senses (First year)

Stimulation of the senses should start at birth. Spend part of every day helping your child become more aware of himself and the world around him. Above all, try always to have a smile on your face when you are with your child. A smile is the best signal there is that you love your child and are happy with him.

Important Note:

Children like to do things in their own time. Respect a child's sense of time. Do not expect him to be "getting somewhere" each Let's-Play-to-Grow session. The Special child takes great pleasure in doing one thing again and again until he finds what he is looking for in that activity. Often we do not know what the child is trying to do. But he does. His pattern of play is his own and holds the secret to his spirit.

The following activities go from the simplest to the more complex — from lying in the crib to walking, climbing and jumping. Many children with severe impairments may not be able to perform these movements without help. You can do a lot to strengthen their bodies and minds by guiding and encouraging different kinds of movement and urging them with love and patience to stretch beyond the limits of their present abilities.

Find time to stimulate each of the five senses every day by doing some of the following simple activities. These are only examples. Use your own imagination in opening up the windows of your child's senses.

1. Touch

Rub different parts of your child's body with your hands or with material of different texture, for example, with:

a. a wash cloth dry or with soap and warm water
b. a soft diaper
c. a cotton shirt or towel
d. a woolen cloth or sweater
e. a soft baby brush

Smile, talk to your child or sing while you are stroking or rubbing. Move your head so that your baby's eyes can follow yours.

...RUB WITH A CLOTH

2 Seeing

a. Hang a toy over the crib, or hang brightly-colored objects on the sides of the crib or bed.
b. Swing a brightly-colored object or a rattle several inches above your baby's eyes for a few minutes each day.

c. Turn your child's head towards the object and wait until he looks at it.
d. Move the object slowly back and forth to stimulate eye movement and to encourage reaching and stretching.
e. Allow the child to pull the object to him. If he puts it in his hand, let him play with it.
f. Make funny faces. Pull out both sides of your mouth. Make a funny noise. Your child will laugh. From 9 months to a year he will try to imitate you.

3. Hearing

a. Talk and sing to your child while holding or rocking him.
b. Hang crib toys with bells.
c. Move around so that your child hears you from different directions.
d. Shake a rattle close by your child's left ear (or right). Do it until he turns his head. Then do it near the other ear. Repeat until he turns his head toward you in both directions.
e. Play phonograph records or a radio.
f. Make and play simple rhythm instruments such as sticks, coffee cans, measuring spoons.

SENSORY-MOTOR EXPERIENCES FOR THE HOME: A MANUAL FOR PARENTS

This material is taken from *Sensory-Motor Experiences for the Home,* a manual for parents developed in 1978 by Janet A. Seaman and Karen P. DePauw. All rights to this material are reserved.

Sensory-Motor Experiences for the Home A Manual for Parents

Janet A. Seaman, P.E.D.   Karen P. DePauw, M.S.

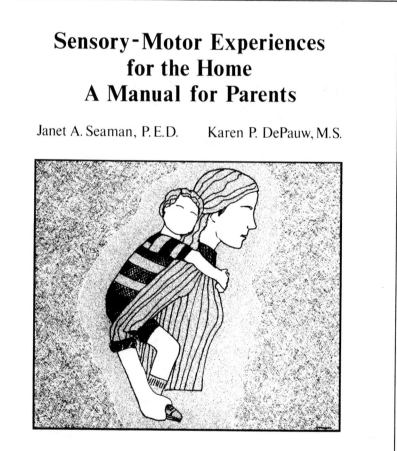

Printed by
Trident Shop
California State University, Los Angeles

11

The Vestibular and Proprioceptive Systems

Vestibular input is an extremely powerful source of sensory stimulation. Once received and organized, vestibular stimulation can be used to enhance balance and equilibrium responses. Proprioceptive input provides stimulation which helps the youngster utilize information about where his body is in space and also serves to enhance balance.

Vestibular Stimulation

1. Swinging: Can provide valuable motion experiences. At a higher level, have your child try swinging on his/her stomach, hold onto his/her arms to give a push.

   (a) Swinging in a hammock or inner tube swing is likewise important.

   (b) Have your child swing in as many different positions as possible. Challenge him/her to find every position possible; upside down, sidewards, backwards, tucked, open, on stomach, on back, etc.

   (c) Requiring him/her to perform some task, as hitting a target with a ball, while swinging, makes the experience even more integrative.

2. Sliding: Especially sliding on the stomach, can be useful stimulation.

3. Playground Equipment: Equipment which rocks or twirls around provides vestibular input, as do amusement park rides. Allow the child to decide for himself/herself if he/she wants this type of stimulation and how much.

4. Cruising: This motion provided through roller skates, a skateboard, a bicycle or a scooter is useful, again, especially when some additional task is required so that the vestibular stimulation accompanies the movement.

5. Airplane: Holding the child by one arm and leg, lift him/her from the ground and spin him/her around in a circle.

6. Trampoline: Provides motion stimulation as well as requiring many adaptive equilibrium responses. Small trampolines have now been made available for home use.

7. Rocking: Slow vestibular input, as that gained from a rocking chair or a slow rocking horse, can be a quiet and relaxing experience.

APPENDIX

EQUIPMENT THAT CAN BE MADE

TACTILE EXPERIENCES

Barrel Roller

Barrel of any size with carpet, burlap, sheep skin, or other fabrics attached inside and out. Stitch pieces together to cover and line barrel, then punch holes near top and bottom rims and sew to barrel using nylon cord and overhand stitch.

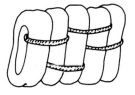

Innertube "Tube"

Inflate 4-5 innertubes and tie together in twos.

Incline Mat

Wedge-shaped construction with 3/4'' plywood top and sides. Top should be padded or carpeted. Supporting ribs of 1x2s should be equally spaced inside for durability.

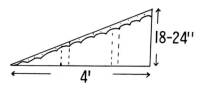

18-24''

4'

VESTIBULAR EXPERIENCES

Balance Beam

2''x4''x10' of hardwood board can be used flat on the floor or on supports made from same material. Notches in supports are 2'' and 4'' to hold beam flat or on edge for variations in balance challenges. A third support

may be used in the center for heavier, older children.

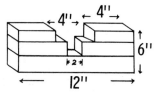

4''   4''

6''

2

12''

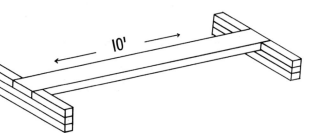

10'

LUNCHTIME: THE ALTERNATIVE TO THE M & M: OR, HOW TO TEACH SELF-FEEDING SKILLS TO THE PROFOUNDLY HANDICAPPED

This material is excerpted (with the permission of the author) from *Lunchtime: The Alternative to the M & M,* a manual written by Linda M. Osborn, a Special Education Teacher. The complete manual may be obtained from Osborn: 3136 Carfax Avenue, Long Beach, California 90808.

Introduction

Teachers and the students will benefit from the training guide in several ways. Besides accessibility, teachers will have an efficient, systematic and sequential method to use to teach self-feeding skills. The guide will help teachers to learn task analysis and create a bank of learning objectives that can be used with many students. And, most important of all, the burden of the teacher manually feeding students can be diminished. The time spent at mealtimes now takes a large part of the day, but the newly learned skills will allow for more time so teachers will be free to work with other students.

Methods for Teaching Self-Feeding

Before starting any new self-feeding program . . . a formal assessment is important. . . To augment any of the formal assessment tools, I suggest that you design an assessment of your own. . . Be aware of those special behaviors that he/she might be manifesting during playtime or mealtime that will assist you in determining the starting point for the training.

Listed below are a few such behaviors to look for when you begin to design a program for teaching self-feeding.

Quick Assessment

1. Does the student pick up objects?
2. Does student take objects when presented with them?
3. Can student hold an object from 10 - 20 seconds without dropping it?
4. Does student pick up object using palm and all fingers?
5. Does student put objects into mouth?
6. Will student finger feed?
7. Does student take food from others when placed at the table?
8. What hand does the student use most of the time when picking up objects?
9. Does the student exhibit thumb and/or finger sucking?
10. Does the student visually track objects? Does the student hear well (optional)?

STUDENT: OBJECTIVE: S will scoop food from a scoop dish with
                                                       minimal assistance during feeding training
                                           CRITERION: 80% of 20 trials for five consecutive days

STEP	STIMULUS	PROMPT	RESPONSE	CONSEQUENCE CORRECT RESPONSE	SCHEDULE	CONSEQUENCE INCORRECT RESPONSE
1.	T sits in front of S and presents S with spoon and scoop dish. T says "Scoop."	T places hand over S hand and scoops food	S scoops	Primary (Meal) Secondary (Nice scooping)	Continuous	T takes food and spoon away from S and waits 5 seconds before repeating Step #1
2.	Same as #1	Same as #1 except T lifts spoon with S to within 2" from S mouth and fades prompt	S scoops food and brings to mouth	Same as #1	Same as #1	Same as #1 except repeat Step #2
3.	Same as #1	Same as #1 except T fades prompt within 4" of S mouth	Same as #2	Same as #1	Same as #1	T says "No" takes food away and waits five seconds to repeat step
4.	Same as #1	T places S hand on spoon and begins the scooping process	S scoops food and brings to mouth	Same as #1	Same as #1	T puts S hand on spoon and scoops food as in Step 1. Repeat for 5 trials then repeat #4
5.	Same as Step 1	T touches S hand	Same as #1	Same as #1	Continuous	T says "No" and repeats Step 4 for 5 trials, then repeats Step 5
6.	Same as Step 1	None	Same as #1	Same as #1	Continuous	T says "No" and repeats Step 5 for 5 trials before moving to Step 6
7.	Same as Step 1	None	Same as #1	Primary reinforcer always be present	Change secondary schedule to suit	Same as above except repeat 6 for 5 trials before moving on to Step 7

BIBLIOGRAPHY OF REFERENCES FOR PARENTS

Brancato, R. F. *Winning.* New York: Knopf, 1977.

Brown, G. *Suggestions for Parents.* Larkspur, California: CANHC Literature Center (P.O. Box 710, Larkspur, CA), n.d.

Chaney, C. *Pointers for Parents.* Larkspur, California: CANHC Literature Center, n.d.

Cliff, S., Gray, J., and Nyman, C. *Mothers Can Help.* El Paso, Texas: El Paso Rehabilitation Center, 1974.

Coe, M. *Neurologically Handicapped Child: One Parent to Another.* Larkspur, California: CANHC Literature Center, n.d.

Crook, W. *Can Your Child Read? Is He Hyperactive?* Larkspur, California: CANHC Literature Center, n.d.

Eareckson, J., with Musser, J. *Joni.* Grand Rapids, Michigan: Zondervan, 1976.

Frey, M. *ABC's for Parents: Aid to Management of the Slow Child at Home.* Larkspur, California: CANHC Literature Center, n.d.

Gordon, T. *Parent Effectiveness Training.* New York: David McKay, 1970.

Johnson, G. *Parents in Crisis.* Larkspur, California: CANHC Literature Center, n.d.

Karnes, M. *Helping Young Children Develop Language Skills.* Larkspur, California: CANHC Literature Center, n.d.

Kennedy, The Joseph P., Jr. Foundation. *Let's-Play-to-Grow.* Washington, D.C.: The Joseph P. Kennedy, Jr., Foundation, 1978.

Krents, H. *To Race the Wind.* New York: G. P. Putnam's Sons, 1972.

Patterson, G. R. *Living with Children.* Champaign, Illinois: Research Press, 1968.

Seaman, J. A., and DePauw, K. P. *Sensory-Motor Experiences for the Home.* Los Angeles: Trident Shop, 1979.

Smith, B. *Feelings Are a Family Affair.* Larkspur, California: CANHC Literature Center, n.d.

Index